ASPECTS of
WESTERN
CIVILIZATION

ASPECTS of WESTERN CIVILIZATION

Problems and Sources in History

Volume II

Edited by

PERRY M. ROGERS

The Ohio State University

Prentice Hall, Englewood Cliffs, New Jersey 07632

LIBRARY OF CONGRESS
Library of Congress Cataloging-in-Publication Data

Aspects of Western civilization : problems and sources in history /
    edited by Perry M. Rogers.
        p.   cm.
    Contents: v. 1. The ancient world through the age of Reformation -
- v. 2. The age of Reformation through the contemporary world.
    ISBN 0-13-048976-X (v. 1).   ISBN 0-13-048968-9 (v. 2)
    1. Civilization, Occidental--History.   2. Civilization,
Occidental--History--Sources.   I. Rogers, Perry McAdow.
CB245.A86 1988
909'.09821--dc19

                                            87-32701
                                               CIP

Cover design: *George Cornell*
Manufacturing buyer: *Ed O'Dougherty*

Cover art: "The Proportions of Man" by
Leonardo da Vinci, courtesy of Accademia, Venice.

© 1988 by Prentice-Hall, Inc.
A Division of Simon & Schuster
Englewood Cliffs, New Jersey 07632

Printed in the United States of America
10 9 8 7 6 5 4 3 2 1

ISBN 0-13-048968-9   01

Prentice-Hall International (UK) Limited, *London*
Prentice-Hall of Australia Pty. Limited, *Sydney*
Prentice-Hall Canada Inc., *Toronto*
Prentice-Hall Hispanoamericana, S.A., *Mexico*
Prentice-Hall of India Private Limited, *New Delhi*
Prentice-Hall of Japan, Inc., *Tokyo*
Simon & Schuster Asia Pte. Ltd., *Singapore*
Editora Prentice-Hall do Brasil, Ltda., *Rio de Janeiro*

For Ann
Elisa, Kit, and Tyler

Brief Contents

VOLUME II

Contents

3 "I Am the State": The Absolutism of Louis XIV   *64*

6 Nationalism and Imperialism: The Motives and Methods of Expansion   *196*

10 The Jewish Holocaust *338*

The Evolution of Nazi Jewish Policy *340*

The Final Solution (1941–1945) *351*

Jewish Resistance *364*

Preface

The Roman orator Cicero once remarked that "History is the witness of the times, the torch of truth, the life of memory, the teacher of life, the messenger of antiquity." In spite of these noble words, historians have often labored under the burden of justifying the study of events that are over and done. Human beings are practical, more concerned with their present and future than with their past. And yet the study of history provides us with unique opportunities for self-knowledge. It teaches us what we have done and therefore helps define what we are. On a less abstract level, the study of history enables us to judge present circumstance by drawing on the laboratory of the past. Those who have lived and died, through their recorded attitudes, actions, and ideas, have left a legacy of experience.

One of the best ways to travel through time and perceive the very "humanness" of history is through the study of primary sources. These are the documents, coins, letters, inscriptions, and monuments of past ages. The task of historians is to evaluate this evidence with a critical eye and then construct a narrative that is consistent with the "facts" as they have been established. Such interpretations are inherently subjective and open to dispute. History is thus filled with controversy as historians argue their way toward the truth. The only effective way to understand the past is through personal examination of the primary sources.

Yet, for the beginning student, this poses some difficulties. Such inquiry casts the student adrift from the security of accepting the "truth" as revealed in a textbook. In fact, history is too often presented in a deceptively objective manner; one learns facts and dates in an effort to obtain the right answers for multiple-choice tests. But the student who has wrestled with

primary sources and has experienced voices from the past on a more intimate level accepts the responsibility of evaluation and judgment. He or she
understands that history does not easily lend itself to right answers, but
demands reflection on the problems that have confronted past societies
and are at play even in our contemporary world.

Aspects of Western Civilization offers the student an opportunity to evaluate the primary sources of the past in a structured and organized format.
The documents provided include state papers, secret dispatches, letters,
diary accounts, poems, newspaper articles, papal encyclicals, propaganda
fliers, and even wall graffiti. Occasionally, the assessments of modern historians are included. Yet this two-volume book has been conceived as more
than a simple compilation of sources. The subtitle of the work, *Problems and
Sources in History*, gives true indication of the nature of its premise. Students
learn from the past most effectively when faced with problems that have
meaning for their own lives. In evaluating the material from *Aspects of
Western Civilization*, the student will discover that issues are not nearly as
simple as they may appear at first glance. Historical sources often contradict each other and truth then depends upon logic and upon one's own
experience and outlook on life. Throughout these volumes, the student is
confronted with basic questions regarding historical development, human
nature, moral action, and practical necessity. The text is therefore broad in
its scope, incorporating a wide variety of political, social, economic, religious, intellectual, and scientific issues. It is internally organized around
six major themes that provide direction and cohesion while allowing for
originality of thought in both written and oral analysis:

1. *Imperialism.*   How has imperialism been justified throughout Western
   history, and what are the moral implications of gaining and maintaining empire? Is defensive imperialism a practical foreign policy option?
   This theme is often juxtaposed with subtopics of nationalism, war,
   altruism, and human nature.
2. *Church/State Relationships.*   Is there a natural competition between
   these two controlling units in society? Which is more influential, which
   legacy more enduring? How has religion been used as a means of
   securing political power or of instituting social change? The Judeo-
   Christian heritage of Western Civilization forms the basis of this
   theme.
3. *Systems of Government.*   The student is introduced to the various systems of rule that have shaped Western Civilization: classical democracy, representative democracy (republican government), oligarchy,
   constitutional monarchy, divine-right monarchy, theocracy, and dictatorship (especially fascism and totalitarian rule). What are the advantages and drawbacks to each? This rubric also includes the concepts
   of balance of power and containment, principles of succession, geo-
   politics, and social and economic theories such as capitalism, communism, and socialism.

4. *Revolution.* The text examines the varieties of revolution: political, intellectual, economic, and social. What are the underlying and precipitating causes of political revolution? How essential is the intellectual foundation? Are social demands and spontaneity more important elements in radical action?

5. *Propaganda.* What is the role of propaganda in history? Many sections examine the use and abuse of information, often in connection with absolute government, revolution, imperialism, or genocide. How are art and architecture, as well as the written word, used in the "creation of belief"? This theme emphasizes the relativity of truth and stresses the responsibility of the individual in assessing the validity of evidence.

6. *Historical Change and Transition.* What are the main determinants of change in history? How important is the individual in effecting change, or is society regulated by unseen social and economic forces? What role does chance play? What are the components of civilization and how do we assess progress or decline? Are civilizations biological in nature? Is a crisis/response theory of change valid? This theme works toward providing the student with a philosophy of history and against the tendency to divide history into strict periods. It stresses the close connection between the past and the present.

Structure of the Book

Each chapter begins with a series of quotations from various historians, statesmen, philosophers, literary figures, or religious spokespersons who offer insight on the subject matter of the chapter. These quotations may well be used in conjunction with the study questions at the end of the unit. After the quotations, an introduction provides a brief historical background and identifies the themes or questions to be discussed in the chapter.

Following this general introduction, the primary sources are presented with extensive direction for the student. A headnote explains in more detail the historical or biographical background for each primary source and focuses attention on themes or interrelationships with other sources. Each chapter concludes with a series of study questions that can form the basis of oral discussion or written analysis. They do not seek mere regurgitation of information, but demand a more thoughtful response based on reflective analysis of the primary sources.

Use of the Book

Aspects of Western Civilization offers the instructor a wide variety of didactic applications. The chapters fit into a more or less standard lecture format and are spaced chronologically. An entire chapter may be assigned for oral discussion, or sections from each chapter may satisfy particular interests or requirements. Some of the chapters provide extensive treatment of a broad historical topic ("The Medieval World: Dark Ages?" "The French Revolution and the Rise of Napoleon," "Our Contemporary World: The Progress of Civilization"). In order to make them manageable and effective, they are grouped into topical sections (with correspondingly labeled study questions) that can be utilized separately, if so desired.

The chapters may also be assigned for written analysis. One of the most important concerns of both instructor and student in an introductory class is the written assignment. *Aspects of Western Civilization* has been designed to provide self-contained topics that are problem-oriented, promote reflection and analysis, and encourage responsible citation of particular primary sources. The study questions for each chapter should generally produce an eight- to ten-page paper.

Acknowledgments

I would particularly like to thank friends and colleagues who contributed their expertise and enthusiasm to this book. Professors Alan Beyerchen and Kenneth Andrien of The Ohio State University advised me on particular matters in the initial phases of writing. Jack Guy read drafts of some chapters and offered sterling commentary, and Professor Glenn Janus of Coe College provided me with a detailed review of the entire manuscript that added greatly to the accuracy of the text. Several others also contributed helpful reviews of the manuscript: Professor John Beer, University of Delaware; Professor Donald K. Frank, C. W. Post College of Long Island University; Professor James Friguglietti, Eastern Montana College; Professor Paul Harvey, The Pennsylvania State University; and Professor Kenneth G. Madison, Iowa State University. Sara Shriner typed a difficult manuscript time and again with unfailing determination and good cheer. Stephen Dalphin, History Editor at Prentice Hall, afforded wise direction through the various phases of production. Special thanks to the students of Columbus School for Girls, who "tested" the chapters in this book with their typical diligence and hard work; the final product has benefited greatly from their suggestions and ideas. Finally, I owe an immeasurable debt to my wife, Ann, who suffered all the outrageous fortune and disruption that goes into writing a book of this kind over a period of years—she did it with me.

P. M. R.

1

The Reformation Era

I am more afraid of my own heart than of the pope and all his cardinals. I have within me the great pope—Self.

—Martin Luther

Whatever your heart clings to and confides in, that is really your God.

—Martin Luther

All religions must be tolerated for every man must get to heaven his own way.

—Frederick the Great

During the Middle Ages, the Church was the focal point of society. One's life was inextricably bound to the dictates of religion from the baptism that followed birth to the last rites that accompanied death. But by the sixteenth century, the omnipotence of the Church, both in a spiritual sense and in the political realm, had been called into question. The Church had lost much of the authority that had allowed it, in the eleventh through the thirteenth centuries, to claim superiority in the ongoing struggle between church and state. Crises such as the Babylonian Captivity (1309–1377) and the Great Schism (1378–1417) had strained the loyalty of the faithful and devastated the unity of the Church for over a century. By the middle of the fifteenth century, the papacy was occupied with finding new sources of income that would help it fend off political challenges to its territory and increase its influence in the secular realm. The Renaissance papacy became infamous in its corruption and succumbed to the sensual delights of the world, as well as to the more traditional abuses of simony (the selling of church offices) and pluralism (allowing an individual to hold more than one position). Pope Julius II (1503–1513) was a glaring example of the age as bedecked in armor, he personally led his armies into battle.

These actions resulted in a plenitude of criticism from within the Church and especially from Christian Humanists such as Desiderius Erasmus. Perhaps the most controversial practice of the Church was the sale of indulgences. An indulgence was a piece of paper, signed by the pope, that remitted punishment in Purgatory due to sin. It was based on the theory that all men are by nature sinful and after death will have to undergo a purgation of sin before being allowed to enter the Kingdom of Heaven. The pope, however, controlled an infinite "treasury of grace" that could be dispensed to mortals, thus removing the taint of sin and freeing the soul from Purgatory. By the late fifteenth century, the remission of sin was extended to both the living and the dead, and one could therefore liberate the soul of a relative "trapped" in Purgatory by purchasing an indulgence. The sale of indulgences became a routine affair of peddling forgiveness of purgatorial punishment, and the papacy came to rely on it as a necessary source of income. In 1507, Pope Julius II issued a plenary indulgence in order to obtain funds for the construction of Saint Peter's Basilica in Rome. Leo X renewed the indulgence in 1513 and subcommissioners actively began the sale to the faithful. It was in response to this sale that a young monk named Martin Luther protested and nailed his *Ninety-five Theses* to the door of the Wittenberg church.

It is important to note that although Luther called into question the sale of indulgences, the main issue was salvation. Salvation, he reasoned, was cheap indeed if it could be purchased. Luther was tortured by the demands of God for perfection and worried that his own righteousness was insufficient for salvation in the sight of God. The Church taught that in addition to winning grace through faith, one could also merit God's grace through good works or the remission of sin by indulgence. In fact, the purchase of an indulgence was considered a good work. But to Luther's mind, salvation required more, much more, and had nothing to do with deeds. While studying Saint Paul's *Epistle to the Romans* (1:17), Luther achieved a breakthrough that freed him from his torment: By the grace of God *alone* could one be saved, and this salvation was obtained only through faith in Christ. Neither good works nor indulgences could have anything to do with salvation. This stand called into question the very foundation of established Christian belief. Was the pope the true Vicar of Christ who spoke the words of God? If so, why did he advocate indulgences as a means of salvation? Was he in fact infallible on such matters of faith? The corruption of the papacy was also troubling, yet

Luther's objective was not to overthrow the Church but to reform it from within.

The Church replied to such a challenge with what it considered swift and appropriate action. Luther was excommunicated and his writings condemned as heretical. It became evident to Luther that his desire to reform the Church could only be achieved by defying the authority of the pope and starting a new church. Supported by the Holy Roman Emperor Charles V, the Church sought to eliminate the root of the controversy. However, Luther was hidden, protected by the secular princes in Germany who, because of their location and traditional independence, were willing to defy their emperor and promote a religion that to them served a secular purpose. Yet Luther's movement was spiritual in nature, and he decried such political connections even as he sought the aid of the princes and nobility.

This chapter seeks to explore the spiritual foundations of the Reformation and the Protestant movement, from its inception by Martin Luther through its development under Ulrich Zwingli and John Calvin. The Reformation era must also be viewed in its proper context, noting that during this period the Catholic Church made significant strides toward reform in its own right. The themes presented in this chapter include the role of the individual in changing history and the impact of religion on the political framework and social fabric of the times. The Reformation era was one of transition and instability that eventually led to war and bloodshed as nations fought during the sixteenth and seventeenth centuries in support of the "true religion." This bloody future was far from Martin Luther's mind when he nailed his *Ninety-five Theses* on the Wittenberg church door in 1517 and thus started a movement that shook the spiritual foundations of Christendom and altered the political face of Europe for centuries to come.

The State of the Papacy
Anticlericalism

The Protestant Reformation has often been viewed as a direct response to Church corruption, which was widespread during the fourteenth and fifteenth centuries. Simony (the selling of church offices) was a common practice as Theodoric Vrie, an Augustinian monk, notes in this first selection. Vrie places the lament in the mouth of Christ. The second selection is a papal admonition by Pope Pius II in 1460 to Cardinal Rodrigo Borgia for indulging in sensual pleasures. Borgia fathered several children, a fact that he later used to advantage on becoming Pope Alexander VI. His papacy itself makes a significant statement about corruption in the Church.

Simony (1414)

THEODORIC VRIE

The supreme pontiffs, as I know, are elected through avarice and simony, and likewise the other bishops are ordained for gold. These, in turn, will not ordain those below them, the priests, deacons, sub-deacons and acolytes, except a strict agreement be first drawn up. Of this mammon of unrighteousness the bishops, the real rulers, and the chapters, each has his part. The once accepted proverb, "Freely give for freely ye have received," is now most vilely perverted: "Freely I have not received, nor will I freely give, for I have bought my bishopric for a great price, and I must indemnify myself impiously for my untoward outlay. I will not ordain you as priest except for money. I purchased the sacrament of ordination when I became a bishop and I propose to sell you the same sacred sign and seal of ordination. By beseeching and by gold, I have gained my office, for beseeching and for gold do I sell you your place. Refuse the amount I demand and you shall not become a priest."

If Simon Magus [a magician who offered money to Peter for the Holy Spirit] were now alive he might buy with money not only the Holy Ghost, but God the Father, and Me, the Son of God. But favor is bought from the ungrateful who do not the works of grace, for grace must give freely, but if bought and not given, grace is no longer grace. But why say more? The bishops who take money for ordination become lepers. Those ordained do, by their bribery, condemn themselves to perdition with Simon Magus, to whom Peter said, "Thy money perish with thee."

Scandal in the Church (1460)

POPE PIUS II

Dear Son: We have learned that your Worthiness, forgetfull of the high office with which you are invested, was present from the seventeenth to the twenty-second hour, four days ago, in the gardens of John de Bichis, where there were several women of Siena, women wholly given over to worldly vanities. Your companion was one of your colleagues whom his years, if not the honor of the Apostolic See, ought to have reminded of his duty. We have heard that the dance was indulged in all wantonness; none of the allurements of love were lacking, and you conducted yourself in a wholly worldly manner. Shame forbids mention of all that took place for not only the things themselves but their very names are unworthy of your rank. In

"Simony" is from Theodoric Vrie, *History of the Council of Constance*, in *Translations and Reprints from the Original Sources of European History*, vol. 3, no. 6, ed. James H. Robinson (Philadelphia: University of Pennsylvania, 1898), p. 28.

"Scandal in the Church" is from F. Gregorovius, *Lucretia Borgia* (New York: D. Appleton and Company, 1903), pp. 7–8.

order that your lust might be all the more unrestrained, the husbands, fathers, brothers, and kinsmen of the young women and girls were not invited to be present. You and a few servants were the leaders and inspirers of this orgy. It is said that nothing is now talked of in Siena but your vanity, which is the subject of universal ridicule. Certain it is that here at the baths, where Churchmen and the laity are very numerous, your name is on every one's tongue.

Our displeasure is beyond words, for your conduct has brought the holy state and office into disgrace; the people will say that they make us rich and great, not that we may live a blameless life, but that we may have means to gratify our passions. This is the reason the princes and the powers despise us and the laity mock us; this is why our own mode of living is thrown in our face when we reprove others. Contempt is the lot of Christ's vicar because he seems to tolerate these actions. You, dear son, have charge of the bishopric of Valencia, the most important in Spain; you are a chancellor of the Church, and what renders your conduct all the more reprehensible is the fact that you have a seat among the cardinals, with the Pope, as advisors of the Holy See. We leave it to you whether it is becoming to your dignity to court young women, and to send those whom you love fruits and wine, and during the whole day to give no thought to anything but sensual pleasures.

People blame us on your account, and the memory of your blessed uncle, Calixtus, likewise suffers, and many say he did wrong in heaping honors upon you. If you try to excuse yourself on the ground of your youth, I say to you: you are no longer so young as not to see what duties your offices impose upon you. A cardinal should be above reproach and an example of right living before the eyes of all men, and then we should have just grounds for anger when temporal princes bestow uncomplimentary epithets upon us; when they dispute with us the possession of our property and force us to submit ourselves to their will.

Of a truth we inflict these wounds upon ourselves, and we ourselves are the cause of these troubles, since we by our conduct are daily diminishing the authority of the Church. Our punishment for it in this world is dishonor, and in the world to come well deserved torment. May, therefore, your good sense place a restraint on these frivolities, and may you never lose sight of your dignity; then people will not call you a vain gallant among men.

If this occurs again we shall be compelled to show that it was contrary to our exhortation, and that it caused us great pain; and our censure will not pass over you without causing you to blush. We have always loved you and thought you worthy of our protection as a man of an earnest and modest character. Therefore, conduct yourself henceforth so that we may retain this opinion of you, and may behold in you only the example of a well ordered life. Your years, which are not such as to preclude improvement, permit us to admonish you paternally.

The Criticism of the Northern Humanists

Humanism, the state of mind that formed the cornerstone of the Italian Renaissance, spread to the north in the late fifteenth and sixteenth centuries and became popular in the courts of France and England. The emphasis on the wonder, versatility, and individuality of man was evident in the art and literature of the period. Humanism also fostered scholarship which, in the north especially, tended to be critical of the abuses within the Church. The first selection is a response from the German Humanist Jacob Wimpheling to a letter written by Enea Silvio Piccolomini (a cardinal and later Pope Pius II) that recounts grievances against the Church in 1515, just two years before the Reformation began in earnest. The second piece is a satire written by the most famous of all northern Humanists, Desiderius Erasmus. In it he criticizes abuses within the Church and thereby expresses the hope of promoting a greater spirituality in religion.

The Pope's Special Mission (1515)

JACOB WIMPHELING

The Council of Basel [1431–1449] pointed out that our sacred church fathers had written their canons for the purpose of assuring the Church of good government, and that honor, discipline, faith, piety, love, and peace reigned in the Church as long as these regulations were observed. Later however, vanity and greed began to prevail; the laws of the fathers were neglected, and the Church sank into immorality and depravity, debasement, degradation and abuse of office. This is principally due to papal reservations of prelacies and other ecclesiastical benefices, also to the prolific award of expectancies to future benefices, and to innumerable concessions and other burdens placed upon churches to clergy. To wit:

Church incomes and benefices are given to unworthy men and Italians.

High offices and lucrative posts are awarded to persons of unproven merit and character.

Few holders of benefices reside in their churches, for as they hold several posts simultaneously they cannot reside in all of them at once. Most do not even recognize the faces of their parishioners. They neglect the care of souls and seek only temporal rewards.

The divine service is curtailed.

Hospitality is diminished.

Church laws lose their force.

Ecclesiastical buildings fall into ruin.

The conduct of clerics is an open scandal.

Gerald Strauss, *Manifestations of Discontent in Germany on the Eve of the Reformation* (Bloomington: Indiana University Press, 1971), pp. 43–45. Reprinted by permission of the publisher.

Able, learned, and virtuous priests who might raise the moral and professional level of the clergy abandon their studies because they see no prospect of advancement.

The ranks of the clergy are riven by rivalry and animosity; hatred, envy, and even the wish for the death of others are aroused.

Striving after pluralities of benefices is encouraged.

Poor clerics are maltreated, impoverished, and forced from their posts.

Crooked lawsuits are employed to gather benefices.

Some benefices are procured through simony.

Other benefices remain vacant.

Able young men are left to lead idle and vagrant lives.

Prelates are deprived of jurisdiction and authority.

The hierarchical order of the Church is destroyed.

In this manner, a vast number of violations of divine and human law is committed and condoned. . . . "It is the pope's special mission," writes Enea, "to protect Christ's sheep. He should accomplish this task in such a way as to lead all men to the path of salvation. He must see that the pure Gospel is preached to all, that false doctrines, blasphemies, and unchristian teachings are eradicated, and that all enemies of the faith are driven from the lands of Christendom. He must heal schisms and end wars, abolish robbery, murder, arson, adultery, drunkenness and gluttony, spite, hatred and strife. He must promote peace and order, so that concord might reign among men, and honor and praise be given to God."

So Enea. My questions is: Does a court of ephebes and muleteers and flatterers help the pope prevent schism and abolish blasphemy, wars, robbery, and the other crimes mentioned by Enea? Would he not be better served by men learned in canon law and Scripture, by men who know how to preach and can help the faithful ease their conscience in the confessional? The Council of Basel was surely inspired when it decreed that a third of all benefices should go to men versed in the Bible. . . . If I am not mistaken, the conciliar fathers wished to see the true Gospel of Christ preached everywhere. They wished honor and glory given to God. Ourselves want nothing else. We would rejoice if many men were to praise God, if every priest in his sufficiently endowed benefice were to serve God and celebrate the Eucharist, if popes and emperors, if the whole Church were to draw rich benefit from this holy work, the most efficacious office of them all.

The Praise of Folly (1509)

DESIDERIUS ERASMUS

The next to be placed among the regiment of fools are such as make a trade of telling or inquiring after incredible stories of miracles and pro-

Desiderius Erasmus, *The Praise of Folly* (London: Hamilton Adams and Company, 1887), pp. 90–96, 143–149, 164–169.

digies. Never doubting that a lie will choke them, they will muster up a thousand several strange relations of spirits, ghosts, apparitions, raising of the devil, and such like bugbears of superstition; which the farther they are from being probably true, the more greedily they are swallowed, and the more devoutly believed. And these absurdities do not only bring an empty pleasure and cheap divertisement, but they are a good trade and procure a comfortable income to such priests and friars as by this craft get their gain.

To these again are nearly related such others as attribute strange virtues to the shrines and images of saints and martyrs, and so would make their credulous proselytes believe that if they pay their devotion to St. Christopher in the morning, they shall be guarded and secured the day following from all dangers and misfortunes. If soldiers, when they first take arms, shall come and mumble over such a set prayer before the picture of St. Barbara, they shall return safe from all engagements. Or if any pray to Erasmus on such particular holidays, with the ceremony of wax candles and other fopperies, he shall in a short time be rewarded with a plentiful increase of wealth and riches. The Christians have now their gigantic St. George, as well as the pagans had their Hercules; they paint the saint on horseback, and drawing the horse in splendid trapping very gloriously accoutred, they scarce refrain in a literal sense from worshipping the very beast.

What shall I say of such as cry up and maintain the cheat of pardons and indulgences? That by these compute the time of each soul's residence in purgatory, and assign them a longer or shorter continuance, according as they purchase more or fewer of these paltry pardons and saleable exemptions? Or what can be said bad enough of others, who pretend that by the force of such magical charms, or by the fumbling over their beads in the rehearsal of such, and such petitions; which some religious imposters invented, either for diversion, or, what is more likely, for advantage; they shall procure riches, honor, pleasure, health, long life, a lusty old age, nay, after death a sitting at the right hand of our Saviour in His kingdom.

By this easy way of purchasing pardons, any notorious highwayman, any plundering soldier, or any bribe-taking judge shall disburse some part of their unjust gains, and so think all their grossest impieties sufficiently atoned for. So many perjuries, lusts, drunkenness, quarrels, bloodsheds, cheats, treacheries, shall all be, as it were, struck a bargain for, and such a contract made, as if they had paid off all arrears and might now begin upon a new score.

From the same principles of folly proceeds the custom of each country's challenging their particular guardian-saint. Nay, each saint has his distinct office alloted to him and is accordingly addressed to upon the delivery in childbirth, a third to help persons to lost goods, another to protect seamen in a long voyage, a fifth to guard the farmer's cows and sheep, and so on. For to rehearse all instances would be extremely tedious.

And now for some reflections upon popes, cardinals and bishops, who in pomp and splendour have almost equalled if not [outdone] secular princes.

Now if any one consider that their upper crotchet of white linen is to signify their unspotted purity and innocence; that their forked mitres, with both divisions tied together by the same knot, are to denote the joint knowledge of the Old and New Testament. That their always wearing gloves represents their keeping their hands clean and undefiled from lucre and covetousness; that the pastoral staff implies the care of a flock committed to their charge; that the cross carried before them expresses their victory over all carnal affection. He that considers this, and much more of the like nature, must needs conclude they are entrusted with a very weighty and difficult office. But alas, they think it sufficient if they can but feed themselves, and as to their flock, either commend them to the care of Christ Himself, or commit them to the guidance of some inferior vicars and curates. [They do] not so much as remember what their name of bishop imports, to wit, labor, pains and diligence, but by base simoniacal contracts, they are in a profane sense . . . overseers of their own gain and income.

The popes of Rome . . . pretend themselves Christ's vicars; if they would but imitate His exemplary life . . . an unintermitted course of preaching [and] attendance with poverty, nakedness, hunger and a contempt of this world; if they did but consider the import of the word pope, which signifies a father; or if they did but practice their surname of most holy, what order or degrees of men would be in a worse condition? There would be then no such vigorous making of parties and buying of votes in the conclave upon the vacancy of that see.

And those who, by bribery or other indirect courses, should get themselves elected would never secure their sitting firm in the chair by pistol, poison, force and violence. How much of their pleasure would be abated if they were but endowed with one dram of wisdom? Wisdom, did I say? Nay, with one grain of salt which our Saviour bid them not lose the savor of. All their riches, all their honor, their jurisdictions, their Peter's patrimony, their offices, their dispensations, their licenses, their indulgences, their long train and attendants, see in how short a compass I have abbreviated all their marketing of religion; in a word, all their perquisites would be forfeited and lost; and in their [place] would succeed watchings, fastings, tears, prayers, sermons, hard studies, repenting sighs and a thousand such like severe penalties. . . . The very Head of the Church, the spiritual prince, would then be brought from all his splendour to the poor equipage of a scrip and staff.

The Lutheran Reformation

The Indulgence Controversy

The controversy over the sale of indulgences was the spark that set the Reformation in motion. In 1515, Pope Leo X made an agreement with Archbishop Albert to sell indulgences in Mainz and other areas of northern Germany, with half the proceeds going to support Leo's construction of Saint Peter's Basilica in Rome and half going to pay for the debts that Albert had incurred in securing his church offices. In the first selection, Archbishop Albert gives instructions to those subcommissioners who actually sold the indulgences in 1517. One of the most successful subcommissioners was Johann Tetzel, prior of the Dominican monastery at Leipzig. His oratorical ability is evident in the second passage.

Instructions for the Sale of Indulgences (1517)

ARCHBISHOP ALBERT

Here follow the four principal graces and privileges, which are granted by the apostolic bull, of which each may be obtained without the other. In the matter of these four privileges preachers shall take pains to commend each to believers with the greatest care, and, in-so-far as in their power lies, to explain the same.

The first grace is the complete remission of all sins; and nothing greater than this can be named, since no man who lives in sin and forfeits the favor of God, obtains complete remission by these means and once more enjoys God's favor: moreover, through this remission of sins the punishment which one is obliged to undergo in Purgatory on account of the affront to the divine Majesty, is all remitted, and the pains of Purgatory completely blotted out.

The second grace is a confessional letter containing the most extraordinarily comforting and hitherto unheard of privileges, and which also retains its virtue even after our bull expires at the end of eight years, since the bull says: "they shall be participators now and for ever. . . ."

The third most important grace is the participation in all the possessions of the church universal, which consists herein, that contributors toward the said building, together with their decreased relations, who have departed this world in a state of grace, shall from now and for eternity be partakers in all petitions, intercessions, alms, fasting, prayers, in each and every pilgrimage, even those to the Holy Land; furthermore, in the stations at Rome, in the masses, canonical hours, flagellations, and all other spiritual goods which have brought forth or which shall be brought forth by the universal most holy church militant or by any of its members. Believers will become participants in all these things who purchase confessional letters.

The fourth distinctive grace is for those souls which are in purgatory, and is the complete remission of all sins, which remission the pope brings to pass through his intercession to the advantage of said souls, in this wise; that the same contribution shall be placed in the chest by a living person as one would make for himself. . . . Moreover, preachers shall exert themselves to give this grace the widest publicity, since through the same, help

James H. Robinson, ed., *Translations and Reprints from the Original Sources of European History*, vol. 2, no. 6 (Philadelphia: University of Pennsylvania, 1902), pp. 4–9.

will surely come to departed souls, and the construction of the Church of St. Peter will be abundantly promoted at the same time.

"How Many Sins Are Committed in a Single Day?" (1517)

JOHANN TETZEL

Venerable Sir, I pray you that in your utterances you may be pleased to make use of such words as shall serve to open the eyes of the mind and cause your hearers to consider how great a grace and gift they have had and now have at their very doors. Blessed eyes indeed, which see what they see, because already they possess letters of safe conduct by which they are able to lead their souls through that valley of tears, through that sea of the mad world, where storms and tempests and dangers lie in wait, to the blessed land of Paradise. Know that the life of man upon earth is a constant struggle. We have to fight against the flesh, the world and the devil, who are always seeking to destroy the soul. In sin we are conceived,—alas! what bonds of sin encompass us, and how difficult and almost impossible it is to attain to the gate of salvation without divine aid; since He causes us to be saved, not by virtue of the good works which we accomplish, but through His divine mercy, it is necessary then to put on the armor of God.

You may obtain letters of safe conduct from the vicar of our Lord Jesus Christ, by means of which you are able to liberate your soul from the hands of the enemy, and convey it by means of contrition and confession, safe and secure from all pains of Purgatory, into the happy kingdom. For know that in these letters are stamped and engraven all the merits of Christ's passion there laid bare. Consider, that for each and every mortal sin it is necessary to undergo seven years of penitence after confession and contrition, either in this life or in Purgatory.

How many mortal sins are committed in a day, how many in a week, how many in a month, how many in a year, how many in the whole course of life! They are well-nigh numberless, and those that commit them must needs suffer endless punishment in the burning pains of Purgatory.

But with these confessional letters you will be able at any time in life to obtain full indulgence for all penalties imposed upon you, in all cases except the four reserved to the Apostolic See. Therefore throughout your whole life, whenever you wish to make confession, you may receive the same remission, except in cases reserved to the Pope, and afterwards, at the hour of death, a full indulgence as to all penalties and sins, and your share of all spiritual blessings that exist in the church militant and all its members.

Do you not know that when it is necessary for anyone to go to Rome, or

James H. Robinson, ed., *Translations and Reprints from the Original Sources of European History*, vol. 2, no. 6 (Philadelphia: University of Pennsylvania, 1902), pp. 9–10.

Johannes Tezelus Dominicaner Münch mit sei-
nen Römischen Ablaßkram/welchen er im Jahr Christi 1517. in Deutschen
landen zu marckt gebracht/wie er in der Kirchen zu Pirn in seinem
Vaterland abgemahlet ist.

O ihr deutschen mercket mich recht/
Des heiligen Vaters Papstes Knecht/
Bin ich/vnd vber ing euch ist allein/
Zehn tausent vnd neun hundert carein/
Gnad vnd Ablaß von einer Sünd/
Vor euch/ewer Elter n/Weib vnd Kind/
Sol ein jeder gewehret sein
So viel ihr legt ins Kästelein/
So bald der Gülden im Becken klingt/
Im huy die Seel im Himel springt/

Als Babst Leo der zehend genandt/
Nu mehr fast vnmüglich befand/
Das er das Römisch Jubel Jahr
Kriebet/hat er die faule wahr/
Des Ablaßkrams in Deutschenland/
Durch seine Kramknecht ausgesandt/
Dazu sich denn ohn all verdrieß/
Johann Tetzel gebrauchen ließ/
Der was itzt kaum dem Hencker entlauffen/
Als er wegen Ehebruchs solt ersauffen/
Wo nicht der from Fürst Friederich/,
Seiner het angenommen sich/
Vnd beim Keyser Maximilian/
Ein gnedigste Fürbit gethan/
Hierbey es aber so nicht blieb/
Aus eim Ehebrecher wurd ein Dieb/
Welcher durch vermeint gewalt vnd macht/
Viel Gelds vnd Guts zu weg gebracht/

Als er die blinde Welt bered/
Das er den Himel feil tragen thet/
Wenn man nu Gelt gnug gebe dar/
Hets mit den Menschen kein gefahr/
So bald der Grosch im Kasten klingt/
So bald die Seel in Himel sich schwingt/
Durch diesen Teuffelischen Tandt/
Hat er betrogen sein Vaterland/
Biß ihn Gott hat ins Spiel gesehen/
Durch Doctor Luthern seligen/
Welcher ihm seinen Krämertisch/
Gewaltiglich zu Boden stieß/
Daher/Gott lob/biß auff die zeit/
Der Ablaßkram zerstrewet leit/
So bleibet nun Christi verdienst/
Einig allein vnser Gewinst/
Des Tezels Kram vnd Bapsts Betrug/
Findet bey vns kein recht noch fug.

Caricature of Johann Tetzel, the indulgent preacher who spurred Luther to publish his *Ninety-five Theses*. The last line of the caption reads: "As soon as gold in the basin rings, right then the soul to heaven springs." (*Staatliche Lutherhalle, Wittenberg*) undertake any other dangerous journey, he takes his money to a broker and gives a certain percent—five or six or ten—in order that at Rome or elsewhere he may receive again his funds intact, by means of the letter of this same broker? Are you not willing, then, for the fourth part of a florin, to obtain these letters, by virtue of which you may bring, not your money but your divine and immortal soul safe and sound into the land of Paradise?

Salvation Through Faith Alone

MARTIN LUTHER

Martin Luther's transformation from monk to reformer was not a precon-ceived act; it developed gradually not only as a result of corruption around him, but especially because of a spiritual awakening. Luther struggled with the need to imitate the perfection of Christ, which was important in the eyes of the Church for salvation. Luther realized that because of his nature as a man, he was too sinful, and that no amount of prayer or good works could help him achieve the kingdom of Heaven. After much study and pain, he came to the conclusion that salvation was a free gift of God and that man was saved by his faith in Christ *alone*. In the first selection, Luther explains his enlightenment. The second docu-ment is his answer to the indulgences being sold by Johann Tetzel. When Luther posted the *Ninety-five Theses* on the church in Wittenberg, the Reformation began in earnest.

I, Martin Luther, entered the monastery against the will of my father and lost favor with him, for he saw through the knavery of the monks very well. On the day on which I sang my first mass he said to me, "Son, don't you know that you ought to honor your father?" . . . Later when I stood there during the mass and began the canon, I was so frightened that I would have fled if I hadn't been admonished by the prior. . . .

When I was a monk I was unwilling to omit any of the prayers, but when I was busy with public lecturing and writing I often accumulated my ap-pointed prayers for a whole week, or even two or three weeks. Then I would take a Saturday off, or shut myself in for as long as three days without food and drink, until I had said the prescribed prayers. This made my head split, and as a consequence I couldn't close my eyes for five nights, lay sick unto death, and went out of my senses. Even after I had quickly recovered and I tried again to read, my head went 'round and 'round. Thus our Lord God drew me, as if by force, from that torment of prayers. . . .

Theodore Tappert and H. Lehmann, eds., *Luther's Works*, vol. 54: *Table Talk* (Philadelphia: Fortress Press, 1967), pp. 85, 193–194, 234, 264–265. Copyright © 1967 by Fortress Press. Reprinted by permission of the publisher.

The words "righteous" and "righteousness of God" struck my conscience like lightning. When I heard them I was exceedingly terrified. If God is righteous [I thought], he must punish. But when by God's grace I pondered, in the tower and heated room of this building, over the words, "He who through faith is righteous shall live" [Rom. 1:17] and "the righteousness of God" [Rom. 3:21], I soon came to the conclusion that if we, as righteous men, ought to live from faith and if the righteousness of God should contribute to the salvation of all who believe, then salvation won't be our merit but God's mercy. My spirit was thereby cheered. For it's by the righteousness of God that we're justified and saved through Christ. These words [which had before terrified me] now became more pleasing to me. The Holy Spirit unveiled the Scriptures for me in this tower.

God led us away from all this in a wonderful way; without my quite being aware of it he took me away from that game more than twenty years ago. How difficult it was at first when we journeyed toward Kemberg after All Saints' Day in the year 1517, when I first made up my mind to write against the crass errors of indulgences! Dr. Jerome Schurff advised against this: "You wish to write against the pope? What are you trying to do? It won't be tolerated!" I replied, "And if they have to tolerate it?" Presently Sylvester, master of the sacred palace, entered the arena, fulminating against me with this syllogism: "Whoever questions what the Roman church says and does is heretical. Luther questions what the Roman church says and does, and therefore [he is a heretic]." So it all began.

The Ninety-five Theses (1517)

MARTIN LUTHER

In the desire and with the purpose of elucidating the truth, a disputation will be held on the underwritten propositions at Wittenberg, under the presidency of the Reverend Father Martin Luther, Monk of the Order of St. Augustine, Master of Arts and of Sacred Theology, and ordinary Reader of the same in that place. He therefore asks those who cannot be present and discuss the subject with us orally, to do so by letter in their absence. In the name of our Lord Jesus Christ, Amen. . . .

5. The Pope has neither the will nor the power to remit any penalties except those which he has imposed by his own authority, or by that of the canons.

6. The Pope has no power to remit any guilt, except by declaring and warranting it to have been remitted by God; or at most by remitting cases reserved for himself; in which cases, if his power were [disregarded], guilt would certainly remain. . . .

H. Wace and C. A. Buchheim, eds., *First Principles of the Reformation* (London: John Murray, 1883), pp. 6–13.

20. Therefore the Pope, when he speaks of the plenary remission of all penalties, does not really mean really of all, but only of those imposed by himself.

21. Thus those preachers of indulgences are in error who say that by the indulgences of the Pope a man is freed and saved from all punishment.

22. For in fact he remits to souls in Purgatory no penalty which they would have had to pay in this life according to the canons.

23. If any entire remission of all penalties can be granted to any one it is certain that it is granted to none but the most perfect, that is to very few.

24. Hence, the greater part of the people must needs be deceived by his indiscriminate and high-sounding promise of release from penalties.

25. Such power over Purgatory as the Pope has in general, such has every bishop in his own diocese, and every parish priest in his own parish. . . .

27. They are wrong who say that the soul flies out of Purgatory as soon as the money thrown into the chest rattles.

28. It is certain that, when money rattles in the chest, avarice and gain may be increased, but the effect of the intercession of the Church depends on the will of God alone. . . .

32. Those who believe that, through letters of pardon, they are made sure of their own salvation will be eternally damned along with their teachers.

33. We must especially beware of those who say that these pardons from the Pope are that inestimable gift of God by which man is reconciled to God. . . .

35. They preach no Christian doctrine who teach that contrition is not necessary for those who buy souls (out of Purgatory) or buy confessional licenses.

37. Every true Christian, whether living or dead, has a share in all the benefits of Christ and of the Church, given by God, even without letters of pardon.

42. Christians should be taught that it is not the wish of the Pope that the buying of pardons should be in any way compared to works of mercy.

43. Christians should be taught that he who gives to a poor man, or lends to a needy man, does better than if he bought pardons.

45. Christians should be taught that he who sees any one in need, and, passing him by, gives money for pardons, is not purchasing for himself the indulgences of the Pope but the anger of God. . . .

50. Christians should be taught that, if the Pope were acquainted with the exactions of the Preachers of pardons, he would prefer that the Basilica of St. Peter should be burnt to ashes rather than that it should be built up with the skin, flesh, and bones of his sheep. . . .

62. The true treasure of the Church is the Holy Gospel of the glory and grace of God.

66. The treasures of indulgences are nets, wherewith they now fish for the riches of men.

86. Again; why does not the Pope, whose riches are at this day more ample than those of the wealthiest of the wealthy, build the Basilica of St. Peter with his own money rather than with that of poor believers. . . .

94. Christians should be exhorted to strive to follow Christ their head through pains, deaths, and hells.

95. And thus not trust to enter heaven through many tribulations, rather than in the security of peace.

Breaking with Rome (1520)

Within a period of six months in 1520, Luther finished three important treatises that sealed his break with the Roman Church. Excerpts from two of these treatises are presented below. In the *Address to the Christian Nobility of the German Nation* Luther advocated that the secular authorities in Germany undertake the reform that the Church would not. The treatise *On Christian Liberty* describes the liberating effect that pure faith in Christ has on man. Luther had written an accompanying letter to Pope Leo X stating that his writings were directed at the false doctrine and corruption surrounding the Church and not meant as a personal slight against Leo; nevertheless, the break with Rome was complete, as events in the next year proved.

Address to the Christian Nobility of the German Nation (1520)

MARTIN LUTHER

The Romanists have, with great adroitness, drawn three walls round themselves, with which they have hitherto protected themselves, so that no one could reform them, whereby all Christendom has fallen terribly.

Firstly, if pressed by the temporal power, they have affirmed and maintained that the temporal power has no jurisdiction over them, but on the contrary that the spiritual power is above the temporal.

Secondly, if it were proposed to admonish them with the Scriptures, they objected that no one may interpret the Scriptures but the Pope.

Thirdly, if they are threatened with a Council, they pretend that no one may call a Council but the Pope.

Thus they have secretly stolen our three rods, so that they may be unpunished, and entrenched themselves behind these three walls, to act with all wickedness and malice, as we now see. . . .

H. Wace and C. A. Buchheim, eds., *First Principles of the Reformation* (London: John Murray, 1883), pp. 20–21, 23, 25–26, 28–30. Translation modernized by the editor.

Now may God help us, and give us one of those trumpets, that over-threw the walls of Jericho, so that we may blow down these walls of straw and paper, and that we may set free our Christian rods, for the chastise-ment of sin, and expose the craft and deceit of the devil, so that we may amend ourselves by punishment and again obtain God's favor.

The First Wall

Let us, in the first place, attack the first wall.

It has been devised, that the Pope, bishops, priests and monks are called the Spiritual Estate; Princes, lords, [artisans] and peasants are the Tem-poral Estate; which is a very fine, hypocritical device. But let no one be made afraid by it; and that for this reason: That all Christians are truly of the Spiritual Estate, and there is no difference among them save of office alone. As St. Paul says (I Cor. 12), we are all one body, though each mem-ber does its own work, to serve the others. This is because we have one baptism, one gospel, one faith, and are all Christians alike; for baptism, gospel and faith, these alone make Spiritual and Christian people. . . .

It follows then, that between layman and priests, princes and bishops, or as they call it, between spiritual and temporal persons, the only real dif-ference is one of office and function, and not of estate: for they are all of the same Spiritual Estate, true priests, bishops and Popes, though their functions are not the same: just as among priests and monks every man has not the same functions. . . . Christ's body is not double or twofold, one temporal, the other spiritual. He is one head, and he has one body. . . .

The Second Wall

The second wall is even more tottering and weak: that they alone pretend to be considered masters of the Scriptures; although they learn nothing of them all their life, they assume authority, and juggle before us with impu-dent words, saying that the Pope cannot err in matters of faith, whether he be evil or good; [yet] they cannot prove it be a single letter. That is why the canon law contains so many heretical and unchristian, [even], unnatural laws. . . . If I had not read it, I could never have believed, that the Devil should have put forth such follies at Rome and find a following. . . .

The Third Wall

The third wall falls of itself, as soon as the first two have fallen; for if the Pope acts contrary to the Scriptures, we are bound to stand by the Scrip-tures, to punish and to constrain him, according to Christ's commandment: ["If your brother sins against you, go and tell him his fault. . . . If he does not listen, . . . tell it to the church (Matt. 18. 15–17)."]. . . . If then I am to accuse him before the church, I must collect the church together. Moreover they can show nothing in the Scriptures giving the Pope sole power to call and confirm councils; they have nothing but their own laws; but these hold good only so long as they are not injurious to Christianity and the laws of God. . . .

Therefore when need requires and the Pope is a cause of offence to Christendom, in these cases whoever can best do so, as a faithful member of the whole body, must do what he can to procure a true free council. . . .

And now I hope we have laid the false, lying spectre with which the Romanists have long terrified and stupefied our consciences. And we have shown that, like all the rest of us, they are subject to the temporal sword; that they have no authority to interpret the Scriptures by force without skill; and that they have no power to prevent a council or to pledge it in accordance with their pleasure, or to bind it beforehand, and deprive it of its freedom; and that if they do this, they are verily of the fellowship of Antichrist and the Devil, and have nothing of Christ but the name.

On Christian Liberty (1520)

MARTIN LUTHER

That I may open, then, an easier way for the ignorant—for these alone I am trying to serve—I first lay down these two propositions, concerning spiritual liberty and servitude.

A Christian man is the most free lord of all, and subject to none; a Christian man is the most dutiful servant of all, and subject to every one.

Although these statements appear contradictory, yet, when they are found to agree together, they will be highly serviceable to my purpose. They are both the statements of Paul himself, who says: "Though I be free from all men, yet have I made myself servant unto all" (I Cor. 9.19), and: "Owe no man anything, but to love one another." (Rom. 13.8) Now love is by its own nature dutiful and obedient to the beloved object. Thus even Christ, though Lord of all things, was yet made of a woman; made under the law; at once free and a servant; at once in the form of God and in the form of a servant.

Let us examine the subject on a deeper and less simple principle. Man is composed of a two-fold nature, a spiritual and a bodily. As regards the spiritual nature, which they name the soul, he is called the spiritual, inward, new man; as regards the bodily nature, which they name the flesh, he is called the fleshly, outward, old man. The Apostle speaks of this: "Though our outward man perish, yet the inward man is renewed day by day." (II Cor. 4.16.) The result of this diversity is that in the Scriptures

H. Wace and C. A. Buchheim, eds., *First Principles of the Reformation* (London: John Murray, 1883), pp. 104–125. Translation modernized by the editor.

opposing statements are made concerning the same man; the fact being that in the same man these two men are opposed to one another; the flesh lusting against the spirit, and the spirit against the flesh. (Gal. 5.17.). . . .

And, to cast everything aside, even speculations, meditations, and whatever things can be performed by the exertions of the soul itself, are of no profit. One thing, and one alone, is necessary for life, justification, and Christian liberty; and that is the most holy word of God, the Gospel of Christ, as He says: "I am the resurrection and the life; he that believeth in me shall not die eternally" (John 11.25); and also (John 8.36) "If the Son shall make you free, ye shall be free indeed"; and (Matt. 4.4) "Man shall not live by bread alone."

Let us therefore hold it for certain and firmly established that the soul can do without everything, except the word of God, without which none at all of its wants are provided for. But having the word, it is rich and wants for nothing; since that is the word of life, of truth, of light, of peace, of justification, of salvation, of joy, of liberty, of wisdom, of virtue, of grace, of glory, and of every good thing. . . .

Therefore, the first care of every Christian ought to be, to lay aside all reliance on works, and strengthen his faith alone more and more, and by it grow in the knowledge, not of works, but of Christ Jesus, who has suffered and risen again for him. . . . And yet there is nothing of which I have need—for faith alone suffices for my salvation—unless that, in it, faith may exercise the power and empire of its liberty. This is the inestimable power and liberty of Christians.

Nor are we only kings and the freest of all men, but also priests for ever, a dignity far higher than kingship, because by that priesthood we are worthy to appear before God, to pray for others, and to teach one another mutually the things which are of God. For these are the duties of priests, and they cannot possibly be permitted to any unbeliever. Christ has obtained for us this favor, if we believe in Him, that, just as we are His brethren, and co-heirs and fellow kings with Him, so we should be also fellow priests with Him, and venture with confidence, through the spirit of faith, to come into the presence of God, and cry "Abba, Father!" and to pray for one another, and to do all things which we see done and figured in the visible and corporeal office of priesthood. But to an unbelieving person nothing renders service or works for good. He himself is in servitude to all things, and all things turn out for evil to him, because he used all things in an impious way for his own advantage, and not for the glory of God. And thus he is not a priest, but a profane person, whose prayers are turned into sin; nor does he ever appear in the presence of God, because God does not hear sinners. . . .

Here you will ask: "If all who are in the Church are priests, by what character are those, whom we now call priests, to be distinguished from the laity?" I reply: By the use of these words, "priest," "clergy," "spiritual person," "ecclesiastic," an injustice has been done, since they have been transferred from the remaining body of Christians to those few, who are now, by a hurtful custom, call ecclesiastics. For Holy Scripture makes no distinction between them, except that those, who are now boastfully called popes, bishops, and lords, it calls ministers, servants, and stewards, who are to serve the rest in the ministry of the World, for teaching the faith of Christ and the liberty of believers. For though it is true that we are all equally priests, yet we cannot, nor, if we could, ought we all to minister and teach publicly. Thus Paul says: "Let a man so account of us as of the ministers of Christ, and stewards of the mysteries of God." (I Cor. 4.1)

This bad system has now issued a pompous display of power, and such a terrible tyranny, that no earthly government can be compared to it, as if the laity were something else than Christians. Through this perversion of things it has happened that the knowledge of Christian grace, of faith, of liberty, and altogether of Christ, has utterly perished, and has been succeeded by an intolerable bondage to human works and laws; and, according to the Lamentations of Jeremiah, we have become the slaves of the vilest men on earth, who abuse our misery to all the disgraceful and ignominious purposes of their own will. . . .

True then are these two sayings: Good works do not make a good man, but a good man does good works. Bad works do not make a bad man, but a bad man does bad works. Thus it is always necessary that the substance or person should be good before any good works can be done, and that good works should follow and proceed from a good person. As Christ says: "A good tree cannot bring forth evil fruit, neither can a corrupt tree bring forth good fruit." (Matt. 7.18.) Now it is clear that the fruit does not bear the tree, nor does the tree grow on the fruit; but, on the contrary, the trees bear the fruit and the fruit grows on the trees. . . .

Here is the truly Christian life; here is faith really working by love; when a man applies himself with joy and love to the works of that freest servitude, in which he serves others voluntarily and for naught; himself abundantly satisfied in the fullness and riches of his own faith.

Address at the Diet of Worms (1521)

MARTIN LUTHER

After his excommunication by Leo X in June 1520, Luther was summoned to appear before a Diet (assembly) of prelates and officials of the Holy Roman Empire in the city of Worms to answer questions about his heretical writings. His safe conduct to the meeting was guaranteed by the Holy Roman Emperor Charles V, who presided over the Diet. Accompanied by his secular protector, Frederick the Wise, Elector of Saxony, Luther ap-

J. Pelikan, ed., *Luther's Works*, vol. 2: *Career of the Reformer* (Saint Louis: Concordia Publishing House, 1958), pp. 109–112. Copyright © 1958 by Concordia Publishing House. Used by permission.

Martin Luther by Lucas Cranach the Elder (1521). This picture of Luther was painted in the same year that he defied the Pope and the Holy Roman Emperor at the Diet of Worms. His complete break with Rome ushered in an age of religious reform. (*The Metropolitan Museum of Art, Gift of Robert Lehman, 1955*)

peared on April 17, 1521. When asked whether he wished to defend all his writings or retract some, Luther delivered this famous speech. On April 23, Luther secretly left Worms and was hidden by friends at Wartburg castle. Charles V's edict against Luther is the second selection.

"Most serene emperor, most illustrious princes, most clement lords, obedient to the time set for me yesterday evening, I appear before you, beseeching you, by the mercy of God, that your most serene majesty and your most illustrious lordships may deign to listen graciously to this my cause—which is, as I hope, a cause of justice and truth. If through my inexperience I have either not given the proper titles to some, or have offended in some manner against court customs and etiquette, I beseech you to kindly pardon me, as a man accustomed not to courts but to the cells of monks. I can bear no other witness about myself but that I have taught and written up to this time with simplicity of heart, as I had in view only the glory of God and the sound instruction of Christ's faithful. . . .

"[A] group of my books attacks the papacy and the affairs of the papists as those who both by their doctrines and very wicked examples have laid waste the Christian world with evil that affects the spirit and the body. For no one can deny or conceal this fact, when the experience of all and the complaints of everyone witness that through the decrees of the pope and the doctrines of men the consciences of the faithful have been most miserably entangled, tortured, and torn to pieces. Also, property and possessions, especially in this illustrious nation of Germany, have been devoured by an unbelievable tyranny and are being devoured to this time without letup and by unworthy means. [Yet the papists] by their own decrees . . . warn that the papal laws and doctrines which are contrary to the gospel or the opinions of the fathers are to be regarded as erroneous and reprehensible. If, therefore, I should have retracted these writings, I should have done nothing other than to give strength to this [papal] tyranny and I should have opened not only windows but doors to such great godlessness. It would rage further and more freely than ever it has dared up to this time. Yes, from the proof of such a revocation on my part, their wholly lawless and unrestrained kingdom of wickedness would become still more intolerable for the already wretched people; and their rule would be further strengthened and established, especially if it should be reported that this evil deed had been done by me by virtue of the authority of your most serene majesty and the whole Roman Empire. Good God! What a cover for wickedness and tyranny I should have then become.

"I have written a third sort of book against some private and (as they say) distinguished individuals—those, namely, who strive to preserve the Roman tyranny and to destroy the godliness taught by me. Against these I confess I have been more violent than my religion or profession demands. But then, I do not set myself up as a saint; neither am I disputing about my life, but about the teachings of Christ. It is not proper for me to retract these works, because by this retraction it would again happen that tyranny and godlessness would, with my patronage, rule and rage among the people of God more violently than ever before.

"However, because I am a man and not God, I am not able to shield my books with any other protection than that which my Lord Jesus Christ himself offered for his teaching. When questioned before Annas about his teaching and struck by a servant, he said: 'If I have spoken wrongly, bear witness to the wrong' [John 18:19–23]. If the Lord himself, who knew that he could not err, did not refuse to hear testimony against his teaching, even from the lowliest servant, how much more ought I, who am the lowest scum and able to do nothing except err, desire and expect that somebody should want to offer testimony against my teaching! Therefore, I ask by the mercy of God, may your most serene majesty, most illustrious lordships, or anyone at all who is able, either high or low, bear witness, expose my errors, overthrowing them by the writings of the prophets and the evangelists. Once I have been taught I shall be quite ready to renounce every error, and I shall be the first to cast my books into the fire.

"From these remarks I think it is clear that I have sufficiently considered and weighed the hazards and dangers, as well as the excitement and dissensions aroused in the world as a result of my teachings, things about which I was gravely and forcefully warned yesterday. To see excitement and dissension arise because of the Word of God is to me clearly the most joyful aspect of all in these matters. For this is the way, the opportunity, and the result of the Word of God, just as He [Christ] said, 'I have not come to bring peace, but a sword. For I have come to set a man against his father, etc.' [Matthew 10:34–35]. . . . Therefore we must fear God. I do not say these things because there is a need of either my teachings or my warnings for such leaders as you, but because I must not withhold the allegiance which I owe my Germany. With these words I commend myself to your most serene majesty and to your lordships, humbly asking that I not be allowed through the agitation of my enemies, without cause, to be made hateful to you. I have finished."

When I had finished, the speaker for the emperor said, as if in reproach that I had not answered the question, that I ought not call into question those things which had been condemned and defined in councils; therefore what was sought from me was not a horned response, but a simple one, whether or not I wished to retract.

Here I answered:

"Since then your serene majesty and your lordships seek a simple answer, I will give it in this manner, neither horned nor toothed: Unless I am convinced by the testimony of the Scriptures or by clear reason (for I do not trust either in the pope or in councils alone, since it is well known that they have often errored and contradicted themselves), I am bound by the Scriptures I have quoted and my conscience is captive to the Word of God. I cannot and I will not retract anything, since it is neither safe nor right to go against conscience.

"I cannot do otherwise, here I stand, may God help me, Amen."

The Edict of Worms (1521)

EMPEROR CHARLES V

In view of . . . the fact that Martin Luther still persists obstinately and perversely in maintaining his heretical opinions, and consequently all pious and God-fearing persons abominate and abhor him as one mad or possessed by a demon . . . we have declared and made known that the said Martin Luther shall hereafter be held and esteemed by each and all of us as a limb cut off from the Church of God, an obstinate schismatic and manifest heretic. . . .

And we publicly attest by these letters that we order and command each and all of you, as you owe fidelity to us and the Holy Empire, and would escape the penalties of the crime of treason, and the ban and over-ban of the Empire, and the forfeiture of all regalia, fiefs, privileges, and immunities, which up to this time you have in any way obtained from our predecessors, ourself, and the Holy Roman Empire—commanding, we say, in the name of the Roman and imperial majesty, we strictly order that immediately after the expiration of the appointed twenty days, terminating on the fourteenth day of May, you shall refuse to give the aforesaid Martin Luther hospitality, lodging, food, or drink; neither shall any one, by word or deed, secretly or openly, succor or assist him by counsel or help; but in whatever place you meet him, you shall proceed against him; if you have sufficient force, you shall take him prisoner and keep him in close custody; you shall deliver him, or cause him to be delivered, to us or at least let us know where he may be captured. In the meanwhile you shall keep him closely imprisoned until you receive notice from us what further to do, according to the direction of the laws. And for such holy and pious work we will indemnify you for your trouble and expense. . . .

And in order that all this may be done and credit given to this document we have sealed it with our imperial seal, which has been affixed in our imperial city of Worms, on the eighth day of May, after the birth of Christ 1521, in the second year of our reign over the Roman Empire, and over our other lands the sixth.

By our lord the emperor's own command.

Social and Political Aspects of the Lutheran Reformation

The Lutheran Reformation was not simply spiritual or corrective in nature, for it had many political and social repercussions as well. In response to the celibacy demanded of priests by the Church, Luther

James H. Robinson, ed., *Readings in European History*, vol. 2 (Boston: Ginn and Company, 1906), pp. 87–88.

advocated that clergy be allowed to marry. He himself married a former nun. Such defiance in one sphere was confusing for certain elements of society that saw Luther as their champion as well. In 1524, a major peasant revolt broke out in Germany as social and economic conflicts came to a head. The peasants demanded freedom from the long-standing feudal obligations of serfdom. Luther understood that the survival of his movement depended on the political influence and protection of the nobility. Although Luther sympathized with the peasants, he clearly sided with the nobility, and they savagely crushed the revolt.

On Celibacy and Marriage

MARTIN LUTHER

First, not every priest can do without a woman, not only on account of the weakness of the flesh but much more because of the needs of the household. If, then, he is to keep a woman, and the pope grants him permission to do so, but he may not have her in marriage, what is this but leaving a man and a woman alone and forbidding them to fall? It is like putting fire and straw together and commanding that there shall be neither smoke nor fire. Secondly, the pope has as little power to give this command as he has to forbid eating, drinking, the natural process of bodily elimination or becoming fat. No one, therefore, is in duty bound to keep this commandment and the pope is responsible for all the sins that are committed against this ordinance, for all the souls lost thereby, and for all the consciences thereby confused and tortured. Consequently, he undoubtedly has deserved long ago that someone should drive him out of the world, so many souls has he strangled with this devilish snare; although I hope that God has been more gracious to many of them at their end than the pope had been during their life. Nothing good has ever come out of the papacy and its laws, nor ever will.

Listen! In all my days I have not heard the confession of a nun, but in the light of Scripture I shall hit upon how matters fare with her and know I shall not be lying. If a girl is not sustained by great and exceptional grace, she can live without a man as little as she can without eating, drinking, sleeping, and other natural necessities. Nor, on the other hand, can a man dispense with a wife. The reason for this is that procreating children is an urge planted as deeply in human nature as eating and drinking. That is why God has given and put into the body the organs, arteries, fluxes, and everything that serves it. Therefore what is he doing who would check this process and keep nature from running its desired and intended course? He is attempting to keep nature from being nature, fire from burning, water from wetting, and a man from eating, drinking, and sleeping.

E. M. Plass, ed., *What Luther Says*, vol. 2 (Saint Louis: Concordia Publishing House, 1959), pp. 888–889, 891. Copyright © 1959 by Concordia Publishing House. Used by permission.

Whoever intends to enter married life should do so in faith and in God's name. He should pray that it may prosper according to His will and that marriage may not be treated as a matter of fun and folly. It is a hazardous matter and as serious as anything on earth can be. Therefore we should not rush into it as the world does, in keeping with its frivolousness and wantonness and in pursuit of its pleasure; but before taking this step we should consult God, so that we may lead our married life to His glory. Those who do not go about it in this way may certainly thank God if it turns out well. If it turns out badly, they should not be surprised; for they did not begin it in the name of God and did not ask for His blessing.

Condemnation of the Peasant Revolt (1524)

MARTIN LUTHER

In my preceding pamphlet [on the "Twelve Articles"] I had no occasion to condemn the peasants, because they promised to yield to law and better instruction, as Christ also demands (Matt. 7.1). But before I can turn around, they go out and appeal to force, in spite of their promises and rob and pillage and act like mad dogs. From this it is quite apparent what they had in their false minds, and that what they put forth under the name of the gospel in the "Twelve Articles" was all vain pretense. In short, they practice mere devil's work, and it is the arch-devil himself who reigns at Muhlhausen, indulging in nothing but robbery, murder, and bloodshed; as Christ says of the devil in John 8.44, "he was a murderer from the beginning." Since, therefore, those peasants and miserable wretches allow themselves to be led astray and act differently from what they declared, I likewise must write differently concerning them; and first bring their sins before their eyes, as God commands (Isa. 58.1; Ezek. 2.7), whether perchance some of them may come to their senses; and, further, I would instruct those in authority how to conduct themselves in this matter.

With threefold horrible sins against God and men have these peasants loaded themselves, for which they have deserved a manifold death of body and soul.

First, they have sworn to their true and gracious rulers to be submissive and obedient, in accord with God's command (Matt. 22.21), "Render therefore unto Caesar the things which are Caesar's," and (Rom. 13.1), "Let every soul be subject unto the higher powers." But since they have deliberately and sacreligiously abandoned their obedience, and in addition have dared to oppose their lords, they have thereby forfeited body and soul, as perfidious, perjured, lying, disobedient wretches and scoundrels are wont to do. Wherefore St. Paul judges them saying (Rom. 13.2), "And they that resist shall receive to themselves damnation." The peasants will incur this sentence, sooner or later; for God wills that fidelity and allegiance shall be sacredly kept.

James H. Robinson, ed., *Readings in European History* (Boston: Ginn and Company, 1904), pp. 106–108.

Second, they cause uproar and sacreligiously rob and pillage monasteries and castles that do not belong to them, for which, like public highwaymen and murderers, they deserve the twofold death of body and soul. It is right and lawful to slay at the first opportunity a rebellious person, who is known as such, for he is already under God's and the emperor's ban. Every man is at once judge and executioner of a public rebel; just as, when a fire starts, he who can extinguish it first is the best fellow. Rebellion is not simply vile murder, but is like a great fire that kindles and devastates a country; it fills the land with murder and bloodshed, makes widows and orphans, and destroys everything, like the greatest calamity. Therefore, whosoever can, should smite, strangle, and stab, secretly or publicly, and should remember that there is nothing more poisonous, pernicious, and devilish than a rebellious man. Just as one must slay a mad dog, so, if you do not fight the rebels, they will fight you, and the whole country with you.

Third, they cloak their frightful and revolting sins with the gospel, call themselves Christian brethren, swear allegiance, and compel people to join them in such abominations. Thereby they become the greatest blasphemers and violators of God's holy name, and serve and honor the devil under the semblance of the gospel, so that they have ten times deserved death of body and soul, for never have I heard of uglier sins. And I believe also that the devil forsees the judgment day, that he undertakes such an unheard-of measure; as if he said, "It is the last and therefore it shall be the worst; I'll stir up the dregs and knock the very bottom out." May the Lord restrain him! Lo, how mighty a prince is the devil, how he holds the world in his hands and can put it to confusion: who else could so soon capture so many thousands of peasants, lead them astray, blind and deceive them, stir them to revolt, and make them the willing executioners of his malice. . . .

And should the peasants prevail (which God forbid!),—for all things are possible to God, and we know not but that he is preparing for the judgment day, which cannot be far distant, and may purpose to destroy, by means of the devil, all order and authority and throw the world into wild chaos,—yet surely they who are found, sword in hand, shall perish in the wreck with clear consciences, leaving to the devil the kingdom of this world and receiving instead the eternal kingdom. For we are come upon such strange times that a prince may more easily win heaven by the shedding of blood than others by prayers.

In the Wake of Luther

Ulrich Zwingli and the Swiss Reformation

Another major figure of this period was the leader of the Swiss reform efforts, Ulrich Zwingli. Influenced by northern Humanists such as Erasmus, Zwingli became the people's priest in the Great Minster of Zurich. Zwingli composed his *Sixty-seven Articles* as a basis for discussing his objections to the mass, compulsory fasting, pilgrimages, clerical celibacy, indulgences, confessions, and purgatory, among other issues. Over six hundred men assembled in the Zurich town hall for the discussion and enthusiastically approved the teachings for promotion throughout the area. Most are compatible with Lutheran theology; however, Luther and Zwingli remained at odds over the nature of the Eucharist and transubstantiation. The Catholic Church taught that the bread and wine were actually transformed by the priest into the body and blood of Christ; Luther accepted the "Real Presence" of Christ in the ceremony, but Zwingli maintained that the bread and wine were only a symbolic presence. As a result, Luther regarded Zwingli as a dangerous radical and refused to support his Protestant movement.

The Sixty-seven Articles (1523)

ULRICH ZWINGLI

The articles and opinions below, I, Ulrich Zwingli, confess to have preached in the worthy city of Zurich as based upon the Scriptures which are called inspired by God, and I offer to protect and conquer with the said articles, and where I have not now correctly understood said Scriptures I shall allow myself to be taught better, but only from said Scriptures.

3. Christ is the only way to salvation for all who ever were, are and shall be.

6. For Jesus Christ is the guide and leader, promised by God to all human beings, which promise was fulfilled.

7. He is an eternal salvation and head of all believers, who are his body, but which is dead and can do nothing without him.

15. For in the faith rests our salvation, and in unbelief our damnation; for all truth is clear to Him.

16. In the gospel one learns that human doctrines and decrees do not aid in salvation.

About the Pope

17. That Christ is the only eternal high priest, wherefrom it follows that those who have called themselves high priests have opposed the honor and power of Christ, yea, cast it out.

About the Intercession of Saints

20. That God desires to give us all things in His name, whence it follows that outside of this life we need no mediator except Himself.

Samuel Macauley Jackson, ed., *Selected Works of Huldreich Zwingli (1484–1531)* (Philadelphia: University of Pennsylvania, 1901), pp. 111–117.

21. That when we pray for each other on earth, we do so in such fashion that we believe that all things are given to us through Christ alone.

Concerning Clerical Property

23. That Christ scorns the property and pomp of this world, whence. . . . it follows that those who attract wealth to themselves in His name slander Him terribly when they make Him a pretext for their avarice and wilfullness.

About the Marriage of Ecclesiasts

28. That all which God has allowed or not forbidden is righteous, hence marriage is permitted to all human beings.
30. That those who promise chastity [outside of matrimony] take foolishly or childishly too much upon themselves, whence is learned that those who make such vows do wrong to the pious being.
49. Greater offence I know not than that one does not allow priests to have wives, but permits them to hire prostitutes. Out upon the shame!

About Remittance of Sin

50. God alone remits sin through Jesus Christ, His Son and alone our Lord.
52. Hence the confession which is made to the priest or neighbor shall not be declared to be a remittance of sin, but only a seeking for advice.
54. Christ has borne all our pains and labor. Hence whoever assigns to works of penance what belongs to Christ errs and slanders God.
56. Whoever remits an sin only for the sake of money is the . . . real messenger of the devil personified.

John Calvin and the Genevan Reformation

Although Lutheranism formed the basis of the Reformation, by the mid-sixteenth century, it had lost much of its energy and was confined to Germany and Scandinavia. The movement was spread throughout Europe by other reformers, the most influential of whom was John Calvin (1509–1564).

A trained lawyer and classical scholar, Calvin had been a convert to Luther's ideas, and this forced him to leave France and settle in Geneva in the 1530s. There in the 1540s he established a very structured society that can best be described as a theocracy. His doctrines were primarily Lutheran in nature, but Calvin went a step beyond and stressed the doctrine of predestination: One's salvation had already been determined by God, and those elect who had been "chosen" gave evidence of their calling by living exemplary lives. Calvinism became popular in the Netherlands and Scotland and it formed the core of the Puritan belief that was to be so influential in the colonization of America. The following excerpts reveal Calvin's concept of predestination and his strict regulation of lives and beliefs in Geneva.

Predestination: Institutes of the Christian Religion (1536)

JOHN CALVIN

The covenant of life is not preached equally to all, and among those to whom it is preached, does not always meet with the same reception. This diversity displays the unsearchable depth of the divine judgment, and is without doubt subordinate to God's purpose of eternal election. But it is plainly owing to the mere pleasure of God that salvation is spontaneously offered to some, while others have no access to it, great and difficult questions immediately arise, questions which are inexplicable, when just views are not entertained concerning election and predestination. . . .

By predestination we mean the eternal decree of God, by which he determined with himself whatever he wished to happen with regard to every man. All are not created on equal terms, but some are preordained to eternal life, others to eternal damnation; and, accordingly, as each has been created for one or other of these ends, we say that he has been predestined to life or to death. . . .

We say, then, that Scripture clearly proves this much, that God by his eternal and immutable counsel determined once for all those whom it was his pleasure one day to admit to salvation, and those whom, on the other hand, it was his pleasure to doom to destruction. We maintain that this counsel, as regards the elect, is founded on his free mercy, without any respect to human worth, while those whom he dooms to destruction are excluded from access to life by a just and blameless, but at the same time incomprehensible judgment. In regard to the elect, we regard calling as the evidence of election, and justification as another symbol of its manifestation, until it is fully accomplished by the attainment of glory. But as the Lord seals his elect by calling and justification, so by excluding the reprobate either from the knowledge of his name or the sanctification of his Spirit, he by these marks in a manner discloses the judgment which awaits them. I will here omit many of the fictions which foolish men have devised to everthrow predestination. There is no need of refuting objections which the moment they are produced abundantly betray their hollowness. I will dwell only on those points which either form the subject of dispute among the learned, or may occasion any difficulty to the simple. . . .

John Calvin, *Institutes of the Christian Religion,* vol. 2, trans. Henry Beveridge (Edinburgh: Calvin Translation Society, 1845), pp. 529, 534, 540.

Genevan Catechism (1541):
Concerning the Lord's Supper

JOHN CALVIN

The minister.   Have we in the supper simply a signification of the things above mentioned, or are they given to us in reality?

The child.   Since Jesus Christ is truth itself there can be no doubt that the promises he has made regarding the supper are accomplished, and that what is figured there is verified there also. Wherefore according as he promises and represents I have no doubt that he makes us partakers of his own substance, in order that he may unite us with him in one life.

The minister.   But how may this be, when the Body of Jesus Christ is in heaven, and we are on this early pilgrimage?

The child.   It comes about through the incomprehensible power of his spirit, which may indeed unite things widely separated in space.

The minister.   You do not understand then that the body is enclosed in the bread, or the blood in the cup?

The child.   No. On the contrary, in order that the reality of the sacrament be achieved our hearts must be raised to heaven, where Jesus Christ dwells in the glory of the Father, whence we await him for our redemption; and we are not to seek him in these corruptible elements.

The minister.   You understand then that there are two things in this sacrament: the natural bread and wine, which we see with the eye, touch with the hand and perceive with the taste; and Jesus Christ, through whom our souls are inwardly nourished?

The child.   I do. In such a way moreover that we have there the very witness and so say a pledge of the resurrection of our bodies; since they are made partakers in the symbol of life.

Ordinances for the Regulation of Churches (1547)

JOHN CALVIN

Blasphemy

Whoever shall have blasphemed, swearing by the body or by the blood of our Lord, or in similar manner, he shall be made to kiss the earth for the first offence; for the second to pay 5 sous, and for the third 6 sous, and for the last offence be put in the pillory for one hour.

"Genevan Catechism" is from James H. Robinson, ed., *Translations and Reprints from the Original Sources of European History,* vol. 3 (Philadelphia: University of Pennsylvania, 1902), pp. 8–9

"Ordinances for the Regulation of Churches" is from James H. Robinson, ed., *Translations and Reprints from the Original Sources of European History,* vol. 3 (Philadelphia: University of Pennsylvania, 1902), pp. 10–11.

Drunkeness

1. That no one shall invite another to drink under penalty of 3 sous.
2. That taverns shall be closed during the sermon, under penalty that the tavern-keeper shall pay 3 sous, and whoever may be found therein shall pay the same amount.
3. If any one be found intoxicated he shall pay for the first offence 3 sous and shall be remanded to the consistory; for the second offence he shall be held to pay the same sum of 6 sous, and for the third 10 sous and be put in prison.

Songs and Dances

If any one sing immoral, dissolute or outrageous songs, or dance the *virollet* or other dance, he shall be put in prison for three days and then sent to the consistory.

Usury

That no one shall take upon interest or profit more than five percent, upon penalty of confiscation of the principal and of being condemned to make restitution as the case may demand.

Games

That no one shall play at any dissolute game or at any game whatsoever it may be, neither for gold nor silver nor for any excessive stake, upon penalty of 5 sous and forfeiture of stake played for.

How soon Marriage must be Consummated after the Promise is Made

After the promise is made the marriage shall not be deferred more than six weeks; otherwise the parties shall be called before the consistory, in order that they may be admonished. If they do not obey they shall be remanded to the council and be constrained to celebrate the marriage.

Concerning the Celebration of the Marriage

That the parties at the time when they are to be married shall go modestly to the church, without drummers and minstrels, preserving an order and gravity becoming to Christians; and this before the last stroke of the bell, in order that the marriage blessing may be given before the sermon. If they are negligent and come too late they shall be sent away.

Of the Common Residence of Husband and Wife

That the husband shall have his wife with him and they shall live in the same house, maintaining a common household, and if it should happen that one should leave the other to life apart they shall be summoned in order that they may be remonstrated with and constrained to return, the one to the other.

The Catholic Reformation

The Society of Jesus

During the Protestant movement, the Catholic Church was active in its own efforts to reform from within. The Society of Jesus (Jesuits) was a religious order founded by Ignatius Loyola in 1540. Loyola (1491–1556) was a soldier who had turned to religion while recovering from wounds. Under Loyola's firm leadership, the Jesuits became a disciplined organization that was dedicated to serving the pope with unquestioned loyalty. The next two selections from the constitutions of the society and the famous spiritual exercises of Loyola demonstrate the purity and determination of these Catholic reformers.

Constitution (1540)

He who desires to fight for God under the banner of the cross in our society,—which we wish to distinguish by the name of Jesus,—and to serve God alone and the Roman pontiff, his vicar on earth, after a solemn vow of perpetual chastity, shall set this thought before his mind, that he is a part of a society founded for the especial purpose of providing for the advancement of souls in Christian life and doctrine and for the propagation of faith through public preaching and the ministry of the word of God, spiritual exercises and deeds of charity, and in particular through the training of the young and ignorant in Christianity and through the spiritual consolation of the faithful of Christ in hearing confessions; and he shall take care to keep first God and next the purpose of this organization always before his eyes. . . .

All the members shall realize, and shall recall daily, as long as they live, that this society as a whole and in every part is fighting for God under faithful obedience to one most holy lord, the pope, and to other Roman pontiffs who succeed him. And although we are taught in the gospel and

James H. Robinson, ed., *Readings in European History* (Boston: Ginn and Company, 1904), pp. 162–163.

through the orthodox faith to recognize and steadfastly profess that all the faithful of Christ are subject to the Roman pontiff as their head and as the vicar of Jesus Christ, yet we have adjudged that, for the special promotion of greater humility in our society and the perfect mortification of every individual and the sacrifice of our own wills, we should each be bound by a peculiar vow, in addition to the general obligation, that whatever the present Roman pontiff, or any future one, may from time to time decree regarding the welfare of souls and the propagation of the faith, we are pledged to obey without evasion or excuse, instantly, so far as in us lies, whether he send us to the Turks or any other infidels, even to those who inhabit the regions men call the Indies; whether to heretics or schismatics, or, on the other hand, to certain of the faithful.

Spiritual Exercises (1548)

IGNATIUS LOYOLA

1. Always to be ready to obey with mind and heart, setting aside all judgement of one's own, the true spouse of Jesus Christ, our holy mother our infallible and orthodox mistress, the Catholic Church, whose authority is exercised over us by the hierarchy.

2. To commend the confession of sins to a priest as it is practised in the Church; the reception of the Holy Eucharist once a year, or better still every week, or at least every month, with the necessary preparation.

4. To have a great esteem for the religious orders, and to give the preference to celibacy or virginity over the married state.

5. To approve of the religious vows of chastity, poverty, perpetual obedience, as well as the other works of perfection and supererogation. Let us remark in passing, that we must never engage by vow to take a state (such e.g. as marriage) that would be an impediment to one more perfect. . . .

6. To praise relics, the veneration and invocation of Saints: also the stations, and pious pilgrimages, indulgences, jubilees, the custom of lighting candles in the churches, and other such aids to piety and devotion.

9. To uphold especially all the precepts of the Church, and not censure them in any manner; but, on the contrary, to defend them promptly, with reasons drawn from all sources, against those who criticize them.

10. To be eager to commend the decrees, mandates, traditions, rites and conduct; although there may not always be the uprightness of conduct that there ought to be, yet to attack or revile them in private or in public tends to scandal and disorder. Such attacks set the people against their princes and pastors; we must avoid such reproaches and never attack supe-

Henry Bettenson, ed., *Documents of the Christian Church*, 2nd ed. (London: Oxford University Press, 1963), pp. 364–365. Reprinted by permission of the publisher.

riors before inferiors. The best course is to make private approach to those who have power to remedy the evil.

The Council of Trent (1545–1563)

The Council of Trent was an involved effort by the Catholic Church to clarify its doctrine and bring about internal reform. The Church sought to make its own stand in the face of the Protestant threat, and thus its traditional doctrinal views are set forth with a firmness and confidence, as the first excerpt indicates. The second excerpt is from the oration by Bishop Jerome Ragozonus, which was delivered during the last session of the Council of Trent and summarized its accomplishments. One of the most significant actions of Trent was its reorganization and codification of laws concerning censorship and the prohibition of books. The last selection, published after the Council closed, sets out some of the restrictions. These general rules were in force until they were replaced with new decrees in 1897.

The Profession of Faith

I profess . . . that true God is offered in the Mass, a proper and propitiatory sacrifice for the living and the dead, and that in the most Holy Eucharist there are truly, really and substantially the body and blood together with the soul and divinity of Our Lord Jesus Christ, and that a conversion is made of the whole substance of bread into his body and of the whole substance of wine into his blood, which conversion the Catholic Church calls transubstantiation. I also confess that the whole and entire Christ and the true sacrament is taken under the one species alone.

I hold unswervingly that there is a purgatory and that the souls there detained are helped by the intercessions of the faithful; likewise also that the Saints who reign with Christ are to be venerated and invoked; that they offer prayers to God for us and that their relics are to be venerated. I firmly assert that the images of Christ and of the ever-Virgin Mother of God, as also those of the older Saints, are to be kept and retained, and that due honour and veneration is to be accorded them; and I affirm that the power of indulgences has been left by Christ in the Church, and that their use is very salutary for Christian people.

I recognize the Holy Catholic and Apostolic Roman Church as the Mother and mistress of all churches; and I vow and swear true obedience to the

Henry Bettenson, ed., *Documents of the Christian Church*, 2nd ed. (London: Oxford University Press, 1963), pp. 364–365. Reprinted by permission of the publisher.

Roman Pontiff, the successor of blessed Peter, the chief of the Apostles and the representative [*vicarius*] of Jesus Christ.

I accept and profess, without doubting the traditions, definitions and declarations of the sacred Canons and Oecumenical Councils and especially those of the holy Council of Trent. . . .

The Closing Oration at Trent (1563)

BISHOP JEROME RAGOZONUS

"Hear these things, all you nations; give ear all inhabitants of the world!"

The Council of Trent which was begun long ago, was for a time suspended, often postponed and dispersed, now at last through a singular favor of almighty God and with a complete and wonderful accord of all ranks and nations has come to a close. This most happy day has dawned for the Christian people; the day in which the temple of the Lord, often shattered and destroyed, is restored and completed, and this one ship, laden with every blessing and buffeted by the worst and most relentless storms and waves, is brought safely into port. Oh, that those for whose sake this voyage was chiefly undertaken had decided to board it with us; that those who caused us to take this work in hand had participated in the erection of this edifice! Then indeed we would now have reason for greater rejoicing. But it is certainly not through our fault that it so happened.

For that reason we chose this city, situated at the entrance to Germany, situated almost at the threshold of their homes. We have, in order to give them no ground for suspicion that the place is not entirely free, employed no guard for ourselves; we granted them that public security which they requested and which they themselves had drawn up. For a long time we awaited them and never did we cease to exhort them and plead with them to come here and learn the truth. Indeed, even in their absence we were, I think, sufficiently concerned about them. In a twofold respect medicine had to be applied to their weak and infirm spirits, one, the explanation and confirmation of the teaching of the Catholic and truly evangelical faith in those matters upon which they had cast doubt and which at this time appeared opportune for the dispersion and destruction of all the darkness of errors; the other, the restoration of ecclesiastical discipline, the collapse of which they claim was the chief cause of their severance from us. We have amply accomplished both so far as the conditions of the times would permit.

At the beginning, [the Council of Trent] . . . made a profession of faith, in order to lay a foundation, as it were, for subsequent transactions and to point out by what witnesses and evidence the definition of articles of faith must be supported. . . . Through this most extraordinary decree in the memory of man, well-nigh all heresies are strangled and, as darkness be-

J. Barry Colman, ed., *Readings in Church History*, rev. ed., vol. 2 (Westminster, Md.: Christian Classics, Inc., 1985), pp. 699–703.

fore the sun, dispersed and dissipated, and the truth appears with such clearness and splendor that no one can any longer pretend not to see so great a light.

[Most esteemed fathers,] you have thereby removed from the celebration of the Mass all superstition, all greed for lucre and all irreverence; forbidden vagrant, unknown and depraved priests to offer this holy sacrifice; removed its celebration from private homes and profane places to holy and consecrated sanctuaries. You have banished from the temple of the Lord the more effeminate singing and musical compositions, promenades, conversations and business transactions; you have thus prescribed for each ecclesiastical rank such laws as leave no room for the abuse of the orders divinely conferred. You have likewise removed some matrimonial impediments which seemed to give occasion for violating the precepts of the Church, and to those who do not enter the conjugal union legitimately, you have closed the easy way of obtaining forgiveness. And what shall I say about furtive and clandestine marriages? For myself I feel that if there had been no other reason for convoking the council, and there were many and grave reasons, this one alone would have provided sufficient ground for its convocation. For since this is a matter that concerns all, and since there is no corner of the earth which this plague has not invaded, provision had to be made by which this common evil might be remedied by common deliberation. By your clear-sighted and well-nigh divine direction, most holy fathers, the occasion for innumerable and grave excesses and crimes has been completely removed, and the government of the Christian commonwealth most wisely provided for. To this is added the exceedingly salutary and necessary prohibition of many abuses connected with purgatory, the veneration and invocation of the saints, images and relics, and also indulgences, abuses which appeared to defile and deform in no small measure the beautiful aspect of these objects.

The other part, in which was considered the restoration of the tottering and well-nigh collapsed ecclesiastical discipline, was most carefully performed and completed. In the future only those who are known for their virtues, not for their ambition, who will serve the interests of the people, not their own, and who desire to be useful rather than invested with authority, will be chosen for the discharge of ecclesiastical offices. The word of God, which is more penetrating than any two-edged sword, will be more frequently and more zealously preached and explained.

The bishops and others to whom the *cura animarum* [care of the soul] has been committed, will remain with and watch over their flocks and not wander about outside the districts entrusted to them. Privileges will no longer avail anyone for an impure and wicked life or for evil and pernicious teaching; no crime will go unpunished, no virtue will be without its reward. The multitude of poor and mendicant priests have been very well provided for; everyone will be assigned to a definite church and to a prescribed field of labor whence he may obtain sustenance.

Avarice, than which there is no vice more hideous, especially in the house of God, will be absolutely banished therefrom, and the sacraments, as is proper, will be dispensed gratuitously. From one Church many will be established and from many One, according as the welfare of the people and circumstances demand. Questors of alms, as they are called, who seeking their own and not the things of Jesus Christ, have brought great injury, great dishonor upon our religion, will be completely removed from the memory of men, which must be regarded as a very great blessing. For from this our present calamity took its beginning; from it an endless evil did not cease to creep in by degrees and daily take a wider course, nor have precautionary and disciplinary measures of many councils thus far been able to suppress it. Wherefore, who will not agree that for this reason it was a very prudent undertaking to cut off this member, on whose restoration to health much labor had been vainly spent, lest it corrupt the remainder of the body?

Moreover, divine worship will be discharged more purely and promptly, and those who carry the vessels of the Lord will be so chastened that they will move others to follow their example. In connection with this point plans were skillfully devised whereby those who are to be promoted to sacred orders might in every church be from their youth up instructed in the habits of Christian life and knowledge, so that in this way a sort of seminary of all virtues might be established. In addition, . . . visitations [were] reintroduced for the welfare of the people, not for the disturbance and oppression of them; greater faculties granted to the pastors for guiding and feeding their flocks; . . . plurality of benefices abolished; the hereditary possession of the sanctuary of God prohibited; excommunication restricted and the manner of its imposition determined; . . . a sort of bridle put on the luxury, greed and licentiousness of all people, particularly the clergy, which cannot be easily shaken off; kings and princes diligently reminded of their duties, and other things of a similar nature were enacted with the greatest discernment. . . .

Let [the Protestant Reformers] read with humility, as becomes a Christian, what we have defined concerning our faith, and if some light should come upon them, let them not harden their hearts, and if they should wish to return to the common embrace of mother Church from which they severed themselves, they may rest assured that every indulgence and sympathy will be extended to them. . . .

The Tridentine Index of Books (1564)

The holy council in the second session, celebrated under our most holy Lord, Pius IV, commissioned some fathers to consider what ought to be done concerning various censures and books either suspected or pernicious and to report to this holy council. . . .

J. Barry Colman, ed., *Readings in Church History*, rev. ed., vol. 2 (Westminster, Md.: Christian Classics, Inc., 1985), pp. 705–706, 708.

1. All books which have been condemned either by the supreme pontiffs or by ecumenical councils before the year 1515 and are not contained in this list, shall be considered condemned in the same manner as they were formerly condemned.

2. The books of those heresiarchs, who after the aforesaid year originated or revived heresies, as well as of those who are or have been the heads or leaders of heretics, as Luther, Zwingli, Calvin, Balthasar Friedberg, Schwenkfeld, and others like these, whatever may be their name, title or nature or their heresy, are absolutely forbidden. The books of other heretics, moreover, which deal professedly with religion are absolutely condemned. Those on the other hand, which do not deal with religion and have by order of the bishops and inquisitors been examined by Catholic theologians and approved by them, are permitted. Likewise, Catholic books written by those who afterward fell into heresy, as well as by those who after their fall returned to the bosom of the Church, may be permitted if they have been approved by the theological faculty of a Catholic university or by the general inquisition.

3. The translations of writers, also. ecclesiastical, which have till now been edited by condemned authors, are permitted provided they contain nothing contrary to sound doctrine. Translations of the books of the Old Testament may in the judgment of the bishop be permitted to learned and pious men only. . . . Translations of the New Testament made by authors of the first class of this list shall be permitted to no one, since great danger and little usefullness usually results to readers from their perusal. . . .

4. Since it is clear from experience that if the Sacred Books are permitted everywhere and without discrimination in the vernacular, there will by reason of the boldness of men arise therefrom more harm than good, the matter is in this respect left to the judgment of the bishop or inquisitor, who may with the advice of the pastor or confessor permit the reading of the Sacred Books translated into the vernacular by Catholic authors to those who they know will derive from such reading no harm but rather an increase of faith and piety, which permission they must have in writing. Those, however, who presume to read or possess them without such permission may not receive absolution from their sins until they have handed them over to the authorities. . . .

5. Those books which sometimes produce the works of heretical authors, in which these add little or nothing of their own but rather collect therein the sayings of others, as lexicons, concordances, apothegms, parables, tables of contents and such like, are permitted if whatever needs to be eliminated in the additions is removed and corrected in accordance with the suggestions of the bishop, the inquisitor and Catholic theologians.

7. Books which professedly deal with, narrate or teach things lascivious or obscene are absolutely prohibited, since not only the matter of faith but also that of morals, which are usually easily corrupted through the reading of such books, must be taken into consideration, and those who possess them are to be severely punished by the bishops. Ancient books written by

heathens may by reason of their elegance and quality of style be permitted, but may by no means be read to children.

8. Books whose chief contents are good but in which things have incidentally been inserted which have reference to heresy, ungodliness, divination or superstition, may be permitted if by the authority of the general inquisition they have been purged by Catholic theologians. . . .

Finally, all the faithful are commanded not to presume to read or possess any books contrary to the prescriptions of these rules or the prohibition of this list. And if anyone should read or possess books by heretics or writings by any author condemned and prohibited by reason of heresy or suspicion of false teaching, he incurs immediately the sentence of excommunication. . . .

The Abdication of Charles V (1556)

Charles V, King of Spain and Holy Roman Emperor, had opposed the Protestant movement since its inception when he first ascended the throne in 1519. In 1556, he abdicated, a tired and disappointed man. The speech that follows gives insight into his life and some political consequences of the Reformation.

"The Wretched Condition of the Christian State"

EMPEROR CHARLES V

Soon came the death of my grandfather Maximilian, in my nineteenth year [1519], and although I was still young, they conferred upon me in his stead the imperial dignity. I had no inordinate ambition to rule a multitude of kingdoms, but merely sought to secure the welfare of Germany, to provide for the defence of Flanders, to consecrate my forces to the safety of Christianity against the Turk and to labor for the extention of the Christian religion. But although such zeal was mine, I was unable to show so much of it as I might have wished, on account of the troubles raised by the heresies of Luther and the other innovators of Germany and on account of serious war into which the hostility and envy of neighboring princes had driven me, and from which I have safely emerged, thanks to the favor of God.

This is the fourth time that I go to Spain, there to bury myself. I wish to say to you that nothing I have ever experienced has given me so much pain or rested so heavily upon my soul as that which I experience in parting from you today, without leaving behind me that peace and quiet which I so

James H. Robinson, ed., *Readings in European History*, vol. 2 (Boston: Ginn and Company, 1906), pp. 165–167.

much desired. . . . I am no longer able to attend to my affairs without great bodily fatigue and consequent detriment to the affairs of the state. The cares which so great a responsibility involves; the extreme dejection it causes; my health already ruined; all these leave me no longer the strength sufficient for governing the states which God has confided to me. The little strength that remains to me is rapidly disappearing. So I should long ago have put down the burden if my son's immaturity and my mother's incapacity had not forced both my spirit and my body to sustain the weight until this hour.

The last time that I went to Germany I had determined to do what you see me do today, but I could not bring myself to do it when I saw the wretched condition of the Christian state, a prey to such a multitude of disturbances, of innovations, of singular opinions as to faith, of worse than civil wars, and fallen finally into so many lamentable disorders. I was turned from my purpose because my ills were not yet so great, and I hoped to make an end of all these things and restore the peace. In order that I might not be wanting in my duty I risked my strength, my goods, my repose and my life for the safety of Christianity and the defence of my subjects. From this struggle I emerged with a portion of the things I desired. . . .

I have carried out what God has permitted, since the outcome of our efforts depends upon the will of God. We human beings act according to our powers, our strength, our spirit, and God awards the victory and permits defeat. I have ever done as I was able, and God has aided me. I return to Him boundless thanks for having succored me in my greatest trials and in all my dangers.

I am determined then to retire to Spain, to yield to my son Philip the possessions of all my states, and to my brother, the king of the Romans, the Empire. I particularly commend to you my son, and I ask of you in remembrance of me, that you extend to him the love which you have always borne towards me; moreover I ask you to preserve among yourselves the same affection and harmony. Be obedient towards justice, zealous in the observance of the laws, preserve for all that merits it, and do not refuse to grant authority the support of which it stands in need.

Above all, beware of infection from the sects of neighboring lands. Extirpate at once the germs, if they appear in your midst, for fear lest they may spread abroad and utterly overthrow your state, and lest you may fall into the direst calamities.

STUDY QUESTIONS

1. Discuss the abuses within the Church during the fifteenth and sixteenth centuries. What specifically are the criticisms of Jacob Wimpheling and Desiderius Erasmus? Is there any evidence that the Church tried to reform itself during this period?
2. Why were indulgences so detested by critics of the Church? Can you construct a logical argument in support of indulgences with which the

Church could have satisfactorily defended itself against criticism? Is the principle of indulgences at issue here, or just the manner in which they were sold?

3. What would you identify as the underlying causes for the Reformation and what is the "spark" that set things in motion? To what extent was Martin Luther's action directed against abuses within the Church?

4. What do you consider the most significant passages from Luther's *Address to the Christian Nobility of the German Nation* and treatise *On Christian Liberty?* Why? What was Luther trying to accomplish by writing them? Why did Luther finally break completely with the Roman Church?

5. What were Luther's arguments against the peasants in 1524? Are they persuasive? What does Luther's condemnation of the Peasant's Revolt tell you about his reform movement? Do you regard Luther as a hypocrite or not?

6. Note the *Sixty-seven Articles* by Ulrich Zwingli. To what extent are they in keeping with established Lutheran doctrine? Do you see any variance?

7. Analyze the primary sources of Calvinism. Why is the concept of pre-destination so efficient as a device for controlling a congregation? What is the basis for the success of the Calvinist movement?

8. Read carefully the selection on the Society of Jesus and the Council of Trent. What specifically do Loyola and the Council of Trent demand from the Catholic faithful? Does the closing oration at the Council of Trent seem to be progressive in its message? Why then does the Tridentine Index of Books seem so repressive? Can faith be enforced in this manner? Some historians have called the Catholic reform movement the "Counter Reformation." Do you think a reformation of the Church would have occurred without Martin Luther? How important was Luther in changing history?

9. A critical issue of the Reformation era centered on the diverse means of attaining salvation. How is this issue reflected in the sources? According to Luther, Zwingli, Calvin, Loyola, and the Catholic Church, how is one saved? Be specific in your documentation.

10. One of the most important questions of this period which separated the reformers from the Church centered on religious authority. In spiritual matters, did religious authority rest in the Church (as dictated by the Pope), in Church councils (such as Trent), in scripture, or in individual conscience? How is this problem reflected in the sources?

11. Some historians have maintained that without people such as Charles V, the Reformation would never have been the success it was. What do they mean by this argument? Would you agree?

12. Edward Bulwer-Lytton once said, "A reform is a correction of abuses; a revolution is a transfer of power." Under this definition, would you consider the Protestant Reformation to be a revolution?

2

Science and the Church: The Condemnation of Galileo

Reason is the greatest enemy that faith has. It never comes to the aid of spiritual things, but . . . struggles against the divine Word, treating with contempt all that emanates from God.

—Martin Luther

I respect faith, but doubt is what gets you an education.

—Wilson Mizner

He who desires to have understanding must be free in mind.

—Alcinous

The real and legitimate goal of the sciences, is the endowment of human life with new inventions and riches.

—Francis Bacon

Science has done more for the development of western civilization in one hundred years than Christianity has done in eighteen hundred years.

—John Burroughs

Portrait of Galileo Galilei. (*AIP Niels Bohr Library*)

The political history of the sixteenth and seventeenth centuries is filled with conflict between the developing states of Europe, especially over the issue of religion. The Thirty Years War (1618–1648) is an example of the mindless struggle to ensure the dominance of either the Protestant or Catholic faith. In truth, there are usually a number of complex causes of war, but the competition for souls and territory engendered by the Protestant Reformation gave new resolve and commitment to the warring factions of Europe.

Juxtaposed with the chaos of religious warfare and its attendant destruction was an intellectual attempt during the sixteenth and seventeenth centuries to progress in the realm of science. Sweeping changes took place in man's conception of the universe and of his place in it. Although the movement has been called the Scientific Revolution, the changes neither were rapid nor involved large numbers of people. On the contrary, the revolution evolved slowly, through experimentation, often in makeshift laboratories. Yet great thinkers such as Sir Isaac Newton, René Descartes, and Francis Bacon attempted to discover the physical and natural laws of the universe and to organize and criticize that diverse body of knowledge.

One of the most important and fundamental areas of investigation was astronomy. For centuries, man had subscribed to a geocentric theory that placed earth at the center of the universe with all the planets orbiting around it. This theory, ascribed to the Egyptian astronomer Ptolemy (fl. A.D. 150) and supported by Aristotelian physics, maintained that the earth had to be the center of the universe because of its heaviness and that the stars and other planets existed in surrounding crystalline spheres. Beyond these crystalline spheres lay the realm of God and the angels. This view was supported by the Catholic Church, which saw man as the central focus of God's creation and therefore at the epicenter of all existence. Biblical support for the geocentric theory included Psalm 104: "Thou didst set the earth on its foundation, so that it should never be shaken." Still, there were mathematical problems associated with this theory. For one, it was difficult to explain the motion of the planets, which seemed to be moving in noncircular patterns around the earth. At times the planets actually appeared to be going backward. This was explained by epicycles. Ptolemy maintained that planets make a second revolution in an orbit tangent to the first. It was therefore difficult to predict the location of a planet at any given time. A Polish astronomer named Nicholaus Copernicus (1473–1543) attempted to eliminate many of the mathematical inconsistencies by proposing that the sun, not the earth, was the center of the universe. In most other ways, including the acceptance of epicycles and the circular orbit of planets, Copernicus' system was still Ptolemaic. Yet Copernicus freed scientists from a rigid conception of cosmic structure and in essence proposed the empirical evidence of mathematics as the cornerstone of scientific thought. After Copernicus, the quest for rational truth was continued by Tycho Brahe, who compiled accurate tables of astronomical observations, and Johannes Kepler, who analyzed these tables and posited the elliptical orbits of planets. And yet this progress in scientific thought was to encounter various roadblocks beyond the difficulties of gathering and interpreting data. For the Catholic Church, the question was not one of empirical evidence and rational inquiry but rather of faith and authority.

The Protestant Reformation of the sixteenth century changed forever the religious orientation of Europe. No longer could the pope claim unquestioned authority over a Christian Europe that had since been split between Protestants and Roman Catholics. The Catholic Church now had to direct its energies toward maintaining the loyalty of its flock and toward remedying the abuses within the Church that had led to Martin Luther's defiance and the initiation of the Protestant Reformation.

During the sixteenth century, the Church established an organization that was designed to maintain purity of doctrine and authority over the faithful. The Inquisition, as it came to be called, was administered by Dominican friars whose responsibilities had always involved the explanation of doctrine to those who had strayed from the path. Now they were actively to seek out those whose deeds and ideas seemed to contradict established Catholic doctrine.

The term "Inquisition" is filled with pejorative connotations because this institution used harsh methods to elicit acceptance of Church teachings. The Inquisition was a vehicle for reform through coercion, with allegiance being obtained through argument, intimidation, and torture if necessary. During the seventeenth century, the Church found itself embroiled in events that again threatened its established authority. The attack was now centered on the new scientific theories that challenged Catholic doctrine and were being pursued and advocated independently of Church control. At the forefront of the controversy was one of the most influential scientists in history—Galileo Galilei.

Galileo was born in Pisa, Italy, in the year of Shakespeare's birth and Michelangelo's death (1564). He had much in common with these great men since he played the lute, painted, wrote poetry, and enjoyed polemics and satire. In 1592, Galileo was appointed professor of mathematics at the University of Padua, and he remained in this position for eighteen years, supporting a mistress, two daughters, a son, and a widowed mother on a small income supplemented by tutoring. During this time, Galileo came to doubt the teachings of Aristotle and other ancient philosophers and scientists which were accepted by the Church as being consistent with Catholic doctrine. Galileo had admired the mathematical aesthetics of the Copernican theory and became even more confirmed in his support of this thesis after viewing the heavens through a new instrument that he had recently improved—the telescope. Galileo considered himself a devout and obedient son of the Church, but he believed that the Bible conveyed truth figuratively as well as literally. He argued that scientific facts must first be discovered, then interpreted according to observation. As Galileo noted, "The Bible shows the way to go to Heaven, not the way the heavens go." No one, not even the pope, could alter the facts.

This chapter deals with several themes that recur throughout history: the confrontation between religion and science, the conflicting demands of faith and observed reality, and, most especially, the friction between established authority and its defiant opposition. Does progress in civilization occur as a reconciliation between these opposing elements? Is such a reconciliation even possible? The topic is as real and relevant today as it was for Galileo 350 years ago. Should Darwinism be taught in modern science classes as a "theory" of creation or as the scientific explanation for human development supported by scientific method and observation? Or should the creation epic as described in the book of Genesis be accepted as the true word of God and therefore unalterable fact? Is the solution as simple as "creationists were created and evolutionists evolved"? Or must there be one truth? The Catholic Church in the seventeenth century argued that there could only be one truth where matters of science and religion were concerned. The Inquisition was founded to enforce orthodox beliefs. Galileo was condemned for heresy and finally recanted his scientific beliefs in order to satisfy the demands of a church that was clearly trying to survive as an institution of faith and authority. Only in the 1980s, under Pope John Paul II, is Galileo's case being reviewed. The jury is still out.

The Seed of Conflict

One of the most important figures of the Scientific Revolution was Sir Francis Bacon (1561–1626). He was not a scientist except in an amateur sense, but he attacked the Scholastic belief that most truth had already been discovered and just required explanation. Bacon believed that through examination of empirical evidence and experimentation, human knowledge could progress and aid in the improvement of the human condition. The first selection from *The Advancement of Learning* (1605) contains some of his thoughts about the relationship between religion and scientific inquiry.

The second selection is the simple statement by Copernicus proposing the heliocentric theory; it is excerpted from a letter entitled *Commentariolus*, written sometime after 1520. In 1543, Copernicus published *On the Revolutions of the Heavenly Spheres*. The last excerpt is from the preface of that work and was addressed to Pope Paul III. In it, Copernicus explains why he questioned the geocentric theory.

The Advancement of Learning (1605)

SIR FRANCIS BACON

Lastly, some are weakly afraid lest a deeper search into nature should transgress the permitted limits of sober-mindedness, wrongfully wresting and transferring what is said in Holy Writ against those who pry into sacred mysteries to the hidden things of nature, which are barred by no prohibition. Others, with more subtlety, surmise and reflect that if the secondary causes are unknown, everything can be more readily referred to divine hand and rod—a point in which they think religion greatly concerned; which is, in fact, nothing else but to seek to gratify God with a lie. Others

James H. Robinson and Charles A. Beard, eds., *Readings in Modern European History*, vol. 1 (Boston: Ginn and Company, 1908), p. 176.

fear from past example that movements and changes in philosophy will end in assaults on religion; and others again appear apprehensive that in the investigation of nature something may be found to subvert, or at least shake, the authority of religion, especially with the unlearned.

But these two last fears seem to me to savor utterly of carnal wisdom; as if men in the recesses and secret thoughts of their hearts doubted and distrusted the strength of religion, and the empire of faith over the senses, and therefore feared that the investigation of truth in nature might be dangerous to them. But if the matter be truly considered, natural philosophy is, after the word of God, at once the surest medicine against superstition and the most approved nourishment for faith; and therefore she is rightly given to religion as her most faithful handmaid, since the one displays the will of God, the other his power.

The Heliocentric Statement (ca. 1520)
COPERNICUS

What appears to us as motions of the sun arise not from its motion but from the motion of the earth and our sphere, with which we revolve about the sun like any other planet. The earth has, then, more than one motion.

On the Movement of the Earth (1543)
COPERNICUS

I may well presume, most Holy Father, that certain people, as soon as they hear that in this book about the Revolutions of the Spheres of the Universe I ascribe movement to the earthly globe, will cry out that, holding such views, I should at once be hissed off the stage. . . .

So I should like your Holiness to know that I was induced to think of a method of computing the motions of the spheres by nothing else than the knowledge that the mathematicians [who had previously considered the problem] are inconsistent in these investigations.

For, first, the mathematicians are so unsure of the movements of the Sun and Moon that they cannot even explain or observe the constant length of the seasonal year. Secondly, in determining the motions of these and of the other five planets, they use neither the same principles and hypotheses nor the same demonstrations of the apparent motions and revolutions. . . . Nor have they been able thereby to discern or deduce the

"The Heliocentric Statement" is from Copernicus, *Three Copernican Treatises*, trans. Edward Rosen (New York: Columbia University Press, 1939), p. 58. © 1939, Columbia University Press. Reprinted by permission.

"On the Movement of the Earth" is from Copernicus, *De Revolutionibus Orbium Caelestium* (1543), trans. John F. Dobson and Selig Brodetsky, published in *Occasional Notes of the Royal Astronomical Society*, vol. 2, no. 1 (London: Royal Astronomical Society, 1947), excerpts from the preface and Book I.

principal thing—namely the shape of the Universe and the unchangeable symmetry of its parts. . . .

I pondered long upon this uncertainty of mathematical tradition in establishing the motions of the system of the spheres. At last I began to chafe that philosophers could by no means agree on any one certain theory of the mechanism of the Universe, wrought for us by a supremely good and orderly Creator. . . . I therefore took pains to read again the works of all the philosophers on whom I could lay hand to seek out whether any of them had even supposed that the motions of the spheres were other than those demanded by the [Ptolemaic] mathematical schools. I found first in Cicero that Hicetas [of Syracuse, fifth century B.C.] had realized that the Earth moved. Afterwards I found in Plutarch that certain others had held the like opinion. . . .

Thus assuming motions, which in my work I ascribe to the Earth, by long and frequent observations I have at last discovered that, if the motions of the rest of the planets be brought into relation with the circulation of the Earth and be reckoned in proportion to the circles of each planets, . . . the orders and magnitudes of all stars and spheres, nay the heavens themselves, become so bound together that nothing in any part thereof could be moved from its place without producing confusion of all the other parts of the Universe as a whole.

Letter to Galileo: "Come Out Publicly" (1597)

JOHANNES KEPLER

In 1597, the great German astronomer Johannes Kepler sent Galileo a manuscript copy of his *New Astronomy*. Galileo explained that he too had held the Copernican belief for some time but dared not reveal this for fear of being "derided and dishonored." Kepler's response follows.

I could only have wished that you, who have so profound an insight, would choose another way. You advise us . . . to retreat before the general ignorance and not to expose ourselves or heedlessly to oppose the violent attacks of the mobs of scholars. . . . But after a tremendous task has been begun in our time, first by Copernicus and then by many very learned mathematicians, and when the assertion that the Earth moves can no longer be considered something new, would it not be much better to pull the wagon to its goal by our joint efforts, now that we have got it under way, and gradually, with powerful voices, to shout down the common herd? . . . Be of good cheer, Galileo, and come out publicly. If I judge correctly, there

Giorgio de Santillana, *The Crime of Galileo* (Chicago: University of Chicago Press, 1955), pp. 11, 14–15. Copyright 1955 by The University of Chicago. Reprinted by permission of the publisher.

are only a few of the distinguished mathematicians of Europe who would part company with us, so great is the power of truth. If Italy seems less a favorable place for your publication. . . perhaps Germany will allow us this freedom.

Criticism and Response

Galileo began encountering opposition from conservative theologians and academicians shortly after the publication of his first work on astronomy in 1610. They charged that the ideas of Copernicus contradicted the Bible. Some of the main objections to Galileo's writing were stated by Cardinal Bellarmine in a letter of April 12, 1615, to a priest who had just written a book supporting the Copernican-Galilean system. Galileo's response to such charges is contained in the "Letter to the Grand Duchess of Tuscany," written in 1615, but published in Germany 21 years later in 1636.

Objections Against Galileo (1615)

CARDINAL BELLARMINE

I have gladly read the letter in Italian and the essay in Latin that Your Reverence has sent me, and I thank you for both, confessing that they are filled with ingenuity and learning. But since you ask my opinion, I shall give it to you briefly, as you have little time for reading and I for writing.

First. I say that it appears to me that Your Reverence and Sig. Galileo did prudently to content yourselves with speaking hypothetically and not positively, as I have always believed Copernicus did. For to say that assuming the earth moves and the sun stands still saves all the appearances better than eccentrics and epicycles is to speak well. This has no danger in it, and it suffices for mathematicians. But to wish to affirm that the sun is really fixed in the center of the heavens and merely turns upon itself without traveling from east to west, and that the earth is situated in the third sphere and revolves very swiftly around the sun, is a very dangerous thing, not only by irritating all the theologians and scholastic philosophers, but also by injuring our holy faith and making the sacred Scripture false. Your Reverence has indeed demonstrated many ways of expounding the Bible, but you have not applied them specifically, and doubtless you would have had a great deal of difficulty if you had tried to explain all the passages that you yourself have cited.

Second. I say that, as you know, the Council [of Trent] would prohibit

A. Lossky, ed., *The Seventeenth Century* (New York: The Free Press, 1967), pp. 94–95. Reprinted by permission of The Free Press, a Division of Macmillan, Inc.

expounding the Bible contrary to the common agreement of the holy Fathers. And if Your Reverence would read not only all their works, but the commentaries of modern writers on Genesis, Psalms, Ecclesiastes, and Joshua, you would find that all agree in expounding literally that the sun is in the heavens and travels swiftly around the earth, while the earth is far from the heavens and remains motionless in the center of the world.

Third. I say that if there were a true demonstration that the sun was in the center of the universe and the earth in the third sphere, and that the sun did not go around the earth but the earth went around the sun, then it would be necessary to use careful consideration in explaining the Scriptures that seemed contrary, and we should rather have to say that we do not understand them than to say that something is false which had been proven. But I do not think there is any such demonstration, since none has been shown to me. To demonstrate that the appearances are saved by assuming the sun at the center and the earth in the heavens is not the same thing as to demonstrate that in fact the sun is in the center and the earth in the heavens. I believe that the first demonstration may exist, but I have very grave doubts about the second; and in case of doubt one may not abandon the Holy Scriptures as expounded by the holy Fathers. I add that the words *The sun also riseth, and the sun goeth down, and hasteneth to the place where he ariseth* [Ecclesiastes 1:5] were written by Solomon, who not only spoke by divine inspiration, but was a man wise above all others, and learned in the human sciences and in the knowledge of all created things, which wisdom he had from God; so it is not very likely that he would affirm something that was contrary to demonstrated truth, or truth that might be demonstrated.

Science and the Bible: Letter to the Grand Duchess of Tuscany (1615)

GALILEO GALILEI

Some years ago, as Your Serene Highness well knows, I discovered in the heavens many things that had not been seen before our own age. The novelty of these things, as well as some consequences which followed from them in contradiction to the physical notions commonly held among academic philosophers, stirred up against me no small number of professors—as if I had placed these things in the sky with my own hands in order to upset nature and overturn the sciences. . . .

Showing a greater fondness for their own opinions than for truth, they sought to deny and disprove the new things which, if they had cared to look for themselves, their own senses would have demonstrated to them. To this end they hurled various charges and published numerous writings filled with vain arguments, and they made the grave mistake of sprinkling these with passages taken from places in the Bible which they had failed to understand properly, and which were ill suited to their purposes. . . .

Persisting in their original resolve to destroy me and everything mine by any means they can think of, these men . . . know that as to the arrangement of the parts of the universe, I hold the sun to be situated motionless in the center of the revolution of the celestial orbs while the earth rotates on its axis and revolves about the sun. They know also that I support this position not only by refuting the arguments of Ptolemy and Aristotle, but by producing many counter-arguments; in particular, some which relate to physical effects whose causes can perhaps be assigned in no other way. In addition there are astronomical arguments derived from many things in my new celestial discoveries that plainly confute the Ptolemaic system while admirably agreeing with and confirming the contrary hypothesis. . . . These men have resolved to fabricate a shield for their fallacies out of the mantle of pretended religion and the authority of the Bible. These they apply, with little judgment, to the refutation of arguments that they do not understand and have not even listened to.

First they have endeavored to spread the opinion that such propositions in general are contrary to the Bible and are consequently damnable and heretical. . . . Next, becoming bolder, and hoping (though vainly) that this seed which first took root in their hypocritical minds would send out branches and ascend to heaven, they began scattering rumors among the people that before long this doctrine would be condemned by the supreme authority. . . .

They go about invoking the Bible, which they would have minister to their deceitful purposes. Contrary to the sense of the Bible and the intention of the holy Fathers, if I am not mistaken, they would extend such authorities until even in purely physical matters—where faith is not involved—they would have us altogether abandon reason and the evidence of our senses in favor of some biblical passage, though under the surface meaning of its words this passage may contain a different sense. . . .

I think in the first place that it is very pious to say and prudent to affirm that the holy Bible can never speak untruth—whenever its true meaning is understood. But I believe nobody will deny that it is often very abstruse, and may say things which are quite different from what its bare words signify. . . .

This being granted, I think that in discussions of physical problems we ought to begin not from the authority of scriptural passages, but from sense-experiences and necessary demonstrations; for the holy Bible and the phenomena of nature proceed alike from the divine Word, the former as the dictate of the Holy Ghost and the latter as the observant executrix of God's commands. It is necessary for the Bible, in order to be accommodated to the understanding of every man, to speak many things which appear to differ from the absolute truth so far as the bare meaning of the words is concerned. But Nature, on the other hand, is inexorable and immutable; she never transgresses the laws imposed upon her, or cares a whit whether her abstruse reasons and methods of operation are understandable to men. For that reason it appears that nothing physical which sense-experience sets before our eyes, or which necessary demonstrations prove to us, ought to be called in question (much less condemned) upon the testimony of biblical passages which may have some different meaning beneath their words. For the Bible is not chained in every expression to conditions as strict as those which govern all physical effects; nor is God any less excellently revealed in Nature's actions than in the sacred statements of the Bible. . . .

From this I do not mean to infer that we need not have an extraordinary esteem for the passages of holy Scripture. On the contrary, having arrived at any certainties in physics, we ought to utilize these as the most appropriate aids in the true exposition of the Bible and in the investigation of those meanings which are necessarily contained therein for these must be concordant with demonstrated truths. I should judge the authority of the Bible was designed to persuade men of those articles and propositions which, surpassing all human reasoning, could not be made credible by science, or by any other means than through the very mouth of the Holy Spirit. . . .

But I do not feel obliged to believe that the same God who has endowed us with senses, reason, and intellect has intended to forgo their use and by some other means to give us knowledge which we can attain by them.

Condemnation by the Inquisition

When Galileo wrote the above letter to the Grand Duchess of Tuscany in 1615, Copernicanism was being actively investigated by the Inquisition as philosophically foolish and absurd. However, on February 23, 1616, the heliocentric theory was condemned as formally heretical. By this time, Galileo had already traveled to Rome to defend his views in front of a group of prelates led by the chief prosecutor, Cardinal Bellarmine. The following are selections from the proceedings beginning on February 25, 1616, which resulted in Galileo's condemnation.

The Hearings of 1616

Thursday, 25th February, 1616. The Lord Cardinal Mellini notified to the Reverend Fathers . . . of the Holy Office [of the Inquisition], that the cen-

Karl von Gebler, *Galileo Galilei and the Roman Curia* (London: C.K. Paul and Company 1879), pp. 77, 82–85.

sure passed by the theologians upon the propositions of Galileo—to the effect particularly that the sun is the center of the world, and immovable from its place, and that the earth moves, and also with a diurnal motion— had been reported [to the Pope]; and His Holiness [Paul V] has directed the Lord Cardinal Bellarmine to summon before him the said Galileo, and admonish him to abandon the said opinion, and in case of his refusal to obey, that the Commissary is to intimate to him, before a notary and witnesses, a command to abstain altogether from teaching or defending this opinion and doctrine, and even from discussing it; and if he do not acquiesce therein, that he is to be imprisoned.

3rd March, 1616. The Lord Cardinal Bellarmine having reported that Galileo Galilei, mathematician, had in terms of the order of the Holy Congregation [of the Inquisition] been admonished to abandon the opinion he has hitherto held, that the sun is the center of the spheres and immovable, and that the earth moves, and had acquiesced therein; and the decree of the Congregation of the Index [of forbidden books] having been presented, prohibiting and suspending . . . the writings of Nicholas Copernicus. . . .—His Holiness ordered this edict of prohibition and suspension . . . to be published by the Master of the Palace.

Decree of the Index

5th March 1616. And whereas it has also come to the knowledge of the said Congregation [of the Index] that the . . . doctrine—which is false and altogether opposed to Holy Scripture—of the motion of the earth, and the quiescence of the sun, which is also taught by Nicholas Copernicus in *De Revolutionibus Orbium Caelestium* . . . is now being spread abroad and accepted by many. . . . Therefore, in order that this opinion may not insinuate itself any further to the prejudice of Catholic truth, the Holy Congregation [of the Index] has decreed that the said Nicholas Copernicus, *De Revolutionibus Orbium* . . . be suspended until [it] be corrected.

The Trial of 1633

After his hearings in 1616, Galileo left Rome on cordial terms with the pope. It had been made clear to him that he could not openly advocate Copernicanism. Still, Galileo got involved in various disputes and succeeded in antagonizing the Jesuits who had supported him earlier in 1616 against the Dominicans who ran the Inquisition. The new pope, Urban VIII, was an old admirer of Galileo and actually encouraged the idea of a major work, though he warned that it must be hypothetical in nature and could not advocate opinions of Galileo that would constrain "the infinite power and wisdom of God." The book, entitled *Dialogues on the Two*

Karl von Gebler, *Galileo Galilei and the Roman Curia* (London: C.K. Paul and Company 1879), pp. 202–204.

Great Systems of the World, appeared in 1632 and actually passed the scrutiny of the Church's censors. But it did advocate Copernicanism as something more than just a hypothesis. Galileo was summoned before the Inquisition and the trial began in April 1633; he was nearly seventy years old. The following selections present the transcript of the trial, Galileo's sentence, and his recantation of his views.

Galileo: Respecting the controversy which had arisen on the aforesaid opinion that the sun is stationary, and the earth moves, it was decided by the Holy Congregation of the Index, that such an opinion, considered as established fact, contradicted Holy Scripture, and was only admissible as a conjecture. . . .

Inquisitor: Was this decision then communicated to you, and by whom?

Galileo: This decision . . . was made known to me by Cardinal Bellarmine.

Inquisitor: You must state what his Eminence Cardinal Bellarmine told you about the aforesaid decision, and whether he said anything else on the subject, and what?

Galileo: Signor Cardinal Bellarmine signified to me that the aforesaid opinion of Copernicus might be held as a conjecture, as it had been held by Copernicus, and his eminence was aware that, like Copernicus, I only held that opinion as a conjecture. . . .

In accordance with this I possess a certificate of the said Signor Cardinal Bellarmine . . . of which certificate I herewith submit a copy. . . .

Inquisitor: Was any other command communicated to you on this subject . . . and what?

Galileo: It may be that a command was issued to me that I should not hold nor defend the opinion in question, but I do not remember it, for it is several years ago.

Inquisitor: If what was then said and enjoined upon you as a command were read aloud to you, would you remember it?

[A document was then read to Galileo which, the Inquisitors claimed, was dated 1616 and had forbidden him to defend or to teach the doctrine "in any way whatsoever." Galileo replied that he could not remember the phrases "not to teach" or "in any way." In fact, the Inquisitors had actually forged the document. Galileo, however, conceded inadvertent guilt, as the next selection indicates.]

[At the second hearing:]

Galileo: In the course of some days' continuous and attentive reflection on the interrogations put to me . . . it occurred to me to re-peruse my printed dialogue, which for three years I had not seen, in order carefully to note whether, contrary to my most sincere intention, there had, by inadvertence, fallen from my pen anything from which a reader or the authorities might infer not only some taint of disobedience on my part, but also other particulars which might induce the belief that I had contravened the orders of the Holy Church. . . . I [had] resorted to . . . the natural complacency which every man feels with regard to his own subtleties and in showing himself more skillful than the generality of men, in devising, even in favour of false propositions, ingenious and plausible arguments. . . . My error, then, has been—and I confess it—one of vainglorious ambition, and of pure ignorance and inadvertence

[The final hearing got under way after the pope ordered Galileo to be questioned, under threat of torture, concerning his adherence to Copernicanism.]

Galileo: A long time ago, that is, before the decision of the Holy Congregation of the Index, and before the Inquisition was intimated to me, I was indifferent, and regarded both opinions, namely, that of Ptolemy and that of Copernicus, as open to discussion, inasmuch as either one or the other might be true in nature; but after the said decision, assured of the wisdom of the authorities, I ceased to have any doubt; and I held, as I still hold, as most true and indisputable, the opinion of Ptolemy, that is to say, the stability of the earth and the motion of the sun. . . .

As regards the writing of the published dialogue, my motive in so doing was not because I held the Copernican doctrine to be true, but simply thinking to confer a common benefit, I have set forth the proofs from nature and astronomy which may be adduced on either side; my object being to make it clear that neither the one set of arguments nor the other has the force of conclusive demonstration in favour of this opinion or of that; and that therefore, in order to proceed with certainty we must have recourse to the decisions of higher teaching, as may be clearly seen from the large number of passages in the dialogue in question. I affirm, therefore, on my conscience, that I do not now hold the condemned opinion, and have not held it since the decision of the authorities.

[The Inquisitor threatened that "appropriate remedies of the law" would be applied if Galileo did not speak the truth. Galileo's reply:]

Galileo: I do not hold, and have not held this opinion of Copernicus since the command was intimated to me that I must abandon it; for the rest, I am here in your hands,—do with me what you please.

[The Inquisitor then threatened torture. Galileo's final reply:]

Galileo: 1 am here to obey, and I have not held this opinion since the decision was pronounced, as I have stated.

The Sentence of the Cardinals

We. . . by the grace of God, cardinals of the Holy Roman Church, Inquisitors General, by the Holy Apostolic See specially deputed, against heretical depravity throughout the whole Christian Republic.

Whereas you, Galileo . . . were in the year 1615 denounced to this Holy Office for holding as true the false doctrine taught by many, that the sun is the centre of the world and immovable, and that the earth moves, and also with a diurnal motion; for having disciples to whom you taught the same doctrines; for holding correspondence with certain mathematicians of Germany concerning the same; for have printed certain letters, entitled "On the Solar Spots," wherein you developed the same doctrine as true; and for replying to the objections from the Holy Scriptures, which from time to time were urged against it, by glossing the said Scriptures according to your own meaning. . . .

This Holy Tribunal being therefore desirous of proceeding against the disorder and mischief thence resulting, which went on increasing to the prejudice of the Holy Faith, by command of his Holiness and of the most eminent Lords Cardinals of this supreme and universal Inquisition, the two propositions of the stability of the sun and the motion of the earth were by the theological "Qualifiers" qualified as follows:

The Proposition that the sun is the centre of the world and does not move from its place is . . . formally heretical. . . .

The proposition that the earth is not the centre of the world and immovable, but that it moves, and also with a diurnal motion, is . . . theologically considered, at least erroneous in faith.

But whereas it was desired at that time to deal leniently with you . . . the command was intimated to you . . . that you were altogether to abandon the said false opinion, and not in future to defend or teach it in any way whatsoever, neither verbally nor in writing; and upon your promising to obey you were dismissed.

And . . . a decree was issued by the Holy Congregation of the Index, prohibiting the books which treat of this doctrine, and declaring the doctrine itself to be false and wholly contrary to sacred and divine Scripture.

And whereas a book appeared here recently . . . the title of which shows that you were the author, this title being: *Dialogues of Galileo Galilei;* and whereas the Holy Congregation was afterwards informed that through the publication of the said book, the false opinion of the motion of the earth and the stability of the sun was daily gaining ground; the said book was taken into careful consideration, and in it there was discovered a patent violation of the aforesaid injunction that had been imposed upon you, for in this book you have defended the said opinion previously condemned and to your face declared to be so, although in the said book you strive by

Karl von Gebler, *Galileo Galilei and the Roman Curia* (London: C.K. Paul and Company 1879), pp. 214–216.

various devices to produce the impression that you leave it undecided, and in express terms as possible: which however is a most grievous error, as an opinion can in no wise be probable which has been declared and defined to be contrary to Divine Scripture:

Therefore by our order you were cited before this Holy Office, where . . . you . . . confessed that the writing of the said book is in various places drawn up in such a form that the reader might fancy that the arguments brought forward on the false side are rather calculated by their cogency to compel conviction than to be easy of refutation. . . .

And whereas it appeared to us that you had not stated the full truth with regard to your intention, we thought it necessary to subject you to a rigorous examination, at which (without prejudice, however, to the matters confessed by you . . .) you answered like a good Catholic. Therefore, having seen and maturely considered the merits of this your cause . . . we have arrived at the underwritten final sentence against you:—

We say, pronounce, sentence, declare, that you, the said Galileo, by reasons of the matters adduced in process, and by you confessed as above, have rendered yourself in the judgment of this Holy Office vehemently suspected of heresy, namely, of having believed and held the doctrine— which is false and contrary to the sacred and divine Scriptures—that the sun is the centre of the world and does not move from east to west, and that the earth moves and is not the centre of the world; and that an opinion may be held and defended as probable after it has been declared and defined to be contrary to Holy Scripture; and that consequently you have incurred all the censures and penalities imposed and promulgated in the sacred canons and other constitutions, general and particular, against such first, with a sincere heart, and unfeigned faith, you abjure, curse, and detest the aforesaid errors and heresies . . . in the form to be prescribed by us.

And in order that this your grave and pernicious error and transgression may not remain altogether unpunished, and that you may be more cautious for the future, and an example to others . . . we ordain that the book of the *"Dialogues of Galileo Galilei"* be prohibited by public edict.

We condemn you to the formal prison of this Holy Office during our pleasure and by way of salutary penance, we enjoin that for three years to come you repeat once a week the seven penitential Psalms. . . .

So we the undersigned Cardinals pronounce.

Recantation

GALILEO GALILEI

And by God's help will for the future believe, all that is held, preached, and taught by the Holy Catholic and Apostolic Roman Church. But whereas . . .

Karl von Gebler, *Galileo Galilei and the Roman Curia* (London: C.K. Paul and Company 1879), pp. 226–227.

I wrote and printed a book in which I discuss this [heliocentric] doctrine already condemned, and adduce arguments of great cogency in its favour, without presenting any solution of these; and for this cause I have been pronounced by the Holy Office to be vehemently suspected of heresy, that is to say, of having held and believed that the sun is the centre of the world and immovable, and that the earth is not the centre and moves:—

Therefore, desiring to remove from the minds of your Eminences, and of all faithful Christians, this strong suspicion, reasonably conceived against me, with sincere heart and unfeigned faith I abjure, curse, and detest the aforesaid errors and heresies . . . and I swear that in future I will never again say or assert, verbally or in writing, anything that might furnish occasion for a similar suspicion regarding me. . . .

I, the said Galileo Galilei, have abjured, sworn, promised, and bound myself as above.

Galileo's Condemnation Reconsidered (1983)

On October 22, 1980, Pope John Paul II summoned a synod of bishops to deliberate on the future. Archbishop Paul Poupard, head of the Secretariat for Non-Believers, announced that the pope wanted to reexamine Galileo's case "with full objectivity." A year earlier, John Paul II had joined in honoring another great scientist, Albert Einstein, who once described Galileo as possessing "the passionate will, the intelligence, and the courage to stand up as the representative of rational thinking against the host of those who, relying on the ignorance of the people and the indolence of teachers in priest's and scholar's garb, maintain and defend their positions of authority."

On May 9, 1983, Pope John Paul II spoke to an international symposium of scientists on the occasion of the 350th anniversary of the publication of Galileo's *Dialogues on the Two Great Systems of the World*. The following is an excerpt from his discourse that gives indication of the progress made on the case.

"A Fruitful Concord Between Science and Faith"

POPE JOHN PAUL II

We cast our minds back to an age when there had developed between science and faith grave incomprehension, the result of misunderstandings

Pope John Paul II, "The Responsibility of Service," in *The Pope Speaks*, vol. 28, no. 3 (Fall 1983), pp. 245–249. Reprinted by permission of Our Sunday Visitor, Inc.

or errors, which only humble and patient reexamination succeeded in gradually dispelling. So we should rejoice together that the world of science and the Catholic Church have learned to go beyond those moments of conflict, understandable no doubt, but nonetheless regrettable. This was the result of a more accurate appreciation of the methods proper to the different orders of knowledge and the fruit of bringing to research a more rigorous attitude of mind.

The Church and science itself have reaped great profit from this and have discovered through reflection and sometimes painful experience the paths that lead to truth and objective knowledge.

To you who are preparing to mark the 350th anniversary of the publication of Galileo Galilei's great work [*Dialogues on the Two Great Systems of the World*], I would like to say that the Church's experience, during the Galileo affair and after it, has led to a more mature attitude and to a more accurate grasp of the authority proper to it. I repeat before you what I stated before the Pontifical Academy of Sciences on Nov. 17, 1979: "I hope that theologians, scholars and historians, animated by a spirit of sincere collaboration, will study the Galileo case more deeply and, in frank recognition of wrongs, from whichever side they come, will dispel the mistrust which still forms an obstacle, in the minds of many, to a fruitful concord between science and faith, between the Church and the world. I give all my support to this task, which will be able to honor the truth of faith and of science and open the door to future collaboration."

As you know, I have asked for the formation of an interdisciplinary research team for the careful study of the whole question. Its work is progressing very encouragingly, and there are good grounds for hoping that it will make an important contribution to the examination of the whole matter.

The Church itself learns by experience and reflection, and it now understands better the meaning that must be given to freedom of research, as I said to the representatives of the Spanish universities on Nov. 3, 1982:

"The Church upholds freedom of research, which is one of the most noble attributes of man. It is through research that man attains to Truth— one of the most beautiful names that God has given himself. That is why the Church is convinced that there can be no real contradiction between science and faith, for the reason that the whole of reality ultimately comes from God the Creator. This is what is stated by the Second Vatican Council. I have stated this myself on a number of occasions in addressing men and women of science. It is certain that science and faith represent two different orders of knowledge, autonomous in their processes, but finally converging upon the discovery of reality in all its aspects, which has its origin in God.

One thus perceives more clearly that divine revelation, of which the Church is the guarantor and witness, does not of itself involve any particular scientific theory, and the assistance of the Holy Spirit in no way lends itself to guaranteeing explanations that we would wish to profess concerning the physical constitution of reality.

The fact that the Church has been able only with difficulty to make advances in such a complex sphere should neither surprise nor scandalize us. The Church, founded by Christ who called himself the Way, the Truth and the Life, still remains made up of individuals who are limited and who are closely bound up with the culture of the time they live in. So it is that it declares that it is always interested in research concerning the knowledge of the universe, whether physical, biological or psychological. It is only through humble and assiduous study that it learns to dissociate the essentials of faith from the scientific systems of a given age, especially when a culturally influenced reading of the Bible seems to be linked to an obligatory cosmogony.

The Case of Galileo

To return to the case of Galileo, we certainly recognize that he suffered from departments of the Church. In his time, however, there were no lack of Catholic centers which were already cultivating with great competence, over and above theology and philosophy, disciplines such as history, geography, archaeology, physics, mathematics, astronomy and astrophysics; and these studies were considered necessary for a better knowledge of the historical evolution of man and of the secrets of the universe. Brilliant forerunners had even put Catholics on their guard, urging them not to set up an opposition between science and faith. This is what I wished to affirm, Dec. 15, 1979, at the Gregorian University, whose researches and professors were known, in his own time, to Galileo:

"And while we must recognize that students of that time were not unaffected by their cultural milieu, we can, nevertheless, note that there were brilliant forerunners and freer minds, like St. Robert Bellarmine in the case of Galileo Galilei, who wished that useless tensions and harmful rigidities between faith and science could be avoided."

These facts confirm us in the indispensable need for a frank and open dialogue between theologians, scientific specialists and those who exercise leadership in the Church.

Better Understanding

Hence we can see that the age-old relationships between the Church and science have brought Catholics to a more correct understanding of the sphere of their faith, to a sort of intellectual purification and to a conviction that scientific study deserves a commitment to unbiased research which, in the final analysis, is a service to truth and to man himself. We should add that the Church recognizes with gratitude all that it owes to research and science. I had occasion to say this to the Pontifical Council for Culture Jan. 18, 1983:

"Let us think of how the results of scientific research help us to know the universe better, to understand better the mystery of man; think of the advantages which the new means of communication and contact among people offer to society and to the Church; let us think of the ability to produce incalculable economic and cultural wealth, and especially to promote the education of the masses, and to cure diseases previously thought incurable. What admirable achievements! All this is to man's credit. And all this has greatly benefitted the Church itself, in its life, its organization, its work and its own activity."

A New Dimension

If we address ourselves now, more directly to the scientific world, does one not see today how the greater sensitivity of scholars and researchers to spiritual and moral values brings to your disciplines a new dimension and a more generous openness to what is universal? This attitude has greatly facilitated and enriched the dialogue between science and the church. . . .

Moreover, the scientific world, having now become one of the principal sectors of activity in modern society, is itself discovering, in the light of reflection and experience, the extent and at the same time the seriousness of its responsibilities. Modern science and the technology that derives from it have become a veritable power and form the object of socio-economic policies or strategies, which are not neutral as regards the future of man. . . .

Ladies and gentlemen, you enjoy immense moral influence in order to assert the properly humanistic and cultural objectives of science. Strive to defend man and his dignity at the centers of decision making which govern scientific policies and social planning. You will always find an ally in the Church each time that you strive to promote man and his authentic development.

Church's Concern

It is also assuredly from within that the Church concerns itself with your work. For none of the things that can deepen knowledge of man, nature and the universe can leave us indifferent. All scientific progress, pursued with rectitude, honors humanity and is a tribute to the Creator of all things. Your investigations constitute an extension of the marvelous revelation which God gives us in His work of creation. The Church does not first turn to your discoveries in order to draw from them facile apologetic arguments for strengthening its beliefs. Rather it seeks, thanks to you, to expand the horizon of its contemplation and of its admiration for the clarity with which the infinitely powerful God shines through His creation.

For the believer, the most specialized research can thus become a highly ethical and spiritual act. For the saints, study was prayer and contemplation.

Yes, the Church appeals to your capacities for research in order that no limit may be placed upon our common quest for knowledge. Your specialization, of course, imposes upon you certain rules and indispensable limitations in investigation; but beyond these epistemological limits, let the inclination of your spirit carry you toward the universal and the absolute. More than ever before, our world needs intellects capable of grasping the whole picture and of enabling knowledge to advance toward humanistic understanding and toward wisdom. In a word, your knowledge must blossom into wisdom, that is, it must become the growth of man and of the whole man. Open your minds and hearts fully to the imperatives of today's world, which aspire to justice and to dignity founded on truth. You yourselves, be ready to seek all that is true, convinced that the realities of the spirit form part of what is real and part of the whole Truth.

Ladies and gentlemen, your task is noble and very great. The world looks to you and expects from you a service which matches your intellectual capacities and ethical responsibilities.

May God, the Creator of all things, who is present in the immensity of the universe and in each of our hearts, accompany you in your work and inspire your admirable work.

STUDY QUESTIONS

1. Read Copernicus' statement on the movement of the sun and earth. What reasons does he give for supporting the heliocentric theory? Is he convincing? Why is it significant that Copernicus refers to ancient authors like Cicero and Plutarch?

2. What were Galileo's specific ideas regarding the relationship between science and the Bible? Be particular in your analysis of the primary documents. Why were Galileo's ideas considered dangerous by the Inquisition? Did the Inquisition do the Church more harm than good?

3. What methods did the Inquisition employ to elicit obedience from Galileo? Did Galileo defend himself well? Why did he recant his position? Do you view Galileo as a hypocrite who was not committed to the principles of science that he advocated? Or do you see the Church at fault?

4. Consider the Martin Luther quote at the beginning of this chapter: "Reason is the greatest enemy that faith has. It never comes to the aid of spiritual things, but . . . struggles against the divine Word, treating with contempt all that emanates from God." Does it surprise you that this statement comes from the leader of the Protestant Reformation?

5. The heresies of Galileo have been studied by a papal commission since 1980. Why is this happening now? Read the address by John Paul II. What is his opinion of the relationship between religion and science? Note that the pope gives no hint of whether the Church will eventually reverse its decision on Galileo. What is at risk should its condemnation be upheld?

6. What are some of the current areas of tension between science and religion? Are these two areas naturally antagonistic or can they truly be compatible? In man's quest for knowledge and understanding about the world around him and his place in it, must one choose between the mind and the spirit? What does Francis Bacon say about this? Do you agree with him?

3

"I Am the State": The Absolutism of Louis XIV

It is atheism and blasphemy to dispute what God can do; so it is presumption and contempt to dispute what a king can do, or say that a king cannot do this or that.

—James I

It is in my person alone that ultimate power resides. It is from me alone that my courts derive their authority. It is to me alone that the power to make law belongs, without any dependence and without any division. The whole public order comes from me, and the rights and interests of the nation are necessarily joined with mine and rest only in my hands.

—Louis XIV

Resistance on the part of people to the supreme legislative power of the state is never legitimate; it is the duty of the people to bear any abuse of the supreme power.

—Immanuel Kant

It has often been said that the primary purpose of government is to create and maintain a stable domestic environment. Only through such stability and domestic tranquility can a government establish a strong defense against threatening foes and also pursue a successful foreign policy.

When the state is divided against itself into several political, social, or economic factions, it is weak and thus susceptible to invasion or revolution. This is a rather conservative opinion, and others throughout the years have argued that a state based primarily on efficiency and security does not tolerate new ideas or respond quickly to the needs of its citizens; in essence, such a state is not progressive in outlook, but seeks only to maintain the status quo. At the root of these different ideas lies a basic problem: To what extent are citizens of a state able to rule themselves? Is democracy a "noble experiment" that errs by ascribing extraordinary possibilities to ordinary people? Indeed, is progress best served when a citizen body is directed and controlled by a monarch or even a dictator who uses all the resources of the state to achieve his goals? These questions form the basis of political theory in the western world. How best should humans organize society in order to provide stability, security, and happiness?

During the fifteenth through the eighteenth centuries, these questions were of fundamental importance. As the Middle Ages blended into the Renaissance, decentralized feudalism gave way to more structured monarchies in France, England, and Spain. The modern state was forming under the control of kings who had relatively few restrictions on their authority. The major exception to this was England, whose monarch had coexisted since the thirteenth century with a developing Parliament, or representative body, and was beholden to certain laws and decrees (such as the Magna Carta of 1215), which guaranteed basic civil rights for Englishmen. It is perhaps because of this long tradition of more or less shared power and responsibilities that England was the first major state to experience the conflicts that inevitably resulted from such an arrangement.

Between 1603 and 1715, England experienced the most tumultuous years of its long history. The glorious reign of Queen Elizabeth I (1558–1603) gave way to increasing religious dissension under her successor, James I (1603–1625). The new king, who hailed from Scotland, lacked tact and was ignorant of English institutions. More seriously, he was an advocate of absolute, divine-right monarchy. According to this theory, the authority of a king was unlimited and could not be challenged because it was sanctioned by God. The reign of James I began a breach between the monarchy and Parliament that was eventually to result in a civil war (1642–1646) between supporters of the Parliament (Roundheads) and those of the king (Cavaliers). The victory of Parliament was crowned with the beheading of King Charles I (1649), an act without precedent in English history. After this, the government was controlled first by Parliament alone and then under the direction of Oliver Cromwell, who was determined to give England efficient rule as Lord Protector (1653–1658). On Cromwell's death the monarchy was restored under Charles II (1660–1685), but it was conciliatory to the will of Parliament.

The final breach occurred when King James II (1685–1688) once again tried to assert authority as an absolute monarch. Parliament deposed him, banned his Catholic relatives from succession, and invited the popular Dutch Protestant leader William of Orange and his wife Mary to rule as monarchs (1688). This "Glorious Revolution" was bloodless and resulted in a Bill of Rights that limited the powers of the monarchy; henceforward the king would rule with the consent of Parliament.

Seventeenth-century France, in contrast to England, saw representative government crushed by the success of absolute monarchy. It was Henry IV (1589–1610) who began the process of establishing a strong centralized state by curtailing the privileges of the nobility and restricting provincial governors and regional councils called *parlements*. Henry and his finance minister, the Duke of Sully (1560–1641), also sought to control the finances of the state by establishing government monopolies on gunpowder, mines, and salt. When Henry IV was assassinated in 1610, he was succeeded by his son, Louis XIII (1610–1643). Since Louis was only nine years old at the time of his father's death, France was ruled by his mother, Marie de Medici, who sought internal security by promoting Cardinal Richelieu (1585–1642) as chief advisor to the king. Richelieu, an efficient and shrewd counselor, sought to make France the dominant European power by consolidating the domestic authority of the king. There was to be but one law—that of the king. To this end, Richelieu imprisoned and executed recalcitrant nobles; indeed, the French nobility eventually became docile in their subservience at court. Richelieu was succeeded in 1642 by another cardinal named Mazarin (1602–1661), who acted as regent for the young monarch, Louis XIV. It is because of the strict policies of Richelieu and Mazarin that Louis XIV inherited a basic foundation for absolute rule.

The reign of Louis XIV (1643–1714) was of fundamental importance for the establishment of France both as the supreme political power on the Continent and as the dominant cultural influence throughout Europe. The sun shone brightly on the fortunes of France in the seventeenth and eighteenth centuries, and Louis, or the "Sun King" as he was called, became the model of stable, secure rule. His control over his subjects was absolute, subject to no authority except that of God. God had appointed Louis, and God alone could judge his actions. Thus, all political, social, economic, and military decisions were made by the king and his various advisors without interference or input from the people of France. Collectively, his subjects were Louis' children and as such were expected to follow the policies of their "father." Louis' famous comment, "I am the state," was the essence of French divine-right monarchy.

This period of history, however, was not in any sense tranquil. For over half a century before Louis' accession, France had been disrupted by religious wars between Catholics, whom the French monarchy supported, and the Huguenots or French Protestants. The wars had secured certain political and military privileges for the Huguenots that were scarcely compatible with the ideal of a strong, centralized monarchy. When Louis assumed control of the government in 1661 after his eighteen-year minority, the Huguenots were still an independent religious group, officially tolerated by the crown, but an embarrassment nonetheless. Finally, in 1685, Louis demanded conformity to Catholic doctrine and revoked the Edict of Nantes (1598), which had granted religious toleration to the Huguenots.

Another major threat to the tranquility of the state and the supremacy of royal power came from the nobility. During the minority of Louis XIV, France had lapsed into civil war, fomented by nobles who were jealous of the increasing power of the monarchy and particularly its close financial support from an active middle class. To many, the chaos of such disturbances was a greater fear than the existence of a strong, centralized monarchy that could ensure domestic tranquility and external security. This fear of chaos and desire for order probably lay behind popular support of Louis' divine-right monarchy. The longevity and relative harmony of his reign demonstrates Louis' successful disarming of the nobility. His magnificent palace at Versailles, testimony to his pursuit of order, not only was an enduring artistic legacy of his reign, but also served a practical purpose: Louis could house all his important nobles at the palace and thus maintain close control over their activities. Louis reserved high government positions for hand-picked members of the aristocracy and aspiring middle class, who thus owed their success to him; this in turn assured their loyalty.

In the late seventeenth and early eighteenth centuries, France was the envy and terror of Europe, its most powerful state and cultural center. Other monarchs imitated Louis' court at Versailles and even the palace itself. His army was perhaps the best trained and best supplied military force of its day, and his diplomatic service proved to be a model of excellence. The French language became accepted as the common tongue among diplomats. French dominance of European affairs was cultural as well as political.

The purpose of this chapter is to examine the theory and practice of absolute rule, especially as it was applied by Louis XIV. Is absolute monarchy a natural form of government, in keeping with man's desire to follow, and to be taken care of? Or do you resist this idea? To what extent is absolutism, whether justified by God or by force of arms, different from tyranny? Louis XIV was an aggressive ruler who sought glory in foreign wars and domestic stability under the motto, "one King, one law, one faith." The formula is simplistic, yet the policy was effective. To his admirers, Louis represented the quintessential monarch. Yet, the Sun King was certainly not without his critics. Such voices must also be heard for a balanced evaluation of his reign.

The Theory of Absolute Monarchy

The English Model: Leviathan (1651)

Thomas Hobbes was one of the great political philosophers of the seventeenth century. His major work, entitled *Leviathan*, was published in 1651 and reflects the insecurity and fear of the English Revolution that had resulted in civil war (1642–1646) and had just seen the decapitation of a sovereign monarch, Charles I, in 1649. Hobbes himself, because of his aristocratic associations, had been forced to flee England. Not surprisingly, *Leviathan* is a treatise that advocates political absolutism. Its theme is power, and it justifies absolute monarchy as necessary in order to subdue man's violent nature and promote a reasonable existence. For Hobbes, the authority of the absolute monarch did not lie in hereditary right or in divine sanction, but only in his ability to achieve power and maintain it. In this sense, Hobbes borrowed much from the Renaissance political philosopher Niccolò Machiavelli. But Hobbes went much further by providing an integrated social and political philosophy of government.

The Life of Man: "Brutish and Short"

THOMAS HOBBES

Nature has made men so equal, in the faculties of the body and mind; as that though there be found one man sometimes manifestly stronger in body, or of quicker mind than another; yet when all is reckoned together, the differences between man and man, is not so considerable. . . . For as to the strength of body, the weakest has strength enough to kill the strongest, either by secret machination, or by confederacy with others, that are in the same danger with himself.

And as to the faculties of the mind . . . I find yet a greater equality among men, than that of strength. . . . Such is the nature of men, that howsoever they may acknowledge many others to be more witty, or more eloquent, or more learned; yet they will hardly believe there are many so wise as themselves; for they see their own wit at hand, and other men's at a distance. . . .

From this equality of ability, arises equality of hope in the attaining of our ends. And therefore if any two men desire the same thing, which nevertheless they cannot both enjoy, they become enemies; and in the way to their end, which is principally their own conservation . . . endeavour to destroy, or subdue one another. And from hence it comes to pass, that . . . an invader has no more to fear than another man's single power; if one

W. Molesworth, ed., *The English Works of Thomas Hobbes*, vol. 3 (London: John Bohn, 1839), from chapters 13 and 17, pp. 110–113, 153, 157–158. Text modernized by the editor.

plant, sow, build, and possess a convenient seat, others may probably be expected to come prepared with forces united, to disspossess, and deprive him, not only of the fruit of his labour, but also of his life, or liberty. And the invader again is in the like danger of another. . . . [Thus], men have no pleasure, but on the contrary a great deal of grief, in keeping company, where there is no power able to over-awe them all. . . .

So that in the nature of man, we find three principal causes of quarrel. First, competition; secondly, insecurity; thirdly, glory.

The first, makes men invade for gain; the second, for safety; and the third, for reputation. The first use violence, to make themselves master of other men's persons, wives, children, and cattle; the second, to defend them; the third, for trifles, as a word, a smile, a different opinion, and any other sign of undervalue, either direct in their persons, or by reflection in their kindred, their friends, their nation, their profession, or their name.

[Therefore, it is clear] that during the time men live without a common power to keep them all in awe, they are in that condition which is called war; and such a war is of every man, against every man. . . . In such condition, there is no place for industry; because the fruit thereof is uncertain: and consequently no culture of the earth; no navigation, nor use of the commodities that may be imported by sea; no commodious building; no instruments of moving, and removing, such things as require much force; no knowledge of the face of the earth; no account of time; no arts; no letters; no society; and which is worst of all, continual fear, and danger of violent death; and the life of man, solitary, poor, nasty, brutish, and short. . . .

The final cause, end, or design of men, who naturally love liberty, and dominion over others, [is] the introduction of that restraint upon themselves, [by] which we see them live in commonwealths. . . . The only way to erect such a common power, as may be able to defend them from the invasion of foreigners, and the injuries of one another, and thereby to secure them in such sort, as that by their own industry, and by the fruits of the earth, they may nourish themselves and live contentedly; is, to confer all their power and strength upon one man, or upon one assembly of men, that may reduce all their wills, by plurality of voices, unto one will. . . . [All men shall] submit their wills . . . to his will, and their judgments, to his judgment. This is more than consent, or concord; it is a real unity of them all, in one and the same person, made by covenant of every man with every man, in such manner, as if every man should say to every man, *I authorize and give up my right of governing myself, to this man, or to this assembly of men, on this condition, that you give up your right to him, and authorize all his actions in like manner.* This done, the multitude so united in one person, is called a COMMONWEALTH. . . . This is the generation of that great LEVIATHAN, or rather, to speak more reverently, of that *mortal god,* to which we own under the *immortal God,* our peace and defence. For by this authority, given him by every particular man in the commonwealth, he hath the use of so much power and strength conferred on him, that by terror thereof, he is enabled to perform the wills of them all, to peace at home, and mutual aid against their enemies abroad. And in him consists the essence of the commonwealth; which, to define it, is *one person of whose acts a great multitude, by mutual covenants one with another, have made themselves every one the author, to the end he may use the strength and means of them all, as he shall think expedient, for their peace and common defence.*

And . . . this person, is called SOVEREIGN, and said to have *sovereign power;* and every one besides, his SUBJECT.

The Development of Absolutism in France

The stable monarchy that Louis XIV inherited was largely the product of two master political craftsmen, Cardinals Richelieu and Mazarin. These statesmen actually ran the day-to-day affairs of the French state under Louis XIII and during Louis XIV's minority, respectively. Under their strict control, the French nobility was subdued and made to realize that the king was absolute in his authority and would tolerate no defiance. It was under their direction from 1610–1661 that political absolutism was advanced out of the realm of theory and made a part of the practical life of France.

The first selection, entitled "The Ideal Prince," is a panegyric of Louis XIII by Jean-Louis de Guez de Balzac (1594–1654). In it, Balzac (a rhetorician and partisan of Cardinal Richelieu) presents the major justification for absolutism: the establishment of order. The second selection is by Claude Joly (1607–1700), a famous jurist who opposed Cardinal Mazarin. Joly believed that the king of France should rule within prescribed limits of legal tradition and Christian morality. Needless to say, Joly's appeal went unheeded by Louis XIV.

The Ideal Prince (1631)
JEAN-LOUIS DE GUEZ DE BALZAC

For ten years he [Louis XIII] has watched over us and has been almost constantly on horseback, travelling wherever public necessity calls him. Although he well knows that kings and realms may not enjoy the same repose, he is content to assume the difficulties and dangers to himself and to leave peace and security to France. His white hair has resulted from the noble and glorious anxiety that has brought tranquillity to his people. Every winter the rain and snow beat down on the first head in the world. In

William F. Church, ed. and trans., *The Impact of Absolutism in France: National Experience Under Richelieu, Mazarin and Louis XIV* (New York: John Wiley & Sons, 1969), pp. 35–36. Copyright © 1969 John Wiley & Sons, Inc. Reprinted by permission of John Wiley & Sons, Inc.

the greatest heat of the summer, when we use all possible means to keep cool and find shade, his face is burned by the sun of Languedoc, . . . subject to injury from air and season. Some of his predecessors found it more difficult to bestir themselves and move from their quarters to the council chamber than he does in going from one end of the realm to the other. He makes his inspections from Paris to Guyenne and Dauphine, and there is no afflicted area of his state whose wounds and ills do not immediately feel the relief that his presence brings wherever he shows himself. . . .

Let us not speak ungratefully of our prosperity. Let us not contradict public sentiment. Let us not weaken the truth by malicious exceptions and limited praise. Let us at least confess our obligations to the king even though we cannot comprehend them. There never was a ruler so well-disposed to do right as urged by political philosophers; never were there greater promises for the future. We no longer fear the ruin of our state; we have unending hope. All parts of this superb body that was wracked so long [by dissention] are again strengthened. Everything is encompassed by an admirable justice; hardly a stone is out of place; nothing offends our sensibilities. For the first time slander is nowhere to be heard. There are no faults to uncover and almost no wishes to make.

I can hardly believe my own eyes and impressions, when I consider the present and recall the past. It is no longer the France that recently was so torn apart, ill and decrepit. No longer are the French enemies of their [own] country, slothful in the service of their prince and despised by other nations. Behind their faces I see other men and in the same realm another state. The form remains, but the interior has been renewed. There has occurred a moral revolution, a change of spirit, a most agreeable progress from evil to good. The king has restored the good repute of his subjects, communicated his strength and vigor to the state, and corrected the faults of the previous century; he has eliminated both indolence and recklessness from public affairs.

True Maxims of Government (1663)

CLAUDE JOLY

Although Cardinal Mazarin is incompetent in all things but the infamous art of deceit, it has not been difficult for him to imitate the earlier corruptors of princes who preceeded him, since he found himself, after the death of King Louis XIII (of glorious memory), in possession of the mind of the Queen [Marie de Medici], then Regent, and later that of her son [Louis XIV], both because of her influence and the new title of superintendent of his majesty's education, which Mazarin gave himself in order to possess this young royal mind more easily. . . .

William F. Church, ed. and trans., *The Impact of Absolutism in France: National Experience Under Richelieu, Mazarin and Louis XIV* (New York: John Wiley & Sons, 1969), pp. 46–52. Copyright © 1969 John Wiley & Sons, Inc. Reprinted by permission of John Wiley & Sons, Inc.

Although it seems that the principal reason for seeking the permanent banishment of this alien minister is our deliverance from our present ills, . . . nevertheless the greatest and most pressing reason . . . is our well-founded fear that this pernicious superintendent of our young monarch's education will in time pervert all his good inclinations toward virtue and the welfare and relief of his subjects. . . .

That is why it is most important to ensure that the corrupt doctrine that this bad preceptor has given the king will not penetrate his heart, the place from which come evil thoughts capable of raising tempests. For this purpose, it is most appropriate to inform his majesty of the truths that are contrary to the falsehoods with which he has been imbued so as to instruct him concerning what he may and should do, and still more what he may not and should not do. . . .

The power of kings is not absolute and without limits. And since it is important to instruct them . . . it is necessary to begin by establishing this maxim that carries with it many others, for example, that the power of kings is bounded and limited, and that they may not dispose of their subjects according to their will and pleasure. . . .

However, the flattery of courtiers has advanced to such a degree of audacity and extravagance that some impertinent men attempt to persuade kings that they may rightfully dispose of their subjects' lives and goods at will. . . . This pretended right is a weak foundation for the absolute and tyrannical power with which ministers and courtiers delude the kings in order to solidify their positions and subject the people to a blind obedience that would be greater than that which we give to God who demands from us only a reasonable obedience. . . .

Moreover, it is a very great error, against which kings should be warned, that politics and Christian piety are incompatible and that it is impossible to accommodate the laws of the state to those of the Gospel. This most dangerous opinion is sometimes insinuated into their minds and not only does great damage to their consciences but is particularly detrimental to a King of France because it may cause him to do many things that would completely tarnish his beautiful name of Most Christian. . . .

Certain persons who are badly informed concerning the rights of the sovereign believe that the people were made for kings, whereas on the contrary it is true that kings were made only for the people. There have always been people without kings, but never kings without people.

Because of this, and because the people cannot live without justice, it is entirely correct to say that kings were created to render justice to their people. It was owing to their need of justice that the people resolved to erect a king over themselves. . . .

From this, it should not be difficult to prove that kings are bound by law, for that which does not conform to approved and accepted law may not be regarded as just. . . .

It is a dangerous falsehood, which avaricious ministers and ambitious persons have sought to insinuate into the minds of kings, that they are absolute masters of the lives and goods of their subjects and that, consequently, all that belongs to us is theirs to take and distribute to others at will whenever they please.

Now, I entirely disapprove of calling the king our master unless we understand this to be a mere figure of speech, implying nothing that is not intended by the word "king." I myself have used the term "master" in this sense in this book, indicating the profound respect and veneration that I own royal majesty. But when it is a question of proper and exact terms, I say that the word "master" is the diametrical opposite of "king." For persons who are completely different from a master, such as slaves or domestics, are made for the master, . . . but it is the king who is made for his subjects. . . .

From this it follows that if kings, speaking strictly and not in terms of respect and honor, cannot be called our masters, it is impossible to urge the untenable proposition that they are masters of our lives and goods. On the contrary, we must conclude with all assurance that since they are not masters of our goods, they have no right to take them nor to levy taxes from us without our will and consent. . . .

It is God who punishes bad kings and punishes them most rigorously; very rarely does He neglect to punish them in this world. . . . Princes should be taught that they have a great obligation to God. He may punish them in this world, using this temporal punishment to lessen the eternal punishment, which is more severe for kings and princes than for others.

I have occasionally reflected on the words of the Son of God where He teaches us that when He comes in his majesty at the day of the last judgment, He will admit to his Father's realm only those who have performed acts of mercy toward the poor, to whom He seems principally to attach the salvation of all men, and will condemn to eternal flames those who have neglected the poor. And I have thought that by this teaching, He attributes the cause of damnation to a single sin of omission.

This passage of Scripture is truly capable of astonishing everyone, but it should particularly cause kings to tremble in terror as well as all who have the power to do good or evil. For if it is true that God punishes so rigorously those who have failed to make use of their resources to aid the poor, how horrible will be the hell and punishment of princes who, because of bad conduct, nonchalance, uncontrolled passion, concern for small matters of honor, or unfounded authority . . . levy taxes and wage cruel, barbarous wars with which they ruin their people, reducing them from riches to poverty and to inconceivable need and misery?

Divine-Right Monarchy: Louis XIV

The practical rule of any government must be justified through some doctrine, whether it be a devotion to the principles of democracy or to the more blatant dictum, "might makes right." Louis XIV justified his absolutism through the belief that God so willed it. Such a "divine-right" monarch ruled with the authority of God and was beholden to no power except that of God. For his part, the king was accountable to God and was expected to rule with the best interests of his people at heart.

The following selections explain the theoretical basis of Louis' absolutism. The first is by Jean Domat (1624–1696), one of the most renown jurists and legal scholars of his age. He was responsible for a codification of French law that was sponsored by the king himself. The selection presented is from his treatment of French public law and may be regarded as the official statement of divine-right absolutism. The second excerpt is from a treatise by Jacques Benique Bossuet (1627–1704), bishop and tutor to Louis XIV's heir. An eloquent political writer, Bossuet justified divine-right monarchy by basing his support on direct evidence from the Bible. The treatise, entitled *Politics Drawn from the Very Words of Scripture,* was directed specifically at Louis' son and successor, the Dauphin.

The Ideal Absolute State (1697)

JEAN DOMAT

All men being equal by nature because of the humanity that is their essence, nature does not cause some to be inferior to others. But in this natural equality, they are separated by other principles that render their conditions unequal and give rise to relationships and dependencies that determine their varying duties toward others and render government necessary. . . .

The first distinction that subjects some persons to others is that which birth introduces between parents and children. . . . The second distinction among persons is that which requires different employments in society and unites all in the body of which each is a member. . . . And it is these varying occupations and dependencies that create the ties that form society among men, as those of its members form a body. This renders it necessary that a head coerce and rule the body of society and maintain order among those who should give the public the benefit of the different contributions that their stations require of them. . . .

Since government is necessary for the common good and God himself established it, it follows that those who are its subjects must be submissive and obedient. For otherwise they would resist God, and the government which should be the source of the peace and unity that make possible the public good would suffer from dissention and trouble that would destroy it. . . .

As obedience is necessary to preserve the order and peace that unite the

William F. Church, ed. and trans., *The Impact of Absolutism in France: National Experience Under Richelieu, Mazarin and Louis XIV* (New York: John Wiley & Sons, 1969), pp. 377–381. Copyright © 1969 John Wiley & Sons, Inc. Reprinted by permission of John Wiley & Sons, Inc.

head and members of the body of the state, it is the universal obligation of all subjects in all cases to obey the ruler's orders without assuming the liberty of judging them. For otherwise each man would be master because of his right to examine what might be just or unjust, and this liberty would favor sedition. Thus every man owes obedience even to unjust laws and orders, provided that he may execute and obey them without injustice. And the only exception that may exempt him from this obligation is limited to cases in which he may not obey without violating divine law. . . .

According to these principles, which are the natural foundations of the authority of those who govern, their power should have two essential attributes: first, to cause justice to rule without exception and, second, to be as absolute as the rule of justice, that is, as absolute as the rule of God Himself who is justice, rules according to its principles, and desires rulers to do likewise. . . .

Since the power of princes comes to them from God and is placed in their hands as an instrument of his providence and his guidance of the states that He commits to their rule, it is clear that princes should use their power in proportion to the objectives that providence and divine guidance seek . . . and that power is confided to them to this end. This is without doubt the foundation and first principle of all the duties of sovereigns that consist of causing God Himself to rule, that is, regulating all things according to His will, which is nothing more than justice. The rule of justice should be the glory of the rule of princes. . . .

The power of sovereigns includes the authority to exercise the functions of government and to use the force that is necessary to their ministry. For authority without force would be despised and almost useless, while force without legitimate authority would be mere tyranny. . . .

There are two uses of sovereign power that are necessary to the public tranquillity. One consists of constraining the subjects to obey and repressing violence and injustice, the other of defending the state against the aggressions of its enemies. Power should be accompanied by the force that is required for these two functions.

The use of force for the maintenance of public tranquillity within the state includes all that is required to protect the sovereign himself from rebellions that would be frequent if authority and force were not united, and all that is required to keep order among the subjects, repress violence against individuals and the general public, execute the orders of the sovereign, and effect all that is required for the administration of justice. Since the use of force and the occasions that require it are never-ending, the government of the sovereign must maintain the force that is needed for the rule of justice. This requires officials and ministers in various functions and the use of arms whenever necessary. . . .

One should include among the rights that the law gives the sovereign that of acquiring all the evidences of grandeur and majesty that are needed to bring renown to the authority and dignity of such great power and to instill awe in the minds of the subjects. For although the latter should view royal power as from God and submit to it regardless of tangible indications of grandeur, God accompanies his own power with a visible majesty that extends over land and sea. . . . When He wishes to exercise his august power as lawgiver, He proclaims his laws with prodigies that inspire reverence and unspeakable terror. He is therefore willing that sovereigns enhance the dignity of their power . . . in such manner as to win the respect of the people. . . .

The general duties . . . of those who have sovereign authority include all that concern the administration of justice, the general polity of the state, public order, tranquillity of the subjects, security of families, attention to all that may contribute to the general good, the choice of skillful ministers who love justice and truth . . . discrimination between justice and clemency whenever justice might suffer from relaxation of its rigor, wise distribution of benefits, rewards, exemptions, privileges and other concessions, wise administration of the public funds, prudence regarding foreigners, and all that may render government agreeable to the good, terrible to the wicked, and entirely worthy of the divine function of ruling men by wielding power that comes only from God and is a participation in his own.

As the final duty of the sovereign, one may add the following which stems from the administration of justice and includes all others. Although his power seems to place him above the law, since no man has the right to call him to account for his conduct, he should observe the laws that concern himself not only because he should be an example to his subjects and render their duty pleasant but because he is not dispensed from his own duty by his sovereign power. On the contrary, his rank obliges him to subordinate his personal interests to the general good of the state, which it is his glory to regard as his own.

Politics and Scripture (1679)

JACQUES BENIQUE BOSSUET

Monarchical government is the best form: If it is the most natural, it is therefore the most enduring, and in consequence the strongest form of government.

It is also the best defense against division, which is the deadliest disease of states, and the most certain cause of their downfall. "Every kingdom divided against itself is brought to desolation; and every city or house divided against itself shall not stand." . . . [Matt. 12:25]

The purpose of founding states is unity, and there is no greater unity than being under one ruler. There is also no greater strength, for all [the wills] concur. . . .

Reprinted with permission of The Free Press, a Division of Macmillan, Inc., from *The Seventeenth Century*, edited by Andrew Lossky, section *Bossuet*, translated by Geoffrey W. Symcox, pp. 221–222, 224–225, 227, 229, 233–234, 250. Copyright © 1967 by The Free Press.

Kings should respect their powers and only employ them for the general good: Since their power comes from above, as has been stated, they should not believe that they are masters of it and may use it just as they please; they should exercise it with fear and restraint, as a thing conferred on them by God, for which they are answerable to Him. "Hear therefore, O ye Kings, and understand; learn, ye that be judges of the ends of the earth. Give ear, ye that rule the people, and glory in the multitude of nations. For power is given you of the Lord, and sovereignty from the Highest, who shall try your works and search out your counsels. Because, being ministers of His kingdom, ye have not judged aright, not kept the law, nor walked after the counsel of God. Horribly and speedily shall He come upon you: for a sharp judgment shall be to them that are in high places. . . ." [Wis. 6]

Kings should therefore tremble to exercise the power which God has given to them, and remember how terrible a sacrilege it is to abuse the power which comes from God.

We have seen kings seated on the throne of the Lord, holding in their hand the sword which He has committed to their charge. What blasphemy and presumption it is for an unjust ruler to occupy the throne of God and give judgments contrary to His law, to wield the sword which He has placed in their hands to oppress and destroy His children!

There is no higher judgment than that of the prince: Kings are gods, and partake in some measure of the independence of God: "I have said, Ye are gods; and all of you are children of the most High." [Ps. 82:6]

From this we conclude that he who refuses obedience to the prince is not to be referred to another judgment, but condemned to death without appeal, as an enemy of the public peace and of human society. . . .

The prince can correct himself, when he knows that he has erred; but against his authority there can be no redress save in that authority itself.

Kings are not therefore above the law: Kings are therefore, as others, subject to the equity of the laws, both because they are bound to act justly, and because they owe it to the people to set an example of fairness. But they are not liable to the penalties of the law: or, in the language of theology, princes are subject to the laws in their directive, but not in their coercive function.

Definition of majesty: Nothing is more majestic than all-embracing goodness: and there is no greater debasement of majesty than misery brought upon subjects by the prince. . . .

God is the essence of holiness, goodness, power, reason. In these consists the divine majesty. In their reflection consists the majesty of the prince.

So great is this majesty that its source cannot be found to reside in the prince: it is borrowed from God, who entrusts it to the prince for the good of his people, to which end it is well that it be restrained by a higher power. . . .

O kings, be bold therefore in the exercise of your power; for it is divine and beneficial to the human race; but wield it with humility. It is conferred on you from without. It leaves you in the end weak and mortal, it leaves you still sinners: and it lays upon you a heavier charge to render to God.

On arbitrary government which is not found among us in well-ordered states: It is one thing for a government to be absolute, and quite another for it to be arbitrary. It is absolute in that it is not liable to constraint, there being no other power capable of coercing the sovereign, who is in this sense independent of all human authority. But it does not follow from this that the government is arbitrary, for besides the fact that all is subject to the judgment of God (which is also true of those governments we have just called arbitrary), there are also [fundamental] laws, in such empires, so that whatever is done contrary to them is null in a legal sense: moreover, there is always an opportunity for redress, either at other times or in other conditions. Thus each man remains the legitimate owner of his property. . . .

This is what is termed legitimate government, by its very nature the opposite of arbitrary government.

The Practice of Absolute Rule

Letters to His Heirs:
"Allow Good Sense to Act"

KING LOUIS XIV

In this selection, drawn from Louis' memoirs, the king himself gives practical advice to his heirs concerning the demands and duties of absolute monarchy.

Two things without doubt were absolutely necessary: very hard work on my part, and a wise choice of persons capable of seconding it.

As for work, it may be, my son, that you will begin to read these Memoirs at an age when one is far more in the habit of dreading than loving it, only too happy to have escaped subjection to tutors and to have your hours regulated no longer, nor lengthy and prescribed study laid down for you.

On this heading I will not warn you solely that it is none the less toil *by which* one reigns, and *for which* one reigns, and that the conditions of royalty, which may seem to you sometimes hard and vexatious in so lofty a position, would appear pleasant and easy if there was any doubt of your reaching it.

Jean Longnon, ed., *A King's Lessons in Statecraft: Louis XIV*, trans. H. Wilson, (London: T. Fisher Unwin Ltd., 1924), pp. 48–53, 149.

Portrait bust of Louis XIV by Giovanni Lorenzo Bernini. (*National Gallery of Art, Samuel H. Kress Collection*)

There is something more, my son, and I hope that your own experience will never teach it to you: nothing could be more laborious to you than a great amount of idleness if you were to have the misfortune to fall into it through beginning by being disgusted with public affairs, then with pleasure, then with idleness itself, seeking everywhere fruitlessly for what can never be found, that is to say, the sweetness of repose and leisure without having the preceding fatigue and occupation.

I laid a rule on myself to work regularly twice every day, and for two or three hours each time with different persons, without counting the hours which I passed privately and alone, nor the time which I was able to give on particular occasions to any special affairs that might arise. There was no moment when I did not permit people to talk to me about them, provided that they were urgent; with the exception of foreign ministers who sometimes find too favourable moments in the familiarity allowed to them, either to obtain or to discover something, and whom one should not hear without being previously prepared.

I cannot tell you what fruit I gathered immediately I had taken this resolution. I felt myself, as it were, uplifted in thought and courage; I found myself quite another man, and with joy reproached myself for having been too long unaware of it. This first timidity, which a little self-judgment always produces and which at the beginning gave me pain, especially on occasions when I had to speak in public, disappeared in less than no time. The only thing I felt then was that I was King, and born to be one. I experienced next a delicious feeling, hard to express, and which you will not know yourself except by tasting it as I have done. For you must not imagine, my son, that the affairs of State are like some obscure and thorny path of learning which may possibly have already wearied you, wherein the mind strives to raise itself with effort above its purview, more often to arrive at no conclusion, and whose utility or apparent utility is repugnant to us as much as its difficulty. The function of Kings consists principally in allowing good sense to act, which always acts naturally and without effort. What we apply ourselves to is sometimes less difficult than what we do only for our amusement. Its usefullness always follows. A King, however skillful and enlightened be his ministers, cannot put his own hand to the work without its effect being seen. Success, which is agreeable in everything, even in the smallest matters, gratifies us in these as well as in the greatest, and there is no satisfaction to equal that of noting every day some progress in glorious and lofty enterprises, and in the happiness of the people which has been planned and thought out by oneself. All that is most necessary to this work is at the same time agreeable, for; in a word, my son, it is to have one's eyes open to the whole earth; to learn each hour the news concerning every province and every nation, the secrets of every court, the mood and the weaknesses of each Prince and of every foreign minister; to be well-informed on an infinite number of matters about which we are supposed to know nothing; to elicit from our subjects what they hide from us with the greatest care; to discover the most remote opinions of our own courtiers and the most hidden interests of those who come to us with quite contrary professions. I do not know of any other pleasure we would not renounce for that, even if curiousity alone gave us the opportunity. . . .

.   .   .

I gave orders to the four Secretaries of State no longer to sign anything whatsoever without speaking to me; likewise to the Controller, and that he should authorise nothing as regards finance without its being registered in a book which must remain with me, and being noted down in a very abridged abstract form in which at any moment, and at a glance, I could see the state of the funds, and past and future expenditure. . . .

· · ·

Regarding the persons whose duty it was to second my labours, I resolved at all costs to have no prime minister; and if you will believe me, my son, and all your successors after you, the name shall be banished for ever from France, for there is nothing more undignified than to see all the administration on one side, and on the other, the mere title of King.

To effect this, it was necessary to divide my confidence and the execution of my orders without giving it entirely to one single person, applying these different people to different spheres according to their diverse talents, which is perhaps the first and greatest gift that Princes can possess.

I also made a resolution on a further matter. With a view the better to unite in myself alone all the authority of a master, although there must be in all affairs a certain amount of detail to which our occupations and also our dignity do not permit us to descend as a rule, I conceived the plan, after I should have made choice of my ministers, of entering sometimes into matters with each one of them, and when they least expected it, in order that they might understand that I could do the same upon other subjects and at any moment. Besides, a knowledge of some small detail acquired only occasionally, and for amusement rather than as a regular rule, is instructive little by little and without fatigue, on a thousand things which are not without their use in general resolutions, and which we ought to know and do ourselves were it possible that a single man could know and do everything.

· · ·

I have never failed, when an occasion has presented itself, to impress upon you the great respect we should have for religion, and the deference we should show to its ministers in matters specially connected with their mission, that is to say, with the celebration of the Sacred Mysteries and the preaching of the doctrine of the Gospels. But because people connected with the Church are liable to presume a little too much on the advantages attaching to their profession, and are willing sometimes to make use of them in order to whittle down their most rightful duties, I feel obliged to explain to you certain points on this question which may be of importance.

The first is that Kings are absolute *seigneurs*, and from their nature have full and free disposal of all property both secular and ecclesiastical, to use it as wise dispensers, that is to say, in accordance with the requirements of their State. . . .

The Revocation of the Edict of Nantes (1685)

KING LOUIS XIV

On October 22, 1685, Louis XIV annulled the Edict of Nantes, which had provided political and religious freedom for the French Protestants or Huguenots since 1598. Louis was determined to control a nation that was unified politically under his rule and religiously under his faith; Catholicism was to be the only accepted religion for the French people. The revocation was hailed by Catholics, but was not without its critics even at court, as reflected in the opinion of the Duke of Saint-Simon, which follows the text of the treaty.

I. Be it known that [with] . . . our certain knowledge, full power, and royal authority, we have, by this present perpetual and irrevocable edict, suppressed and revoked . . . the edict of our said grandfather, [Henry IV], null and void, together will all concessions . . . in favor of the said persons of the [Reformed religion], . . . and it is our pleasure, that all the temples of those of the said [Reformed religion] situate in our kingdom, countries, territories, and the lordships under our crown, shall be demolished without delay.

II. We forbid our subjects of the [Reformed religion] to meet any more for the exercise of the said religion in any place or private house, under any pretext whatever. . . .

III. We likewise forbid all noblemen . . . to hold such religious exercises in their houses or fiefs, under penalty . . . of imprisonment and confiscation.

IV. We enjoin all ministers of the said [Reformed religion], who do not choose to become converts and to embrace the Catholic, apostolic, and Roman religion, to leave our kingdom and the territories subject to us within a fortnight of the publication of our present edict . . . on pain of being sent to the galleys.

VII. We forbid private schools for the instruction of children of the said [Reformed religion], and in general all things whatever which can be regarded as a concession of any kind in favor of the said religion.

VIII. As for children who may be born of persons of the said [Reformed religion], we desire that from henceforth they be baptized by the parish priests. We enjoin parents to send them to the churches for that purpose, under penalty of five hundred livres fine . . . and thereafter the children shall be brought up in the Catholic, apostolic, and Roman religion, which we expressly enjoin the local magistrates to see done.

X. We repeat our most express prohibition to all our subjects of the said

James H. Robinson, ed., *Readings in European History*, vol. 2 (Boston: Ginn and Company, 1906), pp. 289–291.

[Reformed religion], together with their wives and children, against leaving our kingdom, lands, and territories subject to us, or transporting their goods and effects therefrom under penalty, as respects the men, of being sent to the galleys, and as respects the women, of imprisonment and confiscation.

XII. As for the rest, liberty is granted to the said persons of the [Reformed religion], pending the time when it shall please God to enlighten them as well as others to remain in the cities and places of our kingdom, lands, and territories subject to us, and there to continue their commerce, and to enjoy their possessions, without being subjected to molestation ... on condition of not engaging in the exercise of the said religion. ...

"A Frightful Plot": Results of the Revocation

THE DUKE OF SAINT-SIMON

The revocation of the Edict of Nantes, without the slightest pretext of necessity, and the various proscriptions that followed it, were the fruits of a frightful plot, in which the new spouse was one of the chief conspirators, and which depopulated a quarter of the realm; ruined its commerce; weakened it in every direction; gave it up for a long time to the public and avowed pillage of the dragoons; authorized torments and punishments by which many innocent people of both sexes were killed by thousands; ruined a numerous class; tore in pieces a world of families; armed relatives against relatives, so as to seize their property and leave them to die in hunger; banished our manufactures to foreign lands; made those lands flourish and overflow at the expense of France, and enabled them to build new cities; gave to the world the spectacle of a prodigious population proscribed without crime, stripped, fugitive, wandering, and seeking shelter far from their country; sent to the galleys nobles, rich old men, people carefully nurtured, weak, and delicate;—and all solely on account of religion. ...

The king congratulated himself on his power and his piety. He believed himself to have brought back the days of the apostles, and attributed to himself all the honor. The bishops wrote panegyrics of him; the Jesuits made the pulpit resound with his praise. All France was filled with horror and confusion; and yet there was never such triumph and joy, such boundless laudation of the king.

James H. Robinson, ed., *Readings in European History*, vol. 2 (Boston: Ginn and Company, 1906), pp. 291–293.

The Sighs of Enslaved France (1690)

PIERRE JURIEU

As a result of the revocation of the Edict of Nantes, the persecution of Huguenots began in earnest. The author of the following memoirs cannot be positively identified, but they are probably from the pen of Pierre Jurieu, a Calvinist pastor who had fled to Holland. Louis endured much criticism from such dissidents in exile. Jurieu's memoirs are among the most provocative because they characterize Louis' absolutism as oppressive and responsible for many of the ills of France.

The oppression of the people is caused primarily by the prodigious number of taxes and excessive levies of money that are everywhere taken in France. Taxes and finance are a science today, and one must be skilled to speak knowledgeably of them, but it suffices for us to relate what we all feel and what the people know of the matter. There are the personal and [land taxes]. There are taxes on salt, wine, merchandise, principal, and revenue. This miserable century has produced a flood of names [of taxes], most of which were unknown to our ancestors or, if some were known, they were not odious because of the moderation with which they were imposed and levied. . . . It does not serve my purpose to acquaint you with the details of these taxes so that you may feel their weight and injustice. It will suffice to enable you to understand the horrible oppression of these taxes by showing (1) the immense sums that are collected, (2) the violence and abuses that are committed in levying them, (3) the bad use that is made of them, and (4) the misery to which the people are reduced.

First, dear unfortunate compatriots, you should realize that the taxes that are taken from you comprise a sum perhaps greater than that which all the other princes of Europe together draw from their states. One thing is certain, that France pays two hundred million in taxes of which about three-fourths go into the coffers of the king and the rest to expenses of collection, tax-farmers, officials, keepers, receivers, the profits of financiers, and new fortunes that are created in almost a single day. For the collection of the salt tax alone, there is a great army of officers and constables. . . .

If tyranny is clear and evident in the immense sums that are levied in France, it is not less so in the manner of collecting them. Kings were established by the people to preserve their persons, lives, liberty, and properties. But the government of France has risen to such excessive tyranny that the prince today regards everything as belonging to him alone. He imposes taxes at will without consulting the people, the nobles, the Estates, or the Parlements. I shall tell you something that is true and that thousands

William F. Church, ed. and trans., *The Impact of Absolutism in France: National Experience Under Richelieu, Mazarin and Louis XIV* (New York: John Wiley & Sons, 1969), pp. 102–105. Copyright © 1969 John Wiley & Sons, Inc. Reprinted by permission of John Wiley & Sons, Inc.

know but most Frenchmen do not. During Colbert's ministry [supervisor of the royal finances] it was discussed whether the king should take immediate possession of all real and personal property in France and reduce it to royal domain, to be used and assigned to whomever the court judged appropriate without regard for former possession, heredity, or other rights. . . .

How much abuse and violence is committed in the collection of taxes? The meanest agent is a sacred person who has absolute power over gentlemen, the judiciary, and all the people. A single blow is capable of ruining the most powerful subject. They confiscate houses, furnishings, cattle, money, grain, wine, and everything in sight. The prisons are full of wretches who are responsible for sums that they impose upon other wretches who cannot pay what is demanded of them. Is there anything more harsh and cruel than the salt tax? They make you buy for ten or twelve *sous* per pound something that nature, the sun, and the sea provide for nothing and may be had for two farthings. Under pretext of exercising this royal right, the realm is flooded with a great army of scoundrels called constables of the gabelle [salt tax] who enter houses, penetrate the most secret places with impunity, and do not fail to find unauthorized salt wherever they think there is money. They condemn wretches to pay huge fines, cause them to rot in prison, and ruin families. They force salt upon people everywhere and give each family more than three times as much as they can consume. In the provinces by the sea, they will not permit a poor peasant to bring home salt water; they break jugs, beat people, and imprison them. In a word, every abuse is committed in levying this and other taxes which is done with horrible expense, seizures, imprisonments, and legal cases before the collectors and courts with costs far above the sums involved. . . .

This is how all of France is reduced to the greatest poverty. In earlier reigns, that is, during the ministries of Cardinal Richelieu and Cardinal Mazarin, France was already burdened with heavy taxes. But the manner of collecting them, although not entirely just, nevertheless exhausted the realm much less than the way in which they are collected today. . . . The government of today has changed all of this. M. de Colbert made a plan to reform the finances and applied it to the letter. But what was this reformation? It was not the diminution of taxes in order to relieve the people. . . . He increased the king's revenue by one half. . . .

After this, if we examine the use that is made of these immense sums that are collected with such abuses and extortion, we shall find all the characteristics of oppression and tyranny. It sometimes happens that princes and sovereigns exact levies that appear excessive and greatly inconvenience individuals, but are required by what are called the needs and necessities of the state. In France there is no such thing. There are neither *needs* nor *state*. As for the *state*, earlier it entered into everything; one spoke only of the interests of the *state*, the needs of the *state*, the preservation of the *state*, and the service of the *state*. To speak this way today would literally be a crime of *lese majesty* [treason]. The king has taken the place of the state.

It is the service of the *king,* the interest of the *king,* the preservation of the provinces and wealth of the *king.* Therefore the king is all and the state nothing. And these are no mere figures of speech but realities. At the French court, no interest is considered but the personal interest of the king, that is, his grandeur and glory. He is the idol to which are sacrificed princes, great men and small, families, provinces, cities, finances and generally everything. Therefore, it is not for the good of the state that these horrible exactions are made, since there is no more state. . . .

This money is used solely to nourish and serve the greatest self-pride and arrogance that ever existed. It is so deep an abyss that it would have swallowed not only the wealth of the whole realm but that of all other states if the king had been able to take possession of it as he attempted to do. The king has caused himself to receive more false flattery than all the pagan demi-gods did with true flattery. Never before was flattery pushed to this point. Never has man loved praise and vainglory to the extent that this prince has sought them. In his court and around himself he supports a multitude of flatterers who constantly seek to outdo each other. He not only permits the erection of statues to himself, on which are inscribed blasphemies in his honor and below which all the nations of the earth are shown in chains; he causes himself to be represented in gold, silver, bronze, copper, marble, silk, in paintings, arches of triumph, and inscriptions. He fills all Paris, all his palaces, and the whole realm with his name and his exploits, as though he far surpassed the Alexanders, the Caesars, and all the heroes of antiquity.

Louis XIV: The Sun King

The Memoirs of the Duke of Saint-Simon

The Duke of Saint-Simon (1675–1755) was a rather indifferent soldier and diplomat, but he was a passionate observer of affairs at Louis' court and has provided us with our most vivid account of the king and his activities. Saint-Simon was typical of the feudal nobility that Louis was trying to control and thus his account was by no means free from prejudice.

Portrait of the King

Louis XIV was made for a brilliant Court. In the midst of other men, his figure, his courage, his grace, his beauty, his grand mien, even the tone of his voice and the majestic and natural charm of all his person, dis-

Bayle St. John, ed., *The Memoirs of the Duke of Saint-Simon,* vol. 2 (New York: James Pott and Co., 1901), pp. 202–203, 214–219, 226–227, 231–232, 273–276.

tinguished him till his death as the King Bee, and showed that if he had only been born a simple private gentleman, he would equally have excelled in fetes, pleasures, and gallantry, and would have had the greatest success in love. . . . Vanity, this unmeasured and unreasonable love of admiration, was his ruin. His ministers, his generals, his mistresses, his courtiers, soon perceived his weakness. They praised him with emulation and spoiled him. Praises, or to say the truth, flattery, pleased him to such an extent, that the coarsest was well received, the vilest even better relished. It was the sole means by which you could approach him. Those whom he liked owed his affection for them, to their untiring flatteries. This is what gave his ministers so much authority, and the opportunities they had for adulating him, of attributing everything to him, and of pretending to learn everything from him. Suppleness, meanness, an admiring, dependent, cringing manner—above all, an air of nothingness—were the sole means of pleasing him. . . .

Though his intellect, as I have said, was beneath mediocrity, it was capable of being formed. He loved glory, was fond of order and regularity; was by disposition prudent, moderate, discreet, master of his movements and his tongue. Will it be believed? He was also by disposition good and just! God had sufficiently gifted him to enable him to be a good King; perhaps even *a tolerably great King!* All the evil came to him from elsewhere. His early education was so neglected that nobody dared approach his apartment. He has often been heard to speak of those times with bitterness, and even to relate that, one evening he was found in the basin of the Palais Royale garden fountain, into which he had fallen! He was scarcely taught how to read or write, and remained so ignorant, that the most familiar historical and other facts were utterly unknown to him! He fell, accordingly, and sometimes even in public, into the grossest absurdities. . . .

Louis XIV took great pains to be well informed of all that passed everywhere; in the public places, in the private houses, in society and familiar intercourse. His spies and tell-tales were infinite. He had them of all species; many who were ignorant that their information reached him; others who knew it; others who wrote to him direct, sending their letters through channels he indicated; and all these letters were seen by him alone, and always before everything else; others who sometimes spoke to him secretly in his cabinet, entering by the back stairs. These unknown means ruined an infinite number of people of all classes, who never could discover the cause; often ruined them very unjustly; for the King, once prejudiced, never altered his opinion, or so rarely, that nothing was more rare. He had, too, another fault, very dangerous for others and often for himself, since it deprived him of good subjects. He had an excellent memory; in this way, that if he saw a man who, twenty years before, perhaps, had in some manner offended him, he did not forget the man, though he might forget the offence. This was enough, however, to exclude the person from all favour. The representations of a minister, of a general, of his confessor even, could not move the King. He would not yield.

The most cruel means by which the King was informed of what was passing—for many years before anybody knew it—was that of opening letters. The promptitude and dexterity with which they were opened passes understanding. He saw extracts from all the letters in which there were passages that the chiefs of the post-office, and then the minister who governed it, thought ought to go before him; entire letters, too, were sent to him, when their contents seemed to justify the sending. Thus the chiefs of the post, nay, the principal clerks were in a position to suppose what they pleased and against whom they pleased. A word of contempt against the King or the government, a joke, a detached phrase, was enough. It is incredible how many people, justly or unjustly, were more or less ruined, always without resource, without trial, and without knowing why. The secret was impenetrable; for nothing ever cost the King less than profound silence and dissimulation. . . .

The King loved air and exercise very much, as long as he could make use of them. He had excelled in dancing, and at tennis and mall. On horseback he was admirable, even at a late age. He liked to see everything done with grace and address. To acquit yourself well or ill before him was a merit or fault. He said that with things not necessary it was best not to meddle, unless they were done well. He was very fond of shooting, and there was not a better or more graceful shot than he. . . .

He liked splendour, magnificence, and profusion in everything: you pleased him if you shone through the brilliancy of your houses, your clothes, your table, your equipages. Thus a taste for extravagance and luxury was disseminated through all classes of society; causing infinite harm, and leading to general confusion of rank and to ruin.

The King's Day

At eight o'clock the chief *valet de chambre* on duty, who alone had slept in the royal chamber, and who had dressed himself, awoke the King. The chief physician, the chief surgeon, and the nurse (as long as she lived), entered at the same time. The latter kissed the King; the others rubbed and often changed his shirt, because he was in the habit of sweating a great deal. At the quarter, the grand chamberlain was called (or, in the absence, the first gentleman of the chamber), and those who had what was called the *grandes entrees*. The chamberlain (or chief gentleman) drew back the curtains which had been closed again, and presented the holy-water from the vase, at the head of the bed. . . . Then all passed into the cabinet of the council. A very short religious service being over, the King called, they re-entered. The same officer gave him his dressing-gown; immediately after, other privileged courtiers entered, and then everybody, in time to find the King putting on his shoes and stockings, for he did almost everything himself and with address and grace. Every other day we saw him shave himself; and he had a little short wig in which he always appeared, even in bed, and on medicine days. He often spoke of the chase, and sometimes said a word to somebody. No toilette table was near him; he had simply a mirror held before him.

As soon as he was dressed, he prayed to God, at the side of his bed, where all the clergy present knelt, the cardinals without cushions, all the laity remaining standing; and the captain of the guards came to the balustrade during the prayer, after which the King passed into his cabinet.

He found there, or was followed by all who had the *entree,* a very numerous company, for it included everybody in any office. He gave orders to each for the day; thus within a half a quarter of an hour it was known what he meant to do; and then all this crowd left directly. The bastards, a few favorites, and the valets alone were left. It was then a good opportunity for talking with the King; for example, about plans of gardens and buildings; and conversation lasted more or less according to the person engaged in it. . . .

On Sunday, and often on Monday, there was a council of state; on Tuesday a finance council; on Wednesday council of state; on Saturday finance council. Rarely were two held in one day or any on Thursday or Friday. Once or twice a month there was a council of despatches on Monday morning. . . .

The dinner was always *au petit couvert,* that is the King ate by himself in his chamber upon a square table in front of the middle window. It was more or less abundant, for he ordered in the morning whether it was to be "a little," or "very little" service. But even at this last, there were always many dishes, and three courses without counting the fruit.

The King's Diet

As during the last year of his life the King became more and more costive, Fagon [the court physician] made him eat at the commencement of his repasts many iced fruits, that is to say, mulberries, melons, and figs rotten from ripeness; and at his dessert many other fruits, finishing with a surprising quantity of sweetmeats. All the year round he ate at supper a prodigious quantity of salad. His soups, several of which he partook of morning and evening, were full of gravy, and were of exceeding strength, and everything that was served to him was full of spice, to double the usual extent, and very strong also. . . .

This summer he redoubled his regime of fruits and drinks. At last the former clogged his stomach, taken after soup, weakened the digestive organs and took away his appetite, which until then had never failed him all his life, though however late dinner might be delayed he never was hungry or wanted to eat. But after the first spoonfuls of soup, his appetite came, as I have several times heard him say, and he ate so prodigiously and so solidly morning and evening that no one could get accustomed to see it. So much water and so much fruit unconnected by anything spiritous, turned his blood into gangrene; while those forced night sweats diminshed its strength and impoverished it; and thus his death was caused, as was seen by the opening of his body. The organs were found in such good and healthy condition that there is reason to believe he would have lived beyond his hundredth year. His stomach above all astonished, and also his bowels by their volume and extent, double that of the ordinary, whence it came that he was such a great yet uniform eater.

The King's Death

Friday, August the 30th, was a bad day preceded by a bad night. The King continually lost his reason. About five o'clock in the evening Madame de Maintenon left him, gave away her furniture to the domestics, and went to Saint-Cyr never to leave it.

On Saturday, the 31st of August, everything went from bad to worse. The gangrene had reached the knee and all the thigh. Towards eleven o'clock at night the King was found to be so ill that the prayers for the dying were said. This restored him to himself. He repeated the prayers in a voice so strong that it rose above all the other voices. At the end he recognised Cardinal de Rohan, and said to him, "These are the last favours of the Church." This was the last man to whom he spoke. He repeated several times, *Nunc et in hora mortis,* then said, "Oh, my God, come to my aid: hasten to succour me."

These were his last words. All the night he was without consciousness and in a long agony, which finished on Sunday, the 1st September, 1715, at a quarter past eight in the morning, three days before he had accomplished his seventy-seventh year, and in the seventy-second of his reign. He had survived all his sons and grandsons, except the King of Spain. Europe never saw so long a reign or France a King so old.

Impressions of the Palace at Versailles

In 1661, Louis XIV began construction on his famous palace at Versailles, about twenty miles from Paris. By 1668, two shifts of laborers were working constantly, and by 1682, enough of the palace had been completed to warrant Louis' move from Paris. Amid the construction that continued until 1710, Louis lived, along with most of the French aristocracy, entertaining lavishly and administering the affairs of state. The palace at Versailles was both admired and reviled, as is noted in the following excerpts, but it served its purpose as a monument to the glory of the "Sun King."

"A Fine Chateau" (1664)

SEBASTIANO LOCATELLI

Sebastiano Locatelli was an Italian priest who visited France in 1664, and described the palace in these terms:

Versailles is a fine chateau begun by Louis XIII and completed by the reigning king. There is plentiful game in the vicinity. An aviary constructed of copper wire contains, I think, an example of every bird known to man. Indeed, I was shown more than forty species which I had never yet seen or even heard of. As regards the buildings, hunting facilities, comfort and pleasure, Versailles excels all the King's other chateaux, even Fountainbleau.

Three great roadways leading from the Cours la Reine in Paris to Versailles have already been started and will gradually be improved. They will be twenty-one miles in a straight line, planted with four lines of trees and divided into three pathways: the central pathway, to be paved for the use of carriages, will be four perches wide; the two flanking pathways, each a perch wide, will be raised, so forming a sort of levee. All this will cost the King a great sum of money, for this region is very hilly, and these hills must be levelled out over a distance of seven miles; it is true that they are not very high, and contain no stones. If these roadways are ever completed they will surely be unparalleled throughout the world.

A Celebration of Greatness (1665)

JEAN COLBERT

The expense of the palace was indeed a concern, especially to Jean Colbert, who supervised the royal finances. Still, in 1665, Colbert did not doubt that such a venture was an essential component of Louis' monarchy. In the second selection, Louis himself reveals the necessity of a palace on such a scale as Versailles. Other impressions of the palace follow.

If Your Majesty desires to discover where in Versailles are the more than 500,000 ecus spent there in two years, he will have great difficulty in finding them. Will he also deign to reflect that the Accounts of the Royal Buildings will always record the evidence that, during the time he has lavished such vast sums on this mansion, he has neglected the Louvre, which is assuredly the most superb palace in the world and the one worth-

"A Fine Chateau" is from Gilette Ziegler, ed., *The Court of Versailles in the Reign of Louis XIV*, trans. Simon Watson Taylor (London: George Allen and Unwin, Ltd., 1966), p. 25. Reprinted by permission of the publisher.

"A Celebration of Greatness" is from Gilette Ziegler, ed., *The Court of Versailles in the Reign of Louis XIV*, trans. Simon Watson Taylor (London: George Allen and Unwin, Ltd., 1966), p. 26. Reprinted by permission of the publisher.

A full view of Versailles as it appeared after its expansion from a hunting lodge to the royal residence and seat of government (ca. 1682). A center of culture, the palace also served as propaganda, being symbolic of the absolute authority of the "Sun King." (*The New York Public Library, Art and Architecture Room*)

iest of Your Majesty's greatness. . . . And God forbid that those many occasions which may impel him to go to war, and thus deprive him of the financial means to complete this superb building, should give him lasting occasion for regret at having lost the time and opportunity.

Your Majesty knows that, apart from glorious actions of war, nothing celebrates so advantageously the greatness and genius of princes than buildings, and all posterity measures them by the yardstick of these superb edifices which they have erected during their life. O what pity were the greatest and most virtuous of kings, of that real virtue which makes the greatest princes, to be measured by the scale of Versailles!

Visible Majesty

KING LOUIS XIV

Those who imagine that these are merely matters of ceremony are gravely mistaken. The peoples over whom we reign, being able to apprehend the basic reality of things, usually derive their opinion from what they can see with their eyes.

Glory Secured (1684)

SIEUR DES COMBES

Italy must now yield to France the prize and garland which it has borne away hitherto from all the nations of the earth, in what regards the excellency of architecture, the beauty of the carving, the magnificence of painting, and the invention of aqueducts. . . . Versailles alone suffices to secure forever to France the glory it has at present, in surpassing all other kingdoms in the science of building: and it is beholding for this high esteem to the grandeur and magnificence of Louis the Great.

The Bad Taste of Versailles

THE DUKE OF SAINT-SIMON

As for the King himself, nobody ever approached his magnificence. His buildings, who could number them? At the same time, who was there who did not deplore the pride, the caprice, the bad taste seen in them? He built nothing useful or ornamental in Paris, except the Pont Royal, and that simply by necessity; so that despite its incomparable extent, Paris is inferior

"Visible Majesty" is from Gilette Ziegler, ed., *The Court of Versailles in the Reign of Louis XIV,* trans. Simon Watson Taylor (London: George Allen and Unwin, Ltd., 1966), p. 26. Reprinted by permission of the publisher.

"Glory Secured" is from Sieur des Combes (Laurent Morellet), *An Historical Explication of What There Is Most Remarkable in That Wonder of the World, the French King's House at Versailles* (London, 1684).

"The Bad Taste of Versailles" is from Bayle St. John, ed., *The Memoirs of the Duke of Saint-Simon,* vol. 2 (New York: James Pott and Co., 1901), pp. 232–233.

to many cities of Europe. Saint-Germains, a lovely spot, with a marvellous view, rich forest, terraces, gardens, and water he abandoned for Versailles; the dullest and most ungrateful of all places, without prospect, without wood, without water, without soil; for the ground is all shifting sand or swamp, the air accordingly bad.

But he liked to subjugate nature by art and treasure. He built at Versailles, on and on, without any general design, the beautiful and the ugly, the vast and the mean, all jumbled together. His own apartments and those of the Queen, are inconvenient to the last degree, dull, close, stinking. The gardens astonish by their magnificence, but cause regret by their bad taste. You are introduced to the freshness of the shade only by a vast torrid zone, at the end of which there is nothing for you but to mount or descend; and with the hill, which is very short, terminate the gardens. The violence everywhere done to nature repels and wearies us despite ourselves. The abundance of water, forced up and gathered together from all parts, is rendered green, thick, muddy; it disseminates humidity, unhealthy and evident; and an odour still more so. I might never finish upon the monstrous defects of a palace so immense and so immensely dear, with its accomplishments, which are still more so.

But the supply of water for the fountains was all defective at all moments, in spite of those seas of reservoirs which had cost so many millions to establish and to form upon the shifting sands and marsh. Who could have believed it? This defect became the ruin of the infantry which was turned out to do the work. . . . How many men were years in recovering from the effects of the contagion! How many never regained their health at all!

STUDY QUESTIONS

1. Discuss the ideas of Thomas Hobbes contained in the excerpt entitled *Leviathan*. What is his view of human nature, and how does he justify absolute monarchy? Be specific in your assessment. What are the advantages of absolute rule as detailed by Guez de Balzac? How would you say that the statements of Balzac and Hobbes are mutually supportive?

2. What are Claude Joly's main ideas regarding absolutist rule? Do you find his arguments persuasive? Compare these with the ideas of Jean Domat on "The Ideal Absolute State" and Jacques Benique Bossuet on "Politics and Scripture." How do their arguments differ specifically? Which is more compelling and why?

3. Louis XIV was a divine-right monarch. What does this mean, and how did Louis use religion to strengthen his political position in the state?

4. What is the difference between tyranny and the absolutism of Louis XIV's monarchy? What were the advantages and disadvantages of absolute rule for the different classes of French society? Who profited the most?

5. Analyze the Edict of Nantes. Why was it invoked in 1598 and why did Louis XIV revoke it? Was this a wise move politically? Are you persuaded

by the Duke of Saint-Simon's criticism? If you accept his criticism as valid, then how would you characterize the absolute rule of Louis XIV? Was he a tyrant—or a wise monarch?

6. Was Louis XIV a responsible monarch? From the accounts in his own memoirs and those of the Duke of Saint-Simon, do you think that Louis worked hard at his job? How did he view his duties as king? Do the criticisms of Pierre Jurieu in "The Sighs of Enslaved France" seem valid to you? Why should a historian be somewhat careful in the judgments drawn from this evidence?

7. Look closely at the picture of Louis' palace at Versailles at the beginning of the section. In what ways did this structure reflect the character of Louis' monarchy? According to the comments contained in the section on Versailles, was the palace an effective propaganda medium? Why?

8. To what extent do you think absolute rule is a "natural" form of government, generally acceptable to most people, especially if it is benign or even enlightened so that the best interests of citizens are promoted? Do people want a government that provides for their security and happiness but do not care about the participation and personal responsibility that a democracy demands? What are your own opinions on the subject?

4

Liberty, Equality, Fraternity! The French Revolution and the Rise of Napoleon

I hold that a little rebellion now and then is a good thing, and as necessary to the political world as storms in the physical. The tree of liberty must be refreshed from time to time with the blood of patriots and tyrants. It is its natural manure.

—Thomas Jefferson

The greatest dangers to liberty lurk in insidious encroachment by men of zeal—well-meaning, but without understanding.

—Justice Louis D. Brandeis

Inferiors revolt in order that they may be equal, and equals that they may be superior. Such is the state of mind that creates revolution.

—Aristotle

What is the throne?—a bit of wood gilded and covered with velvet. I am the state—I alone am the representative of the people. . . . France has more need of me than I of France.

—Napoleon Bonaparte (1814)

Do you know what astounds me most about the world? It is the impotence of force to establish anything. In the end, the sword is always conquered by the mind.

—Napoleon Bonaparte (1808)

Men of genius are meteors destined to be consumed in lighting up their
century.

—Napoleon Bonaparte (1791)

One of the most exciting periods of change and development in Western
Civilization occurred during the seventeenth and eighteenth centuries.
The attitudes and ideas that flourished during this time have formed the
intellectual and political bases of our modern western world.

The eighteenth century, in particular, has been called the Age of Reason or the Enlightenment. The writers and thinkers of this time were
convinced that natural laws governed the universe and that man, being
essentially a rational creature, could discover and apply those laws to the
world around him. Thus did Sir Isaac Newton seek to explain motion in
the universe through observation, experimentation, and deduction. Others endeavored to explain human relationships through such rational
thought. These intellectuals, called the *philosophes,* examined and challenged the political institutions and economic theories of the day. The
philosophes were diverse in their thought and often contended among
themselves, but they were united by the conviction that man had natural
rights (defined by political philosopher John Locke as life, liberty, and
property) and that man must control his own destiny for the sole purpose
of a better life on earth. Thus the political divine-right absolutism of King
Louis XIV (1643–1715), although providing security, could not be tolerated by many *philosophes* because it curtailed individual liberty. Similarly, the *philosophes* were generally opposed to the accepted economic
theory of mercantilism, which sought complete government control of
the national economy, and especially promoted the establishment of
foreign trading monopolies. The production and distribution of goods in
colonial markets were therefore regulated for the benefit of the mother
country. Adam Smith, in his treatise *The Wealth of Nations* (1776), argued that such a rigid policy restricted individual initiative and the natural pursuit of profit. Thus was born the theory of capitalism. In spiritual
matters as well, the *philosophes* regarded religion, especially Christianity, as fantasy that drew humanity away from the rational world into a
realm of hope and belief in a nonexistent life beyond. The spiritual world
was not subject to reason or proof and therefore drew scorn from the
philosophes. Indeed, they contended that organized religion sought to
control thought and was therefore anathema to true intellectual freedom.

Although the *philosophes* generally advocated intellectual freedom
and political equality, it should be stressed that the Enlightenment was
not initially a concerted effort, but took shape in individual minds over
several generations; it did not become a conscious movement until about

1750. Yet the ideas of such important figures as John Locke, the Baron de Montesquieu, Voltaire, Denis Diderot, and Jean Jacques Rousseau were to be influential apart from the theoretical and abstract world of thought. They were to give philosophical justification to the notion that it was proper and desirable to remove a monarch who was incompetent or inattentive to the needs of the people. Revolution often requires philosophical inspiration in order to succeed; without the underlying attitude that revolution can be a proper and progressive act, perhaps the French middle class would not have been motivated to lead a revolt against the established order.

And yet the French Revolution in 1789 did not simply happen as a result of intellectual committment to abstract principles. In fact, there existed more tangible evidence that revolution could succeed and produce desired results. The precedents were clear. In 1649, the English executed their monarch, Charles I, for his autocratic behavior, and in 1688, Parliament established itself as the supreme depository of law and the "popular will" by restricting monarchical authority. It should be remembered, however, that the English had a long tradition of representative government and monarchical limitation dating back most importantly to the Magna Carta in 1215. The French lacked this tradition and their representative institution, the Estates-General, had not met in 175 years. More recent precedent for French revolutionary action existed in the American example. In 1776, the American colonies declared their independence from Britain and were supported in this venture by the French government itself.

There were also economic problems that moved France toward revolution. The wars and extravagance of Louis XIV had sent France to the brink of bankruptcy by 1715, and Louis was a competent and diligent administrator. His heirs, on the other hand, were not particularly dedicated to the governance of France. Louis XV (1715–1774) was poorly educated and preferred to allow his mistresses (one of whom had been a Parisian prostitute) to control the politics of state. Louis XVI (1774–1792) was well educated but more interested in hunting than in administration. From 1715 to 1789, the French economy spiraled into chaos. With the nobility and church exempt from taxation, the burden fell upon the Third Estate.

The French Revolution drew much of its support from the Third Estate, a conglomeration of middle-class professionals, artisans, and peasants. As a group the middle class or *bourgeoisie* was ambitious, educated, and competent. Could they be expected to sit idly by while the nobility held offices that should have been theirs? Inspired by philosophical ideals as well as by potential economic and social advantages, they provided the leadership for the revolution. Lower members of the Third Estate, the artisans and peasants, generally could not read and were not concerned with philosophical justifications. It was the peasantry that labored under intolerable taxes, rents, and *corvees* (feudal services), which they were forced to undertake by the nobility without payment. What were their demands in 1789? Did their needs justify revolution?

The first part of this chapter will explore some of the ideological and social origins of the French Revolution, as well as some of its most important events, such as the storming of the Bastille, the execution of Louis XVI, and the Terror. Revolutions generally go through conservative and radical phases. Differences among revolutionaries often result in violence. The path toward freedom or despotism is littered with bodies and bloodshed. And in the power vacuum created by such chaos, the door is left open for a transfer of power. During the French Revolution, an individual seized the initiative, filled the power vacuum, and altered its course. His name was Napoleon Bonaparte.

The mere name of Napoleon (1769–1821) evokes a wide array of emotions. As is the case with most influential individuals, he inspires controversy. Some historians have described him as a force for good, a lawgiver and reformer who spread revolutionary ideals throughout Europe. Others have viewed him as an egomaniac whose lust for conquest overshadowed any other secondary achievements. Whatever final judgment one may make, it is clear that Napoleon Bonaparte had a brilliant mind, equally at home in the context of law and military strategy.

Napoleon was born in 1769 to a poor family of lesser nobility on the island of Corsica. The "little Corsican," as he was called, went to French schools and obtained a commission as a French artillery officer. He was enthusiastic about the revolution of 1789 and was rewarded for his military service against the British with a promotion to brigadier general. After the fall of Robespierre in 1794, Napoleon's radical political associations threatened his career, but he was able to convince the new government of his loyalty. This government was called the Directory, and it was composed of people who had benefited from the recent revolution and whose major goal was to perpetuate their own rule. Their chief opposition came from royalists who supported a monarch as head of France and who had won a majority of the seats in the legislature in 1797. With the aid of Napoleon, the Directory succeeded in overthrowing the elected officials and placed their own supporters in the legislature. Napoleon then received a command against the Austrians and Sardinians that resulted in a swift victory for the French and eventual annexation of Italy. Napoleon was hailed as a hero and decided to sail to Egypt, there to fight the British fleet and hopefully cut off British contact and trade with her colonies in the East. However, the invasion of Egypt (1798) was a failure for the French; Napoleon abandoned his troops and returned to Paris, where he overthrew the Directory that he had once championed (November 10, 1799). Establishing a new government called the Consulate, he then issued the Constitution for the Year VIII (December 1799), which promoted liberal ideas such as universal manhood suffrage and a system of governmental checks and balances, but in reality granted Napoleon virtual dictatorial power as First Consul. His position was confirmed by a plebiscite that approved the new constitution by a vote of 3,011,077 to 1,567. Both the middle and lower classes seemed satisfied to accept the security that Napoleon offered.

Napoleon then quickly consolidated his rule by achieving peace with Austria and Britain and by restoring order at home. In 1801, he concluded a concordat with the Catholic Church, which in fact resulted in the subordination of the church to the state; there would be no controversy between secular and religious authority in Napoleonic France. So satisfied were French citizens that in 1802 they voted Napoleon Consul for Life. In 1804, there was simply no one with enough authority to grant him the final accolade, so Napoleon crowned himself Napoleon I, Emperor of the French. The pope sat nearby, watching the ceremony. Napoleon had achieved the ultimate authority, which had escaped even Charlemagne.

In his decade as emperor, Napoleon conquered most of Europe, spreading France's revolutionary ideals. It was at this time too that he paid great attention to domestic concerns and soon instituted reforms and programs including a codification of laws known as the Napoleonic Code. His glory came to an end in 1814 when he was finally defeated by a coalition of European powers. Napoleon's brief return from exile was unsuccessful and resulted in his defeat by Lord Wellington at Waterloo. The victors agreed at the Congress of Vienna in 1815 that no single state should dominate Europe—power must be balanced. Another Napoleon would not be tolerated. The great general was ingloriously exiled to St. Helena, an isolated and inaccessible rock in the Atlantic. He died there in 1821 of stomach cancer or, as some modern researchers advocate, the victim of gradual poisoning. Even in death, Napoleon remains a controversial figure.

In the second part of this chapter, we will look at Napoleon's rise to power and especially his reforms and attempts to consolidate his position. Napoleon was certainly a military leader of genius, but his achievements inspire more philosophical thoughts about the nature of power and the ability of the individual to change the course of history. Is history motivated by social and economic forces over which individuals have no control? Or does the "hero" actually change history by force of personality and ability? Did Napoleon make France a great nation through his reforms and conquests? If so, does progress come about because of the imposition of reforms upon a people? Was Napoleon, who overthrew the legitimate, elected government of France and who installed a dictatorship, necessary for the progress of a revolution dedicated to liberty and equality? The French Revolution presents historians with complex problems of great importance. This chapter will focus on the components of revolution, the relationship between power and progress and factors of historical change. Finally, did the French Revolution succeed in realizing its ideals of liberty, equality, and fraternity?

SECTION I: THE FRENCH REVOLUTION

Justification for Revolution

The following selections discuss the theoretical basis for revolution and present justification for the elimination of absolute monarchy. John Locke (1632–1704) was an English political philosopher whose *Second Treatise of Civil Government* (1690) later influenced both the French and American Revolutions. It is also the first philosophical statement of liberalism, a doctrine that sought the limitation of the arbitrary power of government and the establishment of legal equality, religious toleration, and freedom of the press. The Baron de Montesquieu (1689–1755) was one of the most penetrating political analysts of his age. The selection from *The Spirit of the Laws* was published in 1748, about forty years before the French Revolution broke out. The third selection is from *The Social Contract* (1762) by Jean Jacques Rousseau (1712–1778). Although Rousseau spent much of his life in intimate contact with the *philosophes*, he rejected their attitude that man is a rational creature and that man's confidence in reason would result in liberty and equality. Rousseau advocated the elimination of political despotism and the introduction of a new social order in which only the authority of the "general will" of the governed placed limits on individual freedom. His ideas provided the most inspirational justification for revolutionary action during the eighteenth century.

Second Treatise of Civil Government (1690)

JOHN LOCKE

Political power, then, I take to be a right of making laws with penalties of death, and consequently all less penalties, for the regulating and preserving of property, and of employing the force of the community, in the execution of such laws, and in the defence of the commonwealth from foreign injury; and all this only for the public good.

John Locke, *The Treatises of Government* (London, 1694).

Chapter II: Of the State of Nature

To understand political power right, and derive it from its original, we must consider what state all men are naturally in, and that is, a state of perfect freedom to order their actions and dispose of their possessions and persons, as they think fit, within the bounds of the law of nature; without asking leave, or depending upon the will of any other man.

A state also of equality, wherein all the power and jurisdiction is reciprocal, no one having more than another; there being nothing more evident, than that creatures of the same species and rank, promiscuously born to all the same advantages of nature, and the use of the same faculties, should also be equal one amongst another without subordination or subjection; unless the lord and master of them all should, by any manifest declaration of his will, set one above another, and confer on him, by an evident and clear appointment, an undoubted right to dominion and sovereignty. . . .

But though this be a state of liberty, yet it is not a state of license: though man in that state has an uncontrollable liberty to dispose of his person or possessions, yet he has not liberty to destroy himself, or so much as any creature in his possession, but where some nobler use than its bare preservation call for it. The state of nature has a law of nature to govern it, which obliges every one: and reason, which is that law, teaches all mankind, who will but consult it, that being equal and independent, no one ought to harm another in his life, health, liberty, or possessions: for men being all the workmanship of one omnipotent and infinitely wise Maker; all the servants of one sovereign master, sent into the world by his order, and about his business; they are his property, whose workmanship they are, made to last during his, not another's pleasure: and being furnished with like faculties, sharing all in one community of nature, there cannot be supposed any such subordination among us, that may authorize us to destroy another, as if we were made for one another's uses, as the inferior ranks of creatures are for ours. Every one, as he is bound to preserve himself, . . . ought he, as much as he can, to preserve the rest of mankind, and may not, unless it be to do justice to an offender, take away or impair the life, or what tends to the preservation of life, the liberty, health, limb, or goods of another.

And that all men may be restrained from invading others' rights, and from doing hurt to one another, and the law of nature be observed, which willeth the peace and preservation of all mankind, the execution of the law of nature is, in that state, put into every man's hands, whereby every one has a right to punish the transgressors of that law to such a degree as may hinder its violation: for the law of nature would, as all other laws that concern men in this world, be in vain, if there were nobody that in the state of nature had a power to execute the law, and thereby preserve the innocent and restrain offenders. And if any one in the state of nature may punish another for any evil he has done, every one may do so: for in that state of perfect equality, where naturally there is no superiority or jurisdiction of one over another, what any may do in prosecution of that law, every one must needs have a right to do.

And thus, in the state of nature, "one man comes by a power over another"; but yet this is not an absolute or arbitrary power. . . .

Chapter III: Of the State of War

[It is reasonable and just that . . .] I should have a right to destroy that which threatens me with destruction; for, by the fundamental law of nature, man being to be preserved as much as possible, when all cannot be preserved, the safety of the innocent is to be preferred: and one may destroy a man who makes war upon him, or has discovered an enmity to his being, for the same reason that he may kill a wolf or a lion; because such men are not under the ties of the common law of reason, have no other rule, than that of force and violence, and so may be treated as beasts of prey, those dangerous and noxious creatures, that will be sure to destroy him whenever he falls into their power.

And hence it is, that he who attempts to get another man into his absolute power, does thereby put himself into a state of war with him; it being to be understood as a declaration of a design upon his life: for I have reason to conclude, that he who would get me into his power without my consent, would use me as he pleased when he got me there, and destroy me too when he had a fancy to it; for nobody can desire to have me in his absolute power, unless it be to compel me by force to that which is against the right of my freedom, i.e., make me a slave. To be free from such force is the only security of my preservation; and reason bids me look on him, as an enemy to my preservation, who would take away that freedom which is the fence to it; so that he who makes an attempt to enslave me, thereby puts himself into a state of war with me. He that, in the state of nature, would take away the freedom that belongs to any one· in that state, must necessarily be supposed to have a design to take away everything else, that freedom being the foundation of all the rest; as he that, in the state of society, would take away the freedom belonging to those of that society or commonwealth, must be supposed to design to take away from them every thing else, and so be looked on as in a state of war. . . .

Chapter IV: Of Slavery

The natural liberty of man is to be free from any superior power on earth, and not to be under the will or legislative authority of man, but to have only the law of nature for his rule. The liberty of man, in society, is to be under no other legislative power, but that established, by consent, in the commonwealth; nor under the dominion of any will, or restraint of any law, but what that legislative shall enact, according to the trust put in it. Freedom then is not what Sir Robert Filmer tells us, "a liberty for every one to do what he lists, to live as he pleases, and not to be tied by any laws": but freedom of men under government is, to have a standing rule to live by, common to every one of that society, and made by the legislative power erected in it; a liberty to follow my own will in all things, where the rule prescribes not; and not to be subject to the inconstant, uncertain, unknown, arbitrary will of another man: as freedom of nature is, to be under any other restraint but the law of nature.

This freedom from absolute, arbitrary power, is so necessary to, and closely joined with a man's preservation, that he cannot part with it, but by what forfeits his preservation and life together.

Chapter VIII: Of the Beginning of Political Societies

Men being, as has been said by nature, all free, equal, and independent, no one can be put out of this estate, and subjected to the political power of another, without his own consent. The only way, whereby any one divests himself of his natural liberty, and puts on the bonds of civil society, is by agreeing with other men to join and unite into a community, for their comfortable, safe, and peaceable living one amongst another, in a secure enjoyment of their properties, and a greater security against any, that are not of it. This any number of men may do, because it injures not the freedom of the rest; they are left as they were in the liberty of the state of nature. When any number of men have so consented to make one community or government they are thereby presently incorporated, and make one body politic, wherein the majority have a right to act and conclude the rest.

For, when any number of men have, by the consent of every individual, made a community, they have thereby made that community one body, with a power to act as one body, which is only by the will and determination of the majority: . . . or else it is impossible that it should act or continue as one body, one community, which the consent of every individual that united into it, agreed that it should; and so every one is bound by that consent to be concluded by the majority. . . .

And thus every man, by consenting with others to make one body politic under one government, puts himself under an obligation, to every one of that society, to submit to the determination of the majority, and to be concluded by it; or else this original compact, whereby he with others incorporate into one society, would signify nothing, and be no compact, if he be left free, and under no other ties than he was in before in the state of nature.

Chapter IX: Of the Ends of Political Society and Government

If man in the state of nature be so free, as has been said: if he be absolute lord of his own person and possessions, equal to the greatest, and subject to nobody, why will he part with his freedom? why will he give up his empire, and subject himself to the dominion and control of any other power? To which it is obvious to answer, that though in the state of nature he hath such a right, yet the enjoyment of it is very uncertain, and constantly exposed to the invasion of others; for all being kings as much as he, every man his equal, and the greater part no strict observers of equity and justice, the enjoyment of the property he has in this state is very unsafe, very unsecure. This makes him willing to quit a condition, which however free, is full of fears and continual dangers: and it is not without reason, that he seeks out, and is willing to join in society with others, who are already united, or have a mind to unite, for the mutual preservation of their lives, liberties, and estates, which I call by the general name, property.

The great and chief end, therefore, of men's uniting into commonwealths, and putting themselves under government, is the preservation of their property. To which in the state of nature there are many things wanting. . . .

Chapter XV: Of Despotical Power

Despotical power is an absolute, arbitrary power one man has over another, to take away his life whenever he pleases; and this is a power which neither Nature gives, for it has made no such distinction between one man and another, nor compact can convey. . . . For having quitted reason, which God has given to be the rule betwixt man and man, and the peaceable ways which that teaches, and made use of force to compass his unjust ends upon another where he has no right, he renders himself liable to be destroyed by his adversary whenever he can, as any other noxious and brutish creature that is destructive to his being. . . .

Chapter XIX: Of the Dissolution of Government

The reason why men enter into society, is the preservation of their property; and the end why they choose and authorize a legislative, is, that there may be laws made, and rules set, as guards and fences to the properties of all the members of the society: to limit the power, and moderate the dominion, of every part and member of the society: for since it can never be supposed to be the will of the society, that the legislative should have a power to destroy that which every one designs to secure by entering into society, and for which the people submitted themselves to legislators of their own making; whenever the legislators endeavour to take away and destroy the property of the people, or to reduce them to slavery under arbitrary power, they put themselves into a state of war with the people, who are thereupon absolved from any farther obedience, and are left to the common refuge, which God hath provided for all men, against force and violence. Whensoever therefore the legislative shall transgress this fundamental rule of society; and either by ambition, fear, folly or corruption, endeavour to grasp themselves, or put into the hands of any other, an absolute power over the lives, liberties, and estates of the people, by this breach of trust they forfeit the power the people had put into their hands for quite contrary ends, and it devolves to the people, who have a right to resume their original liberty, and, by the establishment of a new legislative, (such as they shall think fit) provide for their own safety and security, which is the end for which they are in society. What I have said here, concerning the legislative in general holds true also concerning the supreme executor, who having a double trust put in him, both to have a part in the legislative, and the supreme execution of the law, acts against both, when he goes about to set up his own arbitrary will as the law of the society. . . .

Whosoever uses force without right, as every one does in society, who does it without law, puts himself into a state of war with those against whom he so used it; and in that state all former ties are cancelled, all other rights cease, and every one has a right to defend himself, and to resist the aggressor.

The Spirit of the Laws (1748)

THE BARON DE MONTESQUIEU

When the legislative and executive powers are united in the same person, or in the same body of magistrates, there can be no liberty; because apprehensions may arise lest the same monarch or senate should enact tyrannical laws to execute then in a tyrannical manner.

Again there is no liberty if the power of judging be not separated from the legislative and executive powers. Were it joined with the legislature, the life and liberty of the subject would be exposed to arbitrary control; for the judge would be then the legislator. Were it joined to the executive power, the judge might behave with all the violence of an oppressor.

There would be an end of everything were the same man or the same body, whether of the nobles or of the people, to exercise those three powers, that of enacting the laws, that of executing the public resolutions, and that of judging the crimes or differences of individuals.

Most kingdoms of Europe enjoy a moderate government because the prince who is invested with the two first powers leaves the third to his subjects. In Turkey, where these three powers are united in the sultan's person, the subjects groan under the weight of the most frightful oppression.

In the republics of Italy, where these three powers are united, there is less liberty than in our monarchies. Hence their government is obliged to have recourse to as violent methods for its support as even that of the Turks; witness the state inquisitors (at Venice), and the lion's mouth into which every informer may at all hours throw his written accusations.

What a situation must the poor subjects be in, under those republics!

Baron de Montesquieu (Charles de Secondat), *The Spirit of the Laws*, 2 vols. (London, 1758), pp. 216–217.

The same body of magistrates are possessed, as executors of the laws, of the whole power they have given themselves in quality of legislators. They may plunder the state by their general determination, and as they have likewise the judiciary power in their hands, every private citizen may be ruined by their particular decisions.

The whole power is here united in one body; and though there is no external pomp that indicates a despotic sway, yet the people feel the effects of it every moment.

Hence it is that many of the princes of Europe, whose aim has been levelled at arbitrary power, have constantly set out with uniting in their own persons all the branches of magistracy, and all the great offices of the state.

The Social Contract (1762)

JEAN JACQUES ROUSSEAU

Of the Social Compact

We will suppose that men in a state of nature are arrived at that crisis when the strength of each individual is insufficient to defend him from the attacks he is subject to. This primitive state can therefore subsist no longer; and the human race must perish, unless they change their manner of life.

As men cannot create for themselves new forces, but merely unite and direct those which already exist, the only means they can employ for the preservation is to form by aggregation an assemblage of forces that may be able to resist all assaults, be put in motion as one body, and act in concert upon all occasions.

This assemblage of forces must be produced by the concurrence of many: as the force and the liberty of a man are the chief instruments of his preservation, how can he engage them without danger, and without neglect the care which is due to himself? This doubt, which leads directly to my subject, may be expressed in these words:

"Where shall we find a form of association which will defend and protect with the whole aggregate force the person and the property of each individual; and by which every person, while united with ALL, shall obey only HIMSELF, and remain as free as before the union? Such is the fundamental problem, of which the Social Contract gives the solution.

The articles of this contract are so unalterably fixed by the nature of the act, that the least modification renders them vain and of no effect. They are the same everywhere, and are everywhere understood and admitted, even though they may never have been formally announced: so that, when once the social pact is violated in any instance, all obligations it created

Jean Jacques Rousseau, *An Inquiry into the Nature of the Social Contract* (London, 1791), pp. 33–49.

cease; and each individual is restored to his original rights, and resumes native liberty, as the consequence of losing that conventional liberty for which he exchanged them.

All the articles of the social contract will, when clearly understood, be found reducible to this single point—THE TOTAL ALIENATION OF EACH ASSOCIATE, AND ALL HIS RIGHTS, TO THE WHOLE COMMUNITY. For every individual gives himself up entirely—the condition of every person is alike; and being so, it would not be the interest of anyone to render himself offensive to others.

Moreover, the alienation is made without any reserve; the union is as complete as it can be, and no associate has a claim to anything; for if any individual was to retain rights not enjoyed in general by all, as there would be no common superior to decide between him and the public, each person being in some points his own proper judge, would soon pretend to be so in everything; and thus would the state of nature be revived, and the association become tyrannical or be annihilated.

Finally, each person gives himself to ALL, but not to any INDIVIDUAL: and as there is no one associate over whom the same right is not acquired which is ceded to him by others, each gains an equivalent for what he loses, and finds his force increased for preserving that which he possesses.

If, therefore, we exclude from the social compact all that is not essentially necessary, we shall find it reduced to the following terms:

"We each of us place, in common, his person, and all his power, under the supreme direction of the general will; and we receive into the body each member as an indivisible part of the whole."

From that moment, instead of so many separate persons as there are contractors, this act of association produces a moral collective body, composed of as many members as there are voices in the assembly; which from this act receives its unity, its common self, its life, and its will. This public person, which is thus formed by the union of all the private persons, took formerly the name of *city*, and now takes that of *republic* or *body politic*. It is called by its members *state* when it is passive, and *sovereign* when in activity: and whenever it is spoken of with other bodies of a similar kind, it is denominated *power*. The associates take collectively the name of *people*, and separately that *citizens*, as participating in the sovereign authority: they are also styled *subjects*, because they are subjected to the laws. But these terms are frequently confounded, and used one for the other; and a man must understand them well to distinguish when they are properly employed.

Of the Sovereign Power

It appears from this form that the act of association contains a reciprocal engagement between the public and individuals; and that each individual contracting as it were with himself, is engaged under a double character that is, as a part of the *sovereign power* engaging with individuals, and as a member of the *state* entering into a compact with the *sovereign power*. But we cannot apply here the maxim of civil right, that no person is bound by any engagement which he makes with himself; for there is a material difference between an obligation contracted towards *one's self* individually, and towards a collective body of *which one's self* constitutes a part.

It is necessary to observe here that the will of the public, expressed by a majority of votes—which can enforce obedience from the subjects to the sovereign power in consequence of the double character under which the members of that body appear—cannot bind the sovereign power to itself; and that it is against the nature of the body politic for the sovereign power to impose any one law which it cannot alter. Were they to consider themselves as acting under one character only, they would be in the situation of individuals forming each a contract with himself: but this is not the case; and therefore there can be no fundamental obligatory law established for the body of the people, not even the social contract. But this is of little moment, as that body could not very well engage itself to others in any manner which would not derogate from the contract. With respect to foreigners, it becomes a single being, an individual only.

But the body politic, or sovereign power, which derives its existence from the sacredness of the contract, can never bind itself, even towards others, in any thing that would derogate from the original act; such as alienating any portion of itself, or submitting to another sovereign; for by violating the contract its own existence would be at once annihilated, and by nothing nothing can be performed.

As soon as the multitude is thus united in one body, you cannot offend one of its members without attacking the whole; much less can you offend the whole without incurring the resentment of all the members. Thus duty and interest equally oblige the two contracting parties to lend their mutual aid to each other; and the same men must endeavour to unite under this double character all the advantages which attend it.

The sovereign power being formed only of the individuals which compose it, neither has, or can have, any interest contrary to theirs; consequently the sovereign power requires no guarantee towards its subjects, because it is impossible that the body should seek to injure all its members: and shall see presently that it can do no injury to any individual. The sovereign power by its nature must, while it exists, be everything it ought to be: it is not so with subjects towards the sovereign power; to which, notwithstanding the common interest subsisting between them, there is nothing to answer for the performance of their engagements, if some means is not found of ensuring their fidelity.

In fact, each individual may, as a man, have a private will, dissimilar contrary to the general will which he has as a citizen. His own particular interest may dictate to him very differently from the common interest; his mind, naturally and absolutely independent, may regard what he owes to the common cause as a gratuitous contribution, the omission of which would be less injurious to others than the payment would be burdensome to himself; and considering the moral person which constitutes the state as a creature of the imagination, because it is not a man, he may wish to enjoy the rights of a citizen, without being disposed to fulfill the duties of a subject: an injustice which would in its progress cause the ruin of the body politic.

In order therefore to prevent the social compact from becoming an empty formula, it tacitly includes this premise, which alone can give effect to the others—That whoever refuses to obey the general will, shall be compelled to it by the whole body, which is in fact only forcing him to be free; for this is the condition which guarantees his absolute personal independence to every citizen of the country: a condition which gives motion and effect to the political machine; which alone renders all civil engagements legal; and without which they would be absurd, tyrannical, and subject to the most enormous abuses.

Of the State

The passing from a state of nature to a civil state, produces in man a very remarkable change, by substituting justice for instinct, and giving to his actions a moral character which they wanted before.

It is at the moment of that transition that the voice of duty succeeds to physical impulse; and a sense of what is right, to the incitements of appetite. The man who had till then regarded none but himself, perceives that he must act on other principles, and learns to consult his reason before he listens to his propensities.

The Influence of Philosophy

THE MARQUIS D'ARGENSON

In 1688, England was in the midst of political turmoil. The monarch, James II, had sought absolute control over the affairs of his realm, and Parliament reacted by deposing him. The monarchy was not eliminated, but Parliament took a more assertive role in the governance of the state. John Locke's *Second Treatise on Government* (1690) was a reaction to and a commentary on these dynamic events. The "spirit of revolt" was spreading to Europe, as the following excerpts indicate. The first is from the *Memoirs* of the Marquis d'Argenson (1694–1757), Minister of Foreign Affairs under the French king Louis XV. The second offers commentary from a conservative Paris newspaper, dated June 12, 1778.

A philosophical wind is blowing from England; one hears the murmur of the words *liberty* and *republicanism;* they are already in people's minds, and

E. L. Higgins, ed., *The French Revolution as Told by Contemporaries* (Boston: Houghton Mifflin, 1966), p. 29. Copyright © 1938, renewed 1966 by Houghton Mifflin Company. Used by permission of the publisher.

we know how public opinion rules the world. The times of adoration have passed; the name of master, so dear to our ancestors, sounds unpleasant to our ears. For all one knows, there is a new conception of government in certain heads that will emerge in battle array at the first occasion. Perhaps the revolution will be accomplished with less opposition than one thinks; there will be no need of princes of the blood, great lords, or religious fanaticism; all will be accomplished by acclamation, as in the election of popes at times. Today all classes are discontented: the military disbanded by the peace; the clergy offended in its privileges; the *parlements*, corporate bodies, provincial governments, debased in their functions; the lower classes crushed by taxes, and racked by misery; the financiers alone triumphant and reviving the reign of the Jews. Combustible matters everywhere. A riot might become a revolt, and a revolt a complete revolution; bringing real tribunes of the people, consuls, and commissaries; and depriving the king and his ministers of their excessive power for harm.

"The Origin of the Evil" (1778)

The origin of the evil must be looked for in the spirit of revolt and irreligion caused by the flood of infamous writings which circulate not only in the upper classes, but descend today even to the dwellings of the people.

From top to bottom of the social body, in the palace as in the cottage, imbecile ragamuffins, whom a wise government would do well to have whipped in the public square, set themselves up for philosophers and cultivate blasphemy. . . .

Elsewhere a flock of peddlers, unwatched by the police, disseminate in the country districts the infectious writings of Voltaire, of the materialist Diderot, of the dangerous misanthrope of Geneva [Rousseau], and those of Helvetius, the most fanatical of the unbelievers and the most ignoble apostle of pleasure.

All these books do not preach the disdain of religion and of right customs alone; they preach revolt against the royal authority and sap the base of all the conservative principles of the state.

Conditions of Society on the Eve of Revolution

France was composed of three main classes, which were divided on the basis of occupation and ancient privilege. The First Estate consisted of the clergy, the Second Estate of the nobility, and the Third Estate of everyone

E. L. Higgins, ed., *The French Revolution as Told by Contemporaries* (Boston: Houghton Mifflin, 1966), pp. 29–30. Copyright © 1938, renewed 1966 by Houghton Mifflin Company. Used by permission of the publisher.

else. Within the estates themselves there were also social divisions. The following selections relate many of the problems and criticisms of the time.

The Nobility

Corruption of the French Court

THE MARQUIS D'ARGENSON

[The Marquis D'Argenson was Minister of Foreign Affairs under Louis XV. He claimed he "loved both royalty and the people."]

The court! The court! In that single word lies all the nation's misfortune. . . . It is the court that corrupts the morals of the nation by its luxury, its extravagance, its artificial manners, its ignorance, and its intrigue in place of emulation. All places, positions, and grades in the army go to the courtiers through favoritism; hence there is no longer any attempt to rise by merit.

In the finances everything is sold; all the money of the provinces goes to Paris never to return; all the people go there to make fortunes by intrigue. . . .

Justice cannot be administered with integrity; the judges fear the grandees, and base their hopes only upon favor. In short, the king no longer reigns, and disregards even the virtues that he has.

Those are the fruits of the establishment by Louis XIV of a capital at Versailles expressly for the court. He was still powerful and gave authority to his ministers. But these are not supported under Louis XV, who distrusts them and prefers his courtiers and favorites. There is, as a result, anarchy and an oligarchy of satraps. Favor means influence, and the possession of favor is more important than the rights of authority.

"Ancient Oaks Mutilated by Time"

THE MARQUIS DE BOUILLE

[The Marquis de Bouille was a noble, general, governor, and trusted advisor to Louis XVI.]

The nobility had undergone still greater changes; it had lost, not only its ancient splendor, but almost its existence, and had entirely decayed. There had been in France nearly eighty thousand noble families. . . . Included in this numerous nobility were about a thousand families whose origin dated from the earliest times of the monarchy. Among these there were scarcely two or three hundred who had escaped poverty and misfortune. There could still be found at court a few great names which brought to mind the noted personages who had made them illustrious, but which too often were brought into disrepute by the vices of those who had inherited them. There were a few families in the provinces who had continued to exist and command respect. . . . The remainder of this ancient nobility languished in poverty, and resembled those ancient oaks mutilated by time, where nothing remains except the ravaged trunks. No longer convoked either for military service or for the provincial or national assemblies, they had lost their ancient hierarchy. If honorary titles remained to some illustrious or ancient families, they were also held by a multitude of newly created nobles who had acquired by their riches the right to assume them arbitrarily. . . . The nobility, in short, were not distinguishable from the other classes of citizens, except by the arbitrary favors of the court, and by the exemptions from imposts, less useful to them than onerous to the state and shocking to the people. They had conserved nothing of their ancient dignity and consideration; they retained only the hate and jealousy of the plebeians. Such was the situation of the nobility of the kingdom.

The Indifferent Nobility

THE COMPTE DE SEGUR

[The Compte de Segur was a liberal noble in favor at Louis XVI's court, a diplomatist, and a historian.]

The heads of the old noble families, believing themselves as unshakable as the monarchy, slept without fear upon a volcano. The exercise of their charges; royal promotions, favors, or rebuffs; and the nomination or dismissal of ministers, were the sole objects of their attention, the motives of their movements, and the subjects of their conversations. Indifferent to the real affairs of state as to their own they allowed themselves to be governed, some by the intendants of the provinces, others by their own intendants; but they regarded with a chagrined and scornful eye the changes in costumes which were being introduced, the abandonment of liveries, the vogue of dress-coats and English styles.

E. L. Higgins, ed., *The French Revolution as Told by Contemporaries* (Boston: Houghton Mifflin, 1966), pp. 19–20. Copyright © 1938, renewed 1966 by Houghton Mifflin Company. Used by permission of the publisher.

The Superficial Education of the Nobility
MME. DE STAEL

[Mme. de Stael was an author and a liberal member of the nobility.]

The great nobles in France were not very well informed, because they had nothing to gain by being so. Grace in conversation, which would please at court, was the surest means of arriving at honors. This superficial education was one cause of the downfall of the nobles: they could no longer fight against the intelligence of the third estate; they should have tried to surpass it. The great lords would have by degrees gained supremacy in the primary assemblies through their knowledge of administration, as formerly they had acquired it by their swords; and the public mind would have been prepared for the establishment of free institutions in France.

The Clergy

"Luxury, Debauchery, and Lavish Expenditure"
THE MARQUIS DE FERRIERES

[The Marquis de Ferrieres was a conservative noble, yet still a severe critic of the monarchy, the nobility, and revolutionaries.]

There were dioceses which contained fifteen hundred square leagues, and others which contained only twenty; parishes which were ten leagues in circumference, and others which had scarcely fifteen families. Among the priests there were some whose allowances scarcely reached seven hundred livres; while in their neighborhood were benefices of ten and twelve thousand livres income, possessed of ecclesiastics who performed no function in the cult and who, residing elsewhere, carried away the revenue of these benefices, dissipating it in luxury, debauchery, and lavish expenditure. . . . Inasmuch as the appointment of bishops had been concentrated in the hands of the king, or rather in the hands of the ministers, too often the choice fell, not upon him who possessed the most apostolic virtues, but upon him whose family enjoyed the greatest influence. What evils have not resulted from this! Most of the bishops, incapable of fulfilling their duties, entered upon them with insuperable distaste. This distaste extended even to the places where they were to exercise their functions, and had become so general that the small number of prelates who remained were cited as models. The same abuses reigned in the selection of the grand vicars: all thought more of soliciting favors than of deserving them. Totally abandoned by those who were supposed to administer them, the dioceses remained in the hands of obscure secretaries.

The Peasantry

Beggars, Rags, and Misery

ARTHUR YOUNG

[Arthur Young was an English writer on agricultural subjects who traveled through France before and during the Revolution.]

1787

The same wretched country continues to La Loge; the fields are scenes of pitiable management, as the houses are of misery. Yet all this country is highly improveable, if they knew what to do with it: the property, perhaps, of some of those glittering beings, who figured in the procession the other day at Versailles. Heaven grant me patience while I see a country thus neglected—and forgive me the oaths I swear at the absence and ignorance of the possessors. . . .

Pass Payrac, and meet many beggars, which we had not done before. All the country, girls and women, are without shoes or stockings; and the ploughmen at their work have neither sabots nor feet to their stockings. This is a poverty, that strikes at the root of national prosperity; a large consumption among the poor being of more consequence than among the rich the wealth of a nation lies in its circulation and consumption; and the case of poor people abstaining from the use of manufacturers of leather and wool ought to be considered as an evil of the first magnitude. It reminded me of the misery of Ireland.

1788

To Montauban. The poor people seem poor indeed; the children terribly ragged, if possible worse clad than if with no cloaths at all; as to shoes and

Arthur Young, *Travels in France during the Years 1781, 1788, 1789,* 3rd ed. (London: George Bell and Sons, 1889), pp. 19, 27.

stockings they are luxuries. A beautiful girl of six or seven years playing with a stick, and smiling under such a bundle of rags as made my heart ache to see her: they did not beg and when I gave them any thing seemed more surprized than obliged. One third of what I have seen of this province seems uncultivated, and nearly all of it in misery. What have kings, and ministers, and parliaments, and states, to answer for their prejudices, seeing millions of hands that would be industrious, idle and starving, through the execrable maxims of despotism, or the equally detestable prejudices of a feudal nobility. . . .

"Well Clothed and Plenty of Food"

THOMAS JEFFERSON

[Traveling in France in 1787, Jefferson wrote the following letter to a friend in Nice.]

In the great cities I go to see what travelers think alone worthy of being seen; but I make a job of it and generally gulp it all down in a day. On the other hand, I am never satiated with rambling through the fields and farms, examining the culture and cultivators with a degree of curiosity which makes some take me for a fool, and others to be much wiser that I am. I have been pleased to find among the people a less degree of physical misery than I had expected. They are generally well clothed and have a plenty of food,—not animal, indeed, but vegetable, which is just as wholesome. Perhaps they are overworked, the excess of the rent required by the landlord obliging them to too many hours of labor in order to produce that and wherewith to feed and clothe themselves. The soil of Burgundy and Champagne I have found more universally good than I had expected; and as I could not help making a comparison with England, I found that comparison more unfavorable to the latter than is generally admitted. The soil, the climate, and the productions are superior to those of England, and the husbandry as good except in one point, that of manure.

From the first olive fields of Pierrelatte to the orangeries of Hieres has been continued rapture to me. . . . You must ferret the people out of their hovels, as I have done, look into their kettles, eat their bread, loll on their beds under pretense of resting yourself, but in fact to find if they are soft. You will feel a sublime pleasure in the course of this investigation, and a sublimer one hereafter, when you shall be able to apply your knowledge to

James H. Robinson and Charles A. Beard, eds., *Readings in Modern European History*, vol. 1 (Boston: Ginn and Company, 1908), p. 234.

the softening of their beds or the throwing a morsel of meat into their kettle of vegetables.

The Outbreak of Revolution (1789–1791)

"What Is the Third Estate?" (January 1789)

THE ABBÉ SIEYÈS

By August 1788, Louis XVI had decided to summon the Estates-General, a convocation of the three estates which had not met since 1614, in order to solve the government's financial problems. Louis was in debt and he wanted the Estates-General to raise new taxes. This pamphlet by the Abbé Sieyès (1748–1836) was issued in January 1789, before the Estates-General met. It was intended to unite the various interests within the Third Estate toward a common cause: reform of the unequal voting procedure that gave advantage to the first two estates.

What Does the Third Estate Demand? To Become Something

The true petitions of this order may be appreciated only through the authentic claims directed to the government by the large municipalities of the kingdom. What is indicated therein? That the people wishes to be *something*, and, in truth, the very least that is possible. It wishes to have real representatives in the Estates General, that is to say, deputies *drawn from its order*, who are competent to be interpreters of its will and defenders of its interests. But what will it avail it to be present at the Estates General if the predominating interest there is contrary to its own! Its presence would only consecrate the oppression of which it would be the eternal victim. Thus, it is indeed certain that it cannot come to vote at the Estates General unless it is to have in that body *an influence at least equal to that of the privileged classes;* and it demands a number of representatives equal to that of the first two orders together. Finally, this equality of representation would become completely illusory if every chamber voted separately. The third estate demands, then, that votes be taken *by head and not by order.* This is the essence of those claims so alarming to the privileged classes, because they believed that thereby the reform of abuses would become inevitable. The real inten-

Reprinted with permission of Macmillan Publishing Company from *A Documentary Survey of the French Revolution*, edited by John Hall Stewart, pp. 46, 51–52. Copyright 1951 by Macmillan Publishing Company, renewed 1979 by John Hall Stewart.

tion of the third estate is to have an influence in the Estates General equal to that of the privileged classes. I repeat, can it ask less?

What Remains to Be Done: Development of Some Principles

The time is past when the three orders, thinking only of defending themselves from ministerial despotism, were ready to unite against the common enemy. . . .

.   .   .

The third estate awaits, to no purpose, the meeting of all classes, the restitution of its political rights, and the plenitude of its civil rights; the fear of seeing abuses reformed alarms the first two orders far more than the desire for liberty inspires them. Between liberty and some odious privileges, they have chosen the latter. Their soul is identified with the favors of servitude. Today they dread this Estates General which but lately they invoked so ardently. All is well with them; they no longer complain, except of the spirit of innovation. They no longer lack anything; fear has given them a constitution.

The third estate must perceive in the trend of opinions and circumstances that it can hope for nothing except from its own enlightenment and courage. Reason and justice are in its favor; . . . there is no longer time to work for the conciliation of parties. What accord can be anticipated between the energy of the oppressed and the rage of the oppressors?

They have dared pronounce the word secession. They have menaced the King and the people. Well! Good God! How fortunate for the nation if this desirable secession might be made permanently! How easy it would be to dispense with the privileged classes! How difficult to induce them to be citizens!

.   .   .

In vain would they close their eyes to the revolution which time and force of circumstances have effected; it is none the less real. Formerly the third estate was serf, the noble order everything. Today the third estate is everything, the nobility but a word. . . .

In such a state of affairs, what must the third estate do if it wishes to gain possession of its political rights in a manner beneficial to the nation? There are two ways of attaining this objective. In following the first, the third estate must assemble apart: it will not meet with the nobility and the clergy at all; it will not remain with them, either by *order* or by *head*. I pray that they will keep in mind the enormous difference between the assembly of the third estate and that of the other two orders. The first represents 25,000,000 men, and deliberates concerning the interests of the nation. The two others, were they to unite, have the powers of only about 200,000 individuals, and think only of their privileges. The third estate alone, they say, cannot constitute the *Estates General*. Well! So much the better! It will form a *National Assembly*.

The Tennis Court Oath (June 20, 1789)

From the outset, the Estates-General was hampered by organizational disputes. After several weeks of frustration, the Third Estate invited the clergy and nobility to join them in organizing a new legislative body. Only a few of the lower clergy accepted, but the National Assembly was thus formed on June 17, 1789. Three days later they were accidently locked out of their usual meeting place and marched to a nearby tennis court, where they took an oath to draft a new constitution for France. This is one of the most important documents of the Revolution. The oath was taken orally and individually with but one vote in dissension. The president of the National Assembly was barely able to save the dissenter from bodily harm.

The National Assembly, considering that it has been summoned to establish the constitution of the kingdom, to effect the regeneration of public order, and to maintain the true principles of monarchy; that nothing can prevent it from continuing its deliberations in whatever place it may be forced to establish itself; and, finally, that wheresoever its members are assembled, *there* is the National Assembly;

Decrees that all members of this Assembly shall immediately take a solemn oath not to separate, and to reassemble wherever circumstances require, until the constitution of the kingdom is established and consolidated upon firm foundations; and that, the said oath taken, all members and each one of them individually shall ratify this steadfast resolution by signature.

The Fall of the Bastille (July 14, 1789)

The Bastille was a fortress built to protect the eastern gates of Paris. It had also been used as a prison for political offenders of the Old Regime. Hence, it served as a symbol of monarchical despotism. On July 14, 1789, a mob, irritated at the dismissal of a popular minister of the king,

"The Tennis Court Oath" is reprinted with permission of Macmillan Publishing Company from *A Documentary Survey of the French Revolution*, edited by John Hall Stewart, p. 88. Copyright 1951 by Macmillan Publishing Company, renewed 1979 by John Hall Stewart.

"The Fall of the Bastille" is from E. L. Higgins, ed., *The French Revolution as Told by Contemporaries* (Boston: Houghton Mifflin, 1966), pp. 98–100. Copyright © 1938, renewed 1966 by Houghton Mifflin Company. Used by permission of the publisher.

The Oath of the Tennis Court by Jacques Louis David. Having pledged their cooperation in the establishment of the National Assembly, members from the different estates took the famous oath to write a new constitution for France. (*Giraudon/Art Resource*)

paraded through the streets of Paris, searching for arms and clashing with the military. They stormed the Bastille and slaughtered many of its small garrison. Although this act yielded few political prisoners of the king, the event would provide a catalyst to the Revolution and is commemorated today in France with special reverence. Louis XVI, however, did not view it with such import. The entry in his diary for July 14, 1789, was "rien" (nothing), signifying that he failed to kill any game in his hunt that day. The following accounts of the fall of the Bastille are drawn from various witnesses and contemporaries of the event.

The Surrender

It was then that M. de Launay [commander of the forces of the Bastille] asked the garrison what course should be followed, that he saw no other than to blow himself up rather than to expose himself to having his throat cut by the people, from the fury of which they could not escape; that they must remount the towers, continue to fight, and blow themselves up rather than surrender.

The soldiers replied that it was impossible to fight any longer, that they would resign themselves to everything rather than destroy such a great number of citizens, that it was best to put the drummer on the towers to beat the recall, hoist a white flag, and capitulate. The governor, having no flag, gave them a white handkerchief. An officer wrote out the capitulation and passed it through the hole, saying that they desired to render themselves and lay down their arms, on condition of a promise not to massacre the troop; there was a cry of, "Lower your bridge; nothing will happen to you!"

. . .

The little drawbridge of the fort being first opened, Elie [one of the leaders of the attacking force] entered with his companions, all brave and honorable men, and fully determined to keep his word. On seeing him the governor went up to him, embraced him, and presented him with his sword, with the keys of the Bastille.

"I refused his sword," said Elie to me, "and took only the keys." His companions received the staff and the officers of the garrison with the same cordiality, swearing to serve them as guard and defense; but they swore in vain.

As soon as the great bridge was let down (and it is not known by what hand that was done) the people rushed into the court of the castle and, full of fury, seized on the troop of Invalides. Elie and the honest men who had entered with him exerted all their efforts to tear from the hands of the people the victims which they themselves had delivered to it. Ferocity held obstinately attached to its prey. Several of these soldiers, whose lives had been promised them, were assassinated; others were dragged like slaves through the street of Paris. Twenty-two were brought to the Greve, and, after humiliations and inhuman treatment, they had the affliction of seeing two of their comrades hanged. When they were presented at the Hotel de Ville, a furious madman said to them: "You deserve to be hanged; and you shall be so presently." De Launay, torn from the arms of those who wished to save him, had his head cut off under the walls of the Hotel de Ville. In the midst of his assassins, he defended his life with the courage of despair; but he fell under their number. De Losme-Salbray, his major, was murdered in the same manner. The adjutant, Mirai, had been so, near the Bastille. Pernon, an old lieutenant of the Invalides, was assassinated on the wharf Saint-Paul, as he was going to the hall. Another lieutenant, Caron, was covered with wounds. The head of the Marquis de Launay was carried about Paris by this same populace that he would have crushed had he not been moved to pity. Such were the exploits of those who have since been called the heroes and conquerors of the Bastille.

The King Informed of the Fall of the Bastille

When M. de Liancourt had made known to the king the total defection of his guards, the taking of the Bastille, the massacres that had taken place, the rising of two hundred thousand men, after a few moments' silence the king said, "It is then a revolt." "No, Sire," replied the duke. "It is a revolution."

Declaration of the Rights of Man (August 27, 1789)

The Declaration of the Rights of Man, issued by the National Assembly on August 27, 1789, served as a preamble to the French constitution, which was as yet unwritten. Its articles detail abuses of the Old Regime and was imitative of American bills of rights that had been attached to state constitutions. The Declaration in turn influenced several European constitutions in the nineteenth century.

The representatives of the French people, organized as a National Assembly, believing that the ignorance, neglect, or contempt of the rights of man are the sole causes of public calamities and of the corruption of governments, have determined to set forth in a solemn declaration the natural, inalienable, and sacred rights of man, in order that this declaration, being constantly before all the members of the social body, shall remind them continually of their rights and duties; in order that the acts of the legislative power, as well as those of the executive power, may be compared at any

James H. Robinson and Charles A. Beard, eds., *Readings in Modern European History*, vol. 1 (Boston: Ginn and Company, 1908), pp. 260–262.

moment with the objects and purposes of all political institutions and may thus be more respected; and, lastly, in order that the grievances of the citizens, based hereafter upon simple and incontestable principles, shall tend to the maintenance of the constitution and redound to the happiness of all. Therefore the National Assembly recognizes and proclaims, in the presence and under the auspices of the Supreme Being, the following rights of man and of the citizen:

Article 1. Men are born and remain free and equal in rights. Social distinctions may be founded only upon the general good.

2. The aim of all political association is the preservation of the natural and imprescriptible rights of man. These rights are liberty, property, security, and resistance to oppression.

3. The principle of all sovereignty resides essentially in the nation. No body nor individual may exercise any authority which does not proceed directly from the nation.

4. Liberty consists in the freedom to do everything which injures no one else; hence the exercise of the natural rights of each man has no limits except those which assure to the other members of the society the enjoyment of the same rights. These limits can only be determined by law.

5. Law can only prohibit such actions as are hurtful to society. Nothing may be prevented which is not forbidden by law, and no one may be forced to do anything not provided for by law.

6. Law is the expression of the general will. Every citizen has a right to participate personally, or through his representative, in its formation. It must be the same for all, whether it protects or punishes. All citizens, being equal in the eyes of the law, are equally eligible to all dignities and to all public positions and occupations, according to their abilities, and without distinction except that of their virtues and talents.

7. No person shall be accused, arrested, or imprisoned, except in the cases and according to the forms prescribed by law. Any one soliciting, transmitting, executing, or causing to be executed, any arbitrary order, shall be punished. But any citizen summoned or arrested in virtue of the law shall submit without delay, as resistance constitutes an offense.

8. The law shall provide for such punishments only as are strictly and obviously necessary, and no one shall suffer punishment except it be legally inflicted in virtue of a law passed and promulgated before the commission of the offense.

9. As all persons are held innocent until they shall have been declared guilty, if arrest shall be deemed indispensable, all harshness not essential to the securing of the prisoner's person shall be severely repressed by law.

10. No one shall be disquieted on account of his opinions, including his religious views, provided their manifestation does not disturb the public order established by law.

11. The free communication of ideas and opinions is one of the most precious of the rights of man. Every citizen may, accordingly, speak, write,

and print with freedom, but shall be responsible for such abuses of this freedom as shall be defined by law.

12. The security of the rights of man and of the citizen requires public military forces. These forces are, therefore, established for the good of all and not for the personal advantage of those to whom they shall be intrusted.

13. A common contribution is essential for the maintenance of the public forces and for the cost of administration. This should be equitably distributed among all the citizens in proportion to their means.

14. All the citizens have a right to decide, either personally or by their representatives, as to the necessity of the public contribution; to grant this freely; to know to what uses it is put; and to fix the proportion, the mode of assessment and of collection and the duration of the taxes.

15. Society has the right to require of every public agent an account of his administration.

16. A society in which the observance of the law is not assured, nor the separation of powers defined, has no constitution at all.

17. Since property is an inviolable and sacred right, no one shall be deprived thereof except where public necessity, legally determined, shall clearly demand it, and then only on condition that the owner shall have been previously and equitably indemnified.

Reflections on the Revolution (1790)

EDMUND BURKE

Edmund Burke (1729–1797) was a respected member of the English Parliament who gained extraordinary influence in public affairs through his writings. The following selection from his most famous work, *Reflections on the Revolution in France* (1790), gives evidence of his regret concerning the changes that had taken place during the first year of the Revolution. Burke left a legacy of conservative thought that proved a solace to many whose status was jeopardized by revolutionary action. Burke's contributions to conservative political theory would provide a serious challenge to liberalism in the nineteenth century.

When I see the spirit of liberty in action, I see a strong principle at work; and this, for a while, is all I can possibly know of it. The wild *gas*, the fixed air is plainly broke loose: but we ought to suspend our judgment until the first effervescence is a little subsided, till the liquor is cleared, and until we see something deeper than the agitation of a troubled and frothy surface. I must be tolerably sure, before I venture publicly to congratulate men upon a blessing, that they have really received one. Flattery corrupts both the

Edmund Burke, *Reflections on the Revolution in France*, in *The Works of the Right Honourable Edmund Burke*, vol. 2 (London: Henry G. Bohn, 1864), pp. 515–516.

receiver and the giver; and adulation is not of more service to the people than to kings. I should therefore suspend my congratulations on the new liberty of France, until I was informed how it had been combined with government; with public force; with the discipline and obedience of armies; with the collection of an effective and well-distributed revenue; with morality and religion; with the solidity for property; with peace and order; with civil and social manners. All these (in their way) are good things too; and, without them, liberty is not a benefit while it lasts, and is not likely to continue long. The effect of liberty to individuals is, that they may do what they please: we ought to see what it will please them to do, before we risk congratulations, which may soon be turned into complaints. Prudence would dictate this in the case of separate insulated private men; but liberty, when men act in bodies, is *power.* Considerate people, before they declare themselves, will observe the use which is made of *power;* and particularly of so trying a thing as *new* power in *new* persons, of whose principles, tempers, and dispositions, they have little or no experience, and in situations where those who appear the most stirring in the scene may possibly not be the real movers. . . .

The age of chivalry is gone.—That of sophisters, economists, and calculators, has succeeded; and the glory of Europe is extinguished for ever. Never, never more, shall we behold that generous loyalty to rank and sex, that proud submission, that dignified obedience, that subordination of the heart, which kept alive, even in servitude itself, the spirit of an exalted freedom. The unbought grace of life, the cheap defence of nations, the nurse of manly sentiment and heroic enterprize is gone! It is gone, that sensibility of principle, that chastity of honour, which felt a stain like a wound, which inspired courage while it mitigated ferocity, which ennobled whatever it touched, and under which vice itself lost half its evil, by losing all its grossness. . . .

But now all is to be changed. All the pleasing illusions, which made power gentle, and obedience liberal, which harmonized the different shades of life, and which, by a bland assimilation, incorporated into politics the sentiments which beautify and soften private society, are to be dissolved by this new conquering empire of light and reason. All the decent drapery of life is to be rudely torn off. All the super-added ideas, furnished from the wardrobe of a moral imagination, which the heart owns, and the understanding ratifies, as necessary to cover the defects of our naked shivering nature, and to raise it to dignity in our own estimation, are to be exploded as a ridiculous, absurd, and antiquated fashion.

On this scheme of things, a king is but a man; a queen is but a woman; a woman is but an animal; and an animal not of the highest order. . . . On the scheme of this barbarous philosophy, which is the offspring of cold hearts and muddy understandings, and which is as void of solid wisdom, as it is destitute of all taste and elegance, laws are to be supported only by their own terrors, and by the concern, which each individual may find in them, from his own private speculations, or even spare to them from his own private interests. In the groves of *their* academy, at the end of every vista, you see nothing but the gallows. . . . When the old feudal and chivalrous spirit of *Fealty*, which, by freeing kings from fear, freed both kings and subjects from the precautions of tyranny, shall be extinct in the minds of men, plots and assassinations will be anticipated by preventive murder and preventive confiscation, and that long roll of grim and bloody maxims, which form the political code of all power, not standing on its own honour, and the honour of those who are to obey it. Kings will be tyrants from policy when subjects are rebels from principle. . . .

To make a government requires no great prudence. Settle the seat of power; teach obedience: and the work is done. To give Freedom is still more easy. It is not necessary to guide; it only requires to let go the rein. But to form a *free government;* that is, to temper together these opposite elements of liberty and restraint in one consistent work, requires much thought, deep reflection, a sagacious, powerful, and combining mind. This I do not find in those who take the lead in the National Assembly. Perhaps they are not so miserably deficient as they appear. I rather believe it. It would put them below the common level of human understanding. But when the leaders choose to make themselves bidders at an auction of popularity, their talents, in the construction of the state, will be of no service. They will become flatterers instead of legislators; the instruments, not the guides, of the people. If any of them should happen to propose a scheme of liberty, soberly limited, and defined with proper qualifications, he will be immediately outbid by his competitors, who will produce something more spendidly popular. Suspicions will be raised of his fidelity to his cause. Moderation will be stigmatized as the virtue of cowards; and compromise as the prudence of traitors; until, in hopes of preserving the credit which may enable him to temper, and moderate, on some occasions, the popular leader is obliged to become active in propagating doctrines, and establishing powers, that will afterwards defeat any sober purpose at which he ultimately might have aimed.

The improvements of the National Assembly are superficial, their errors fundamental.

The Clerical Oath of Loyalty (November 27, 1790)

The serious financial crisis that had existed before the Revolution and had actually resulted in the calling of the Estates-General persisted. In order to pay off the national debt, the Assembly took decisive action and confiscated church lands. Such a radical act required an ecclesiastical reconstruction. In July 1790, the National Assembly issued the Civil Constitution of the Clergy. This placed the Roman Catholic Church under the direct control of the secular state. Bishops and priests were reduced in number and became salaried employees of the state. In this move, the Assembly consulted neither the pope nor the French clergy. It was a major blunder that divided the clergy and brought the condemnation of the pope; many devout Catholics were then forced to choose between their loyalty to the Revolution and that to the Church. This domination of the French state over the Catholic Church was to continue under Napoleon and resulted in a papal offensive against liberalism throughout the nineteenth century. The following selection is a decree that was designed to test the loyalty of the clergy to the religious reorganization of the state.

Bishops and former archbishops and *curés* maintained in office, [directors of seminaries, . . . teachers in seminaries and colleges, and all other ecclesiastical public functionaries], shall be required to take, if they have not done so, the oath to which they are subject by article 39 of the decree . . . concerning the Civil Constitution of the Clergy. Accordingly, by virtue of this latter decree, they shall swear to watch carefully over the faithful of the diocese or parish entrusted to them, to be faithful to the nation, to the law, and to the King, and to maintain with all their power the Constitution decreed by the National Assembly and accepted by the King. . . .

In case the said bishops, former archbishops, *curés,* and other ecclesiastical public functionaries, after having taken their respective oaths, fail therein, either by refusing to obey the decrees of the National Assembly accepted or sanctioned by the King, or by constituting or instigating opposition to their execution, they shall be prosecuted in the district courts as rebels resisting the law, and punished by deprivation of their stipend, and, moreover, they shall be declared to have forfeited the rights of active citizenship and to be ineligible for any public office. Consequently, provision shall be made for their replacement, according to the said decree [Civil Constitution of the Clergy]. . . .

All ecclesiastical or lay persons who unite to contrive a refusal to obey the decrees of the National Assembly accepted or sanctioned by the King, or to constitute or instigate opposition to the execution thereof, likewise shall be prosecuted as disturbers of public order, and punished according to the rigor of the laws.

Letter from Louis XVI to Foreign Courts (April 23, 1791)

The following selection is a letter issued by Louis XVI's Minister of Foreign Affairs. It was designed to calm foreign monarchs who feared that the example of the French Revolution might jeopardize their own thrones. Its tacit purpose, however, was to conceal the king's prepara-

Reprinted with permission of Macmillan Publishing Company from *A Documentary Survey of the French Revolution,* edited by John Hall Stewart, pp. 201–202. Copyright 1951 by Macmillan Publishing Company, renewed 1979 by John Hall Stewart.

tions for leaving France. On June 20, 1791, the royal family managed to get out of Paris. Traveling in disguise with false passports, they were detained and arrested in Varennes, about 150 miles from Paris. The king was disgraced and the monarchy suffered a humiliating blow.

What is called the Revolution is only the destruction of a multitude of abuses accumulated over centuries through the errors of the people or the power of the ministers, which has never been the power of the kings. These abuses were no less calamitous to the nation than to the monarch; during happy reigns authority had not ceased to attack them without being able to destroy them. They no longer exist. The sovereign nation now has only citizens equal in rights, no despot but the law, no agencies but the public functionaries, and the King is the first of these functionaries. Such is the French Revolution.

It was bound to have as enemies all who, in a first moment of error, lamented the abuses of the former government because of self-interest. Hence the apparent division which has manifested itself within the kingdom, and which daily grows weaker; hence, perhaps, some severe laws and circumstances which time will correct. But the King, whose real force is indivisible from that of the nation, who has no other ambition than the welfare of the people, no other real power than that which is delegated to him, the King was obliged to adopt without hesitation a favorable constitution which would regenerate, at one and the same time, his authority, the nation, and the monarchy. All his power has been preserved, except the formidable power to make laws; he remains in charge of negotiations with foreign powers and of the task of defending the kingdom and repulsing its enemies; but henceforth the French nation will no longer have any external enemies save its aggressors. It no longer has internal enemies except those who, still nourishing themselves on foolish hopes, believe that the will of twenty-four million men, restored to their natural rights, after having organized the kingdom so that there remain only memories of the old forms and former abuses, is not an immutable, an irrevocable constitution.

The most dangerous of these enemies are those who have a predilection for spreading doubts concerning the intentions of the monarch. These men are entirely culpable or entirely blinded; they believe themselves the friends of the King—they are the only enemies of the monarchy. They would have deprived the monarch of the love and confidence of a great nation if his principles and integrity had not been so well known. Ah! What has the King not done to show that he counted the French Revolution and the Constitution also among his titles to glory? After having accepted and sanctioned all the laws, he has not neglected any means of having them put into effect. As early as the month of February of last year, in the midst of the National Assembly, he promised to maintain them; he took oath thereto in the midst of the universal federation of the kingdom. Honored with the title of Restorer of French Liberty, he will transmit more than a crown to his son; he will bequeath him a constitutional monarchy.

The enemies of the Constitution do not cease to repeat that the King is not happy; as if there might exist for a king any happiness other than that of the people! They say that his authority is debased; as if authority founded upon force were not less powerful and less certain than the authority of the law! Finally, that the King is not free: atrocious calumny, if it be supposed that his will might be forced; absurd one, if they take for default of liberty the consent His Majesty has several times expressed to remain among the citizens of Paris. . . .

Signed: Montmorin

The King's Declaration (June 20, 1791)

LOUIS XVI

Upon his flight from Paris to Varennes, Louis XVI left behind the following declaration, which reveals his true feelings about the French Revolution. After Louis' arrest, the declaration was read aloud to the National Assembly and firmly established the king's duplicity.

As long as the King could hope to see order and the welfare of the kingdom regenerated by the means employed by the National Assembly, and by his residence near that assembly in the capital of the kingdom, no sacrifice mattered to him; . . . but today, when his sole recompense for so many sacrifices consists of seeing the monarchy destroyed, all powers disregarded, property violated, personal security everywhere endangered, crimes unpunished, and total anarchy taking the place of law, while the semblance of authority provided by the new Constitution is insufficient to repair a single one of the ills afflicting the kingdom, the King, having solemnly protested against all the acts issued during his captivity, deems it his duty to place before Frenchmen and the entire universe the picture of his conduct and that of the government which has established itself in the kingdom. . . .

Let us, then, examine the several branches of the government.

Justice. The King has no share in making the laws; he has only the right to obstruct, until the third legislature, matters which are not regarded as constitutional, and to request the National Assembly to apply itself to such and such matters, without possessing the right to make a formal proposal thereon. Justice is rendered in the name of the King . . . ; but it is only a matter of form. . . .

Internal Administration. There is entirely too much authority in the hands of the departments, districts, and municipalities, which impede the working of the machine, and may often thwart one another. All these bodies are elected by the people, and are not under the jurisdiction of the government. . . .

Foreign Affairs. Appointment to ministerial posts at foreign courts and the conduct of negotiations have been reserved to the King; but the King's liberty in such appointments is as void as for those of officers in the army; . . . The revision and confirmation of treaties, which is reserved to the National Assembly, and the nomination of a diplomatic committee absolutely nullify [this] provision. . . .

Finances. . . . There is still no exact statement of receipts and expenditures. . . . The ordinary taxes are at present greatly in arrears, and the extraordinary expedient of the first one billion, two hundred millions in *assignats* is almost exhausted. . . . The regulation of funds, the collection of taxes, the assessment among the departments, the rewards for services rendered, all have been removed from the King's supervision. . . .

The King does not think it possible to govern a kingdom of such great extent and importance as France through the means established by the National Assembly, as they exist at present. His Majesty, in granting to all decrees, without distinction, a sanction which he well knew could not be refused, was influenced by a desire to avoid all discussion, which experience has shown to be useless to say the least; he feared, moreover, that he would be suspected of wishing to retard or to bring about the failure of the efforts of the National Assembly, in the success of which the nation took so great an interest. . . .

Frenchmen, . . . would you want the anarchy and despotism of the clubs to supplant the monarchical government under which the nation has prospered for fourteen hundred years? Would you want to see your King overwhelmed with insults and deprived of his liberty, while he devotes himself entirely to the establishment of yours?

Love for their kings is one of the virtues of Frenchmen, and His Majesty has personally received too many touching proofs thereof ever to be able to forget them. The rebels are well aware that, so long as this love abides, their work can never succeed; they know, likewise, that in order to enfeeble it, it is necessary, if possible, to destroy the respect which has always accompanied it; and that is the source of the outrages which the King has experienced during the past two years, and of all the ills which he has suffered. . . .

In view of all these facts and the King's present inability to effect the good and prevent the evil that is perpetrated, is it astonishing that the King has sought to recover his liberty and to place himself and his family in safety?

Frenchmen, and especially you Parisians, you inhabitants of a city which the ancestors of His Majesty were pleased to call the good city of Paris, distrust the suggestions and lies of your false friends. Return to your king; he will always be your father, your best friend. What pleasure will he not take in forgetting all his personal injuries, and in beholding himself again in your midst, when a constitution, freely accepted by him, shall cause our holy religion to be respected, the government to be established upon a firm foundation and made useful by its functioning, the property and position of every person no longer to be disturbed, the laws no longer to be violated with impunity, and, finally, liberty to be established on firm and immovable foundations.

Signed, LOUIS

The Radicalization of the Revolution (1792–1794)

The Fall of Louis XVI

The months following the king's flight from Paris were tense and saw the eventual erosion of Royalist support and the abolition of the monarchy in September 1792. Louis was indicted on December 11, 1792. The first selection indicates that he was being tried for treason. The king denied most of the charges and blamed the rest on others. Nevertheless, a small majority of votes in the Assembly sent him to the guillotine. The second excerpt is an eyewitness account of the execution by Henry Edgeworth de Firmont, the king's confessor, who accompanied Louis to the scaffold. Justification for regicide came later in the day by way of a proclamation of the government to the French people. The last selection is from the memoirs of Mme. Roland, a guiding spirit of the revolutionary Girondist faction who was eventually imprisoned and sent to the guillotine herself.

The Indictment of Louis XVI (December 11, 1792)

Louis, the French people accuses you of having committed a multitude of crimes in order to establish your tyranny by destroying its liberty.

1. On 20 June, 1789, you attacked the sovereignty of the people by suspending the assemblies of its representatives and by driving them by violence from the place of their sessions. . . .
2. On 23 June you wished to dictate laws to the nation; you surrounded its representatives with troops; you presented them with two royal declarations, subversive of every liberty, and you ordered them to separate. Your declarations and the minutes of the Assembly establish these outrages undeniably.

Reprinted with permission of Macmillan Publishing Company from *A Documentary Survey of the French Revolution*, edited by John Hall Stewart, pp. 386–389, 391. Copyright 1951 by Macmillan Publishing Company, renewed 1979 by John Hall Stewart.

3. You caused an army to march against the citizens of Paris; your satellites caused their blood to flow, and you withdrew this army only when the capture of the Bastille and the general insurrection apprised you that the people were victorious. . . .

6. For a long time you contemplated flight; . . . but on 21 June you made your escape with a false passport; you left a declaration against those same constitutional articles; you ordered the ministers not to sign any documents emanating from the National Assembly, and you forbade the Minister of Justice to deliver the Seals of State. The people's money was wasted in achieving the success of this treason. . . .

7. On 14 September you apparently accepted the Constitution; your speeches announced a desire to maintain it, and you worked to overthrow it before it even was achieved.

15. Your brothers, enemies of the state, have rallied the *émigrés* [French nobility in self-imposed exile] under their colors; they have raised regiments, borrowed money, and contracted alliances in your name; you disavowed them only when you were quite certain that you could not harm their plans. . . .

30. You tried to bribe, with considerable sums, several members of the Constituent and Legislative Assemblies. . . .

31. You allowed the French nation to be disgraced in Germany, in Italy, and in Spain, since you did nothing to exact reparation for the ill treatment which the French experienced in those countries.

32. On 10 August you reviewed the Swiss Guards at five o'clock in the morning; and the Swiss Guards fired first on the citizens.

33. You caused the blood of Frenchmen to flow.

The Execution of Louis XVI (January 23, 1793)

HENRY EDGEWORTH DE FIRMONT

The carriage arrived . . . in the greatest silence, at the Place Louis XV, and came to a halt in the middle of a large empty space that had been left around the scaffold. This space was bordered with cannon; and beyond, as far as the eye could reach, was a multitude in arms. . . .

As soon as the king descended from the carriage, three executioners surrounded him and wished to take off his coat. He repulsed them with dignity and took it off himself. The executioners, whom the proud bearing of the king had momentarily disconcerted, seemed then to resume their audacity and, surrounding him again, attempted to tie his hands. "What are you trying to do?" asked the king, withdrawing his hands abruptly.

"Tie you," replied one of the executioners.

"Tie me!" returned the king in an indignant tone. "No, I will never consent; do what you are ordered to do, but I will not be tied; renounce that idea." The executioners insisted, they lifted their voices, and seemed about to call for help in order to use force. . . .

"Sire," I said to him with tears, "in this new outrage I see only a final resemblance between Your Majesty and the Saviour who is to reward you."

At these words he lifted his eyes to heaven with a sorrowing look that I cannot describe . . . and, turning to the executioners, said: "Do what you wish; I will drain the cup to the dregs."

The steps that led to the scaffold were extremely steep in ascent. The king was obliged to hold to my arm, and by the pains he seemed to take, feared that his courage had begun to weaken; but what was my astonishment when, upon arriving at the last step, I saw him escape, so to speak, from my hands, cross the length of the scaffold with firm step to impose silence, by a single glance, upon ten or fifteen drummers who were in front of him, and with a voice so strong that it could be heard at the Pont-Tournant, distinctly pronounce these words forever memorable: "I die innocent of all the crimes imputed to me. I pardon the authors of my death, and pray God that the blood you are about to shed will never fall upon France."

. . .

The executioners seized him, the knife struck him, his head fell at fifteen minutes after ten. The executioners seized it by the hair, and showed it to the multitude, whose cries of "Long live the Republic!" resounded to the very bosom of the Convention, whose place of meeting was only a few steps from the place of execution.

Thus died, at the age of thirty-eight years, four months, and twenty-eight days, Louis, sixteenth of his name, whose ancestors had reigned in France for more than eight hundred years. . . .

Immediately after the execution, the body of Louis was transported to the cemetery of the ancient Church of the Madeleine. It was placed in a pit six feet square, close to the wall of the Rue d'Anjou, and dissolved instantly by a great quantity of quicklime with which they took the precaution to cover it.

Proclamation of the Convention to the French People (January 23, 1793)

Citizens, the tyrant is no more. For a long time the cries of the victims, whom war and domestic dissensions have spread over France and Europe, loudly protested his existence. He has paid his penalty, and only acclamations for the Republic and for liberty have been heard from the people.

E. L. Higgins, ed., *The French Revolution as Told by Contemporaries* (Boston: Houghton Mifflin, 1966), p. 392. Copyright © 1938, renewed 1966 by Houghton Mifflin Company. Used by permission of the publisher.

We have had to combat inveterate prejudices, and the superstition of centuries concerning monarchy. Involuntary uncertainties and inevitable disturbances always accompany great changes and revolutions as profound as ours. This political crisis has suddenly surrounded us with contradictions and tumults.

But the cause has ceased, and the motives have disappeared; respect for liberty of opinion must cause these tumultuous scenes to be forgotten; only the good which they have produced through the death of the tyrant and of tyranny now remains, and this judgment belongs in its entirety to each of us, just as it belongs to the entire nation. The National Convention and the French people are now to have only one mind, only one sentiment, that of liberty and civic fraternity.

Now, above all, we need peace in the interior of the Republic, and the most active surveillance of the domestic enemies of liberty. Never did circumstances more urgently require of all citizens the sacrifice of their passions and their personal opinions concerning the act of national justice which has just been effected. Today the French people can have no other passion than that for liberty.

Reflections on Louis XVI

MME. ROLAND

Louis XVI was not exactly the man they were interested in painting in order to discredit him. He was neither the stupid imbecile that they presented for the disdain of the people, nor the fine, judicious, virtuous man that his friends described. Nature had made him an ordinary man, who would have done well in some obscure station. He was ruined in being educated for the throne, and lost through mediocrity in a difficult period when he could have been saved only through genius and strength. An ordinary mind, brought up near the throne and taught from infancy to dissemble, acquires many advantages for dealing with people; the art of letting each see only what is suitable for him to see is for it only a habit to which practice gives an appearance of cleverness: one would have to be an idiot to appear stupid in such a situation. Louis XVI had moreover, a good memory and much activity; he never remained idle, and read a great deal. He knew well the various treaties made by France with the neighboring powers, and he was the best geographer in his kingdom. The knowledge of names, the exact application to the faces of the court personages to whom they belonged, of anecdotes personal to them, had been extended by him to all the individuals who appeared in some manner in the Revolution. But Louis XVI, without elevation of soul without boldness of mind, without

E. L. Higgins, ed., *The French Revolution as Told by Contemporaries* (Boston: Houghton Mifflin, 1966), pp. 13–14. Copyright © 1938, renewed 1966 by Houghton Mifflin Company. Used by permission of the publisher.

strength of character, still had his ideas narrowed and his sentiments perverted, so to say, by religious prejudices and jesuitical principles. . . . If he had been born two centuries earlier, and if he had had a reasonable wife, he would have made no more noise in the world than many other princes of his race who have passed across the stage without having done much good or much harm.

The Reign of Terror

One of the most dramatic personalities of the French Revolution was Maximilien Robespierre (1758–1794), who dominated the principal policy-making body in the state, the Committee of Public Safety. An ardent democrat, Robespierre believed in a republic of virtue that demanded selfless adherence to republican ideals. Those who supported the monarchy or were more moderate in their republican zeal became threats to the success of the Revolution and had to be eliminated. Terror, according to Robespierre, was "swift, inflexible justice" and therefore virtuous. The Reign of Terror, which lasted from 1793 to 1794, saw the execution by the guillotine of more then 25,000 people, from both the political left and right, many without proper trials.

The aims of the revolution are presented in the first selection by Robespierre. The second document is a law that transferred the administration of the Terror from the official government (called the Convention) to the Committee of Public Safety. This enactment provided a general definition of an "enemy of the Republic" and increased the number of victims sacrificed to the purity of the Revolution. Historians generally agree that this law not only damaged the ideals of the French Revolution, but also was the ultimate cause of Robespierre's downfall. He fell victim to colleagues who feared his menacing power and was himself executed a month and a half after the law was ratified. With Robespierre's death, the Terror came to an end. The Revolution continued, but without the bloodshed that had devoured its own children.

"Virtue and Terror": Speech to the Convention (February 5, 1794)

MAXIMILIEN ROBESPIERRE

What is the aim we want to achieve? The peaceful enjoyment of liberty and equality, the reign of that eternal justice whose laws have been engraved,

Richard W. Lyman and Lewis W. Spitz, eds., *Major Crises in Western Civilization*, vol. 2 (New York: Harcourt, Brace & World, 1965), pp. 71–72.

not in stone and marble, but in the hearts of all men, even in the heart of the slave who forgets them or of the tyrant who denies them.

We want a state of affairs where all despicable and cruel passions are unknown and all kind and generous passions are aroused by the laws; when ambition is the desire to deserve glory and to serve the fatherland; where distinctions arise only from equality itself; where the citizen submits to the magistrate, the magistrate to the people and the people to justice; where the fatherland guarantees the well-being of each individual, and where each individual enjoys with pride the prosperity and the glory of the fatherland; where all souls elevate themselves through constant communication of republican sentiments and through the need to deserve the esteem of a great people; where the arts are the decorations of liberty that ennobles them, where commerce is the source of public wealth and not only of the monstrous opulence of a few houses.

In our country we want to substitute morality for egoism, honesty for honor, principles for customs, duties for decorum, the rule of reason for the tyranny of custom, the contempt of vice for the contempt of misfortune, pride for insolence, magnanimity for vanity, love of glory for love of money, good people for well-bred people, merit for intrigue, genius for wit, truth for pompous action, warmth of happiness for boredom of sensuality, greatness of man for pettiness of the great; a magnanimous, powerful, happy people for a polite, frivolous, despicable people—that is to say, all the virtues and all the miracles of the Republic for all the vices and all the absurdities of the monarchy.

In one word, we want to fulfill the wishes of nature, accomplish the destiny of humanity, keep the promises of philosophy, absolve Providence from the long reign of crime and tyranny.

What kind of government can realize these marvels? Only a democratic or republican government.

But what is the fundamental principle of the democratic or popular government, that is to say, the essential strength that sustains it and makes it move? It is virtue: I am speaking of the public virtue which brought about so many marvels in Greece and Rome and which must bring about much more astonishing ones yet in republican France; of that virtue which is nothing more than love of the fatherland and of its laws.

If the strength of popular government in peacetime is virtue, the strength of popular government in revolution is both virtue and terror; terror without virtue is disastrous, virtue without terror is powerless. Terror is nothing but prompt, severe, and inflexible justice; it is thus an emanation of virtue; it is less a particular principle than a consequence of the general principle of democracy applied to the most urgent needs of the fatherland. It is said that terror is the strength of despotic government. Does ours then resemble despotism? Yes, as the sword that shines in the hands of the heroes of liberty resemble the one with which the satellites of tyranny are armed. Let the despot govern his brutalized subjects through terror; he is right as a despot. Subdue the enemies of liberty through terror and you will be right as founders of the Republic. The government of revolution is the despotism of liberty against tyranny.

The Administration of Terror (June 10, 1794)

1. In the Revolutionary Tribunal there shall be a president and four vice-presidents, one public prosecutor, four substitutes for the public prosecutor, and twelve judges.

2. The jurors shall be fifty in number.

4. The Revolutionary Tribunal is instituted to punish the enemies of the people.

5. The enemies of the people are those who seek to destroy public liberty, either by force or by cunning.

6. The following are deemed enemies of the people: those who have instigated the re-establishment of monarchy, or have sought to disparage or dissolve the National Convention and the revolutionary and republican government of which it is the center;

Those who have betrayed the Republic in the command of places and armies, or in any other military function, carried on correspondence with the enemies of the Republic, labored to disrupt the provisioning or the service of the armies;

Those who have supported the designs of the enemies of France, either by countenancing the sheltering and the impunity of conspirators and aristocracy, by persecuting and calumniating patriotism, by corrupting the mandataries of the people, or by abusing the principles of the Revolution or the laws or measures of the government by false and perfidious applications;

Those who have deceived the people or the representatives of the people, in order to lead them into undertakings contrary to the interests of liberty;

Those who have sought to inspire discouragement, in order to favor the enterprises of the tyrants leagued against the Republic;

Those who have disseminated false news in order to divide or disturb the people;

Those who have sought to mislead opinion and to prevent the instruction of the people, to deprave morals and to corrupt the public conscience, to impair the energy and the purity of revolutionary and republican principles, or to impede the progress thereof, either by counter-revolutionary or insidious writings, or by any other machination; . . .

Finally, all who are designated in previous laws relative to the punishment of conspirators and counter-revolutionaries, and who, by whatever means or by whatever appearances they assume, have made an attempt against the liberty, unity, and security of the Republic, or labored to prevent the strengthening thereof.

7. The penalty provided for all offences under the jurisdiction of the Revolutionary Tribunal is death.

8. The proof necessary to convict enemies of the people comprises every kind of evidence, whether material or moral, oral or written, which can naturally secure the approval of every just and reasonable mind; the rule of judgments is the conscience of the jurors, enlightened by love of the *Patrie;* their aim, the triumph of the Republic and the ruin of its enemies; the procedure, the simple means which good sense dictates in order to arrive at a knowledge of the truth, in the forms determined by law.

9. Every citizen has the right to seize conspirators and counter-revolutionaries, and to arraign them before the magistrates. He is required to denounce them as soon as he knows of them.

The Execution of Robespierre (July 28, 1794)

DURAND DE MAILLANE

Robespierre's turn had come at last. By fawning upon the people he had become their idol, and this will happen to any man who declaims against the rich, causing the people to hope for a division of the spoils. Through the populace, he ruled the Jacobin Club; through the Jacobin Club, the Convention and through the Convention, France. He dictated decrees and directed the administration. Nothing was done except by his orders or with his approval. His caprices were flattered, and his very manias were praised. The tribunal beheaded those he designated without investigation. His power seemed too terrible to his accomplices as it did to his victims. A number had been sacrificed already and others feared the same fate. They banded together to pull down the idol they themselves had set up.

. . .

[The committee of general security] ordered that he [Robespierre] be taken to the prison of the Conciergerie. His trial was short. On the following day he was guillotined, together with Saint-Just, Couthon, and his other accomplices. It was quite a distance from the Palais de Justice to the scaffold, and the immensity of the long Rue Saint-Honore had to be traversed.

E. L. Higgins, ed., *The French Revolution as Told by Contemporaries* (Boston: Houghton Mifflin, 1966), pp. 346, 361. Copyright © 1938, renewed 1966 by Houghton Mifflin Company. Used by permission of the publisher.

Along the whole course, the people pursued Robespierre with hoots and maledictions. He had been given a conspicuous place in the tumbril, his face half covered by a dirty, bloodstained cloth which enveloped his jaw. It may be said that this man, who had brought so much anguish to others, suffered during these twenty-four hours all the pain and agony that a mortal can experience.

SECTION II: THE NAPOLEONIC ERA
The Rise of Napoleon
Napoleon Achieves Power (1799–1802)

After the Reign of Terror, the French Revolution entered a moderate period that retreated from the violent radicalism of Robespierre. A new government called the Directory was formed, and it governed the French Republic rather ineffectively until 1799. In this year, Napoleon Bonaparte, who had supported the Directory and had earned fame as the military protector of the Republic, returned to Paris from his Egyptian campaign and promptly overthrew the government. In its place he established the Consulate. Napoleon, as First Consul, was given significant power over his other two colleagues. On December 15, 1799, the Consulate proclaimed the end of the French Revolution. The ideals that founded the Republic ostensibly had not changed, but the leadership certainly had. The first excerpt is from a conversation Napoleon had with one of his confidants in 1796, three years before coming into power. The second document is a proclamation to the French people that explains Napoleon's role in the overthrow of the Directory and the establishment of the Consulate. It is a fine example of effective propaganda. Both excerpts reveal much about Napoleon's ambition.

On the Realities of Power (1796)
NAPOLEON

What I have done so far is nothing. I am but at the opening of the career I am to run. Do you suppose that I have gained my victories in Italy in order

Memoires of Miot de Melito, in James H. Robinson, ed., *Translations and Reprints from the Original Sources of European History,* revised ed., vol. 2, pt. 2 (Philadelphia: University of Pennsylvania Press, 1900), pp. 2–3.

to advance the lawyers of the Directory? Do you think, either, that my object is to establish a Republic? What a notion! A republic of thirty million people, with our morals and vices! How could that ever be? It is a chimera with which the French are infatuated but which will pass away in time like all others. What they want is glory and the gratification of their vanity; as for liberty, of that they have no conception. Look at the army! The victories which we have just gained have given the French soldier his true character. I am everything to him. Let the Directory attempt to deprive me of my command and they will see who is master. The nation must have a head, a head rendered illustrious by glory and not by theories of government, fine phrases, or the talk of idealists, of which the French understand not a whit. Let them have their toys and they will be satisfied. They will amuse themselves and allow themselves to be led, provided the goal is cleverly disguised.

The First Consul: "A Citizen Devoted to the Republic" (November 10, 1799)

NAPOLEON

On my return to Paris [from Egypt] I found division among all authorities, and agreement upon only one point, namely, that the Constitution was half destroyed and was unable to save liberty.

All parties came to me, confided to me their designs, disclosed their secrets, and requested my support; I refused to be the man of a party.

The Council of Elders summoned me; I answered its appeal. A plan of general restoration had been devised by men whom the nation has been accustomed to regard as the defenders of liberty, equality, and property; this plan required an examination, calm, free, exempt from all influence and all fear. Accordingly, the Council of Elders resolved upon the removal of the Legislative Body to Saint-Cloud; it gave me the responsibility of disposing the force necessary for its independence. I believe it my duty to my fellow citizens, to the soldiers perishing in our armies, to the national glory acquired at the cost of their blood, to accept the command.

The Councils assembled at Saint-Cloud; republican troops guaranteed their security from without, but assassins created terror within. Several deputies of the Council of Five Hundred, armed with stilettos and firearms, circulated threats of death around them.

The plans which ought to have been developed were withheld, the majority disorganized, the boldest orators disconcerted, and the futility of every wise proposition was evident.

I took my indignation and grief to the Council of Elders. I besought it to assure the execution of its generous designs; I directed its attention to the evils of the *Patrie* [Fatherland] . . .; it concurred with me *by new* evidence of its steadfast will.

I presented myself at the Council of Five Hundred, alone, unarmed, my head uncovered, just as the Elders had received and applauded me; I came to remind the majority of its wishes, and to assure it of its power.

The stilettos which menaced the deputies were instantly raised against their liberator; twenty assassins threw themselves upon me and aimed at my breast. The grenadiers of the Legislative Body whom l had left at the door of the hall ran forward, placed themselves between the assassins and myself. One of these brave grenadiers had his clothes pierced by a stiletto. They bore me out.

At the same moment cries of "Outlaw" were raised against the defender of the law. It was the fierce cry of assassins against the power destined to repress them.

They crowded around the president, uttering threats, arms in their hands; they commanded him to outlaw me; I was informed of this: I ordered him to be rescued from their fury, and six grenadiers of the Legislative Body secured him. Immediately afterwards some grenadiers of the Legislative Body charged into the hall and cleared it.

The factions, intimidated, dispersed and fled. The majority, freed from their attacks, returned freely and peaceably into the meeting hall, listened to the proposals on behalf of public safety, deliberated, and prepared the salutary resolution which is to become the new and provisional law of the Republic.

Frenchmen, you will doubtless recognize in this conduct the zeal of a soldier of liberty, a citizen devoted to the Republic. Conservative, tutelary, and liberal ideas have been restored to their rights through the dispersal of the rebels who oppressed the Councils.

Napoleon's Consolidation of His Rule

In order to consolidate the new regime, Napoleon sought to control the flow of information in the state. In the first document, note the reasons given for suppression of the newspapers. Between July 1801 and April 1802 Napoleon sought to reorganize the religious institutions of France. The second document is the agreement between France and the papacy, which controlled the position of the Roman Catholic Church in France until 1905. The third selection is a legislative act of state that was promulgated without the pope's consent, but enforced nevertheless. There were other similar pronouncements for Protestants (1802) and Jews (1808).

Suppression of the Newspapers (1800)

The consuls of the Republic, considering that a part of the newspapers which are printed in the department of the Seine are instruments in the hands of the enemies of the Republic; that the government is particularly charged by the French people to look after their security, orders as follows:

1. The minister of police shall permit to be printed, published, and circulated during the whole course of the war only the following newspapers: . . . [Here follows the names of thirteen newspapers], and newspapers devoted exclusively to science, arts, literature, commerce, announcements and notices.

2. The minister of the general police shall immediately make a report upon all the newspapers that are printed in the other departments.

3. The minister of the general police shall see that no new newspaper be printed in the department of the Seine, as well as in all the other departments of the Republic.

4. The proprietors and editors of the newspapers preserved by the present order shall present themselves to the minister of the police in order to attest their character as French citizens, their residences and signatures, and they shall promise fidelity to the constitution.

5. All newspapers which shall insert articles opposed to the respect that is due to the social compact, to the sovereignty of the people and the glory of the armies, or which shall publish invectives against the governments and nations who are the friends or allies of the Republic, even when these articles may be extracts from foreign periodicals, shall be immediately suppressed.

6. The minister of the general police is charged with the execution of the present order, which shall be inserted in the *Bulletin of the Laws.*

Reorganization of Religion: Convention Between the French Government and His Holiness Pope Pius VII (1802)

The government of the French Republic recognizes that the Roman, catholic and apostolic religion is the religion of the great majority of French citizens.

His Holiness likewise recognizes that this same religion has derived and in this moment again expects the greatest benefit and grandeur from the establishment of catholic worship in France and from the personal profession of it which the consuls of the Republic make.

"Suppression of the Newspapers" is from Frank M. Anderson, *The Constitutions and Other Illustrative Documents of the History of France*, 2nd ed., revised (New York: Russell and Russell, 1908), p. 282.

"Reorganization of Religion" is from Frank M. Anderson, *The Constitutions and Other Illustrative Documents of the History of France*, 2nd ed., revised (New York: Russell and Russell, 1908), pp. 296–297.

In consequence, after this mutual recognition, as well for the benefit of religion as for the maintenance of internal tranquility, they have agreed as follows:

1. The catholic, apostolic and Roman religion shall be freely exercised in France: its worship shall be public, and in conformity with the police regulations which the government shall deem necessary for the public tranquility.

4. The First Consul of the Republic shall make appointments, within the three months which shall follow the publication of the bull of His Holiness to the archbishoprics and bishoprics of the new circumscription. His Holiness shall confer the canonical institution, following the forms established in relation to France before the change of government.

6. Before entering upon their functions, the bishops shall take directly, at the hands of the First Consul, the oath of fidelity which was in use before the change of government, expressed in the following terms:

"I swear and promise to God, upon the holy scriptures, to remain in obedience and fidelity to the government established by the constitution of the French Republic. I also promise not to have any intercourse, nor to assist by any counsel, nor to support any league, either within or without, which is inimical to the public tranquility; and if, within my diocese or elsewhere, I learn that anything to the prejudice of the state is being contrived, I will make it known to the government."

Articles for the Catholic Church (1802)

1. No bull, brief, rescript, decree, injunction, provision, signature serving as a provision, nor other documents from the court of Rome, even concerning individuals only, can be received, published, printed, or otherwise put into effect, without the authorization of the government.

4. No national or metropolitan council, no diocesan synod, no deliberative assembly, shall take place without the express permission of the government.

6. There shall be recourse to the Council of State in every case of abuse on the part of the Superiors and other ecclesiastical persons.

The cases of abuse are usurpation or excess of power, contravention of the laws and regulations of the Republic, infraction of the rules sanctioned by the canons received in France, attack upon the liberties, privileges and customs of the Gallican church, and every undertaking or any proceeding which in the exercise of worship can compromise the honor of the citizens, disturb arbitrarily their consciences, or degenerate into oppression or injury against them or into public scandal.

Frank M. Anderson, *The Constitutions and Other Illustrative Documents of the History of France,* 2nd ed., revised (New York: Russell and Russell, 1908), p. 299.

Consul for Life (1802)

On May 8, 1802, Napoleon's ten-year term as First Consul of the Republic was extended by the senate for another ten years. Reasons for this vote of confidence are given in the first selection. Napoleon's reply to this action follows. His term of office was further extended for life just three months later. This accumulation of so much power in so short a time is extraordinary. The third selection is Napoleon's oath of office.

Reelection as Consul (May 8, 1802)

Considering that, under the circumstances in which the Republic finds itself, it is the duty of the Conservative Senate to employ all the means which the constitution has put in its power in order to give to the government the stability which alone multiplies resources, inspires confidence abroad, establishes credit within, reassures allies, discourages secret enemies, turns away the scourge of war, permits the enjoyment of the fruits of peace, and leaves to wisdom time to carry out whatever it can conceive for the welfare of a free people;

Considering, moreover, that the supreme magistrate who, after having so many times led the republican legions to victory, delivered Italy, triumphed in Europe, in Africa, in Asia, and filled the world with his renown, has preserved France from the horrors of anarchy which were menacing it, broken the revolutionary sickle, dispersed the factions, extinguished civil discords and religious disturbances, added to the benefits of liberty those of order and of security, hastened the progress of enlightenment, consoled humanity, and pacified the continent and the seas, has the greatest right to the recognition of his fellow citizens, as well as the admiration of posterity;

That the wish of the Tribunate, which has come to the Senate in the sitting of this day, under these circumstances, can be regarded as that of the French nation;

That the Senate cannot express more solemnly to the First Consul the recognition of the nation than in giving him a striking proof of the confidence which he has inspired in the French people;

Considering, finally, that the second and the third consuls have worthily seconded the glorious labors of the First Consul of the Republic;

In consequence of all these motives, and the votes having been collected by secret ballot;

The Senate decrees as follows:

1. The Conservative Senate, in the name of the French people, testifies to its recognition of the consuls of the Republic.

Frank M. Anderson, *The Constitutions and Other Illustrative Documents of the History of France,* 2nd ed., revised (New York: Russell and Russell, 1908), p. 324.

2. The Conservative Senate re-elects Citizen Napoleon Bonaparte, First Consul of the French Republic for the ten years which shall immediately follow the ten for which he has been appointed by article 39 of the constitution.

Reply to the Senate (May 11, 1802)

NAPOLEON

Senators:

The honorable proof of esteem contained in your resolution of [May 8th] will ever be graven upon my heart.

The suffrage of the people has invested me with the supreme magistracy. I should not think myself assured of their confidence, if the act which retained me there was not again sanctioned by their suffrage.

In the three years which have just passed away fortune has smiled upon the Republic; but fortune is inconstant, and how many men whom it had crowned with its favors have lived on some years too many.

The interest of my glory and that of my happiness would seem to have marked the termination of my public life at the moment in which the peace of the world is proclaimed.

But the glory and happiness of the citizen must be silent, when the interest of the state and the public well-being summon him.

You deem that I owe to the people a new sacrifice: I will make it, if the wish of the people commands what your suffrage authorises.

Signed, Bonaparte

Oath as Consul for Life (August 4, 1802)

NAPOLEON

"I swear to maintain the constitution, to respect liberty of conscience, to oppose a return to feudal institutions, never to make war except for the defence and glory of the Republic, and to employ the authority with which I shall be invested only for the good of the people, from whom and for whom I shall have received it."

"Reply to the Senate" is from Frank M. Anderson, *The Constitutions and Other Illustrative Documents of the History of France,* 2nd ed., revised (New York: Russell and Russell, 1908), p. 325.

"Oath as Consul for Life" is from Frank M. Anderson, *The Constitutions and Other Illustrative Documents of the History of France,* 2nd ed., revised (New York: Russell and Russell, 1908), p. 331.

Napoleon's Reforms and Institutions

Although Napoleon's rise was extraordinary and, some would say, not in keeping with the spirit of a free republic, it is true that the programs he advocated were progressive and contributed to the stability and morale of the French state. Of the many reforms and institutions created by Napoleon, the provisions for education and the Legion of Honor are among the most characteristic and enduring.

General Provisions on Education

143. The Imperial University and its grand master, charged exclusively by us with the care of education and public instruction in all the empire, shall aim without respite to improve the instruction of all sorts, and to favor the composition of classical works; they shall particularly take care that the instruction of the sciences shall always be upon the level of acquired knowledge and that the spirit of system shall never arrest their progress.

The Legion of Honor

Each person admitted to the legion shall swear upon his honor to devote himself to the service of the Republic, to the preservation of its territory in its integrity, to the defence of its government, its laws and the properties which they have consecrated; to combat with all the means that justice, reason and the laws authorise, every undertaking having a tendency to reestablish the feudal regime, or to reproduce the titles and qualities which were symbolical of it; lastly, to assist with all his power in the maintenance of liberty and equality.

All military men who have received arms of honor are members of the legion.

The military men who have rendered important services to the state in the war for liberty;

The citizens who by their knowledge, their talents or their virtues, have contributed to the establishment or defence of the principles of the Republic, or have made justice or the public administration loved and respected shall be eligible for appointment.

In times of peace one must have had twenty-five years of military service in order to be appointed a member of the legion; the years of service in

"General Provisions on Education" is from Frank M. Anderson, *The Constitutions and Other Illustrative Documents of the History of France*, 2nd ed., revised (New York: Russell and Russell, 1908), p. 323.

"The Legion of Honor" is from Frank M. Anderson, *The Constitutions and Other Illustrative Documents of the History of France*, 2nd ed., revised (New York: Russell and Russell, 1908), p. 337.

Napoleon as Emperor by Jacques Louis David. Having executed King Louis XVI in 1793 in support of republican government, the French overwhelmingly accepted Napoleon as Emperor in 1804. Did France have more need of Napoleon than did he for France? (*Alinari/Art Resource*)

time of war shall count double and each campaign of the last war shall count for four years.

Great services rendered to the state in legislative functions, diplomacy, administration, justice or the sciences, shall also be titles for admission, provided the person who shall have rendered them has made part of the national guard of the place his domicile.

Napoleon Becomes Emperor (1804)

Five years after Napoleon became head of the French government as First Consul, he moved to expand his power, and on May 18, 1804, the Senate decreed that he should be made Emperor of the French. The people of France overwhelmingly approved of this measure through a plebiscite. Napoleon now had complete control of France's government and fate. In the following statement, before the legislative body of December 31, 1804, Napoleon recounts the reasons for establishing the government of the Empire in place of the Consulate. Note the importance of having the pope "officiate" at the coronation. In fact, Napoleon crowned himself emperor since he did not recognize the pope's authority as superior to his own. But why did the French people willingly submit to the despotism of Napoleon? In the second selection, the Comtesse de Rémusat (1780–1821), lady-in-waiting to Napoleon's wife Josephine and the author of some lively memoirs, gives her assessment. Appropriately, Napoleon found divine sanction for his power. The third offering recounts a catechism written during the reign of Louis XIV and modified to meet Napoleon's particular needs. Its questions and answers address the duties of French citizens toward their emperor.

Reasons for Establishing the Empire
(December 1804)

NAPOLEON

The internal situation of France is to-day as calm as it has ever been in the most peaceful periods. There is no agitation to disturb the public tranquility, no suggestion of those crimes which recall the Revolution. Everywhere useful enterprises are in progress, and the general improvements, both public and private, attest the universal confidence and sense of security. . . .

A plot conceived by an implacable government was about to replunge

James H. Robinson and Charles A. Beard, eds., *Readings in Modern European History*, vol. 1 (Boston: Ginn and Company, 1908), pp. 334–336.

France into the abyss of civil war and anarchy. The discovery of this horrible crime stirred all France profoundly, and anxieties that had scarcely been calmed again awoke. Experience has taught that a divided power in the state is impotent and at odds with itself. It was generally felt that if power was delegated for short periods only, it was so uncertain as to discourage any prolonged undertakings or wide-reaching plans. If vested in an individual for life, it would lapse with him, and after him would prove a source of anarchy and discord. It was clearly seen that for a great nation the only salvation lies in hereditary power, which can alone assure a continuous political life which may endure for generations, even for centuries.

The Senate, as was proper, served as the organ through which this general apprehension found expression. The necessity of hereditary power in a state as vast as France had long been perceived by the First Consul. He had endeavored in vain to avoid this conclusion; but the public solicitude and the hopes of our enemies emphasized the importance of his task, and he realized that his death might ruin his whole work. Under such circumstances, and with such a pressure of public opinion, there was no alternative left to the First Consul. He resolved, therefore, to accept for himself, and two of his brothers after him, the burden imposed by the exigencies of the situation.

After prolonged consideration, repeated conferences with the members of the Senate, discussion in the councils, and the suggestions of the most prudent advisers, a series of provisions was drawn up which regulate the succession to the imperial throne. These provisions were decreed by a *senatus consultus* of the 28th Floreal last. The French people, by a free and independent expression, then manifested its desire that the imperial dignity should pass down in a direct line through the legitimate or adopted descendants of Napoleon Bonaparte, or through the legitimate descendants of Joseph Bonaparte, or of Louis Bonaparte.

From this moment Napoleon was, by the most unquestioned of titles, emperor of the French. No other act was necessary to sanction his right and consecrate his authority. But he wished to restore in France the ancient forms and recall those institutions which divinity itself seems to have inspired. He wished to impress the seal of religion itself upon the opening of his reign. The head of the Church, in order to give the French a striking proof of his paternal affection, consented to officiate at this august ceremony. What deep and enduring impressions did this leave on the mind of Napoleon and in the memory of the nation! What thoughts for future races! What a subject of wonder for all Europe!

In the midst of this pomp, and under the eye of the Eternal, Napoleon pronounced the inviolable oath which assures the integrity of the empire, the security of property, the perpetuity of institutions, the respect for Law, and the happiness of the nation. The oath of Napoleon shall be forever the terror of the enemies of France. If our borders are attacked, it will be repeated at the head of our armies, and our frontiers shall never more fear foreign invasion.

Why the French Submitted to Napoleon's Rule (1804)

THE COMTESSE DE RÉMUSAT

I can understand how it was that men worn out by the turmoil of the Revolution, and afraid of that liberty which had long been associated with death, looked for repose under the dominion of an able ruler on who Fortune was seemingly resolved to smile. I can conceive that they regarded his elevation as a decree of destiny and fondly believed that in the irrevocable they should find peace. I may confidently assert that those persons believed quite sincerely that Bonaparte, whether as Consul or Emperor, would exert his authority to oppose the intrigues of faction and would save us from the perils of anarchy.

None dared to utter the word "republic," so deeply had the Terror stained that name; and the government of the Directory had perished in the contempt with which its chiefs were regarded. The return of the Bourbons could only be brought about by the aid of a revolution; and the slightest disturbance terrified the French people, in whom enthusiasm of every kind seemed dead. Besides, the men in whom they had trusted had one after the other deceived them; and as, this time, they were yielding to force, they were at least certain they were not deceiving themselves.

The belief, or rather the error, that only despotism could at that epoch maintain order in France was very widespread. It became the mainstay of Bonaparte; and it is due to him to say that he also believed it. The factions played into his hands by imprudent attempts which he turned to his own advantage. He had some grounds for his belief that he was necessary; France believed it, too; and he even succeeded in persuading foreign sovereigns that he constituted a barrier against republican influences, which, but for him, might spread widely. At the moment when Bonaparte placed the imperial crown upon his head there was not a king in Europe who did not believe that he wore his own crown more securely because of that event. Had the new emperor granted a liberal constitution, the peace of nations and of kings might really have been forever secured.

The Imperial Catechism (April 1806)

Question: What are the duties of Christians toward those who govern them, and what in particular are our duties towards Napoleon I, our emperor?

"Why the French Submitted to Napoleon's Rule" is from James H. Robinson and Charles A. Beard, eds., *Readings in Modern European History*, vol. 1 (Boston: Ginn and Company, 1908), pp. 333–334.

"The Imperial Catechism" is from James H. Robinson and Charles A. Beard, eds., *Readings in Modern European History*, vol. 1 (Boston: Ginn and Company, 1908), pp. 351–352.

Answer: Christians owe to the princes who govern them, and we in particular owe to Napoleon I, our emperor, love, respect, obedience, fidelity, military service, and the taxes levied for the preservation and defense of the empire and of his throne. We also owe him fervent prayers for his safety and for the spiritual and temporal prosperity of the state.

Question: Why are we subject to all these duties toward our emperor?

Answer: First, because God, who has created empires and distributes them according to his will, has, by loading our emperor with gifts both in peace and in war, established him as our sovereign and made him the agent of his power and his image on earth. To honor and serve our emperor is therefore to honor and serve God himself. Secondly, because our Lord Jesus Christ himself, both by his teaching and his example, has taught us what we owe to our sovereign. Even at his very birth he obeyed the edict of Caesar Augustus; he paid the established tax; and while he commanded us to render to God those things which belong to God, he also commanded us to render unto Caesar those things which are Caesar's.

Question: Are there not special motives which should attach us more closely to Napoleon I, our emperor?

Answer: Yes, for it is he whom God has raised up in trying times to reestablish the public worship of the holy religion of our fathers and to be its protector; he has reestablished and preserved public order by his profound and active wisdom; he defends the state by his mighty arm; he has become the anointed of the Lord by the consecration which he has received from the sovereign pontiff, head of the Church universal.

Question: What must we think of those who are neglecting their duties toward our emperor?

Answer: According to the apostle Paul, they are resisting the order established by God himself, and render themselves worthy of eternal damnation.

The Hero in History

Beginning in 1792 and continuing throughout much of the Revolution, France was at war against various coalitions of European nations. Revolutionary ideology was exportable and threatened the very foundation of enlightened despotism. As the French revolutionaries attacked the Church, monarchy, and aristocracy, most of Europe, including Great Britain, reacted by repressing liberal reform movements. These wars at once threatened the Revolution, but also granted it purpose and unity. Napoleon, a military commander of genius and overreaching ambition, capitalized on this French "spirit of the times" and sought to dominate Europe both militarily and culturally from 1803 to his final defeat at Waterloo in 1815. In the process, he inspired France and certainly changed the course of history. Napoleon believed that his actions were directed toward a destiny that he was compelled to achieve by fate. The first selection is a good example of this belief. It is an address to Dutch representatives upon the annexation of Holland to the French empire in 1810.

Yet, what is the role of the "great man" or "hero" in history? Can the course of history be changed by a dynamic individual of ability and resolve? Or does history progress by uncontrollable economic and social "forces"? The second selection is by G. W. F. Hegel, a German philosopher who believed that "heroes" such as Caesar, Alexander, and Napoleon were unconscious instruments of a "world spirit" (*Zeitgeist*) that lay behind the development of human history. The chosen passage reveals Hegel's thoughts about how heroes could change the course of history. Hegel is representative of the romantic belief, current in the early nineteenth century, that human history was connected with much larger spiritual forces.

The last selection is an excerpt from the memoirs of Stanislaus Girardin (1762–1827), a French politician. As he and the then First Consul Napoleon stood by the grave of Jean Jacques Rousseau, Napoleon reflected on the influence of this great political philosopher.

"An End to the Woes of Anarchy" (1810)

NAPOLEON

When Providence elevated me to the first throne in the world it became my duty, while establishing forever the destinies of France, to determine the fate of all those people who formed a part of the empire, to insure for all the benefits of stability and order, and to put an end everywhere to the woes of anarchy. I have done away with the uncertainty in Italy by placing upon my head the crown of iron. . . .

I gave you a prince of my own blood to govern you. . . . I have opened the continent to your industry, and the day will come when you shall bear my eagles upon the seas which your ancestors have rendered illustrious. You will then show yourself worthy of them and of me. . . .

The Role of Great Men in History

G. W. F. HEGEL

Such are all great historical men—whose own particular aims involve those large issues which are the will of the World-Spirit. They may be called

"An End to the Woes of Anarchy" is from James H. Robinson and Charles A. Beard, eds., *Readings in Modern European History*, vol. 1 (Boston: Ginn and Company, 1908), pp. 355–356.

"The Role of Great Men in History" is from G. W. F. Hegel, *The Philosophy of History*, trans. by J. Sibree (New York: Dover, 1956), pp. 30–31. Reprinted by permission of the publisher.

Heroes, inasmuch as they have derived their purposes and their vocation, not from the calm, regular course of things, sanctioned by the existing order: but from a concealed fount—one which has not attained to phenomenal, present existence—from that inner Spirit, still hidden beneath the surface, which, impinging on the outer world as on a shell, bursts it in pieces, because it is another kernel than that which belonged to the shell in question. They are men, therefore, who appear to draw the impulse of their life from themselves; and whose deeds have produced a condition of things and a complex of historical relations which appear to be only their interest, and their work.

Such individuals had no consciousness of the general idea they were unfolding, while prosecuting those aims of theirs; on the contrary, they were practical, political men. But at the same time they were thinking men, who had an insight into the requirements of the time—what was ripe for development. This was the very Truth for their age, for their world: the species next in order, so to speak, and which was already formed in the womb of time. It was theirs to know this nascent principle; the necessary, directly sequent step in progress, which their world was to take; to make this their aim, and to expend their energy in promoting it. World-historical men—the Heroes of an epoch—much, therefore, be recognized as its clear-sighted ones: their deed, their words are the best of that time.

Napoleon on Rousseau

STANISLAUS GIRARDIN

When he reached the poplar island, Bonaparte stepped in front of Jean-Jacques' tomb and said, "It would have been better for the peace of France if this man had never lived."—"And why, Citizen Consul?"—"It was he who prepared the French Revolution."—"I should have thought, Citizen Consul, that it was not for you to complain of the Revolution."—"Well," Napoleon replied, "the future will tell us whether it would not have been better if neither I nor Rousseau had ever lived." And he resumed his walk with a thoughtful air.

STUDY QUESTIONS

Section I: The French Revolution

1. What are the arguments used by Locke, Montesquieu, and Rousseau to justify revolution? Who or what is the "sovereign power" Rousseau mentions? Comment in particular on Rousseau's belief that "whoever refuses to obey the general will shall be compelled to it by the whole body." Isn't this a form of tyranny?

J. Christopher Herold, ed. and trans., *The Mind of Napoleon* (New York: Columbia University Press, 1955), p. 67. Reprinted by permission of the publisher.

2. Note the excerpts under the section, "The Influence of Philosophy." In order to be enduring, must revolutions have precedents for action (like the Glorious Revolution or the American Revolution)? Must they have some philosophical justification?

3. What is a revolution? How do you distinguish it from a riot or a rebellion? What political, social, or economic conditions existed in eighteenth-century France that contributed to the French Revolution? Compare especially the accounts of Arthur Young and Thomas Jefferson. What do they tell you? In a general sense, do you think that difficult conditions precede any successful revolution?

4. What were the specific demands made by the Third Estate? Do they seem reasonable to you?

5. Read the Tennis Court Oath carefully. Does it call for radical action? Why is it considered to be one of the most important documents of the French Revolution?

6. Why was the fall of the Bastille such an important event? After reading the pertinent selections, discuss how important violence is in a revolution. Do most successful revolutions promote violence to some degree?

7. What are the most important ideas contained in the Declaration of the Rights of Man? Why was it essential to the French Revolution? What does it tell you about the Old Regime of Louis XVI and his predecessors? Do you believe (as did most of the *philosophes*) that there are "natural rights" for all human beings and that a government should protect these rights? How is this "natural rights" argument reflected in the various documents of the Revolution?

8. What were Edmund Burke's main criticisms of the Revolution in France? Why did Burke anticipate plots, assassinations, and a "long roll of bloody maxims"? Was he right?

9. Compare Louis XVI's "Letter to Foreign Courts" with his "Declaration" of June 20, 1791. Do you find his arguments in the Declaration to be legitimate and effective? Is the "Indictment of Louis XVI" a truthful or exaggerated account of the king's actions? To what extent then were the revolutionaries justified in executing Louis XVI as a tyrant and traitor to the revolution?

10. Analyze the speech of Robespierre. How did he justify the use of terror in the promotion of revolution? Note, in particular, the juxtaposition of virtue and terror. In an ethical sense, can virtue ever be promoted by terror?

Section II: The Napoleonic Era

11. How did Napoleon come to power in 1799? Carefully read the statement he made on becoming consul. Pay particular attention to the vocabulary. How did Napoleon justify his overthrow of the Directory? Balance this public statement with the attitude found in the preceding excerpt on the "Realities of Power." What does this say about Napoleon's commitment to democratic ideals? At the time though, to progress as a nation did

France need less ideal and more practical inspiration and leadership? Was Napoleon a hypocrite who saved France from chaos? If so, do you condemn him for his hypocrisy?

12. On becoming First Consul, Napoleon consolidated his position by suppressing the newspapers and reorganizing the state's religious institutions. Read these selections. Are these actions consistent with democratic government? From Napoleon's perspective, why were these actions essential to the stability of the state?

13. In 1802, Napoleon was voted Consul for Life. In practical terms, what does this title mean? How did the senate justify its decision to elect Napoleon to this position? Examine Napoleon's reply to the senate. Why did he decide to accept the position?

14. Look carefully at the statements concerning the reform of education and establishing the Legion of Honor. What special traits or characteristics of French citizens was Napoleon trying to reward or inspire in these measures? Were these reforms progressive and healthy for the French state? Why?

15. In 1804, Napoleon became Emperor of the French by decree of the senate. How does this position differ from that of First Consul for Life? Compare the reasons that Napoleon gives for assuming this position with those given when he became First Consul and Consul for Life. Is there any pattern of justification? Note that the people of France approved of Napoleon's rise to power and his assumption of titles by supporting him with plebiscites. Were they in fact limiting their own freedom? Is freedom, most importantly, just a state of mind? Does progress often depend on a restriction of freedom in the interests of stability and security?

16. Compare the provisions for Napoleon's reorganization of the Church in 1806 with the imperial catechism of 1808. What comment can you make regarding Napoleon and religion? Was he a divine-right monarch? What role did religion play in the establishment of Napoleon's political power? In this sense, note also the Clerical Oath of Loyalty (1790). Why is it essential in time of revolution for the state to control religious organization?

17. Was Napoleon an absolute monarch in the tradition of Louis XIV? Was he a democrat, or the first of the "modern dictators" in the fascist mold of Mussolini and Hitler? Does the distinction between a democrat and a dictator blur when one is trying to achieve and consolidate power?

18. Note Napoleon's view of his destiny, entitled "An End to the Woes of Anarchy." Was he a progressive or destructive force in French history? Did he embody Hegel's conception of the term "hero"? How? Was the philosophy of Jean Jacques Rousseau every bit as much a force for the promotion of historical change as were the actions of Napoleon Bonaparte?

5

The Industrial Revolution

Two nations between whom there is no intercourse and no sympathy; who are as ignorant of each other's habits, thoughts and feelings as if they were . . . inhabitants of different planets; who are formed by a different breeding, are fed by a different food, are ordered by different manners, and are not governed by the same laws—the rich and the poor.

—Benjamin Disraeli

The inherent vice of capitalism is the unequal sharing of blessings; the inherent virtue of socialism is the equal sharing of miseries.

—Winston Churchill

The worth of a State, in the long run, is the worth of the individuals composing it.

—John Stuart Mill

Man is born free and everywhere he is in chains.

—Jean Jacques Rousseau

The word revolution implies drastic change, most often of a political nature, which results in a new form of government. There are other types of revolution as well. From the late eighteenth century to the late nineteenth century, Europe underwent a social and economic revolution that was the result of technological progress inspired by inventive minds. No longer would man be harnessed to the land, completely dependent on the vicissitudes of nature for his livelihood; a new world was dawning, based on the city and filled with the prospect of employment and new lives. But this was not a move toward economic independence, for man would soon be harnessed to an even more exacting master than the land—the machine.

Historically, the process of industrialization was a gradual one. The first stage of the Industrial Revolution began slowly, about 1760, and was made possible by several factors. First, Europe had reaped the benefits of an age of discovery during the sixteenth and seventeenth centuries. This fostered a commercial revolution that resulted in substantial economic growth. Indeed, the economic benefits of exploration were evident as nations sought to organize and compete on a grand scale. In addition, the English and French political revolutions of the seventeenth and eighteenth centuries began the ascendency of the middle class, which furnished the investment capital and expansive leadership necessary for the inception of the Industrial Revolution. At the same time, the population of Europe was growing dramatically, so much so that a rural-based economy simply could not support the growing tax requirements of governments and employ all who sought jobs.

These conditions were especially evident in England, where rural unemployment had been exacerbated by a conscious decision on the part of the wealthy land owners and the government itself to "enclose" farmland, release the tenantry from the security of farm labor, and use the land as pasture for sheep. Great profits were to be made in the textile trade, but the resulting displacement of the yeoman farmer added to the rural dilemma.

Yet England in the mid-eighteenth century was generally prosperous since it had developed a solid colonial foundation that provided ready markets for its goods. These markets were served by a maritime commercial and military fleet without peer and were supported by growing domestic production. This increase in the productive capacity of domestic industry resulted in large part from English ingenuity. The development of the "flying shuttle," "spinning jenny," "power loom," and "cotton gin" in the mid-eighteenth century bespoke English technical superiority and advancement. The English had other natural advantages as well. Blessed with the existence of large quantities of coal and iron in close proximity, the English developed techniques for reducing the impurities in iron, thereby stimulating production; this eventually led to the development of the railroad in the mid-nineteenth century.

These new technologies were harnessed and organized in the factory. Men, women, and children were employed to keep the machines running, and the "factory system" was established to provide the greatest efficiency of material and labor, at the least expensive cost.

To many, industrialization became synonymous with progress. In-creased production of goods meant greater potential for export, and this in turn created greater profit for the individual and government alike. The cultivation of new markets inspired competition among nations, explora-tion of new lands, and efficient management of time and labor. Yet industrialization, for all its glorification of the genius of the human mind, was never without its critics. It solved certain problems, but created others. What, for instance, was to be done with those people who moved to the city in search of factory employment and found themselves among the "technologically unemployed," looking for jobs that simply did not exist? And what of those who were fortunate enough to find work in the mills or the mines? The dull monotony and danger of their occupations, not to mention their subsistence living conditions, made life depressing. The factory worker dreaded unemployment, yet could do little to change his condition. As long as competition, efficiency, and profit were the primary catalysts of the Industrial Revolution, the laborer would have to be sacrificed.

The conflicts raised by industrialization were all the more bewildering because they were unprecedented. How, for example, was government to respond to the complex problems created by industrial progress? This question was of primary importance for Britain, the first industrial area and the subject of this chapter. British industrialization was stimulated in the nineteenth century by the needs of national defense in view of the threat imposed by Napoleon. Criticism by reformers was not tolerated by the government, which viewed such acts as unpatriotic and incendiary. By the 1820s, however, tentative reforms were made that led to a rather prolonged debate resulting in the Reform Bill of 1832. This ensured that most middle-class British subjects would receive parliamentary represen-tation and opened the franchise to some of the new industrial towns whose populations had never before been represented. In the following years, further reforms were legislated, such as the Factory Act of 1833, that limited the working hours of women and children in the textile mills and provided government inspection of the workplace. Still, reform was not won without struggle. In the 1830s and 1840s, writers and literary figures such as Charles Dickens and historian Thomas Carlyle and politi-cal organizations such as the Chartists advocated constitutional and so-cial change. Liberalism was born as a political philosophy, and intellec-tuals such as John Stuart Mill (1806–1873) advocated workers' cooperatives, unions, and even women's suffrage.

Change was advocated from other directions as well. It was during this time that Karl Marx and Friedrich Engels observed the conditions of the working class in England and composed one of the most influential docu-ments of the modern world—the *Communist Manifesto* (1848). Accord-ing to Marx, the true revolutionary force in society was the workers (proletarians) who were dominated and abused by capitalists interested in profit at the workers' expense. As Marx wrote: "Let the ruling classes tremble at a Communist revolution. The proletarians have nothing to lose but their chains. They have a world to win." Other socialists less radical than Marx preached the need and inevitability of change to a more balanced society, based less on privilege and more on equality of opportunity.

The Industrial Revolution can thus be viewed in two ways: as a force for progress, an example of man's ability to mold his environment, and as a demonstration of man's abuse of man, for the Industrial Revolution intensified class animosities and provided the catalyst for social change. The questions that emerge from this chapter are thus philosophical in nature yet practical in application. In order for civilization to progress, to move forward technologically, must there always be a price to pay in human suffering or abuse? And if that is the case, is it worth it? What indeed constitutes "progress"? The twentieth century has experienced some of the greatest technological change, from the invention of the automobile to the exploration of space. Have we too paid a price?

The Factory System: Working Conditions

Sybil (1845)

BENJAMIN DISRAELI

One of the most ardent reformers who criticized working conditions was Benjamin Disraeli. A novelist and politician, he served as Prime Minister of Britain from 1867 to 1868 and from 1874 to 1880. His most famous novel, *Sybil, or the Two Nations,* vividly describes working and living conditions in factory towns. Disraeli hoped to gain working-class support for a group of reforming aristocrats in his Tory party. The following selection from this novel demonstrates the power of his prose.

They come forth: the mine delivers its gang and the pit its bondsmen, the forge is silent and the engine is still. The plain is covered with the swarming multitude: bands of stalwart men, broad-chested and muscular, wet with the toil, and black as the children of the tropics; troops of youth, alas! of both sexes, though neither their raiment nor their language indicates the difference; all are clad in male attire; and oaths that men might shudder at issue from lips born to breathe words of sweetness. Yet these are to be, some are, the mothers of England! But can we wonder at the hideous coarseness of their language, when we remember the savage rudeness of

Benjamin Disraeli, *Sybil, or the Two Nations* (New York: M. Walter Dunne, 1904), pp. 199–200.

their lives? Naked to the waist, an iron chain fastened to a belt of leather runs between their legs clad in canvas trousers, while on hands and feet an English girl, for twelve, sometimes for sixteen hours a day, hauls and hurries tubs of coals up subterranean roads, dark, precipitous, and plashy; circumstances that seem to have escaped the notice of the Society for the Abolition of Negro Slavery. Those worthy gentlemen, too, appear to have been singularly unconscious of the sufferings of the little trappers, which was remarkable, as many of them were in their own employ.

See, too, these emerge from the bowels of the earth! Infants of four and five years of age, many of them girls, pretty and still soft and timid; entrusted with the fulfillment of responsible duties, the very nature of which entails on them the necessity of being the earliest to enter the mine and the latest to leave it. Their labour indeed is not severe, for that would be impossible, but it is passed in darkness and in solitude. They endure that punishment which philosophical philanthropy has invented for the direst criminals, and which those criminals deem more terrible than the death for which it is substituted. Hour after hour elapses, and all that reminds the infant trappers of the world they have quitted, and that which they have joined, is the passage of the coal-wagons for which they open the air-doors of the galleries, and on keeping which doors constantly closed, except at this moment of passage, the safety of the mine and the lives of the persons employed in it entirely depend.

Testimony Before the Sadler Committee (1832)

In 1831 and 1832, the British government was under popular pressure to regulate factories and protect men, women, and children from abusive working conditions. The Sadler Committee was established and heard testimony from both workers and factory owners. The following selection clearly describes working conditions in a flax mill.

What age are you?—Twenty-three.

Where do you live?—At Leeds.

What time did you begin to work at a factory?—When I was six years old.

At whose factory did you work?—At Mr. Busk's.

What kind of mill is it?—Flax-mill.

What was your business in that mill?—I was a little doffer.

What were your hours of labour in that mill?—From 5 in the morning till 9 at night, when they were thronged.

For how long a time together have you worked that excessive length of time?—For about half a year.

Parliamentary Papers, Reports from Committees, XV, "Labour of Children in Factories 1831–1832" (London, 1832).

What were your usual hours of labour when you were not so thronged?—From 6 in the morning till 7 at night.

What time was allowed for your meals?—Forty minutes at noon.

Had you any time to get your breakfast or drinking?—No, we got it as we could.

And when your work was bad, you hardly had anytime to eat at all?— No; we were obliged to leave it or take it home, and when we did not take it, the overlooker took it, and gave it to his pigs.

Do you consider doffing a laborious employment?—Yes.

Explain what it is you had to do?—When the frames are full, they have to stop the frames, and take the flyers off, and take the full bobbins off, and carry them to the roller; and then put empty ones on, and set the frame going again.

Does that keep you constantly on your feet?—Yes, there are so many frames, and they run so quick.

Your labour is very excessive?—Yes; you have not time for anything.

Suppose you flagged a little, or were too late, what would they do?— Strap us.

Are they in the habit of strapping those who are last in doffing?—Yes.

Constantly?—Yes.

Have you ever been strapped?—Yes.

Severely?—Yes.

Is the strap used so as to hurt you excessively?—Yes, it is.

Were you strapped if you were too much fatigued to keep up with the machinery?—Yes; the overlooker I was under was a very severe man, and when we have been fatigued and worn out, and had not baskets to put the bobbins in, we used to put them in the window bottoms, and that broke the panes sometimes, and I broke one one time, and the overlooker strapped me on the arm, and it rose a blister, and I ran home to my mother.

How long did you work at Mr. Busk's?—Three or four years.

Where did you go to then?—Benyon's factory.

That was when you were about 10 years?—Yes.

What were you then?—A weigher in the card-room.

How long did you work there?—From half-past 5 till 8 at night.

Was that the ordinary time?—Till 9 when they were thronged.

What time was allowed for meals at that mill?—Forty minutes at noon.

Any time at breakfast or drinking?—Yes, for the card-rooms, but not for the spinning-rooms, a quarter of an hour to get their breakfast.

And the same for their drinking?—Yes.

So that the spinners in that room worked from half-past 5 till 9 at night?—Yes.

Having only forty minutes' rest?—Yes.

The carding-room is more oppressive than the spinning department?— Yes, it is so dusty they cannot see each other for dust.

It is on that account they are allowed a relaxation of those few minutes?—Yes; the cards get so soon filled up with waste and dirt, they are obliged to stop them, or they would take fire.

There is a convenience in that stoppage?—Yes, it is as much for their benefit as for the working people.

When it was not necessary no such indulgence was allowed?—No.

Never?—No.

Were the children beat up to their labour there?—Yes.

With what?—A strap; I have seen the overlooker go to the top end of the room, where the little girls hug the can to the backminders; he has taken a strap, and a whistle in his mouth, and sometimes he has got a chain and chained them, and strapped them all down the room.

All the children?—No, only those hugging the cans.

What was his reason for that?—He was angry.

Had the children committed any fault?—They were too slow.

Were the children excessively fatigued at that time?—Yes, it was in the afternoon.

Were the girls so struck as to leave marks upon their skin?—Yes, they have had black marks many times, and their parents dare not come to him about it, they were afraid of losing their work.

If the parents were to complain of this excessive ill-usage, the probable consequence would be the loss of the situation of the child?—Yes.

In what part of the mill did you work?—In the card-room.

It was exceedingly dusty?—Yes.

Did it affect your health?—Yes; it was so dusty, the dust got upon my lungs, and the work was so hard; I was middling strong when I went there, but the work was so bad; I got so bad in health, that when I pulled the baskets down, I pulled my bones out of their places.

You dragged the baskets?—Yes; down the rooms to where they are worked.

And as you had been weakened by excessive labour, you could not stand that labour?—No.

It has had the effect of pulling your shoulders out?—Yes; it was a great basket that stood higher than this table a good deal.

How heavy was it?—I cannot say; it was a very large one, that was full of weights up-heaped, and pulling the basket pulled my shoulders out of its place, and my ribs have grown over it.

You continued at that work?—Yes.

You think that work is too much for children?—Yes.

It is woman's work, not fit for children?—Yes.

Is that work generally done by women?—Yes.

How came you to do it?—There was no spinning for me.

Did they give you women's wages?—They gave me 5s. and the women had 6s. 6d.

What wages did you get as a spinner?—Six shillings.

Did you perceive that many other girls were made ill by that long labour?—Yes, a good many of them.

So that you were constantly receiving fresh hands to supply the places of those that could no longer bear their work?—Yes, there were fresh hands every week; they could not keep their hands.

Did they all go away on account of illness?—They were sick and ill with the dust.

Do you know whether any of them died in consequence of it?—No, I cannot speak to that.

You do not know what became of them?—No, we did not know that.

If a person was to take an account of a mill, and the hands in it that were ill, they would know very little of those who had suffered from their labour; they would be elsewhere?—Yes.

But you are sure of this, that they were constantly leaving on account of the excessive labour they had to endure?—Yes.

And the unhealthy nature of their employment?—Yes.

Did you take any means to obviate the bad effects of this dust?—No.

Did it make you very thirsty?—Yes, we drank a deal of water in the room.

Were you heated with your employment at the same time?—No, it was not so very hot as in the summer time; in the winter time they were obliged to have the windows open, it made no matter what the weather was, and sometimes we got very severe colds in frost and snow.

You were constantly exposed to colds, and were made ill by that cause also?—Yes.

You are considerably deformed in your person in consequence of this labour?—Yes, I am.

At what time did it come on?—I was about 13 years old when it began coming, and it has got worse since. . . .

Do you know of any body that has been similarly injured in their health?—Yes, in their health, but not many deformed as I am.

You are deformed in the shoulders?—Yes.

It is very common to have weak ankles and crooked knees?—Yes, very common indeed.

That is brought on by stopping the spindle?—Yes.

Do you know anything of wet-spinning?—Yes, it is very uncomfortable; I have stood before the frame till I have been wet through to my skin; and in winter time, when we have gone home, our clothes have been frozen, and we have nearly caught our death of cold.

Child Labor

Children were an integral part of the factory system. Mine owners depended on small boys to enter and work in restrictive areas that could not

John Saville, ed., *Working Conditions in the Victorian Age* (Westmead, England: Gregg International Publishers Limited, 1973), pp. 130–132, 378–380. Reprinted by permission of the publisher.

accommodate adults. The mills were common sources of employment for children who were good with their hands. Many parents condoned this and often forced their children to work, since they depended on their children's wages to live at subsistence level. The following accounts were excerpted from various liberal journals such as the *Edinburgh Review,* the *Westminster Review,* and *Fraser's Magazine;* they reveal the social conscience of Victorian England.

With regard to the hours of work, the commissioners state, that when the work-people are in full employment, the regular hours of work for children and young persons are rarely less than eleven; more often they are twelve; in some districts they are thirteen; and in one district they are generally fourteen and upwards. Certainly, unless upon the ample testimony produced by the Commission, it would not be credible that there is one district in the centre of England in which children are regularly required to pursue the labours of the mine for fourteen and sixteen hours daily; but in Derbyshire, south of Chesterfield, from thirteen to sixteen hours are considered a day's work; from eleven to twelve hours are reckoned three quarters of a day's work; and eight hours make half a day's work.

"John Hawkins, eight years of age:—'Has worked in Sissons Pit, a year and a half; lives a mile from the pit; goes down from five to nine;' that is, this child, eight years old, is employed in the pit at work from five o'clock in the morning to nine at night, a period of 16 hours.—John Houghton, nine years old:—'Goes down from six to eight—it has been ten:' that is, this child is regularly employed at work in the pits 14 hours, and occasionally 16 hours.—Ephraim Riley, eleven years old:—'Had three miles to walk to the pit; left home at five o'clock, winter and summer, and did not get home again until nine o'clock at night (16 hours); his legs and thighs hurt him so with working so much that he remains in bed on Sunday mornings.'—John Chambers, thirteen years old:—'Has worked in pits since he was seven; works from six to nine or ten (from 15 to 16 hours). When first he worked in a pit he felt so tired, and his legs, arms, and back ached so much, that his brother has had to help him home many times. He could not go to school on a Sunday morning, he has been so stiff; he felt these pains until about a year since; he now feels tired, but his limbs do not ache as they did.'— James Creswell, fourteen years old:—'Has worked in pits four or five years; goes down at half-past six to nine, has this winter been after ten; half-days half-past six to three or four.'

"Of the fatigue of such labour, so protracted and carried on in such places of work, the following evidence exhibits a striking picture, and it will be observed that the witnesses of every class, children, young persons, colliers, underground stewards, agents, parents, teachers, and ministers of religion, all concur in making similar statements.

"John Bostock, aged seventeen, Babbington:—'Has often been made to work until he was so tired as to lie down on his road home until 12 o'clock, when his mother has come and led him home; he has done so many times when he first went to the pits; he has sometimes been so fatigued that he could not eat his dinner, but has been beaten and made to work until night; he never thought to play, was always too anxious to get to bed; is sure this is all true.'—John Leadbeater, aged eighteen, Babbington:—'Has two miles to go to the pit, and must be there before six, and works until eight; he has often worked all night, and been made by the butties to work as usual the next day; has often been so tired that he has lain in bed all Sunday. He knows no work so bad as that of a pit lad.'—Samuel Radford, aged nineteen, New Birchwood:—'Has been a week together and never seen daylight but on a Sunday, and not much then, he was so sleepy.'

An imperfect abstract from the registration of deaths for the year 1838, gives a total, in England alone, of 349 deaths by violence in coal mines, and shows the most common causes of them:—

Cause of death	Under 13 years of age	13 and not exceeding 18 years of age	Over 18 years of age
Fell down the shafts	13	12	31
Fell down the shaft from the rope breaking	1	—	2
Fell out when ascending	—	—	3
Drawn over the pulley	3	—	3
Fall of stone out of a skip down the shaft	1	—	3
Drowned in the mines	3	4	15
Fall of stones, coal, and rubbish in the mines	14	14	69
Injuries in coal-pits, the nature of which is not specified	6	3	32
Crushed in coal-pits	—	1	1
Explosion of gas	13	18	49
Suffocation by choke-damp	—	2	6
Explosion of gunpowder	—	1	3
By tram-wagons	4	5	12
Total	58	62	229

We proceed now to notice the great *Metal Manufactures* and their influence upon the health and well being of the children and youths employed in them. . . . In the blast-furnaces, mills, and forges, great numbers of children and youths are employed in night sets, between 6 P.M. and 6 A.M.; and in the miscellaneous trades overtime is very common, a great number of children working as long as the men, viz. from 6 A.M. to 11 P.M. Little girls are employed in bellows-blowing (very hard work for children) for fourteen hours a-day, standing on platforms to enable them to reach the handle of the bellows. Night work, overtime, and the very nature of the employment, cannot but have a very disastrous influence on their health. The foundry-boys, it is admitted by the masters themselves, commence work at much too early an age, and are taxed far beyond their strength; and the children who work at home, in the various domestic manufactures, are so injured by premature labour, often commencing from the age of seven, that, as a rule, they are stunted, dwarfed, or deformed. An instance is given of a father having worked his three young boys from four in the morning until twelve at night for weeks together, until the other men 'cried shame upon him'. . . . Two girls, nine and ten years of age, were working as 'strikers' and a little girl of eight, occasionally relieved by a still younger one of six, was working the bellows. The gross earnings of this man amounted to two guineas per week. It may be doubted whether the world could not produce a more revolting instance of parental oppression than the spectacle of these two young girls, whose little hands would have been appropriately employed in hemming a kerchief or working a sampler, begrimed with the smoke, stifled with the heat and stunned with the din morning till night. A single instance of oppression has often had a greater effect in rousing indignation than the most powerful denunciation of a general wrong. The picture of these little Staffordshire girls thus unsexed by an imperious taskmaster, and that taskmaster their parent, is well adapted to expose for universal reprobation a system under which such an enormity could be possible, and to prove the necessity of immediate legislative interference.

Living Conditions

The living conditions of workers in urban industrial settings were a popular subject for reformers. One of the most important reformers, Friedrich Engels (1820–1895), was born to a family of German textile manufacturers. Engels was a keen observer of society and a talented, urbane writer. His close friendship and collaboration with Karl Marx was instrumental in the dissemination and success of communist ideology. In the first selection, Engels describes the condition of the working class in Manchester, the primary manufacturing town in England. A second view of Manchester is afforded by William Dodd, a reformer who sought to expose the moral degradation of industrial life.

The Condition of the Working Class in England (1844)
FRIEDRICH ENGELS

Above Ducie Bridge, the left bank grows more flat and the right bank steeper, but the condition of the dwellings on both banks grows worse

Friedrich Engels, *The Condition of the Working Class in England in 1844* (London: Sonnenschein & Co., 1892), pp. 51–53.

rather than better. He who turns to the left here from the main street, Long Millgate, is lost; he wanders from one court to another, turns countless corners, passes nothing but narrow, filthy nooks and alleys, until after a few minutes he has lost all clue, and knows not whither to turn. Everywhere half or wholly ruined buildings, some of them actually uninhabited, which means a great deal here; rarely a wooden or stone floor to be seen in the houses, almost uniformly broken, ill-fitting windows and doors, and a state of filth! Everywhere heaps of debris, refuse, and offal; standing pools for gutters, and a stench which alone would make it impossible for a human being in any degree civilised to live in such a district. The newly-built extension of the Leeds railway, which crosses the Irk here, has swept away some of these courts and lanes, laying others completely open to view. Immediately under the railway bridge there stands a court, the filth and horrors of which surpass all the others by far, just because it was hitherto so shut off, so secluded that the way to it could not be found without a good deal of trouble. I should never have discovered it myself, without the breaks made by the railway, though I thought I knew this whole region thoroughly. Passing along a rough bank, among stakes and washing-lines, one penetrates into this chaos of small one-storied, one-roomed huts, in most of which there is no artificial floor; kitchen, living and sleeping-room all in one. In such a hole, scarcely five feet long by six broad, I found two beds—and such bedsteads and beds!—which, with a staircase and chimney-place, exactly filled the room. In several others I found absolutely nothing, while the door stood open, and the inhabitants leaned against it. Everywhere before the doors refuse and offal; that any sort of pavement lay underneath could not be seen but only felt, here and there with the feet. This whole collection of cattle-sheds for human beings was surrounded on two sides by houses and a factory, and on the third by the river, and besides the narrow stair up the bank, a narrow doorway alone led out into another almost equally ill-built, ill-kept labyrinth of dwellings. . . .

Such is the Old Town of Manchester, and on re-reading my description, I am forced to admit that instead of being exaggerated, it is far from black enough to convey a true impression of the filth, ruin, and uninhabitableness, the defiance of all considerations of cleanliness, ventilation, and health which characterise the construction of this single district, containing at least twenty to thirty thousand inhabitants. And such a district exists in the heart of the second city of England, the first manufacturing city of the world. If any one wishes to see in how little space a human being can move, how little air—and *such* air!—he can breathe, how little civilisation he may share and yet live, it is only necessary to travel hither. True, this is the *Old* Town, and the people of Manchester emphasise the fact whenever any one mentions to them the frightful condition of this Hell upon Earth; but what does that prove? Everything which here arouses horror and indignation is of recent origin, belongs to the *industrial epoch*.

The Factory System Illustrated (1842)

WILLIAM DODD

The impressions which Manchester, and its teeming population made upon my mind, are so similar to those they produced upon the mind of Dr. Kay, formerly a physician here, and the author of a pamphlet on the condition of the working classes, that I shall endeavour to fortify my opinions by a few extracts from his work.

"Visiting Manchester, the metropolis of the commercial system, a stranger regards with wonder the ingenuity and comprehensive capacity which, in the short space of half a century, have here established the staple manufacture of this kingdom. He beholds with astonishment the establishments of its merchants, the masses of capital which have been accumulated by those who crowd upon its mart, and the restless spirit which has made every part of the known world the scene of their enterprise. When he turns from the great capitalists, he contemplates the strength of that labouring population, which lies like a slumbering giant at their feet. He has heard of the turbulent riots of the people—of machine-breaking—of the secret and sullen organization which has suddenly lit the torch of incendiarism, or well nigh uplifted the arm of rebellion in the land. He remembers that political desperadoes have ever loved to tempt this population to the hazards of the swindling game of revolution, and have scarcely failed. In the midst of so much affluence, however, he has disbelieved the cry of need."

The streets and lanes, in which are the dwellings of the working classes, are generally narrow, and dirty; very little attention seems to be paid to the comfort of the people living in these crowded neighbourhoods. The dwellings of vast numbers of the poor people have been erected without any care for the health of those who were destined to live in them. In the first place, the ground has not been properly prepared, there being no sewers or drainage in many of the streets; nor has the slightest regard been paid to the warmth, ventilation, and convenience of the houses; many of them are built back to back, so that the admission of a fresh current of air through them is impossible. The rooms are so small, and the ceilings so low, that they are not capable of admitting a sufficient quantity of air to support healthy respiration.

There is no boiler, oven, wash-house, or any convenience needed by a family. The sleeping rooms are not sufficient for decency, or even morality, to say nothing of salubrity. Frequently there is only one out-office in common to several tenements, and that always partially, and often altogether open and exposed. In short, houses built not only without regard to the ordinary comforts, and the common decencies of civilized society, but even without regard to the primary and essential requisites to life and health.

William Dodd, *The Factory System Illustrated* (London: John Murray, 1842), pp. 96–99, 101.

The inhabitants of these loathsome dwellings take but little care of their health and comfort; for in many of the streets we find heaps of filth, and pools of stagnant water; sufficient of themselves to breed fevers and diseases, by the poisonous exhalations arising from decaying vegetable matter, and other filth which ought to be removed. In the centre of the town there is a mass of buildings inhabited by the very lowest orders; these are again intersected by narrow streets, and close courts, defiled with every description of refuse.

Dr. Kay thus describes the houses in the crowded parts of the town, and the manner in which a great proportion of the operatives are accomodated in them.

"The houses in such situations are uncleanly, ill-provided with furniture; an air of discomfort, if not of squalid and loathsome wretchedness, pervades them; they are often dilapidated, badly drained, damp, and the habits of their tenants are gross. They are ill-fed, ill-clothed, and uneconomical, at once spendthrifts and destitute; denying themselves the comforts of life, in order that they may wallow in the unrestrained license of animal appetite."

"Instructed in the fatal secret of subsisting on what is barely necessary to life, the labouring classes have ceased to entertain a laudable pride in furnishing their houses, and in multiplying the decent comforts which minister to happiness."

"Without distinction of age or sex, careless of all decency, they are crowded in small and wretched apartments; the same bed receiving a succession of tenants, until too offensive even for their unfastidious senses."

"A whole family is often accommodated on a single bed, and sometimes a heap of filthy straw and a covering of old sacking, hide them in one undistinguished heap, defaced alike by a penury, want of economy, and dissolute habits. . . ."

I have now, my Lord, to introduce a passage from Dr. Kay's pamphlet, to which I desire to call your Lordship's special attention. What a state of suffering is here exhibited!

"These artisans are frequently subject to a disease, in which the sensibility of the stomach and bowels is morbidly excited; the alvine secretions are deranged, and the appetite impaired. Whilst this state continues, the patient loses flesh, his features are sharpened, the skin becomes pale, leaden-coloured, or of the yellow hue which is observed in those who have suffered from the influence of tropical climates."

"The strength fails, all the capacities of physical enjoyment are destroyed, and the paroxysms of corporeal suffering are aggravated by the horrors of a disordered imagination, till they lead to gloomy apprehension, to the deepest depression, and almost to despair. We cannot wonder that the wretched victim of this disease, invited by those haunts of misery and crime, the gin-shop and the tavern, as he passes to his daily labour, should endeavor to cheat his suffering of a few minutes, by the false excitement procured by ardent spirits. . . ."

Defense of the Factory System

The Philosophy of Manufactures (1835)

ANDREW URE

The factory system was not without its advocates. One of the most influential was Andrew Ure, a professor of applied science at the University of Glasgow. He was supportive of the efficiency and productive capabilities of mechanized manufacturing. Note how the major criticisms of the reformers (child labor, degrading and unhealthy work conditions, etc.) are methodically countered. Ure argued that the owners of the mills and mines were not devils, but were actually abused themselves by the demands of the workers.

Proud of the power of malefaction, many of the cotton-spinners, though better paid, as we have shown, than any similar set of artisans in the world, organized the machinery of strikes through all the gradations of their people, *terrifying* or *cajoling* the timid or the passive among them to join their vindictive union. They boasted of possessing a dark tribunal, by the mandates of which they could paralyze every mill whose master did not comply with their wishes, and so bring ruin on the man who had given them profitable employment for many a year. By flattery or intimidation, they levied contributions from their associates in the privileged mills, which they suffered to proceed, in order to furnish spare funds for the maintenance of the idle during the decreed suspension of labour. In this extraordinary state of things, when the inventive head and the sustaining heart of trade were held in bondage by the unruly lower members, a destructive spirit began to display itself among some partisans of the union. Acts of singular atrocity were committed, sometimes with weapons fit only for demons to wield, such as the corrosive oil of vitriol, dashed in the faces of most meritorious individuals, with the effect of disfiguring their persons, and burning their eyes out of the sockets with dreadful agony.

The true spirit of turn-outs [strikes] among the spinners is well described in the following statement made on oath to the Factory Commission, by Mr. George Royle Chappel, a manufacturer of Manchester, who employs 274 hands, and two steam-engines of sixty-four horse power.

"I have had several turn-outs, and have heard of many more, but never heard of a turn-out for short time. I will relate the circumstances of the last turn-out, which took place on the 16th October, 1830, and continued till the 17th January, 1831. The whole of our spinners, whose average (weekly) wages were 2£. 13s. 5d., turned out at the instigation, as they told us at the time, of the delegates of the union. They said they had no fault to find with their wages, their work, or their masters, but the union obliged them to

Andrew Ure, *The Philosophy of Manufactures* (London: Charles Knight, 1835), pp. 282–284, 290, 300–301, 309–311, 398–399.

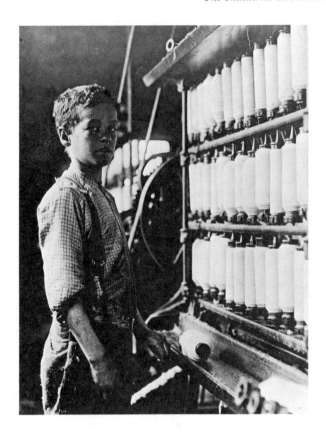

"[The children] seemed always to be cheerful and alert, taking pleasure in the light play of their muscles, enjoying the mobility natural to their age."—Andrew Ure, *The Philosophy of Manufactures* (1835). (*Library of Congress*)

turn out. The same week three delegates from the spinners' union waited upon us at our mill, and dictated certain advances in wages, and other regulations, to which, if we would not adhere, they said neither our own spinners not any other should work for us again! Of course we declined, believing our wages to be ample, and our regulations such as were necessary for the proper conducting of the establishment. The consequences were, they set watches on every avenue to the mill, night and day, to prevent any fresh hands coming into the mill, an object which they effectually attained, by intimidating some, and promising support to others (whom I got into the mill in a caravan), if they would leave their work. Under these circumstances, I could not work the mill, and advertised it for sale, without any applications, and I also tried in vain to let it. At the end of twenty-three weeks the hands requested to be taken to the mill again on the terms that they had left it, declaring, as they had done at first, that the union alone had forced them to turn out. . . .

Nothing shows in a clearer point of view the credulity of mankind in general, and of the people of these islands in particular, than the ready faith which was given to the tales of cruelty exercised by proprietors of cotton-mills towards young children. The systems of calumny somewhat resembles that brought by the Pagans against the primitive Christians, of enticing children into their meetings in order to murder and devour them. . . .

No master would wish to have any wayward children to work within the walls of his factory, who do not mind their business without beating, and he therefore usually fines or turns away any spinners who are known to maltreat their assistants. Hence, ill-usage of any kind is a very rare occurrence. I have visited many factories, both in Manchester and in the surrounding districts, during a period of several months, entering the spinning rooms, unexpectedly, and often alone, at different times of the day, and I never saw a single instance of corporal chastisement inflicted on a child, nor indeed did I ever see children in ill-humour. They seemed to be always cheerful and alert, taking pleasure in the light play of their muscles, enjoying the mobility natural to their age. The scene of industry, so far from exciting sad emotions in my mind, was always exhilarating. It was delightful to observe the nimbleness with which they pieced the broken ends, as the mule-carriage began to recede from the fixed roller-beam, and to see them at leisure, after a few seconds' exercise of their tiny fingers, to amuse themselves in any attitude they chose, till the stretch and winding-on were once more completed. The work of these lively elves seemed to resemble a sport, in which habit gave them a pleasing dexterity. Conscious of their skill, they were delighted to show it off to any stranger. As to exhaustion by the day's work, they evinced no trace of it on emerging from the mill in the evening; for they immediately began to skip about any neighbouring playground, and to commence their little amusements with the same alacrity as boys issuing from a school. It is moreover my firm conviction, that if children are not ill-used by bad parents or guardians, but receive in food and raiment the full benefit of what they earn, they would thrive better when employed in our modern factories, than if left at home in apartments too often ill-aired, damp, and cold. . . .

Of all the common prejudices that exist with regard to factory labour, there is none more unfounded than that which ascribes to it excessive tedium and irksomeness above other occupations, owing to its being carried on in conjunction with the "unceasing motion of the steam-engine." In an establishment for spinning or weaving cotton, all the hard work is performed by the steam-engine, which leaves for the attendant no hard labour at all, and literally nothing to do in general; but at intervals to perform some delicate operation, such as joining the threads that break, taking the cops off the spindle, &c. And it is so far from being true that the work in a factory is incessant, because the motion of the steam-engine is incessant, that the fact is, that the labour is not incessant on that very count, because it is performed in conjunction with the steam-engine. Of all manufacturing employments, those are by far the most irksome and incessant in which steam-engines are not employed, as in lace-running and stocking-weaving; and the way to prevent an employment from being incessant, is to introduce a steam-engine into it. These remarks certainly apply more especially to the labour of children in factories. Three-fourths of the children so employed are engaged in piecing at the mules. "When the carriages of these have receded a foot and a half or two feet from the rollers," says Mr. Tufnell, "nothing is to be done, not even attention is required from either spinner or piecer." Both of them stand idle for a time, and in fine spinning particularly, for three-quarters of a minute, or more. Consequently, if a child remains at this business twelve hours daily, he has nine hours of inaction. And though he attends two mules, he has still six hours of non-exertion. Spinners sometimes dedicate these intervals to the perusal of books. The scavengers, who, in Mr. Sadler's report, have been described as being "constantly in a state of grief, always in terror, and every moment they have to spare stretched all their length upon the floor in a state of perspiration," may be observed in cotton factories idle for *four* minutes at a time, or moving about in a sportive mood, utterly unconscious of the tragical scenes in which they were dramatized. . . .

Mr. Hutton, who has been in practice as a surgeon at Stayley Bridge upwards of thirty-one years, and, of course, remembers the commencement, and has had occasion to trace the progress and effect, of the factory system, says that the health of the population has much improved since its introduction, and that they are much superior in point of comfort to what they were formerly. He also says that fever has become less common since the erection of factories, and that the persons employed in them were less attacked by the influenza in 1833, than other classes of work-people. Mr. Bott, a surgeon, who is employed by the operatives in Messrs. Lichfield's mills to attend them in all cases of sickness or accident, at the rate of one halfpenny a week (a sum which indicates pretty distinctly their small chances of ailment), says that the factory workmen are not so liable to epidemics as other persons; and that though he has had many cases of typhus fever in the surrounding district, nearly all the mill-hands have escaped, and not one was attacked by the cholera during its prevalence in the neighbourhood.

Reaction and Reform

The Iron Law of Wages (1817)

DAVID RICARDO

The Industrial Revolution began to develop in England while the economic practice of mercantilism was still widespread. Proponents of mer-

David Ricardo, *The Principles of Political Economy and Taxation* (London: J. M. Dent & Sons, Ltd., 1911), pp. 57, 61–63.

cantilism argued that colonies existed for the benefit of the mother country, and indeed all economic activity should be regulated by the state for the good of the state. This concept was not in harmony with the rise of industrial capitalism. Adam Smith, in his important treatise *The Wealth of Nations* (1776), advocated the economic doctrine of *laissez faire*. He contended that every human being is motivated primarily by self-interest and that the marketplace is regulated by its own competitive laws of supply and demand, profit and loss. Therefore, the market must be left alone (hence the name *laissez faire*) and free from government controls and monopolies. Adam Smith soon became the "Patron Saint of Free Enterprise" and capitalism as a theory was born.

Two of the most important "Classical Economists" who subscribed to Smith's ideas were Thomas Malthus (1766–1834) and David Ricardo (1772–1823). Malthus employed statistics to develop the Malthusian Doctrine: the world's population, unless checked by war, disease, famine, late marriage, or moral restraint, grows at a higher rate than the means of subsistence, resulting in a doubling of the population every twenty-five years. His prediction for world famine was pessimistic indeed. David Ricardo, who had made a fortune on the London Stock Exchange, developed a theory, based to some extent on Malthus' analysis, that later came to be called the Iron Law of Wages. Ricardo believed that the wages of laborers must necessarily remain at a subsistence level because of the working class's unchecked rate of reproduction that would continuously keep the supply of labor excessive. Ricardo advocated a restriction of "poor laws" that were enacted by Parliament in the early nineteenth century to relieve the poor through governmental assistance. Ricardo thus became a champion of the rising industrial capitalists. A selection from his treatise *The Principles of Political Economy and Taxation* (1817) follows.

The friends of humanity cannot but wish that in all countries the labouring classes should have a taste for comforts and enjoyments, and that they should be stimulated by all legal means in their exertions to procure them. There cannot be a better security against a superabundant population. In those countries where the labouring classes have the fewest wants, and are contented with the cheapest food, the people are exposed to the greatest vicissitudes and miseries. They have no place or refuge from calamity; they cannot seek safety in a lower station; they are already so low that they can fall no lower. On any deficiency of the chief article of their subsistence there are few substitutes of which they can avail themselves and dearth to them is attended with almost all the evils of famine.

In the natural advance of society, the wages of labour will have a tendency to fall, as far as they are regulated by supply and demand; for the supply of labourers will continue to increase at the same rate, while the demand for them will increase at a slower rate. . . . I say that, under these circumstances, wages would fall if they were regulated only by the supply and demand of labourers; but we must not forget that wages are also regulated by the prices of the commodities on which they are expended.

As population increases, these necessaries will be constantly rising in price, because more labour will be necessary to produce them. If, then, the money wages of labour should fall, while every commodity on which the wages of labour were expended rose, the labourer would be doubly affected, and would be soon totally deprived of subsistence. . . . These, then, are the laws by which wages are regulated, and by which the happiness of far the greatest part of every community is governed. Like all other contracts, wages should be left to the fair and free competition of the market, and should never be controlled by the interference of the legislature.

The clear and direct tendency of the poor laws is in direct opposition to those obvious principles: it is not, as the legislature benevolently intended, to amend the condition of the poor, but to deteriorate the condition of both poor and rich; instead of making the poor rich, they are calculated to make the rich poor; and while the present laws are in force, it is quite in the natural order of things that the fund for the maintenance of the poor should progressively increase till it has absorbed all the net revenue of the country, or at least so much of it as the state shall leave to us, after satisfying its own never-failing demands for the public expenditure.

This pernicious tendency of these laws is no longer a mystery, since it has been fully developed by the able hand of Mr. Malthus; and every friend to the poor must ardently wish for their abolition. Unfortunately, however, they have been so long established, and the habits of the poor have been so formed upon their operation, that to eradicate them with safety from our political system requires the most cautious and skillful management. It is agreed by all who are most friendly to a repeal of these laws that, if it be desirable to prevent the most overwhelming distress to those for whose benefit they were erroneously enacted, their abolition should be effected by the most gradual steps.

It is a truth which admits not a doubt that the comforts and well-being of the poor cannot be permanently secured without some regard on their part, or some effort on the part of the legislature, to regulate the increase of their numbers, and to render less frequent among them early and improvident marriages. The operation of the system of poor laws has been directly contrary to this. They have rendered restraint superfluous, and have invited imprudence, by offering it a portion of the wages of prudence and industry.

The nature of the evil points out the remedy. By gradually contracting the sphere of the poor laws; by impressing on the poor the value of independence, by teaching them that they must look not to systematic or casual charity, but to their own exertions for support, that prudence and forethought are neither unnecessary nor unprofitable virtues, we shall by degrees approach a sounder and more healthful state.

No scheme for the amendment of the poor laws merits the least attention which has not their abolition for its ultimate object; and he is the best friend of the poor, and to the cause of humanity, who can point out how this end can be attained with the most security, and at the same time with the least violence. It is not by raising in any manner different from the present the fund from which the poor are supported that the evil can be mitigated. It would not only be no improvement, but it would be an aggravation of the distress which we wish to see removed, if the fund were increased in amount or were levied according to some late proposals, as a general fund from the country at large. . . . If by law every human being wanting support could be sure to obtain it, and obtain it in such a degree as to make life tolerably comfortable, theory would lead us to expect that all other taxes together would be light compared with the single one of poor rates. The principle of gravitation is not more certain than the tendency of such laws to change wealth and power into misery and weakness; . . . to confound all intellectual distinction; to busy the mind continually in supplying the body's wants; until at last all classes should be infected with the plague of universal poverty. Happily these laws have been in operation during a period of progressive prosperity, when the funds for the maintenance of labour have regularly increased, and when an increase of population would be naturally called for. But if our progress should become more slow; if we should attain the stationary state, from which I trust we are yet far distant, then will the pernicious nature of these laws become more manifest and alarming; and then, too, will their removal be obstructed by many additional difficulties.

On Liberty (1859)

JOHN STUART MILL

The Classical Economists, such as Adam Smith and David Ricardo, stressed the need for free enterprise in the marketplace and defied regulation by government. Other theoreticians accepted these principles of self-interest and self-determination and yet applied them more specifically to the social and political world. Jeremy Bentham (1748–1832) advocated a principle called "utilitarianism," whereby all things could be judged on twin concepts of utility and happiness. The best government, for example, was one that ensured the greatest happiness for the greatest number of people. These utilitarians were also referred to as "philosophical radicals" because they lacked all reverence for tradition and believed that political, social, and economic problems could be addressed rationally, without reference to privilege or special interests. They were popularly characterized as unemotional intellectuals without a practical understanding of humanity. Yet their most distinguished spokesman went far in moderating this image. John Stuart Mill (1806–1878) was groomed by his father to carry on "the movement," but rebelled against the rigid educa-

John Stuart Mill, *On Liberty* (New York: John B. Alden, 1885), pp. 302–303, 305, 307.

tional system imposed on him. Mill believed, as did the Classical Economists, that human beings were motivated principally by self-interest and that individual freedom was a cherished necessity. Still, he had a true social conscience and believed in the dignity of the working class. Mill favored the education of workers as a means of social progress, the reform of working conditions, the establishment of unions, and women's suffrage. His distinguished presence and ideas gave legitimacy to the liberalization of English democracy. The following excerpt is from his work *On Liberty* (1859) and is representative of his concern for the rights of the individual in the state.

Of the Limits to the Authority of Society over the Individual

What, then, is the rightful limit to the sovereignty of the individual over himself? Where does the authority of society begin? How much of human life should be assigned to individuality, and how much to society?

Each will receive its proper share, if each has that which more particularly concerns it. To individuality should belong the part of life in which it is chiefly the individual that is interested; to society, the part which chiefly interests society.

Though society is not founded on a contract, and though no good purpose is answered by inventing a contract in order to deduce social obligations from it, every one who receives the protection of society owes a return for the benefit, and the fact of living in society renders it indispensable that each should be bound to observe a certain line of conduct towards the rest. This conduct consists, first, in not injuring the interests of one another; or rather certain interests, which, either by express legal provision or by tacit understanding, ought to be considered as rights; and secondly, in each person's bearing his share (to be fixed on some equitable principle) of the labours and sacrifices incurred for defending the society or its members from injury and molestation. These conditions society is justified in enforcing, at all costs to those who endeavour to withhold fulfilment. Nor is this all that society may do. The acts of an individual may be hurtful to others, or wanting in due consideration for their welfare, without going to the length of violating any of their constituted rights. The offender may then be justly punished by opinion, though not by law. As soon as any part of a person's conduct affects prejudicially the interests of others, society has jurisdiction over it, and the question whether the general welfare will or will not be promoted by interfering with it, becomes open to discussion. But there is no room for entertaining any such question when a person's conduct affects the interests of no persons besides himself, or needs not affect them unless they like (all the persons concerned being of full age, and the ordinary amount of understanding). In all such cases, there should be perfect freedom, legal and social, to do the action and stand the consequences.

It would be a great misunderstanding of this doctrine to suppose that it is one of selfish indifference, which pretends that human beings have no business with each other's conduct in life, and that they should not concern themselves about the well-doing or well-being of one another, unless their own interest is involved. Instead of any diminution, there is need of a great increase of disinterested exertion to promote the good of others. . . . Human beings owe to each other help to distinguish the better from the worse, and encouragement to choose the former and avoid the latter. They should be for ever stimulating each other to increased exercise of their higher faculties, and increased direction of their feelings and aims toward wise instead of foolish, elevating instead of degrading, objects and contemplations. But neither one person, nor any number of persons, is warranted in saying to another human creature of ripe years, that he shall not do with his life for his own benefit what he chooses to do with it. He is the person most interested in his own well-being: the interest which any other person, except in cases of strong personal attachment, can have in it, is trifling, compared with that which he himself has: the interest which society has in him individually (except as to his conduct to others) is fractional, and altogether indirect; while the respect to his own feelings and circumstances, the most ordinary man or woman has means of knowledge immeasurably surpassing those that can be possessed by any one else. The interference of society to overrule his judgment and purposes in what only regards himself must be grounded on general presumptions; which may be altogether wrong, and even if right, are as likely as not to be misapplied to individual cases, by persons no better acquainted with the circumstances of such cases than those are who look at them merely from without. In this department, therefore, of human affairs, Individuality has its proper field of action. In the conduct of human beings towards one another it is necessary that general rules should for the most part be observed, in order that people may know what they have to expect: but in each person's own concerns his individual spontaneity is entitled to free exercise. Considerations to aid his judgment, exhortations to strengthen his will, may be offered to him, even obtruded on him, by others: but he himself is the final judge. All errors which he is likely to commit against advice and warning are far outweighed by the evil of allowing others to constrain him to what they deem is good. . . .

The distinction here pointed out between the part of a person's life which concerns only himself, and that which concerns others, many persons will refuse to admit. How (it may be asked) can any part of the conduct of a member of society be a matter of indifference to the other members? No person is an entirely isolated being; it is impossible for a person to do anything seriously or permanently hurtful to himself, without mischief reaching at least to his near connections, and often far beyond them. If he injures his property, he does harm to those who directly or indirectly derived support from it, and usually diminishes, by a greater or less amount, the general resources of the community. If he deteriorates his bodily or mental faculties, he not only brings evil upon all who depended on him for any portion of their happiness, but disqualifies himself for rendering the services which he owes to his fellow creatures generally; perhaps becomes a burden on their affection or benevolence; and if such conduct were very frequent, hardly any offence that is committed would detract more from the general sum of good. Finally, if by his vices or follies a person does no direct harm to others, he is nevertheless (it may be said) injurious by his example; and ought to be compelled to control himself, for the sake of those whom the sight or knowledge of his conduct might corrupt or mislead.

And even (it will be added) if the consequences of misconduct could be confined to the vicious or thoughtless individual, ought society to abandon to their own guidance those who are manifestly unfit for it? If protection against themselves is confessedly due to children and persons under age, is not society equally bound to afford it to persons of mature years who are equally incapable of self-government? If gambling, or drunkenness, or incontinence, or idleness, or uncleanliness, are as injurious to happiness, and as great a hindrance to improvement, as many or most of the acts prohibited by law, why (it may be asked) should not law, so far as is consistent with practicability and social convenience, endeavour to repress these also? And as a supplement to the unavoidable imperfections of law, ought not opinion at least to organize a powerful police against these vices, and visit rigidly with social penalties those who are known to practise them? There is no question here (it may be said) about restricting individual experiments in living. The only things it is sought to prevent are things which have been tried and condemned from the beginning of the world until now; things which experience has shown not to be useful or suitable to any person's individuality. There must be some length of time and amount of experience after which a moral or prudential truth may be regarded as established: and it is merely desired to prevent generation after generation from falling over the same precipice which has been fatal to their predecessors. . . .

But the strongest of all the arguments against the interference of the public with purely personal conduct is that, when it does interfere, the odds are that it interferes wrongly, and in the wrong place. On questions of social morality, of duty to others, the opinion of the public, that is, of an overruling majority, though often wrong, is likely to be still oftener right; because on such questions they are only required to judge of their own interests; of the manner in which some mode of conduct, if allowed to be practised, would effect themselves. But the opinion of a similar majority, imposed as a law on the minority, on questions of selfregarding conduct, is quite as likely to be wrong as right; for in these cases public opinion means, at the best, some people's opinion of what is good or bad for other people; while very often it does not even mean that; the public, with the most perfect indifference, passing over the pleasure or convenience of those whose conduct they censure, and considering only their own preference. . . . It is easy for any one to imagine an ideal public which leaves the freedom and choice of individuals in all uncertain matters undisturbed, and only requires them to abstain from modes of conduct which universal experience has condemned. But where has there been seen a public which set any such limit to its censorship? or when does the public trouble itself about universal experience? In its interferences with personal conduct it is seldom thinking of anything but the enormity of acting or feeling differently from itself; and this standard of judgment, thinly disguised, is held up to mankind as dictate of religion and philosophy, by nine-tenths of all moralists and speculative writers. These teach that things are right because they are right; because we tell them to be so. They tell us to search in our own minds and hearts for laws of conduct binding on ourselves and on all others. What can the poor public do but apply these instructions, and make their own personal feelings of good and evil, if they are tolerably unanimous in them, obligatory on all the world?

A Middle-Class Perspective (1859)

SAMUEL SMILES

For many members of the middle class, the Victorian Age was not characterized by the slums of Glasgow or the dirt of industry. To their thinking, perseverance and hard work resulted in a better life and was always rewarded. In his book *Self-Help* (1859), Samuel Smiles emphasized this principle through a series of biographies of men who had risen to fame and fortune. The guiding idea was that "the most important results in daily life are to be obtained, not through the exercise of extraordinary powers, such as genius and intellect, but through the energetic use of simple means and ordinary qualities with which nearly all human individuals have more or less been endowed." Man was responsible for his own fate; it was up to the individual to change his situation if so desired.

The object of the book briefly is, to re-inculcate these old-fashioned but wholesome lessons—which perhaps cannot be too often urged,—that youth must work in order to enjoy,—that nothing creditable can be accomplished without application and diligence,—that the student must not be daunted by difficulties, but conquer them by patience and perserverance,—and that, above all, he must seek elevation of character, without which capacity is worthless and worldly success is naught. If the author has not succeeded in illustrating these lessons, he can only say that he has failed in his object.

"Heaven helps those who help themselves" is a well-tried maxim, embodying in a small compass the results of vast human experience. The spirit of self-help is the root of all genuine growth in the individual; and, exhib-

Samuel Smiles, *Self-Help* (London: John Murray, 1882), pp. v, 1, 4.

ited in the lives of many, it constitutes the true source of national vigour and strength. Help from without is often enfeebling in its effects, but help from within invariably invigorates. Whatever is done *for* men or classes, to a certain extent takes away the stimulus and necessity of doing for themselves; and where men are subjected to over-guidance and over-government, the inevitable tendency is to render them comparatively helpless.

Even the best institutions can give a man no active help. Perhaps the most they can do is, to leave him free to develop himself and improve his individual condition. But in all times men have been prone to believe that their happiness and well-being were to be secured by means of institutions rather than by their own conduct. Hence the value of legislation as an agent in human advancement has usually been much over-estimated. To constitute the millionth part of a Legislature, by voting for one or two men once in three or five years, however conscientiously this duty may be performed, can exercise but little active influence upon any man's life and character. Moreover, it is every day becoming more clearly understood, that the function of Government is negative and restrictive, rather than positive and active; being resolvable principally into protection—protection of life, liberty, and property. Laws, wisely administered, will secure men in the enjoyment of the fruits of their labour, whether of mind or body, at a comparatively small personal sacrifice; but no laws, however, stringent, can make the idle industrious, the thriftless provident, or the drunken sober. Reforms can only be effected by means of individual action, economy, and self-denial; better habits, rather than by greater rights. . . .

Daily experience shows that it is energetic individualism which produces the most powerful effects upon the life and action of others, and really constitutes the best practical education. Schools, academies, and colleges, give but the merest beginnings of culture in comparison with it. Far more influential is the life-education daily given in our homes, in the streets, behind counters, in workshops, at the loom and the plough, in counting-houses and manufactories, and in the busy haunts of men. This is that finishing instruction as members of society, which Schiller designated "the education of the human race," consisting in action, conduct, self-culture, self-control,—all that tends to discipline a man truly, and fit him for the proper performance of the duties and business of life,—a kind of education not to be learnt from books, or acquired by any amount of mere literary training. With his usual weight of words Bacon observes, that "Studies teach not their own use; but that is a wisdom without them, and above them, won by observation;" a remark that holds true of actual life, as well as of the cultivation of the intellect itself. For all experience serves to illustrate and enforce the lesson, that a man perfects himself by work more than by reading,—that it is life rather than literature, action rather than study, and character rather than biography, which tend perpetually to renovate mankind.

Utopian Socialism (1816)

ROBERT OWEN

One of the great personal success stories of the nineteenth century was Robert Owen. Born the son of a saddlemaker, Owen left school at the age of nine and went to work in a draper's shop. At the age of eighteen, he borrowed money and set up a small cotton mill in Manchester. Within ten years, he was very wealthy and was joint owner of the New Lanark mills, the largest textile operation in Scotland. But Robert Owen was possessed with a desire to improve the lot of humanity. He provided higher wages and better working conditions for his employees and established free schools for their children. The New Lanark mills also returned a handsome profit. Owen sought government intervention and regulation to change conditions in industry. He could not understand why all factories could not be run on his utopian model. He is generally accepted in England as the founder of British socialism. The following address was delivered in 1816 on the opening of an "Institution for the Formation of Character" at New Lanark. Note the emphasis on morality as an essential ingredient of change.

Every society which exists at present, as well as every society which history records, has been formed and governed on a belief in the following notions, assumed as *first principles:*

First,—That it is in the power of every individual to form his own character.

Hence the various systems called by the name of religion, codes of law, and punishments. Hence also the angry passions entertained by individuals and nations towards each other.

Second,—That the affections are at the command of the individual.

Hence insincerity and degradation of character. Hence the miseries of domestic life, and more than one-half of all the crimes of mankind.

Third,—That it is necessary that a large portion of mankind should exist in ignorance and poverty, in order to secure to the remaining part such a degree of happiness as they now enjoy.

Hence a system of counteraction in the pursuits of men, a general opposition among individuals to the interests of each other, and the necessary effects of such a system,—ignorance, poverty, and vice.

Facts prove, however—

First,—That character is universally formed *for*, and not *by*, the individual.

Second,—That *any* habits and sentiments may be given to mankind.

Third,—That the affections are *not* under the control of the individual.

Fourth,—That every individual may be trained to produce far more

Excerpt from *Socialist Thought* by Albert Fried and Ronald Sanders, pp. 172–175. Copyright ©1964 by Albert Fried and Ronald Sanders. Reprinted by permission of Doubleday & Company, Inc.

than he can consume, while there is a sufficiency of soil left for him to cultivate.

Fifth,—That nature has provided means by which population may be at all times maintained in the proper state to give the greatest happiness to every individual, without one check of vice or misery.

Sixth,—That any community may be arranged, on a due combination of the foregoing principles, in such a manner, as not only to withdraw vice, poverty, and, in a great degree, misery, from the world, but also to place *every* individual under circumstances in which he shall enjoy more permanent happiness than can be given to *any* individual under the principles which have hitherto regulated society.

Seventh,—That all the assumed fundamental principles on which society has hitherto been founded are erroneous, and may be demonstrated to be contrary to fact. And—

Eighth,—That the change which would follow the abandonment of those erroneous maxims which bring misery into the world, and the adoption of principles of truth, unfolding a system which shall remove and for ever exclude that misery, may be effected without the slightest injury to any human being.

Here is the groundwork,—these are the data, on which society shall ere long be re-arranged; and for this simple reason, that it will be rendered evident that it will be for the immediate and future interest of every one to lend his most active assistance gradually to reform society on this basis. I say *gradually*, for in that word the most important considerations are involved. Any sudden and coercive attempt which may be made to remove even misery from men will prove injurious rather than beneficial. Their minds must be gradually prepared by an essential alteration of the circumstances which surround them, for any great and important change and amelioration in their condition. They must be first convinced of their blindness: this cannot be effected, even among the least unreasonable, or those termed the best part of mankind, in their present state, without creating some degree of irritation. This irritation, must then be tranquillized before another step ought to be attempted; and a general conviction must be established of the truth of the principles on which the projected change is to be founded. Their introduction into practice will then become easy,—difficulties will vanish as we approach them,—and, afterwards, the desire to see the whole system carried immediately into effect will exceed the means of putting it into execution.

The principles on which this practical system is founded are not new; separately, or partially united, they have been often recommended by the sages of antiquity, and by modern writers. But it is not known to me that they have ever been thus combined. Yet it can be demonstrated that it is only by their being *all brought into practice together* that they are to be rendered beneficial to mankind; and sure I am that this is the earliest period in the history of man when they could be successfully introduced into practice.

The Communist Manifesto (1848)

KARL MARX

The Communist Manifesto, written by Karl Marx (1818–1883) and Friedrich Engels in 1848, is the fundamental declaration of communist ideology. Marx was concerned with the process of change in history (dialectic). A keen observer of the industrial world around him, Marx saw the oppression of the working man (proletarian) by those who owned the means of production (bourgeoisie). Marx advocated a society that was devoid of capitalistic oppression, a society in which workers actually controlled the factories and regulated their own working conditions and environment. His call to revolution had little influence on the protests of 1848, but his ideas would serve as the foundation for the Russian Revolution in 1917 and are of great importance today.

Bourgeoisie and Proletariat

The history of all hitherto existing society is the history of class struggles.

Freeman and slave, patrician and plebian, lord and serf, guildmaster and journeyman, in a word, oppressor and oppressed, stood in constant opposition to one another, carried on an uninterrupted, now hidden, now open fight, a fight that each time ended, either in a revolutionary re-constitution of society at large, or in the common ruin of the contending classes.

In the earlier epochs of history, we find almost everywhere a compli-cated arrangement of society into various orders, a manifold graduation of social rank. In ancient Rome we have patricians, knights, plebians, slaves; in the Middle Ages, feudal lords, vassals, guildmasters, journeymen, ap-prentices, serfs; in almost all of these classes, again, subordinate gradations.

The modern bourgeois society that has sprouted from the ruins of feudal society, has not done away with class antagonisms. It has but estab-lished new classes, new conditions of oppression, new forms of struggle in place of the old ones.

Our epoch, the epoch of the bourgeoisie, possesses, however, this dis-tinctive feature: it has simplified the class antagonisms. Society as a whole is more and more splitting up into two great hostile camps, into two great classes directly facing each other: Bourgeoisie and Proletariat. . . .

Each step in the development of the bourgeoisie was accompanied by a corresponding political advance of the class. An oppressed class under the sway of the feudal nobility, an armed and self-governing association in the medieval commune, here independent urban republic (as in Italy and Ger-many), there taxable "third estate" of the monarchy (as in France), after-wards, in the period of manufacture proper, serving either the semi-feudal or the absolute monarchy as a counterpoise against the nobility, and in fact,

Karl Marx and Friedrich Engels, *The Communist Manifesto,* trans. Samuel Moore (New York: Socialist Labor Party, 1888).

corner stone of the great monarchies in general, the bourgeoisie has at last, since the establishment of Modern Industry and of the world-market, conquered for itself, in the modern representative State, exclusive political sway. The executive of the modern State is but a committee for managing the common affairs of the whole bourgeoisie. . . .

The need of a constantly expanding market for its products chases the bourgeoisie over the whole surface of the globe. It must nestle everywhere, establish connections everywhere. . . .

The bourgeoisie, during its rule of scarce one hundred years, has created more massive and more colossal productive forces than have all preceding generations together. Subjection of Nature's forces to man, machinery, application of chemistry to industry and agriculture, steam-navigation, railways, electric telegraphs, clearing of whole continents for cultivation, canalization of rivers, whole populations conjured out of the ground—what earlier century had even a presentiment that such productive forces slumbered in the lap of social labor? . . .

In proportion as the bourgeoisie, i.e., capital, is developed, in the same proportion is the proletariat, the modern working-class, developed, a class of laborers, who live only so long as they find work, and who find work only so long as their labor increases capital. These laborers, who must sell themselves piecemeal, are a commodity, like every other article of commerce, and are consequently exposed to all the vicissitudes of competition, to all the fluctuations of the market.

Owing to the extensive use of machinery and to division of labor, the work of the proletarians has lost all individual character, and, consequently, all charm for the workman. He becomes an appendage of the machine, and it is only the most simple, most monotonous, and most easily acquired knack that is required of him. Hence, the cost of production of a workman is restricted, almost entirely, to the means of subsistence that he requires for his maintenance, and for the propagation of his race. But the price of commodity, and also of labor, is equal to its cost of production. In proportion, therefore, as the repulsiveness of the work increases, the wage decreases. Nay more, in proportion as the use of the machinery and division of labor increases, in the same proportion the burden of toil also increases, whether by prolongation of the working hours, by increase of the work enacted in a given time, or by increased speed of the machinery, etc.

Modern industry has converted the little workshop of the patriarchal master into the great factory of the industrial capitalist. Masses of laborers, crowded into the factory, are organized like soldiers. As privates of the industrial army they are placed under the command of a perfect hierarchy of officers and sergeants. Not only are they the slaves of the bourgeois class, and of the bourgeois State, they are daily and hourly enslaved by the machine, by the over-looker, and, above all, by the individual bourgeois manufacturer himself. The more openly despotism proclaims gain to be its end and aim, the more petty, the more hateful and the more embittering it is.

The less the skill and exertion or strength implied in manual labor, in other words, the more modern industry becomes developed, the more is the labor of men superseded by that of women. Differences of age and sex have no longer any distinctive social validity for the working class. All are instruments of labor, more or less expensive to use, according to their age and sex.

No sooner is the exploitation of the laborer by the manufacturer, so far at an end, that he receives his wages in cash, than he is set upon by the other portions of the bourgeoisie, the landlord, the shopkeeper, the pawn-broker, etc. . . .

But with the development of industry the proletariat not only increases in number, it becomes concentrated in greater masses, its strength grows, and it feels that strength more. The various interests and conditions of life within the ranks of the proletariat are more and more equalized, in proportion as machinery obliterates all distinctions of labor, and nearly everywhere reduces wages to the same low level. The growing competition among the bourgeois, and the resulting commercial crises, make the wages of the workers ever more fluctuating. The unceasing improvement of machinery, ever more rapidly developing, makes their livelihood more and more precarious; the collisions between individual workmen and individual bourgeois take more and more the character of collisions between two classes. Thereupon the workers begin to form combinations (Trades' Unions) against the bourgeois; they club together in order to keep up the rate of wages; they found permanent associations in order to make provision beforehand for these occasional revolts. Here and there the contest breaks out into riots.

Now and then the workers are victorious, but only for a time. The real fruit of their battles lies, not in the immediate result, but in the ever expanding union of the workers. This union is helped on by the improved means of communications that are created by modern industry, and that place the workers of different localities in contact with one another. It was just this contact that was needed to centralize the numerous local struggles, all of the same character, into one national struggle between classes. But every class struggle is a political struggle. . . .

This organization of the proletarians into a class, and consequently into a political party, is continually being upset again by the competition between the workers themselves. But it ever rises up again, stronger, firmer, mightier. It compels legislative recognition of particular interests of the workers, by taking advantage of the divisions among the bourgeoisie itself. Thus the ten-hour bill in England was carried. . . .

The essential condition for the existence, and for the sway of the bourgeois class, is the formation and augmentation of capital; the condition for capital is wage-labor. Wage-labor rests exclusively on competition between the laborers. The advance of industry, whose involuntary promoter is the bourgeoisie, replaces the isolation of the laborers, due to competition, by their revolutionary combination, due to association. The development of Modern Industry, therefore, cuts from under its feet the very foundation on which the bourgeoisie produces and appropriates products. What the bourgeoisie therefore produces, above all, are its own gravediggers. Its fall and the victory of the proletariat are equally inevitable.

Proletarians and Communists

In what relation do the Communists stand to the proletarians as a whole?

The Communists do not form a separate party opposed to other working class parties.

They have no interests separate and apart from those of the proletariat as a whole.

They do not set up any sectarian principles of their own, by which to shape and mould the proletarian movement.

The Communists are distinguished from the other working class parties by this only: 1. In the national struggles of the proletarians of the different countries, they point out and bring to the front the common interests of the entire proletariat independently of all nationality. 2. In the various stages of development which the struggle of the working class against the bourgeoisie has to pass through, they always and everywhere represent the interests of the movement as a whole.

The Communists, therefore, are on the one hand, practically, the most advanced and resolute section of the working class parties of every country, that section which pushes forward all other; on the other hand, theoretically, they have over the great mass of the proletariat the advantage of clearly understanding the line of march, the conditions, and the ultimate general results of the proletarian movement.

The immediate aim of the Communists is the same as that of all the other proletarian parties: formation of the proletariat into a class, overthrow of the bourgeois supremacy, conquest of political power by the proletariat.

The theoretical conclusions of the Communists are in no way based on ideas or principles that have been invented, or discovered, by this or that would-be universal reformer.

They merely express, in general terms, actual relations springing from an existing class struggle, from a historical movement going on under our very eyes. The abolition of existing property relations is not at all a distinctive feature of Communism.

All property relations in the past have continually been subject to historical change consequent upon the change in historical conditions.

The French Revolution, for example, abolished feudal property in favor of bourgeois property.

The distinguishing feature of Communism is not the abolition of property generally, but the abolition of bourgeois property. But modern bourgeois private property is the final and most complete expression of the system of producing and appropriating products, that is based on class antagonism, on the exploitation of the many by the few.

In this sense, the theory of the Communists may be summed up in the single sentence: Abolition of private property. . . .

The Communist revolution is the most radical rupture with traditional property-relations; no wonder that its development involves the most radical rupture with traditional ideas.

But let us have done with the bourgeois objections to Communism.

We have seen above, that the first step in the revolution by the working class, is to raise the proletariat to the position of ruling class, to win the battle of democracy.

The proletariat will use its political supremacy, to wrest, by degrees, all capital from the bourgeoisie, to centralize all instruments of production in the hands of the State, i.e., of the proletariat organized as the ruling class; and to increase the total of productive forces as rapidly as possible.

Of course, in the beginning, this cannot be effected except by means of despotic inroads on the rights of property, and on the conditions of bourgeois production; by means of measures, therefore, which appear economically insufficient and untenable, but which, in the course of the movement, outstrip themselves, necessitate further inroads upon the old social order, and are unavoidable as a means of entirely revolutionizing the mode of production.

These measures will of course be different in different countries.

Nevertheless in the most advanced countries the following will be pretty generally applicable:

1. Abolition of property in land and application of all rents of land to public purposes.
2. A heavy progressive or graduated income tax.
3. Abolition of all rights of inheritance.
4. Confiscation of the property of all emigrants and rebels.
5. Centralization of credit in the hands of the state, by means of a national bank with State capital and an exclusive monopoly.
6. Centralization of the means of communication and transport in the hands of the State.
7. Extension of factories and instruments of production owned by the State; the bringing into cultivation of waste lands, and the improvement of the soil generally in accordance with a common plan.
8. Equal liability of all to labor. Establishment of industrial armies, especially for agriculture.
9. Combination of agriculture with manufacturing industries; gradual abolition of the distinction between town and country, by a more equable distribution of population over the country.
10. Free education for all children in public schools. Abolition of chil-

dren's factory labor in its present form. Combination of education with industrial production, etc., etc.

When, in the course of development, class distinctions have disappeared, and all production has been concentrated in the hands of a vast association of the whole nation, the public power will lose its political character. Political power, properly so called, is merely the organized power of one class for oppressing another. If the proletariat during its contest with the bourgeoisie is compelled, by the force of circumstances, to organize itself as a class, if, by means of a revolution, it makes itself the ruling class, and, as such, sweeps away by force the old conditions of production, then it will, along with these conditions, have swept away the conditions for the existence of class antagonisms, and of class generally, and will thereby have abolished its own supremacy as a class.

In place of the old bourgeois society, with its classes and class antagonisms, we shall have an association, in which the free development of each is the condition for the free development of all. . . .

In short, the Communists everywhere support every revolutionary movement against the existing social and political order of things.

In all these movements they bring to the front, as the leading question in each, the property question, no matter what its degree of development at the time.

Finally, they labor everywhere for the union and agreement of the democratic parties of all countries.

The Communists disdain to conceal their views and aims. They openly declare that their ends can be attained only by the forcible overthrow of all existing social conditions. Let the ruling classes tremble at a Communistic revolution. The proletarians have nothing to lose but their chains. They have a world to win.

Workers of the world, unite!

Fabianism (1889)

SIDNEY WEBB

In response to the fervent appeal of Marxism, there were competing ideologies that stressed moderation and gradual change. Fabianism was an English movement founded in 1884 and dedicated to the gradual implementation of socialist policies. It was led by such intellectuals as George Bernard Shaw, H. G. Wells, and Sidney Webb (1859–1947). The following is an excerpt from Webb's "Fabian Essays."

Sidney Webb, "Fabian Essays" in *Fabian Essays in Socialism*, ed. G. Bernard Shaw (London: Walter Scott, 1889), pp. 34–35.

In the present Socialist movement these two streams are united: advocates of social reconstruction have learnt the lesson of Democracy, and know that it is through the slow and gradual turning of the popular mind to new principles that social reorganization bit by bit comes. All students of society who are abreast of their time, Socialists as well as Individualists, realize that important organic changes can only be (1) democratic, and thus acceptable to a majority of the people, and prepared for in the minds of all; (2) gradual, and thus causing no dislocation, however rapid may be the rate of progress; (3) not regarded as immoral by the mass of the people, and thus not subjectively demoralizing to them; and (4) in this country at any rate, constitutional and peaceful. Socialists may therefore be quite at one with Radicals in their political methods. Radicals, on the other hand, are perforce realizing that mere political levelling is insufficient to save a State from anarchy and despair. Both sections have been driven to recognize that the root of the difficulty is economic; and there is every day a wider census that the inevitable outcome of Democracy is the control by the people themselves, not only of their own political organization, but, through that, also of the main instruments of wealth production; the gradual substitution of organized cooperation for the anarchy of the competitive struggle; and the consequent recovery, in the only possible way, of what John Stuart Mill calls "the enormous share which the possessors of the instruments of industry are able to take from the produce." The economic side of the democratic ideal is, in fact, Socialism itself.

Rerum Novarum (1891)

POPE LEO XIII

One of the more influential associations against the abuses of industrialism was the Christian Socialist movement. It began in England about 1848 and stressed that one could overcome the evils of industrialism by following Christian principles: brotherly love was preferable to ruthless competition and exploitation. Quite apart from this movement, but adhering to the same basic principles, was the Catholic Church. Pope Leo XIII was an active commentator on political power and human liberty. In 1891, he issued the encyclical *Rerum Novarum,* which addressed the continuing struggle between capitalists and workers. This official opinion of the pope demonstrates the Church's continuing interest in the affairs of the secular world.

Rights and Duties of Capital Labor

That the spirit of revolutionary change, which has long been disturbing the nations of the world, should have passed beyond the sphere of politics and

Claudia Carlen Ihm, ed., *The Papal Encyclicals,* 1878–1903, vol. 2 (New York: McGrath Publishing Company, 1981), pp. 241–242, 244–246, 248, 255–256.

made its influence felt in the cognate sphere of practical economics is not surprising. The elements of the conflict now raging are unmistakable, in the vast expansion of industrial pursuits and the marvelous discoveries of science; in the changed relations between masters and workmen; in the enormous fortunes of some few individuals, and the utter poverty of the masses; in the increased self-reliance and closer mutual combination of the working classes; as also, finally, in the prevailing moral degeneracy. The momentous gravity of the state of things now obtaining fills every mind with painful apprehension; wise men are discussing it; practical men are proposing schemes; popular meetings, legislatures, and rulers of nations are all busied with it—actually there is no question which has taken a deeper hold on the public mind.

Therefore, . . . We thought it expedient now to speak on the condition of the working classes. It is a subject on which We have already touched more than once, incidentally. But in the present letter, the responsibility of the apostolic office urges Us to treat the question of set purpose and in detail, in order that no misapprehension may exist as to the principles which truth and justice dictate for its settlement. The discussion is not easy, nor is it void of danger. It is no easy matter to define the relative rights and mutual duties of the rich and of the poor, of capital and of labor. And the danger lies in this, that crafty agitators are intent on making use of these differences of opinion to pervert men's judgments and to stir up the people to revolt.

In any case we clearly see, and on this there is general agreement, that some opportune remedy must be found quickly for the misery and wretchedness pressing so unjustly on the majority of the working class: for the ancient working-men's guilds were abolished in the last century, and no other protective organization took their place. . . . Hence, by degrees it has come to pass that working men have been surrendered, isolated and help-less, to the hardheartedness of employers and the greed of unchecked competition. The mischief has been increased by rapacious usury, which, although more than once condemned by the Church, is nevertheless, un-der a different guise, but with like injustice, still practiced by covetous and grasping men. To this must be added that the hiring of labor and the conduct of trade are concentrated in the hands of comparatively few; so that a small number of very rich men have been able to lay upon the teeming masses of the laboring poor a yoke little better than that of slavery itself.

To remedy these wrongs the socialists, working on the poor man's envy of the rich, are striving to do away with private property, and contend that individual possessions should become the common property of all, to be administered by the State or by municipal bodies. They hold that by thus transferring property from private individuals to the community, the pre-sent mischievous state of things will be set to rights, inasmuch as each citizen will then get his fair share of whatever there is to enjoy. But their contentions are so clearly powerless to end the controversy that were they carried into effect the working man himself would be among the first to suffer. They are, moreover, emphatically unjust, for they would rob the lawful possessor, distort the functions of the State, and create utter confusion in the community.

It is surely undeniable that, when a man engages in remunerative labor, the impelling reason and motive of his work is to obtain property, and thereafter to hold it as his very own. If one man hires out to another his strength or skill, he does so for the purpose of receiving in return what is necessary for the satisfaction of his needs; he therefore expressly intends to acquire a right full and real, not only to the remuneration, but also to the disposal of such remuneration, just as he pleases. Thus, if he lives sparingly, saves money, and, for greater security, invests his savings in land, the land, in such case, is only his wages under another form; and, consequently, a working man's little estate thus purchased should be as completely at his full disposal as are the wages he receives for his labor. But it is precisely in such power of disposal that ownership obtains, whether the property consist of land or chattels. Socialists, therefore, by endeavoring to transfer the possessions of individuals to the community at large, strike at the interests of every wage-earner, since they would deprive him of the liberty of disposing of his wages, and thereby of all hope and possibility of increasing his resources and of bettering his condition in life.

What is of far greater movement, however, is the fact that the remedy they propose is manifestly against justice. For, every man has by nature the right to possess property as his own. This is one of the chief points of distinction between man and the animal creation, for the brute has no power of self-direction, but is governed by two main instincts, which keep his powers on the alert, impel him to develop them in a fitting manner, and stimulate and determine him to action without any power of choice. One of these instincts is self-preservation, the other the propagation of the species. Both can attain their purpose by means of things which lie within range; beyond their verge the brute creation cannot go, for they are moved to action by their senses only, and in the special direction which these suggest. But with man it is wholly different. He possesses, on the one hand, the full perfection of the animal being, and hence enjoys at least as much as the rest of the animal kind, the fruition of things material. But animal nature, however perfect, is far from representing the human being in its completeness, and is in truth but humanity's humble handmaid, made to serve and to obey. It is the mind, or reason, which is the predominate element in us who are human creatures; it is this which renders a human being human, and distinguishes him essentially from the brute. And on this very account—that man alone among the animal creation is endowed with reason—it must be within his right to possess things not merely for temporary and momentary use, as other living things do, but to have and to hold them in stable and permanent possession. . . .

The contention, then, that the civil government should at its option intrude into and exercise intimate control over the family and the household is a great and pernicious error. True, if a family finds itself in exceeding distress, utterly deprived of the counsel of friends, and without any prospect of extricating itself, it is right that extreme necessity be met by public aid, since each family is a part of the commonwealth. In like manner, if within the precincts of the household there occur grave disturbance of mutual rights, public authority should intervene to force each party to yield to the other its proper due; for this is not to deprive citizens of their rights, but justly and properly to safeguard and strengthen them. But rulers of the commonwealth must go no further; here, nature bids them stop. Paternal authority can be neither abolished nor absorbed by the State; for it has the same source as human life itself. . . . The socialists, therefore, in setting aside the parent and setting up a State supervision, act against natural justice, and destroy the structure of the home. . . .

The great mistake in regard to the matter now under consideration is to take up with the notion that class is naturally hostile to class, and that the wealthy and the working men are intended by nature to live in mutual conflict. So irrational and so false is this view that the direct contrary is the truth. Just as the symmetry of the human frame is the result of the suitable arrangement of the different parts of the body, so in a State is it ordained by nature that these two classes should dwell in harmony and agreement, so as to maintain the balance of the body politic. Each needs the other: capital cannot do without labor, nor labor without capital. Mutual agreement results in the beauty of good order, while perpetual conflict necessarily produces confusion and savage barbarity. Now, in preventing such strife as this, and in uprooting it, the efficacy of Christian institutions is marvelous and manifold. First of all, there is no intermediary more powerful than religion (whereof the Church is the interpreter and guardian) in drawing the rich and the working class together, by reminding each of its duties to the other, and especially of the obligations of justice.

Of these duties, the following bind the proletarian and the worker: fully and faithfully to perform the work which has been freely and equitably agreed upon; never to injure the property, nor to outrage the person, of an employer; never to resort to violence in defending their own cause, nor to engage in riot or disorder; and to have nothing to do with men of evil principles, who work upon the people with artful promises of great results, and excite foolish hopes which usually end in useless regrets and grievous loss. The following duties bind the wealthy owner and the employer: not to look upon their work people as their bondsmen, but to respect in every man his dignity as a person ennobled by Christian character. They are reminded that, according to natural reason and Christian philosophy, working for gain is creditable, not shameful, to a man, since it enables him to earn an honorable livelihood; but to misuse men as though they were things in the pursuit of gain, or to value them solely for their physical powers—that is truly shameful and inhuman. Again justice demands that, in dealing with the working man, religion and the good of his soul must be kept in mind. Hence, the employer is bound to see that the worker has time for his religious duties; that he be not exposed to corrupting influences and dangerous occasions; and that he be not led away to neglect his home and family, or to squander his earnings. Furthermore, the employer must never tax his work people beyond their strength, or employ them in work unsuited to their sex and age. His great and principal duty is to give every one what is just. Doubtless, before deciding whether wages are fair, many things have to be considered; but wealthy owners and all masters of labor should be mindful of this—that to exercise pressure upon the indigent and the destitute for the sake of gain, and to gather one's profit out of the need of another, is condemned by all laws, human and divine. To defraud any one of wages that are his due is a great crime which cries to the avenging anger of Heaven. . . .

Were these precepts carefully obeyed and followed out, would they not be sufficient of themselves to keep under all strife and all its causes?. . .

[It must not] be supposed that the solicitude of the Church is so preoccupied with the spiritual concerns of her children as to neglect their temporal and earthly interests. Her desire is that the poor, for example, should rise above poverty and wretchedness, and better their condition in life; and for this she makes a strong endeavor. By the fact that she calls men to virtue and forms them to its practice she promotes this in no slight degree. Christian morality, when adequately and completely practiced, leads of itself to temporal prosperity, for it merits the blessing of that God who is the source of all blessings; it powerfully restrains the greed of possession and the thirst for pleasure—twin plagues, which too often make a man who is void of self-restraint miserable in the midst of abundance; it makes men supply for the lack of means through economy, teaching them to be content with frugal living, and further, keeping them out of the reach of those vices which devour not small incomes merely, but large fortunes, and dissipate many a goodly inheritance. . . .

To sum up, then, We may lay it down as a general and lasting law that working men's associations should be so organized and governed as to furnish the best and most suitable means for attaining what is aimed at, that is to say, for helping each individual member to better his condition to the utmost in body, soul, and property. It is clear that they must pay special and chief attention to the duties of religion and morality, and that social betterment should have this chiefly in view; otherwise they would lose wholly their special character, and end by becoming little better than those societies which take no account whatever of religion. What advantage can it be to a working man to obtain by means of a society material well-being, if he endangers his soul for lack of spiritual food? "What doth it profit a man, if he gains the whole world and suffer the loss of his soul?" This, as our Lord teaches, is the mark of character that distinguishes the Christian from the heathen. . . . Let the working man be urged and led to the worship of God, to the earnest practice of religion. . . . Let him learn to reverence and love holy Church, the common Mother of us all; and hence to obey the precepts of the Church, . . . since they are the means ordained by God for obtaining forgiveness of sin and for leading a holy life. . . .

STUDY QUESTIONS

1. What was the "factory system"? How and why did it originate? What was it intended to do?
2. Do the descriptions of child labor and the testimony about degrading working conditions constitute a realistic and accurate portrayal of urban life during the Industrial Revolution? Or is this portrait an exaggeration? How does Andrew Ure defend the factory system? What specific points does he address? Are his arguments persuasive? Why or why not?
3. Discuss David Ricardo's ideas on the wages of laborers. Why were the poor laws to be regarded as destructive to the basic economic health of the state? Do you find his argument logical and compelling? Can you apply it to our contemporary society?
4. Discuss John Stuart Mill's ideas on liberty. Is the state ever legitimate in restricting individual liberty? To what extent should a person be free in society?
5. What was the attitude of Samuel Smiles toward the plight of the working class? Why would this opinion be considered "middle class"? What do you think of the principle of "self-help"?
6. What do you consider to be the most important ideas or statements that can be found in the excerpt on the *Communist Manifesto*? How does Marx's solution to society's ills differ from those of Robert Owen or the Fabians?
7. What is Pope Leo XIII's basic argument concerning the relationship between capital and labor? What specific measures does he advocate? How do his ideals compare with those of Karl Marx or Robert Owen?
8. How do you view the Industrial Revolution? Was it a progressive time that demonstrated the creativity of man, or was it born of man's greed and exploitation of others who were less fortunate or less conscientious and determined to succeed? Is there always a price to pay in human suffering for a civilization to progress? How can you apply your ideas to our contemporary age?

6

Nationalism and Imperialism: The Motives and Methods of Expansion

No other factor in history, not even religion, has produced so many wars as has the clash of national egotisms sanctified by the name of patriotism.

—Preserved Smith

Lust for dominion inflames the heart more than any other passion.

—Tacitus

The Englishman does everything on principle. He fights you on patriotic principles; he robs you on business principles; he enslaves you on imperial principles. . . . His watchword is always Duty; and he never forgets that the nation which lets its duty get on the side opposite to its interest is lost.

—Napoleon Bonaparte

The right of conquest has no foundation other than the right of the strongest.

—Jean Jacques Rousseau

Nationalism and imperialism were two of the most important factors that shaped the nineteenth century. These terms, however, are difficult to define and have been used so loosely as nearly to deprive them of meaning. Nationalism involves devotion, a patriotism that implies unity and constructive action in the service of one's country. Imperialism is a policy of extending a nation's authority by establishing political or economic control over another area or people. It is important to note that nationalism need not cause imperialism, but it promotes domestic unity, which is a necessity for successful expansion. The term "expansion" is basically benign, connoting progress and dedication, but "imperialism" is often pejorative in connotation and recalls economic exploitation, racial prejudice, and even war. This chapter will seek to define more clearly the nature of nationalism and imperialism and to demonstrate how the two were inextricably linked during the nineteenth century.

Imperialism and nationalism were certainly not introduced in the nineteenth century. During the Renaissance and Reformation eras in the fifteenth and sixteenth centuries, countries such as Spain, France, and England, which had heretofore been decentralized feudal areas, were united under the leadership of strong monarchs. Although this unity was often achieved initially by the sword, the benefits of centralized rule soon became apparent. Unity fostered pride and cooperation among countrymen and soon provided the energy and direction that made possible an age of exploration and discovery.

In essence, the establishment of colonial empires was profitable and patriotic. But by the nineteenth century, the age of colonial empire building was at an end. Spain, Portugal, and France had lost much of their old empires, Great Britain had lost her American colonies, and Germany was too divided internally to attempt to acquire new territory. Of the continental powers, only France under Napoleon was somewhat successful in establishing overseas colonies but realized only small gains. From 1800 to 1870, Britain acquired New Zealand, central Canada, and western Australia; however, these territories generally were contiguous to areas Britain already held. There was a great deal of missionary activity from Christian organizations but little overt government support.

This period of relative disinterest did not last long. Suddenly, between 1870 and 1900, there was a general outburst of imperialistic activity among the nations of Europe. France, Belgium, Britain, and Portugal made extensive gains, especially in Africa. By 1871, both Italy and Germany were born as nations under the aggressive political and military leadership of Camillo Cavour (1810–1861) and Giuseppe Garibaldi (1807–1882) in the case of Italy, and Otto von Bismarck (1815–1898), the first Chancellor of the German Empire. Appealing to abstractions such as "fate" and "duty," politicians immediately sought new territories that would keep them economically and politically competitive with the other nations of Europe. It has been estimated that in this thirty-year period from 1870 to 1900, Europeans expanded their colonial empires by over ten million square miles and nearly one hundred fifty million people.

These intense economic rivalries were often expressed as well in political alliances. In 1882, the Triple Alliance was formed between Germany, Austria-Hungary, and Italy and, in 1907, the Triple Entente between Great Britain, France, and Russia. Such organized competition resulted in a polarization of European nations that contributed to the outbreak of World War I in 1914.

This drive for colonial acquisition was not limited to European powers, however. The United States had come of age in the mid-nineteenth century by expanding to its "natural boundaries" of Mexico and the Pacific. Impelled by the dictates of a policy called "manifest destiny," American settlers moved west in quest of new lives as farmers or in pursuit of the gold of California. They were supported militarily by the American government and ideologically by Christian missionaries who saw westward expansion as the fulfillment of the destiny of the United States, so ordained by God. Thus were Indians dehumanized and sent to reservations, and thus was Texas taken from Mexico in 1845. This expansion, however, was essentially "domestic." The United States did not become involved in foreign adventures until 1898 when the Spanish-American War resulted in the cession of the Philippines. The same arguments used by Europeans to legitimate their rule were now employed by the United States.

The imperialism of the late nineteenth century differed somewhat from the colonialism of the fifteenth to the eighteenth centuries. Earlier, nations had seized land with the intention of settling it with colonists or using it as a base from which to exploit the area economically. The "New Imperialism," as it was called, retained some of these goals, but also introduced new ones. European nations now invested capital in a "backward region" and set about building productive enterprises while also improving the area with hygienic and transportation facilities. In so doing, the colonial powers employed native labor and made cooperative arrangements with local rulers (through either enrichment or intimidation). Their main purpose was to control the region, and if such arrangements proved inadequate the colonial power had other options, which frequently resulted in full annexation.

Our twentieth century has also seen its share of imperialism. Determined to secure Germany's "place in the sun," Kaiser Wilhelm II led Germany to war in 1914. Adolf Hitler resurrected a moribund German people, reminded them of their national heritage, gave them respect, and promised them more living space (*Lebensraum*) through expansion to "natural boundaries." Hitler's territorial demands could not be satisfied and became one of the primary causes of World War II. After Hitler's defeat in 1945, the Soviet Union and the United States moved from their role as allies to rivals in the scramble for territory and influence in the remains of war-ravaged Europe. In a more contemporary setting, the United States fought a war in Vietnam to maintain "principles of democracy" in a country 7500 miles from home. In 1979, the Soviet Union invaded Afghanistan and offered as justification the explanation that it was "asked in" by the Afghan people. In 1982, the Israelis invaded southern Lebanon in an attempt to eliminate dangerous Palestinian bases in the area; they ended up controlling Beirut itself. The United States in 1983 not only rescued American students from the perils of a coup d'état on the Caribbean island of Grenada, but also stayed to ensure the establishment of a democratic regime. The questions abound: What are the responsibilities of great powers? Impelled by their conception of rightness and geopolitical advantage, are they civilizing elements or obstructions to the principle of self-determination? These questions have been asked since the sixteenth century. It is important to achieve the perspective that history can offer.

Nationalism

The Unification of Italy

The Duties of Man

GIUSEPPE MAZZINI

Before Italy finally became a single, independent state under the pragmatic leadership of Count Camillo Cavour, unification was an ideal kept alive through the liberal beliefs of advocates such as Giuseppe Mazzini. Active in the 1830s and 1840s, Mazzini, through his writings, helped define a basis for unification and proved influential in establishing a liberal constitutional monarchy in Italy by 1870. The following selection is from his address to Italian workers.

Your first duties—first as regards importance—are, as I have already told you, towards Humanity. You are *men* before you are either citizens or fathers. Embrace the whole human family in your affection. Bear witness to your belief in the Unity of that family, consequent upon the Unity of God, and in that fraternity among the peoples which is destined to reduce that unity of action. . . .

But what can each of you, singly, *do* for the moral improvement and progress of Humanity? You can from time to time give sterile utterance to your belief; you may, on some rare occasions, perform some act of charity towards a brother man not belonging to your own land;—no more. But

Emilie Ashurst Venturi, *Joseph Mazzini: A Memoir* (London: Alexander and Shepherd, 1875), pp. 312–315.

charity is not the watchword of the Faith of the Future. The watchword of the faith of the future is *Association*, and fraternal co-operation of all towards a common aim; and this is as far superior to all *charity*, as the edifice which all of you should unite to raise would be superior to the humble hut each one of you might build alone, or with the mere assistance of lending, and borrowing stone, mortar, and tools.

But, you tell me, you cannot attempt united action, distinct and divided as you are in language, customs, tendencies, and capacity. The individual is too insignificant, and Humanity too vast. . . .

This means was provided for you by God when he gave you a country; when, even as a wise overseer of labour distributes the various branches of employment according to the different capacities of the workmen, he divided Humanity into distinct groups or nuclei upon the face of the earth, thus creating the germ of Nationalities. Evil governments have disfigured the divine design. Nevertheless you may still trace it, distinctly marked out. . . . They have disfigured it by their conquests, their greed, and their jealousy even of the righteous power of others; disfigured it so far that if we except England and France—there is not perhaps a single country whose present boundaries correspond to that design.

These governments did not, and do not, recognise any country save their own families or dynasty, the egotism of caste. But the Divine design will infallibly be realized. Natural divisions, and the spontaneous, innate tendencies of the peoples, will take the place of the arbitrary divisions sanctioned by evil governments. The map of Europe will be re-drawn. The countries of the Peoples, defined by the vote of free men, will arise upon the ruins of the countries of kings and privileged castes, and between these countries harmony and fraternity will exist. And the common work of Humanity, of general amelioration and the gradual discovery and application of its Law of life, being distributed according to local development and advance. Then may each one of you, fortified by the power and the affection of many millions, all speaking the same language, gifted with the same tendencies, and educated by the same historical tradition, hope, even by your own single effort, to be able to benefit all Humanity.

O my brothers, love your Country! Our country is our Home, the house that God has given us, placing therein a numerous family that loves us, and whom we love; a family with whom we sympathise more readily, and whom we understand more quickly than we do others; and which, from its being centered round a given spot, and from the homogeneous nature of its elements, is adapted to a special branch of activity. Our country is our common workshop, whence the products of our activity are sent forth for the benefit of the whole world; wherein the tools and implements of labour we can most usefully employ are gathered together: nor may we reject them without disobeying the plan of the Almighty, and diminishing our own strength.

Proclamation for the Liberation of Sicily (1860)

GIUSEPPE GARIBALDI

One of Mazzini's most devoted disciples was Giuseppe Garibaldi (1807–1882). A man of action, he was also an adventurer of military ability who succeeded in gaining military support for the King of Piedmont, Victor Emmanuel. In 1860, he organized a volunteer force to invade Sicily and offered the following appeal to the people. Note the emphasis on goals that transcend the individual boundaries and responsibilities of the small regions that heretofore composed Italy. Garibaldi was successful in gaining control of both Sicily and Naples.

Italians!—The Sicilians are fighting against the enemies of Italy, and for Italy. It is the duty of every Italian to succour them with words, money, and arms, and, above all, in person.

The misfortunes of Italy arise from the indifference of one province to the fate of the others.

The redemption of Italy began from the moment that men of the same land ran to help their distressed brothers.

Left to themselves, the brave Sicilians will have to fight, not only the mercenaries of the Bourbon, but also those of Austria and the Priest of Rome.

Let the inhabitants of the free provinces lift their voices in behalf of their struggling brethren, and impel their brave youth to the conflict.

Let the Marches, Umbria, Sabina, Rome, the Neapolitan, rise to divide the forces of our enemies.

Where the cities suffice not for the insurrection, let them send bands of their bravest into the country.

The brave man finds an arm everywhere. Listen not to the voice of cowards, but arm, and let us fight for our brethren, who will fight for us tomorrow.

A band of those who fought with me the country's battles marches with me to the fight. Good and generous, they will fight for their country to the last drop of their blood, nor ask for other reward than a clear conscience.

"Italy and Victor Emmanuel!" they cried, on passing the Ticino. "Italy and Victor Emmanuel!" shall re-echo in the blazing caves of Mongibello.

At this cry, thundering from the great rock of Italy to the Tarpeian, the rotton Throne of tyranny shall crumble, and, as one man, the brave descendants of Vespro shall rise.

To Arms! Let me put an end, once and for all, to the miseries of so many centuries. Prove to the world that it is no lie that Roman generations inhabited this land.

Public Documents, *The Annual Register, 1860* (London: 1861), pp. 281–282.

Address to Parliament (1871)

VICTOR EMMANUEL

Through years of idealistic and impassioned speeches by people like Giuseppe Mazzini, diplomatic maneuvering by Camillo Cavour, and the exercise of military might by Giuseppe Garibaldi, Italy became a unified, independent state in 1870 under the leadership of Victor Emmanuel (1820–1878), former King of Piedmont. This excerpt from his address to the Italian Parliament in 1871 discusses some of the challenges that a new nation must face.

Senators and Deputies, gentlemen!

The work to which we consecrated our life is accomplished. After long trials of expiation Italy is restored to herself and to Rome. Here, where our people, after centuries of separation, find themselves for the first time solemnly reunited in the person of their representatives: here where we recognize the fatherland of our dreams, everything speaks to us of greatness; but at the same time it all reminds us of our duties. The joy that we experience must not let us forget them. . . .

We have proclaimed the separation of Church and State. Having recognized the absolute independence of the spiritual authority, we are convinced that Rome, the capital of Italy, will continue to be the peaceful and respected seat of the Pontificate. . . .

Economic and financial affairs, moreover, claim our most careful attention. Now that Italy is established, it is necessary to make it prosperous by putting in order its finances; we shall succeed in this only by persevering in the virtues which have been the source of our national regeneration. Good finances will be the means of re-enforcing our military organization. Our most ardent desire is for peace, and nothing can make us believe that it can be troubled. But the organization of the army and the navy, the supply of arms, the works for the defense of the national territory, demand long and profound study. . . .

Senators and deputies, a vast range of activity opens before you; the national unity which is today attained will have, I hope, the effect of rendering less bitter the struggles of parties, the rivalry of which will have henceforth no other end than the development of the productive forces of the nation.

I rejoice to see that our population already gives unequivocal proofs of its love of work. The economic awakening is closely associated with the political awakening. The banks multiply, as do the commercial institutions, the expositions of the products of art and industry, and the congresses of the learned. We ought, you and I, to favor this productive movement while

Christine Walsh, ed., *Prologue: A Documentary History of Europe: 1846–1960.* Originally published by Cassell Australia Ltd. (1968), pp. 103–104. Reprinted by permission of Macmillan Publishing Company.

giving to professional and scientific education more attention and efficiency, and opening to commerce new avenues of communication and new outlets. . . .

A brilliant future opens before us. It remains for us to respond to the blessings of Providence by showing ourselves worthy of bearing among the nations the glorious names of Italy and Rome.

The Unification of Germany

The People and the Fatherland (1807–1808)

JOHANN GOTTLIEB FICHTE

Like Italy, Germany did not achieve unification until 1871. But there were those who provided the philosophical and idealistic foundation for later policies that would prove more practical. Johann Gottlieb Fichte delivered a series of addresses in 1807–1808 that disclose the frustration of German disunity and presage the intense nationalism that was to erupt in the latter part of the nineteenth century, propelling Germany toward what Kaiser Wilhelm II would later call her "place in the sun."

Our oldest common ancestors, the original people of the new culture, the Teutons, called Germans by the Romans, set themselves bravely in opposition to the overwhelming worldwide rule of the Romans. Did they not see with their own eyes the finest blossom of the Roman provinces beside them, the finer enjoyment in the same, together with laws, courts of justice, lictors' staves and axes in superabundance? Were not the Romans ready and generous enough to let them share in all these benefits? Did they not see proof of the famous Roman clemency in the case of several of their own princes, who allowed themselves to think that war against such benefactors of the human race was rebellion? For the compliant were decorated with the title of king and rewarded with posts of importance as leaders in the Roman army, with Roman sacrificial wreaths; and when they were expelled by their countrymen, the Romans furnished them with a refuge and support in their colonies. Had they no appreciation of the advantages of Roman culture, for better organization of their armies, for example, in which even Arminius himself did not refuse to learn the art of war? It cannot be charged against them that in any one of these respects they were ignorant. Their descendants have appropriated that culture, as soon as they could do so without loss of their own freedom, and as far as it was possible without loss of their distinctive character. Wherefore, then, have they fought for so many generations in bloody wars which have been repeatedly renewed with

Guy Carelton Lee, ed., *The World's Orators*, vol. 2 (New York: G. P. Putnam's Sons, 1900), pp. 190–193.

undiminished fury? A Roman writer represents their leaders as asking if anything else remained for them but to maintain their freedom or to die before they became slaves. Freedom was their possession, that they might remain Germans, that they might continue to settle their own affairs independently and originally and in their own way, and at the same time to advance their culture and to plant the same independence in the hearts of their posterity. Slavery was what they called all the benefits which the Romans offered them, because through them they would become other than Germans, they would have to become semi-Romans. It was perfectly clear, they assumed, that every man, rather than become this, would die, and that a true German could wish to live only to be and to remain a German, and to have his sons the same.

They have not all died; they have not seen slavery; they have bequeathed freedom to their children. To their constant resistance the whole new world owes that it is as it is. Had the Romans succeeded in subjugating them also, and, as the Romans everywhere did, destroying them as a nation, the entire development of the human race would have taken a different direction, and it cannot be thought a better one. We who are the nearest heirs of their land, their language, and their sentiments, owe to them that we are still Germans, that the stream of original and independent life still bears us on; to them we owe that we have since then become a nation; to them, if now perhaps it is not at an end with us and the last drops of blood inherited from them are not dried in our veins, we owe all that which we have become. To them, even the other tribes, who have become to us aliens but through them our brethren, owe their existence; when they conquered eternal Rome, there were no others of all those peoples present; at that time was won for them the possibility of their future origin. . . .

These orations have attempted, by the only means remaining after others have been tried in vain, to prevent this annihilation of every noble action that may in the future arise among us, and this degradation of our entire nation. They have attempted to implant in your minds the deep and immovable foundations of the true and almighty love of the fatherland, in the conception of our nation as eternal and the people as citizens of our own eternity through the education of all hearts and minds.

Speech to the Reichstag (1888)

OTTO VON BISMARCK

In 1862, Otto von Bismarck was appointed Prime Minister of Prussia. At that time he declared that German unity would be realized "not by speeches and majorities . . . but by blood and iron." By 1871, after

From pp. 290–293 of *The Age of Bismarck: Documents and Interpretations*, edited by T. S. Hamerow. Copyright © 1973 by T. S. Hamerow. Reprinted by permission of Harper & Row, Publishers, Inc.

several wars, Bismarck had formed the unified fatherland of which Fichte had dreamed: the nation of Germany existed under the leadership of Kaiser Wilhelm I. The following excerpt is from Bismarck's speech to the Reichstag (parliament) in 1888. Unity demands great goals.

Great complications and all kinds of coalitions, which no one can foresee, are constantly possible, and we must be prepared for them. We must be so strong, irrespective of momentary conditions, that we can face any coalition with the assurance of a great nation which is strong enough under circumstances to take her fate into her own hands. We must be able to face our fate placidly with that self reliance and confidence in God which are ours when we are strong and our cause is just. And the government will see to it that the German cause will be just always.

We must, to put it briefly, be as strong in these times as we possibly can be, and we can be stronger than any other nation of equal numbers in the world. I shall revert to this later—but it would be criminal if we were not to make use of our opportunity. If we do not need our full armed strength, we need not summon it. The only problem is the not very weighty one of money—not very weighty I say in passing, because I have no wish to enter upon a discussion of the financial and military figures, and of the fact that France has spent three milliards for the improvement of her armaments these last years, while we have spent scarcely one and one half milliards, including what we are asking of you at this time. But I leave the elucidation of this to the minister of war and the representatives of the treasury department.

When I saw that it is our duty to endeavor to be ready at all times and for all emergencies, I imply that we must make greater exertions than other people for the same purpose, because of our geographical position. We are situated in the heart of Europe, and have at least three fronts open to an attack. France has only her eastern, and Russia only her western frontier where they may be attacked. We are also more exposed to the dangers of a coalition than any other nation, as is proved by the whole development of history, by our geographical position, and the lesser degree of cohesiveness, which until now has characterized the German nation in comparison with others. God has placed us where we are prevented, thanks to our neighbors, from growing lazy and dull. He has placed by our side the most warlike and restless of all nations, the French, and He has permitted warlike inclinations to grow strong in Russia, where formerly they existed to a lesser degree. Thus we are given the spur, so to speak, from both sides, and are compelled to exertions which we should perhaps not be making otherwise. The pikes in the European carp-pond are keeping us from being carps by making us feel their teeth on both sides. They also are forcing us to an exertion which without them we might not make, and to a union among us Germans, which is abhorrent to us at heart. By nature we are rather tending away, the one from the other. But the Franco-Russian press within which we are squeezed compels us to hold together, and by pressure our cohesive force is greatly increased. This will bring us to that state of being inseparable which all other nations possess, while we do not yet enjoy it. But we must respond to the intentions of Providence by making ourselves so strong that the pikes can do nothing but encourage us. . . .

If we Germans wish to wage a war with the full effect of our national strength, it must be a war which satisfies all who take part in it, all who sacrifice anything for it, in short the whole nation. It must be a national war, a war carried on with the enthusiasm of 1870, when we were foully attacked. I still remember the earsplitting, joyful shouts in the station at Köln. It was the same all the way from Berlin to Köln, in Berlin itself. The waves of popular approval bore us into the war, whether or not we wished it. That is the way it must be, if a popular force like ours is to show what it can do. . . . A war into which we are not borne by the will of the people will be waged, to be sure, if it has been declared by the constituted authorities who deemed it necessary; it will even be waged pluckily, and possibly victoriously, after we have once smelled fire and tasted blood, but it will lack from the beginning the nerve and enthusiasm of a war in which we are attacked. In such a one the whole of Germany from Memel to the Alpine Lakes will flare up like a powder mine; it will be bristling with guns, and no enemy will dare to engage this *furor teutonicus* which develops when we are attacked. We cannot afford to lose this factor of preeminence even if many military men—not only ours but others as well—believe that today we are superior to our future opponents. Our own officers believe this to a man, naturally. Every soldier believes this. He would almost cease to be a useful soldier if he did not wish for war, and did not believe that we would be victorious in it. If our opponents by any chance are thinking that we are pacific because we are afraid of how the war may end, they are mightily mistaken. We believe as firmly in our victory in a just cause as any foreign lieutenant in his garrison, after his third glass of champagne, can believe in his, and we probably do so with greater certainty. It is not fear, therefore, which makes us pacific, but the consciousness of our strength. We are strong enough to protect ourselves, even if we should be attacked at a less favorable moment, and we are in a position to let divine providence determine whether a war in the meanwhile may not become unnecessary after all.

I am, therefore, not in favor of any kind of an aggressive war, and if war could result only from our attack—somebody must kindle a fire, we shall not kindle it. Neither the consciousness of our strength, which I have described, nor our confidence in our treaties, will prevent us from continuing our former endeavors to preserve peace. In this we do not permit ourselves to be influenced by annoyances or dislikes. The threats and insults, and the challenges, which have been made have, no doubt, excited also with us a feeling of irritation, which does not easily happen with Germans, for they are less prone to national hatred than any other nation. We are, however, trying to calm our countrymen, and we shall work for peace with our neighbors, especially with Russia, in the future as in the past. . . .

We are easily influenced—perhaps too easily—by love and kindness, but quite surely never by threats! We Germans fear God, and naught else in the world! It is this fear of God which makes us love and cherish peace. If in spite of this anybody breaks the peace, he will discover that ardent patriotism . . . has today become the common property of the whole German nation. Attack the German nation anywhere, and you will find it armed to a man, and every man with the firm belief in his heart: God will be with us.

Motives for Imperialism

Racism and Social Darwinism

In general, imperialistic nations have felt compelled to justify their actions by explaining why they have taken control of territory or populations. One of the most popular justifications has been the policy of Social Darwinism, a vulgarization of the scientific theory of Charles Darwin contained in *The Origin of Species* (1859). Social Darwinists held that only the fittest peoples would survive and that "lesser breeds" would of necessity perish or be taken over. Indeed, some argued that an empire was a living organism that must either grow or die. Racism, therefore, provided a potent thrust to imperial expansion. The first selection, by American clergyman Josiah Strong (1847–1916), is typical of the racist argument. The second excerpt is from a lecture delivered in 1900 by the German scientist Karl Pearson; in it he presents racism as being consistent with the directives of nature. The last account is by Sir Henry Johnston, British explorer and administrator in Central and East Africa at the turn of the century.

Our Country (1885)

JOSIAH STRONG

God, with infinite wisdom and skill, is training the Anglo-Saxon race for an hour sure to come in the world's future. Heretofore there has always been in the history of the world a comparatively unoccupied land westward, into

Josiah Strong, *Our Country* (New York: The Baker and Taylor Publishing Company, 1885), pp. 174–178.

which the crowded countries of the East have poured their surplus populations. But the widening waves of migration, which millenniums ago rolled east and west from the valley of the Euphrates meet to-day on our Pacific coast. There are no more new worlds. . . . The time is coming when the pressure of population on the means of subsistence will be felt here as it is now felt in Europe and Asia. Then will the world enter upon a new stage of its history—*the final competition of races, for which the Anglo-Saxon is being schooled.* Long before the thousand millions are here, the mighty *centrifugal* tendency, inherent in this stock and strengthened in the United States, will assert itself. Then this race of unequaled energy, with all the majesty of numbers and the might of wealth behind it—the representative, let us hope, of the largest liberty, the purest Christianity, the highest civilization—having developed peculiarly aggressive traits calculated to impress its institutions upon mankind, will spread itself over the earth. If I read not amiss, this powerful race will move down upon Mexico, down upon Central and South America, out upon the islands of the sea, over upon Africa and beyond. And can any one doubt that the result of this competition of races will be the "survival of the fittest"? . . . Nothing can save the inferior race but a ready and pliant assimilation. Whether the feebler and more abject races are going to be regenerated and raised up, is already very much of a question. What if it should be God's plan to people the world with better and finer material? Certain it is, whatever expectations we may indulge, that there is a tremendous overbearing surge of power in the Christian nations, which, if the others are not speedily raised to some vastly higher capacity, will inevitably submerge and bury them forever. . . . To this result no war of extermination is needful; the contest is not one of arms, but of vitality and of civilization. "At the present day," says Mr. Darwin, "civilized nations are everywhere supplanting barbarous nations. . . ."

Some of the stronger races, doubtless, may be able to preserve their integrity; but, in order to compete with the Anglo-Saxon, they will probably be forced to adopt his methods and instruments, his civilization and his religion. . . . The contact of Christian with heathen nations is awakening the latter to new life. Old superstitions are loosening their grasp. The dead crust of fossil faiths is being shattered by the movements of life underneath. In Catholic countries, Catholicism is losing its influence over educated minds, and in some cases the masses have already lost all faith in it. Thus, while on this continent God is training the Anglo-Saxon race for its mission, a complemental work has been in progress in the great world beyond. God has two hands. Not only is He preparing in our civilization the die with which to stamp the nations, but . . . he is preparing mankind to receive our impress.

Is there room for reasonable doubt that this race, unless devitalized by alcohol and tobacco, is destined to dispossess many weaker races, assimilate others, and mold the remainder, until, in a very true and important sense, it has Anglo-Saxonized mankind?

The Standpoint of Science (1900)

KARL PEARSON

How many centuries, how many thousand of years, have the Kaffir or the Negro held large districts in Africa undisturbed by the white man? Yet their intertribal struggles have not yet produced a civilization in the least comparable with the Aryan. Educate and nurture them as you will, I do not believe that you will succeed in modifying the stock. History shows me one way, and one way only, in which a high state of civilization has been produced, namely, the struggle of race with race, and the survival of the physically and mentally fitter race. If you want to know whether the lower races of man can evolve a higher type, I fear the only course is to leave them to fight it out among themselves, and even then the struggle for existence between individual and individual, between tribe and tribe, may not be supported by that physical selection due to a particular climate on which probably so much of the Aryan's success depended.

If you bring the white man into contact with the black, you too often suspend the very process of natural selection on which the evolution of a higher type depends. You get superior and inferior races living on the same soil, and that coexistence is demoralizing for both. They naturally sink into the position of master and servant, if not admittedly or covertly into that of slave-owner and slave. Frequently they inter-cross, and if the bad stock be raised the good is lowered. Even in the case of Eurasians, of whom I have met mentally and physically fine specimens, I have felt how much better they would have been had they been pure Asiatics or pure Europeans. Thus it comes about that when the struggle for existence between races is suspended, the solution of great problems may be unnaturally postponed; instead of the slow, stern processes of evolution, cataclysmal solutions are prepared for the future. Such problems in suspense, it appears to me, are to be found in the Negro population of the Southern States of America, in the large admixture of Indian blood in some of the South American races, but, above all, in the Kaffir factor in South Africa.

You may possibly think that I am straying from my subject, but I want to justify natural selection to you. I want you to see selection as something which renders the inexorable law of heredity a source of progress which produces the good through suffering, an infinitely greater good which far outbalances the very obvious pain and evil. Let us suppose the alternative were possible. Let us suppose we could prevent the white man, if we liked, from going to lands of which the agricultural and mineral resources are not worked to the full; then I should say a thousand times better for him that he should not go than that he should settle down and live alongside the inferior race. The only healthy alternative is that he should go and com-

Karl Pearson, *National Life from the Standpoint of Science,* 2nd ed. (Cambridge: Cambridge University Press, 1907), pp. 21–25.

pletely drive out the inferior race. That is practically what the white man has done in North America. . . . The civilization of the white man is a civilization dependent upon free white labour, and when that element of stability is removed it will collapse like those of Greece and Rome. I venture to assert, then, that the struggle for existence between white and red man, painful and even terrible as it was in its details, has given us a good for outbalancing its immediate evil. In place of the red man, contributing practically nothing to the work and thought of the world, we have a great nation, mistress of many arts, and able, with its youthful imagination and fresh, untrammelled impulses, to contribute much to the common stock of civilized man. Against that we have only to put the romantic sympathy for the Red Indian generated by the novels of Cooper and the poems of Longfellow, and then—see how little it weighs in the balance! . . .

You will see that my view—and I think it may be called the scientific view of a nation—is that of an organized whole, kept up to a high pitch of internal efficiency by insuring that its numbers are substantially recruited from the better stocks, and kept up to a high pitch of external efficiency by contest, chiefly by way of war with inferior races, and with equal races by the struggle for trade-routes and for the sources of raw material and of food supply. This is the natural history view of mankind, and I do not think you can in its main features subvert it. Some of you may refuse to acknowledge it, but you cannot really study history and refuse to see its force. Some of you may realize it, and then despair of life; you may decline to admit any glory in a world where the superior race must either eject the inferior, or, mixing with it, or even living alongside it, degenerate itself. What beauty can there be when the battle is to the stronger, and the weaker must suffer in the struggle of nations and in the struggle of individual men? You may say: Let us cease to struggle; let us leave the lands of the world to the races that cannot profit by them to the full; let us cease to compete in the markets of the world. Well, we could do it, if we were a small nation living off the produce of our own soil, and a soil so worthless that no other race envied it and sought to appropriate it. We should cease to advance; but then we should naturally give up progress as a good which comes through suffering. I say it is impossible for a small rural community to stand apart from the world-contest and to stagnate, if no more powerful nation wants its possessions.

The Backward Peoples (1920)

SIR HARRY JOHNSTON

[L]et us proceed to define who and what these backward or unprogressive peoples are and to what extent they may be considered to be retrograde

Sir Harry Johnston, *The Backward Peoples and Our Relations with Them* (London: Oxford University Press, 1920), pp. 7–9.

and ineffective as compared with the dominating white race. The chief and obvious distinction between the backward and forward peoples is that the former, with the exception of about 20,000,000 in the Mediterranean basin and the Near East, are of coloured skin; while the latter are white-skinned, or, as in the case of the Japanese and the inhabitants of Northern China, nearly white.

I think if we took all the factors into consideration—religion, education (especially knowledge concerning the relations between this planet and the universe of which it is a minute speck, the history and geography of the planet, the sciences that are a part of earth-study), standard of living, respect for sanitation, infant death rate, bodily strength, manner of government, regard for law and order, position in agriculture and manufactures,—we might appraise mathematically, according to the following ratio, the principal nations and peoples into which humanity is divided:

100 per cent.

1. Great Britain and Ireland, Canada and Newfoundland, White Australia, New Zealand, White South Africa (south of the Zambezi), Malta and Mauritius, United States, France, Corsica, much of Algeria and Tunis, Belgium and Luxembourg, Holland, Germany, Austria, Chekho-Slovakia, Italy, Switzerland, Hungary, Norway, Sweden, Denmark and Iceland, Finland, Estonia, Spain, Chile, Argentina, Japan

98 per cent.

2. Poland and Lithuania, Serbia and Croatia, Bulgaria, Rumania, Portugal, Greece, Cyprus, Brazil, Peru, Columbia, British Guiana, French and Dutch Guiana, British and French West Indies, Cuba and Puerto Rico, Hawaii, Uruguay

97 per cent.

3. Russia, Russian Siberia, Russian Central Asia, the Caucasus, Egypt, British India, French Indo-China, Siam, British Malaysia, Mexico, Central America, Bolivia, Venezuela, Ecuador, Paraguay, Java, . . . Armenia

95 per cent.

4. Albania, Asia Minor, Morocco, Southern Algeria, Tripoli, Palestine, Syria, Persia, China, Tibet, Afghanistan, Zanzibar

90 per cent.

5. Madagascar, Black South Africa, French West Africa, British West Africa, Uganda, British Central and East Africa, Sumatra, Borneo, the Philippines, the Anglo-Egyptian Sudan, Angola, Santo Domingo

80 per cent.

6. Abyssina, Arabia, Portuguese East Africa, the Belgian Congo, Portuguese Congo, Liberia, Haiti, Celebes, Timor, New Caledonia, British Papas

75 per cent.

7. Dutch New Guinea and New Hebrides, Portuguese Guinea, French Central Africa

This rough estimate of civilization and culture does not imply that the nations or peoples which are classed together resemble one another in all their stages of culture. Some will excel in one direction, some in another. In certain directions a people may be very forward, coupled with retrograde features which reduce their average value.

Obviously, the foremost nations in the world at the present day are Britain and the regions of the British Empire in which the white race predominates; the United States; France; and Germany,—not only by the numbers of their peoples and the degree of their national wealth, but by their industry, commerce and the proportion of educated to uneducated people in the population. In all elements of greatness, but not in potency of numbers, Denmark, Sweden, Norway, Finland, Holland, Luxembourg and Belgium, are on an equal footing. From their magnificent parts in history one would like to class Spain, Portugal and Italy with these powers of the first rank. . . .

It is the peoples of 95 per cent. to 90 per cent. that may be put in the unprogressive or retrograde class, unable at present to govern themselves in a manner conducive to progress; while those that are graded 80 to 75 per cent. still contain in their midst elements of sheer savagery. Such regions, if left alone by the controlling white men, might easily relapse into the unprofitable barbarism out of which they have been lifted with the white man's efforts during the past fifty years.

For God and Country

The Mandate System: Britain's Duty in Egypt (1890)

JOSEPH CHAMBERLAIN

The British in the late nineteenth century often justified their imperialism on the premise of duty. As a civilized power, it was imperative that they spread God's word and the fruits of civilization to those peoples who were not sufficiently advanced to develop them on their own. In essence, Britain held a nation "in trust" until the backward peoples could be educated and made ready to assume the responsibilities of self-government. The "mandate system," as it came to be called, is described in the following excerpt by the liberal statesman Joseph Chamberlain (1836–1914). The motive for British expansion in Egypt was not completely

Joseph Chamberlain, *Foreign and Colonial Speeches* (London: George Routledge and Sons, 1897), pp. 41–44.

altruistic, however. Britain also wanted to protect the strategic Suez Canal, which controlled access to the riches of Britain's empire in India and the Far East. In 1882, Britain occupied Cairo and set about reorganizing the country. Chamberlain's address to Parliament must also be viewed in this light.

I want to say a word or two to you about the future. I am going to make a confession. I admit I was one of those—I think my views were shared by the whole Cabinet of Mr. Gladstone—who regretted the necessity for the occupation of Egypt. I thought that England had so much to do, such enormous obligations and responsibilities, that we might well escape, if we could, this addition to them; and, when the occupation was forced upon us, I looked forward with anxiety to an early, it might be even, to an immediate evacuation. The confession I have to make is that having seen what are the results of this occupation, having seen what is the nature of the task we have undertaken, and what progress we have already made towards its accomplishment, I have changed my mind. (Cheers.) I say it would be unworthy of this great nation if we did not rise to the full height of our duty, and complete our work before we left the country. (Cheers.) We have no right to abandon the duty which has been cast upon us, and the work which already shows so much promise for the advantage of the people with whose destinies we have become involved.

This great alteration is due to the influence of a mere handful of your fellow-countrymen. . . . They, by their persevering devotion, and their single-minded honesty, have wrought out this great work, and have brought Egypt from a condition which may fairly be described as one of ruin, to the promise of once more being restored to its ancient prosperity. I hear sometimes of pessimists who think the work of England is accomplished, who will tell you that we have lost the force and the capacity to govern. No; that is not true; and as long as we can spare from our abundance men like these, who, after all, are only ordinary Englishmen—men like these, who are able and willing to carry their zeal and their intelligence wherever it may conduce to the service of humanity, and to the honour of their native land—so long as we can do that we need not despair of the future of the United Kingdom. (Cheers.) But we owe it to them, we owe it to ourselves, that their work shall not be in vain. You cannot revolutionise a country like Egypt— you cannot reform all that is wrong in her system, all that is poor and weak in the character of the people—in a few minutes, or a few years. Egypt has been submitted for centuries to arbitrary despotism. I believe there is hardly any time in her history, even if you go back to almost prehistoric ages, when she has not been in the grasp of some foreign ruler; and, under these circumstances, you cannot expect to find ready to your hands a self-governing people. They are not able—they cannot be able—to stand alone; and they do not wish to stand alone. They ask for your support and assistance, and without it, it is absolutely impossible that their welfare can be secured. If you were to abandon your responsibility, your retirement would be followed by an attempt once more to restore the old arbitrary methods and the old abuses, which in turn would no doubt be followed by anarchy and disorder; and then in time there would be again a foreign intervention, this time the intervention of some other European country. I have too much confidence in the public spirit of the country to believe that it will ever neglect a national duty. (Hear, hear.) A nation is like an individual; it has duties which it must fulfill, or else it cannot live honoured and respected as a nation. (Loud cheers.)

American Imperialism in the Philippines (1900)

ALBERT J. BEVERIDGE

Through much of the nineteenth century, the United States was involved with establishing its own borders "from sea to shining sea," but did not try to expand internationally. In 1898, however, because of the Spanish-American War, the United States inaugurated a policy of foreign imperialism. One of the Spanish colonies ceded to the United States was the Philippine Islands. There was a strong independence movement in the islands, however, and actual warfare broke out in 1899 between Filipinos and American forces. Congress was divided about setting up a government for the newly acquired territory. One of the champions of imperialism was Albert J. Beveridge, senator from Indiana. In January 1900, he addressed Congress in support of a resolution that decreed that the United States "establish and maintain such government control throughout the archipelago as the situation may demand."

Mr. President, the times call for candor. The Philippines are ours forever, "territory belonging to the United States," as the Constitution calls them. And just beyond the Philippines are China's illimitable markets. We will not retreat from either. We will not repudiate our duty in the archipelago. We will not abandon our opportunity in the Orient. We will not renounce our part in the mission of our race, trustee under God, of the civilization of the world. And we will move forward to our work, not howling our regrets like slaves whipped to their burdens, but with gratitude for a task worthy of our strength, and thanksgiving to Almighty God that He has marked us as His chosen people, henceforth to lead in the regeneration of the world. . . .

Senators, it would be better to abandon this combined garden and Gibraltar of the Pacific, and count our blood and treasure already spent a profitable loss, than to apply any academic arrangement of self-government to these children. They are not capable of self-government. How could they be? They are not of a self-governing race. They are Orientals, Malays, instructed by Spaniards in the latter's worst estate.

They know nothing of practical government except as they have wit-

Congressional Record, vol. 33 (1900), pp. 704–705, 708, 710–712.

nessed the weak, corrupt, cruel, and capricious rule of Spain. What magic will anyone employ to dissolve in their minds and characters those impressions of governors and governed which three centuries of misrule have created? What alchemy will change the Oriental quality of their blood and set the self-governing currents of the American pouring through their Malay veins? How shall they, in the twinkling of an eye, be exalted to the heights of self-governing peoples which required a thousand years for us to reach, Anglo-Saxon though we are? . . .

Mr. President, self-government and internal development have been the dominant notes of our first century; administration and the development of other lands will be the dominant notes of our second century. And administration is as high and holy a function as self-government, just as the care of a trust estate is as sacred an obligation as the management of our own concerns. . . .

The Declaration of Independence does not forbid us to do our part in the regeneration of the world. If it did, the Declaration would be wrong, just as the Articles of Confederation, drafted by the very same men who signed the Declaration, were found to be wrong. The Declaration has no application to the present situation. It was written by self-governing men for self-governing men. . . .

Mr. President, this question is deeper that any question of party politics; deeper than any question of the isolated policy of our country even; deeper even than any question of constitutional power. It is elemental. It is racial. God has not been preparing the English-speaking and Teutonic peoples for a thousand years for nothing but vain and idle self-contemplation and self-admiration. No! He has made us the master organizers of the world to establish system where chaos reigns. He has given the spirit of progress to overwhelm the forces of reaction throughout the earth. He has made us adepts in government that we may administer government among savage and senile peoples. Were it not for such a force as this the world would relapse into barbarism and night. And of all our race He has marked the American people as His chosen nation to finally lead in the regeneration of the world. This is the divine mission of America, and it holds for us all the profit, all the glory, all the happiness possible to man. We are trustees of the world's progress, guardians of its righteous peace. The judgment of the Master is upon us: "Ye have been faithful over a few things; I will make you ruler over many things."

What shall history say of us? Shall it say that we renounced that holy trust, left the savage to his base condition, the wilderness to the reign of waste, deserted duty, abandoned glory, forgot our sordid profit even, because we feared our strength and read the charter of our powers with the doubter's eye and the quibbler's mind? Shall it say that, called by events to captain and command the proudest, ablest, purest race of history in history's noblest work, we declined that great commission? Our fathers would not have had it so. No! They founded no paralytic government, incapable of the simplest acts of administration. They planted no sluggard people, passive while the world's work calls them. They established no reactionary nation. They unfurled no retreating flag. . . .

Blind indeed is he who sees not the hand of God in events so vast, so harmonious, so benign. Reactionary indeed is the mind that perceives not that this vital people is the strongest of the saving forces of the world; that our place, therefore, is at the head of the constructing and redeeming nations of the earth; and that to stand aside while events march on is a surrender of our interests, a betrayal of our duty as blind as it is base. Craven indeed is the heart that fears to perform a work so golden and so noble; that dares not win a glory or immortal. . . .

Mr. President and Senators, adopt the resolution offered, that peace may quickly come and that we may begin our saving, regenerating, and uplifting work. . . . Reject it, and the world, history, and the American people will know where to forever fix the awful responsibility for the consequences that will surely follow such failure to do our manifest duty. How dare we delay when our soldiers' blood is flowing?

The White Man's Burden (1899)

RUDYARD KIPLING

In commemoration of successful U.S. imperialism in the Philippines, the great British poet Rudyard Kipling wrote "The White Man's Burden" in 1899. It reflects a devotion to the demands of empire and the duty of civilized nations. In Kipling's eyes, imperialism was a nationalistic venture—a heroic necessity.

Take up the White Man's burden—
Send forth the best ye breed—
Go bind your sons to exile
To serve your captive's need;
To wait in heavy harness,
On fluttered folk and wild—
Your new-caught, sullen peoples,
Half-devil and half-child.

Take up the White Man's burden—
In patience to abide,
To veil the threat of terror
And check the show of pride;
By open speech and simple,
An hundred times made plain
To seek another's profit,
And work another's gain.

Rudyard Kipling, *Collected Verse* (New York: Doubleday and Page, 1911), pp. 215–217.

Take up the White Man's burden—
The savage wars of peace—
Fill full the mouth of Famine
And bid the sickness cease;
And when your goal is nearest
The end for others sought,
Watch sloth and heathen Folly
Bring all your hopes to nought.

Take up the White Man's burden—
No tawdry rule of kings,
But toil of serf and sweeper—
The tale of common things.
The ports ye shall not enter,
The roads ye shall not tread,
Go mark them with your living,
And mark them with your dead.

Take up the White Man's burden—
And reap his old reward:
The blame of those ye better,
The hate of those ye guard—
The cry of hosts ye humour
(Ah, slowly!) toward the light:—
'Why brought he us from bondage,
Our loved Egyptian night?

Take up the White Man's burden—
Ye dare not stoop to less—
Nor call too loud on Freedom
To cloke your weariness;
By all ye cry or whisper,
By all ye leave or do,
The silent, sullen peoples
Shall weigh your gods and you.

Take up the White Man's burden—
Have done with childish days—
The lightly proferred laurel,
The easy, ungrudged praise.
Comes now, to search your manhood
Through all the thankless years,
Cold, edged with dear-bought wisdom,
The judgment of your peers!

The Economic Argument

Probably the most obvious motive for imperialism is in the economic profit to be made from the colonization of territory and the subjugation of people. Sir Frederick Lugard, British soldier and administrator of some of Britain's colonial possessions in the late nineteenth century, analyzes the "scramble for Africa."

"A Natural Inclination to Submit to a Higher Authority" (1893)

SIR FREDERICK DEALTRY LUGARD

The Chambers of Commerce of the United Kingdom have unanimously urged the retention of East Africa on the grounds of commercial advantage. The Presidents of the London and Liverpool chambers attended a deputation to her Majesty's Minister for Foreign Affairs to urge "the absolute necessity, for the prosperity of this country, that new avenues for commerce such as that in East Equatorial Africa should be opened up, in view of the hostile tariffs with which British manufacturers are being everywhere confronted." Manchester followed with a similar declaration; Glasgow, Birmingham, Edinburgh, and other commercial centres gave it as their opinion that "there is practically no middle course for this country, between a reversal of the freetrade policy to which it is pledged, on the one hand, and a prudent but continuous territorial extension for the creation of new markets, on the other hand. . . .

The "Scramble for Africa" by the nations of Europe—an incident without parallel in the history of the world—was due to the growing commercial rivalry, which brought home to civilised nations the vital necessity of securing the only remaining fields for industrial enterprise and expansion. It is well, then, to realise that it is for our *advantage*—and not alone at the dictates of duty—that we have undertaken responsibilities in East Africa. It is in order to foster the growth of the trade of this country, and to find an outlet for our manufactures and our surplus energy, that our far-seeing statesmen and our commercial men advocate colonial expansion. . . .

There are some who say we have no *right* in Africa at all, that "it belongs to the natives". I hold that our right is the necessity that is upon us to provide for our ever-growing population—either by opening new fields for emigration, or by providing work and employment which the development of over-sea extension entails—and to stimulate trade by finding new markets, since we know what misery trade depression brings at home.

While thus serving our own interests as a nation, we may, by selecting

Sir Frederick Dealtry Lugard, *The Rise of Our East African Empire*, vol. 1 (London: William Blackwood and Sons, 1893), pp. 379–382.

men of the right stamp for the control of new territories, bring at the same time many advantages to Africa. Nor do we deprive the natives of their birthright of freedom, to place them under a foreign yoke. It has ever been the key-note of British colonial method to rule through and by the natives, and it is this method, in contrast to the arbitrary and uncompromising rule of Germany, France, Portugal, and Spain, which has been the secret of our success as a colonising nation, and has made us welcomed by tribes and peoples in Africa, who ever rose in revolt against the other nations named. In Africa, moreover, there is among the people a natural inclination to submit to a higher authority. That intense detestation of control which animates our Teutonic races does not exist among the tribes of Africa, and if there is any authority that we replace, it is the authority of the Slavers and Arabs, or the intolerable tyranny of the "dominant tribe."

Power and Pride

The next three selections provide another motive for imperialism. The desire for power can be justified through the pride that one has in one's nation. Nationalism and imperialism seem to be intimately connected. The first excerpt is from a speech made by the German Kaiser Wilhelm II in 1901. The second selection, by John Louis O'Sullivan, promotes the concept of "manifest destiny," which legitimized the American annexation of land as settlers moved west. The fulfillment of the "destiny" of the nation necessarily involved the sacrifice of Mexican and Indian populations in Texas and throughout the plains.

Germany's Place in the Sun (1901)

KAISER WILHELM II

In spite of the fact that we have no such fleet as we should have, we have conquered for ourselves a place in the sun. It will now be my task to see to it that this place in the sun shall remain our undisputed possession, in order that the sun's rays may fall fruitfully upon our activity and trade in foreign parts, that our industry and agriculture may develop within the state and our sailing sports upon the water, for our future lies upon the water. The more Germans go out upon the waters . . . whether it be in journeys across the ocean, or in the service of the battleflag, so much the better will it be for us. For when the German has once learned to direct his glance upon what is distant and great, the pettiness which surrounds him in daily life on all sides will disappear. . . .

As head of the empire I therefore rejoice over every citizen, whether from Hamburg, Bremen, or Lubeck, who goes forth with this large outlook and seeks new points where we can drive in the nail on which to hang our armour.

Manifest Destiny: The Annexation of Texas (1845)

JOHN LOUIS O'SULLIVAN

Texas is now ours. . . . It is wholly untrue, and unjust to ourselves, the pretence that the Annexation has been a measure of spoliation, unrightful and unrighteous—of military conquest under forms of peace and law—of territorial aggrandizement at the expense of justice, and justice due by a double sanctity to the weak. This view of the question is wholly unfounded, and has been before so amply refuted in these pages, as well as in a thousand other modes, that we shall not again dwell upon it. The independence of Texas was complete and absolute. It was an independence, not only in fact but of right. . . .

Texas has been absorbed into the Union in the inevitable fulfillment of the general law which is rolling our population westward; the connection of which with that ratio of growth in population which is destined within a hundred years to swell our numbers to the enormous population of two hundred and fifty millions (if not more), is too evident to leave us in doubt of the manifest design of Providence in regard to the occupation of this continent. It was disintegrated from Mexico in the natural course of events, by a process perfectly legitimate on its own part, blameless on ours; and in which all the censures due to wrong, perfidy and folly, rest on Mexico alone. And possessed as it was by a population which was in truth but a colonial detachment from our own, and which was still bound by myriad ties of the very heartstrings to its old relations, domestic and political, their incorporation into the Union was not only inevitable, but the most natural, right and proper thing in the world—and it is only astonishing that there should be any among ourselves to say it nay. . . .

California will, probably, next fall away from the loose adhesion which, in such a country as Mexico, holds a remote province in a slight equivocal kind of dependence on the metropolis. Imbecile and distracted, Mexico never can exert any real governmental authority over such a country. A population will soon be in actual occupation of California, over which it will be idle for Mexico to dream of dominion. They will necessarily become independent. Whether they will then attach themselves to our Union or not, is not to be predicted with any certainty. Unless the projected railroad across the continent to the Pacific be carried into effect, perhaps they may not; though even in that case, the day is not distant when the Empires of

John Louis O'Sullivan, *The United States Magazine and Democratic Review*, vol. 17, no. 85, 1845.

the Atlantic and Pacific would again flow together into one, as soon as their inland border should approach each other. . . .

Away then with all idle French talk of balances of power on the American Continent. There is no growth in Spanish America! Whatever progress of population there may be in the British Canada, is only for their own early severance of their present colonial relation to the little island three thousand miles across the Atlantic; soon to be followed by Annexation, and destined to swell the still accumulating momentum of our progress. And whosoever may hold the balance, though they should cast into the opposite scale all the bayonets and cannon, not only of France and England, but of Europe entire, how would it kick the beam against the simple solid weight of the two hundred millions—destined to gather beneath the flutter of the stripes and stars, in the fast hastening year of the Lord 1945!

A Criticism of British Imperialism (1900)

WILFRID SCAWEN BLUNT

The next selections are entries in the diary of Wilfrid Scawen Blunt (1840–1922), a diplomat and poet who ardently opposed British imperialism in Egypt, India, and Ireland. He was one of several who resisted the attractions of power and glory and advocated the right of national self-determination.

22nd Dec., 1900—The old century is very nearly out, and leaves the world in a pretty pass, and the British Empire is playing the devil in it as never an empire before on so large a scale. We may live to see its fall. All the nations of Europe are making the same heel upon earth in China, massacring and pillaging and raping in the captured cities as outrageously as in the Middle Ages. The Emperor of Germany gives the word for slaughter and the Pope looks on and approves. In South Africa our troops are burning farms under Kitchener's command, and the Queen and the two houses of Parliament, and the bench of bishops thank God publicly and vote money for the work. The Americans are spending fifty millions a year on slaughtering Filipinos; the King of the Belgians has invested his whole fortune on the Congo, where he is brutalizing the Negroes to fill his pockets. The French and Italians for the moment are playing a less prominent part in the slaughter, but their inactivity grieves them. The whole white race is reveling openly in violence, as though it had never pretended to be Christian. God's equal curse be on them all! So ends the famous nineteenth century into which we were so proud to have been born. . . .

31st Dec., 1900—I bid good-bye to the old century, may it rest in peace as it has lived in war. Of the new century I prophesy nothing except that it will

Wilfrid Scawen Blunt, *My Diaries: Being a Personal Narrative of Events 1888–1914,* vol. 1 (New York: Alfred A. Knopf, 1921), pp. 375–377. Reprinted by permission of the publisher.

see the decline of the British Empire. Other worse empires will rise perhaps in its place, but I shall not live to see the day. It all seems a very little matter here in Egypt, with the pyramids watching us as they watched Joseph, when, as a young man four thousand years ago, perhaps in this very garden, he walked and gazed at the sunset behind them, wondering about the future just as I did this evening. And so, poor wicked nineteenth century, farewell!

Interpretations of Imperialism

This section is composed of classic interpretations of imperialism and seeks to investigate why man, in an abstract sense, is seemingly determined to take over territory at the expense of others. Is it a part of human nature to possess what is not yours? Or is nationalism, which promotes unity and energy, the root of imperialism? Or is the primary motive the desire for economic gain? More specifically, does capitalism, by its very nature, cause imperialism? To what extent is war a concomitant of imperialism, a factor in the progress of civilization? The following opinions span a wide chasm of interpretation from Marxist thought to that of the Social Darwinists. The first two selections are by the English economist John Hobson (1858–1940), whose analysis of imperialism became the standard of comparison. V. I. Lenin (1870–1924), a disciple of Karl Marx and leader of the Russian revolution of 1917, attacked imperialism as "a special stage of capitalism" in his much debated analysis. The next selection is by Joseph Schumpeter, an Austrian-born economist, who argued that imperialism was an essential aspect of human nature. Finally, Charles Morris, a popularizer of Social Darwinist theories, discusses war as a progressive force in civilization.

Nationalism and Imperialism (1902)

JOHN HOBSON

Nationalism is a plain highway to internationalism, and if it manifests divergence we may well suspect a perversion of its nature and its purpose. Such a perversion is imperialism, in which nations trespassing beyond the limits of facile assimilation transform the wholesome stimulative rivalry of varied national types into the cutthroat struggle of competing empires.

   Not only does aggressive imperialism defeat the movement toward internationalism by fostering animosities among competing empires: its attacks upon the liberties and the existence of weaker or lower races stimulate in

John Hobson, *Imperialism: A Study*, 3rd ed. (London: George Allen and Unwin, 1938), pp. 9–10. Reprinted by permission of the publisher.

them a corresponding excess of national self-consciousness. A nationalism that bristles with resentment and is all astrain with the passion of self-defense is only less perverted from its natural genius than the nationalism which glows with the animus of greed and self-aggrandisement at the expense of others. From this aspect aggressive imperialism is an artificial stimulation of nationalism in peoples too foreign to be absorbed and too compact to be permanently crushed. We have welded Africanderdom into just such a strong dangerous nationalism, and we have joined with other nations in creating a resentful nationalism hitherto unknown in China. The injury to nationalism in both cases consists in converting a cohesive, pacific, internal force into an exclusive, hostile force, a perversion of the true power and use of nationality. The worst and most certain result is the retardation of internationalism. The older nationalism was primarily an inclusive sentiment; its natural relation to the same sentiment in another people was lack of sympathy, not open hostility; there was no inherent antagonism to prevent nationalities from growing and thriving side by side. Such in the main was the nationalism of the earlier nineteenth century, and the politicians of free trade had some foundation for their dream of a quick growth of effective, profitable, intercommunication of goods and ideas among nations recognizing a just harmony of interests in free peoples. . . .

Economics and Imperialism (1902)

JOHN HOBSON

What is the direct economic outcome of imperialism? A great expenditure of public money upon ships, guns, military and naval equipment and stores, growing and productive of enormous profits when a war, or an alarm of war, occurs; new public loans and important fluctuations in the home and foreign bourses; more posts for soldiers and sailors and in the diplomatic and consular services; improvement of foreign investments by the substitution of the British flag for a foreign flag; acquisition of markets for certain classes of exports, and some protection and assistance for trades representing British houses in these manufactures; employment for engineers, missionaries, speculative miners, ranchers, and other emigrants. . . .

In all the professions, military and civil, the army, diplomacy, the church, the bar, teaching and engineering, Greater Britain serves for an overflow, relieving the congestion of the home market and offering chances to more reckless or adventurous members, while it furnishes a convenient limbo for damaged characters and careers. The actual amount of profitable employment thus furnished by our recent acquisitions is inconsiderable, but it arouses that disproportionate interest which always

John Hobson, *Imperialism: A Study*, 3rd ed. (London: George Allen and Unwin, 1938), pp. 48, 51, 85–86, 88–89, 93, 109. Reprinted by permission of the publisher.

attaches to the margin of employment. To extend this margin is a powerful motive in imperialism.

These influences, primarily economic, though not unmixed with other sentimental motives, are particularly operative in military, clerical, academic, and civil service circles, and furnish an interested bias toward imperialism throughout the educated classes. . . .

Thus we reach the conclusion that imperialism is the endeavor of the great controllers of industry to broaden the channel for the flow of their surplus wealth by seeking foreign markets and foreign investments to take off the goods and capital they cannot sell or use at home.

The fallacy of the supposed inevitability of imperial expansion as a necessary outlet for progressive industry is now manifest. It is not industrial progress that demands the opening up of new markets and areas of investment, but maldistribution of consuming power which prevents the absorption of commodities and capital within the country. The oversaving which is the economic root of imperialism is found by analysis to consist of rents, monopoly profits, and other unearned or excessive elements of income, which, not being earned by labor of head or hand, have no legitimate *raison d'être*. Having no natural relation to effort of production, they impel their recipients to no corresponding satisfaction of consumption: they form a surplus wealth, which, having no proper place in the normal economy of production and consumption, tends to accumulate as excessive savings. Let any turn in the tide of politico-economic forces divert from these owners their excess of income and make it flow, either to the workers in higher wages, or to the community in taxes, so that it will be spent instead of being saved, serving in either of these ways to swell the tide of consumption—there will be no need to fight for foreign markets or foreign areas of investment. . . .

There is no necessity to open up new foreign markets; the home markets are capable of indefinite expansion. Whatever is produced in England can be consumed in England, provided that the "income," or power to demand commodities, is properly distributed. This only appears untrue because of the unnatural and unwholesome specialization to which this country has been subjected, based upon a bad distribution of economic resources, which had induced an overgrowth of certain manufacturing trades for the express purpose of effecting foreign sales. . . . An economy that assigns to the "possessing" classes an excess of consuming power which they cannot use, and cannot convert into really serviceable capital, is a dog-in-the-manger policy. The social reforms which deprive the possession classes of their surplus will not, therefore, inflict upon them the real injury they dread; they can only use this surplus by forcing on their country a wrecking policy of imperialism. The only safety of nations lies in removing the unearned increments of income from the possessing classes, and adding them to the wage income of the working classes or to the public income, in order that they may be spent in raising the standard of consumption. . . . It is idle to attack imperialism or militarism as political expedients or policies unless the axe is laid at the economic root of the tree, and the classes for whose interest imperialism works are shorn of the surplus revenues which seek this outlet.

Imperialism with its wars and its armaments is undeniably responsible for the growing debts of the Continental nations, and while the unparalleled industrial prosperity of Great Britain and the isolation of the United States have enabled these great nations to escape this ruinous competition during the recent decades, the period of their immunity is over; both, committed as they seem to an imperialism without limit, will succumb more and more to the money-lending classes dressed as imperialists and patriots.

Imperialism: The Highest Stage of Capitalism (1916)

V. I. LENIN

The enormous dimensions of finance capital concentrated in a few hands and creating an extremely extensive and close network of ties and relationships which subordinate not only the small and medium, but also even the very small capitalists and small masters, on the one hand, and the intense struggle waged against other national state groups of financiers for the division of the world and domination over other countries, on the other hand, cause wholesale transition of the possessing classes to the side of imperialism. The signs of the times are a "general" enthusiasm regarding its prospects, a passionate defence of imperialist ideology also penetrates the working class. There is no Chinese Wall between it and the other classes. The leaders of the so-called "Social-Democratic" Party of Germany are today justly called "social-imperialists," that is, socialists in words and imperialists in deeds; but as early as 1902, Hobson noted the existence of "Fabian Imperialists" who belonged to the opportunist Fabian Society in England.

Bourgeois scholars and publicists usually come out in defence of imperialism in a somewhat veiled form, and obscure its complete domination and its profound roots; they strive to concentrate attention on partial and secondary details and do their very best to distract attention from the main issue by means of ridiculous schemes for "reform," such as police supervision of the trusts and banks, etc. Less frequently, cynical and frank imperialists speak out and are bold enough to admit the absurdity of the idea of reforming the fundamental features of imperialism. . . .

The question as to whether it is possible to reform the basis of imperialism, whether to go forward to the accentuation and deepening of the antagonisms, which it engenders, or backwards, towards allaying these antagonisms, is a fundamental question in the critique of imperialism. As a

V. I. Lenin, *Imperialism: The Highest Stage of Capitalism* (New York: International Publishers Co., 1939), pp. 109–111, 123–124. Reprinted by permission of the publisher.

consequence of the fact that the political features of imperialism are reaction all along the line, and increased national oppression, resulting from the oppression of the financial oligarchy and the elimination of free competition, a petty-bourgeois–democratic opposition has been rising against imperialism in almost all imperialist countries since the beginning of the twentieth century. . . .

In the United States, the imperialist war waged against Spain in 1898 stirred up the opposition of the "anti-imperialists," the last of the Mohicans of bourgeois democracy. They declared this war to be "criminal"; they denounced the annexation of foreign territories as being a violation of the Constitution, and denounced the "Jingo treachery" by means of which Aguinaldo, leader of the native Filipinos, was deceived (the Americans promised him the independence of his country, but later they landed troops and annexed it). They quoted the words of Lincoln: "When the white man governs himself, that is self-government, but when he governs himself and also governs another man, that is more than self-government—that is despotism."

But while all this criticism shrank from recognising the indissoluble bond between imperialism and the trusts, and, therefore, between imperialism and the very foundations of capitalism; while it shrank from joining up with the forces engendered by large-scale capitalism and its development—it remained a "pious wish." . . .

We have seen that the economic quintessence of imperialism is monopoly capitalism. This very fact determines its place in history, for monopoly that grew up on the basis of free competition, and precisely out of free competition, is the transition from the capitalist system to a higher social-economic order. We must take special note of the four principal forms of monopoly, or the four principal manifestations of monopoly capitalism, which are characteristic of the epoch under review.

Firstly, monopoly arose out of the concentration of production at a very advanced stage of development. This refers to the monopolist capitalist combines, cartels, syndicates and trusts. We have seen the important part that these play in modern economic life. At the beginning of the twentieth century, monopolies acquired complete supremacy in the advanced countries. And although the first steps towards the formation of the cartels were first taken by countries enjoying the protection of high tariffs (Germany, America), Great Britain, with her system of free trade, was not far behind in revealing the same basic phenomenon, namely, the birth of monopoly out of the concentration of production.

Secondly, monopolies have accelerated the capture of the most important sources of raw materials, especially for the coal and iron industries, which are the basic and most highly cartelised industries in capitalist society. The monopoly of the most important sources of raw materials has enormously increased the power of big capital, and has sharpened the antagonism between cartelised and non-cartelised industry.

Thirdly, monopoly has sprung from the banks. The banks have developed from modest intermediary enterprises into the monopolists of finance capital. Some three to five of the biggest banks in each of the foremost capitalist countries have achieved the "personal union" of industrial and bank capital, and have concentrated in their hands the disposal of thousands upon thousands of millions which form the greater part of the capital and income of entire countries. A financial oligarchy, which throws a close net of relations of dependence over all the economic and political institutions of contemporary bourgeois society without exception—such is the most striking manifestation of this monopoly.

Fourthly, the monopoly has grown out of colonial policy. To the numerous "old" motives of colonial policy, finance capital has added the struggle for the sources of raw materials, for the export capital, for "spheres of influence," i.e., for spheres for profitable deals, concessions, monopolist profits and so on; in fine, for economic territory in general. When the colonies of the European powers in Africa, for instance, comprised only one-tenth of that territory (as was the case in 1876), colonial policy was able to develop by methods other than those of monopoly—by the "free grabbing" of territories, so to speak. But when nine-tenths of Africa had been seized (approximately by 1900), when the whole world had been divided up, there was inevitably ushered in a period of colonial monopoly and, consequently, a period of particularly intense struggle for the division and the redivision of the world.

The extent to which monopolist capital has intensified all the contradictions of capitalism is generally known. It is sufficient to mention the high cost of living and the oppression of the cartels. This intensification of contradictions constitutes the most powerful driving force of the transitional period of history, which began from the time of the definite victory of world finance capital.

Monopolies, oligarchy, the striving for domination instead of the striving for liberty, the exploitation of an increasing number of small or weak nations by an extremely small group of the richest or most powerful nations—all these have given birth to those distinctive characteristics of imperialism which compel us to define it as parasitic or decaying capitalism. . . .

The receipt of high monopoly profits by the capitalists in one of the numerous branches of industry, in one of numerous countries, etc., makes it economically possible for them to corrupt certain sections of the working class, and for a time a fairly considerable minority, and win them to the side of the bourgeoisie of a given industry or nation against all other. The intensification of antagonisms between imperialist nations for the division of the world increases this striving. And so there is created that bond between imperialism and opportunism, which revealed itself first and most clearly in England, owing to the fact that certain features of imperialist development were observable there much earlier than in other countries. . . .

From all that has been said . . . on the economic nature of imperialism, it follows that we must define it as capitalism in transition, or, more precisely, as moribund capitalism.

Imperialism and Capitalism (1919)

JOSEPH SCHUMPETER

The competitive system [capitalism] absorbs the full energies of most of the people at all economic levels. Constant application, attention, and concentration of energy are the conditions of survival within it, primarily in the specifically economic professions, but also in other activities organized on their model. There is much less excess energy to be vented in war and conquest than in any precapitalist society. What excess energy there is flows largely into industry itself, accounts for its shining figures—the type of the captain of industry—and for the rest is applied to art, science, and the social struggle. In a purely capitalist world, what was once energy for war becomes simply energy for labor of every kind. Wars of conquest and adventurism in foreign policy in general are bound to be regarded as troublesome distractions, destructive of life's meaning, a diversion from the accustomed and therefore "true" task.

A purely capitalist world therefore can offer no fertile soil to imperialist impulses. That does not mean that it cannot still maintain an interest in imperialist expansion. . . . The point is that its people are likely to be essentially of an unwarlike disposition. Hence we must expect that anti-imperialist tendencies will show themselves wherever capitalism penetrates the economy and, through the economy, the mind of modern nations—most strongly, of course, where capitalism itself is strongest. . . . The facts that follow are cited to show that this expectation, which flows from our theory, is in fact justified.

1. Throughout the world of capitalism, and specifically among the elements formed by capitalism in modern social life, there has arisen a fundamental opposition to war, expansion, cabinet diplomacy, armaments, and socially entrenched professional armies. This opposition had its origin in the society that first turned capitalist—England—and arose coincidentally with that country's capitalist development. . . . True, pacifism as a matter of principle had existed before, though only among a few small religious sects. But modern pacifism, in its political foundations if not its derivation, is unquestionably a phenomenon of the capitalist world.

2. Wherever capitalism penetrated, peace parties of such strength arose that virtually every war meant a political struggle on the domestic

Joseph Schumpeter, *Imperialism and Social Classes* (Cambridge, Mass.: Harvard University Press, 1951), pp. 90–96. Copyright © 1951 by the Trustees of Elizabeth B. Schumpeter. Reprinted by permission of the President and Fellows of Harvard College and the Harvard University Press.

scene. . . . In the distant past, imperialism had needed no disguise whatever, and in the absolute autocracies only a very transparent one; but today imperialism is carefully hidden from public view. . . . Every expansionist urge must be carefully related to a concrete goal. All this is primarily a matter of political phraseology, to be sure. But the necessity for this phraseology is a symptom of the popular attitude. . . .

3. The type of industrial worker created by capitalism is always vigorously anti-imperialist. In the individual case, skillful agitation may persuade the working masses to approve or remain neutral—a concrete goal or interest in self-defense always playing the main part—but no initiative for a forcible policy of expansion ever emanates from this quarter. . . .

4. Despite manifest resistance on the part of powerful elements, the capitalist age has seen the development of methods for preventing war, for the peaceful settlement of disputes among states. . . .

5. Among all capitalist economies, that of the United States is least burdened with precapitalist elements, survivals, reminiscences, and power factors. Certainly we cannot expect to find imperialist tendencies altogether lacking even in the United States, for the immigrants came from Europe with their convictions fully formed, and the environment certainly favored the revival of instincts of pugnacity. But we can conjecture that among all countries the United States is likely to exhibit the weakest imperialist trend. This turns out to be the truth. . . . [T]he United States was the first advocate of disarmament and arbitration. It was the first to conclude treaties concerning arms limitations (1817) and arbitral courts (first attempt in 1797). . . . Since 1908 such treaties have been concluded with twenty-two states. In the course of the nineteenth century, the United States had numerous occasions for war, including instances that were well calculated to test its patience. It made almost no use of such occasions. . . .

These facts are scarcely in dispute. And since they fit into the picture of the mode of life which we have recognized to be the necessary product of capitalism . . . it follows that capitalism is by nature anti-imperialist. Hence we cannot readily derive from it such imperialist tendencies as actually exist, but must evidently see them only as alien elements, carried into the world of capitalism from the outside, supported by non-capitalist factors in modern life.

War and Civilization (1895)

CHARLES MORRIS

It may seem to many readers absurd to speak of war as a helpful agency in civilization. It is the general impression that a state of profound peace, with its consequent agricultural and mechanical industries, is most conducive to

Charles Morris, "War As a Factor in Civilization," *Popular Science Monthly* 47 (1895), pp. 823, 826.

human advancement. Warfare is usually looked upon as simply destructive, and as destitute of any redeeming feature; and yet I venture to claim
that all the civilizations to-day existing were in their origin largely the
results of ancient wars; and that peace, in the long past of the human race,
was almost a synonym for social and intellectual stagnation. . . .

If we ask what is the philosophy of this, the answer may not be difficult
to reach. Unlike the fixed conservatism of peace, war introduces new conditions, new foundations for human thought, on which the edifice of future civilization may be erected; and, breaking up the isolation of peace, it
spreads these conditions throughout the world, making distant nations
participants in their influences. The progress of mankind means simply the
development of the human mind. Ideas are the seeds of civilization, and
under whatever form it appears the idea must be born first, the embodi-
ment must come afterward. In seeking for the causes of advancement,
then, we must seek for the sources of new ideas; but, as experience lies at
the root of ideas, new ideas can only arise from new experiences. Whence,
then, do we derive our experiences? No isolated individual can learn much
of himself. His own powers of observation and thought are limited. Our
minds can only rapidly develop when we avail ourselves of the experience
of others. In this way only can they become storehouses of new thoughts.
There is a common stock of such thought abroad in the world, from which
we derive the great mass of the ideas which we call our own. And, obviously, that mind will be most developed which comes into contact with
and assimilates the greatest number of these thoughts.

The same holds good with nations. An isolated nation is in the same
position as an isolated individual. Its experiences are limited, its ideas few
and narrow in range. Its thoughts move in one fixed channel, and the
other powers of its mind are apt to become virtually aborted. An isolated
nation, then, is not likely rapidly to gain new ideas. Yet peace, in all barbarian and semi-civilized nations, seems to tend strongly toward this condition
of isolation; and such isolation in its conservative influence is a fatal bar to
any wide or continuous progress. The long persistence of one form of
government, of one condition of social customs, of one line of thought,
tends to produce that uniformity of character which is so fatally opposed to
any width of development of breadth of mental grasp. From uniformity
arises stagnation. Its final result is a dead pause in mental advancement.
Variety of influences and conditions alone can yield a healthy and vigorous
growth of thought. The movement of the national mind in any one line
must soon cease. Its limit is quickly reached, unless it be aided by development in other directions.

STUDY QUESTIONS

1. What are the main ideas contained in Giuseppe Mazzini's address "The
   Duties of Man"? This piece was directed toward Italian workers. How
   does it appeal to them specifically? How does Garibaldi's speech to the

Italians differ from that of Mazzini? How is Garibaldi *using* nationalism?

2. Why does Johann Gottlieb Fichte refer to Rome and the Germanic tribes to such an extent? What specifically does he demonstrate by these examples? How does he define the German "people"?

3. According to Bismarck, why must Germany be armed? Does Bismarck advocate imperialism? How does he use God in his arguments? How does this relate to nationalism? How is religion (specifically Christianity) used in other sources as justification for imperial expansion?

4. Explain Social Darwinism and give several specific examples from the reading selections that demonstrate its practice and use as justification for imperial expansion. What phrases and ideas are consistently used? What are some of Karl Pearson's arguments? Are they compelling?

5. Discuss the "mandate system." What was it and how is it evident in the speech by Joseph Chamberlin regarding Britain's duty in Egypt? Cite specific phrases in this regard.

6. Analyze Senator Beveridge's speech on American control of the Philippines. What does he advocate and what are the specific arguments he uses to justify his beliefs? Note especially how he uses the abstraction of "history." Is this a *logical,* if not satisfying, argument? Why would it be appealing to many? How does Kipling's poem "The White Man's Burden" complement Beveridge's statements? How do this source and other sources in this chapter define imperialism as an agent of "progress and civilization"?

7. How does Sir Frederick Lugard connect nationalism with the economic argument for imperialism? How does he respond to the arguments presented by critics of imperialism? How does he justify his support of imperial expansion?

8. Explain the concept of "manifest destiny." What is "Providence" and how is it used to justify expansion into Indian lands and the annexation of Texas? What other arguments does O'Sullivan use for justification?

9. What does Wilfrid Blunt have to say about the civility of British imperialism or American or European imperialism, for that matter? What specific justifications for imperialism, presented in earlier accounts, do his comments attack?

10. Discuss the various interpretations of imperialism. In your opinion, based on the evidence provided, does nationalism necessarily cause imperialism, or is economic profit a more important factor? What are Hobson's and Lenin's thoughts on the subject? Compare these with Schumpeter's beliefs. Which are more firmly grounded in the evidence and therefore more persuasive? Do you agree or disagree with the arguments of Charles Morris on war as a factor of civilization? Why?

7

The Great War (1914–1918)

The next dreadful thing to a battle lost is a battle won.

—Arthur Wellesley, Duke of Wellington

There never was a good war or a bad peace.

—Benjamin Franklin

Only a general who was a barbarian would send his men to certain death against the concentrated power of my new gun.

—Hiram Maxim (Inventor of the Machine Gun)

Diplomats are just as essential to starting a war as soldiers are for finishing it. . . . You take diplomacy out of war and the whole thing would fall flat in a week.

—Will Rogers

After the defeat of Napoleon at the Battle of Waterloo in 1815, it was decided by the victors at the Congress of Vienna that Europe had to be governed by a policy of deterrence that resisted dominance by any one country. Nations required comparable strength in order to maintain the balance of power and thus preserve the peace. Great Britain led the way and applied this policy successfully throughout the nineteenth century. During this time, however, Europe was changing. The Industrial Revolution had increased the demand for trade, and various countries sought markets in Africa and the East, establishing hegemony over a region by military force. Imperialism and competition abroad affected the sense of security and the balance of power that were crucial to the preservation of peace at home. In addition, new factors were being introduced that further threatened to disrupt the balance.

The first serious threat to the *Pax Britannica* of the nineteenth century came from the expansion of industry and the accompanying scientific progress. In the first decade of the twentieth century, new weapons were being developed, as were more rapid forms of communication and transportation, including the telegraph, the automobile, the railway, and the steamship. These technological advancements presented new possibilities for highly mobilized warfare that could be better coordinated and managed.

The second serious threat to the balance of European power in the late nineteenth century was Germany. By 1870, the Prussians had unified north and west Germany through a policy of "blood and iron." The various regions of Germany had always been disunited, defying such masters as the Romans, Charlemagne, the Holy Roman Emperors, and Napoleon. But Kaiser Wilhelm I of Prussia (1797–1888), together with his master statesman, Otto von Bismarck (1815–1898), and his general, Count Helmut von Moltke, made highly effective use of the military capabilities of a thoroughly disciplined and well-supported army. To achieve unification, Prussia had beaten and humiliated the French in 1870 and succeeded in forging a unified German Reich. The balance of power had been upset and the lesson was clear: No nation in Europe could feel secure without training all of its young men for war, establishing a system of reserves, and creating a general staff that would prepare plans for potential wars and oversee a scheme for mobilization.

The concept of mobilization is very important in understanding why Europe and the world went to war. By 1914, every continental power had a complex plan and timetable for mobilizing against the most likely opponent or combination of enemies. When a country mobilized for war, its reserve troops were called to active duty, placed in the field, and supported with necessary rations, equipment, and armament. Timing was essential. Full mobilization took weeks, and it was important to get the process started before your enemy was ready to commit to such a policy. Hence the beginning of hostilities came when the various chiefs of state were convinced that military "necessity" required a mobilization order and that further delay would spell defeat by allowing the opponent to gain a military advantage that could not be overcome. Since mobilization involved a radical shift of the economy to maximum production and since troop movements could be detected by other nations within hours, the mobilization order could not be rescinded without the prospect of diplomatic and economic disaster. William H. McNeill, in *The Rise of the West*, notes that "the first weeks of World War I presented the amazing spectacle of vast human machines operating in a truly inhuman fashion and moving at least approximately according to predetermined and irreversible plans. The millions of persons composing the rival machines behaved almost as though they had lost individual will and intelligence." The "predetermined and irreversible" plans were centered on a military theory by Karl von Clausewitz that was accepted by all the general staffs of Europe: A swift and decisive battle that led to the initial destruction of the enemy's forces would achieve ultimate success. None planned for a long war—three or four months at best.

Thus, the nations of Europe were powderkegs waiting to go off when in June 1914 the heir to the Austro-Hungarian Empire, the Archduke Franz Ferdinand, was assassinated at Sarajevo. The diplomats talked and then the armies mobilized one by one. The "guns of August" soon enveloped Europe in a war that was to last not four months but four years. Over 8.5 million people were killed, with a total casualty count of over 37.5 million.

This chapter seeks to give an overall picture of World War I, or what has been more accurately called the Great War. This was war on a world scale, involving hostilities in Africa and the Balkans, as well as an American presence. And it was war on some of the cruelest terms. Rules were changing. There were no longer strict orders to exempt the civilian population from harm. Nor were there moral constraints on the use of submarines, machine guns, and poisonous gas; all became permanent fixtures. The Great War stands unequaled in terms of blood sacrificed for miserable accomplishment. To die for a "victory" of 100 yards of land needed justification, which was rarely forthcoming. The questions are disturbing and perhaps unanswerable: Why did commanders send their men repeatedly "over the top" of the trenches, across "no man's land," and into the bloody rain of machine gun fire? Why was this slaughter of human life condoned by the diplomats and even the soldiers themselves? Why had Europe lost an entire generation of men?

When the war ended in 1918, the world of the nineteenth century had been forever altered. The thin veneer of civilization had been shattered and the nations of Europe had difficulty defining what had happened and why. Europe would be led out of this abyss of disillusionment and despair by those promising order and respect: Benito Mussolini and Adolf Hitler.

The Road to War

Assassination at Sarajevo

For decades the Balkan areas of Bosnia and Serbia had been in turmoil, causing the neighboring Austro-Hungarian empire great anxiety. The Serbs had their own language and customs and had always been wary of

Austrian attempts to unify the region politically and culturally. Several extremist organizations, inspired by patriotic idealism, sought to eliminate the Austro-Hungarian presence through terror and violence. Among these organizations was the pan-Serbian nationalist group "Union or Death," also known as "The Black Hand." Statutes of this representative group are included in the first selection.

The second selection recounts the famous assassination of the heir to the Austro-Hungarian throne, Archduke Franz Ferdinand. The murderer, a nineteen-year-old Serb student named Gavrilo Princip, was a member of a patriotic society similar to "The Black Hand," called *Narodna Odbrana*. One of the leaders of this organization who was arrested along with Princip gave this first-hand account of the assassination, an event that propelled the world to war.

Statutes of "The Black Hand"

Article 1. This organization has been created with the object of realising the national ideal: The union of all the Serbs. All Serbs without distinction of sex, religion, place of birth, and all who are sincerely devoted to this cause, may become members.

Article 2. This organization prefers terrorist action to intellectual propaganda and for this reason must be kept absolutely secret from persons who do not belong to it.

Article 3. This organization bears the name "Union or Death."

Article 4. To accomplish its task, the organization:

1. Brings influence to bear on Government circles, on the various social classes and on the whole social life of the Kingdom of Serbia, regarded as Piedmont.
2. Organises revolutionary action in all territories inhabited by Serbs.
3. Outside the frontiers of Serbia uses every means available to fight the adversaries of this idea.
4. Maintains amicable relations with all states, peoples, organisations, and individuals who entertain feelings of friendship towards Serbia and the Serbian element.
5. Lends help and support in every way possible to all people and all organisations struggling for their national liberation and for their union.

Article 5. A central Committee having its headquarters at Belgrade is at the head of this organisation and exercises executive authority. . . .

From p. 309 of *Readings in European International Relations* by W. Henry Cooke and Edith P. Stickney. Copyright, 1931, by Harper & Row, Publishers, Inc.; renewed 1959 by W. Henry Cooke. Reprinted by permission of Harper & Row, Publishers, Inc.

Article 25. Members of the organisation are not known to each other personally. It is only the members of the Central Committee who are known to one another.

Article 26. In the organisation itself the members are known by numbers. Only the Central Committee at Belgrade is to know their names. . . .

Article 31. Anyone who once enters the organisation may never withdraw from it. . . .

Article 33. When the Central Committee at Belgrade has pronounced penalty of death [on one of the members] the only matter of importance is that the execution take place without fail. . . .

The Plot and Murder (June 28, 1914)

A tiny clipping from a newspaper, mailed without comment from a secret band of terrorists in Zagreb, capital of Croatia, to their comrades in Belgrade, was the torch which set the world afire with war in 1914. That bit of paper wrecked old, proud empires. It gave birth to new, free nations.

I was one of the members of the terrorist band in Belgrade which received it.

The little clipping declared that the Austrian Archduke Francis Ferdinand would visit Sarajevo, the capital of Bosnia, June 28, to direct army maneuvers in the neighboring mountains.

It reached our meeting place, the cafe called Zeatna Moruna, one night the latter part of April, 1914. To understand how great a sensation that little piece of paper caused among us when it was passed from hand to hand almost in silence, and how greatly it inflamed our hearts, it is necessary to explain just why the *Narodna Odbrana* existed, the kind of men that were in it, and the significance of that date, June 28, on which the Archduke dared to enter Sarajevo.

As every one knows, the old Austrio-Hungarian Empire was built by conquest and intrigues, by sales and treacheries, which held in subjugation many peoples who were neither Austrian nor Hungarian. It taxed them heavily; it diverted the products of their toil to serve the wealth of the master state. It interfered in their old freedom by a multiplicity of laws administered with arrogance.

Several years before the war, a little group of us, thirty-five in all, living in several Bosnian and Herzegovinian cities and villages, formed the *Narodna Odbrana,* the secret society, the aim of which was to work for freedom from Austria and a union with Serbia. So strict was the police vigilance in Bosnia and Herzegovina that we set up our headquarters in Belgrade, the capital of our mother country.

The men who were terrorists in 1914 embraced all classes. Most of them were students. Youth is the time for the philosophy of action. There were

New York World, June 28, 1924, the North American Newspaper Alliance.

also teachers, tradesmen and peasants, artisans and even men of the upper classes were ardent patriots. They were dissimilar in everything except hatred of the oppressor.

Such were the men into whose hands the tiny bit of newsprint was sent by friends in Bosnia that April night in Belgrade. At a small table in a very humble cafe, beneath a flickering gas jet we sat and read it. There was no advice nor admonition sent with it. Only four letters and two numerals were sufficient to make us unanimous, without discussion, as to what we should do about it. They were contained in the fateful date, June 28.

How dared Francis Ferdinand, not only the representative of the oppressor but in his own person an arrogant tyrant, enter Sarajevo on that day? Such an entry was a studied insult.

June 28 is a date engraved deep in the heart of every Serb, so that the day has a name of its own. It is called the *vidovnan* [St. Vitus Day]. It is the day on which the old Serbian kingdom was conquered by the Turks at the battle of Amselfelde in 1389. It is also the day on which in the second Balkan War the Serbian armies took glorious revenge on the Turk for his old victory and for the years of enslavement. . . .

As we read that clipping in Belgrade we knew what we would do to Francis Ferdinand. We would kill him to show Austria there yet lived within its borders defiance of its rule. We would kill him to bring once more to the boiling point the fighting spirit of the revolutionaries and pave the way for revolt.

Our decision was taken almost immediately. Death to the tyrant!

Then came the matter of arranging it. To make his death certain twenty-two members of the organization were selected to carry out the sentence. At first we thought we would choose the men by lot. But here Gavrilo Princip intervened. . . . From the moment Ferdinand's death was decided upon, he took an active leadership in its planning. Upon his advice we left the deed to members of our band, who were in and around Sarajevo, under his direction and that of Gabrinovic, a linotype operator on a Serbian newspaper. Both were regarded as capable of anything in the cause. . . .

The fateful morning dawned. Two hours before Francis Ferdinand arrived in Sarajevo all the twenty-two conspirators were in their allotted positions, armed and ready. They were distributed five hundred yards apart over the whole route along which the Archduke must travel from the railroad station to the town hall.

When Francis Ferdinand and his retinue drove from the station they were allowed to pass the first two conspirators. The motor cars were driving too fast to make an attempt feasible and in the crowd were many Serbians; throwing a grenade would have killed many innocent people.

When the car passed Chabrinovic, the compositor, he threw his grenade. It hit the side of the car, but Francis Ferdinand with presence of mind threw himself back and was uninjured. Several officers riding in his attendance were injured.

The cars sped to the Town Hall and the rest of the conspirators did not interfere with them. After the reception in the Town Hall General Potiorek, the Austrian Commander, pleaded with Francis Ferdinand to leave the city, as it was seething with rebellion. The Archduke was persuaded to drive the shortest way out of the city and to go quickly.

The road to the maneuvers was shaped like the letter V, making a sharp turn at the bridge over the River Nilgacka. Francis Ferdinand's car could go fast enough until it reached this spot but here it was forced to slow down for the turn. Here Princip had taken his stand.

As the car came abreast he stepped forward from the curb, drew his automatic pistol from his coat and fired two shots. The first struck the wife of the Archduke, the Archduchess Sofia, in the abdomen. She was an expectant mother. She died instantly.

The second bullet struck the Archduke close to the heart.

He uttered only one word, "Sofia"—a call to his stricken wife. Then his head fell back and he collapsed. He died almost instantly.

The officers seized Princip. They beat him over the head with the flat of their swords. They knocked him down, they kicked him, scraped the skin from his neck with the edges of their swords, tortured him, all but killed him.

The next day they put chains on Princip's feet, which he wore till his death. . . .

I was placed in the cell next to Princip's, and when Princip was taken out to walk in the prison yard I was taken along as his companion.

By Oct. 12, the date of Princip's trial, his prison sufferings had worn him to a skeleton.

His sentence was twenty years imprisonment at hard labor, the death sentence being inapplicable because he was a minor.

Awakened in the middle of the night and told that he was to be carried off to another prison, Princip made an appeal to the prison governor:

"There is no need to carry me to another prison. My life here is already ebbing away. I suggest that you nail me to a cross and burn me alive. My flaming body will be a torch to light my people on their path to freedom."

Diplomatic Maneuvers

For several years Europe had been diplomatically divided into two rival camps. The Triple Alliance was formed in 1882 between Germany, Italy, and Austria-Hungary. In 1907, the Triple Entente was established between Great Britain, France, and Russia. Both organizations were pledged by treaty to support their respective allies militarily should their mutual interests or existence be threatened. Thus, the European world was shocked by the assassination of Archduke Franz Ferdinand. Poised on the brink of crisis, each nation took stock of its diplomatic commitments, its military arsenal, and its long-range goals. Such a slap in the face of the powerful Austro-Hungarian empire by Serbian terrorists had wide-ranging implications. Response had to be quick in order to preserve the honor and integrity of the throne and to assure that such action would not invite further insolence, which could lead to outright revolt. There were other factors to consider as well. How would Russia react to a severe stand against the Serbs? Russia, after all, was a Slavic nation and was promoting a policy that advocated the independence and cultural integrity of Balkan Slavs.

Count Leopold von Berchtold, the Austro-Hungarian Foreign Minister, sought German support in his plans to punish Serbia for the assassination of the Austrian heir. Germany would be an important ally in countering the potential hostility of Russia. On July 6, 1914, the German Kaiser, Wilhelm II, and his Chancellor, Theobold von Bethmann-Hollweg, sent the following dispatch to Vienna. Berchtold regarded this telegram as a "blank check" that guaranteed German support for whatever punishment he decided to inflict upon Serbia.

The Austrians, thus secure in their relationship with Germany, sent an ultimatum to Serbia demanding the dissolution of nationalist societies, the suppression of anti-Austrian propaganda, and permission to allow Austrian officials to aid in suppressing disorders in Serbia. The Serbian government agreed to all conditions except the last, noting that this violated Serbia's sovereignty as a nation. Austria thereupon rejected Serbia's reply, declared war, and started mobilizing her military forces.

The "Blank Check" Telegram (July 6, 1914)

CHANCELLOR THEOBOLD VON BETHMANN-HOLLWEG

His Majesty sends his thanks to the Emperor Francis Joseph for his letter and would soon answer it personally. In the meantime His Majesty desires to say that he is not blind to the danger which threatens Austria-Hungary and thus the Triple Alliance as a result of the Russian and Serbian Pan-Slavic agitation. . . . As far as concerns Serbia, His Majesty, of course, cannot interfere in the dispute now going on between Austria-Hungary and that country, as it is a matter not within his competence. The Emperor Francis Joseph may, however, rest assured that His Majesty will faithfully stand by Austria-Hungary, as is required by the obligations of his alliance and of his ancient friendship.

Max Montgelas and Walter Schucking, eds., *Outbreak of the European War: Documents Collected by Karl Kautsky* (New York: Oxford University Press, 1924), p. 79. Reprinted by permission of the Carnegie Endowment for International Peace.

Austro-Hungarian Declaration of War on Serbia (July 28, 1914)

COUNT LEOPOLD VON BERCHTOLD

[Telegraphic]

Vienna, July 28, 1914

The Royal Serbian Government not having answered in a satisfactory manner the note of July 23, 1914, presented by the Austro-Hungarian Minister at Belgrade, the Imperial and Royal Government are themselves compelled to see to the safeguarding of their rights and interests, and, with this object, to have recourse to force of arms. Austria-Hungary consequently considers herself henceforward in state of war with Serbia.

Telegram: Kaiser to Tsar (July 29, 1:45 A.M.)

KAISER WILHELM II

The Great War was, in some ways, an intensely personal war. The monarchs of Great Britain, Germany, and Russia were all cousins and had been on rather good terms for years. Personal relationships, however, were being strained as Europe drifted closer to war. The following telegrams reflect a confidence that personal communication between cousin "Willy" and cousin "Nicky" might salvage the deteriorating relationship between Germany and Russia. However, the secret telegram from the Russian Minister of Foreign Affairs, Sergei Sazonoff, to Paris suggests that war was fast becoming inevitable despite the private and perhaps naive attempts of the monarchs to control the situation.

It is with the gravest concern that I hear of the impression which the action of Austria against Serbia is creating in your country. The unscrupulous agitation that has been going on in Serbia for years has resulted in the outrageous crime, to which Archduke Francis Ferdinand fell a victim. The spirit that led Serbians to murder their own king and his wife still dominates the country. You will doubtless agree with me that we both, you and I, have a common interest as well as all Sovereigns to insist that all the persons morally responsible for the dastardly murder should receive their deserved punishment. In this case politics plays no part at all.

On the other hand, I fully understand how difficult it is for you and your Government to face the drift of your public opinion. Therefore, with regard to the hearty and tender friendship which binds us both from long

"Austro-Hungarian Declaration of War" is from Great Britain Foreign Office, *Collected Documents Relating to the Outbreak of the European War*, 1915: Serbian Blue Book, no. 45, p. 392.

"Telegram: Kaiser to Tsar" and "Telegram: Tsar to Kaiser" are from Max Montgelas and Walter Schucking, eds., *Outbreak of the European War: Documents Collected by Karl Kautsky* (New York: Oxford University Press, 1924), pp. 295–297. Reprinted by permission of the Carnegie Endowment for International Peace.

ago with firm ties, I am exerting my utmost influence to induce the Austrians to deal straightly to arrive to a satisfactory understanding with you. I confidently hope that you will help me in my efforts to smooth over difficulties that may still arise.

Your very sincere and devoted friend and cousin,

WILLY

Telegram: Tsar to Kaiser (July 29, 8:20 P.M.)

TSAR NICHOLAS II

Am glad you are back. In this serious moment, I appeal to you to help me. An ignoble war has been declared to a weak country. The indignation in Russia shared fully by me is enormous. I foresee that very soon I shall be overwhelmed by the pressure forced upon me and be forced to take extreme measures which will lead to war. To try and avoid such a calamity as a European war I beg you in the name of our old friendship to do what you can to stop your allies from going too far.

NICKY

Secret Telegram of the Russian Minister of Foreign Affairs to the Russian Ambassador at Paris (July 29, 1914)

SERGEI SAZONOFF

No. 1551 Urgent

Saint Petersburg, July 29, 1914

Communicate to London

The German Ambassabor informed me today of the decision of his Government to mobilize its forces if Russia did not stop its military preparations. Now, these preparations have been begun by us only as a consequence of the mobilization of eight corps which the Austrians have already effected and of the evident unwillingness on the part of the Austrians to accept any means of arriving at a peaceful settlement of their differences with Serbia. As we cannot comply with the wishes of Germany, we have no alternative but to hasten on our own military preparations and to envisage the inevitable eventuality of war. Please inform the French Government and at the same time express to it our sincere gratitude for the declaration which the French Ambassador made to me on its behalf, to the effect that

From pp. 370–371 of *Readings in European International Relations* by W. Henry Cooke and Edith P. Stickney. Copyright, 1931, by Harper & Row, Publishers, Inc.; renewed 1959 by W. Henry Cooke. Reprinted by permission of Harper & Row, Publishers, Inc.

we could count fully upon the support of France. In the present circumstances this declaration is particularly valuable to us. It will be extremely desirable that England join France without loss of time, for only in this way can she succeed in anticipating a dangerous rupture of the European equilibrium.

Russia Enters the War

Kaiser Wilhelm II was known for his bellicose personality. He dearly loved his military forces and felt a personal responsibility as a self-styled divine-right monarch. The following excerpt from a speech delivered two days after his telegram to Nicholas reveals his intentions. On August 1, Germany declared war on Russia.

Speech from the Balcony of the Royal Palace (July 31, 1914)

KAISER WILHELM II

A momentous hour has struck for Germany. Envious rivals everywhere force us to legitimate defense. The sword has been forced into our hands. I hope that in the event that my efforts to the very last moment do not succeed in bringing our opponents to reason and in preserving peace, we may use the sword, with the help of God, so that we may sheathe it again with honor. War will demand enormous sacrifices by the German people, but we shall show the enemy what it means to attack Germany. And so I commend you to God. Go forth into the churches, kneel down before God, and implore his help for our brave army.

The German Declaration of War on Russia (August 1, 1914)

The Imperial German Government have used every effort since the beginning of the crisis to bring about a peaceful settlement. In compliance with a wish expressed to him by His Majesty the Emperor of Russia, the German Emperor had undertaken, in concert with Great Britain, the part of mediator between the Cabinets of Vienna and St. Petersburg; but Russia, without waiting for any result, proceeded to a general mobilisation of her forces

---

"Speech from the Balcony" is from Louis L. Snyder, eds., *Historic Documents of World War I* (Princeton: Van Nostrand, 1958), p. 80. Reprinted by permission of Louis Snyder.

"The German Declaration" is from Great Britain Foreign Office, *Collected Diplomatic Documents Relating to the Outbreak of the European War*, 1915: Russian Orange Book, no. 76, pp. 294–295.

both on land and sea. In consequence of this threatening step, which was not justified by any military proceedings on the part of Germany, the German Empire was faced by a grave and imminent danger. If the German Government had failed to guard against this peril, they would have compromised the safety and the very existence of Germany. The German Government were, therefore, obliged to make representations to the Government of His Majesty the Emperor of All the Russians and to insist upon a cessation of the aforesaid military acts. Russia having refused to comply with this demand, and having shown by this refusal that her action was directed against Germany, I have the honor, on the instruction of my Government, to inform your Excellency as follows:

His Majesty the Emperor, by august Sovereign, in the name of the German Empire, accepts the challenge, and considers itself at war with Russia.

The Question of Belgian Neutrality

On August 1, Germany declared war on Russia. At the same time, France began to mobilize her forces, and Germany declared war on August 3. The British, removed from the fray by the English Channel, could not long remain out of the conflict. On August 2, Germany issued an ultimatum that Belgium allow German troops to pass through her territory in order to invade France. Belgium refused and appealed to Britain to intervene diplomatically in order "to safeguard the integrity of Belgium." The British Parliament responded favorably and demanded that Germany withdraw its ultimatum. She refused and Britain declared war on August 4, 1914.

The following speech was by the German Chancellor, Bethmann-Hollweg, who admitted that the violation of Belgian neutrality was unjust but necessary to ensure German security. The second selection is another of Kaiser Wilhelm's militaristic speeches. The European world was now at war.

German Defense for Invading Belgium (August 4, 1914)

CHANCELLOR THEOBOLD VON BETHMANN-HOLLWEG

A stupendous fate is breaking over Europe. For forty-four years, since the time we fought for and won the German Empire and our position in the world, we have lived in peace and have protected the peace of Europe. In the works of peace we have become strong and powerful, and have thus aroused the envy of others. With patience we have faced the fact that,

Great Britain Foreign Office, *Collected Diplomatic Documents Relating to the Outbreak of the European War,* 1915: German White Book, pp. 436–439.

under the pretense that Germany was desirous of war, enmity has been awakened against us in the East and the West, and chains have been fashioned for us. The wind then sown has brought forth the whirlwind which has now broken loose. We wished to continue our work of peace, and, like a silent vow, the feeling that animated everyone from the Emperor down to the youngest soldier was this: Only in defense of a just cause shall our sword fly from its scabbard.

The day has now come when we must draw it, against our wish, and in spite of our sincere endeavors. Russia has set fire to the building. We are at war with Russia and France—a war that has been forced upon us.

From the first moment of the Austro-Serbian conflict we declared that this question must be limited to Austria-Hungary and Serbia, and we worked with this end in view. All governments, especially that of Great Britain, took the same attitude. Russia alone asserted that she had to be heard in the settlement of this matter.

Thus the danger of a European crisis raised its threatening head.

As soon as the first definite information regarding the military preparations in Russia reached us, we declared at St. Petersburg in a friendly but emphatic manner that military measures against Austria would find us on the side of our ally, and that military preparations against ourselves would oblige us to take countermeasures; but that mobilization would come very near to actual war.

Russia assured us in the most solemn manner of her desire for peace, and declared that she was making no military preparations against us.

In the meantime, Great Britain, warmly supported by us, tried to mediate between Vienna and St. Petersburg.

On July 28th the Emperor telegraphed to the Tsar asking him to take into consideration the fact that it was both the duty and the right of Austria-Hungary to defend herself against the Pan-Serb agitation, which threatened to undermine her existence.... About the same time, and before receipt of this telegram, the Tsar asked the Emperor to come to his aid and to induce Vienna to moderate her demands. The emperor accepted the role of mediator.

But scarcely had active steps on these lines begun, when Russia mobilized all her forces directed against Austria, while Austria-Hungary had mobilized only those of her corps which were directed against Serbia. To the north she has mobilized only two of her corps, far from the Russian frontier. The Emperor immediately informed the Tsar that this mobilization of Russian forces against Austria rendered the role of mediator, which he accepted at the Tsar's request, difficult, if not impossible.

The Emperor ordered that the French frontier was to be unconditionally respected. This order, with one single exception, was strictly obeyed. France, who mobilized at the same time as we did, assured us that she would respect a zone of ten kilometers on the frontier. What really happened? Aviators dropped bombs, and cavalry patrols and French infantry detachments appeared on the territory of the Empire! Though war had not been declared, France thus broke the peace and actually attacked us. . . .

Gentlemen, we are now in a state of necessity (*Notwehr*), and necessity (*Not*) knows no law. Our troops have occupied Luxembourg and perhaps have already entered Belgian territory.

Gentlemen, that is a breach of international law. It is true that the French government declared at Brussels that France would respect Belgian neutrality as long as her adversary respected it. We knew, however, that France stood ready for an invasion. France could wait, we could not. A French attack on our flank on the lower Rhine might have been disastrous. Thus we were forced to ignore the rightful protests of the governments of Luxemburg and Belgium. The wrong—I speak openly—the wrong we thereby commit we will try to make good as soon as our military aims have been attained.

Gentlemen, we stand shoulder to shoulder with Austria-Hungary.

Gentlemen, so much for the facts. I repeat the words of the Emperor: "With a clear conscience we enter the lists." We are fighting for the fruits of our works of peace, for the inheritance of a great past and for our future. The fifty years are not yet past during which Count Moltke said we should have to remain armed to defend the inheritance that we won in 1870. Now the great hour of trial has struck for our people. But with clear confidence we go forward to meet it. Our army is in the field, our navy is ready for battle—behind them stands the entire German nation—the entire German nation united to the last man.

"The Sword Is Drawn!" (August 18, 1914)

KAISER WILHELM II

Former generations as well as those who stand here today have often seen the soldiers of the First Guard Regiment and My Guards at this place. We were brought together then by an oath of allegiance which we swore before God. Today all have gathered to pray for the triumph of our weapons, for now that oath must be proved to the last drop of blood. The sword, which I have left in its scabbard for decades, shall decide.

I expect My First Guard Regiment on Foot and My Guards to add a new page of fame to their glorious history. The celebration today finds us confident in God in the Highest and remembering the glorious days of Leuthen, Chlum, and St. Privat. Our ancient fame is an appeal to the German people and their sword. And the entire German nation to the last man has grasped the sword. And so I draw the sword which with the help of God I have kept in its scabbard for decades. [*At this point the Kaiser drew his sword from its scabbard and held it high above his head.*]

Louis L. Snyder, ed., *Historic Documents of World War I* (Princeton: Van Nostrand, 1958), pp. 80–81. Reprinted by permission of Louis Snyder.

The sword is drawn, and I cannot sheathe it again without victory and honor. All of you shall and will see to it that only in honor is it returned to the scabbard. You are my guarantee that I can dictate peace to my enemies. Up and at the enemy! Down with the enemies of Brandenburg!
Three cheers for our army!

"They Shall Not Pass": The War

The Horror of Battle

The German strategy in August 1914 had been planned long in advance by Count Alfred von Schlieffen, German Chief of Staff until 1905. The essence of the strategy was to sweep through Belgium and overwhelm French defenses in one swift onslaught; about 90 percent of the German army would be used for that purpose, while the remaining fraction, together with the Austrians, would hold off Russia. Once France was defeated, Germany and Austria-Hungary could concentrate their forces against the Russian army. Quite unexpectedly, however, the Belgians put up a gallant resistance, and the German attack was stalled long enough to upset the timetable. The British were able to land troops in Europe, and the war degenerated into a struggle for position that was characterized by trench warfare. New weapons such as the machine gun, the tank, and barbed wire eliminated thousands of men as attacks failed and comrades were left to die in the region between the trenches called "No Man's Land."

The following accounts of soldiers testify to the horrors of ceaseless shelling and destruction. The Battle of Verdun in 1916 raged for ten months, resulting in a combined total of about one million casualties. The Battle of the Somme lasted five months, with well over 1 million killed or wounded. Very little ground or tactical advantage was gained. Battle cries such as the French "They Shall Not Pass" were indicative of the stalemated defensive war. In such a situation, propaganda leaflets dropped into enemy trenches by balloons attempted to gain advantage in what was as much psychological as physical combat.

The Battle of Verdun (February–December 1916)

During three days (February 26–29th) after their initial advance over devastated and useless ground, they assaulted with the greatest dash and determination the main French positions. But the defenders were now in strength; and the French guns at length took matters in hand. The German

Charles F. Horne, ed., *Source Records of the Great War*, vol. IV (Indianapolis: The American Legion, 1931), pp. 45, 54–57. Reprinted by permission of The American Legion.

assaulting waves dashed themselves in vain against the Talou heights, the Pepper ridge, and the Vaux position. They were ripped open with cannon, broken by the French bayonets, and driven back with fearful slaughter, time and again. Finally the mauled and battered German columns collapsed, and they were withdrawn from the fray; the casualties of the assailants for the first full week of uninterrupted fighting being estimated, on the lowest computation, at 60,000.

For such heavy sacrifice the enemy technically had won nothing, although, as usual, he indulged in much boasting and he magnified tremendously the barren results he had obtained from the action—an insignificant and useless gain of ground, a few prisoners, and some disabled guns; this was really all he could show as the outcome of his plan which was meant to open to him the gates of Verdun and to place him in possession of the Heights of the Meuse. The French, who had lost 20,000 men, continued to hold Verdun and the main positions surrounding it. . . .

Thousands of projectiles are flying in all directions, some whistling, others howling, others moaning low, and all uniting in one infernal roar. From time to time an aerial torpedo passes, making a noise like a gigantic motor car. With a tremendous thud a giant shell bursts quite close to our observation post, breaking the telephone wire and interrupting all communication with our batteries.

A man gets out at once for repairs, crawling along on his stomach through all this place of bursting mines and shells. It seems quite impossible that he should escape in the rain of shell, which exceeds anything imaginable; there has never been such a bombardment in war. Our man seems to be enveloped in explosions, and shelters himself from time to time in the shell craters which honeycomb the ground; finally he reaches a less stormy spot, mends his wires, and then, as it would be madness to try to return, settles down in a big crater and waits for the storm to pass.

Beyond, in the valley, dark-masses are moving over the snow-covered ground. It is German infantry advancing in packed formation along the valley to the attack. They look like a big gray carpet being unrolled over the country. We telephone through to the batteries and the ball begins. The sight is hellish. In the distance, in the valley and upon the slopes, regiments spread out, and as they deploy fresh troops come pouring in.

There is a whistle over our heads. It is our first shell. It falls right in the middle of the enemy infantry. We telephone through, telling our batteries of their hit, and a deluge of heavy shells is poured on the enemy. Their position becomes critical. Through glasses we can see men maddened, men covered with earth and blood, falling one upon the other. When the first wave of the assault is decimated, the ground is dotted with heaps of corpses, but the second wave is already pressing on. Once more our shells carve awful gaps in their ranks. Nevertheless, like an army of rats the Boches [Germans] continue to advance in spite of our "marmites." Then our heavy artillery bursts forth in fury. The whole valley is turned into a volcano, and its exit is stopped by the barrier of the slain.

Despite the horror of it, despite the ceaseless flow of blood, one wants to see. One's soul wants to feed on the sight of the brute Boches falling. I stopped on the ground for hours, and when I closed my eyes I saw the whole picture again. The guns are firing at 200 and 300 yards, and shrapnel is exploding with a crash, schything them down. Our men hold their ground; our machine guns keep to their work, and yet they advance.

The Boches are returning again massed to the assault, and they are being killed in bulk. It makes one think that in declaring war the Kaiser had sworn the destruction of his race, and he would have shown good taste in doing so. Their gunfire is slackening now, and ours redoubles. The fort has gone, and if under its ruins there are left a few guns and gunners the bulk of the guns are firing from outside. The machine guns are coming up and getting in position, and our men are moving on in numerous waves.

I find a rifle belonging to a comrade who has fallen and join the Chasseurs with the fifty cartridges that I have left. What a fight it is, and what troops! From time to time a man falls, rises, shoots, runs, shoots again, keeps on firing, fights with his bayonet, and then, worn out, falls, to be trampled on without raising a cry. The storm of fire continues. Everything is on fire—the wood near by, the village of Douaumont, Verdun, the front of Bezonvaux, and the back of Thiaumont. There is fire everywhere. The acid smell of carbonic acid and blood catches at our throats, but the battle goes on.

They are brave, but one of our men is worth two of theirs, especially in hand-to-hand fighting. . . . Our reenforcements continue to arrive. We are the masters.

The Battle of the Somme (July–November 1916)

The German Command was not thinking much about the human suffering of its troops. It was thinking, necessarily, of the next defensive line upon which they would have to fall back if the pressure of the British offensive could be maintained. . . . It was getting nervous. Owing to the enormous efforts made in the Verdun offensive the supplies of ammunition were not adequate to the enormous demand.

The German gunners were trying to compete with the British in continuity of bombardments and the shells were running short. Guns were wearing out under this incessant strain, and it was difficult to replace them. General von Gallwitz received reports of "an alarmingly large number of bursts in the bore, particularly in the field guns."

In all the letters written during those weeks of fighting and captured by us from dead or living men there is one great cry of agony and horror.

Charles F. Horne, ed., *Source Records of the Great War*, vol. IV (Indianapolis: The American Legion, 1931), pp. 248–251. Reprinted by permission of The American Legion.

"I stood on the brink of the most terrible days of my life," wrote one of them. "They were those of the battle of the Somme. It began with a night attack on August 13th–14th. The attack lasted till the evening of the 18th, when the English wrote on our bodies in letters of blood: 'It is all over with you.' A handful of half-mad, wretched creatures, worn out in body and mind, were all that was left of a whole battalion. We were that handful."

In many letters this phrase was used. The Somme was called the "Bath of Blood" by the German troops who waded across its shell-craters, and in the ditches which were heaped with their dead. But what I have described is only the beginning of the battle, and the bath was to be filled deeper in the months that followed.

It was in no cheerful mood that men went away to the Somme battlefields. Those battalions of gray-clad men entrained without any of the old enthusiasm with which they had gone to earlier battles. Their gloom was noticed by the officers.

"Sing, you sheep's heads, sing!" they shouted.

They were compelled to sing, by order.

"In the afternoon," wrote a man of the 18th Reserve Division, "we had to go out again: we were to learn to sing. The greater part did not join in, and the song went feebly. Then we had to march round in a circle, and sing, and that went no better."

"After that we had an hour off, and on the way back to billets we were to sing '*Deutschland über Alles*,' but this broke down completely. One never hears songs of the Fatherland any more."

They were silent, grave-eyed men who marched through the streets of French and Belgian towns to be entrained for the Somme front, for they had forebodings of the fate before them. Yet none of their forebodings were equal in intensity of fear to the frightful reality into which they were flung.

No Man's Land

J. KNIGHT-ADKIN

No Man's Land is an eerie sight
At early dawn in the pale gray light.
Never a house and never a hedge
In No Man's Land from edge to edge,
And never a living soul walks there
To taste the fresh of the morning air.
Only some lumps of rotting clay,
That were friends or foemen yesterday.

W. Reginald Wheeler, ed., *A Book of Verse of the Great War* (New Haven: Yale University Press, 1917), pp. 90–91. Reprinted by permission of *The Spectator*.

What are the bounds of No Man's Land?
You can see them clearly on either hand,
A mound of rag-bags gray in the sun,
Or a furrow of brown where the earth works run
From the eastern hills to the western sea,
Through field or forest o'er river and lea;
No man may pass them, but aim you well
And Death rides across on the bullet or shell.

But No Man's Land is a goblin sight
When patrols crawl over at dead o' night;
Boche or British, Belgian or French,
You dice with death when you cross the trench.
When the "rapid," like fireflies in the dark,
Flits down the parapet spark by spark,
And you drop for cover to keep your head
With your face on the breast of the four months' dead.

The man who ranges in No Man's Land
Is dogged by the shadows on either hand
When the star-shell's flares, as it bursts o'erhead,
Scares the great gray rats that feed on the dead,
And the bursting bomb or the bayonet-snatch
May answer the click of your safety-catch.
For the lone patrol, with his life in his hand,
Is hunting for blood in No Man's Land.

Life in the Trenches

ROBERT GRAVES

Those were early days of trench warfare, the days of the jamtin bomb and the gas-pipe trench mortar: still innocent of Lewis or Stokes guns, steel helmets, telescopic rifle-sights, gas-shells, pillboxes, tanks, well-organized trench-raids, or any of the later refinements of trench warfare.

After a meal of bread, bacon, rum, and bitter stewed tea sickly with sugar, we went through the broken trees to the east of the village and up a long trench to battalion headquarters. The wet and slippery trench ran through dull red clay. I had a torch with me, and saw that hundreds of field mice and frogs had fallen into the trench but found no way out. The light dazzled them, and because I could not help treading on them, I put the torch back in my pocket. We had no mental picture of what the trenches would be like, and were almost as ignorant as a young soldier who joined us

Robert Graves, *Goodbye to All That,* 3rd ed. (London: Cassell & Co., 1961), pp. 84–85, 115–116. Reprinted by permission of A. P. Watt Ltd. on behalf of The Executors of the Estate of Robert Graves.

"A rifle bullet, even when fired blindly always seemed purposefully aimed. . . . When we were in a trench, the bullets made a tremendous crack as they went over the hollow." (*Wide World Photos*)

a week or two later. He called out excitedly to old Burford, who was cooking up a bit of stew in a dixie, apart from the others: 'Hi, mate, where's the battle? I want to do my bit.'

We now came under rifle-fire, which I found more trying than shell-fire. The gunner, I knew, fired not at people but at map-references—crossroads, likely artillery positions, houses that suggested billets for troops, and so on. Even when an observation officer in an aeroplane or captive balloon or on a church spire directed the guns, it seemed random, somehow. But a rifle-bullet, even when fired blindly, always seemed purposely aimed. And whereas we could usually hear a shell approaching, and take some sort of cover, the rifle-bullet gave no warning. So, though we learned not to duck a rifle-bullet because, once heard, it must have missed, it gave us a worse feeling of danger. Rifle-bullets in the open went hissing into the grass without much noise, but when we were in a trench, the bullets made a tremendous crack as they went over the hollow. Bullets often struck the barbed wire in front of the trenches, which sent them spinning with a head-over-heels motion—ping! rockety-ockety-ockety into the woods behind.

I went on patrol fairly often, finding that the only thing respected in young officers was personal courage. Besides, I had cannily worked it out like this. My best way of lasting through to the end of the war would be to get wounded. The best time to get wounded would be at night and in the open, with the rifle fire more or less unaimed and my whole body exposed. Best, also, to get wounded when there was no rush on the dressing-station services, and while the back areas were not being heavily shelled. Best to get wounded, therefore, on a night patrol in a quiet sector. One could usually manage to crawl into a shell hole until help arrived.

Still, patrolling had its peculiar risks. If a German patrol found a wounded man, they were as likely as not to cut his throat. The bowie-knife was a favourite German patrol weapon because of its silence. . . . The most important information that a patrol could bring back was to what regiment and division the troops opposite belonged. So if it were impossible to get a wounded enemy back without danger to oneself, he had to be stripped of his badges. To do that quickly and silently, it might be necessary to cut his throat or beat in his skull.

Like everyone else, I had a carefully worked out formula for taking risks. In principle, we would all take any risk, even the certainty of death, to save life or to maintain an important position. To take life we would run, say, a one-in-five risk, particularly if there was some wider object than merely reducing the enemy's manpower; for instance, picking off a well-known sniper, or getting fire ascendancy in trenches where the lines came dangerously close.

French Propaganda Leaflet

Pass this along!

German War Comrades!

Think about this:

1. Only greedy rulers want war. The people want peace, and work, and bread.

2. Only the German Kaiser with his militarists, Junkers, and arms manufacturers wanted war, prepared for it, and brought it on. No one wanted to fight Germany, no one opposed her desires for a "place in the sun."

3. If a murderer shoots a revolver on the street, it is the duty of every peace-loving, dutiful citizen to hurry to the aid of the fallen. For that reason Italy, Rumania, and the United States went to war against Germany; to free Belgium, Serbia, and France from the clutches of the murderer. . . .

10. Stop [*fighting*]! Turn your cannons around! Come over to us. Shoot anyone who wants to hinder you from coming.

YOUR DEMOCRATIC GERMAN COMRADES IN FRENCH PRISONS

George G. Bruntz, *Allied Propaganda and the Collapse of the German Empire in 1918,* Hoover War Library Publication No. 13 (Stanford: Stanford University Press, 1938), pp. 98. Reprinted by permission of the publisher.

What Are You Fighting for, Michel?

They tell you that you are fighting to secure victory for your Fatherland. But have you ever thought about what you are fighting for?

You are fighting for the glory of, and for the enrichment of the Krupps. You are fighting to save the Kaiser, the Junkers and the War Lords who caused the war from the anger of the people.

The Junkers [German nobility] are sitting at home with their bejewelled wives and mistresses. Their bank accounts are constantly growing, accounts to which you and your comrades pay with your lives. For your wives and brides there are no growing bank accounts. They are at home working and starving, sacrifices like yourselves to the greed of the ruling class to whose pipes you have to dance.

What a dance! The dance of death. But yesterday you marched over the corpses of your comrades against the English cannon. Tomorrow another German soldier will march over your corpse.

You have been promised victory and peace. You poor fool! Your comrades were also promised these things more than three years ago. Peace indeed they have found—deep in the grave. But victory did not come.

Your Kaiser has adorned the glorious Hindenburg with the Iron Cross with golden beams. What has the Kaiser awarded to you? Ruin, suffering, poverty, hunger for your wives and children, misery, disease, and tomorrow the grave.

It is for the Fatherland, you say, that you go out as a brave patriot to death for the Fatherland.

But of what does your Fatherland consist? Is it the Kaiser with his fine speeches? Is it the Crown Prince with his jolly companions, who sacrificed 600,000 men at Verdun? Is it [Field Marshall] Hindenburg, who sits with [General] Ludendorf, both covered with medals many kilometers behind you and who plans how he can furnish the English with still more cannon fodder. Is it Frau Bertha Krupp for whom through year after year of war you pile up millions upon millions of marks? Is it the Prussian Junkers who cry out over your dead bodies for annexation?

No, the Fatherland is not any of these. You are the Fatherland, Michel! You and your sisters and your wives and your parents and your children. You, the common people are the Fatherland. And yet it is you and your comrades who are driven like slaves into the hell of English cannon-fire, driven by the command of the feelingless slave-drivers.

When your comrades at home were striking, they were shot at with machine guns. If you, after the war, strike a blow for your rights, the machine guns will be turned upon you, for you are fighting only to increase the power of your lords.

George G. Bruntz, *Allied Propaganda and the Collapse of the German Empire in 1918*, Hoover War Library Publication No. 13 (Stanford: Stanford University Press, 1938), pp. 99. Reprinted by permission of the publisher.

Do you perhaps believe your rulers who love war as you hate it? Of course not. They love war for it brings them advancement, honor, power, profit. The longer the war lasts, the longer they will postpone the revolution.

They promise you that you can compel the English to beg for peace. Do you really believe that? You have advanced a few kilometers but for every Englishman whom you have shot down, six Germans have fallen. And all America is still to come.

Your commanders report to you wonderful stories of English losses. But did they tell you that Germany in the first five days of battle lost 315,000 men?

Arrayed against Germany in battle today stands the entire world because it knows that German rulers caused the war to serve their own greedy ambition. The entire power of the Western World stands behind England and France and America. Soon it will go forth to battle. Have you thought of that, Michel?

The Red Baron: Glory in the Skies?

BARON MANFRED VON RICHTHOFEN

While the infantryman was exposed to the frustration and chaos of land combat, there was another war that existed with less restriction. By 1916, airplanes had been developed for combat, and the sky became the haven for men who relished the opportunity to test individual skill in "dog-fights" high above the earth. The romantic notion of the solitary warrior, with scarf flying high in the wind, was established by men who played by their own rules of honor and death in the air. Baron Manfred von Richthofen, a member of the Prussian aristocracy, became the ace of the war, shooting down eighty planes within two years before he himself was felled. In spite of his romantic aura, Richthofen was a methodical killer, a hunter with a morbid curiosity for death, who flew with his brains and not with the innocent courage of other pilots. The Red Baron discriminated between a sportsman and a butcher: "The latter shoots for fun. When I have shot down an Englishman, my hunting passion is satisfied for a quarter of an hour. If one of them comes down, I have a feeling of complete satisfaction. Only much much later I have overcome my instinct and have become a butcher." The first excerpt is from his autobiography, *The Red Battle Flyer;* the second selection is an assessment of the Red Baron by one of his fellow pilots.

Manfred von Richthofen, *The Red Battle Flyer* (New York: McBride Co., 1918), pp. 131–133.

My First English Victim (September 17, 1915)

We were all at the butts trying our machine guns. On the previous day we had received our new aeroplanes and the next morning Boelcke was to fly with us. We were all beginners. None of us had had a success so far. Consequently everything that Boelcke told us was to us gospel truth. Every day, during the last few days, he had, as he said, shot one or two Englishmen for breakfast.

Slowly we approached the hostile squadron. It could not escape us. We had intercepted it, for we were between the Front and our opponents. If they wished to go back they had to pass us. We counted the hostile machines. They were seven in number. We were only five. All the Englishmen flew large bomb-carrying two-seaters. In a few seconds the dance would begin.

Boelcke had come very near the first English machine but he did not yet shoot. I followed. Close to me were my comrades. The Englishman nearest to me was traveling in a large boat painted with dark colors. I did not reflect very long but took my aim and shot.

Apparently he was no beginner, for he knew exactly that his last hour had arrived at the moment when I got at the back of him. At that time I had not yet the conviction "He must fall!" which I have now on such occasions, but on the contrary, I was curious to see whether he would fall. There is a great difference between the two feelings. When one has shot down one's first, second or third opponent, then one begins to find our how the trick is done.

In a fraction of a second I was at his back with my excellent machine. I give a short series of shots with my machine gun. I had gone so close that I was afraid I might dash into the Englishman. Suddenly, I nearly yelled with joy for the propeller of the enemy machine had stopped turning. I had shot his engine to pieces; the enemy was compelled to land, for it was impossible for him to reach his own lines.

The Englishman landed close to the flying ground of one of our squadrons. I was so excited that I landed also and my eagerness was so great that I nearly smashed up my machine. The English flying machine and my own stood close together. I rushed to the English machine and saw that a lot of soldiers were running towards my enemy. When I arrived I discovered that my assumption had been correct. I had shot the engine to pieces and both the pilot and observer were severely wounded. The observer died at once and the pilot while being transported to the nearest dressing station. I honored the fallen enemy by placing a stone on his beautiful grave.

English and French Flying (February 1917)

The great thing in air fighting is that the decisive factor does not lie in trick flying but solely in the personal ability and energy of the aviator. A flying man may be able to loop and do all the stunts imaginable and yet he may not succeed in shooting down a single enemy. In my opinion the aggressive spirit is everything and that spirit is very strong in us Germans. Hence we shall always retain the domination of the air.

The French have a different character. They like to put traps and to attack their opponents unawares. That cannot easily be done in the air. Only a beginner can be caught and one cannot set traps because an aeroplane cannot hide itself. The invisible aeroplane has not yet been discovered. Sometimes, however, the Gaelic blood asserts itself. The Frenchmen will then attack. But the French attacking spirit is like bottled lemonade. It lacks tenacity.

The Englishmen, on the other hand, one notices that they are of Germanic blood. Sportsmen easily take to flying, and Englishmen see in flying nothing but a sport. They take a perfect delight in looping the loop, flying on their back, and indulging in other stunts for the benefit of our soldiers in the trenches. All these tricks may impress people who attend a Sports Meeting, but the public at the battle-front is not as appreciative of these things. It demands higher qualifications than trick flying. Therefore, the blood of English pilots will have to flow in streams.

An Assessment of the Red Baron

ERNST UDET

What a man he was! The others, admittedly, were doing their share, but they had wives at home, children, a mother or a profession. And only on rare occasions could they forget it. But Richthofen always lived on the other side of the boundary which we crossed only in our great moments. When he fought, his private life was thrust ruthlessly behind him. Eating, drinking and sleeping were all he granted life, and then only the minimum that was necessary to keep flesh and blood in working order. He was the simplest man I ever met. He was a Prussian through and through. A great soldier.

It Is Sweet and Proper to Die for One's Country

Wilfred Owen, a poet and soldier who was killed a week before the war ended, wrote that the "Lie" of the conflict lay in the belief that it was honorable and proper to give your life for the benefit of your country (Dulce et decorum est pro patria mori). Indeed, the war seemed to people an absurd and tragic event. Why were they fighting? Why did old men send young men off to die "for their country"? How could poisonous gas,

Ernst Udet, *Ace of the Black Cross*, trans. Kenneth Kirkness (London: Newnes, 1937), p. 72.

"This is the way the world ends, not with a bang, but a whimper."—T. S. Eliot. (*Library of Congress*)

which burned out the lungs and led to a painfully slow death, be justified—or submarines, which destroyed under cover, thus eliminating a
"fair fight"? The rules of war had changed. Disillusionment was evident
in mutinies and in the poetry written in the trenches and in the letters sent
home. It was not enough to be complimented by your general for victory
in battle.

Order of the Day
(Battle of the Marne, September 1914)
GENERAL JOSEPH JOFFRE

September 11th

The battle which we have been fighting for the last five days has ended in
an undoubted victory. The retreat of the 1st, 2nd, and 3rd German Armies
before our left and center becomes more and more marked. The enemy's

"Order of the Day" is from Charles F. Horne, ed., *Source Records of the Great War*, vol. II (Indianapolis: The American Legion, 1931), p. 281. Reprinted by permission of the American Legion.

4th Army in its turn has begun to withdraw to the north of Vitry and Sermaise.

Everywhere the enemy has left on the field numerous wounded and a quantity of munitions. Everywhere we have made prisoners while gaining ground. Our troops bear witness to the intensity of the fight, and the means employed by the Germans in their endeavors to resist our *elan*. The vigorous resumption of the offensive has determined our success.

Officers, non-commissioned officers, and men! You have all responded to my appeal; you have all deserved well of your country.

Five Souls

W. N. EWER

FIRST SOUL—
I was a peasant of the Polish plain;
I left my plow because the message ran:
Russia, in danger, needed every man
To save her from the Teuton; and was slain.
I gave my life for freedom—this I know;
For those who bade me fight had told me so.

SECOND SOUL—
I was a Tyrolese, a mountaineer;
I gladly left my mountain home to fight
Against the brutal, treacherous Muscovite;
And died in Poland on a Cossack spear.
I gave my life for freedom—this I know;
For those who bade me fight had told me so.

THIRD SOUL—
I worked in Lyons at my weaver's loom,
    When suddenly the Prussian despot hurled
    His felon blow at France and at the world;
Then I went forth to Belgium and my doom.
I gave my life for freedom—this I know;
For those who bade me fight had told me so.

FOURTH SOUL—
I owned a vineyard by the wooded Main,
    Until the Fatherland, begirt by foes
    Lusting her downfall, called me, and I rose
Swift to the call—and died in fair Lorraine.
I gave my life for freedom—this I know;
For those who bade me fight had told me so.

W. Reginald Wheeler, ed., *A Book of Verse of the Great War* (New Haven: Yale University Press, 1917), pp. 46–47. Reprinted by permission.

FIFTH SOUL—
> I worked in a great shipyard by the Clyde,
> There came a sudden word of wars declared,
> Of Belgium, peaceful, helpless, unprepared,
> Asking our aid; I joined the ranks, and died.
> *I gave my life for freedom—this I know;*
> *For those who bade me fight had told me so.*

German Student's War Letter

RICHARD SCHMIEDER, Student of Philosophy, Leipzig
Born January 24th, 1888.
Killed July 14th, 1916, near Bethenville.

In the Trenches near Vaudesincourt, March 13th, 1915.

Anybody who, like myself, has been through the awful days near Penthy
since the 6th of February, will agree with me that a more appalling struggle
could not be imagined. It has been a case of soldier against soldier, equally
matched and both mad with hate and anger, fighting for days on end over
a single square of ground, till the whole tract of country is one blood-
soaked, corpse-strewn field. . . .

On February 27th, tired out and utterly exhausted in body and mind, we
were suddenly called up to reinforce the VIIIth Reserve Corps, had to
reoccupy our old position at Ripont, and were immediately attacked by the
French with extraordinary strength and violence. It was a gigantic murder,
by means of bullets, shells, axes, and bombs, and there was such a thundering, crashing, bellowing and screaming as might have heralded the Day of
Judgment.

In three days, on a front of about 200 yards, we lost 909 men, and the
enemy casualties must have amounted to thousands. The blue French cloth
mingled with the German grey upon the ground, and in some places the
bodies were piled so high that one could take cover from shell-fire behind
them. The noise was so terrific that orders had to be shouted by each man
into the ear of the next. And whenever there was a momentary lull in the
tumult of battle and the groans of the wounded, one heard, high up in the
blue sky, the joyful song of birds! Birds singing just as they do at home in
spring-time! It was enough to tear the heart out of one's body!

Don't ask about the fate of the wounded! Anybody who was incapable of

German Students' War Letters, translated and arranged from the original edition of Dr.
Philipp Witkop by A. F. Wedd (New York: E. P. Dutton, 1929), pp. 208–209. Reprinted by
permission of Methuen and Company.

walking to the doctor had to die a miserable death; some lingered in agony for hours, some for days, and even for a week. And the combatants stormed regardlessly to and fro over them: 'I can't give you a hand,—You're for the Promised Land,—My Comrade good and true.' A dog, dying in the poorest hovel at home, is enviable in comparison.

There are moments when even the bravest soldier is so utterly sick of the whole thing that he could cry like a child. When I heard the birds singing at Ripont, I could have crushed the whole world to death in my wrath and fury. If only those gentlemen—Grey, Asquith, and Poincare—could be transported to this spot, instead of the war lasting ten years, there would be peace tomorrow!

Dulce et Decorum Est

WILFRED OWEN

Bent double, like old beggars under sacks,
Knocked-kneed, coughing like hags, we cursed through sludge,
Till on the haunting flares we turned our backs
And towards our distant rest began to trudge.
Men marched asleep. Many had lost their boots
But limped on, blood-shod. All went lame; all blind;
Drunk with fatigue; deaf even to the hoots
Of tired, outstripped Five-Nines that dropped behind.

Gas! Gas! Quick boys!—An ecstasy of fumbling,
Fitting the clumsy helmets just in time;
But someone still was yelling out and stumbling
And flound'ring like a man in fire or lime. . . .
Dim, through the misty panes and thick green light,
As under a green sea, I saw him drowning.
In all my dreams, before my helpless sight,
He plunges at me, guttering, choking, drowning.

If in some smothering dreams you too could pace
Behind the wagon that we flung him in,
And watch the white eyes writhing in his face,
His hanging face, like a devil's sick of sin;
If you could hear, at every jolt, the blood
Come gargling from the froth-corrupted lungs,
Obscene as cancer, bitter as the cud

Wilfred Owen, *Collected Poems*, p. 55. Copyright © 1963 by Chatto & Windus. Reprinted by permission of New Directions Publishing Corporation.

Of vile, incurable sores on innocent tongues,—
My friend, you would not tell with such high zest
To children ardent for some desperate glory,
The old Lie: Dulce et decorum est
Pro patria mori.

Stirrings of Peace

In January 1917, Germany informed the United States that she intended to resume unrestricted submarine warfare. Consequently, three American merchant ships were sunk, and at President Woodrow Wilson's request Congress declared war with Germany on April 6. As fresh American troops arrived in Europe, German resistance became increasingly tenuous. The papacy took an important role in establishing a climate for peace, as the first selection demonstrates. Pope Benedict XV's proposals attracted much popular attention but went unheeded. Still, the attempt gave indication of the growing spiritual and moral influence of the modern papacy. It was left to President Wilson to provide the framework for a peace treaty. In his address to Congress, he proposed a fourteen-point plan, which is excerpted in the second selection.

Peace Proposals (August 1, 1917)

POPE BENEDICT XV

To the heads of the belligerent peoples.

From the beginning of our pontificate, amid the horrors of the terrible war unleashed upon Europe, we have kept before our attention three things above all: to preserve complete impartiality in relation to all the belligerents as is appropriate to him who is the common father and who loves all his children with an equal affection; to endeavor constantly to do to all the most possible good, without personal exceptions and without national or religious distinctions, a duty which the universal law of charity, as well as the supreme spiritual charge entrusted to us by Christ, dictates to us; finally, as our peace-making mission equally demands, to leave nothing undone within our power, which could assist in hastening the end of this calamity, by trying to lead the peoples and their heads to more moderate frames of mind and to the calm deliberations of peace, of a "just and lasting" peace.

Sidney Z. Ehler and John B. Morrall, trans. and eds., *Church and State Through the Centuries* (Westminster, Md.: Newman Press, 1954), pp. 374–377.

Whoever has followed our work during the three unhappy years which have just elapsed, has been able to recognize with ease that if we have always remained faithful to our resolution of absolute impartiality and to our practical policy of welldoing, we have never ceased to urge the belligerent peoples and governments to become brothers once more, even though publicity has not been given to all which we have done to attain the most noble end.

Towards the end of the first year of war, we addressed to the conflicting nations the most lively exhortations, and in addition we indicated the way to follow in order to arrive at a lasting and honorable peace for all. Unhappily, our appeal was not heeded; and the war continued bitterly for two more years, with all its horrors; it even became more cruel and spread over land and sea, even in the air; desolation and death were seen to fall upon defenseless cities, peaceful villages and their innocent populations. And at the present moment no one can imagine how the sufferings of all may increase and become more intense, if further months, or still worse, further years are added to these bloodstained three years. Will the civilized world then become nothing but a field of death? And will Europe, so glorious and so flourishing before, rush, as if driven on by a universal folly, to the abyss and be the agent of her own suicide?

In so agonizing a situation, in face of so great a danger, we who have no special aim, who pay no attention to the suggestions of the interests of either of the belligerent groups, but are moved only by the feeling of our lofty duty as common father of the faithful and by the solicitations of our children who beg for our intervention and our peace-making word, we raise anew a cry for peace and we renew an urgent appeal to those who hold in their hands the destinies of nations. But so as not to confine ourselves any longer to general terms, as circumstances have advised us in the past, we now wish to descend to more concrete and practical propositions, and to invite the governments of the belligerent peoples to reach agreement on the following points, which seem to be the basis of a just and lasting peace, leaving to them the task of making them more precise and of completing them.

First of all, the fundamental point should be that for the material force of arms should be substituted the moral force of law; hence a just agreement by all for the simultaneous and reciprocal reduction of armaments, according to rules and guarantees to be established to the degree necessary and sufficient for the maintenance of public order in each state; then, instead of armies, the institution of arbitration, with its lofty peace-making function according to the standards to be agreed upon and with sanctions to be decided against the state which might refuse to submit international questions to arbitration or to accept its decisions.

Once the supremacy of law has been established, let every obstacle to the ways of communication between the peoples be removed, by insuring through rules to be fixed in similar fashion, the true freedom and common use of the seas. This would, on the one hand, remove many reasons for conflict and, on the other, would open new sources of prosperity and progress to all.

With regard to reparations for damage and to the expenses of the war, we see no way of settling the question other than by laying down as a general principle, a complete and reciprocal condonation, justified by the immense benefits to be drawn from disarmament, and all the more because one could not understand the continuation of slaughter solely for reasons of an economic nature. If, however, in certain cases there exist special reasons, let them be pondered with justice and equity.

But pacifying agreements, with the advantages flowing from them, are not possible without the reciprocal restitution of territories actually occupied. In consequence, on the part of Germany, there should be total evacuation of Belgium, with a guarantee of its full political, military and economic independence *vis-à-vis* any power whatsoever; similarly the evacuation of French territory. On the side of the other belligerent parties, there should be a corresponding restitution of the German colonies.

With regard to territorial questions, such as those disputed between Italy and Austria, and between Germany and France, there is ground for hope that in consideration of the immense advantages of a lasting peace with disarmament, the conflicting parties will examine them in a conciliatory frame of mind, taking into account . . . the aspirations of the peoples and co-ordinating, according to circumstances, particular interests with the general good of the great human society.

The same spirit of equity and justice should direct the examination of other territorial and political questions, notably those relating to Armenia, the Balkan States and the territories composing the ancient kingdom of Poland, for which especially its noble historical traditions and the sufferings which it has undergone, particularly during the present war, ought rightly to enlist the sympathies of the nations.

Such are the principal foundations upon which we believe the future reorganization of peoples should rest. They are of a kind which would make impossible the recurrence of such conflicts and would pave the way for a solution of the economic questions, so important for the future and the material welfare of all the belligerent states. Thus, in presenting them all to you who preside at this tragic hour over the destinies of the belligerent nations, we are animated by a sweet hope, that of seeing them accepted and thus of seeing the earliest possible end to the fearful struggle which has the ever-increasing appearance of a useless massacre. Everybody recognizes, furthermore, that on both sides the honor of arms has been satisfied. Give attention, then, to our entreaty, accept the paternal invitation which we address to you in the name of the divine redeemer, Prince of Peace. Reflect on your very grave responsibility before God and before men; on your decisions depend the rest and joy of countless families, the life of thousands of young people, in short, the happiness of the peoples, whose well-being it is your overriding duty to procure. May the Lord inspire you with decisions agreeable to his most holy will. May heaven bring it about that, by earning the applause of your contemporaries, you will also gain for yourselves the beautiful name of peacemakers among future generations.

As for us, closely united in prayer and penitence to all faithful souls who sigh for peace, we implore for you from the Divine Spirit light and counsel.

The Fourteen Points (January 8, 1918)

WOODROW WILSON

Gentlemen of the Congress:

It will be our wish and purpose that the processes of peace, when they are begun, shall be absolutely open and that they shall involve and permit henceforth no secret understandings of any kind. The day of conquest and aggrandizement is gone by; so is also the day of secret covenants entered into in the interest of particular governments and likely at some unlooked-for moment to upset the peace of the world. It is this happy fact, now clear to the view of every public man whose thoughts do not still linger in an age that is dead and gone, which makes it possible for every nation whose purposes are consistent with justice and the peace of the world to avow now or at any other time the objects it has in view.

We entered this war because violations of right had occurred which touched us to the quick and made the life of our own people impossible unless they were corrected and the world secured once for all against their recurrence. What we demand in this war, therefore, is nothing peculiar to ourselves. It is that the world be made fit and safe to live in; and particularly that it be made safe for every peace-loving nation which, like our own, wishes to live its own life, determine its own institutions, be assured of justice and fair dealing by the other peoples of the world as against force and selfish aggression. All the peoples of the world are in effect partners in this interest, and for our own part we see very clearly that unless justice be done to others it will not be done to us. The program of the world's peace, therefore, is our program; and that program, the only possible program, as we see it, is this:

1. Open covenants of peace, openly arrived at, after which there shall be no private international understandings of any kind but diplomacy shall proceed always frankly and in the public view.

2. Absolute freedom of navigation upon the seas. . . .

4. Adequate guarantees given and taken that national armaments will be reduced to the lowest point consistent with domestic safety.

5. A free, open-minded, and absolutely impartial adjustment of all colonial claims, based upon a strict observance of the principle that in determining all such questions of sovereignty the interests of the populations concerned must have equal weight with the equitable claims of the government whose title is to be determined.

Congressional Record (January 8, 1918), vol. 56, pt. 1, p. 691.

6. The evacuation of all Russian territory and such a settlement of all questions affecting Russia as will secure . . . the independent determination of her own political development and national policy and assure her of a sincere welcome into the society of free nations under institutions of her own choosing. . . .

7. Belgium, the whole world will agree, must be evacuated and restored, without any attempt to limit the sovereignty which she enjoys in common with all other free nations. No other single act will serve as this will serve to restore confidence among the nations in the laws which they have themselves set and determined for the government of their relations with one another. Without this healing act the whole structure and validity of international law is forever impaired.

8. All French territory should be freed and the invaded portions restored, and the wrong done to France by Prussia in 1871 in the matter of Alsace-Lorraine, which has unsettled the peace of the world for nearly fifty years, should be righted, in order that peace may once more be made secure in the interest of all.

10. The peoples of Austria-Hungary, whose place among the nations we wish to see safeguarded and assured, should be accorded the freest opportunity of autonomous development.

11. Rumania, Serbia, and Montenegro should be evacuated; occupied territories restored; Serbia accorded free and secure access to the sea. . . .

13. An independent Polish state should be erected which should include the territories inhabited by indisputably Polish populations. . . .

14. A general association of nations must be formed under specific covenants for the purpose of affording mutual guarantees of political independence and territorial integrity to great and small states alike.

In regard to these essential rectifications of wrong and assertions of right we feel ourselves to be intimate partners of all the governments and peoples associated together against the Imperialists. We cannot be separated in interest or divided in purpose. We stand together until the end.

For such arrangements and covenants we are willing to fight and to continue to fight until they are achieved; but only because we wish the right to prevail and desire a just and stable peace such as can be secured only by removing the chief provocations to war, which this program does not remove. We have no jealousy of German greatness, and there is nothing in this program that impairs it. We grudge her no achievement or distinction of learning or of pacific enterprise such as have made her record very bright and very enviable. We do not wish to injure her or to block in any way her legitimate influence or power. We do not wish to fight her either with arms or with hostile arrangements of trade if she is willing to associate herself with us and the other peace-loving nations of the world in covenants of justice and law and fair dealing. We wish her only to accept a place of equality among the peoples of the world,—the new world in which we now live,—instead of a place of mastery.

Neither do we presume to suggest to her any alteration or modification of her institutions. But it is necessary, we must frankly say, and necessary as a preliminary to any intelligent dealings with her on our part, that we should know whom her spokesmen speak for when they speak to us, whether for the Reichstag majority or for the military party and the men whose creed is imperial domination.

We have spoken now, surely, in terms too concrete to admit to any further doubt or question. An evident principle runs through the whole program of justice to all peoples and nationalities, and their right to live on equal terms of liberty and safety with one another, whether they be strong or weak. Unless this principle be made its foundation no part of the structure of international justice can stand. The people of the United States could act upon no other principle; and to the vindication of this principle they are ready to devote their lives, their honor, and everything that they possess. The moral climax of this, the culminating and final war for human liberty has come, and they are ready to put their own strength, their own highest purpose, their own integrity and devotion to the test.

The Aftermath of War

On November 9, 1918, the German Kaiser abdicated his throne and fled the country. The armistice, which ended the war, was signed on November 11. The European world of 1914 had been shattered, people were changed, and the foremost question was, how to begin again?

The first selection is from the diary of Anna Eisenmenger, an Austrian whose son returned home after the armistice a changed man. The next two selections argue similar viewpoints, but *The Great Illusion* was written in 1910, four years before the war, and *The International Anarchy* was written in 1926. The authors were struggling with the relationship between war and civilization. The final piece is an excerpt from a poem by T. S. Eliot. Where is the bluster and confidence that gave rise to the Great War?

A German Soldier Returns Home: "A Complete Stranger"

ANNA EISENMENGER

Karl looked very ill. He had no underlinen or socks. His uniform was dirty and in rags. "Mother, I am famished!" he said, and walking straight into the kitchen without waiting for me to bring him something he began to

Anna Eisenmenger, *Blockade: The Diary of an Austrian Middle-Class Woman, 1914–1924* (London: Constable Publishers, 1932), pp. 39–42. Reprinted by permission of the publisher.

devour our rations of bread and jam. "Forgive me, Mother, but we have got into the habit of taking what we can find." He only greeted us very casually and did not notice until much later that Erni, who had come in to welcome him on Liesbeth's arm, was wounded. "Hullo! So it's caught you too!" and then, still hurriedly chewing and swallowing: "Well, just wait! We'll pay them out yet, the war profiteers and parasites. We've grown wiser out there in the trenches, far wiser than we were. Everything must be changed, utterly changed."

I got ready the bath and clean underlinen. After his bath Karl went straight to bed, but he was too excited to sleep, although it was almost 11 o'clock at night. He telephoned to Edith, and then he made us all come to his bedside, for he wanted to tell us about himself. He told us that . . . the Italians had gone on attacking in spite of the Armistice. For another whole day they had fired on our retreating columns in the Fellathal and had captured several divisions. That, however, was the only victory they had won. It was contemptible, but war made every one base and contemptible. He had become so too. . . . After the proclamation of the Armistice all military discipline went to pieces. Everyone was intent only on getting home and made for home by the way that seemed to him quickest and surest. The men trampled down whatever stood in their way, even if the obstacle were their own officers. Woe to the officers who were unpopular with their men. . . . In the next war there would be no one foolish enough to risk his life, they would see to that. . . . Karl was evidently in a nervous, over-exited state, but he went on talking, and only after I had entreated him several times did he consent to try to get to sleep.

"We are all tired, Karl, and it is already past midnight. . . ."

"Do you know, Mother, how I feel here? In a clean bed, washed and fed? As if I were in heaven. . . . Oh no, there is no heaven so beautiful. . . . As if I were in a beautiful dream . . . and in that dream I shall try to find sleep."

We left Karl's room in order to go to bed ourselves. As I was helping Erni undress, he said: "Mother, Karl seems to me like a complete stranger."

Although I was nervously and physically exhausted, sleep refused to close my eyelids. For a long, long time I lay awake, agitated by the horrors of the War. I found myself marvelling that civilised human beings could live through all the brutalities which war entailed for themselves and others without going utterly to pieces. . . .

The Great Illusion (1910)

NORMAN ANGELL

What are the fundamental motives that explain the present rivalry of armaments in Europe, notably the Anglo-German? Each nation pleads the need

Norman Angell, *The Great Illusion* (New York: G. P. Putnam's Sons, 1913), pp. IX–XIIIff, 381–382.

for defence; but this implies that someone is likely to attack, and has therefore a presumed interest in so doing. What are the motives which each State thus fears its neighbors may obey?

They are based on the universal assumption that a nation, in order to find outlets for expanding population and increasing industry, or simply to ensure the best conditions possible for its people, is necessarily pushed to territorial expansion and the exercise of political force against others. . . . It is assumed that a nation's relative prosperity is broadly determined by its political power; that nations being competing units, advantage in the last resort goes to the possessor of preponderant military force, the weaker goes to the wall, as in the other forms of the struggle for life. The author challenges this whole doctrine. . . .

War has no longer the justification that it makes for the survival of the fittest; it involves the survival of the less fit. The idea that the struggle between nations is a part of the evolutionary law of man's advance involves a profound misreading of the biological analogy.

The warlike nations do not inherit the earth; they represent the decaying human element. . . .

Are we, in blind obedience to primitive instincts and old prejudices, enslaved by the old catchwords and that curious indolence which makes the revision of old ideas unpleasant, to duplicate indefinitely on the political and economic side a condition from which we have liberated ourselves on the religious side? Are we to continue to struggle, as so many good men struggled in the first dozen centuries of Christendom—spilling oceans of blood, wasting mountains of treasure—to achieve what is at bottom a logical absurdity, to accomplish something which, when accomplished, can avail us nothing, and which, if it could avail us anything, would condemn the nations of the world to never-ending bloodshed and the constant defeat of all those aims which men, in their sober hours, know to be alone worthy of sustained endeavor?

The International Anarchy (1926)

G. LOWES DICKINSON

I have written, consciously and deliberately, to point a moral. I believe, with most instructed people, that modern war, with all the resources of science at its disposal, has become incompatible with the continuance of civilization. If this be true, it is a mistake to look back upon the course of history and say: There has always been war, and yet civilization has survived. At the best, what has survived is a poor thing compared to what might have been, had there been no war. But even such poor survival cannot be counted upon in the future. . . .

G. Lowes Dickinson, *The International Anarchy, 1904–1914* (London: Allen & Unwin, 1926), pp. V, 47–48.

My thesis is, that whenever and wherever the anarchy of armed states exists, war becomes inevitable. That was the condition in ancient Greece, in republican Rome, in medieval Italy, and in Europe for several centuries after its emergence from the feudal chaos. That chaos also involved war. But such war is not properly to be called civil or international; and with that particular condition we are not now concerned. International war, in our own age as in the others referred to, is a clash between sovereign armed States. It arises in consequence of the international anarchy. . . .

States armed, and therefore a menace to one another; policies ostensibly defensive, but really just as much offensive; these policies pursued in the dark by a very few men who, because they act secretly, cannot act honestly; and this whole complex playing upon primitive passions, arousable at any moment by appropriate appeals from a Press which has no object except to make money out of the weaknesses of men—that is the real situation of the world under the conditions of the international anarchy.

These conditions are commonly regarded as unalterable. Hence the view that war is a fate from which we cannot escape. I will cite in illustration the words of a typical militarist which express, I believe, the real opinion of most soldiers, sailors, politicians, journalists, and plain men: "Possibly in the future great coalitions of Powers will be able to keep the peace for long epochs and to avoid conflict with arms; but this will not be possible in permanence. The life of man is unbroken combat in every form; eternal peace, unfortunately, a Utopia in which only philanthropists ignorant of the world believe. A nation which lays down its arms thereby seals its fate."

Those who hold this philosophy also devoted their lives to making sure that it shall come true; for it is impossible to hold any view about life without thereby contributing to its realization. The confusion, in the passage quoted, between military conflict and other forms of struggle is patent to any one who can think. The same philosophy should conclude that civil war also is an eternal fact, a conclusion to which militarists are usually much averse. But this much is certainly true, that until men lay down their arms, and accept the method of peaceable decision of their disputes, war can never cease.

The Hollow Men (1925)

T. S. ELIOT

A penny for the Old Guy

We are the hollow men
We are the stuffed men
Leaning together

Headpiece filled with straw. Alas!
Our dried voices, when
We whisper together
Are quiet and meaningless
As wind in dry grass
Or rats' feet over broken glass
In our dry cellar

Shape without form, shade without colour,
Paralysed force, gesture without motion;

Those who have crossed
With direct eyes, to death's other Kingdom
Remember us—if at all—not as lost
Violent souls, but only
As the hollow men
The stuffed men.

.   .   .

For Thine is
Life is
For Thine is the

This is the way the world ends
This is the way the world ends
This is the way the world ends
Not with a bang but a whimper.

STUDY QUESTIONS

1. In any conflict there are underlying tensions within countries or between countries that depend on a precipitating action to upset the status quo. What was the "spark" that ignited the Great War, and what were the underlying causes for the conflict? Do you regard the German dispatch to the Austro-Hungarian government as a "blank check" supporting any Austrian action against Serbia?

2. Note the speech of German Chancellor Bethmann-Hollweg in which he defends the German violation of Belgian neutrality. What are his arguments and is his defense a convincing one?

3. Did the diplomats and other personalities of the time do enough to try to prevent war? On the basis of the evidence at your disposal, do you think war could have been avoided? If so, how? Or was it inevitable? What is your reaction to the quote by Will Rogers at the beginning of this chapter?

4. What are your most vivid impressions from the personal accounts of combat under the section "The Horrors of War"? Granted that all wars are horrible, what made this war unique? What makes the propaganda leaflet an effective weapon?

5. Apart from the physical differences, how was war in the air different from war on land? Is killing more palatable when it is romanticized? Do you find the Red Baron an exciting or intriguing personality?

6. Evaluate the statement, "It is sweet and proper to die for one's country." Is it an "Old Lie" as Wilfred Owen said? Was this war a game started by the old, fought by the young, and suffered by the innocent? What about patriotism and honor? Were they hollow concepts in this war? How about in World War II or in Vietnam?

7. In his Fourteen Points and at the Paris Peace Conference (1919), President Woodrow Wilson advocated idealistic principles: self-determination for nationalities, open diplomacy, disarmament, and the establishment of an international organization to discuss the concerns of the world community. Would these measures have helped stop the war? What do Norman Angell and G. Lowes Dickinson advocate? Does the fact that their books were written before and after the war say anything about political leadership in the early decades of the twentieth century?

8. In 1864, the English prelate John Henry Cardinal Newman said, "There is such a thing as legitimate warfare: war has its laws; there are things which may fairly be done, and things which may not be done." Do you agree or disagree? Did war have its laws in 1914? How about in our contemporary world?

9. The Great War has sometimes been viewed as the logical outcome of the intense nationalism and imperialism of the late nineteenth century. Do you agree with this view? What evidence exists in this chapter that indicates that nationalism and imperialism played a role in the Great War?

10. Although terrible in its ferocity, can the Great War be viewed as an agent of change and progress in civilization? Can you find evidence of this in the sources?

8

The Russian Revolution

Even if for every hundred correct things we did, we committed ten thousand mistakes, our revolution would still be—and it will be in the judgment of history—great and invincible; for this is the first time that the working people are themselves building a new life.

—V. I. Lenin

The Russian dictatorship of the proletariat has made a farce of the whole Marxist vision: developing a powerful, privileged ruling class to prepare for a classless society, setting up the most despotic state in history so that the state may *wither away*, establishing by force a colonial empire to combat imperialism and unite the workers of the world.

—Herbert J. Muller

A proletarian revolution is never proletarian.

—Will Durant

The events of the year 1917 remain among the most significant in the history of the twentieth century. The world was in the midst of a war that could no longer be viewed as glorious and patriotic, but had degenerated in people's minds to what war really is—suffering, destruction, and death. In such a crisis, it is important for governments to justify their actions, inspire soldiers, and assuage the populace. Statesmen require domestic stability in order to focus attention on the war effort. However,

Russia was not afforded this tranquility, and the monarchy of Tsar Nicholas II fell in March 1917, a prelude to a power struggle that by November of that year would see the imposition of a new regime, born of Marxist revolutionary philosophy and led by Vladimir Ulyanov, better known as Lenin (1870–1924). This was a complex revolution, and any simplification distorts the intricacy of events and political philosophies. Yet, for our purposes, it can be divided into three separate but related phases: the revolution of 1905, the March revolution of 1917, and the Bolshevik revolution of November 1917. This chapter seeks to unravel the conditions and pressures that led to the overthrow of the Romanov dynasty and the eventual Bolshevik seizure of power.

As in the French and American revolutions, social and economic conditions, as well as ideology, played an important role in providing the underlying causes and inspiration for revolution. Tsar Nicholas II was heir to a long tradition of autocracy that regarded change as dangerous to the stability of the dynasty. In the nineteenth century alone, Tsar Alexander I (1801–1825) continued the longstanding policy of absolutism, and his successor, Nicholas I (1825–1855), became Europe's most reactionary monarch with the slogan, "Autocracy, Orthodoxy and National Unity." Under Nicholas' leadership, Russia became a closed society. Nicholas employed a secret police and a network of paid informers that successfully exiled over 150,000 persons to the frigid wastes of Siberia. And yet there existed reform movements. Alexander Herzen (1812–1870), called the "father of Russian liberalism," advocated moderate socialist policies. But other dissidents were not so polite. Michail Bakunin (1814–1876) founded the anarchist movement and advocated the use of terror to effect change. Tsar Alexander II (1855–1881) instituted a series of liberal measures, including the emancipation of Russian serfs (1861), and reforms of the judiciary, army, and local and municipal governments. Yet his actions, though revolutionary for the absolutist government of Russia, were incomplete, and his failure to provide a constitution led to growing opposition and a populist movement (*Narodnik*), which preached revolution to the peasant masses and was suppressed by the Tsar. On March 13, 1881, Alexander II was assassinated by the terrorist group "People's Will"—ironically on the very day he had signed a decree that was to lead to constitutional reform. His son, Alexander III (1881–1894), refused to conform to the decree and set about reimplementing a policy of reactionary oppression. Thus when Nicholas II came to the throne in 1894, a long tradition of violent repression and terrorist response already existed.

One of the most influential philosophies that gave inspiration to the Russian Revolution was Marxism. Karl Marx and Friedrich Engels published the *Communist Manifesto* in 1848. In it they advocated a classless society that would come about through struggle between the exploiting *bourgeoisie* or middle-class capitalists and the working class, or proletariat. Marx intoned, "Workers of the world unite! You have nothing to lose but your chains!'' Marx's ideas became popular among the Russian revolutionary ''intelligentsia,'' and converts met in secret societies throughout Europe and Russia to discuss and plan action. One of his most dedicated disciples was Lenin. By 1905, Tsar Nicholas II's political opposition was more firmly organized. The Social Democratic party had been formed among industrial workers and was truly Marxist in philosophy. Yet party members differed among themselves; the Menshevik faction was more moderate and wanted to concentrate on improving the lot of the industrial worker, instead of concentrating on the world revolution that Marx predicted would become a reality. The other faction of the Social Democrats, the Bolsheviks, were led by Lenin and were more extreme in their insistence on a core of ''professional revolutionaries,'' dedicated to the immediate overthrow of capitalist society. Other political groups existed in 1905 as well, including the Constitutional Democratic party (Cadets) and the Social Revolutionary party, which sought agricultural land reform.

Although Russian tsars had long resisted demands for basic civil rights, equality before the law and representative government, Nicholas II especially seemed to live in a vacuum—his own world of yachts and tennis, crystal and caviar. He remained unaware of the plight of the Russian peasantry, half-starved and oppressed by landlords who often confiscated their land, or of the urban worker who was burdened by low wages and long hours. Following the massacre of Russian workers during a peaceful demonstration in January 1905 (called ''Bloody Sunday''), the popular outcry forced the tsar to establish an Imperial Duma, or representative assembly, and to provide a new constitution, guaranteeing civil rights for the people. The first phase of the Russian Revolution had taken place. Still, the Duma had no real authority over the tsar and its liberal recommendations were stifled. From 1906 to 1907, Nicholas merely dismissed Dumas that sought to encroach upon his power. From 1907 to 1916, the Dumas were controlled by the tsar through voting restrictions and altered election laws.

In the summer of 1914, Europe gravitated toward disaster. When Germany declared war on Russia (August 1, 1914), France supported her Russian ally. On August 4, Great Britain also joined in the struggle against Germany and Austria. The Great War had begun. Conditions among the Russian people deteriorated as thousands died in battle or as victims of disease or famine. The refugee problem was acute and people wandered homeless throughout Russia. The government was simply not able to cope with the economic and logistic demands of military mobilization and war. In March of 1917, the tsar was persuaded to abdicate, hoping that such action would assure Russia's continued participation in the war. This action came as a surprise to almost everyone. Even the most vitriolic detractors of the tsarist regime, notably Lenin in Switzerland, were caught off-guard. The second phase of the revolution had just begun.

With the fall of the tsar, a power vacuum existed and the competition to fill it was intense. A Provisional Government was chosen from members of the sitting Imperial Duma. The Provisional Government generally was made up of liberals and moderate socialists who promised an elected Constituent Assembly that was representative of the Russian people; they also pledged to draw up a new constitution that guaranteed civil liberties. However, the Provisional Government also supported Russia's continuation of the war. The other competitor for power was the Petrograd Soviet of Workers and Soldier's Deputies. A soviet was simply a council of elected representatives that advocated reforms for the working classes. The soviets were generally composed of Social Revolutionaries, Mensheviks, and initially only a minority of Bolsheviks. They regarded the war as a struggle between capitalists at the expense of the working classes (proletariat) and therefore wanted Russia to cease hostilities immediately. However, the Petrograd Soviet did not advocate armed rebellion against the Provisional Government. On the contrary, some members of the Soviet even believed that they held a kind of dual power with it. No one proposed a government of national unity, and this lack of cooperation was to prove fatal to political stability.

Perhaps too much was expected of the Provisional Government. Soldiers wanted an end to the war, peasants needed more land, the workers in the cities demanded better living conditions, the national and religious minorities of Russia wanted official recognition, as well as political and cultural autonomy, and the Allies wanted Russia's continued support in the war. For a temporary government composed of people who lacked experience and an organized plan of action, the burden was too great.

Lenin arrived in Petrograd in April and started organizing the opposition. As leader of the more radical Bolshevik faction of the Social Democratic party, he denounced the Provisional Government and worked independently of the other socialist groups in an effort to seize control. Lenin proclaimed "all power to the soviets" and in July led a premature uprising that failed. Several Bolsheviks were arrested (including Lenin's brilliant associate Leon Trotsky), but Lenin escaped to Finland. Bolshevik fortunes changed when the leader of the Provisional Government, Alexander Kerensky (1881–1970), was confronted with a military rebellion— a right-wing revolt led by General Lavr Kornilov that was quelled only with the assistance of the Petrograd Soviet. In November 1917, Lenin, against the judgment of some of his colleagues, made another attempt to topple the Provisional Government. This time he was successful and his Bolshevik faction of radical socialists was able to maintain its power. This third phase of the Russian Revolution established a regime of a very different order.

The Provisional Government failed for many reasons. The members had little experience in government and administration and could not counter the effective propaganda of Lenin, which offered "Peace, Bread, and Land." Kerensky believed that he had an obligation to act in a legal, democratic fashion, to demonstrate that his leadership was progressive and superior to that of the tsar. Lenin played by his own rules and would not share power. His organization and insistence in the rightness of his ideas, coupled with a measure of luck, produced a revolution that indeed shook the world.

Lenin's Bolshevik government survived a counterrevolutionary threat from supporters of the tsar as the Civil War came to an end in 1921. Lenin had started the transition toward Marx's conception of a Communist society, but fell ill in 1922 and died two years later. His position as leader of the revolution would eventually be assumed by Joseph Stalin (1879–1953). Under Stalin's brutal direction, and the leadership of his successors, the Soviet Union emerged as a formidable political, military, and ideological adversary to the United States in the late twentieth century. We live today under a cloud of mutual suspicion, fostered by intense propaganda, massive nuclear arsenals, and geopolitical competition. Viewed from this perspective, the Russian Revolution of 1917 remains one of the most significant political events of the modern world.

The Fall of the Monarchy

Bloody Sunday (January 1905)

Successful revolutions often depend on an incident or immediate crisis that serves as a rallying point for mass protest and outrage. It is at this moment that underlying problems between rulers and governed are brought into focus and the revolution given justification and incentive. Just such an incident occurred on January 22, 1905, when elite Russian troops called Cossacks attacked unarmed workers who were protesting in a peaceful demonstration. The workers wanted to address the tsar regarding civil rights, popular representation, and the needs of the Russian laborer. A correspondent of the *London Times* dispatched the first account below of the massacre. The second account was telegraphed to the Paris newspaper, *Le Matin*, by its correspondent.

Report of the *London Times*

A more perfect and lovely day never dawned. The air was crisp and the sky almost cloudless. The gilded domes of the cathedrals and churches, bril-

James H. Robinson and Charles A. Beard, eds., *Readings in Modern European History*, vol. II (Boston: Ginn & Company, 1909), pp. 373–374.

Bloody Sunday (January 1905). Russian Cossacks fire on a group of protesting workers. This incident became a rallying point for governmental reform. (*Sovfoto*)

liantly illuminated by the sun, formed a superb panorama. I noticed a significant change in the bearing of the passers-by. They were all wending their way, singly or in small groups, in the direction of the Winter Palace. Joining in the stream of workingmen, I proceeded in the direction of the Winter Palace. No observer could help being struck by the look of sullen determination on every face. Already a crowd of many thousands had collected, but was prevented from entering the square by mounted troops drawn up across the thoroughfare. The cavalry advanced at a walking pace, scattering the people right and left.

Event has succeeded event with such bewildering rapidity that the public is staggered and shocked beyond measure. The first trouble began at 11 o'clock, when the military tried to turn back some thousands of strikers at one of the bridges. The same thing happened almost simultaneously at other bridges, where the constant flow of workmen pressing forward refused to be denied access to the common rendezvous in the Palace Square.

The Cossacks at first used their knouts, then the flat of their sabers, and finally they fired. The strikers in the front ranks fell on their knees and implored the Cossacks to let them pass, protesting that they had no hostile intentions. They refused, however, to be intimidated by blank cartridges, and orders were given to load with ball.

The passions of the mob broke loose like a bursting dam. The people, seeing the dead and dying carried away in all directions, the snow on the streets and pavements soaked with blood, cried aloud for vengeance. Meanwhile the situation at the Palace was becoming momentarily worse. The troops were reported to be unable to control the vast masses which were constantly surging forward. Reenforcements were sent, and at 2 o'clock here also the order was given to fire. Men, women, and children fell at each volley, and were carried away in ambulances, sledges, and carts. The indignation and fury of every class were aroused. Students, merchants, all classes of the population alike were inflamed. At the moment of writing, firing is going on in every quarter of the city.

Father Gapon, marching at the head of a large body of workmen, carrying a cross and other religious emblems, was wounded in the arm and shoulder. The two forces of workmen are now separated. Those on the other side of the river were arming with swords, knives, and smiths' and carpenters' tools, and are busy erecting barricades. The troops are apparently reckless, firing right and left, with or without reason. The rioters continue to appeal to them, saying, "You are Russians! Why play the part of bloodthirsty butchers?"

Dreadful anxiety prevails in every household where any members are absent. Distracted husbands, fathers, wives, and children are searching for those missing. The surgeons and Red Cross ambulances are busy. A night of terror is in prospect.

Report of *Le Matin*

The soldiers of the Preobrazhensky regiment, without any summons to disperse, shoot down the unfortunate people as if they were playing at bloodshed. Several hundred fall; more than a hundred and fifty are killed. They are almost all children, women, and young people. It is terrible. Blood flows on all sides. At 5 o'clock the crowd is driven back, cut down and repelled on all sides. The people, terror-stricken, fly in every direction. Scared women and children slip, fall, rise to their feet, only to fall again farther on. At this moment a sharp word of command is heard and the

James H. Robinson & Charles A. Beard, eds., *Readings in Modern European History*, vol. II (Boston: Ginn and Company, 1909, pp. 374–375.

victims fall *en masse*. There had been no disturbances to speak of. The whole crowd is unarmed and has not uttered a single threat.

As I proceeded, there were everywhere troops and Cossacks. Successive discharges of musketry shoot down on all sides the terrorized mob. The soldiers aim at the people's heads and the victims are frightfully disfigured. A woman falls almost at my side. A little farther I slip on a piece of brain. Before me is a child of eight years whose face is no longer human. Its mother is kneeling in tears over its corpse. The wounded, as they drag themselves along, leave streams of blood on the snow.

Duma and Constitution

The public outcry following the massacre on Bloody Sunday contributed to a more responsive attitude on the part of the tsar. Nicholas decided to institute a Duma, or representative assembly, which was to exist as a testament to reform, but with no real power to change conditions. The Duma convened in May 1906; it tried to direct the tsar's attention to liberal reforms, but was dismissed as a consequence (1906). In all, there were four Dumas from 1905 to 1917. The first two selections recall the institution and dismissal of the first Duma. Note the tsar's reasons for his actions. The last document excerpts articles from the Russian Imperial Constitution of April 1906. Has Nicholas compromised on his autocracy?

Manifesto for the First Duma (August 1905)

TSAR NICHOLAS II

The empire of Russia is formed and strengthened by the indestructible union of the Tsar with the people and the people with the Tsar. This concord and the union of the Tsar and the people is the great moral force which has created Russia in the course of centuries by protecting her from all misfortunes and all attacks, and has constituted up to the present time a pledge of unity, independence, integrity, material well-being, and intellectual development in the present and in the future.

In our manifesto of February 26, 1903, we summoned all faithful sons of the fatherland in order to perfect, through mutual understanding, the organization of the State, founding it securely on public order and private welfare. We devoted ourselves to the task of coordinating local elective

James H. Robinson and Charles A. Beard, eds., *Readings in Modern European History*, Vol. II (Boston: Ginn & Company, 1909), pp. 375–377.

bodies [zemstvos] with the central authorities, and removing the disagreements existing between them, which so disturbed the normal course of the national life. Autocratic Tsars, our ancestors, have had this aim constantly in view, and the time has now come to follow out their good intentions and to summon elected representatives from the whole of Russia to take a constant and active part in the elaboration of laws, adding for this purpose to the higher State institutions a special consultative body entrusted with the preliminary elaboration and discussion of measures and with the examination of the State Budget. It is for this reason that, while preserving the fundamental law regarding autocratic power, we have deemed it well to form a *Gosundarstvennaia* Duma (i.e. State Council) and to approve regulations for elections to this Duma, extending these laws to the whole territory of the empire, with such exceptions only as may be considered necessary in the case of some regions in which special conditions obtain. . . .

We are convinced that those who are elected by the confidence of the whole people, and who are called upon to take part in the legislative work of the government, will show themselves in the eyes of all Russia worthy of the imperial trust in virtue of which they have been invited to cooperate in this great work; and that in perfect harmony with the other institutions and authorities of the State, established by us, they will contribute profitably and zealously to our labors for the well-being of our common mother, Russia, and for the strengthening of the unity, security, and greatness of the empire, as well as for the tranquillity and prosperity of the people.

In invoking the blessing of the Lord on the labors of the new assembly which we are establishing, and with unshakable confidence in the grace of God and in the assurance of the great historical destinies reserved by Divine Providence for our beloved fatherland, we firmly hope that Russia with the help of God Almighty, and with the combined efforts of all her sons, will emerge triumphant from the trying ordeals through which she is now passing, and will renew her strength in the greatness and glory of her history extending over a thousand years.

Given at Peterhof on the nineteenth day of August, in the year of grace 1905, and the eleventh year of our reign.

Dissolution of the Duma (July 1906)

TSAR NICHOLAS II

We summoned the representatives of the nation by our will to the work of productive legislation. Confiding firmly in divine clemency and believing in the great and brilliant future of our people, we confidantly anticipated benefits for the country from their labors. We proposed great reforms in all departments of the national life. We have always devoted our greatest

James H. Robinson and Charles A. Beard, eds., *Readings in Modern European History*, Vol. II (Boston: Ginn & Company, 1909), pp. 377–378.

care to the removal of the ignorance of the people by the light of instruction, and to the removal of their burdens by improving the conditions of agricultural work.

A cruel disappointment has befallen our expectations. The representatives of the nation, instead of applying themselves to the work of productive legislation, have strayed into spheres beyond their competence, and have been making inquiries into the acts of local authorities established by ourselves, and have been making comments upon the imperfections of the fundamental laws, which can only be modified by our imperial will. In short, the representatives of the nation have undertaken really illegal acts, such as the appeal by the Duma to the nation.

The peasants, disturbed by such anomalies, and seeing no hope of the amelioration of their lot, have resorted in a number of districts to open pillage and the destruction of other people's property, and to disobedience of the law and of the legal authorities. But our subjects ought to remember that an improvement in the lot of the people is only possible under conditions of perfect order and tranquillity. We shall not permit arbitrary or illegal acts, and we shall impose our imperial will on the disobedient by all the power of the State.

In dissolving the Duma we confirm our immutable intention of maintaining this institution, and in conformity with this intention we fix March 5, 1907 as the date of the convocation of a new Duma. With unshakable faith in divine clemency and in the good sense of the Russian people, we shall expect from the new Duma the realization of our efforts and their promotion of legislation in accordance with the requirements of a regenerated Russia.

Faithful sons of Russia, your Tsar calls upon you as a father upon his children to unite with him for the regeneration of our holy fatherland. We believe that giants in thought and action will appear, and that, thanks to their assiduous efforts, the glory of Russia will continue to shine.

Russian Imperial Constitution (April 1906)

Art. 4. The supreme autocratic power is vested in the Tsar of all the Russias. It is God's command that his authority should be obeyed not only through fear but for conscience' sake.

Art. 5. The person of the Tsar is sacred and inviolable.

Art. 7. The Tsar exercises the legislative power in conjunction with the Council of the Empire and the imperial Duma.

Art. 8. The initiative in all branches of legislation belongs to the Tsar. Solely on his initiative may the fundamental laws of the empire be subjected to a revision in the Council of the Empire and the imperial Duma.

James H. Robinson and Charles A. Beard, eds., *Readings in Modern European History*, Vol. II (Boston: Ginn & Company, 1909), pp. 379–381.

Art. 9. The Tsar approves the laws, and without his approval no law can come into existence.

Art. 10. All governmental powers in their widest extent throughout the whole Russian empire are vested in the Tsar. . . .

Art. 62. The established and ruling faith of the Russian Empire is the Christian, Orthodox Catholic, Eastern faith.

Art. 64. The Tsar as Christian ruler is the supreme defender and upholder of the doctrines of the ruling faith, the protector of the true belief, and of every ordinance in the holy Church.

Art. 66. All those subjects of the Russian State who do not belong to the ruling Church, natives as well as the inhabitants of annexed districts, foreigners in the Russian service, or temporary sojourners in Russia, enjoy the free exercise of their respective faiths and religious services according to their particular usages.

Art. 73. No one shall be arrested except in the cases determined by law.

Art. 74. No one shall be brought into court or punished for an offense which was not a crime according to the law when committed.

Art. 75. The dwelling of every one is inviolable.

Art. 76. Every Russian subject is entitled freely to choose his residence and occupation.

Art. 77. Property is inviolable. Property shall be taken only for public use and after just compensation.

Art. 78. Russian subjects are entitled to meet peacably and without arms for such purposes as are not contrary to law.

Art. 79. Within the limits fixed by law every one may express his thoughts by word or writing and circulate them by means of the press or otherwise.

What Is to Be Done? *(1902)*

The above question was asked time and again by revolutionaries who fought against the autocracy of the Russian monarchy during the nineteenth century. The famous solution written in 1902 came from Vladimir Ulyanov (Lenin), who was a disciple of Karl Marx but was rather impatient with the disorganization and amateurism of his fellow revolutionaries. Lenin saw the Communist revolution as an all-consuming goal, to be obtained only by hard work and commitment to the cause of revolution itself. Lenin advocated the strict organization of a party composed of "professional revolutionaries." In this he went far beyond Marx's conception of revolution as "eventual." Lenin's answer to the question, "What is to be done?" marks the beginning of Leninism as a distinct political philosophy.

"We Shall Overturn Russia!"

V. I. LENIN

Without a revolutionary theory there can be no revolutionary movement. This thought cannot be insisted upon too strongly at a time when the fashionable preaching of opportunism goes hand in hand with an infatuation for the narrowest forms of practical activity. . . . Our Party is only in process of formation, its features are only just becoming outlined, and it is yet far from having settled accounts with other trends of revolutionary thought, which threaten to divert the movement from the correct path. . . . The national tasks of Russian Social-Democracy are such as have never confronted any other socialist party in the world. . . . *The role of vanguard fighter can be fulfilled only by a party that is guided by the most advanced theory.* . . .

The strikes of the nineties represented the class struggle in embryo, but only in embryo. Taken by themselves, these strikes were simply trade union struggles, but not yet Social-Democratic struggles. They testified to the awakening antagonisms between workers and employers, but the workers were not, and could not be, conscious of the irreconcilable antagonism of their interests to the whole of the modern political and social system, i.e., theirs was not yet Social-Democratic consciousness. In this sense, the strikes of the nineties in spite of the enormous progress they represented as compared with the "riots," remained a purely spontaneous movement.

I assert: 1) that no revolutionary movement can endure without a stable organization of leaders that maintains continuity; 2) that the wider the masses spontaneously drawn into the struggle, forming the basis of the movement and participating in it, the more urgent the need of such an organization, and the more solid this organization must be (for it is much easier for demagogues to sidetrack the more backward sections of the masses); 3) that such an organization must consist chiefly of people professionally engaged in revolutionary activity; 4) that in an autocratic state, the more we *confine* the membership of such an organization to people who are professionally engaged in revolutionary activity and to have been professionally trained in the art of combatting the political police, the more difficult will it be to wipe out such an organization, and 5) the *greater* will be the number of people of the working class of the other classes of society who will be able to join the movement and perform active work in it. . . .

Our chief sin with regard to organization is that *by our amateurishness we have lowered the prestige of revolutionaries in Russia.* A person who is flabby and shaky in questions of theory, who has a narrow outlook, who pleads the spontaneity of the masses as an excuse for his own sluggishness, who resembles a trade union secretary more than a people's tribune, who is unable to conceive of a broad and bold plan that would command the respect

Robert V. Daniels, *A Documentary History of Communism*, vol. 1 (Hanover, N.H.: University Press of New England, 1984), pp. 8, 12–13. Reprinted by permission of the publisher.

even of opponents, and who is inexperienced and clumsy in his own professional art—the art of combatting the political police—why, such a man is
not a revolutionary but a wretched amateur!

Let no active worker take offense at these frank remarks, for as far as
insufficient training is concerned, I apply them first and foremost to myself. I used to work in a circle that set itself very wide, all-embracing tasks;
and all of us, members of that circle, suffered painfully, acutely from the
realization that we were proving ourselves to be amateurs at a moment in
history when we might have been able to say, paraphrasing a well-known
epigram: "Give us an organization of revolutionaries, and we shall overturn Russia!" And the more I recall the burning sense of shame I then
experienced, the more bitter are my feelings towards those pseudo Social-
Democrats whose teachings "bring disgrace on the calling of a revolutionary," who fail to understand that our task is not to champion the degrading
of the revolutionary to the level of an amateur, but to *raise* the amateurs to
the level of revolutionaries. . . .

War and the Abdication of the Tsar

The following selections range in time from August 1914, when Russia
entered the Great War, to March 1917, when Nicholas abdicated the
throne. They recount the reasons given for Russia's entrance into the war,
the problems associated with the abdication of the tsar, and the debate
over the continued existence of the Romanov dynasty.

Imperial Manifesto for Entrance (August 2, 1914)

TSAR NICHOLAS II

Compelled, by the force of circumstances thus created, to adopt the necessary measures of precaution, We commanded that the army and the navy
be put on a war footing, but, at the same time, holding the blood and the
treasure of Our subjects dear, We made every effort to obtain a peaceable
issue of the negotiations that had been started.

In the midst of friendly communications, Austria's Ally, Germany, contrary to our trust in century-old relations of neighborliness, and paying no
heed to Our assurances that the measures We had adopted implied no
hostile aims whatever, insisted upon their immediate abandonment, and,
meeting with a rejection of this demand, suddenly declared war on Russia.

We have now to intercede not only for a related country, unjustly attacked, but also to safeguard the honor, dignity, and integrity of Russia,

Frank A. Golder, ed., *Documents of Russian History (1914–1917)*, trans. Emanuel Aronsberg
(New York: The Century Company, 1927), pp. 29–30.

and her position among the Great Powers. We firmly believe that all Our loyal subjects will rally self-sacrificingly and with one accord to the defense of the Russian soil.

At this hour of threatening danger, let domestic strife be forgotten. Let the union between the Tsar and His people be stronger than ever, and let Russia, rising like one man, repel the insolent assault of the enemy.

With a profound faith in the justice of Our cause, and trusting humbly in Almighty Providence, We invoke prayerfully the Divine blessing for Holy Russia and our valiant troops.

Given at Saint Petersburg, on the second day of August, in the year of Our Lord one thousand nine hundred and fourteen, and the twentieth year of Our reign.

The Refugee Problem (August 17, 1915)

[Discussion in a meeting of the Council of Ministers]

Of all the grave consequences of the war this one [refugee] is the most unexpected, the most serious and the most difficult to remedy. . . . It has been worked out by the wise strategists to frighten the enemy. . . . Misery, sickness, sorrow and poverty go with them [refugees] all over Russia. They create panics wherever they go and put out whatever still remains of the ardor of the first days of the war. They move like a wall, knocking down the grain, trampling down the plowed fields and destroying the forests. . . . Their trail is like that of the flight of locusts or the band of Tamerlane on the warpath. The railways are choked, and pretty soon it will be impossible to move war freight and food supplies. . . . I have an idea that the Germans watch with pleasure the result of this attempt to repeat the tactics of 1812. If on the one hand they [Germans] are deprived of certain local provisions, they are, on the other hand, freed from the care of the population and have full freedom of action in the depopulated areas. . . . In my capacity as member of the Council of Ministers I should like to say that this undertaking of Headquarters to bring about a second migration of peoples will lead Russia into darkness, revolution and ruin.

Abdication of the Russian Throne (March 15, 1917)

TSAR NICHOLAS II

In the midst of the great struggle against a foreign foe, who has been striving for three years to enslave our country, it has pleased God to lay on Russia a new and painful trial. Newly arisen popular disturbances in the

"The Refugee Problem" is from Frank A. Golder, ed., *Documents of Russian History (1914–1917)*, trans. Emanuel Aronsberg (New York: The Centur~ Company, 1927), p. 182.

"Abdication of the Russian Throne" is from Frank A. Golder, ed., *Documents of Russian History (1914–1917)*, trans. Emanuel Aronsberg (New York: The Century Company, 1927), pp. 297–298.

interior imperil the successful continuation of the stubborn fight. The fate of Russia, the honor of our heroic army, the welfare of our people, the entire future of our dear land, call for the prosecution of the conflict, regardless of the sacrifices, to a triumphant end. The cruel foe is making his last effort and the hour is near when our brave army, together with our glorious Allies, will crush him.

In these decisive days in the life of Russia, we deem it our duty to do what we can to help our people to draw together and unite all their forces with the State Duma, think it best to abdicate the throne of the Russian State and to lay down the Supreme Power.

Not wishing to be separated from our beloved son, we hand down our inheritance to our brother, Grand Duke Michael Alexandrovich, and give him our blessing on mounting the throne of the Russian Empire.

We enjoin our brother to govern in union and harmony with the representatives of the people on such principles as they shall see fit to establish. He should bind himself to do so by an oath in the name of our beloved country.

We call on all faithful sons of the Fatherland to fulfil their sacred obligations to their country by obeying the Tsar at this hour of national distress, and to help him and the representatives of the people to take the path of victory, well-being, and glory.

May the Lord God help Russia!

March 15, 1917, 3 P.M.
City of Pskov

Shall the Romanov Dynasty Remain? (March 15, 1917)

[Newspaper editorial from *Izvestiia*]

The revolutionary people should carry through to the end the revolution and the democratization of its political and social organization. To return to the old is unthinkable. The revolutionary people should organize the State in the way that will best satisfy its interests, strength and great zeal, and will make impossible a new attempt on its rights and liberty. This can be done by handing the power over to the people, that is to say, by forming a democratic republic, in which the officers of government are elected by universal equal, secret, and direct suffrage. All the revolutionary elements in Russia, who have made tremendous sacrifices in the fight and the forging of freedom, should strive for such a government.

If the power were entrusted to a monarch, one, with his responsible ministry, the latter might make an attempt on the liberty of the people and bind it with chains of slavery. Then again, in a constitutional monarchy

Frank A. Golder, ed., *Documents of Russian History (1914–1917)*, trans. Emanuel Aronsberg (New York: The Century Company, 1927), pp. 296–297.

there is the right of succession which again creates the possibility of rulers of the type of Nicholas, the Last.

In a constitutional monarchy, the army serves not the people, but the monarch, giving him great power, which he could use to harm the people. The Romanov dynasty is now overthrown. . . . There must be no going back to it. The revolutionary people will find enough strength to form a new republican government, which will guarantee its rights and freedom.

Last Address to the Army (March 21, 1917)

TSAR NICHOLAS II

I appeal to you for the last time, my beloved troops. After the abdication of myself and my son, all the authority has passed into the hands of the Provisional Government, formed by the State Duma. So may God help them lead Russia on the way to prosperity and glory!

And you, my valiant troops, God help you to defend our country against the cruel foe! For two and a half years you have daily and hourly borne on your shoulders the heavy burden of war. Much blood has been shed; many efforts have been made; and the day is near when Russia, closely united to her gallant allies in their common aspiration to victory, will break the resistance of the enemy. This war, unprecedented in history, must be continued and brought to a victorious end. Any one who dreams of peace at the present moment is a traitor to his country. I know that every honest soldier thinks so. Go on fulfilling your duty; stand to guard your glorious fatherland; obey the Provisional Government and your chiefs. Do not forget that all disorder, all weakening of discipline, are so many assets for the foe.

I firmly believe that the love for your great country is, and ever will be, alive in your hearts. God will give you his blessing, and St. George, the Victorious, will help you to triumph over the foe!

The Provisional Government

After the abdication of the tsar in March 1917, a temporary body called the Provisional Government was installed to maintain stability in the country until a representative constituent assembly could be elected by the Russian people. The Petrograd Soviet, an elected council of workers and soldiers, immediately threatened the authority of the Provisional Government. Lenin, who had just arrived in Petrograd from Switzerland,

Frank A. Golder, ed., *Documents of Russian History (1914–1917)*, trans. Emanuel Aronsberg (New York: The Century Company, 1927), pp. 53–54.

reasserted leadership of the Bolshevik party and set forth his demands in the last selection, the famous "April Theses."

First Declaration of the Provisional Government (March 19, 1917)

Citizens of Russia:

A great event has taken place. By the mighty assault of the Russian people, the old order has been overthrown. A new, free Russia is born. The great revolution crowns long years of struggle. By the act of October 17, [30] 1905, under the pressure of the awakened popular forces, Russia was promised constitutional liberties. Those promises, however, were not kept. The First State Duma, interpreter of the nation's hopes, was dissolved. The Second Duma suffered the same fate, and the Government, powerless to crush the national will, decided, by the act of June 3, [16] 1907, to deprive the people of a part of those rights of participation in legislative work which had been granted.

In the course of nine long years, there were taken from the people, step by step, all the rights that they had won. Once more the country was plunged into an abyss of arbitrariness and despotism. All attempts to bring the Government to its senses proved futile, and the titanic world struggle, into which the country was dragged by the enemy, found the Government in a state of moral decay, alienated from the people, indifferent to the fate of our native land, and steeped in the infamy of corruption. Neither the heroic efforts of the army, staggering under the crushing burdens of internal chaos, nor the appeals of the popular representatives who had united in the face of the national peril, were able to lead the former Emperor and his Government into the path of unity with the people. And when Russia, owing to the illegal and fatal actions of her rulers, was confronted with gravest disasters, the nation was obliged to take the power into its own hands.

The unanimous revolutionary enthusiasm of the people, fully conscious of the gravity of the moment, and the determination of the State Duma, have created the Provisional Government, which considers it to be its sacred and responsible duty to fulfill the hopes of the nation, and lead the country out onto the bright path of free civic organization.

The Government trusts that the spirit of lofty patriotism, manifested during the struggle of the people against the old regime, will also inspire our valiant soldiers on the field of battle. For its own part, the Government will make every effort to provide our army with everything necessary to bring the war to a victorious end.

Frank A. Golder, ed., *Documents of Russian History (1914–1917)*, trans. Emanuel Aronsberg (New York: The Century Company, 1927), pp. 311–313.

The Government will sacredly observe the alliances which bind us to other powers, and will unswervingly carry out the agreements entered into by the Allies. While taking measures to defend the country against the foreign enemy, the Government will, at the same time, consider it to be its primary duty to make possible the expression of the popular will as regards the form of government, and will convoke the Constituent Assembly within the shortest time possible, on the basis of universal, direct, equal, and secret suffrage, also guaranteeing participation in the elections to the gallant defenders of our native land, who are now shedding their blood on the fields of battle.

The Constituent Assembly will issue the fundamental laws, guaranteeing to the country the inalienable rights of justice, equality, and liberty. Conscious of the heavy burden which the country suffers because of the lack of civic rights, which lack stands in the way of its free, creative power at this time of violent national commotion, the Provisional Government deems it necessary, at once, before the convocation of the Constituent Assembly, to provide the country with laws for the safeguard of civic liberty and equality, in order to enable all citizens freely to apply their spiritual forces to creative work for the benefit of the country. The Government will also undertake the enactment of legal provisions to assure to all citizens, on the basis of universal suffrage, an equal share in the election of local governments.

At this moment of national liberation, the whole country remembers with reverent gratitude those who, in the struggle for their political and religious convictions, fell victims to the vindictive old regime, and the Provisional Government will regard it as its joyful duty to bring back from their exile, with full honors, all those who have suffered for the good of the country.

In fulfilling these tasks, the Provisional Government is animated by the belief that it will thus execute the will of the people, and that the whole nation will support it in its honest efforts to insure the happiness of Russia. This belief inspires it with courage. Only in the common effort of the entire nation and the Provisional Government can it see a pledge of triumph of the new order.

March 19, 1917

Policy of the Petrograd Soviet (March 27, 1917)

Comrade-proletarians, and toilers of all countries:

We, Russian workers and soldiers, united in the Petrograd Soviet of Workers' and Soldiers' Deputies, send you warmest greetings and announce the great event. The Russian democracy has shattered in the dust

Frank A. Golder, ed., *Documents of Russian History (1914–1917)*, trans. Emanuel Aronsberg (New York: The Century Company, 1927), pp. 325–326.

the age-long despotism of the Tsar and enters your family [of nations] as an equal, and as a mighty force in the struggle for our common liberation. Our victory is a great victory for the freedom and democracy of the world. The chief pillar of reaction in the world, the "Gendarme of Europe" is no more. May the earth turn to heavy granite on his grave! Long live freedom! Long live the international solidarity of the proletariat, and its struggle for final victory!

Our work is not yet finished: the shades of the old order have not yet been dispersed, and not a few enemies are gathering their forces against the Russian revolution. Nevertheless our achievement so far is tremendous. The people of Russia will express their will in the Constituent Assembly, which will be called as soon as possible on the basis of universal, equal, direct, and secret suffrage. And it may already be said without a doubt that a democratic republic will triumph in Russia. The Russian people now possess full political liberty. They can now assert their mighty power in the internal government of the country and in its foreign policy. And, appealing to all people who are being destroyed and ruined in the monstrous war, we announce that the time has come to start a decisive struggle against the grasping ambitions of the governments of all countries; the time has come for the people to take into their own hands the decision of the question of war and peace.

Conscious of its revolutionary power, the Russian democracy announces that it will, by every means, resist the policy of conquest of its ruling classes, and it calls upon the peoples of Europe for concerted, decisive action in favor of peace.

We are appealing to our brother-proletarians of the Austro-German coalition, and, first of all, to the German proletariat. From the first days of the war, you were assured that by raising arms against autocratic Russia, you were defending the culture of Europe from Asiatic despotism. Many of you saw in this a justification of that support which you were giving to the war. Now even this justification is gone: democratic Russia cannot be a threat to liberty and civilization.

We will firmly defend our own liberty from all reactionary attempts from within, as well as from without. The Russian revolution will not retreat before the bayonets of conquerors, and will not allow itself to be crushed by foreign military force. But we are calling to you: Throw off the yoke of your semi-autocratic rule, as the Russian people have shaken off the Tsar's autocracy; refuse to serve as an instrument of conquest and violence in the hands of kings, landowners, and bankers—and then by our united efforts, we will stop the horrible butchery, which is disgracing humanity and is beclouding the great days of the birth of Russian freedom.

Toilers of all countries: We hold out to you the hand of brotherhood across the mountains of our brothers' corpses, across rivers of innocent blood and tears, over the smoking ruins of cities and villages, over the wreckage of the treasures of civilization;—we appeal to you for the reestablishment and strengthening of international unity. In it is the pledge of our future victories and the complete liberation of humanity.

Proletarians of all countries, Unite!

PETROGRAD SOVIET OF WORKERS'
AND SOLDIERS' DEPUTIES

The April Theses (April 20, 1917)

V. I. LENIN

The class conscious proletariat can consent to a revolutionary war, which would really justify revolutionary defencism, only on condition: (a) that the power of government pass to the proletariat and the poor sections of the peasantry bordering on the proletariat; (b) that all annexations be renounced in deed as well as in words; (c) that a complete and real break be made with all capitalist interests.

In view of the undoubted honesty of the mass of the rank-and-file believers in revolutionary defencism, who accept the war as a necessity only and not as a means of conquest; in view of the fact that they are being deceived by the bourgeoisie, it is necessary thoroughly, persistently and patiently to explain their error to them, to explain the indissoluble connection between capital and the imperialist war, and to prove that *it is impossible* to end the war by a truly democratic, non-coercive peace without overthrow of capital.

The widespread propaganda of this view among the army on active service must be organised.

Fraternisation

(2) The specific feature of the present situation in Russia is that it represents a *transition* from the first stage of the revolution—which owing to the insufficient class consciousness and organisation of the proletariat, led to the assumption of power by the bourgeoisie—*to the second stage,* which must place power in the hands of the proletariat and the poor strata of the peasantry.

This transition is characterised, on the one hand, by a maximum of freedom (Russia is *now* the freest of all the belligerent countries in the world); on the other, by the absence of violence in relation to the masses, and, finally, by the naive confidence of the masses in the government of capitalists, the worst enemies of peace and socialism.

This specific situation demands on our part an ability to adapt ourselves to the specific requirements of Party work among unprecedentedly large masses of proletarians who have just awakened to political life.

Martin McCauley, *The Russian Revolution and the Soviet State* (New York: Barnes & Noble, 1975), pp. 52–54. Permission granted by Barnes & Noble Books, Totowa, New Jersey.

(3) No support must be given to the Provisional Government; the utter falsity of all its promises must be exposed, particularly of those relating to the renunciation of annexations. Exposure, and not the unpardonable illusion-breeding 'demand' that this government, a government of capitalists, should *cease* to be an imperialist government.

(4) The fact must be recognised that in most of the Soviets of Workers' Deputies our Party is in a minority, and so far in a small minority, as against *a bloc of all* the petty-bourgeois opportunist elements, who have yielded to the influence of the bourgeoisie and are the conveyors of its influence to the proletariat. . . .

It must be explained to the masses that the Soviet of Workers' Deputies is the *only possible* form of revolutionary government and that therefore bourgeoisie, to present a patient, systematic, and persistent *explanation* of its errors and tactics, an explanation especially adapted to the practical needs of the masses.

As long as we are in the minority we carry on the work of criticising and exposing errors and at the same time advocate the necessity of transferring the entire power of state to the Soviets of Workers' Deputies, so that the masses may by experience overcome their mistakes.

(5) Not a parliamentary republic—to return to a parliamentary republic from the Soviets of Workers' Deputies would be a retrograde step—but a republic of Soviets of Workers', Agricultural Labourers' and Peasants' Deputies throughout the country, from top to bottom.

Abolition of the police, the army and the bureaucracy.

(6) The agrarian programme must be centered around the Soviets of Agricultural Labourers' Deputies.

Confiscation of All Landed Estates

Nationalisation of *all* lands in the country, the disposal of such *lands* to be in the charge of the local Soviets of Agricultural Labourers' and Peasants' Deputies. The organisation of separate soviets of Deputies of the Poor Peasants. The creation of model farms on each of the large estates. . . .

(7) The immediate amalgamation of all banks in the country into a single national bank, control over which shall be exercised by the Soviet of Workers' Deputies.

(8) Our *immediate* task shall be not the 'introduction of socialism,' but to bring social production and distribution of products at once under the *control* of the Soviet of Workers' Deputies.

(9) Party tasks:
    (a) Immediate summoning of a Party congress.
    (b) Alteration of the Party programme, mainly:
        1. On the question of imperialism and the imperialist war;
        2. On the question of our attitude towards the state and our demand for a 'commune state.'

3. Amendment of our antiquated minimum programme;
(c) A new name for the Party.
(10) A new International.

The November Revolution (November 8, 1917)

The Bolshevik faction, led by Lenin and his very competent colleague Leon Trotsky, had suffered reversals during an abortive uprising in July 1917. Trotsky was imprisoned and Lenin fled to Finland. Finally in November 1917, Lenin persuaded his faction that the time was ripe for a coup. The first selection is Lenin's speech after his successful storming of the Winter Palace in Petrograd. Note the critical editorial from the newspaper *Izvestiia* on November 8. It was the last before the Bolsheviks censored the press. Lenin's seizure of power also included the establishment of a secret police (Cheka), an institution that had been used (in another form) by the autocratic tsar to eliminate opposition.

Speech After the Overthrow of the Provisional Government

V. I. LENIN

Comrades, the workmen's and peasant's revolution, the need of which the Bolsheviks have emphasized many times, has come to pass.

What is the significance of this revolution? Its significance is, in the first place, that we shall have a soviet government, without the participation of bourgeoisie of any kind. The oppressed masses will of themselves form a government. The old state machinery will be smashed into bits and in its place will be created a new machinery of government by the soviet organizations. From now on there is a new page in the history of Russia, and the present, third Russian revolution shall in its final result lead to the victory of Socialism.

One of our immediate tasks is to put an end to the war at once. But in order to end the war, which is closely bound up with the present capitalistic system, it is necessary to overthrow capitalism itself. In this work we shall have the aid of the world labor movement, which has already begun to develop in Italy, England, and Germany.

A just and immediate offer of peace by us to the international democracy will find everywhere a warm response among the international proletariat masses. In order to secure the confidence of the proletariat, it is necessary to publish at once all secret treaties.

Frank A. Golder, ed., *Documents of Russian History, 1914–1917,* trans. Emanuel Aronsberg (New York: The Century Company, 1927), pp. 618–619.

In the interior of Russia a very large part of the peasantry has said: Enough playing with the capitalists; we will go with the workers. We shall secure the confidence of the peasants by one decree, which will wipe out the private property of the landowners. The peasants will understand that their only salvation is in union with the workers.

We will establish a real labor control on production.

We have now learned to work together in a friendly manner, as is evident from this revolution. We have the force of mass organization which has conquered all and which will lead the proletariat to world revolution.

We should now occupy ourselves in Russia in building up a proletarian socialist state.

Long live the world-wide socialistic revolution!

"Little Good Is to Be Expected" (November 8, 1917)

[*Izvestiia* Newspaper Editorial]

Yesterday we said that the Bolshevik uprising is a mad adventure and today, when their attempt is crowned with success, we are of the same mind. We repeat: that which is before us is not a transfer of power to the Soviets, but a seizure of power by one party—the Bolsheviks. Yesterday we said that a successful attempt meant the breaking up of the greatest of the revolution—the Constituent Assembly. Today we add that it means, also, the breaking up of the Congress of Soviets, and perhaps the whole soviet organization. They can call themselves what they please; the fact remains that the Bolsheviks alone took part in the uprising. All the other socialistic and democratic parties protest against it.

How the situation may develop we do not know, but little good is to be expected. We are quite confident that the Bolsheviks cannot organize a state government. As yesterday, so today, we repeat that what is happening will react worst of all on the question of peace.

Censorship of the Press (November 9, 1917)

V. I. LENIN

In the trying critical period of the revolution and the days that immediately followed it the Provisional Revolutionary Committee was compelled to take a number of measures against the counter-revolutionary press of different shades.

Immediately outcries were heard from all sides that the new, socialist power had violated a fundamental principle of its programme by encroaching upon the freedom of the press.

"Little Good Is to Be Expected" is from Frank A. Golder, ed., *Documents of Russian History, 1914–1917*, trans. Emanuel Aronsberg (New York: The Century Company, 1927), p. 619.

"Censorship of the Press" is from Martin McCauley, *The Russian Revolution and the Soviet State* (New York: Barnes & Noble, 1975), pp. 190–191. Permission granted by Barnes & Noble Books, Totowa, New Jersey.

The Workers' and Peasants' Government calls the attention of the population to the fact that what this liberal facade actually conceals is freedom for the propertied classes, having taken hold of the lion's share of the entire press, to poison, unhindered, the minds and obscure the consciousness of the masses.

Every one knows that the bourgeois press is one of the most powerful weapons of the bourgeoisie. Especially at the crucial moment when the new power, the power of workers and peasants, is only affirming itself, it was impossible to leave this weapon wholly in the hands of the enemy, for in such moments it is no less dangerous than bombs and machine-guns. That is why temporary extraordinary measures were taken to stem the torrent of filth and slander in which the yellow and green press would be only too glad to drown the recent victory of the people.

As soon as the new order becomes consolidated, all administrative pressure on the press will be terminated and it will be granted complete freedom within the bounds of legal responsibility, in keeping with a law that will be broadest and most progressive in this respect.

However, being aware that a restriction of the press, even at critical moments, is permissible only within the limits of what is absolutely necessary, the Council of People's Commissars resolves:

General Provisions on the Press

1. Only those publications can be suppressed which (1) call for open resistance or insubordination to the Workers' and Peasants' Government; (2) sow sedition through demonstrably slanderous distortion of facts; (3) instigate actions of an obviously criminal, i.e. criminally punishable, nature.
2. Publications can be proscribed, temporarily or permanently, only by decision of the Council of People's Commissars.
3. The present ordinance is of a temporary nature and will be repealed by a special decree as soon as normal conditions of social life set in.

> Chairman of the Council of People's Commissars,
> VLADIMIR ULYANOV (LENIN).

Establishment of the Secret Police
(December 20, 1917)

V. I. LENIN

The Commission is to be called the All-Russian Extraordinary Commission for the Struggle with Counter-Revolution and Sabotage and is to be attached to the Council of People's Commissars.

Martin McCauley, *The Russian Revolution and the Soviet State* (New York: Barnes & Noble, 1975), pp. 181–182. Permission granted by Barnes & Noble Books, Totowa, New Jersey.

The duties of the Commission are to be as follows:

1. To investigate and nullify all acts of counter-revolution and sabotage throughout Russia, irrespective of origin.
2. To bring before the Revolutionary Tribunal all counter-revolutionaries and saboteurs and to work out measures to combat them.
3. The Commission is to conduct the preliminary investigation only, sufficient to suppress (the counter-revolutionary act). The Commission to be divided into sections: (1) the information (section) (2) the organisation section (in charge of organising the struggle with counter-revolution throughout Russia) with branches, and (3) the fighting section.

The Commission shall be set up finally tomorrow. Then the fighting section of the All-Russian Commission shall start its activities. The Commission shall keep an eye on the press, saboteurs, right Socialist Revolutionaries and strikers. Measures to be taken are confiscation, imprisonment, confiscation of cards, publication of the names of the enemies of the people, etc.

Chairman of the Council of People's Commissars,
V. ULYANOV (LENIN)

Dissolution of the Constituent Assembly (December 1917)

V. I. LENIN

A major responsibility of the Provisional Government had been to organize an election and establish a Constituent Assembly that was truly representative of the Russian people. Lenin, after achieving power through political manipulation and force of arms, decided to hold the election anyway. The results were not encouraging since the Bolsheviks were soundly defeated. Lenin, however, would not concede defeat and chose to dissolve the Constituent Assembly instead. Note Lenin's reasons for his actions. The second document is a questionnaire that all delegates to the Tenth All Russian Congress of the Russian Communist Party had to fill out. This was Lenin's view of himself in 1921.

At its very inception, the Russian revolution produced the Soviets of Workers', Soldiers' and Peasants' Deputies as the only mass organization of all the working and exploited classes capable of giving leadership to the struggle of these classes for their complete political and economic emancipation.

Throughout the initial period of the Russian revolution the Soviets grew

Martin McCauley, *The Russian Revolution and the Soviet State* (New York: Barnes & Noble, 1975), pp. 184–186. Permission granted by Barnes & Noble Books, Totowa, New Jersey.

in number, size and strength, their own experience disabusing them of the illusions regarding compromise with the bourgeoisie, opening their eyes to the fraudulence of the forms of bourgeois-democratic parliamentarism, and leading them to the conclusion that the emancipation of the oppressed classes was unthinkable unless they broke with these forms and with every kind of compromise. Such a break came with the October [November] Revolution, with the transfer of power to the Soviets.

The Constituent Assembly, elected on the basis of lists drawn up before October Revolution, was expressive of the old correlation of political forces, when the conciliators and Constitutional-Democrats were in power.

The working classes learned through experience that old bourgeois parliamentarism had outlived its day, that it was utterly incompatible with the tasks of Socialism, and that only class institutions (such as the Soviets) and not national ones were capable of overcoming the resistance of the propertied classes and laying the foundations of socialist society.

Any renunciation of the sovereign power of the Soviets, of the Soviet Republic won by the people, in favour of bourgeois parliamentarism and the Constituent Assembly would now be a step backwards and would cause a collapse of the entire October Workers' and Peasants' Revolution.

By virtue of generally known circumstances the Constituent Assembly, opening on January 18, gave the majority to the Party of Right-Wing Socialist-Revolutionaries, the party of Kerensky, Avksentev and Chernov. Naturally, this party refused to recognize the programme of Soviet power, to recognize the Declaration of Rights of the Working and Exploited People, to recognize the October Revolution and Soviet power. . . .

Obviously, under such circumstances the Constituent Assembly can only serve as a cover for the struggle of the bourgeois counter-revolution to overthrow the power of the Soviets.

In view of this, the Central Executive Committee resolves:

The Constituent Assembly is hereby dissolved.

A Self-Portrait (March 7, 1921)

V. I. LENIN

Name: Ulyanov (Lenin), Vladimir Ilyich

Party organization: Central Committee, Russian Communist Party

Number of delegate mandate (voting/advisory): No. 21 advisory

By whom elected: Central Committee

No. of Party members represented at meeting at which elected: Central Committee—19 members

Warren B. Walsh, *Readings in Russian History,* 3rd ed. (Syracuse, N.Y.: Syracuse University Press, 1959), pp. 622–623. Reprinted by permission of the publisher.

Which All-Russian Party Congresses have you attended: All except July (August?) 1917

Date of birth—age: 1870—51 years

State of health: Good

Family—no. of members of dependents: Wife and sister

Nationality: Russian

Native tongue: Russian

Knowledge of other languages: English, German, French—poor, Italian— very poor

What parts of Russia do you know well, and how long have you lived there: Know Volga country where I was born best; lived there until age 17

Have you been abroad (when, where, how long): In a number of West European countries—1895, 1900–1905, 1908–1917

Military training: None

Education: Graduate (passed examination as externe) Petrograd University Law Faculty, 1891

Basic occupation before 1917: Writer

Special training: None

Occupation since 1917 besides Party, Soviet, trade union, and similar work: Besides those enumerated, only writing

What trade union do you belong to: Union of Journalists

Positions held since 1917: October 1917 to March 1921; Moscow; Council People's Commissars and Council of Labor and Defense; Chairman

Present position: Since October 1917; Moscow; Chairman, Council of People's Commissars and Council of Labor and Defense.

How long have you been a member of the R.C.P. (Bolsheviks): Since 1894

Have you ever belonged to any other parties: No

Participation in the revolutionary movement before 1917: Illegal Social-Democratic circles; member of the Russian Social-Democrats Workers' Party since its foundation. 1892–3, Samara; 1894–5, St. Petersburg; 1895–7, prison; 1898–1900, Siberia; 1900–05, abroad; 1905–07, St. Petersburg; 1908–1917, abroad.

Penalties incurred for revolutionary activities: 1887 prison; 1895–7 prison; 1898–1900 Siberia; 1900 prison

How long in prison: Several days and 14 months

How long at hard labor: None

Portrait of V. I. Lenin (October, 1918). Could the Russian Revolution have succeeded without Lenin's firm direction? (*Sovfoto*)

How long in exile: Three years

How long a political refugee: 9–10 years

Party functions since 1917: October 1917 to March 1921, Moscow, Member of the Central Committee

Present Party function: as above

Have you ever been tried by the courts of the RSFSR or of the Party: No

Date: March, 1921

Signature of delegate: V. Ulyanov (Lenin)

The Aftermath

The Bolsheviks were thrust into a difficult situation on achieving power. Lenin was true to his slogan, "Peace, Bread, and Land," and took Russia out of the war, negotiating a peace with Germany (Brest-Litovsk) that conceded much Russian territory. Lenin then applied his energies to quelling a civil war that pitted his Red Army (led by Trotsky) against the "White" forces, which consisted of supporters of the tsar or of other anti-Bolshevik elements. The tsar's execution in 1918 removed a possible impediment to the progress of the revolution. The Civil War ended in 1921 and Lenin spent the next three years until his death consolidating his gains and preparing for Russia's transition from a capitalist to a Communist state. In this, Lenin endeavored to apply Marxist theory to the realities of the situation. The first selection, entitled *State and Revolution,* is from a pamphlet written in August 1917, two months before the Bolshevik seizure of power. In it Lenin discusses this crucial period of transition. Events were to move in logical progression: from bourgeois capitalism to the dictatorship of the proletariat, to the "withering away" of the state, and finally to the justice and equality of the purely communist society. But things did not quite go as planned. The chaos of the Civil War and a great drought rendered the socialization of the economic system an unrealistic proposition. Lenin thus allowed a "partial return to capitalism" by permitting the revival of private industry and authorizing the peasantry to produce and trade for profit as part of his New Economic Plan (NEP). Although Russia would still move toward Marx's dream of a truly Communist existence, the journey would take longer than Lenin expected. In any event, the future belonged to a new breed of Communist youth. Lenin appealed to them as noted in the second selection.

When Lenin died, apparently of a stroke, in 1924, Bolshevik leadership was assumed by Trotsky and Stalin. Their shaky relationship resulted in a power struggle that was eventually won by Stalin. Trotsky was exiled and finally executed abroad in 1940. Stalin led the Soviet state toward rapid industrialization, state collectivization of privately owned land, and repression. His execution of over 10 million Soviet dissidents in the collectivization struggle and purges of the 1930s established his reputation as one of the great scourges of history. His imposing figure and totalitarian regime became the model for the repressive world of "Big Brother" in George Orwell's *1984.* Lenin himself doubted Stalin's character, as he revealed in a note written about a year before his death.

State and Revolution: The Transition from Capitalism to Communism (August 1917)

V. I. LENIN

Earlier the question was put thus: to attain its emancipation, the proletariat must overthrow the Bourgeoisie, conquer political power and establish its own revolutionary dictatorship.

V. I. Lenin, *State and Revolution* (New York: International Publishers, 1971), pp. 71–74. Copyright © 1932 and 1943 by International Publishers Co., Inc. Reprinted by permission of the publisher.

Now the question is put somewhat differently: the transition from capitalist society, developing towards Communism, towards a Communist society, is impossible without a "political transition period", and the state in this period can only be the revolutionary dictatorship of the proletariat.

What, then, is the relation of this dictatorship to democracy?

We have seen that the *Communist Manifesto* simply places side by side the two ideas: the "transformation of the proletariat into the ruling class" and the establishment of democracy". On the basis of all that has been said above, one can define more exactly how democracy changes in the transition from capitalism to Communism.

In capitalist society, under the conditions most favourable to its development, we have more or less complete democracy in the democratic republic. But this democracy is always bound by the narrow framework of capitalist exploitation, and consequently always remains, in reality, a democracy for the minority, only for the possessing classes, only for the rich. . . .

Democracy for an insignificant minority, democracy for the rich—that is the democracy of capitalist society. If we look more closely into the mechanism of capitalist democracy, everywhere, both in the . . . details of suffrage (residential qualification, exclusion of women, etc.), and in the technique of the representative institutions . . . on all sides we see restriction after restriction upon democracy. These restrictions, exceptions, exclusions, obstacles for the poor, seem slight, especially in the eyes of one who has himself never known want and has never been in close contact with the oppressed classes in their mass life (and nine-tenths, if not ninety-nine hundredths, of the bourgeois publicists and politicans are of this class), but in their sum total these restrictions exclude and squeeze out the poor from politics and from an active share in democracy.

Marx splendidly grasped this *essence* of capitalist democracy, when . . . he said that the oppressed were allowed once every few years, to decide which particular representatives of the oppressing class should be in parliament to represent and repress them!

But from this capitalist democracy—inevitably narrow, subtly rejecting the poor, and therefore hypocritical and false to the core—progress does not march onward, simply, smoothly and directly, to "greater and greater democracy", as the liberal professors and petty-bourgeois opportunists would have us believe. No, progress marches onward, i.e., towards Communism, through the dictatorship of the proletariat; it cannot do otherwise, for there is no one else and no other way to *break the resistance* of the capitalist exploiters.

But the dictatorship of the proletariat—i.e., the organisation of the vanguard of the oppressed as the ruling class for the purpose of crushing the oppressors—cannot produce merely an expansion of democracy. *Together* with an immense expansion of democracy which *for the first time* becomes democracy for the poor, democracy for the people, and not democracy for the rich folk, the dictatorship of the proletariat produces a series of restrictions of liberty [by itself oppressing] the exploiters, the capitalists. We must crush them in order to free humanity from wage-slavery; their resistance must be broken by force; it is clear that where there is suppression there is also violence, there is no liberty, no democracy.

Engels expressed this splendidly . . . when he said . . . that "as long as the proletariat still *needs* the state, it needs it not in the interests of freedom, but for the purpose of crushing its antagonists; and as soon as it becomes possible to speak of freedom, then the state, as such, ceases to exist."

Democracy for the vast majority of the people, and suppression by force, i.e., exclusion from democracy, of the exploiters and oppressors of the people—this is the modification of democracy during the *transition* from capitalism to Communism.

Only in Communist society, when the resistance of the capitalists has been completely broken, when the capitalists have disappeared, when there are no classes (i.e., there is no difference between the members of society in their relation to the social means of production), *only then* "the state ceases to exist", and "*it becomes possible to speak of freedom.*" Only then a really full democracy, a democracy without any exceptions, will be possible and will be realised. And only then will democracy itself begin to *wither away* due to the simple fact that, free from capitalist slavery, from the untold horrors, savagery, absurdities and infamies of capitalist exploitation, people will gradually *become accustomed* to the observance of the elementary rules of social life that have been known for centuries and repeated for thousands of years in all school books; they will become accustomed to observing them without force, without compulsion, without subordination, without the *special apparatus* for compulsion which is called the state.

The expression "the state *withers away*", is very well chosen, for it indicates both the gradual and the elemental nature of the process. Only habit can, and undoubtedly will, have such an effect; for we see around us millions of times how readily people get accustomed to observe the necessary rules of life in common, if there is no exploitation, if there is nothing that causes indignation, that calls forth protest and revolt and has to be *suppressed.*

Thus, in capitalist society, we have a democracy that is curtailed, poor, false; a democracy only for the rich, for the minority. The dictatorship of the proletariat, the period of transition to Communism, will, for the first time, produce democracy for the people, for the majority, side by side with the necessary suppression of the minority—the exploiters. Communism alone is capable of giving a really complete democracy, and the more complete it is the more quickly will it become unnecessary and wither away of itself. . . .

Again, during the *transition* from capitalism to Communism, suppression is *still* necessary; but it is the suppression of the minority of exploiters by the majority of exploited. . . . Finally, only Communism renders the state absolutely unnecessary, for there is *no one* to be suppressed—"no one" in the sense of a *class,* in the sense of a systematic struggle with a definite section of the population.

The Education of Communist Youth (October 2, 1920)

V. I. LENIN

You must train yourselves to be Communists. It is the task of the Youth League to organise its practical activities in such a way that, by learning, organising, uniting and fighting, its members shall train both themselves and all those who look to it for leadership; it should train Communists. The entire purpose of training, educating and teaching the youth of today should be to imbue them with communist ethics.

But is there such a thing as communist ethics? Is there such a thing as communist morality? Of course, there is. It is often suggested that we have no ethics of our own; very often the bourgeoisie accuse us Communists of rejecting all morality. This is a method of confusing the issue, of throwing dust in the eyes of the workers and peasants.

In what sense do we reject ethics, reject morality?

In the sense given to it by the bourgeoisie, who based ethics on God's commandments. On this point we, of course, say that we do not believe in God, and that we know perfectly well that the clergy, the landowners and the bourgeoisie invoked the name of God so as to further their own interests as exploiters. Or, instead of basing ethics on the commandments of morality, on the commandments of God, they based it on idealist or semi-idealist phrases, which always amounted to something very similar to God's commandments.

We reject any morality based on extra-human and extra-class concepts. We say that this is deception, dupery, stultification of the workers and peasants in the interests of the landowners and capitalists.

We say that our morality is entirely subordinated to the interests of the proletariat's class struggle. Our morality stems from the interests of the class struggle of the proletariat.

The old society was based on the oppression of all the workers and peasants by the land owners and capitalists. We had to destroy all that, and overthrow them but to do that we had to create unity. That is something that God cannot create. . . .

The members of the League should use every spare hour to improve the vegetable gardens, or to organise the education of young people at some factory, and so on. We want to transform Russia from a poverty-stricken

Martin McCauley, *The Russian Revolution and the Soviet State* (New York: Barnes & Noble, 1975), pp. 274–275. Permission granted by Barnes & Noble Books, Totowa, New Jersey.

and wretched country into one that is wealthy. The Young Communist League must combine its education, learning and training with the labour of the workers and peasants, so as not to confine itself to schools or to reading communist books and pamphlets. Only by working side by side with the workers and peasants can one become a genuine Communist. It has to be generally realised that all members of the Youth League are literate people and at the same time are keen at their jobs. When everyone sees that we have ousted the old drill-ground methods from the old schools and have replaced them with conscious discipline, that all young men and women take part in subbotniks [voluntary work programs], and utilise every suburban farm to help the population—people will cease to regard labour in the old way.

It is the task of the Young Communist League to organise assistance everywhere, in village or city block, in such matter as—and I shall take a small example—public hygiene or the distribution of food. How was this done in the old, capitalist society? Everybody worked only for himself and nobody cared a straw for the aged and the sick, or whether housework was the concern only of the women, who, in consequence, were in a condition of oppression and servitude. Whose business is it to combat this? It is the business of the Youth Leagues, which must say: we shall change all this; we shall organise detachments of young people who will help to assure public hygiene or distribute food, who will conduct systematic house-to-house inspections, and work in an organised way for the benefit of the whole society, distributing their forces properly and demonstrating that labour must be organised.

"Stalin Is Too Rude" (January 4, 1923)

V. I. LENIN

Stalin is too rude and this defect, which can be freely tolerated in our midst and in contacts among us Communists, can become an intolerable defect in one holding the position of the Secretary General. Because of this, I proposed that the comrades consider ways and means by which Stalin can be removed from this position and another man selected, a man who, above all, would differ from Com. Stalin in only one quality, namely, attitude toward his comrades, less capricious temper, etc. This circumstance could appear to be a meaningless trifle. I think, however, that from the viewpoint of preventing a split and from the viewpoint of what I have written above concerning the relationship between Stalin and Trotsky, this is not a trifle, or if it is one, then it is a trifle which can acquire a decisive significance.

Warren B. Walsh, *Readings in Russian History,* 3rd ed. (Syracuse, N.Y.: Syracuse University Press, 1959), p. 626. Reprinted by permission of the publisher.

STUDY QUESTIONS

1. Why did Tsar Nicholas institute the first Imperial Duma? Analyze the Imperial Constitution. Would you consider this a liberal constitution presented by a progressive ruler? Why or why not? Consider the "First Declaration of the Provisional Government" in this regard.

2. Even before the events of 1905 and 1906, Lenin opposed the Russian monarchy. He asked the question, "What is to be done?" What was his answer?

3. What reasons does Nicholas give for entering the war? What problems did the Russian people encounter? Compare the manifesto for entrance into the war with the tsar's abdication manifesto and the last address to the troops. Did his perspective change at all?

4. Analyze the demands of the Provisional Government and the Petrograd Soviet just after the abdication of the tsar. How are they similar and what are their differences? Note Lenin's ideas in his "April Theses." What action does he advocate? Is this consistent with his earlier ideas in "What Is to Be Done?"

5. What measures did Lenin take to protect the position of the Bolsheviks once they had achieved power? How does Lenin justify censorship of the press? Do fallacies or inconsistencies exist in his argument? Note especially the vocabulary. For example, how is the phrase, "workmen's and peasants' revolution" used? How was the *Izvestiia* newspaper editorial dangerous to the Bolshevik revolution?

6. What are the duties of the secret police? What elements of society was this organization directed against? The tsar also had an active secret police that protected against "enemies of the monarchy." What is the difference between "enemies of the monarchy" and "enemies of the people"? Is a secret police therefore a necessary instrument for maintaining power, regardless of political philosophy?

7. What arguments do the Bolsheviks give to justify the dissolution of the Constituent Assembly? What gave them the authority to invalidate an assembly that was chosen by vote of the Russian people? Why did the Bolsheviks allow the election to occur in the first place?

8. What social or economic conditions contributed to the outbreak of the Russian Revolution? Although the Russian Revolution involved such strong personalities as Kerensky, Trotsky, and Stalin, it was Lenin who was the guiding spirit. What do his comments on the education of Communist youth tell you about the man? Analyze his self-portrait. What kind of a man emerges? In Marxian theory, the individual is of little or no importance in contributing to the social and economic forces that result in the eventual destruction of capitalism and capitalist society. If so, how then does one explain Lenin? What was his role in the revolution? Without his presence, would the Russian Revolution have succeeded? To what extent can the individual change the course of history?

9

Adolf Hitler and the Nazi Rise to Power

Power is given only to him who dares to stoop and seize it. There is only one thing that matters, just one thing: you have to dare!

—Fyodor Dostoyevsky

Tyranny consists in the desire of universal power beyond its scope; it is the wish to have in one way what can only be had in another.

—Blaise Pascal

Order is the mother of civilization and liberty; chaos is the midwife of dictatorship.

—Will Durant

It is too difficult to think nobly when one only thinks to get a living.

—Jean Jacques Rousseau

There is nothing more terrible than ignorance in action.

—Johann von Goethe

With the end of the war in 1918, Europe entered a new age of change and development. Democratic governments had won the "war to make the world safe for democracy" and the aggressive German monarchy had been abolished. Indeed, most other European nations adopted or maintained democratic institutions. The dominant theme, however, in the political history of Europe from 1919 to 1939 is the decline of these democratic governments. By the beginning of World War II in 1939, authoritarian regimes had been established in Italy, Germany, Spain, and throughout most of central and eastern Europe. The world was introduced to two of the most intriguing and destructive individuals of the twentieth century: Benito Mussolini and Adolf Hitler.

In order to understand the success of Hitler and the Nazis in particular, we must first look at the doctrine of fascism to which Hitler and many other twentieth-century dictators have subscribed. Fascism varies in its particular details of application, but in the simplest of terms, it is a doctrine that sanctifies the interests of the state and minimizes the rights of the individual. Fascism promotes as its great benefit the stability and security of the state.

Nearly all fascist governments have certain features in common. For example, fascism was born in direct opposition to liberal democracy, and as such regards personal freedom as dangerous to the stability of the state. Democracy, according to fascist doctrine, promotes individual expression and self-aggrandizement, which in turn results in disagreement and class conflict. Fascists also oppose socialism and communism since they promote the welfare of the masses over the good of the state. Communism, in fact, with its Leninist emphasis on the immediacy of world revolution, has dangerous potential for destabilization by its very insistence on class warfare. Fascism also depends on extreme nationalism. This goes far beyond the patriotic love of one's nation, but is based on pride in the allegedly unique characteristics and achievements of a "special" people. Therefore, fascist national pride is exclusive and implies a hostility toward other countries that are inferior in their outlook, governmental organization, or national heritage. This hostility is a unifying factor and is often vented against particular minority groups within the state itself. Thus, Hitler promoted hatred of the Jews as a rallying point for his support. This fascist national pride often expresses itself through imperialism, since military and economic expansion actually strengthens the state. Because stability and security of the state are the watchwords of fascism, it is important to implement a strong, highly centralized, and efficient government that only dictatorial rule can provide. One man with total control over the affairs of state ensures coordination and consistency of rule. Such a dictatorship is achieved and maintained through control of the national army, but most practically through paramilitary organizations like secret police, private armies, and bodyguards, which do not hesitate to use violence.

Fascism traditionally derives its support from the "right-wing" or conservative forces of society. The military represents, by its very nature, order and discipline. Big industrialists want to enjoy the lucrative profits that state stability affords; in a fascist society, general workers' strikes, which can often cripple an economy and interrupt production, are forbidden. Socially, fascism derives its mass support from the lower middle class. In general, these are people who have worked hard within the confines of society to attain some measure of self-respect. Sociologically, they are individuals of commitment and pride who harbor dreams of social mobility, have faith in traditional values, and love their country; they have much to lose from instability and chaos. The fascist, totalitarian regime is intended to eliminate class conflict by concentrating the energy of all its members in the service of the state.

Fascism is often born of the frustration and discontent of people who have been in some way humiliated or robbed of their dignity either as individuals or collectively as a nation. According to the philosopher Eric Hoffer, in his book *The True Believer* (New York: Harper & Row, 1951), people who are most susceptible to mass movements are filled with the burden of their present existence and seek inspiration from those who have a vision of a proud and stable future.

Fascism first took hold in Italy during the 1920s, when unemployment greeted returning war veterans and disruptive strikes crippled the economy. Liberal middle-class politicians lost control of the state and four Socialist governments fell in three years. In addition, Italy felt deprived of the "fruits of victory" from her involvement in World War I. She failed to obtain any of the German colonies in Africa and was frustrated in her attempt to acquire Albania as well. Amidst this frustration and dislocation, Benito Mussolini rose to power with his Italian National Fascist party ("Black Shirts"). Mussolini (1883–1945) promised stability and the vision of a "corporate state" in which each individual worked for the welfare of the entire nation. Mussolini guaranteed employment and satisfactory wages for labor but did not permit strikes. He favored industrialists by allowing lucrative profits and gave respect to Italy by closely identifying his regime with the glorious heritage of the ancient Roman Empire. Mussolini succeeded in giving Italy direction and dignity, but he accomplished this through suppression of civil rights and individual liberties. He was, indeed, the quintessential fascist.

But perhaps the most important and influential of the authoritarian regimes in the subsequent history of Europe was established legally in Germany by Adolf Hitler and the National Socialist party.

After the abolition of the aggressive German monarchy in 1918, the Weimar Republic was established amid lofty ideals. Yet it labored under the burden of antirepublican pressures from the army, judiciary, bureaucracy, and even monarchists who wanted to reinstate the Kaiser. Germany had never had a strong democratic tradition and had only been united under a central monarch for about fifty years. The German republic was also weakened because it had been created during a time of national defeat and humiliation. Critics used the Republic as a scapegoat for Germany's ills and accused its democratic leaders of betraying the German armies by making an unacceptable peace. Faced with the threat of communist revolution in Germany and economic dislocation, which was prompted by incredible price inflation and devaluation of currency, the Weimar Republic struggled through the early twenties. Even during a period of relative economic stability after 1924, the leaders of the Republic were unable to foster a coherent program because of the conflicting demands of coalition government.

In the summer of 1929, Germany felt the first effects of the worldwide depression. By the winter of 1929–1930, three million Germans were unemployed, a figure that increased to six million by 1933. The deepening depression made it increasingly difficult for the various parties in the coalition government to work together. In the elections of 1930, the moderate and pro-republican parties suffered a significant defeat; the greatest gains were made by the National Socialist party, headed by Adolf Hitler. The Nazis, as its members were called, had been a small, violent group on the fringes of antirepublican politics during the early twenties. But by 1930, their membership had increased greatly and they were the most dynamic of the antidemocratic parties. Their success and popularity lay in providing, or at least promising, something for everyone. The Nazis promised a renegotiation of peace treaties and reestablishment of German honor and power to those who saw Germany's greatness shattered by the "defeat" in 1918 and the Treaty of Versailles in 1919. They promised efficient authoritarianism to those who were frustrated by the inadequacy of republican politics. The Nazis promised a strong economy to those (especially in the middle class) whose savings were threatened by the depression. Hitler also promised protection to the industrialists whose profits and very existence were jeopardized by the communist movement.

The central doctrine, however, of the National Socialist party was anti-Semitism. In his autobiography, *Mein Kampf (My Struggle)*, and in speeches and party announcements, Hitler blamed the Jews for the economic crises of the twenties. The inflation and depression, he argued, had been caused by Jewish international financiers. The Nazis also believed that the Jews controlled the international communist movement. Jews had to be excluded from German life, they concluded. In the unstable and violent years after 1929, more and more Germans seemed willing to accept this explanation for their difficult times.

As Hitler's influence grew, his followers advocated a violent seizure of power. Although he sanctioned violent political disruption and intimidation, Hitler insisted on attaining power legally. On January 30, 1933, after much political maneuvering, Hitler was appointed chancellor of the Weimar Republic. By July 1934, Hitler had legally altered the Weimar constitution, changed the nature of the Republic, removed all Jews and "politically unreliable" people from the bureaucracy, dissolved all opposition political parties, and purged the army. On August 2, 1934, President von Hindenburg died, and Hitler combined the offices of president and chancellor. The army formally supported these developments by swearing "unconditional obedience to the Fuehrer of the German

Reich and People, Adolf Hitler." Hitler then began fashioning his own dictatorship.

In this chapter, we will look carefully at the political, social, and economic conditions that existed in Germany during the twenties and early thirties in an effort to understand why the Nazis were able to gain power. Themes that will emerge from the material include the use of racism and propaganda in the pursuit of power, as well as the role of the individual in history. Could Hitler have risen to lead Germany had he not been presented with the devastating social and economic conditions of the time? To what extent did Hitler change the course of history? In essence, why did Germany follow the leadership of Adolf Hitler? The complicated political maneuverings are not at issue here. Rather, it is important to try to understand people in crisis.

The Legacy of World War I

"I Resolved Now to Become a Politician"

ADOLF HITLER

On November 11, 1918, German representatives signed terms of sur-render and the Great War came to an end. Although they were clearly beaten militarily, defeat came as a shock to the majority of Germans because they had been told, as late as September, that victory was cer-tain. Adolf Hitler, a corporal at the time, was gassed during the night of October 13, 1918. While recuperating in a military hospital, he heard rumors of German surrender.

But then as the old gentleman tried to continue and began to tell us that now we had to end the long war, that even our fatherland would now be submitted to severe oppressions in the future, that now the War was lost and that we had to surrender to the mercy of the victors . . . that the armi-stice should be accepted with confidence in the generosity of our previous enemies . . . there I could stand it no more. It was impossible for me to stay any longer. While everything began to go black again before my eyes, stumbling, I groped my way back to the dormitory, threw myself on my cot and buried by burning head in the covers and pillows. . . .

Now all had been in vain. In vain all the sacrifices and deprivations, in vain the hunger and thirst of endless months, in vain the hours during which, gripped by the fear of death, we nevertheless did our duty, and in vain the death of two millions who died thereby. Would not the graves of all the hundred of thousands open up, the graves of those who once had

From *Mein Kampf* by Adolf Hitler, translated by Ralph Manheim, pp. 266–269. Copyright 1943 and copyright © renewed 1971 by Houghton Mifflin Company. Reprinted by permis-sion of Houghton Mifflin Company.

marched out with faith in the fatherland, never to return? Would they not open up and send the silent heroes, covered with mud and blood, home as spirits of revenge, to the country that had so mockingly cheated them of the highest sacrifice which in this world man is able to bring to his people? Was it for this that they had died, the soldiers of August and September, 1914, was it for this that the regiments of volunteers followed the old comrads in the fall of the same year? Was it for this that boys of seventeen sank into Flanders Fields? Was that the meaning of the sacrifice which the German mother brought to the fatherland when in those days, with an aching heart, she let her most beloved boys go away, never to see them again? Was it all for this that now a handfull of miserable criminals was allowed to lay hands on the fatherland? . . .

I . . . resolved now to become a politician.

"Stabbed in the Back" (1919)

PAUL VON HINDENBURG

The following is a statement by the German Field Marshal Paul von Hindenburg (1847–1934) to the Committee of Enquiry in November 1919. The Committee was established to investigate charges that Germany had provoked the war and committed war crimes. Hindenburg was one of the most influential German commanders during World War I and later became president of the German Weimar Republic (1925–1934). His statement reveals the dissatisfaction and betrayal that many Germans felt upon surrender.

In spite of the superiority of the enemy in men and materials, we could have brought the struggle to a favourable conclusion if determined and unanimous cooperation had existed between the army and those at home. But while the enemy showed an ever greater will for victory, divergent party interests began to show themselves with us. These circumstances soon led to a breaking up of our will to conquer. . . . Our operations therefore failed, as they were bound to, and the collapse became inevitable; the Revolution was merely that last straw. As an English General has truly said, "The German Army was stabbed in the back." It is plain enough on whom the blame lies.

The Treaty of Versailles (1919)

The Treaty of Versailles, which was signed by Germany on June 28, 1919, was a dictated peace designed to affix blame and to punish. The

"Stabbed in the Back" is from John W. Wheeler-Bennet, *Wooden Titan: Hindenburg in Twenty Years of German History, 1914–34,* pp. 235–236. Copyright © 1950. Reprinted by permission of Macmillan and Co., Ltd., London and Basingstoke.

"The Treaty of Versailles" is from Great Britain, *State Papers,* vol. 112 (1919), pp. 104 ff.

reduction of the army to 100,000 men and the territorial clauses, which eliminated areas abundant in natural resources, were viewed with outrage. The Germans were particularly incensed by the reparation clauses and the statement of German responsibility for the war contained in Article 231.

Article 227. The Allied and Associated Powers publicly arraign William II of Hohenzollern, formerly German Emperor, for a supreme offence against international morality and the sanctity of treaties.

A special tribunal will be constituted to try the accused, thereby assuring him the guarantees essential to the right of defence. It will be composed of five judges, one appointed by each of the following Powers: namely, the United States of America, Great Britain, France, Italy and Japan.

In its decision the tribunal will be guided by the highest motives of international policy, with a view to vindicating the solemn obligations of international undertakings and the validity of international morality. It will be its duty to fix the punishment which it considers should be imposed.

Article 228. The German Government recognises the right of the Allied and Associated Powers to bring before military tribunals persons accused of having committed acts of violation of the laws and customs of war. Such persons shall, if found guilty, be sentenced to punishments laid down by law.

Article 231. The Allied and Associated Governments affirm and Germany accepts the responsibility of Germany and her allies for causing all the loss and damage to which the Allied and Associated Governments and their nationals have been subjected as a consequence of the war imposed upon them by the aggression of Germany and her allies.

Article 232. The Allied and Associated Governments recognise that the resources of Germany are not adequate . . . to make complete reparation for all such loss and damage.

The Allied and Associated Governments, however, require, and Germany undertakes, that she will make compensation for all damage done to the civilian population of the Allied and Associated Powers . . . by such aggression by land, by sea, and from the air. . . .

Article 428. As a guarantee for the execution of the present Treaty by Germany, the German territory situated to the west of the Rhine together with the bridgeheads, will be occupied by Allied and Associated troops for a period of fifteen years from the coming into force of the present Treaty.

Article 430. In case either during the occupation or after the expiration of the fifteen years referred to above the Reparation Commission finds that Germany refuses to observe the whole or part of her obligations under the present Treaty with regard to reparation, the whole or part of the areas specified will be re-occupied immediately by the Allied and Associated forces.

Article 431. If before the expiration of the period of fifteen years Germany complies with all the undertakings resulting from the present Treaty, the occupying forces will be withdrawn immediately.

The Weimar Republic

The Weimar Republic, burdened by the specter of defeat and shame, was impotent to meet the economic and political problems of the twenties. The portion of the constitution that follows reflects the liberal idealism of the Social Democratic, Catholic Center, and Democratic parties that shaped it. Although there was much opposition to these beliefs from the National Socialist (Nazi) party among others, many Germans were still loyal to the Republic, as the second selection reveals.

The Weimar Constitution: Fundamental Rights and Duties of the Germans

Section I: The Individual

Article 109. All Germans are equal before the law. Men and women have the same fundamental civil rights and duties. Public legal privileges or disadvantages of birth or of rank are abolished. Titles of nobility . . . may be bestowed no longer. . . . Orders and decorations shall not be conferred by the state. No German shall accept titles or orders from a foreign government.

Article 110. Citizenship of the Reich and the states is acquired in accordance with the provisions of a Reich law. . . .

Article 111. All Germans shall enjoy liberty of travel and residence throughout the whole Reich. . . .

Article 112. Every German is permitted to emigrate to a foreign country. . . .

Article 114. Personal liberty is inviolable. Curtailment or deprivation of personal liberty by a public authority is permissible only by authority of law.

Persons who have been deprived of their liberty must be informed at the latest on the following day by whose authority and for what reasons they have been held. They shall receive the opportunity without delay of submitting objections to their deprivation of liberty.

Article 115. The house of every German is his sanctuary and is inviolable. Exceptions are permitted only by authority of law. . . .

Louis L. Snyder, ed., *Documents of German History*, pp. 390–392. Copyright © 1985 by Rutgers, the State University. Reprinted by permission of Rutgers University Press.

Article 117. The secrecy of letters and all postal, telegraph, and telephone communications is inviolable. Exceptions are inadmissable by national law.

Article 118. Every German has the right, within the limits of the general laws, to express his opinion freely by word, in writing, in print, in picture form, or in any other way. . . . Censorship is forbidden. . . .

Section II. The General Welfare

Article 123. All Germans have the right to assemble peacefully and unarmed without giving notice and without special permission. . . .

Article 124. All Germans have the right to form associations and societies for purposes not contrary to the criminal law. . . .

Article 126. Every German has the right to petition. . . .

Section III. Religion and Religious Societies

Article 135. All inhabitants of the Reich enjoy full religious freedom and freedom of conscience. The free exercise of religion is guaranteed by the Constitution and is under public protection. . . .

Article 137. There is no state church. . . .

Section IV. Education and the Schools

Article 144. The entire school system is under the supervision of the state. . . .

Article 145. Attendance at school is compulsory. . . .

Section V: Economic Life

Article 151. The regulation of economic life must be compatible with the principles of justice, with the aim of attaining humane conditions of existence for all. Within these limits the economic liberty of the individual is assured. . . .

Article 152. Freedom of contract prevails . . . in accordance with the laws. . . .

Article 153. The right of private property is guaranteed by the Constitution. . . . Expropriation of property may take place . . . by due process of law. . . .

Article 159. Freedom of association for the preservation and promotion of labor and economic conditions is guaranteed to everyone and to all vocations. All agreements and measures attempting to restrict or restrain this freedom are unlawful. . . .

Article 161. The Reich shall organize a comprehensive system of [social] insurance. . . .

Article 165. Workers and employees are called upon to cooperate, on an equal footing, with employers in the regulation of wages and of the conditions of labor, as well as in the general development of the productive forces. . . .

Loyalty to the Weimar Republic

LILO LINKE

A procession was formed, headed by the military band with triangles and drums and clarinets and followed by the members of the movement, two abreast, holding their torches in their upraised hands. We marched through the town, our ghostly magnified shadows moving restlessly over the fronts of the houses.

Never before had I followed the flag of the Republic, which was now waving thirty yards in front of me, spreading its colours overhead, the black melting in one with the night, the red glowing in the light of the torches, and the gold overshining them like a dancing sun. It was not just a torchlight march for me, it was a political confession. I had decided to take part in the struggle for German democracy. I wanted to fight for it although I knew that this meant a challenge to my parents and my whole family, who all lived with their eyes turned towards the past and thought it disloyal and shameful to help the Socialists.

We marched out of the town to the cemetery, where the first President of the Republic, Fritz Ebert, had been buried. Silently we assembled round the grave. Wilhelm Wismar, national leader of the Young Democrats and youngest member of the Reichstag, stepped forward and spoke slowly the oath.

"We vow to stand for the Republic with all our abilities and strength."

"We vow to work for the fulfillment of the promises given to the German people in the Weimar Constitution."

"We vow to shield and defend democracy against all its enemies and attackers whoever they might be."

And out of the night in a rolling echo two thousand citizens of tomorrow answered, repeating solemnly word for word:

"We vow to stand for the Republic with all our abilities and strength."

"We vow to work for the fulfillment of the promises given to the German people in the Weimar Constitution."

"We vow to shield and defend democracy against all its enemies and attackers whoever they might be."

Inflation: "The Boiling Kettle of a Wicked Witch"

LILO LINKE

Inflation, or the decline in the value of currency with the attendant rise in prices, engulfed Germany in the early twenties, reaching a peak in 1923. The following accounts reflect some of the difficulties and frustrations felt by people of the time. The middle classes were especially affected and their hard-earned savings became worthless. Both Lilo Linke and Konrad Heiden witnessed the hardship of these days. Heiden was particularly active against the Nazis in street confrontations as a student at the University of Munich in 1923.

The time for my first excursions into life was badly chosen. Rapidly Germany was precipitated into the inflation, thousands, millions, milliards of marks whirled about, making heads swim in confusion. War, revolution, and the wild years after had deprived everyone of old standards and the possibility of planning a normal life. Again and again fate hurled the helpless individual into the boiling kettle of a wicked witch. Now the inflation came and destroyed the last vestige of steadiness. Hurriedly one had to make use of the moment and could not consider the following day.

The whole population had suddenly turned into maniacs. Everyone was buying, selling, speculating, bargaining, and dollar, dollar, dollar was the magic word which dominated every conversation, every newspaper, every poster in Germany. Nobody understood what was happening. There seemed to be no sense, no rules in the mad game, but one had to take part in it if one did not want to be trampled underfoot at once. Only a few people were able to carry through to the end and gain by the inflation. The majority lost everything and broke down, impoverished and bewildered.

The middle class was hurt more than any other, the savings of a lifetime and their small fortunes melted into a few coppers. They had to sell their most precious belongings for ten milliard inflated marks to buy a bit of food or an absolutely necessary coat, and their pride and dignity were bleeding out of many wounds. Bitterness remained for ever in their hearts. Full of hatred, they accused the international financiers, the Jews and Socialists—their old enemies—of having exploited their distress. They never forgot and never forgave and were the first to lend a willing ear to Hitler's fervent preaching.

In the shop, notices announced that we should receive our salaries in weekly parts; after a while we queued up at the cashier's desk every evening, and before long we were paid twice daily and ran out during the lunch hour to buy a few things, because as soon as the new rate of exchange became known in the early afternoon our money had again lost half its value.

In the beginning I did not concern myself much with these happenings. They merely added to the excitement of my new life, which was all that mattered to me. Living in the east of Berlin and in hard times, I was long accustomed to seeing people around me in hunger, distress, and poverty. My mother was always lamenting that it was impossible for her to make both ends meet, my father—whenever he was at home—always asking what the deuce she had done with all the money he had given her yesterday. A few tears, a few outbreaks more did not make a difference great enough to impress me deeply.

Yet, in the long run, the evil influence of the inflation, financially as well as morally, penetrated even to me. Berlin had become the centre of international profiteers and noisy new rich. For a few dollars they could buy the whole town, drinks and women, horses and houses, virtue and vice, and they made free use of these possibilities.

The Devaluation of Currency

KONRAD HEIDEN

They all stood in lines outside the pay-windows, staring impatiently at the electric wall clock, slowly advancing until at last they reached the window and received a bag full of paper notes. According to the figures inscribed on them, the paper notes amounted to seven hundred thousand or five hundred million, or three hundred and eighty billion, or eighteen trillion marks—the figures rose from month to month, then from week to week, finally from day to day. With their bags the people moved quickly to the doors, all in haste, the younger ones running. They dashed to the nearest food store, where a line had already formed. Again they moved slowly, oh, how slowly, forward. When you reached the store, a pound of sugar might have been obtainable for two millions; but, by the time you came to the counter, all you could get for two millions was half a pound, and the saleswoman said the dollar had just gone up again. With the millions and billions you bought sardines, sausages, sugar, perhaps even a little butter, but as a rule the cheaper margarine—always things that would keep for a week, until next pay-day, until the next stage in the fall of the mark.

Hitler's Response to Germany's Problems

The National Socialist party produced a program in 1920 that formed the basis of Hitler's campaign against the Weimar Republic. The succeeding

From *Der Fuehrer* by Konrad Heiden, translated by Ralph Manheim, p. 126. Copyright 1944 by Konrad Heiden. Copyright © renewed 1971 by Bernhard E. Bartels, Executor of the Estate. Reprinted by permission of the Houghton Mifflin Company.

selections of speeches and rally announcements not only reveal Nazi ideology, but also testify to the dynamism of Nazi propaganda.

The Nazi Program (1920)

The program is the political foundation of the NSDAP [Nazi Party] and accordingly the primary political law of the State. It has been made brief and clear intentionally.

All legal precepts must be applied in the spirit of the party program.

Since the taking over of control, the Fuehrer has succeeded in the realization of essential portions of the Party program from the fundamentals to the detail.

The Party Program of the NSDAP was proclaimed on the 24 February 1920 by Adolf Hitler at the first large Party gathering in Munich and since that day has remained unaltered. Within the national socialist philosophy is summarized in 25 points:

1. We demand the unification of all Germans in the Greater Germany on the basis of the right of self-determination of peoples.

2. We demand equality of rights for the German people in respect to the other nations; abrogation of the peace treaties of Versailles and St. Germain.

3. We demand land and territory [colonies] for the sustenance of our people, and colonization for our surplus population.

4. Only a member of the race can be a citizen. A member of the race can only be one who is of German blood, without consideration of creed. Consequently no Jew can be a member of the race.

5. Whoever has no citizenship is to be able to live in Germany only as a guest, and must be under the authority of legislation for foreigners.

6. The right to determine matters concerning administration and law belongs only to the citizen. Therefore we demand that every public office, of any sort whatsoever, whether in the Reich, the county or municipality, be filled only by citizens. . . .

7. We demand that the state be charged first with providing the opportunity for a livelihood and way of life for citizens. If it is impossible to sustain the total population of the State, then the members of foreign nations (non-citizens) are to be expelled from the Reich.

8. Any further immigration of non-citizens is to be prevented. We demand that all non-Germans, who have immigrated to Germany since the 2 August 1914, be forced immediately to leave the Reich.

9. All citizens must have equal rights and obligations.

"National Socialist Yearbook, 1941," in *Nazi Conspiracy and Aggression*, (Washington, D.C.: Government Printing Office, 1946), vol. 4, pp. 208–211.

10. The first obligation of every citizen must be to work both spiritually and physically. . . .

13. We demand the nationalization of all [previous] associated industries [trusts].

14. We demand a division of profits of all heavy industries.

15. We demand an expansion on a large scale of old age welfare.

16. We demand the creation of a healthy middle class and its conservation. . . .

18. We demand struggle without consideration against those whose activity is injurious to the general interest. Common national criminals, userers . . . and so forth are to be punished with death, without consideration of confession or race.

20. The state is to be responsible for a fundamental reconstruction of our whole national education program, to enable every capable and industrious German to obtain higher education and subsequently introduction into leading positions. . . .

21. The State is to care for the elevating of national health by protecting the mother and child, by outlawing child-labor, by the encouragement of physical fitness, by means of the legal establishment of a gymnastic and sport obligation, by the utmost support of all organizations concerned with the physical instruction of the young.

23. We demand legal opposition to known lies and their promulgation through the press. In order to enable the provision of a German press, we demand, that: a. All writers and employees of the newspapers appearing in the German language be members of the race: b. Non-German newspapers be required to have the express permission of the State to be published. They may not be printed in the German language: c. Non-Germans are forbidden by law any financial interest in German publications, or any influence on them, and as punishment for violations the closing of such a publication as well as the immediate expulsion from the Reich of the non-German concerned. Publications which are counter to the general good are to be forbidden. We demand legal prosecution of artistic and literary forms which exert a destructive influence on our national life, and the closure of organizations opposing the above made demands.

24. We demand freedom of religion for all religious denominations within the state so long as they do not endanger its existence or oppose the moral senses of the Germanic race. The Party as such advocates the standpoint of a positive Christianity without binding itself confessionally to any one denomination. It combats the Jewish-materialistic spirit within and around us, and is convinced that a lasting recovery of our nation can only succeed from within on the framework: common utility precedes individual utility.

25. For the execution of all of this we demand the formation of a strong central power in the Reich. Unlimited authority of the central parliament over the whole Reich and its organizations in general. The forming of state

and profession chambers for the execution of the laws made by the Reich within the various states of the confederation. The leaders of the Party promise, if necessary by sacrificing their own lives, to support the execution of the points set forth above without consideration.

Speech on the Treaty of Versailles (April 17, 1923)

ADOLF HITLER

With the armistice begins the humiliation of Germany. If the Republic on the day of its foundation had appealed to the country: "Germans, stand together! Up and resist the foe! The Fatherland, the Republic expects of you that you fight to your last breath," then millions who are now enemies of the Republic would be fanatical Republicans. Today they are the foes of the Republic not because it is a Republic but because this Republic was founded at the moment when Germany was humiliated, because it so discredited the new flag that men's eyes must turn regretfully towards the old flag.

So long as this Treaty stands there can be no resurrection of the German people; no social reform of any kind is possible! The Treaty was made in order to bring 20 million Germans to their deaths and to ruin the German nation. But those who made the Treaty cannot set it aside. As its foundation our Movement formulated three demands:

1. Setting aside of the Peace Treaty.
2. Unification of all Germans.
3. Land and soil [*Grund* und *Boden*] to feed our nation.

Our movement could formulate these demands, since it was not our Movement which caused the War, it has not made the Republic, it did not sign the Peace Treaty.

There is thus one thing which is the first task of this Movement: it desires to make the German once more National, that his Fatherland shall stand for him above everything else. It desires to teach our people to understand afresh the truth of the old saying: He who will not be a hammer must be an anvil. An anvil are we today, and that anvil will be beaten until out of the anvil we fashion once more a hammer, a German sword!

Norman H. Baynes, trans. and ed., *The Speeches of Adolf Hitler, April 1922–1939*, vol. 1 (London: Oxford University Press, 1942), pp. 56–57. Reprinted by permission of the publisher.

Nazi Political Rally Announcement (February 1921)
NATIONAL SOCIALIST GERMAN WORKERS' PARTY

Fellow Citizens!

A year ago we called you to the Zirkus Krone. For the first time we invited you to a giant protest against making Germany defenseless by disarmament. We declared that this making her defenseless would be the prelude for the loss of Upper Silesia.

For the second time we invite you to resist against the Paris Dictate. We called it the permanent enslavement of Germany. . . .

Poverty no longer begins to appear, it is here. And though one does not feel it in the armchairs of the parliaments and in the soft cushions of our people's leaders it is felt all the more by the millions who have been cheated, by the masses of the people who do not live by cheating, profiteering and usury, but by the sweat of their honest work. But we are not only a poor people, we are also a miserable people.

We have forgotten the millions of our fellow citizens who once, during a long four and a half years, bled for Germany's existence on innumerable battlefields, and of whom our fatherland has been robbed by a cruel fate.

We have forgotten the millions of those Germans who longingly await the day which brings them home to a country that even as the poorest would still present the happiness of being their fatherland. We have forgotten the Rhineland and Upper Silesia, forgotten German-Austria and the millions of our brothers in Czechoslovakia, forgotten Alsace-Lorraine and the Palatinate, and while our beloved Germany thus lies dismembered, powerless and torn, disgracefully robbed, a colony of the international world criminals, there—we dance.

We invite you to come Thursday, February 2, 1921, to a GIANT DEMONSTRATION for a coming GREATER GERMANY to the Zirkus Krone. Engineer Rudolf JUNG, Deputy of the Prague Parliament, and Party Member Adolf HITLER will speak about:
'GERMANY IN HER DEEPEST HUMILIATION'
Beginning 8 p.m., end 10 p.m.   Jews not admitted
To cover expenses of the hall and posters admission M.I. War invalids free.

Fellow citizens, white collar and manual workers, Germans from all countries of our fatherland, come in masses!

[The meeting was attended by more than 7000 persons.]

Nazi Appeal and Victory

Nazi Propaganda

In order to rise to power, an organization or individual must promote ideas, gain converts, and feed on mistakes of the opposition. Where no problems exist, they must be created, and where they are real, they must be exposed and used to advantage. Such is the nature and purpose of propaganda. The first selection is a pamphlet composed in 1930 by Dr. Joseph Goebbels, the future Minister of Propaganda for the Third Reich. It was important to focus on enemies, whether they were cowards, communists, or Jews, since fear and hatred can often unify a people more readily than positive ideas.

Unity must also be achieved through leadership. Above anything else, the Nazis promoted faith over rational thought. The National Socialist program could be reduced to two words: Adolf Hitler. His mythic presence is seen in the second selection, which appeared in the newspaper *Völkischer Beobachter* just before an election on March 13, 1932. As Hitler noted, "The most brilliant propaganda technique must concentrate on a few points and repeat them over and over." He understood that in troubled times, people want a simple explanation for their pain and insecurity—and then they want the pain to go away.

Nationalists, Socialists, and Jews (1930)

JOSEPH GOEBBELS

WHY ARE WE NATIONALISTS?

We are NATIONALISTS because we see in the NATION the only possibility for the protection and the furtherance of our existence.

The NATION is the organic bond of a people for the protection and defense of their lives. He is nationally minded who understands this IN WORD AND IN DEED.

Today, in GERMANY, NATIONALISM has degenerated into BOURGEOIS PATRIOTISM, and its power exhausts itself in tilting at windmills. . . .

Young nationalism has its unconditional demands. BELIEF IN THE NATION is a matter of all the people, not for individuals of rank, a class, or an industrial clique. The eternal must be separated from the contemporary. The maintenance of a rotten industrial system has nothing to do with nationalism. I can love Germany and hate capitalism; not only CAN I do it, I also MUST do it. The germ of the rebirth of our people LIES ONLY IN

Louis L. Snyder, ed., *Documents of German History*, pp. 414–416. Copyright © 1985 by Rutgers, the State University. Reprinted by permission of Rutgers University Press.

THE DESTRUCTION OF THE SYSTEM OF PLUNDERING THE HEALTHY POWER OF THE PEOPLE.

WE ARE NATIONALISTS BECAUSE WE, AS GERMANS, LOVE GERMANY. And because we love Germany, we demand the protection of its national spirit and we battle against its destroyers.

WHY ARE WE SOCIALISTS?

We are SOCIALISTS because we see in SOCIALISM the only possibility for maintaining our racial existence and through it the reconquest of our political freedom and the rebirth of the German state. SOCIALISM has its peculiar form first of all through its comradeship in arms with the forward-driving energy of a newly awakened nationalism. Without nationalism it is nothing, a phantom, a theory, a vision of air, a book. With it, it is everything, THE FUTURE, FREEDOM, FATHERLAND!

It was a sin of the liberal bourgeoisie to overlook THE STATEBUILDING POWER OF SOCIALISM. It was the sin of MARXISM to degrade SOCIALISM to a system of MONEY AND STOMACH.

We are SOCIALISTS because for us THE SOCIAL QUESTION IS A MATTER OF NECESSITY AND JUSTICE, and even beyond that A MATTER FOR THE VERY EXISTENCE OF OUR PEOPLE.

DOWN WITH POLITICAL BOURGEOIS SENTIMENT: FOR REAL NATIONALISM!

DOWN WITH MARXISM: FOR TRUE SOCIALISM!

UP WITH THE STAMP OF THE FIRST GERMAN NATIONAL SOCIALIST STATE!

AT THE FRONT THE NATIONAL SOCIALIST GERMAN WORKERS PARTY! . . .

WHY DO WE OPPOSE THE JEWS?

We are ENEMIES OF THE JEWS, because we are fighters for the freedom of the German people. THE JEW IS THE CAUSE AND THE BENEFICIARY OF OUR MISERY. He has used the social difficulties of the broad masses of our people to deepen the unholy split between Right and Left among our people. He has made two halves of Germany. He is the real cause for our loss of the Great War.

The Jew has no interest in the solution of Germany's fateful problems. He CANNOT have any. FOR HE LIVES ON THE FACT THAT THERE HAS BEEN NO SOLUTION. If we would make the German people a unified community and give them freedom before the world, then the Jew can have no place among us. He has the best trumps in his hands when a people lives in inner and outer slavery. THE JEW IS RESPONSIBLE FOR OUR MISERY AND HE LIVES ON IT.

That is the reason why we, AS NATIONALISTS and AS SOCIALISTS, oppose the Jew. HE HAS CORRUPTED OUR RACE, FOULED OUR MORALS, UNDERMINED OUR CUSTOMS, AND BROKEN OUR POWER.

THE JEW IS THE PLASTIC DEMON OF THE DECLINE OF MANKIND.

THE JEW IS UNCREATIVE. He produces nothing. HE ONLY HANDLES PRODUCTS. As long as he struggles against the state, HE IS A REVOLUTIONARY; as soon as he has power, he preaches QUIET AND ORDER, so that he can consume his plunder at his convenience.

ANTI-SEMITISM IS UN-CHRISTIAN. That means, then, that he is a Christian who looks on while the Jew sews straps around our necks. TO BE A CHRISTIAN MEANS: LOVE THY NEIGHBOR AS THYSELF! MY NEIGHBOR IS ONE WHO IS TIED TO ME BY HIS BLOOD. IF I LOVE HIM, THEN I MUST HATE HIS ENEMIES. HE WHO THINKS GERMAN MUST DESPISE THE JEWS. The one thing makes the other necessary.

WE ARE ENEMIES OF THE JEWS BECAUSE WE BELONG TO THE GERMAN PEOPLE. THE JEW IS OUR GREATEST MISFORTUNE.

It is not true that we eat a Jew every morning at breakfast.

It is true, however, that he SLOWLY BUT SURELY ROBS US OF EVERYTHING WE OWN.

THAT WILL STOP, AS SURELY AS WE ARE GERMANS.

Free Germany! (1932)

The National Socialist movement, assembled, at this hour, as a fighting squad around its leader, today calls on the entire German people to join its ranks, and to pave a path that will bring Adolf Hitler to the head of the nation, and thus

HITLER is the password of all who believe in Germany's resurrection.

HITLER is the last hope of those who were deprived of everything: of farm and home, of savings, employment, survival; and who have but one possession left: their faith in a just Germany which will once again grant to its citizens honor, freedom, and bread.

HITLER is the word of deliverance for millions, for they are in despair, and see only in this name a path to new life and creativity.

HITLER was bequeathed the legacy of the two million dead comrades of the World War, who died not for the present system of the gradual destruction of our nation, but for Germany's future.

Parade through Brandenburg Gate (January 30, 1933). The Nazis celebrated the appointment of Adolf Hitler as Chancellor of the Weimar Republic with a night rally. The dismantling of the Weimar Constitution began almost immediately. (*Bundesarchiva*)

HITLER is the man of the people hated by the enemy because he understands the people and fights for the people.

HITLER is the furious will of Germany's youth, which, in the midst of a tired generation, is fighting for new forms, and neither can nor will abandon its faith in a better German future. Hence Hitler is the password and the flaming signal of all who wish for a German future.

All of them, on March 13, will call out to the men of the old system who promised them freedom, and dignity, and delivered stones and words instead: We have known enough of you. Now you are to know us!

Statistical Evidence

The statistical table on the facing page reveals the increasing popularity of the National Socialist party from 1924, when the Nazis first appeared on a ballot, to 1932, the last free election before Hitler's accession to power. Note the direct relationship of Nazi popularity to the unemployment figures.

Chancellor to Dictator

By 1932, the Nazis had emerged as Germany's strongest single party. Hitler demanded the chancellorship of the Weimar Republic. The president, Paul von Hindenburg, disliked Hitler and resisted entrusting all governmental authority to a single party which "held to such a one-sided attitude toward people with convictions different from theirs." But on January 30, 1933, Hindenburg gave in to political pressure and popular demand and appointed Hitler chancellor. The Nazis were confirmed in power and immediately began to dismantle the Weimar Constitution. On the night of February 27, 1933, the Reichstag building burned. The Nazis blamed the communists and issued the "Decree for the Protection of the People and State," an article of which is presented in the first selection.

The second selection is the famous Enabling Act, which allowed Hitler and his Reich Cabinet to issue laws that could deviate from the established constitution, yet could not practically be challenged by representatives of the Reichstag. Its overwheming passage (444 to 94) gave the destruction of parliamentary democracy an appearance of legality; from then on, the Reichstag became a rubber stamp of approval for Hitler's decrees. The succeeding documents show the conversion of Hitler's chancellorship to a dictatorship.

Elections to the German Reichstag (1924–1932)

	May 4, 1924	December 7, 1924	May 20, 1928	September 14, 1930	July 31, 1932	November 6, 1932
Number of eligible voters (in millions)	38.4	39.0	41.2	43.0	44.2	44.2
Votes cast (in millions)	29.7	30.7	31.2	35.2	37.2	35.7
National Socialist German Workers party (Nazi)	1,918,000 6.6%	908,000 3%	810,000 2.6%	6,407,000 18.3%	13,779,000 37.3%	11,737,000 33.1%
German Nationalist People's party (Conservative)	5,696,000 19.5%	6,209,000 20.5%	4,382,000 14.2%	2,458,000 7%	2,187,000 5.9%	3,131,000 8.8%
Center party (Catholic)	3,914,000 13.4%	4,121,000 13.6%	3,712,000 12.1%	4,127,000 11.8%	4,589,000 12.4%	4,230,000 11.9%
Democratic party (The German State Party)	1,655,000 5.7%	1,921,000 6.3%	1,506,000 4.9%	1,322,000 3.8%	373,000 1%	339,000 1%
Social Democratic party	6,009,000 20.5%	7,886,000 26%	9,153,000 29.8%	8,575,000 24.5%	7,960,000 21.6%	7,251,000 20.4%
Communist party	3,693,000 12.6%	2,712,000 9%	3,265,000 10.6%	4,590,000 13.1%	5,370,000 14.3%	5,980,000 16.9%

Unemployment in Germany (1924–1932)*

1924	1928	1930	July 31, 1932	October 31, 1932
978,000	1,368,000	3,076,000	5,392,000	5,109,000

*The figures are those of annual average unemployment, except for 1932, where some precise end-of-the-month figures are available, and the two dates that coincide with the Reichstag elections are given.

From *The Nazi Years: A Documentary History*, edited by Joachim Remak, p. 44. © 1969. Used by permission of Prentice-Hall, Inc., Englewood Cliffs, N.J.

Decree for the Protection of the People and State (February 28, 1933)

In virtue of Section 48 (2) of the German Constitution, the following is decreed as a defensive measure against Communist acts of violence endangering the state:

ARTICLE 1

Sections 114, 115, 117, 118, 123, 124, and 153 of the Constitution of the German Reich are suspended until further notice. Thus, restrictions on personal liberty, on the right of free expression of opinion, including freedom of the press, on the right of assembly and the right of association, and violations of the privacy of postal, telegraphic, and telephone communications, and warrants for house-searches, orders for confiscations as well as restrictions on property, are also permissible beyond the legal limits otherwise prescribed.

The Enabling Act (March 24, 1933)

The Reichstag has passed the following law, which is, with the approval of the Reichsrat [upper house], herewith promulgated, after it has been established that it satisfies the requirements for legislation altering the Constitution.

Article 1: In addition to the procedure for the passage of legislation outlined in the Constitution, the Reich Cabinet is also authorized to enact Laws.

Article 2: The national laws enacted by the Reich Cabinet may deviate from the Constitution provided they do not affect the position of the Reichstag and the Reichsrat. The powers of the President remain unaffected.

Article 3: The national laws enacted by the Reich Cabinet shall be prepared by the Chancellor and published in the official gazette. They come into effect, unless otherwise specified, upon the day following their publication. Articles 68–77 of the Constitution [concerning the enactment of new legislation] do not apply to the laws enacted by the Reich Cabinet.

Article 4: Treaties of the Reich with foreign states which concern matters of domestic legislation do not require the consent of the bodies participating in legislation. The Reich Cabinet is empowered to issue the necessary provisions for the implementing of these treaties.

Article 5: This law comes into effect on the day of its publication.

"Decree for the Protection of the People and State" is from Office of the U.S. Chief Counsel for Prosecution of Axis Criminality, *Nazi Conspiracy and Aggression* (Washington, D.C.: Government Printing Office, 1946), vol. 1, p. 126 (PS-1390).

"The Enabling Act" is from Jeremy Noakes and Geoffrey Pridham, eds., *Documents on Nazism, 1919–1945*, p. 195. Reprinted by permission of A. D. Peters & Co., Ltd.

Law Against the New Formation of Parties
(July 14, 1933)

The government has passed the following law, which is being proclaimed herewith:

ARTICLE 1

The sole political party existing in Germany is the National Socialist German Workers' Party.

ARTICLE 2

Whoever shall undertake to maintain the organization of another party, or to found a new party, shall be punished with a sentence of hard labor of up to three years, or of prison between six months and three years, unless other regulations provide for heavier punishment.

> The Chancellor
> s. ADOLF HITLER
> The Minister of the Interior
> s. FRICK
> The Minister of Justice
> s. GURTNER

Law Concerning the Head of the German State
(August 1, 1934)

The government has passed the following law, which is being proclaimed herewith:

ARTICLE 1

The office of President shall be combined with that of Chancellor. Thus all the functions heretofore exercised by the President are transferred to the Fuhrer and Chancellor Adolf Hitler. He has the right to appoint his deputy.

Hitler and the Church

After Hitler had established his political control of the government, he sought an agreement with the Papacy that would prohibit participation of

"Law Against the New Formation of Parties" and "Law Concerning the Head of the German State" are from *The Nazi Years: A Documentary History*, edited by Joachim Remak, p. 54. © 1969. Used by permission of Prentice-Hall, Inc., Englewood Cliffs, N.J.

the German clergy in politics and would disband the Catholic Center party. In turn, the Church was to be guaranteed freedom of communication and religious instruction in schools. The first document is the Concordat between Pope Pius XI and the German state. It closely resembles an earlier agreement between the Church and Mussolini's Italy (1929).

Because of these Concordats, it appeared to many Catholics that the Church had given official recognition and even approval to thé fascist regimes of Benito Mussolini and Adolf Hitler. But the agreements were soon broken as the Nazis openly opposed the Catholic press and religious instruction of children. Hitler was in the process of indoctrinating the German youth and could no longer tolerate Catholic interference. In the second selection, Pope Pius XI condemned the Nazi infringement and denounced their actions as un-Christian.

The Concordat Between the Catholic Church and the German Reich (July 20, 1933)

His Holiness Pope Pius XI and the President of the German Reich, led by their common desire to consolidate and enhance the existing friendly relations between the Catholic Church and the State in the whole territory of the German Reich in a stable and satisfactory manner for both parties, have decided to conclude a solemn agreement. . . .

For this purpose: . . .

1. The German Reich guarantees freedom of profession and public practice of the Catholic religion.

It recognizes the right of the Catholic Church to regulate and manage her own affairs independently within the limits of laws applicable to all and to issue—within the framework of her own competence—laws and ordinances binding on her members.

4. The Holy See shall enjoy full freedom in its contact and correspondence with the bishops, clergy and all other members of the Catholic Church in Germany. The same applies to the bishops and other diocesan authorities in their contact with the faithful in all matters of their pastoral office.

Instructions, ordinances, Pastoral Letters, official diocesan gazettes, and other enactments concerning the spiritual guidance of the faithful, issued by the ecclesiastical authorities within the framework of their competence may be published without hindrance and made known to the faithful in the ways heretofore usual.

6. Clerics and religious are exempt from the obligation to undertake public offices and such obligations as are incompatible with their clerical or

Sidney Z. Ehler and John B. Morrall, trans. and eds., *Church and State Through the Centuries* (Westminster, Md.: The Newman Press, 1954), pp. 487–488, 491–493.

religious status. This applies particularly to the office of magistrate, membership of jury in Law Courts, membership of Taxation Committees or membership of the Fiscal Tribunal.

16. Before taking possession of their diocese, the Bishops shall take an oath of loyalty . . . which shall be the following:

"Before God and on the Holy Gospels I swear and promise, as becomes a bishop, loyalty to the German Reich. . . . I swear and promise to respect the Government established according to the Constitution and to cause the clergy of my diocese to respect it. In the due solicitude for the welfare and the interests of the German Reich, I will endeavour, while performing the spiritual office bestowed upon me, to prevent anything which might threaten to be detrimental to it."

21. Catholic religious instruction in primary, vocational, secondary and higher schools is a regular subject of tuition and is to be taught in accordance with the principles of the Catholic Church. In religious instruction the patriotic, civic and social consciousness and sense of duty will be particularly stressed and cultivated, as this is generally done in the school training. The teaching programme of religious education and the selection of textbooks will be settled by agreement with the higher ecclesiastical authorities. These authorities will be given the opportunity to control, in harmony with the school authorities, whether pupils are receiving religious instruction in accordance with the teaching and requirements of the Church.

25. Religious Orders and congregations have the right to establish and run private schools within the limits of the general legislation and conditions laid down by law. The same qualifications as in State schools can be acquired in these private schools if they follow the teaching programme prescribed for State schools. Members of religious Orders and congregations are subject, with regard to their admission to teaching and to their employment in primary schools, to the general conditions applicable to all.

30. On Sundays and Holy days a prayer will be said for the welfare of the German Reich and its people in episcopal, parish, affiliated and conventual churches in the German Reich, immediately after the High Mass and according to the rules of the Church liturgy.

Encyclical Letter on the Church in Germany (March 14, 1937)

POPE PIUS XI

1. With deep anxiety and with ever growing dismay We have for a considerable time watched the Church treading the Way of the Cross and the gradually increasing oppression of the men and women who have

Sidney Z. Ehler and John B. Morrall, trans. and eds., *Church and State Through the Centuries* (Westminster, Md.: The Newman Press, 1954), pp. 519–521, 523–524, 528–529.

remained devoted to her in thought and in act in that country and among that people to whom St. Boniface once brought the light of the Gospel of Christ and of the Kingdom of God.

2. This anxiety of Ours has not been lessened by the reports which the representatives of the reverend Episcopate dutifully and truthfully brought to Us on Our sick-bed. Besides much that is consoling and comforting in the struggle for religion which the faithful are now waging, they could not, in spite of their love for their people and country and their care to express a balanced judgment, pass silently over too much that is bitter and sad. When We heard their reports We could exclaim with the Apostle of Love in the deepest gratitude to God: "I have no greater grace than this, to hear that my children walk in truth" (3 John i,4). But the outspokenness which befits the responsibility of Our Apostolic office and the determination to lay before you and whole Christian world the real truth in all its gravity require Us to add: We have no greater concern and no heavier pastoral anxiety than when We hear that many forsake the way of truth (cf. 2 Pet. ii, 2).

3. When in the summer of 1933, Venerable Brethren, at the request of the German Government We resumed negotiations for a Concordat [and] . . . concluded a solemn agreement, We were moved by the solicitude that is incumbent on Us to safeguard the liberty of the Church in her mission of salvation in Germany and the salvation of the souls entrusted to her—and at the same time by the sincere desire to render an essential service to the peaceful development and welfare of the German people.

4. In spite of many serious misgivings We then brought Ourselves to decide not to withhold Our consent. We wished to spare Our loyal sons and daughters in Germany, as far as was humanly possible, the strain and the suffering which otherwise at that time and in those circumstances must certainly have been expected. By Our act We wished to show to all that, seeking only Christ and the things that are Christ's, We refuse to none who does not himself reject it, the hand of peace of Mother Church.

5. If the tree of peace planted by Us with pure intention in German soil has not borne the fruit We desired in the interests of your people, no one in the world who has eyes to see or ears to hear can say to-day that the fault lies with the Church and with her Supreme Head. The experience of the past years fixes the responsibility. It discloses intrigues which from the beginning had no other aim than a war of extermination. In the furrows in which We had laboured to sow the seeds of true peace, others . . . sowed the tares of suspicion, discord, hatred, calumny, of secret and open fundamental hostility to Christ and His Church, fed from a thousand different sources and making use of every available means. On them and on them alone, and on their silent and vocal protectors, there is to be seen not the rainbow of peace but the threatening storm-clouds of destructive religious wars.

12. God has given His commandments in the manner of a sovereign.

They are independent of time, space, country or nation. As God's sun shines on all the human race without distinction, so His law knows no privileges, no exceptions. Rulers and ruled, crowned and uncrowned, great and small, rich and poor, depend equally on his word. An essential consequence of the fullness of His rights as Creator in His Claim to absolute obedience from individuals in whatsoever society they be. Such a claim to obedience extends to every sphere of life in which moral questions have to be settled in accordance with divine law and therefore with the adjustment of mutable human laws to the structure of the immutable laws of God.

13. Only superficial minds can fall into the error of speaking of a national God, of a national religion, and of making a mad attempt to imprison within the frontiers of a single people, within the pedigree of one single race, God, the Creator of the world, the King, and lawgiver of the peoples before whose greatness the nations are as small as drops in a bucket of water.

15. We thank you, Venerable Brethren, your priests, and all the faithful who have done and are doing their duty as Christians in defending the rights of the divine Majesty against an aggressive neo-paganism which only too often is supported by influential persons. Our thanks are doubly heartfelt and are combined with a recognition and admiration for those who in doing this duty were accounted worthy of enduring temporal sacrifices and temporal sufferings for the cause of God.

23. In your territories, Venerable Brethren, voices are raised in an ever louder chorus, urging men to leave the Church, and preachers arise who from their official position try to create the impression that such a departure from the Church and the consequent infidelity to Christ the King is a particularly convincing and meritorious proof of their loyalty to the present regime. By disguised and by open methods of coercion, by intimidation, by holding out prospects of economic, professional, civil, or other kinds of advantages, the loyalty of Catholics to their faith, and especially of certain classes of Catholic officials, is subjected to a violence which is as unlawful as it is inhuman. With the feelings of a father We are moved and suffer profoundly with those who have paid such a price for their fidelity to Christ and to the Church. . . .

When persons who are not even united in faith in Christ entice you and flatter you with the picture of a "German national church," know that that is nothing but a denial of the one Church of Christ, manifest apostasy from the command of Christ to preach the gospel to the whole world, which can alone be accomplished by a universal Church. The historical development of other national churches, their spiritual torpor, their stifling by, or subservience to, lay power show the hopeless sterility which inevitably attacks the branch that separates itself from the living vine-stem of the Church. Whoever on principle gives to these false developments a watching and unflinching "No" is rendering a service not only to the purity of his own faith, but also to the welfare and vitality of his people.

Conversion and Resistance

The people of Germany were generally enthusiastic about Hitler, his image of a strong, successful fatherland, and his promises of prosperity. Membership in the National Socialist party rose steadily. Some people found that joining the Nazis was even more than a political experience; for them it was almost a religious conversion. The following section presents the experience of two such converts. But it must be remembered that there were still many who were alarmed at Hitler's actions. Among those who refused to support the "Fuehrer" was S. Ricarda Huch, a distinguished novelist and popular historian. In protest to the recent expulsion of writers who were politically or racially undesirable from the Prussian Academy of Arts and Sciences, Huch decided to resign. Her letter to the President of the Academy, Max von Schillings, explains her decision.

"Now I Know Which Road to Take"

JOSEPH GOEBBELS

Someone was standing up and had begun to talk, hesitatingly and shyly at first. . . . Then suddenly the speech gathered momentum. I was caught, I was listening. . . . The crowd began to stir. The haggard grey faces were reflecting hope. . . . Two seats to my left, an old officer was crying like a child. I felt alternately hot and cold. . . . It was as though guns were thundering. . . . I was beside myself. I was shouting hurrah. Nobody seemed surprised. The man up there looked at me for a moment. His blue eyes met my glance like a flame. This was a command. At that moment I was reborn. . . . Now I know which road to take.

[Goebbels became member No. 8,762]

"I Had Given Him My Heart"

KURT LUDECKE

Hitler's words were like a scourge. When he spoke of the disgrace of Germany, I felt ready to spring on any enemy . . . glancing around, I saw that his magnetism was holding these thousands as one. . . . I was a man of 32, weary of disgust and disillusionment, a wanderer seeking a cause . . . a yearner after the heroic without a hero. The intense will of the man, the passion of his sincerity, seemed to flow from him into me. I experienced a feeling that could be likened only to a religious conversion. . . . I felt sure

"Now I Know Which Road to Take" and "I Had Given Him My Heart" are from *Joseph Goebbels*, by Curt Reiss, p. 14. Copyright 1948 by Curt Reiss. Reprinted by permission of Doubleday and Company, Inc.

Nazi propaganda poster: "Youth Serve the Führer. All ten-year-olds in Hitler Youth."
(*Bundesarchiva*)

that no-one who heard Hitler that night could doubt he was the man of
destiny.... I had given him my heart.

A Matter of Principle

S. RICARDA HUCH

Heidelberg, April 9, 1933

Dear President von Schillings:
Let me first thank you for the warm interest you have taken in having me
remain in the Academy. I would very much like you to understand why I
cannot follow your wish. That a German's feelings are German I would
consider to be just about self-evident, but the definition of what is German,
and what acting in a German manner means—those are things where
opinions differ. What the present government prescribes by way of the use
of compulsion, the brutal methods, the defamation of those who hold
different convictions, the boastful self-praise—these are matters which I

From *The Nazi Years: A Documentary History*, edited by Joachim Remak, p. 162. © 1969.
Used by permission of Prentice-Hall, Inc. Englewood Cliffs, N.J.

consider un-German and disastrous. As I consider the divergence between this opinion of mine and that being ordered by the state, I find it impossible to remain in an Academy that is a part of the state. You say that the declaration submitted to me by the Academy would not prevent me from the free expression of my opinions. But "loyal cooperation, in the spirit of the changed historical situation, on matters affecting national and cultural tasks that fall within the jurisdiction of the Academy" requires an agreement with the government's program which in my case does not exist. Besides, I would find no newspaper or magazine that would print an opposition opinion. Thus the right to the free expression of opinion would remain quite theoretical. . . .

I hereby resign from the Academy.

STUDY QUESTIONS

1. Why was the National Socialist party able to rise to power? What were the main political, social, and economic problems of the twenties and early thirties, and what were the solutions offered by the Nazis? Why was the Weimar Republic unable to cope with the major problems facing Germany? Was its destruction inevitable?

2. Compare the constitution of the Weimar Republic with the Nazi program of 1920. How are they similar in outlook and what are the main differences? Pay particular attention to the presentation of specific points and the vocabulary.

3. Analyze the propaganda documents included in this chapter. In particular, what messages does Goebbels promote in "Nationalists, Socialists and Jews"? Is he logical in the presentation of his arguments, or can you find inconsistencies? What emotions does the propaganda exploit? What is the message in "Free Germany!"? Would you call it effective propaganda?

4. Statistics often reveal much after close analysis. What statements about the comparative strength of political parties can you make based on these data? Which party lost the most support from 1924 to 1932? How successful was the Communist party? What relationships do you see between political election and unemployment?

5. Many have viewed the Nazi rise to power as a legitimate act, fully sanctioned by law. Others have called it a revolution in which Hitler seized power. What do you think? To what extent was Hitler justified in stressing the legality of the Nazi assumption of power?

6. Explain Hitler's relationship with the Catholic Church. Was the Concordat that the Church made with Germany a smart move by the Pope, or do you see it as an abrogation of the Church's moral responsibility? In the preceding chapter entitled "Liberty, Equality, Fraternity," note the relationship between church and state during the French Revolution, especially under Napoleon. Is Hitler's treatment of the Church consistent with past actions? What general statement can you make regarding the use of religion during periods of political consolidation?

7. Carefully read the conversion accounts of Joseph Goebbels and Kurt Ludecke. Why did they join the Nazi party? The philosopher Eric Hoffer, in his book *The True Believer* (New York: Harper & Row, 1951, p. 50), described such converts as "permanent misfits." He noted that no achievement can give them a sense of fulfillment; they pursue goals passionately, but never arrive: "The permanent misfits can find salvation only in a complete separation from the self; and they usually find it by losing themselves in the compact collectivity of a mass movement. By renouncing individual will, judgment, and ambition, and dedicating all their powers to the service of an eternal cause, they are at last lifted off the endless treadmill which can never lead them to fulfillment. A rising mass movement attracts and holds a following not by its doctrine or promises, but by the refuge it offers from the anxieties [and] barreness of an individual existence." Do you agree? Why do people give their fanatical devotion to a cause?

8. Was the victory of National Socialism in Germany dependent on Adolf Hitler? How important was he to the Nazi movement? To what extent can the individual mold the events of history? What conditions in a state present the greatest opportunity for individual assertion of will and power?

9. Konrad Heiden, in his book *Der Fuehrer* (New York: Houghton Mifflin, 1944, p. v), stated that "Hitler was able to enslave his own people because he gave them something that even the traditional religions could no longer provide; the belief in a meaning to existence beyond the narrowest self-interest." How do you see this statement reflected in the various sources?

10. During the thirties and forties, Hitler and Germany would lead the world to war, with all its attendant suffering and destruction. Some historians argue that the victory of Adolf Hitler and the National Socialist party was consistent with the racism, militarism, and blind obedience to authority that marks the German national character. Can you describe French, Italian, British, Russian, or American character? Is there even such a thing as "national character," and is it legitimate to explain historical events on the basis of such a characterization?

10

The Jewish Holocaust

I mean the clearing out of the Jews, the extermination of the Jewish race. . . . Most of you must know what it means when 100 corpses are lying side by side, or 500, or 1,000. To have stuck it out and at the same time . . . to have remained decent fellows, that is what has made us hard. This is a page of glory in our history which has never been written and is never to be written. . . .

—Heinrich Himmler to his SS Officers

In spite of everything, I still believe that people are really good at heart.

—Anne Frank

In 1933, Adolf Hitler was appointed Chancellor of the German Weimar Republic, a post of prestige and authority. His National Socialist party was swept into power on the promises made to end the rampant inflation and unemployment that plagued the German economy, and to restore the dignity of the German people, who had been humiliated by the onorous Treaty of Versailles. Germany had to accept the harsh terms of this peace that resolved World War I, and was especially dissatisfied with the stipulation that Germany alone had been responsible for the war. Hitler's program presented a vision of the future, and his speeches inspired a defeated nation. His constant demands for more "living space" (*Lebensraum*) extended the boundaries of Germany, as Austria and the Sudetenland of Czechoslovakia were incorporated. By 1939, Hitler had revived the German economy and set the people back to work building the armaments that were to maintain a strong, united Germany. The other nations of Europe, particularly Great Britain, had generally appeased Hitler and allowed him to incorporate more territory, thinking that each demand would be his last. When Hitler invaded Poland in 1939, he went too far and the world once again went to war.

The road to World War II is, of course, a twisted one, and there are many different aspects to Hitler's rise and ultimate destruction. The name Adolf Hitler has become synonymous with evil. Much of this reputation has been derived from his attempt to commit genocide, to exterminate an entire race of people. One of the more distinctive differences between Italian Fascism under Benito Mussolini (1883–1945) and the Nazi movement was Hitler's use of anti-Semitism. Hitler demanded that Germany be composed of racially pure Aryan stock. The blond, blue-eyed German, untainted by inferior blood, became Hitler's ideal and the image he tried to cultivate in his propaganda. Hitler saw the Jews as the source of all of Germany's trouble. According to Hitler, Jews were cowards who did not support the fatherland in the Great War. They had deep communist sympathies, controlled international finance, and dominated the most important offices in government. Jews also controlled the purse strings of the nation and thus prevented worthier and more talented individuals from holding jobs and contributing to German culture. Indeed, Hitler had once been a frustrated artist in Vienna who blamed his failure on such Jewish influence. Hitler understood that hatred often unifies a nation more readily than does love. In troubled times, people want a simple explanation for their pain and insecurity. For Hitler, and consequently for Germany, that explanation was the Jew.

Anti-Semitism certainly did not originate with Hitler. Jews had been persecuted since the Middle Ages and even blamed for such things as outbreaks of bubonic plague. Still, never before was there such a systematic, methodical attempt to exterminate an entire race.

Although Hitler had exhibited his racism from the early twenties in speeches and writings, and had incorporated it into the philosophy of National Socialism, nothing could be implemented until the Nazis came into power. By 1935, Jews were excluded from citizenship by law in order to preserve German blood and honor. Germany was saturated with propaganda that presented the Jew as an immoral pervert whose presence was a threat to the health and morality of the Germany community. Nazi policy slowly evolved toward deportation and then toward isolation of the Jews in city ghettos. The "Final Solution" to the Jewish problem actually began in June 1941. As Hitler's armies drove into Russia, special mobile killing units (*Einsatzgruppen*) were set up and followed just behind the front lines. For eighteen months, the *Einsatzgruppen* operated and killed over 1,300,000 Jews. The Nazis also built several concentration camps generally designed to house workers and remove Jews from society. The treatment of prisoners was cruel, and hundreds of thousands died of exhaustion, starvation, and disease. The Nazi commitment to Jewish extermination even exceeded the bounds of practicality. Although there was a widespread shortage of labor throughout German-controlled Europe during the war, the Nazis continued to wipe out valuable workers. The camps, run by Hitler's private army called the "SS" (*Schutzstaffel*), often served as holding pens until the inmates were sent by train to six death camps located in Poland. Created solely for the task of killing, the camps at Auschwitz and Treblinka have become infamous—over 2,700,000 Jews were eliminated, one million in Auschwitz alone. Thousands of other undesirable people such as gypsies, Slavs, and even dissident Germans were also killed.

Many questions arise out of the Holocaust that make this a particularly important and relevant historical problem. How could such a violation against humanity have happened? Could it happen again? Can one view the Jewish Holocaust as a precedent that legitimized the dropping of the atomic bomb on Hiroshima and Nagasaki? Can one say, "War is Hell," and let it go at that? How deep and penetrating is the racial argument? Do we all have prejudices, which, if exploited properly, can lead to such results? These questions are ever-present in the world and have great relevance in understanding the policy of apartheid in South Africa or the influence of the Ku Klux Klan; the millions who were murdered by Stalin during Soviet collectivization, industrialization, and the Great Purges of the 1930s; the ruthlessness of the Cambodian dictator Pol Pot; or the maniacal rantings of Idi Amin or Muammar Gaddafi.

Not forgetting is the responsibility of the living.

The Evolution of Nazi Jewish Policy

Anti-Semitism was one of the cornerstones of Nazi dogma. When Hitler became chancellor in 1933, he began the process of excluding Jews from life in the German Reich. Note the charges that are leveled against the Jews in one of Hitler's early speeches. Indeed, Jews felt compelled to defend themselves against accusations that they were in control of international finance and the German government, or that they were cowards who forsook Germany in World War I. With the adoption of the Nuremberg Laws in 1935, Hitler excluded Jews from German citizenship and made provisions to restrict their social relations.

Jewish Responsibility

The Jewish Peril (April 1923)

ADOLF HITLER

The German people was once clear thinking and simple: why has it lost these characteristics? Any inner renewal is possible only if one realizes that this is a question of race: America forbids the yellow peoples to settle there, but this is a lesser peril than that which stretches out its hand over the entire world—the Jewish peril. Many hold that the Jews are not a race, but is there a second people anywhere in the wide world which is so determined to maintain its race?

As a matter of fact the Jew can never become a German however often he may affirm that he can. If he wished to become a German, he must surrender the Jew in him. And that is not possible: he cannot, however much he tries, become a German at heart, and that for several reasons: first because of his blood, second because of his character, thirdly because of his will, and fourthly because of his actions. His actions remain Jewish: he works for the "greater idea" of the Jewish people. Because that is so, because it cannot be otherwise, therefore the bare existence of the Jew as part of another State rests upon a monstrous lie. It is a lie when he pretends to the peoples to be a German, a Frenchman, etc.

What then are the specifically Jewish aims?

To spread their invisible State as a supreme tyranny over all other States in the whole world. The Jew is therefore a disintegrator of peoples. To realize his rule over the peoples he must work in two directions: in economics he dominates peoples when he subjugates them politically and morally: in politics he dominates them through the propagation of the principles of democracy and the doctrines of Marxism—the creed which makes a Proletarian a Terrorist in the domestic sphere and a Pacifist in foreign policy. Ethically the Jew destroys the peoples both in religion and in morals. He who wishes to see that can see it, and him who refuses to see it no one can help.

The Jew, whether consciously or unconsciously, whether he wishes it or not, undermines the platform on which alone a nation can stand.

We are now met by the questions: Do we wish to restore Germany to freedom and power? If "yes": then the first thing to do is to rescue it from him who is ruining our country. Admittedly it is a hard fight that must be fought here. We National Socialists on this point occupy an extreme position: but we know only one people: it is for that people we fight and that is our own people. . . . We want to stir up a storm. Men must not sleep: they

Norman H. Baynes, Translator and Editor, *The Speeches of Adolf Hitler, April, 1922–1939*, Vol 1, pp. 59–60 (London, RIIA/Oxford University Press, 1942). Reprinted by kind permission of the Royal Institute of International Affairs, London.

ought to know that a thunder-storm is coming up. We want to prevent our Germany from suffering, as Another did, the death upon the Cross.

We may be inhumane, but if we rescue Germany we have achieved the greatest deed in the world! We may work injustice, but if we rescue Germany then we have removed the greatest injustice in the world. We may be immoral, but if our people is rescued we have once more opened up the way for morality!

Jewish Defense (1932)

"Not a Single Jew"

Jewish World Finance

Today, capital formation takes place in large industry. Its largest enterprises are almost entirely dominated by non-Jewish interests: Krupp, Vereinigte Stahlwerke, Klockner, Stinnes, Siemeins, Stumm, I. G. Farben, Hugenberg, Hapag, Nordlloyd.

International connections are concentrated most heavily in those industries in which Jews are without influence or altogether unrepresented: the German-French iron cartel, wooden matches trust, oil trust, potash industry, and shipping conventions are all "clean of Jews," and so are the international chemical cartel, nylon production and all the other raw material and key industries in which Jews have no influence either as owners or directors. . . .

Jewish Government

The anti-Semites assert that the German government is full of Jews. The 19 post-war cabinets consisted of 237 ministers of whom three (Preuss and twice Rathenau) were Jews and four (Landsberg, Gradnauer, and twice Hilferding) of Jewish descent. The last few governments have had no Jewish ministers.

In the German provinces, the situation is not different: none of the provincial cabinets contain a Jew. The administration is not full of Jews, either. For example, in Prussia, among the twelve chief presidents, thirty-five government presidents and four hundred provincial counsellors, there is not a single Jew. . . .

The Jews in World War I

Of 538,000 Jews in Germany, more than 96,000 were under arms, including 10,000 volunteers; about 80,000 were on the front lines, 35,000 re-

Raul Hilberg, ed., *Documents of Destruction* (Chicago: Quadrangle Books, 1971), pp. 8–11. Reprinted by permission of the author.

ceived decorations, 23,000 were promoted, including more than 2000 to officer rank (without medical corps). One hundred sixty-eight Jews who volunteered as flyers are known by name. At the top of the list is Lieutenant D. R. Frankl who received the *Pour le merite* [combat medal] and *who like 29* other Jewish flyers was killed in battle.

Twelve thousand Jewish soldiers did not see their homeland again; they *died a hero's death for their German fatherland.* More than 10,000 of their names have now been recorded with personal information, unit, and number. The dead of Hamburg, Alsace-Lorraine and ceded Posen (with its relatively large Jewish population) have not yet been registered.

It is heartless to demand today that the widows and orphans, parents and brothers, brides and relatives of 12,000 fallen Jews be deprived of equality in Germany.

Legal Restriction of the Jews: The Nuremberg Laws (1935)

Law for the Protection of German Blood and German Honor (September 1935)

Entirely convinced that the purity of German blood is essential to the further existence of the German people, and inspired by the uncompromising determination to safeguard the future of the German nation, the Reichstag has unanimously resolved upon the following law, which is promulgated herewith:

Section 1

Marriages between Jews and citizens of German or kindred blood are forbidden. Marriages concluded in defiance of this law are void, even if, for the purpose of evading this law, they were concluded abroad.

Proceedings for annulment may be initiated only by the Public Prosecutor.

Section 2

Sexual relations outside marriage between Jews and nationals of German or kindred blood are forbidden.

Section 3

Jews will not be permitted to employ female citizens of German or kindred blood as domestic servants.

Section 4

Jews are forbidden to display the Reich and national flag or the national colours.

Jeremy Noakes and Geoffrey Pridham, eds., *Documents on Nazism, 1919–1945*, pp. 463–464. Reprinted by permission of A. D. Peters & Co., Ltd.

On the other hand they are permitted to display the Jewish colours. The exercise of this right is protected by the State.

Section 5

A person who acts contrary to the prohibition of Section I will be punished with hard labour.

A person who acts contrary to the prohibition of Section 2 will be punished with imprisonment or with hard labour.

A person who acts contrary to the provisions of Sections 3 or 4 will be punished with imprisonment up to a year and with a fine, or with one of these penalties.

The Reich Citizenship Law (September 1935)

Article I

1. A subject of the State is a person who belongs to the protective union of the German Reich, and who therefore has particular obligations towards the Reich.
2. The status of subject is acquired in accordance with the provisions of the Reich and State Law of Citizenship.

Article 2

1. A citizen of the Reich is that subject only who is of German or kindred blood and who, through his conduct, shows that he is both desirous and fit to serve the German people and Reich faithfully.
2. The right to citizenship is acquired by the granting of Reich citizenship papers.
3. Only the citizen of the Reich enjoys full political rights in accordance with the provision of the laws.

Anti-Jewish Propaganda

In 1936, Germany hosted the Olympic Games, and Hitler ordered the temporary removal of anti-Jewish placards in order to appease foreign opinion. Still, the propaganda continued to flow, especially from *Der Stürmer*, a sensationalistic journal published by Julius Streicher. In the first selection, note the accusation of cannibalism and the misrepresentation of the two Jewish festivals of Purim and Passover, which commemorate not murder but deliverance from oppression. The second excerpt is from a book for older children called *Der Giftpilz (The Poisonous Mush-*

Jeremy Noakes and Geoffrey Pridham, eds., *Documents on Nazism, 1919–1945*, pp. 464–465. Reprinted by permission of A. D. Peters & Co., Ltd.

room), which presented the Jew as an evil deviate who preyed on the innocence of children.

Ritual Murder: *Der Stürmer* (1937)

The murder of the 10 year old Gertrud Lenhoff in Quirschied (Saarpfalz)

* * *   The Jews are our MISFORTUNE!   * * *

Also the numerous confessions made by the Jews show that the execution of ritual murders is a law to the Talmud Jew. The former Chief Rabbi (and later monk) Teofiti declares . . . that the ritual murders take place especially on the Jewish Purim (in memory of the Persian murders) and Passover (in memory of the murder of Christ).

The instructions are as follows:

The blood of the victims is to be tapped by force. On Passover, it is to be used in wine and matzos; thus, a small part of the blood is to be poured into the dough of the matzos and into the wine. The mixing is done by the Jewish head of the family.

The procedure is as follows: the family head empties a few drops of the fresh and powdered blood into the glass, wets the fingers of the left hand with it and sprays (blesses) with it everything on the table. The head of the family then says: "Dam Izzardia chynim heroff dever Isyn porech harbe hossen maschus pohorus" (Exod. 7.12) ("Thus we ask God to send the ten plagues to all enemies of the Jewish faith.") Then they eat, and at the end the head of the family exclaims: "Sfach, chaba, moscho kol hagoym!" ("May all Gentiles perish—as the child whose blood is contained in the bread and wine!")

The fresh (or dried and powdered) blood of the slaughtered is further used by young married Jewish couples, by pregnant Jewesses, for circumcisions, and so on. Ritual murder is recognized by all Talmud Jews. The Jew believes he absolves himself thus of his sins.

The Poisonous Mushroom (1938)

ERNST HIEMER

"It is almost noon," he said, "now we want to summarize what we have learned in this lesson. What did we discuss?"

"Ritual Murder: *Der Stürmer*" is from the Office of the U.S. Chief of Counsel for the Prosecution of Axis Criminality, *Nazi Conspiracy and Aggression* (Washington, D.C.: Government Printing Office, 1947), vol. 5, pp. 372–373 (PS-2699).

"The Poisonous Mushroom" is from the Office of the U.S. Chief of Counsel for the Prosecution of Axis Criminality, *Nazi Conspiracy and Aggression* (Washington, D.C.: Government Printing Office, 1947), vol. 4, pp. 358–359 (PS-1778).

All the children raise their hands. The teacher calls on Karl Scholz, a little boy on the first bench. "We talked about how to recognize a Jew."

"Good! Now tell us about it!"

Little Karl takes the pointer, goes to the blackboard and points to the sketches.

"One usually recognizes a Jew by his nose. The Jewish nose is crooked at the end. It looks like the figure 6. Therefore it is called the "Jewish Six." Many non-Jews have crooked noses, too. But their noses are bent, not at the end but further up. Such a nose is called a hook nose or eagle's beak. It has nothing to do with a Jewish nose."

"Right!" says the teacher. "But the Jew is recognized not only by his nose. . ." The boy continues. The Jew is also recognized by his lips. His lips are usually thick. Often the lower lip hangs down. This is called "sloppy." And the Jew is also recognized by his eyes. His eyelids are usually thicker and more fleshy than ours. The look of the Jew is lurking and sharp.

Then the teacher goes to the desk and turns over the blackboard, on its back is a verse. The children recite it in chorus:

> From a Jew's countenance—the evil devil talks to us,
> The devil, who in every land—is known as evil plague.
> If we shall be free of the Jew—and again will be happy and glad,
> Then the youth must struggle with us—to subdue the Jew devil.

Inge sits in the reception room of the Jew doctor. She has to wait a long time. She looks through the journals which are on the table. But she is almost too nervous to read even a few sentences. Again and again she remembers the talk with her mother. And again and again her mind reflects on the warnings of her leader of the BDM [League of German Girls]: "A German must not consult a Jew doctor! And particularly not a German girl! Many a girl that went to a Jew doctor to be cured, found disease and disgrace!"

When Inge had entered the waiting room, she experienced an extraordinary incident. From the doctor's consulting room she could hear the sound of crying. She heard the voice of a young girl: "Doctor, doctor leave me alone!"

Then she heard the scornful laughing of a man. And then all of a sudden it became absolutely silent. Inge had listened breathlessly.

"What may be the meaning of all this?" she asked herself and her heart was pounding. And again she thought of the warning of her leader in the BDM.

Inge was already waiting for an hour. Again she takes the journals in an endeavor to read. Then the door opens. Inge looks up. The Jew appears. She screams. In terror she drops the paper. Frightened she jumps up. Her eyes stare into the face of the Jewish doctor. And this face is the face of the devil. In the middle of this devil's face is a huge crooked nose. Behind the spectacles two criminal eyes. And the thick lips are grinning. A grinning that expresses: "Now I got you at last, you little German girl!"

And then the Jew approaches her. His fleshy fingers stretch out after her. But now Inge has her wits. Before the Jew can grab hold of her, she hits the fat face of the Jew doctor with her hand. Then one jump to the door. Breathlessly she escapes the Jew house.

The Radicalization of Anti-Semitism (1938–1941)

On November 9–10, 1938, the Nazis, in retaliation for the assassination of a German diplomat, set fire to Jewish synagogues and systematically destroyed 7,500 Jewish stores. The incident became known as *Kristallnacht* (Crystal Night) because of the broken glass that covered the street. A few days later, Reich Marshall Hermann Goering called a meeting of some of the Nazi hierarchy (Reinhard Heydrich and Joseph Goebbels) to place ultimate responsibility for the destruction on the Jews. It was decided that the Jews would have to pay for the damage they "provoked." In the first selection, note the mention of ideas (separate schools, badges, and ghettos) that achieved fruition later as indicated in the second selection. Hitler gave little doubt as to his intentions regarding the Jews in a speech given before the Reichstag in 1939. Joseph Goebbels, the Minister of Propaganda, capitalized on this official anti-Semitic stance of the German government in his tract which blamed the war on the Jews.

Conference on the Jewish Question
(November 12, 1938)

Goering: I should not want to leave any doubt, gentlemen, as to the aim of today's meeting. We have not come together merely to talk again, but to make decisions, and I implore the competent agencies to take all measures for the elimination of the Jew from German economy and to submit them to me, as far as it is necessary. . . .

Furthermore, I advocate that the Jews be eliminated from all positions in public life in which they may prove to be provocative. . . . Jews should not be allowed to sit around in German parks. I am thinking of the whispering campaign on the part of Jewish women in the public gardens at Fehrbelliner Platz. They go and sit with German mothers and their children and begin to gossip and incite. I see in this a particularly grave danger. I think it

Office of the U.S. Chief of Counsel for the Prosecution of Axis Criminality, *Nazi Conspiracy and Aggression* (Washington, D.C.: Government Printing Office, 1947), vol. 4, pp. 426, 432–434 (PS-1816).

is imperative to give the Jews certain public parks, not the best ones—and tell them: "You may sit on these benches," these benches shall be marked, "For Jews only." Besides that they have no business in German parks. Furthermore, Jewish children are still allowed in German schools. That's impossible. It is out of the question that any boy should sit beside a Jewish boy in a German gymnasium and receive lessons in German history. Jews ought to be eliminated completely from German schools; they may take care of their own education in their own communities. . . .

Heydrich: As another means of getting the Jews out, measures for Emigration are to be taken in the rest of the Reich for the next 8 to 10 years. The highest number of Jews we can possibly get out during one year is 8,000 to 10,000. Therefore, a great number of Jews will remain. Because of aryanizing and other restrictions, Jewry will become unemployed. The remaining Jews gradually become proletarians. Therefore, I shall have to take steps; to isolate the Jew so he won't enter into the German normal routine of life. On the other hand, I shall have to restrict the Jew to a small circle of consumers, but I shall have to permit certain activities within professions; lawyers, doctors, barbers, etc. This question shall also have to be examined.

As for the isolation, I'd like to make a few proposals regarding police measures which are important also because of their psychological effect on public opinion. For example, who is Jewish according to the Nuremberg laws shall have to wear a certain insignia. That is a possibility which shall facilitate many other things. I don't see any danger of excuses, and it shall make our relationship with the foreign Jew easier.

Goering: A uniform?

Heydrich: An insignia. This way we could also put an end to it that the foreign Jews who don't look different from ours, are being molested.

Goering: But, my dear Heydrich, you won't be able to avoid the creation of ghettos on a very large scale, in all the cities. They shall have to be created.

Police Decree Concerning the Marking of Jews (September 1941)

Paragraph 1

1. Jews over the age of six are forbidden to show themselves in public without a Jew's star.

From *The Nazi Years: A Documentary History*, edited by Joachim Remak, p. 151. © 1969. Used by permission of Prentice-Hall, Inc., Englewood Cliffs, N.J.

2. The Jew's star consists of a six-pointed star of yellow cloth with black borders, equivalent in size to the palm of the hand. The inscription is to read "JEW" in black letters. It is to be sewn to the left breast of the garment, and to be worn visibly.

Paragraph 2

Jews are Forbidden
a) to leave their area of residence without carrying, on their person, written permission from the local police.
b) to wear medals, decorations, or other insignia. . . .

Speech to the Reichstag (January 30, 1939)
ADOLF HITLER

One thing I should like to say on this day which may be memorable for others as well as for us Germans. In the course of my life I have very often been a prophet, and have usually been ridiculed for it. During the time of my struggle for power it was in the first instance only the Jewish race that received my prophecies with laughter when I said that I would one day take over the leadership of the State, and with it that of the whole nation, and that I would then among other things settle the Jewish problem. Their laughter was uproarious, but I think that for some time now they have been laughing on the other side of their face. Today I will once more be a prophet: if the international Jewish financiers in and outside Europe should succeed in plunging the nations once more into a world war, than the result will not be the Bolshevizing of the earth, and thus the victory of Jewry, but the annihilation of the Jewish race in Europe!

The Jews Are to Blame! (1941)
JOSEPH GOEBBELS

World Jewry's historic guilt for the outbreak and extension of this war has been so abundantly proven that no additional words need to be lost over the matter. The Jews wanted their war. Now they have it. But what is also

"Speech to the Reichstag" is from Norman H. Baynes, Translator and Editor, *The Speeches of Adolf Hitler, April, 1922–1939*, Vol 1, pp. 740–741 (London, RIIA/Oxford University Press, 1942). Reprinted by kind permission of the Royal Institute of International Affairs, London.

"The Jews Are to Blame" is from *The Nazi Years: A Documentary History*, edited by Joachim Remak, pp. 155–156. © 1969. Used by permission of Prentice-Hall, Inc., Englewood Cliffs, N.J.

coming true for them is the Führer's prophecy which he voiced in his Reichstag speech of January 30, 1939. It was that if international financial Jewry succeeded in plunging the nations into another world war, the result would not be the Bolshevization of the world and thus the victory of Jewry, but the destruction of the Jewish race in Europe.

We are now witnessing the acid test of this prophecy, and thus Jewry is experiencing a fate which is hard but more than deserved. Pity or even regrets are entirely out of place here. World Jewry, in starting this war, made an entirely wrong estimate of the forces at its disposal, and is now suffering the same gradual process of destruction which it had planned for us, and which it would apply without hesitation were it to possess the power to do so. It is in line with their own law, "An eye for an eye, a tooth for a tooth," that the ruin of the Jews is now taking place. . . .

So, superfluous though it might be, let me say once more:

1. The Jews are our destruction. They provoked and brought about this war. What they mean to achieve by it is to destroy the German state and nation. This plan must be frustrated.

2. There is no difference between Jew and Jew. Every Jew is a sworn enemy of the German people. If he fails to display his hostility against us, it is merely out of cowardice and slyness, but not because his heart is free of it.

3. Every German soldier's death in this war is the Jew's responsibility. They have it on their conscience; hence they must pay for it.

4. Anyone wearing the Jew's star has been marked as an enemy of the nation. Any person who still maintains social relations with him is one of them, and must be considered a Jew himself and treated as such. He deserves the contempt of the entire nation, which he has deserted in its gravest hour to join the side of those who hate it.

5. The Jews enjoy the protection of the enemy nations. No further proof is needed of their destructive role among our people.

6. The Jews are the messengers of the enemy in our midst. Anyone joining them is going over to the enemy in time of war.

7. The Jews have no claim to pretend to have rights equal to ours. Wherever they want to open their mouths, in the street, in the lines in front of the stores, or on public transportation, they are to be silenced. They are to be silenced not only because they are wrong on principle, but because they are Jews and have no voice in the community.

8. If Jews pull a sentimental act for you, bear in mind that they are speculating on your forgetfullness. Show them immediately that you see right through them and punish them with contempt.

9. A decent enemy, after his defeat, deserves our generosity. But the Jew is no decent enemy. He only pretends to be one.

10. The Jews are to blame for this war. The treatment we give them does them no wrong; they have more than deserved it. . . .

The Final Solution (1941–1945)

By 1940, the Nazis had embarked on a policy that was designed to "cleanse" the German homeland of Jews by confining them to ghettos in cities, especially in Poland. There the Nazis could control them and, upon demand, export them to concentration camps where they would be put to work or die. But in July 1941, preparations were made for a secretive "Final Solution" to the Jewish problem. It was discussed in more detail at the Wansee Conference in January 1942, as the following excerpts indicate.

Official Policy

Decree of the Reich Marshal (July 31, 1941)

HERMANN GOERING

To: The Chief of the Security Police and the Security Service; SS-Gruppenfuehrer Heydrich

Complementing the task that was assigned to you on 24 January 1939, which dealt with the carrying out of emigration and evacuation, a solution of the Jewish problem, as advantageous as possible, I hereby charge you with making all necessary preparations in regard to organizational and financial matters for bringing out a complete solution of the Jewish question in the German sphere of influence in Europe.

Wherever other governmental agencies are involved, these are to cooperate with you.

I charge you furthermore to send me, before long, an overall plan concerning the organizational, factual and material measures necessary for the accomplishment of the desired solution of the Jewish question.

Wansee Conference (January 20, 1942)

II. At the beginning of the meeting the Chief of the Security Police and the SD, SS Lieutenant General Heydrich, reported his appointment by the Reich Marshal to service as Commissioner for the Preparation of the Final

---

"Decree of the Reich Marshal" is from the Office of the U.S. Chief Counsel for Prosecution of Axis Criminality, *Nazi Conspiracy and Aggression* (Washington, D.C.: Government Printing Office, 1947), vol. 3, pp. 525–526 (PS-710).

"Wansee Conference" is from the Nuremberg Military Tribunals, *Trials of War Criminals* (Washington, D.C.: Government Printing Office, 1947–1949), vol. 13, pp. 211–213.

Solution of the European Jewish Problem, and pointed out that the officials had been invited to this conference in order to clear up the fundamental problems. The Reich Marshal's request to have a draft submitted to him on the organizational, factual, and material requirements with respect to the Final Solution of the European Jewish Problem, necessitated this previous general consultation by all the central offices directly concerned, in order that there should be coordination in the policy.

The primary responsibility for the administrative handling of the Final Solution of the Jewish Problem will rest centrally with the Reich Leader SS and the Chief of the German Police (Chief of the Security Police and the SD)—regardless of geographic boundaries.

The Chief of the Security Police and the SD thereafter gave a brief review of the battle conducted up to now against these enemies. The most important are—

    a. Forcing the Jews out of the various fields of the community life of the German people.
    b. Forcing the Jews out of the living space [*Lebensraum*] of the German people.

. . .

Meanwhile, in view of the dangers of emigration during the war and in view of the possibilities in the East, the Reich Leader SS and Chief of the German Police had forbidden the emigrating of the Jews.

III. The emigration program has now been replaced by the evacuation of the Jews to the East as a further solution possibility, in accordance with previous authorization by the Fuehrer.

These actions are of course to be regarded only as a temporary substitute; nonetheless, here already, the coming Final Solution of the Jewish Question is of great importance. In the course of this Final Solution of the European Jewish Problem, approximately 11 million Jews are involved.

Under proper direction the Jews should now in the course of the Final Solution be brought to the East in a suitable way for use as labor. In big labor gangs, with separation of the sexes, the Jews capable of work are brought to these areas and employed in road building, in which task undoubtedly a great part will fall out through natural diminution.

The remnant that finally is able to survive all this—since this is undoubtedly the part with the strongest resistance—must be treated accordingly since these people, representing a natural selection, are to be regarded as the germ cell of a new Jewish development. (See the experience of history.)

In the program of the practical execution of the Final Solution, Europe is combed through from the West to the East.

The evacuated Jews are brought first group by group into the so-called transit ghettos, in order to be transported from these farther to the East.

The Death Camps

The "Final Solution" ordered the implementation of a policy of genocide. Hitler wanted to rid the world of a people whom he found responsible for most of humanity's ills. The following selections present the system of extermination from the trip to the death camp by train through the selection process and the gas chambers. Much of the testimony in this section comes from the Nuremberg trial proceedings in 1946. Hermann Gräbe ("The Pit") was a German construction engineer working in the Ukraine in 1942. Kurt Gerstein ("Gas") was the SS Head of Disinfection Services in early 1942. The gassing of Jews did not take place at concentration or death camps alone, as is noted by the selection entitled "Mobile Killing." This is a top secret dispatch concerning the *Einsatzgruppen* that often followed advancing troops. Excerpts from the autobiography and Nuremberg testimony of Rudolf Hoess are also included. He was commandant of the notorious Auschwitz death camp and was himself executed there in 1947 after being judged guilty of crimes against humanity.

Sites of Nazi Concentration Camps

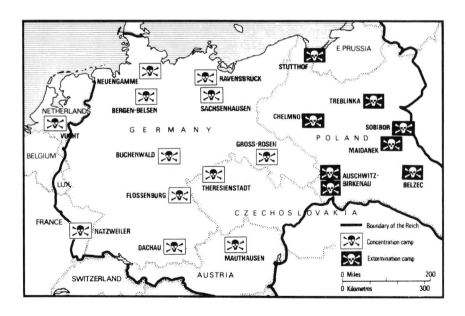

Louis L. Snyder, *Encyclopedia of the Third Reich* (New York: McGraw-Hill Book Company, 1976), p. 57. Reprinted by permission of the publisher.

Arrival: The Death Train

ELIE WIESEL

Indescribable confusion reigned.

Parents searched for their children, children for their parents, and lonely captives for their friends. The people were beset by loneliness. Everyone feared that the outcome of the journey would be tragic and would claim its toll of lives. And so one yearned to have the companionship of someone who would stand by with a word, with a loving glance.

Afterward, an ominous silence fell upon us. We squatted on the soft snow that covered the floor of the railroad car like a carpet, and tried to keep warm by drawing closer to our neighbors.

When the train started to move, no one paid any attention to it. Careworn and burdened with conflicting thoughts, each of us wondered if he was wise to continue on the journey. But in our weariness, whether one died today, tomorrow, a week or a generation later, hardly seemed to matter.

The night dragged on interminably, as though it were to go on to the end of time. When the gray dawn appeared in the east, I felt as though I had spent a night in a tomb haunted by evil spirits. Human beings, defeated and broken, sat like dusty tombstones in the dim light of early dawn. I looked about the subdued throng and tried to distinguish one from another. And, indeed, perhaps there was no distinction.

My gaze fell on one who stared blankly ahead. A wry smile seemed to play on his ice-encrusted face. Those glazed eyes, whether living or dead, seemed to ensnare my gaze. A hundred and twenty captives, shadows of human lives, extinguished flames of burned-out candles lit on the anniversaries of the deaths of their loved ones.

Wrapped in a drenched blanket, his black cap pulled down over his ears, a layer of snow on his shoulders, my father sat beside me. Could it be that he, too, was dead? The thought flashed across my mind. I tried to talk to him. I wanted to shout, but all I could do was mutter. He did not reply, he did not utter a sound. I was certain that from then on I was to be all alone, all alone. Then I was filled with a numbing sense of indifference to everyone and to myself. Well, the Lord giveth and the Lord taketh away. The struggle was over. There was nothing and no one for whom to fight now.

The train ground to an abrupt halt in a snow-covered field. Awakened by the jolt, a few curious captives struggled to their feet to look out. The scene was reminiscent of cattle staring stupidly from a livestock car.

German S. S. guards surrounded the human cargo, shouting, "All the dead are to be thrown out! All the dead are to be thrown out!"

The living were pleased; there would be more space. It would not be as crowded now.

From E. Wiesel, *The World Was Silent*, trans. Moshe Spiegel (Buenos Aires, 1956), in *An Anthology of Holocaust Literature*, ed. J. Glatstein, I. Knox, and S. Margoshes (Philadelphia: The Jewish Publication Society, 1969), pp. 3–5, 10. Reprinted by permission of the publisher.

Halt during railway journey near Jassy: "German S.S. guards surrounded the human cargo shouting, 'All the dead are to be thrown out. All the dead are to be thrown out!'"—Elie Wiesel. *(Yad Vashem, Jerusalem)*

Strong men appeared and examined each one who could not stand up, and rapped out, "Here's one! Get hold of him!"

Whereupon two men would pick the corpse by the shoulders and feet and fling it out of the car like a sack of flour.

From various parts of the car came such cries as, "Here's another—my neighbor! He doesn't move. Help me get rid of him!"

There were some twenty-odd dead in our one car, and after they were stripped of their clothes, which the living snatched up, they were flung out of the car.

This task took several hours. Then the train chugged along, and as icy gusts shrieked about it, it seemed that through the accursed world about us could be heard the far-away, muffled wail of the naked bodies that had been abandoned on Polish snow-covered fields.

The journey was insufferable; and every one who lived through it later questioned the natural laws that their survival seemed to disprove.

We were deprived of even bread and water, and snow was our only source of water. Cramped for space and thoroughly chilled, we were very weak by the third day of the journey. Days were turned into nights, and the nights cast a shadow of doom over our very souls.

The train plodded along for what seemed countless days, and the snow fell, fell, fell incessantly. And the exhausted, travel-weary unfortunates lay huddled for days on end, without uttering a word, eyes closed, waiting for one thing only—the next station, where the new yield of corpses would be got rid of. That was what we looked forward to.

The journey lasted ten interminable days and nights. Each day claimed its toll of victims and each night paid its homage to the Angel of Death.

We passed through German settlements, generally in the early morning hours, only in a few instances. Sometimes men on their way to work would halt in their tracks to glare at us as though we were animals in a kind of demonic circus. Once a German churled a chunk of bread into our car and caused pandemonium break out as scores of famished men fought each other in an effort to pounce upon it. And the German workers eyed the spectacle with sneering amusement.

We arrived at the Buchenwald concentration camp late at night. "Security police" of the camp came forward to unload the human cargo. The dead were left in the cars. Only those who were able to drag their feet got out. Meir Katz was left in the car; like so many others, he had frozen to death a short time before we reached our destination. The journey itself was the worst part of the ordeal. About forty of the deportees were claimed by death on that one day alone. Our car had originally started out with a hundred and twenty souls; twelve—among them my father and I—had survived the ordeal.

Genocide

RUDOLF HOESS

I, Rudolf Franz Ferdinand Hoess, being first duly sworn, depose and say as follows:

1. I am forty-six years old, and have been a member of the NSDAP since 1922; a member of the SS since 1934; a member of the Waffen-SS since 1939. I was a member from 1 December 1934 of the SS Guard Unit, the so-called Deathshead Formation [*Totenkopf Verband*].

2. I have been constantly associated with the administration of concentration camps since 1934, serving at Dachau until 1938; then as Adjutant in Sachenhausen from 1938 to May 1, 1940, when I was appointed Commandant of Auschwitz. I commanded Auschwitz until 1 December 1943, and estimate that at least 2,500,000 victims were executed and exterminated there by gassing and burning, and at least another half million

Office of the U.S. Chief of Counsel for the Prosecution of Axis Criminality, *Nazi Conspiracy and Aggression* (Washington, D.C.: Government Printing Office, 1947), vol. 6, pp. 787–790 (PS-3868).

succumbed to starvation and disease making a total dead of about 3,000,000. This figure represents about 70% of 80% of all persons sent to Auschwitz as prisoners, the remainder having been selected and used for slave labor in the concentration camp industries. Included among the executed and burnt were approximately 20,000 Russian prisoners of war (previously screened out of Prisoner of War cages by the Gestapo) who were delivered at Auschwitz in Wehrmacht transports operated by regular Wehrmacht officers, 100,000 German Jews, and great numbers of citizens, mostly Jewish from Holland, France, Belgium, Poland, Hungary, Czechoslovakia, Greece, or other countries. We executed about 400,000 Hungarian Jews alone at Auschwitz in the summer of 1944. . . .

4. Mass executions by gassing commenced during the summer 1941 and continued until fall 1944. I personally supervised executions at Auschwitz until the first of December 1943 and know by reason of my continued duties . . . that these mass executions continued as stated above. All mass executions by gassing took place under the direct orders, supervisions, and responsibility of RSHA [Reich Security Main Office]. I received all orders for carrying out these mass executions directly from RSHA. . . .

6. The "final solution" of the Jewish question meant the complete extermination of all Jews in Europe. I was ordered to establish extermination facilities at Auschwitz in June 1941. At that time, there were already in the general government three other extermination camps; Belzek, Treblinka, and Wolzek. These camps were under the *Einsatzkommando* of the Security Police and SD. I visited Treblinka to find out how they carried out their extermination. The Camp Commandant at Treblinka told me that he had liquidated 80,000 in the course of one-half year. He was principally concerned with liquidating all the Jews from the Warsaw ghetto. He used monoxide gas and I did not think that his methods were very efficient. So when I set up the extermination building at Auschwitz, I used Cyclon B, which was a crystallized prussic acid which we dropped into the death chamber from a small opening. It took from 3 to 15 minutes to kill the people in the death chamber depending upon climatic conditions. We knew when the people were dead because their screaming stopped. We usually waited about one-half hour before we opened the doors and removed the bodies. After the bodies were removed our special commandos took off the rings and extracted the gold from the teeth of the corpses.

7. Another improvement we made over Treblinka was that we built our gas chambers to accomodate 2,000 people at one time, whereas at Treblinka their 10 gas chambers only accomodated 200 people each. The way we selected our victims was as follows: we had two SS doctors on duty at Auschwitz to examine the incoming transports of prisoners. The prisoners would be marched by one of the doctors who would make spot decisions as they walked by. Those who were fit for work were sent into the Camp. Others were sent immediately to the extermination plants. Children of tender years were invariably exterminated since by reason of their youth

they were unable to work. Still another improvement we made over Treblinka was that at Treblinka the victims almost always knew that they were to be exterminated and at Auschwitz we endeavored to fool the victims into thinking that they were to go through a delousing process. Of course, frequently they realized our true intentions and we sometimes had riots and difficulties due to that fact. Very frequently women would hide their children under their clothes but of course when we found them we would send the children in to be exterminated. We were required to carry out these exterminations in secrecy but of course the foul and nauseating stench from the continuous burning of bodies permeated the entire area and all of the people living in the surrounding communities knew that exterminations were going on at Auschwitz.

8. We received from time to time special prisoners from the local Gestapo office. The SS doctors killed such prisoners by injections of benzine. Doctors had orders to write ordinary death certificates and could put down any reason at all for the cause of death.

9. From time to time we conducted medical experiments on women inmates, including sterilization and experiments relating to cancer. Most of the people who died under these experiments had been already condemned to death by the Gestapo. . . .

I understand English as it is written above. The above statements are true; this declaration is made by me voluntarily and without compulsion; after reading over the statements, I have signed and executed the same at Nuremberg, Germany, on the fifth day of April 1946.

Rudolf Franz Ferdinand Hoess

Subscribed and sworn to before me this 5th day of April 1946, at Nuremberg, Germany
Smith W. Brookhart Jr., Lt. Colonel, IGD

The Pit

HERMANN GRÄBE

On October 5, 1942, when I visited the building office at Dubno, my foreman told me that in the vicinity of the site, Jews from Dubno had been shot in three large pits, each about 30 metres long and 3 metres deep.

Louis L. Snyder, *Documents of German History*, pp. 462–463. Copyright 1958 by Rutgers, The State University. Reprinted by permission of Rutgers University Press.

"I remember and I am afraid."—Elie Wiesel. *(Yad Vashem, Jerusalem)*

About 1,500 persons had been killed daily. All the 5,000 Jews who had still been living in Dubno before the pogrom were to be liquidated. As the shooting had taken place in his presence, he was still much upset.

Thereupon, I drove to the site accompanied by my foreman and saw near it great mounds of earth, about 30 metres long and 2 metres high. Several trucks stood in front of the mounds. Armed Ukrainian militia drove the people off the trucks under the supervision of an S.S. man. The militiamen acted as guards on the trucks and drove them to and from the pit. All these people had the regulation yellow patches on the front and back of their clothes, and thus could be recognized as Jews.

My foreman and I went directly to the pits. Nobody bothered us. Now I heard rifle shots in quick succession from behind one of the earth mounds. The people who had got off the trucks—men, women and children of all ages—had to undress upon the orders of an S.S. man, who carried a riding or dog whip. They had to put down their clothes in fixed places, sorted according to shoes, top clothing and underclothing. I saw a heap of shoes of about 800 to 1,000 pairs, great piles of underlinen and clothing.

Without screaming or weeping, these people undressed, stood around in family groups, kissed each other, said farewells, and waited for a sign from another S.S. man, who stood near the pit, also with a whip in his hand.

During the fifteen minutes that I stood near I heard no complaint or plea for mercy. I watched a family of about eight persons, a man and a woman both about fifty with their children of about one, eight and ten, and two grown-up daughters of about twenty to twenty-nine. An old woman with snow-white hair was holding the one-year-old child in her arms and singing to it and tickling it. The child was cooing with delight. The couple were looking on with tears in their eyes. The father was holding the hand of a boy about ten years old and speaking to him softly; the boy was fighting his tears. The father pointed to the sky, stroked his head, and seemed to explain something to him.

At that moment the S.S. man at the pit shouted something to his comrade. The latter counted off about twenty persons and instructed them to go behind the earth mound. Among them was the family which I have mentioned. I well remember a girl, slim and with black hair, who, as she passed close to me pointed to herself and said "23." I walked around the mound and found myself confronted by a tremendous grave. People were closely wedged together and lying on top of each other so that only their heads were visible. Nearly all had blood running over their shoulders from their heads. Some of the people shot were still moving. Some were lifting their arms and turning their heads to show that they were still alive. The pit was already two-thirds full. I estimated that it already contained about 1,000 people.

Gas

KURT GERSTEIN

In January, 1942, I was named chief of the Waffen SS technical disinfection services, including a section for extremely toxic gases. . . . SS Gruppenfuhrer Globocnik was waiting for us at Lublin. He told us, "This is one of the most secret matters there are, even the most secret. Anybody who talks about it will be shot immediately." He explained to us that there were three installations:

1) Belzec, on the Lublin-Lwow road. A maximum of 15,000 people per day.
2) Sobibor (I don't know exactly where it is), 20,000 people a day.
3) Treblinka, 120 kilometers NNE of Warsaw.
4) Maidanek, near Lublin (under construction).

Leon Poliakov, *Harvest of Hate*, pp. 193–196. Copyright © 1954, The American Jewish Committee. Reprinted by permission.

Globocnik said: "You will have to disinfect large piles of clothing coming from Jews, Poles, Czechs, etc. Your other duty will be to improve the workings of our gas chambers, which operate on the exhaust from a Diesel engine. We need a more toxic and faster working gas, something like prussic acid. . . .

The following morning, a little before seven there was an announcement: "The first train will arrive in ten minutes!" A few minutes later a train arrived from Lemberg: 45 cars with more than 6,000 people. Two hundred Ukrainians assigned to this work flung open the doors and drove the Jews out of the cars with leather whips. A loud speaker gave instructions: Strip, even artificial limbs and glasses. Hand all money and valuables in at the 'valuables window.' Women and young girls are to have their hair cut in the 'barber's hut.' "

Then the march began. Barbed wire on both sides, in the rear two dozen Ukrainians with rifles. They drew near. Wirth and I found ourselves in front of the death chambers. Stark naked men, women, children, and cripples passed by. A tall SS man in the corner called to the unfortunates in a loud minister's voice: "Nothing is going to hurt you! Just breathe deep and it will strengthen your lungs. It's a way to prevent contagious diseases. It's a good disinfectant!" They asked him what was going to happen and he answered: "The men will have to work, build houses and streets. The women won't have to do that, they will be busy with the housework and the kitchen." This was the last hope for some of these poor people, enough to make them march toward the death chambers without resistance. The majority knew everything; the smell betrayed it! They climbed a little wooden stairs and entered the death chambers, most of them silently, pushed by those behind them. A Jewess of about forty with eyes like fire cursed the murderers; she disappeared into the gas chambers after being struck several times by Captain Wirth's whip. . . . All were dead after thirty-two minutes! Jewish workers on the other side opened the wooden doors. They had been promised their lives in return for doing this horrible work, plus a small percentage of the money and valuables collected. The men still standing, like columns of stone, with no room to fall or lean. Even in death you could tell the families, all holding hands. It was difficult to separate them while emptying the rooms for the next batch. The bodies were tossed out, blue, wet with sweat and urine, the legs smeared with excrement and menstrual blood. Two dozen workers were busy checking mouths which they opened with iron hooks. "Gold to the left, no gold to the right." Others checked anus and genitals, looking for money, diamonds, gold, etc. Dentists knocked out gold teeth, bridges and crowns, with hammers. . . .

Then the bodies were thrown into big ditches near the gas chambers, about 100 by 20 by 12 meters. After a few days the bodies swelled and the whole mass rose up 2–3 yards because of the gas in the bodies. When the swelling went down several days later, the bodies matted down again. They told me later they poured Diesel oil over the bodies and burned them on railroad ties to make them disappear.

Mobile Killing

Kiev, 16 May 1942

Field Post Office
No 32704
B Nr 40/42

TOP SECRET

To: SS-Obersturmbannfuehrer Rauff
      Berlin, Prinz-Albrecht-Str. 8

pers.
R/29/5   Pradel n.R

b/R

Sinkkel [?] b.R., p 16/6
  The overhauling of vans by groups D and C is finished. . . .
  I ordered the vans of group D to be camouflaged as housetrailers by putting one set of window shutters on each side of the small van and two on each side of the larger vans, such as one often sees on farm-houses in the country. The vans became so well-known, that not only the authorities, but also the civilian population called the van "death van", as soon as one of these vehicles appeared. It is my opinion, the van cannot be kept secret for any length of time, not even camouflaged. . . .
  I ordered that during application of gas all the men were to be kept as far away from the vans as possible, so they should not suffer damage to their health by the gas which eventually would escape. I should like to take this opportunity to bring the following to your attention: several commands have had the unloading after the application of gas done by their own men. I brought to the attention of the commanders of the *Sonder-Kommando* [special unit] concerning the immense psychological injuries and damages to their health which that work can have for those men, even if not immediately, at least later on. The men complained to me about headaches which appeared after each unloading. Nevertheless prisoners called for that work, could use an opportune moment to flee. To protect the men from these damages, I request orders be issued accordingly.
  The application of gas usually is not undertaken correctly. In order to come to an end as fast as possible, the driver presses the accelerator to the fullest extent. By doing that the persons to be executed suffer death from suffocation and not death by dozing off as was planned. My directions now have proved that by correct adjustment of the levers death comes faster and the prisoners fall asleep peacefully. Distorted faces and excretions, such as could be seen before, are no longer noticed.

  Office of the U.S. Chief Counsel for Prosecution of Axis Criminality, *Nazi Conspiracy and Aggression* (Washington D.C.: Government Printing Office, 1946), vol. 3, pp. 418–419, (PS-501).

Today I shall continue my journey to group B, where I can be reached with further news.

Signed: D. Becker
SS Untersturmfuehrer

Commandant of Auschwitz

RUDOLF HOESS

I must emphasise here that I have never personally hated the Jews. It is true that I looked upon them as the enemies of our people. But just because of this I saw no difference between them and the other prisoners, and I treated them all in the same way. I never drew any distinctions. In any event the emotion of hatred is foreign to my nature. But I know what hate is, and what it looks like. I have seen it and I have suffered it myself.

When the Reichsfuhrer SS modified his original Extermination Order of 1941, by which all Jews without exception were to be destroyed, and ordered instead that those capable of work were to be separated from the rest and employed in the armaments industry, Auschwitz became a Jewish camp. It was a collecting place for Jews, exceeding in scale anything previously known.

Whereas the Jews who had been imprisoned in former years were able to count on being released one day and were thus far less affected psychologically by the hardships of captivity, the Jews in Auschwitz no longer had any such hope. They knew, without exception, that they were condemned to death, that they would live only so long as they could work.

Nor did the majority have any hope of a change in their sad lot. They were fatalists. Patiently and apathetically, they submitted to all the misery and distress and terror. The hopelessness with which they accepted their impending fate made them psychologically quite indifferent to their surroundings. This mental collapse accelerated its physical equivalent. They no longer had the will to live, everything had become a matter of indifference to them, and they would succumb to the slightest physical shock. Sooner or later, death was inevitable. I firmly maintain from what I have seen that the high mortality among the Jews was due not only to the hard work, to which most of them were unaccustomed, and to the insufficient food, the overcrowded quarters and all the severities and abuses of camp life, but principally and decisively to their psychological state. . . .

What I have just written applies to the bulk, the mass of the Jewish prisoners. The more intelligent ones, psychologically stronger and with a keener desire for life, that is to say in most cases those from the western countries, reacted differently.

Rudolf Hoess, *Commandant of Auschwitz: The Autobiography of Rudolf Hoess*, trans. Constantine Fitzgibbon. pp. 147–149, 202–203. Copyright © 1959 by George Weidenfeld & Nicholson, Ltd. Copyright © 1961 by Pan Books, Ltd. Reprinted by permission.

These people, especially if they were doctors, had no illusions concerning their fate. But they continued to hope, reckoning on a change of fortune that somehow or other would save their lives. They also reckoned on the collapse of Germany, for it was not difficult for them to listen to enemy propaganda.

For them the most important thing was to obtain a position which would lift them out of the mass and give them special privileges, a job that would protect them to a certain extent from accidental and mortal hazards, and improve the physical conditions in which they lived.

They employed all their ability and all their will to obtain what can truly be described as a 'living' of this sort. The safer the position the more eagerly and fiercely it was fought for. No quarter was shown, for this was a struggle in which everything was at stake. They flinched from nothing, no matter how desparate, in their efforts to make such safe jobs fall vacant and then to acquire them for themselves. Victory usually went to the most unscrupulous man or woman. Time and again I heard of these struggles to oust a rival and win his job. . . .

So it can be seen that even in a small prison the governor is unable to prevent such behavior; how much more difficult was it in a concentration camp the size of Auschwitz!

I was certainly severe and strict. Often perhaps, when I look at it now, too severe and too strict.

In my disgust at the errors and abuses that I discovered, I may have spoken many hard words that I should have kept to myself. But I was never cruel, and I have never maltreated anyone, even in a fit of temper. A great deal happened in Auschwitz which was done ostensibly in my name, under my authority and on my orders, which I neither knew about nor sanctioned. But all these things happened in Auschwitz and so I am responsible. For the camp regulations say: the camp commandant is *fully* responsible for *everything* that happens in his sphere.

Jewish Resistance

As Hoess noted in his autobiography, many Jews went to their deaths as lambs to slaughter without struggling against their apparent fate. Still, it is misleading to characterize the acts of the condemned under duress as devoid of courage. In fact, there was constant Jewish resistance to the Nazis in the camps and ghettos. A Jewish Fighting Organization was active in the Warsaw ghetto, and resistance continued from January to mid-May 1943, when the Jews were finally defeated. Joseph Goebbels was rather surprised at their tenacity, as the excerpt from his diary indicates. An account by the Nazi SS chief in Warsaw of the destruction of the ghetto follows. The Treblinka death camp was often the final stop for Jews from the Warsaw ghetto. In August 1943, the inmates rebelled.

Although ultimately unsuccessful, the camp was shut down shortly afterward. The last selection is a manifesto of a Jewish resistance organization in the Vilna ghetto dated a month after the revolt at Treblinka.

Nazi Problems in the Warsaw Ghetto (May 1, 1943)

JOSEPH GOEBBELS

Reports from the occupied areas contain no sensational news. The only noteworthy item is the exceedingly serious fights in Warsaw between the police and even a part of our Wehrmacht on the one hand and the rebellious Jews on the other. The Jews have actually succeeded in making a defensive position of the Ghetto. Heavy engagements are being fought there which led even to the Jewish Supreme Command's issuing daily communiques. Of course this fun won't last very long. But it shows what is to be expected of the Jews when they are in possession of arms. Unfortunately, some of their weapons are good German ones, especially machine guns. Heaven only knows how they got them. . . .

The Destruction of the Warsaw Ghetto (May 1943)

JÜRGEN STROOP

On 23 April 1943 the Reichsführer SS issued through the higher SS and Police Führer East at Cracow his order to complete the combing out of the Warsaw Ghetto with the greatest severity and relentless tenacity. I therefore decided to destroy the entire Jewish residential area by setting every block on fire, including the blocks of residential buildings near the armament works. One concern after the other was systematically evacuated and later destroyed by fire. In almost every case, the Jews then emerged from their hiding places and dug-outs. Not infrequently, the Jews stayed in the burning buildings until, because of the heat and the fear of being burned alive, they preferred to jump down from the upper storeys after having thrown mattresses and other upholstered articles into the street from the burning buildings. With their bones broken, they still tried to crawl across the streets into blocks of buildings which had not yet been set on fire or were only partly in flames. Often Jews changed their hiding places during the night, by moving into the ruins of burnt-out buildings, taking refuge there until they were found by our patrols. Their stay in the sewers also ceased to be pleasant after the first week. From the street we could frequently hear loud voices coming through the sewer shafts. Then the men

"Nazi Problems" is from *The Goebbels Diaries* by Louis P. Lochner, pp. 350–351. Copyright 1948 by The Fireside Press, Inc. Reprinted by permission of Doubleday & Company, Inc.

"The Destruction of the Warsaw Ghetto" is from Jeremy Noakes and Geoffrey Pridham, eds., *Documents on Nazism, 1919–1945*, pp. 491–492. Reprinted by permission of A. D. Peters & Co. Ltd.

Warsaw Jews on the way to the Treblinka death camp. (*Yad Vashem, Jerusalem*)

of the Waffen SS, the police or the Wehrmacht engineers courageously climbed down the shafts to bring out the Jews and not infrequently they then stumbled over Jews already dead, or were shot at. It was always necessary to use smoke candles to drive out the Jews. Thus, one day we opened 183 sewer entrance holes and at a fixed time lowered smoke candles into them, so that the bandits fled from what they believed to be gas to the centre of the former Ghetto, where they could then be pulled out of the sewer holes. A great number of Jews, beyond counting, were exterminated by the blowing up of the sewers and dug-outs. . . .

Only through the continuous and untiring work of all involved did we succeed in catching a total of 56,065 Jews, whose extermination can be proved. To this should be added the number of Jews who lost their lives in explosions or fires, whose numbers could not be ascertained.

During the large-scale operation the Aryan population was informed by posters that it was strictly forbidden to enter the former Jewish Ghetto and that anybody caught within the former Ghetto without a valid pass would be shot. At the same time these posters informed the Aryan population again that the death penalty would be imposed on anyone who intentionally gave refuge to a Jew, especially on anyone who lodged, supported or concealed a Jew outside the Jewish residential area. . . .

The large-scale action was terminated on 16 May 1943 with the blowing up of the Warsaw synagogue at 20.15 hours.

The Treblinka Revolt (August 1943)

STANISLAW KOHN

Before I arrived at Treblinka, in other words before October 1, 1942, cases of rebellion on the part of Jews had been reported. Thus, for example, a Jewish youth from Warsaw who worked in one of the death companies, having seen his wife and child escorted to the gas chamber, attacked the S.S. man, Max Bill, with a knife and killed him on the spot. From that day the S.S. barracks bore the name of this Hitlerite "martyr". Neither the plate on the wall of the barracks nor the massacre of Jews after this attack deterred us. This episode encouraged us to fight and take our revenge. The Warsaw youth became our ideal.

A desire for revenge burned within us as we witnessed Hitler's extermination methods, and ripened each day and began to concretize into something precise, particularly from the moment when the fifty-year-old doctor, Choronzicki, of Warsaw, began to be active. The doctor worked in the camps as sanitation adviser, a task invented by the Germans to mock the humiliated victims even more vilely before despatching them to the gas chamber. He was a calm, cautious man who, on the surface, appeared very cold. He wandered around in his white apron with the sign of the Red Cross on his arm as in the olden days in his Warsaw consulting room, and seemed completely disinterested. But beneath his apron beat a warm Jewish heart, burning with desire for revenge. . . .

The date of the revolt was postponed several times for various reasons. And then the last transports of the Warsaw Jews were brought to Treblinka. From them we learned about the ghetto revolt. The Germans treated them with particular savagery; most of the trucks were full of corpses of ghetto combatants who had refused to leave the ghetto alive. Those who now arrived were no longer resigned and indifferent creatures like their predecessors. . . .

The desire for revenge increased continuously. The terror-stricken eyes of the Jews being led to their death, and throngs into the gas chamber, called for revenge.

At last the leader, Galewski, gave the signal for the revolt. The date fixed was for Monday, August 2, 1943, at five o'clock in the afternoon. This was the plan of action: to lay an ambush for the chief murderers, to liquidate them, to disarm the warders, cut the telephone wires and then burn and destroy all the extermination plants so that they could never function again; to free the Poles from the detention camp of Treblinka, to flee into the forest to organize a partisan band. . . .

At two o'clock in the afternoon the distribution of weapons began. It was very difficult to purloin the hand grenades from the armory. . . . Marcus

From *An Anthology of Holocaust Literature*, ed. J. Glatstein, I. Knox, and S. Margoshes (Philadelphia: The Jewish Publication Society, 1969), pp. 319, 321–324. Reprinted by permission of the publisher.

and Salzberg took up the carpets and beat them in front of the armory. The guards were obliged to move away for a while. At that moment the door of the armory was opened with our key [which had been stolen] and Jacek, the Hungarian boy, slipped inside, climbed onto the window sill at the end of the room, cut out a small square in the glass with a diamond and handed out the bombs and other weapons to Jacob Miller who put them on his refuse cart. The arms were carried to the garage. This time the hand grenades acted as a spur.

Spirits grew agitated and no one could keep the secret. The leaders therefore decided to start the revolt an hour before the agreed time.

Punctually at four o'clock in the afternoon messages were sent to all groups with orders to assemble immediately in the garage to fetch their weapons.

Anyone coming to fetch weapons had to give the password, "Death," to which the rely was "life." "Death-Life," "Death-Life!" Cries of enthusiasm arose as the long-hoped-for guns, revolvers and hand grenades were distributed. At the same time the chief murderers of the camp were attacked. Telephonic communication was cut and the watchtowers were set on fire with petrol. The armory was taken by assault and the weapons distributed. We already had two hundred armed men. The others attacked the Germans with axes and spades.

We set fire to the gas chambers, burned the railway station with all the notices. . . . We burned the barracks. . . .

The flames and the reports of the firing roused the Germans who began to arrive from all sides. S.S. and police arrived from Kosow, soldiers from the nearby airfield and finally a special section of the Warsaw S.S. Orders had been given to make for the neighboring forest. Most of our fighters fell but there were many German casualties. Very few of us survived.

Manifesto of the Jewish Resistance in Vilna (September 1943)

Offer armed resistance! Jews, defend yourselves with arms!

The German and Lithuanian executioners are at the gates of the ghetto. They have come to murder us! Soon they will lead you forth in groups through the ghetto door.

Tens of thousands of us were despatched. But we shall not go! We will not offer our heads to the butcher like sheep.

Jews, defend yourselves with arms!

Do not believe the false promises of the assassins or believe the words of the traitors.

From *An Anthology of Holocaust Literature*, ed. J. Glatstein, I. Knox, and S. Margoshes (Philadelphia: The Jewish Publication Society, 1969), pp. 332–333. Reprinted by permission of the publisher.

Anyone who passes through the ghetto gate will go to Ponar! [Death Camp]

And Ponar means death!

Jews, we have nothing to lose. Death will overtake us in any event. And who can still believe in survival when the murderer exterminates us with so much determination? The hand of the executioner will reach each man and woman. Flight and acts of cowardice will not save our lives.

Active resistance alone can save our lives and our honor.

Brothers! It is better to die in battle in the ghetto than to be carried away to Ponar like sheep. And know this: within the walls of the ghetto there are organized Jewish forces who will resist with weapons.

Support the revolt!

Do not take refuge or hide in the bunkers, for then you will fall into the hands of the murderers like rats.

Jewish people, go out into the squares. Anyone who has no weapons should take an ax, and he who has no ax should take a crowbar or a bludgeon!

For our ancestors!

For our murdered children!

Avenge Ponar!

Attack the murderers!

In every street, in every courtyard, in every house within and without the ghetto, attack these dogs!

Jews, we have nothing to lose! We shall save our lives only if we exterminate our assassins.

Long live liberty! Long live armed resistance! Death to the assassins!

The Commander of the F.P.A.

Vilna, the Ghetto, September 1, 1943.

Judgment and Reflection

The Nuremberg Trials (November 1945–October 1946)

In the spring of 1945, Allied troops fought their way into the heart of Nazi Germany. Infamous concentration camps such as Dachau and Buchenwald were liberated by soldiers; the German inhabitants of the area were forced to view the horrors perpetrated by their "neighbors." Judgment was demanded and an international court was established in Nuremberg. Its responsibility was to pass sentence on the various Nazi leaders after first examining documentary evidence and transcripts of oral testimony. No court has ever attained such universal recognition. Transcripts and documents of the proceedings fill forty-two large volumes. The following selection is from the summation of Justice Robert H. Jackson, the chief American prosecutor.

The Crimes of the Nazi Regime

JUSTICE ROBERT H. JACKSON

The Nazi movement will be of evil memory in history because of its persecution of the Jews, the most far-flung and terrible racial persecution of all time. Although the Nazi party neither invented nor monopolized anti-Semitism, its leaders from the very beginning embraced it, and exploited it. They used it as "the psychological spark that ignites the mob." After the seizure of power, it became an official state policy. The persecution began in a series of discriminatory laws eliminating the Jews from the civil service, the professions, and economic life. As it became more intense it included segregation of Jews in ghettos, and exile. Riots were organized by party leaders to loot Jewish business places and to burn synagogues. Jewish property was confiscated and a collective fine of a billion marks was imposed upon German Jewry. The program progressed in fury and irresponsibility to the "final solution." This consisted of sending all Jews who were fit to work to concentration camps as slave laborers, and all who were not fit, which included children under 12 and people over 50, as well as any others judged unfit by an SS doctor, to concentration camps for extermination. . . .

The chief instrumentality for persecution and extermination was the concentration camp, sired by defendant Goering and nurtured under the overall authority of defendants Frick and Kaltenbrunner.

The horrors of these iniquitous places have been vividly disclosed by documents and testified to by witnesses. The Tribunal must be satiated with ghastly verbal and pictorial portrayals. From your records it is clear that the concentration camps were the first and worst weapons of oppression used by the National Socialist State, and that they were the primary means utilized for the persecution of the Christian Church and the extermination of the Jewish race. This has been admitted to you by some of the defendants from the witness stand. In the words of defendant Frank: "A thousand years will pass and this guilt of Germany will still not be erased.". . .

It is against such a background that these defendants now ask this Tribunal to say that they are not guilty of planning, executing, or conspiring to commit this long list of crimes and wrongs. They stand before the record of this trial. . . . If you were to say of these men that they are not guilty, it

Office of the U.S. Chief of Counsel for the Prosecution of Axis Criminality, *Nazi Conspiracy and Aggression* (Washington, D.C.: Government Printing Office, 1947), Supplement A, pp. 15–16, 44.

would be as true to say there has been no war, there are no slain, there has been no crime.

Judgment and Sentence

At Nuremberg, the accused Nazis were indicted on one or more charges: (1) Crimes against Peace (conspiracy), (2) War Crimes, (3) Crimes against Humanity, (4) Membership in a Criminal Organization. The verdict on some of the major Nazi figures of the Holocaust are presented next, followed by an account of the execution of Julius Streicher as described by Kingsbury Smith, European general manager of International News Service. Streicher, a former elementary school Teacher and fanatical Nazi, published *Der Stürmer,* the most violently anti-Semitic journal in the Reich.

Hermann Goering

Goering is indicted on all four Counts. The evidence shows that after Hitler he was the most prominent man in the Nazi regime. He was Commander-in-Chief of the *Luftwaffe.* Plenipotentiary for the Four Year Plan, he had tremendous influence with Hitler, at least until 1943, when their relationship deteriorated, ending in his arrest in 1945. He testified that Hitler kept him informed of all important military and political problems. . . .

Goering persecuted the Jews, particularly after the November 1938 riots, and not only in Germany . . . but in the conquered territories as well. . . . As these countries fell before the German Army, he extended the Reich anti-Jewish laws to them. . . . Although their extermination was in Himmler's hands, Goering was far from disinterested or inactive, despite his protestations in the witness box. By decree of 31 July 1941 he directed Himmler and Heydrich to "bring about a complete solution of the Jewish question in the German sphere of influence in Europe."

There is nothing to be said in mitigation. For Goering was often, indeed almost always, the moving force, second only to his leader. He was the leading war aggressor, both as political and as military leader; he was the director of the slave labor program and the creator of the oppressive program against the Jews and other races, at home and abroad. All of these crimes he frankly admitted. On some specific cases there may be conflict of testimony, but in terms of the broad outline his own admissions are more than sufficiently wide to be conclusive of his guilt. His guilt is unique in its enormity. The record discloses no excuses for this man.

The Tribunal finds the Defendant Goering guilty on all four Counts of the Indictment.

International Military Tribunal, *Nuremberg Trials of the Major War Criminals* (Nuremberg: Allied Central Commission, 1948), vol. 22, pp. 524, 527, 544–549.

Wilhelm Frick

Frick is indicted on all four Counts. Recognized as the chief Nazi administrative specialist and bureaucrat, he was appointed Reich Minister of the Interior in Hitler's first cabinet.

Always rabidly anti-Semitic, Frick drafted, signed, and administered many laws designed to eliminate Jews from German life and economy. His work formed the basis of the Nuremberg Decrees, and he was active in enforcing them. Responsible for prohibiting Jews from following various professions and for confiscating their propety, he signed a final decree in 1943, after the mass destruction of Jews in the East, which placed them "outside the law" and handed them over to the *Gestapo.* These laws paved the way for the "final solution," and were extended by Frick to the incorporated territories and to certain of the occupied territories. While he was Reich Protector of Bohemia and Moravia, thousands of Jews were transferred from the Terezin ghetto in Czechoslovakia to Auschwitz, where they were killed. He issued a decree providing for special penal laws against Jews and Poles in the Governmental General. . . .

During the war nursing homes, hospitals, and asylums in which euthanasia was practised as described elsewhere in this Judgment, came under Frick's jurisdiction. He had knowledge that insane, sick, and aged people, "useless eaters," were being systematically put to death. Complaints of these murders reached him, but he did nothing to stop them. A report of the Czechoslovak War Crimes Commission estimated that 275,000 mentally deficient and aged people, for whose welfare he was responsible, fell victim to it.

The Tribunal finds that Frick is not guilty on Count One. He is guilty on Counts Two, Three and Four.

Julius Streicher

Streicher is indicted on Counts One and Four. One of the earliest members of the Nazi Party, joining in 1921, he took part in the Munich Putsch. From 1925 to 1940 he was Gauleiter of Franconia. Elected to the Reichstag in 1933, he was an honorary general in the SA. His persecution of the Jews was notorious. He was the publisher of *Der Stürmer,* an anti-Semitic weekly newspaper, from 1923 to 1945 and was its editor until 1933. . . .

For his 25 years of speaking, writing, and preaching hatred of the Jews, Streicher was widely known as "Jew-Baiter Number One." In his speeches and articles, week after week, month after month, he infected the German mind with the virus of anti-Semitism and incited the German people to active persecution. Each issue of *Der Stürmer,* which reached a circulation of 600,000 in 1935, was filled with such articles, often lewd and disgusting. . . .

As the war in the early stages proved successful in acquiring more and more territory for the Reich, Streicher even intensified his efforts to incite the Germans against the Jews. In the record are 26 articles from *Der Stürmer*, published between August 1941 and September 1944, 12 by Streicher's own hand, which demanded annihilation and extermination in unequivocal terms. He wrote and published on 25 December 1941:

"If the danger of the reproduction of that curse of God in the Jewish blood is finally to come to an end, then there is only one way—the extermination of that people whose father is the devil." And in February 1944 his own article stated: "Whoever does what a Jew does is a scoundrel, a criminal. And he who repeats and wishes to copy him deserves the same fate: annihilation, death."

With knowledge of the extermination of the Jews in the Occupied Eastern Territories, this defendant continued to write and publish his propaganda of death. Testifying in this Trial, he vehemently denied any knowledge of mass executions of Jews. But the evidence makes it clear that he continually received current information on the progress of the "final solution."

Streicher's incitement to murder and extermination at the time when Jews in the East were being killed under the most horrible conditions clearly constitutes persecution on political and racial grounds in connection with War Crimes, as defined by the Charter, and constitutes a Crime against Humanity.

The Tribunal finds that Streicher is not guilty on Count One, but that he is guilty on Count Four.

The Execution of Julius Streicher (1946)

KINGSBURY SMITH

The only one, however, to make any reference to Nazi ideology was Julius Streicher, that arch Jew-baiter. Displaying the most bitter and enraged defiance of any of the condemned, he screamed "Heil Hitler" at the top of his voice as he was about to mount the steps leading to the gallows.

Streicher appeared in the execution hall, which had been used only last Saturday night for a basketball game by American security guards, at twelve and a half minutes after two o'clock.

As in the case of all the condemned, a warning knock by a guard outside preceded Streicher's entry through a door in the middle of the hall.

An American lieutenant colonel sent to fetch the condemned from the death row of the cell block to the near-by prison wing entered first. He was followed by Streicher, who was stopped immediately inside the door by two

New York Journal-American (October 16, 1946). Reprinted by permission of United Press International, Copyright 1946.

American sergeants. They closed in on each side of him and held his arms while another sergeant removed the manacles from his hands and replaced them with a leather cord.

The first person whom Streicher and the others saw upon entering the gruesome hall was an American lieutenant colonel who stood directly in front of him while his hands were being tied behind his back as they had been manacled upon his entrance.

This ugly, dwarfish little man, wearing a threadbare suit and a well-worn bluish shirt buttoned to the neck but without a tie, glanced at the three wooden scaffolds rising up menacingly in front of him.

Two of these were used alternately to execute the condemned men while the third was kept in reserve.

After a quick glance at the gallows, Streicher glared around the room, his eyes resting momentarily upon the small group of American, British, French, and Russian officers on hand to witness the executions.

By this time Streicher's hands were tied securely behind his back. Two guards, one to each arm, directed him to No. 1 gallows on the left entrance. He walked steadily the six feet to the first wooden step, but his face was twitching nervously. As the guards stopped him at the bottom of the steps for official identification requests, he uttered his piercing scream:

"Heil Hitler!"

His shriek sent a shiver down the back of this International News Service correspondent, who is witnessing the executions as sole representative of the American press.

As its echo died away, another American colonel standing by the steps said sharply:

"Ask the man his name."

In response to the interpreter's query Streicher shouted:

"You know my name well."

The interpreter repeated his request, and the condemned man yelled:

"Julius Streicher."

As he mounted the platform Streicher cried out:

"Now it goes to God!"

After getting up the thirteen steps to the eight-foot-high and eight-foot-square black-painted wooden platform, Streicher was pushed two steps to the mortal spot beneath the hangman's rope.

This was suspended from an iron ring attached to a crossbeam which rested on two posts. The rope was being held back agaist a wooden rail by the American Army sergeant hangman.

Streicher was swung around to face the front.

He glanced again at the Allied officers and the eight Allied correspondents representing the world's press who were lined up against a wall behind small tables directly facing the gallows.

The American officer standing at the scaffold said:

"Ask the man if he has any last words."

When the interpreter had translated, Streicher shouted:

"The Bolsheviks will hang you one day."

As the black hood was being adjusted about his head, Streicher was heard saying:

"Adele, my dear wife."

At that moment the trap was sprung with a loud bang. With the rope snapped taut and the body swinging wildly, a groan could be heard distinctly within the dark interior of the scaffold.

Why?

The most difficult question to answer regarding a genocidal policy is why people participate in such action. In the first selection, Rudolf Hoess, the Commandant of Auschwitz, speaks of the formation of his character. The next sections are from two influential authors who have written books about fanaticism.

"Whatever They Said Was Always Right"

RUDOLF HOESS

I had been brought up by my parents to be respectful and obedient towards all grown-up people, and especially the elderly, regardless of their social status. I was taught that my highest duty was to help those in need. It was constantly impressed upon me in forceful terms that I must obey promptly the wishes and commands of my parents, teachers and priests, and indeed of all grown-up people, including servants, and that nothing must distract me from this duty. Whatever they said was always right.

These basic principles on which I was brought up became part of my flesh and blood. I can still clearly remember how my father, who on account of his fervent Catholicism was a determined opponent of the Reich government and its policy, never ceased to remind his friends that, however strong one's opposition might be, the laws and decrees of the State had to be obeyed unconditionally.

From my earliest youth I was brought up with a strong awareness of duty. In my parents' house it was insisted that every task be exactly and conscientiously carried out. Each member of the family had his own special duties to perform. My father took particular care to see that I obeyed all his instructions and wishes with the greatest meticulousness. I remember to this day how he hauled me out of bed one night, because I had left the saddle-cloth lying in the garden instead of hanging it up in the barn to dry, as he had told me to do. I had simply forgotten all about it. Again and again he impressed on me how great evils almost always spring from small, apparently insignificant misdeeds. At that time I did not fully understand the meaning of this dictum, but in later years I was to learn, through bitter experience, the truth of his words.

I remain, as I have always been, a convinced National-Socialist in my attitude to life. When a man has adhered to a belief and an attitude for nigh on twenty-five years, has grown up with it and become bound to it body and soul, he cannot simply throw it aside because the embodiments of this ideal, the National-Socialist State and its leaders have used their powers wrongly and even criminally, and because as a result of this failure and misdirection his world has collapsed and the entire German people been plunged for decades into untold misery. I, at least, cannot.

From the documents published and from the Nuremberg trials I can see that the leaders of the Third Reich, because of their policy of force, were guilty of causing this vast war and all its consequences. I see that these leaders, by means of exceptionally effective propaganda and of limitless terrorism, were able to make the whole German people so docile and submissive that they were ready, with very few exceptions, to go wherever they were led, without voicing a word of criticism. . . .

In order to disguise a policy of force it is necessary to use propaganda so that a clever distortion of all the facts, the policies and measures of the rulers of the State can be made palatable. Terrorism must be used from the outset, to stifle all doubt and opposition.

The True Believer

ERIC HOFFER

The impulse to fight springs less from self-interest than from intangibles such as tradition, honor (a word), and, above all, hope. Where there is no hope, people either run, or allow themselves to be killed without a fight. They will hang on to life as in a daze. How else explain the fact that millions of Europeans allowed themselves to be led into annihilation camps and gas chambers, knowing beyond doubt that they were being led to death? It was not the least of Hitler's formidable powers that he knew how to drain his opponents (at least in continental Europe) of all hope. His fanatical conviction that he was building a new order that would last a thousand years communicated itself both to followers and antagonists. To the former it gave the feeling that in fighting for the Third Reich they were in league with eternity, while the latter felt that to struggle against Hitler's new order was to defy inexorable fate. . . .

Abridged from pp. 74–76 from *The True Believer* by Eric Hoffer. Copyright, 1951, by Eric Hoffer. Reprinted by permission of Harper & Row, Publishers, Inc.

To rely on the evidence of the senses and of reason is heresy and treason. It is startling to realize how much unbelief is necessary to make belief possible. What we know as blind faith is sustained by innumerable unbeliefs. The fanatical Japanese in Brazil refused to believe for years the evidence of Japan's defeat. The fanatical Communist refuses to believe any unfavorable report or evidence about Russia, nor will he be disillusioned by seeing with his own eyes the cruel misery inside the Soviet promised land.

It is the true believer's ability to "shut his eyes and stop his ears" to facts that do not deserve to be either seen or heard which is the source of his unequaled fortitude and constancy. He cannot be frightened by danger nor disheartened by obstacle nor baffled by contradictions because he denies their existence. Strength of faith . . . manifests itself not in moving mountains but in not seeing mountains move. And it is the certitude of his infallible doctrine that renders the true believer impervious to the uncertainties, surprises and the unpleasant realities of the world around him.

Thus the effectiveness of a doctrine should not be judged by its profundity, sublimity or the validity of the truths it embodies, but by how thoroughly it insulates the individual from his self and the world as it is. What Pascal said of an effective religion is true of any effective doctrine: It must be "contrary to nature, to common sense and to pleasure."

Darkness at Noon

ARTHUR KOESTLER

There are only two conceptions of human ethics, and they are at opposite poles. One of them is Christian and humane, declares the individual to be sacrosanct, and asserts that the rules of arithmetic are not to be applied to human units. The other starts from the basic principle that a collective aim justifies all means, and not only allows, but demands, that the individual should in every way be subordinated and sacrificed to the community—which may dispose of it as an experimentation rabbit or a sacrificial lamb. The first conception could be called anti-vivisection morality, the second, vivisection morality. Humbugs and dilettantes have always tried to mix the two conceptions; in practice, it is impossible. Whoever is burdened with power and responsibility finds out on the first occasion that he has to choose; and he is fatally driven to the second alternative. Do you know, since the establishment of Christianity as a state religion, a single example of a state which really followed a Christian policy? You can't point out one. In times of need—and politics are chronically in a time of need—the rulers were always able to evoke 'exceptional circumstances,' which demanded exceptional measures of defence. Since the existence of nations and classes, they live in a permanent state of mutual self-defence, which forces them to defer to another time the putting into practice of humanism. . . .

Could the Holocaust Happen Again?

One of the formost authorities on the Holocaust is Raul Hilberg. In his book *The Destruction of the European Jews,* he offers some perspective on the possibilities of reoccurrence. The second selection is by Elie Wiesel, himself a survivor of the death camps and now a professor of philosophy and winner of the 1986 Nobel Peace Prize. He wrote this newspaper article in 1974.

The Destruction of the European Jews

RAUL HILBERG

The destruction of the European Jews between 1933 and 1945 appears to us now as an unprecedented event in history. Indeed, in its dimensions and total configuration, nothing like it had ever happened before. Five million people were killed as a result of an organized undertaking in the short space of a few years. The operation was over before anyone could grasp its enormity, let alone its implications for the future.

Yet if we analyze that singularly massive upheaval, we discover that most of what happened in those twelve years had already happened before. The Nazi destruction process did not come out of a void; it was the culmination of a cyclical trend. We have observed the trend in the three successive goals of anti-Jewish administrators. The missionaries of Christianity had said in effect: You have no right to live among us as Jews. The secular rulers who followed had proclaimed: You have no right to live among us. The German Nazis at last decreed: You have no right to live. . . .

As time passes on, the destruction of the European Jews will recede into the background. Its most immediate consequences are almost over, and whatever developments may henceforth be traced to the catastrophe will be consequences of consequences, more and more remote. Already the Nazi outburst has become historical. But this is a strange page in history. Few events of modern times were so filled with unpredicted action and suspected death. A primordial impulse had suddenly surfaced among the Western nations; it had been unfettered through their machines. From this moment, fundamental assumptions about our civilization have no longer stood unchallenged, for while the occurrence is past, the phenomenon remains.

Before the emergence of the 20th century and its technology, a destructive mind could not play in fantasy with the thoughts that the Nazis were to translate into action. The administrator of earlier centuries did not have the tools. He did not possess the network of communications; he did not dispose over rapid small arms fire and quick-working poison gasses. The bureaucrat of tomorrow would not have these problems; already, he is better equipped than the German Nazis were. Killing is not as difficult as it used to be. The modern administrative apparatus has facilities for rapid, concerted movements and for efficient massive killings. These devices not only trap a larger number of victims; they also require a greater degree of specialization, and with that division of labor the moral burden too is fragmented among the participants. The perpetrator can now kill his victims without touching them. He may feel sure of his success and safe from its repercussions. This ever-growing capacity for destruction cannot be arrested anywhere.

Since the end of the Jewish catastrophe, basic decisions have been made about the future. In the Christian world the remaining alternatives are gradually moving toward polar ends. After 2,000 years there is no defensible middle ground. The ancient compromise, with all its contradictions, is weakening day by day. To the Jewish community that growing dichotomy conveys unique opportunities and unprecedented vulnerabilities. Jewry is faced with ultimate weapons. It has no deterrent. The Jews can live more freely now. They can also die more quickly. The summit is within sight. An abyss has opened below.

Ominous Signs and Unspeakable Thoughts

ELIE WIESEL

I admit it sadly: I feel threatened. For the first time in many years I feel that I am in danger. For the first time in my adult life I am afraid that the nightmare may start all over again, or that it has never ended, that since 1945 we have lived in parentheses. Now they are closed.

Could the Holocaust happen again? Over the years I have often put the question to my young students. And they, consistently, have answered yes, while I said no. I saw it as a unique event that would remain unique. I believed that if mankind had learned anything from it, it was that hate and murder reach beyond the direct participants; he who begins by killing others, in the end will kill his own. Without Auschwitz, Hiroshima would not have been possible. The murder of one people inevitably leads to that of mankind.

New York Times (December 28, 1974). Copyright © 1974 by The New York Times Company. Reprinted by permission.

In my naivete I thought, especially in the immediate postwar period, Jews would never again be singled out, handed over to the executioner. That anti-Semitism had received its death-blow long ago, under the fiery skies of Poland. I was somehow convinced that—paradoxically—man would be shielded, protected by the awesome mystery of the Event.

I was wrong. What happened once, could happen again. Perhaps I am exaggerating. Perhaps I am oversensitive. But then I belong to a traumatized generation. We have learned to take threats more seriously than promises.

There are signs and they are unmistakable. The sickening spectacle of a diplomatic gathering wildly applauding a spokesman for killers. The scandalous exclusion of Israel from UNESCO. The arrogant self-righteousness of certain leaders, the cynicism of others. The dramatic solitude of Israel. The anti-Semitic statements made by America's top general. Anti-Semitism has become fashionable once more both in the East and in the West.

No wonder then that suddenly one hears discussions on a subject that many of us had thought buried long ago: Jewish survival. Can Israel—the country, the people—survive another onslaught? How many times must it sacrifice the best of its children? How long can one go on living in a hostile world? Is it conceivable that Hitler could be victorious posthumously?

For those of us who have lived and endured the human and Jewish condition in its ultimate depth know: at this turning point in history, the Jewish people and the Jewish State are irrevocably linked; one cannot survive without the other. As a community, we have rarely been so united. And never so alone.

And so, the idea of another catastrophe is no longer unthinkable. I say it reluctantly. In fact, it is the first time I say it. I have chosen until now to place the Holocaust on a mystical or ontological level, one that defies language and transcends imagination. I have quarreled with friends who built entire theories and doctrines on an event which, in my view, is not to be used or approached casually. If I speak of it now, it is only because of my realization that Jewish survival is being recalled into question.

Hence the fear in me. All of a sudden, I am too much reminded of past experiences. The enemy growing more and more popular. The aggressiveness of the blackmailers, the permissiveness of some leaders and the total submissiveness of others. The overt threats. The complacency and diffidence of the bystanders. I feel as my father must have felt when he was my age.

Not that I foresee the possibility of Jews being massacred in the cities of America or in the forests of Europe. Death-factories will not be built again. But there is a certain climate, a certain mood in the making. As far as the Jewish people are concerned, the world has remained unchanged: as indifferent to our fate as to its own.

And so I look at my young students and tremble for their future; I see myself at their age surrounded by ruins. What am I to tell them?

I would like to be able to tell them that in spite of endless disillusionments one must maintain faith in man and in mankind; that one must never lose heart. I would like to tell them that, notwithstanding the official discourses and policies, our people do have friends and allies and reasons to advocate hope. But I have never lied to them, I am not going to begin now. And yet. . . .

Despair is no solution. I know that. What is the solution? Hitler had one. And he tried it while a civilized world kept silent.

I remember. And I am afraid.

STUDY QUESTIONS

1. What were the main accusations leveled against the Jews by Hitler and the Nazis? Does the Jewish defense seem convincing? Why were the Jews legally restricted?

2. In the conference on the Jewish question (November 12, 1938), the topic concerned the isolation of the Jews. What measures does Heydrich advocate? Why is Goering's solution inevitable?

3. What solutions to the Jewish problem were presented at the Wansee Conference? Based on this evidence and on the directive of Hermann Goering, how would you define the "Final Solution"? What did it entail? Why was there no specific talk of extermination in these documents?

4. After reading through the accounts concerning the death camps, what are your feelings? What statements by Rudolf Hoess in his testimony at Nuremberg and in his autobiography stand out in your mind? Why? How does he free himself from guilt while still accepting it?

5. Granted that Jews were both submissive and resistant to Nazi atrocities during the Holocaust, how do you think you would react under the same stress and abuse?

6. In your opinion, was justice served and the dead avenged by the Nuremberg trials and execution of Nazi leaders?

7. In the opinion of Eric Hoffer, why were the Jews killed and why are people able to commit such acts? Do you agree with him?

8. Comment on another statement of Eric Hoffer's: "It is obvious . . . that in order to be effective, a doctrine must not be understood, but has to be believed in. We can be absolutely certain only about things we do not understand; a doctrine that is understood is shorn of its strength." Do you agree? How can you relate this to the Holocaust?

9. What meaning does Arthur Koestler's message in *Darkness at Noon* have for the Holocaust?

10. After reading the selections by Raul Hilberg, "The Destruction of the European Jews," and Elie Wiesel, "Ominous Signs and Unspeakable Thoughts," do you think such a thing as the Holocaust could happen again? In a way, was the Holocaust the inevitable outcome of the racist and Social Darwinist ideas that were discussed in the chapter on "Na-

tionalism and Imperialism"? Was the Holocaust "conditioned" by the expendability of life that was so characteristic of battles during World War I? Was the Holocaust itself a precedent for the American bombing of Hiroshima? As you look at the world today, give some examples of attitudes, specific organizations, or individuals that might threaten reoccurrence of genocide. What can be done?

11

Our Contemporary World: The Progress of Civilization

The reasonable man adapts himself to the world: the unreasonable one persists in trying to adapt the world to himself. Therefore all progress depends upon the unreasonable man.

—George Bernard Shaw

I have always considered that the substitution of the internal combustion engine for the horse marked a very gloomy milestone in the progress of mankind.

—Winston Churchill

In their worship of the machine, many Americans have . . . confused progress with mechanization.

—Lewis Mumford

Human dignity is best preserved not by developing the capacity to deal destruction, but by refusing to retaliate. If it is possible to train millions in the black art of violence, which is the art of the beast, it is more possible to train them in the white art of non-violence, which is the law of regenerate man.

—Mahatma Gandhi

Progress, far from consisting of change, depends on retentiveness. Those who cannot remember the past are condemned to repeat it.

—George Santayana

The twentieth century has been a most extraordinary time in which to live—extraordinary because the changes that have taken place in science, technology, governmental systems, and especially daily life have occurred in such a short span of time. We live today with computers that can calculate, store, and retrieve information far more quickly and efficiently than is humanly possible. We were amazed in 1969 when man finally walked on the moon, and we still anticipate news from interplanetary probes, which hold out the possibility of discovering other forms of life. Medical research has developed vaccines for dreaded diseases, extended life by transplanting organs, and even unlocked the possibilities of changing the human condition itself through the discovery of DNA and genetic engineering. All these accomplishments bespeak progress. But this progress entails risks that threaten to destroy all that has been created.

There is a curious paradox that technological progress contributes to the ultimate insecurity of mankind. We marvel at the computer revolution, yet fear the specter of "Big Brother," which looms large and threatens personal freedom by controlling information. We in the twentieth century are faced with the ultimate concern: the survival of civilization itself. The obliteration of the human species has never before been within its own power. Those who were born after 1945 have inherited the responsibility of maintaining peace and therefore existence.

So how does one define the word "progress"? Far too often we forget that progress is not necessarily a technological or scientific preserve. Indeed, one must also measure progress on a human scale in terms of moral and ethical considerations. Have we learned anything from history, from the attitudes and mistakes of our ancestors? In 1912, the great ocean liner *Titanic* set sail from Britain to America. It was described as the quintessential expression of human technology—"unsinkable" said its creators. In 1985, the *Titanic* was finally discovered on the bottom of the Atlantic, the victim of a natural disaster on its maiden voyage, when the impact from a collision with an iceberg split the ship in two. More than this, its sinking was symbolic of an ordered world on the path to destruction. Two years after the *Titanic* vanished, the world went to war, a war unparalleled for its ferocity and barbarism. The new technology played its role as machine guns, tanks, airplanes, submarines, and poisonous gas were introduced. This new style of "total war," in which innocents died and thousands of men walked into barbed wire and machine gun fire, must be seen as a retreat from progress on a human scale. The succceeding events of the century—World War II, Hitler's destruction of the Jews, the nuclear devastation of Hiroshima, and the Cold War—have led many to view this less as a century of progress and more as a century of holocaust. And yet, have we in the late twentieth century advanced on an ideal plane of existence toward a more just and equal international community? Is racism generally on the decline? Have we gone beyond totalitarian government and the dictates of imperialism? Can new holocausts be prevented through the force of world opinion?

One needs to question human nature and the value of history in this regard. And what influence does the individual have in all this? His roles in revolution (V. I. Lenin) and destruction (Adolf Hitler and Joseph Stalin) have been confirmed. But how successful has the individual been in promoting peaceful change and coexistence? Mahatma Ghandi, Martin Luther King, Jr., Desmond Tutu, Albert Schweitzer, Elie Wiesel, Albert Einstein, Sister Theresa—have they too made a difference?

Humanity seems to wage a perpetual duel between progress and holocaust. Reasons for this are difficult to discern. The explanation of human action is necessarily fraught with frustration, for humans are ruled more often by their passions than by their intellect. But it is precisely this unpredictability that contributes to the progress of civilization; the new idea, the desire to compete and achieve, the will to give life or take it away—all enter into the equation of success or failure, of progress or destruction. We do not have the benefit of "20/20 hindsight." In fact, we often suffer from the stress of myopia, of not being able to "see the forest for the trees." So the need to understand where we are going in life and what things are of greatest value ceases to be a concern of the historian and becomes more a responsibility of each individual.

This chapter seeks to develop the dichotomy between the desire of humans to progress and coexist and our established record of destruction. It is broken into three separate thematic sections, which can be studied individually or compared for analytic purposes. The role of science and the responsibilities of scientists and politicians are especially at question in this historical problem. But ultimately, responsibility for our own civilization rests in each individual. It is important to understand the problems and progress toward the solutions.

SECTION I: A CENTURY OF PROGRESS

Medical Research

One of the areas in which progress in the twentieth century is most evident is the field of health care. People tend to regard mumps, measles, and whooping cough as childhood diseases of little importance. Yet in the nineteenth century these, as well as tetanus and typhoid, were dangerous and sometimes devastating diseases. Even the bubonic plague (Black Death), which destroyed one-third of the population of Europe in 1348, can be treated today with antibiotics. The first selection is a newspaper account of the appearance of polio vaccine in 1955. Its development freed humanity from the physical ravages of a disease that afflicted even the rich and powerful: Franklin Roosevelt, who was later to become president of the United States, was struck in 1921. As the succeeding accounts reveal, progress in medical research has also led to great advances in heart surgery and even to the potential for changing our very "humanness" through genetic engineering.

Polio Vaccine (1955)

ANN ARBOR, Mich., April 12—The world learned today that its hopes for finding an effective weapon against paralytic polio had been realized.

The triple anti-polio vaccine originated by Dr. Jonas E. Salk works. This was revealed in the long-awaited report on the mass field trials of 1954, largest of their kind in medical history.

In these tests the vaccine, designed to protect against the crippling effects of all three types of virus known to produce paralytic polio, was administered to 440,000 children in forty-four states.

The report, a medical classic, was presented at a special scientific meeting at the University of Michigan by Dr. Thomas Francis Jr. It was he who had directed the evaluation of the vast mass of data provided by the tests, involving the correlation of 144,000,000 separate items of information. . . .

Dr. Salk, who is a member of the faculty at the University of Pittsburgh's School of Medicine, said:

"Theoretically, the new 1955 vaccines and vaccination procedures may lead to 100 per cent protection from paralysis of all those vaccinated. . . ."

While no official figures are available, authorities here said that the effectiveness of most vaccines was in the neighborhood of 90 to 95 per cent. However, it was pointed out, none of them was 90 per cent efficient the first year it was given.

The two most effective vaccines now known are those against smallpox and yellow fever. Both are made of live attenuated virus. Their effectiveness is in the range of 95 per cent. This means that ninety-five out of every 100 vaccinated are protected against the disease if exposed to it. Effective vaccines, in the form known as toxoids, also exist against diptheria, about 90 per cent effective, and tetanus, about 95 per cent effective.

Potent vaccines also exist against whooping cough, typhoid fever, typhus fever, Rocky Mountain spotted fever, rabies and influenza. The vaccine against typhus reduces mortality from the disease to zero. . . .

Heart Transplants (1967)

CAPETOWN, Dec. 3——The world's first successful human heart transplant was announced today.

In a five-hour operation that began at 1 A.M., surgeons at the Groote Schuur Hospital removed the heart of a young woman who died after an automobile crash and placed it in the chest of a 55-year-old man dying because his own heart was damaged, the announcement said.

When the transplanted heart was in place, it was started beating by an electric shock.

Dr. Jan H. Louw, the hospital's chief surgeon, said:

"It was like turning the ignition switch of a car."

The hospital said that the man was in satisfactory condition but that the next few days would be a critical period.

The heart was removed from the body of Denise Ann Darvall, 24, an accounting machine operator, and transferred to Louis Washkansky, a businessman, the hospital said.

Mr. Washkansky was reported fully conscious, with blood pressure normal.

Doctors around the world hailed the transplant achievement but said the crucial question would be whether the man's body would accept the alien heart.

In the first stage of the operation, Mr. Washkansky and the body of Miss Darvall were put on heart-lung machines, each manned by a team of technicians.

In the second stage, the donor's heart was removed and kept going by a pump.

The third stage was the removal of Mr. Washkansky's heart.

The fourth and most intricate stage was the placing of the donor's heart in Mr. Washkansky's body. When the transplant was completed, electrodes were placed against the heart walls, and a high current was switched on for a fraction of a second.

The heart started beating immediately, Dr. Louw said.

Hospital sources said that the transplant almost took place last Wednesday with another donor but was canceled at the last moment because the donor died too soon.

Miss Darvall's kidneys were also removed and taken to the Karl Bremer Hospital for a successful kidney transplant to Jonathan Van Wyk, 10.

The announcement of the transplant to Mr. Washkansky came from Dr. Jacobus G. Burger, medical supervisor of the Groote Schuur Hospital.

"The operation was his only chance," Dr. Burger said. "Washkansky was dying and wouldn't have lived longer than a few days otherwise."

Dr. Burger said the next two or three days would be the critical postoperative period.

"The longer Washkansky goes on, the better," he said, "although that does not mean the heart will not be rejected later. The body could decide in five or 10 years' time that it doesn't want this heart." . . . "Washkansky knew what he was going into, but it was his only chance."

United States surgeons at the Stanford Medical Center in California have performed 200 heart transplants in dogs, with a 60-to-70 per cent survival rate.

Surgeons at the center have been reported by *The Journal of the American Medical Association* to be ready for a heart transplant whenever the ideal donor and ideal recipient appeared at the same time.

Genetic Engineering

TED HOWARD AND JEREMY RIFKIN

Throughout this unfolding process, which we call civilization, scientific and technological progress has never been equally distributed. New discoveries have always been applied selectively, with some group, class, or race using knowledge of the external world to control not only it but their fellow humans as well. As the late C. S. Lewis observed, "Man's power over nature is really the power of some men over others with nature as their instrument."

Now a dramatic new scientific discovery has given some people the power, for the first time, to shift attention from shaping and controlling the external world of matter and energy to shaping and controlling the internal world of life itself. With the discovery of DNA and its workings, scientists have unlocked the very secrets of life. It is now only a matter of a handful of years before biologists will be able to irreversibly change the evolutionary wisdom of billions of years with the creation of new plants, new animals, and new forms of human and post-human beings.

Today, only a tiny handful of people are privy to the secret of life and how to manipulate and change it. Most people are totally unaware of this newfound power. The concept of designing and engineering life, especially human life, is so utterly fantastic that it is difficult even to comprehend its meaning and implications. Yet, even as the public is kept virtually ignorant of this unparalleled new scientific discovery, microbiologists are busy at work in hundreds of laboratories across the country, spending tens of millions of dollars in pursuit of the "mastery of life." . . .

For many years social commentators have looked on nuclear weaponry as the most powerful and dangerous tool at the disposal of humanity. With the development of human genetic engineering, a tool even more awesome is now available. It is true that nuclear weaponry poses the ever-present threat of annihilation of human life on this planet. But with genetic engineering there is a threat of a very different kind: that by calculation and planning, not accident or the precipitous passion of the moment, some people will make conscious and deliberate decisions to irreversibly alter the biological structure of millions of other men and women and their descendants for all time. This is a form of annihilation every bit as deadly as nuclear holocaust, and even more profound—whatever forms of future beings are developed will be forced to live the consequences of the biological designs that were molded for them.

Technological Advance

The following selections contrast the state of technology in the first quarter of this century with the great progress evident in the space exploration of the 1960s. The 1970s and 1980s have continued this advance with the frequent missions of the space shuttles, and probes to Jupiter, Saturn, Uranus, Neptune, and beyond.

The Assembly Line (1922)

HENRY FORD

Along about April 1, 1913, we first tried the experiment of an assembly line. We tried it on assembling the fly-wheel magneto. We try everything in a little way first—we will rip out anything once we discover a better way, but we have to know absolutely that the new way is going to be better than the old before we do anything drastic.

I believe that this was the first moving line ever installed. The idea came in a general way from the overhead trolley that the Chicago packers use in dressing beef. We had previously assembled the fly-wheel magneto in the usual method. With one workman doing a complete job he could turn out from thirty-five to forty pieces in a nine-hour day, or about twenty minutes to an assembly. What he did alone was then spread into twenty-nine operations; that cut down the assembly time to thirteen minutes, ten seconds. Then we raised the height of the line eight inches—this was in 1914—and cut the time to seven minutes. Further experimenting with the speed that the work should move at cut the time down to five minutes. In short, the result is this: by the aid of scientific study one man is now able to do somewhat more than four did only a comparatively few years ago. That line established the efficiency of the method and we now use it everywhere. The assembling of the motor, formerly done by one man, is now divided into eighty-four operations—those men do the work that three times their number formerly did. In a short time we tried out the plan on the chassis.

It must not be imagined, however, that all this worked out as quickly as it sounds. The speed of the moving work had to be carefully tried out. . . . The idea is that a man must not be hurried in his work—he must have every second necessary but not a single unnecessary second. . . .

Manned Space Flight (1962)

GLENN'S TRIP PUTS MAN NEARER MOON

Special to the *New York Times* (February 21, 1962)
CAPE CANAVERAL, Fla.——The three orbit flight around the world by
Lieut. Col. John H. Glenn Jr. today was a dramatic probe that puts man
closer to the moon.

It will probably take something like eight years with continued missile
successes in the interim before an astronaut steps from his planetary craft
onto the surface of the moon. But the successful flight of Colonel Glenn
today is certain to provide valuable information for the next exploratory
probe.

The next step toward the moon will be a "repeat performance" of the
triple orbit, this one by another astronaut, some time within the next eight
weeks, under the present timetable. And before the end of 1963, plans call
for a series of three more triple orbits as well as one flight that will attempt
to surpass the trip taken by Russia's Maj. Gherman S. Titov on Aug. 6 last
year, when the Soviet astronaut circled the globe seventeen times in a little
more than twenty-five hours.

For the next year, the plans include an undetermined number of orbital
flights, each one of them constituting eighteen trips around the earth, that
is, one more than Maj. Titov made. But the emphasis will be not so much
on the competitive aspect as on the need to find out if longer trips will
make the human pilots sick.

Moon Walk (1969)

MEN WALK ON MOON
ASTRONAUTS LAND ON PLAIN;
COLLECT ROCKS, PLANT FLAG

HOUSTON, Monday, July 21—Men have landed and walked on the moon.

Two Americans, astronauts of Apollo 11, steered their fragile four-
legged lunar module safely and smoothly to the historic landing yesterday
at 4:17:40 P.M., Eastern daylight time.

Neil A. Armstrong, the 38-year-old civilian commander, radioed to
earth and the mission control room here.

"Houston, Tranquility Base here. The Eagle has landed."

The first man to reach the moon—Mr. Armstrong and his co-pilot Col. Edwin E. Aldrin Jr. of the Air Force—brought their ship to rest on a level, rock-strewn plain near the southwestern shore of the arid Sea of Tranquility.

About six and a half hours later, Mr. Armstrong opened the landing craft's hatch, stepped slowly down the ladder and declared as he planted the first human footprint on the lunar crust:

"That's one small step for man, one giant leap for mankind."

His first step on the moon came at 10:56:20 P.M., as a television camera outside the craft transmitted his every move to an awed and excited audience of hundreds of millions of people on earth.

Tentative Steps Test Soil

Mr. Armstrong's initial steps were tentative tests of the lunar soil's firmness and of his ability to move about easily in his bulky white spacesuit and backpacks and under the influence of lunar gravity, which is one-sixth that of the earth.

"The surface is fine and powdery," the astronaut reported. "I can pick it up loosely with my toe. It does adhere in fine layers like powdered charcoal to the sole and sides of my boots. I only go in a small fraction of an inch, maybe an eighth of an inch. But I can see the footprints of my boots and the treads in the fine sandy particles.

After 19 minutes of Mr. Armstrong's testing, Colonel Aldrin joined him outside the craft.

The two men got busy setting up another television camera out from the lunar module, planting an American flag into the ground, scooping up soil and rock samples, deploying scientific experiments and hopping and loping about in a demonstration of their lunar agility.

They found walking and working on the moon less taxing than had been forecast. Mr. Armstrong once reported he was "very comfortable."

And the people back on earth found the black-and-white television pictures of the bug-shaped lunar module and the men tramping about it so sharp and clear as to seem unreal, more like a toy and toy-like figures than human beings on the most daring and far-reaching expedition thus far undertaken.

Nixon Telephones Congratulations

During one break in the astronauts' work, President Nixon congratulated them from the White House in what, he said, "certainly has to be the most historic telephone call ever made."

"Because of what you have done," the President told the astronauts, "the heavens have become a part of man's world. And as you talk to us from the

Sea of Tranquility it requires us to redouble our efforts to bring peace and tranquility to earth."

"For one priceless moment in the whole history of man all the people on this earth are truly one—one in their pride in what you have done and one in our prayers that you will return safely to earth."

Mr. Armstrong replied:

"Thank you Mr. President. It's a great honor and privilege for us to be here representing not only the United States but men of peace of all nations, men with interests and a curiosity and men with a vision for the future."

Mr. Armstrong and Colonel Aldrin returned to their landing craft and closed the hatch at 1:12 A.M., 2 hours 21 minutes after opening the hatch on the moon. While the third member of the crew, Lieut. Michael Collins of the Air Force, kept his orbital vigil overhead in the command ship, the two moon explorers settled down to sleep.

Comments on the Moon Landing (1969)

"The necessary has never been man's top priority. The passionate pursuit of the nonessential and the extravagant is one of the chief traits of human uniqueness. Unlike other forms of life, man's greatest exertions are made in the pursuit not of necessities, but of superfluities. Man is the only creature who strives to surpass himself, and yearns for the impossible."

—Eric Hoffer (Longshoreman and Philosopher)

"Only a few generations ago, most men lived and died within a few hundred miles of their birthplace. Now our horizons are virtually limitless. If man can walk on the moon, he can look to the planets and beyond the solar system as Columbus must have looked across a forbidding ocean."

—Henry Ford II

Elements of Peace and International Cooperation

Progress need not be measured in technological terms only. Humans have spent much of their time fighting to survive or to dominate. The cessation of hostilities can be viewed as a progressive act, a victory in and of itself. And humans have struggled to organize and civilize the wars they do fight. The first selection is from the Hague Convention of 1907. This meeting was designed to draft "laws of war," which would control hostilities and promote peaceful coexistence; the Convention was to meet next in 1915, but ironically was canceled because of World War I. The treaty of 1922 concerns regulation of submarine warfare and the use of poisonous gas, both of which had been the subject of controversy in World War I.

Establishing "Laws of War": The Hague Convention (1907)

SECTION II.—HOSTILITIES

Chapter I.—*Means of Injuring the Enemy, Sieges, and Bombardments*

ARTICLE 22

The right of belligerents to adopt means of injuring the enemy is not unlimited.

ARTICLE 23

In addition to the prohibitions provided by special Conventions, it is especially forbidden—

(a.) To employ poison or poisoned weapons;
(b.) To kill or wound treacherously individuals belonging to the hostile nation or army;
(c.) To kill or wound an enemy who, having laid down his arms, or having no longer the means of defence, has surrendered at discretion;

ARTICLE 25

The attack or bombardment, *by whatever means*, of towns, villages, dwellings, or buildings which are undefended is prohibited.

ARTICLE 26

The officer in command of an attacking force must, before commencing a bombardment, except in cases of assault, do all in his power to warn the authorities.

Carnegie Endowment for International Peace, *The Hague Conventions and Declarations of 1899 and 1907* (New York: Oxford University Press, 1915), pp. 116–118.

ARTICLE 27

In sieges and bombardments all necessary steps must be taken to spare, as far as possible, buildings dedicated to religion, art, science, or charitable purposes, *historic monuments,* hospitals, and places where the sick and wounded are collected, provided they are not being used at the time for military purposes.

It is the duty of the besieged to indicate the presence of such buildings or places by distinctive and visible signs, which shall be notified to the enemy beforehand.

ARTICLE 28

The pillage of a town or place, even when taken by assault, is prohibited.

Treaty Concerning Submarines and Poisonous Gases in Warfare (1922)

The United States of America, the British Empire, France, Italy and Japan, hereinafter referred to as the Signatory Powers, desiring to make more effective the rules adopted by civilized nations for the protection of the lives of neutrals and noncombatants at sea in time of war, and to prevent the use in war of noxious gases and chemicals, have determined to conclude a Treaty to this effect:

ARTICLE I

The Signatory Powers declare that among the rules adopted by civilized nations for the protection of the lives of neutrals and noncombatants at sea in time of war, the following are to be deemed an established part of international law:

(1) A merchant vessel must be ordered to submit to visit and search to determine its character before it can be seized.

A merchant vessel must not be attacked unless it refuse to submit to visit and search after warning, or to proceed as directed after seizure.

A merchant must not be destroyed unless the crew and passengers have been first placed in safety.

(2) Belligerent submarines are not under any circumstances exempt from universal rules above stated; and if a submarine can not capture a merchant vessel in conformity with these rules the existing law of nations requires it to desist from attack and from seizure and to permit the merchant vessel to proceed unmolested.

Department of State Bulletin (February 6, 1922).

ARTICLE IV

The Signatory Powers recognize the practical impossibility of using submarines as commerce destroyers without violating, as they were violated in the recent war of 1914–1918, the requirements universally accepted by civilized nations for the protection of the lives of neutrals and noncombatants, and to the end that the prohibition of the use of submarines as commerce destroyers shall be universally accepted as a part of the law of nations, they now accept that prohibition as henceforth binding as between themselves and they invite all other nations to adhere thereto.

ARTICLE V

The use in war of asphyxiating, poisonous or other gases, and all analogous liquids, materials or devices, having been justly condemned by the general opinion of the civilized world and a prohibition of such use having been declared in treaties to which a majority of the civilized Powers are parties.

The Signatory Powers, to the end that this prohibition shall be universally accepted as a part of international law binding alike the prohibitions, agree to be bound thereby as between themselves and invite all other civilized nations to adhere thereto.

The Charter of the United Nations (June 1945)

In June 1945, the Charter of the United Nations was signed. This organization was dedicated to the proposition that international cooperation was not only preferable to war but also possible to attain. The organization has been criticized and applauded throughout the years. Some have seen it as effective in settling disputes and maintaining peace; others have viewed it as impotent and devoid of any authority to enforce its verdicts. The second selection describes another international organization that has gained currency in the 1980s. Amnesty International deals with prisoners of conscience throughout the world.

We the peoples of the United Nations determined to save succeeding generations from the scourge of war, which twice in our lifetime has brought untold sorrow to mankind, and

To reaffirm faith in fundamental human rights, in the dignity and worth of the human person, in the equal rights of men and women and of nations large and small, and

To establish conditions under which justice and respect for the obliga-

Department of State, *The United Nations Conference on International Organization* (Washington, D.C.: Government Printing Office, 1946), pp. 943–944.

tions arising from treaties and other sources of international law can be maintained, and

To promote social progress and better standards of life in larger freedom,

and for these ends to practice tolerance and live together in peace with one another as good neighbors, and

To unite our strength to maintain international peace and security, and

To ensure, by the acceptance of principles and the institution of methods, that armed force shall not be used, save in the common interest, and

To employ international machinery for the promotion of the economic and social advancement of all peoples,

have resolved to combine our efforts to accomplish these aims; accordingly; our respective Governments, through representatives assembled in the city of San Francisco, who have exhibited their full powers found to be in good and due form, have agreed to the present Charter of the United Nations and do hereby establish an international organization to be known as the United Nations.

PURPOSES AND PRINCIPLES

Article 1

The Organization and its Members . . . shall act in accordance with the following Principles.

1. The Organization is based on the principle of the sovereign equality of all its Members.

2. All Members, in order to ensure to all of them the rights and benefits resulting from membership, shall fulfill in good faith the obligations assumed by them in accordance with the present Charter.

3. All Members shall settle their international disputes by peaceful means in such a manner that international peace and security, and justice, are not endangered.

4. All Members shall refrain in their international relations from the threat or use of force against the territorial integrity or political independence of any state, or in any other manner, inconsistent with the Purposes of the United Nations.

5. All Members shall give the United Nations every assistance in any action it takes in accordance with the present Charter, and shall refrain from giving assistance to any state against which the United Nations is taking preventive or enforcement action.

6. The Organization shall ensure that states which are not Members of the United Nations act in accordance with these Principles so far as may be necessary for the maintenance of international peace and security.

7. Nothing contained in the present Charter shall authorize the United Nations to intervene in matters which are essentially within the domestic

jurisdiction of any state or shall require the Members to submit such matters to settlement under the present Charter. . . .

Amnesty International (1982)

Amnesty International plays a specific role in the international protection of human rights. It seeks the immediate and unconditional release of men and women detained anywhere because of their beliefs, colour, sex, ethnic origin, language or religious creed, provided they have not used or advocated violence. These are termed prisoners of conscience. It works for fair and prompt trials for all political prisoners, and works on behalf of such people detained without charge or trial. It opposes the death penalty and torture or other cruel, inhuman or degrading treatment or punishment of all prisoners without reservation. . . . The record shows how much remains to be done.

As the year ended, thousands of men and women were in prison because of their beliefs, many were still held after years without charge or trial. Prisoners were subject to torture, and people had been executed or were under sentence of death in a number of countries, often for politically related offences. Still others were put to death without any pretence of judicial or legal process, selected and killed by governments or their agents.

In many countries men, women and children remained unaccounted for after being taken into custody, often violently, by security forces, or abducted by agents acting with the complicity of governments; they had "disappeared". Their families and friends could gain no information about their fate or whereabouts.

The International Council of Amnesty International, the movement's supreme governing body, stated this year that governments and state security forces who attempt to cover up the abduction and "disappearance" of their political opponents should be made publicly accountable for the fate of the victims. It called for a global publicity campaign to counter this contemporary technique of official repression. This campaign was launched on Human Rights Day, 10 December 1981.

Unlawful and deliberate killings carried out by order of a government or with its complicity have claimed the lives of countless victims. During the year Amnesty International determined to campaign against such killings worldwide. . . .

These two practices which are often related—the "disappearance" of people abducted by the authorities and deliberate killings by governments—represent an outright attack on values and rights which the world community has struggled to establish. These are not new abuses, but the international community must now take effective measures to end them. Governments must not be allowed to evade responsibility when they choose to obliterate suspected opponents. They must accept real accountability by permitting independent investigations, pressing for investigations of complaints in other countries and taking the other actions necessary to expose these abuses.

Human rights transcend the boundaries of nation, race and belief; so does the international responsibility for protecting those rights. The pressure of world public opinion, expressed in the concerted actions of ordinary people from all around the world, must be brought to bear if this principle is to be universally respected. This is the vision which launched Amnesty International. Today, it has more than 325,000 members, subscribers and supporters in over 150 countries and territories committed to that ambition.

The protection of the individual citizen goes beyond the boundaries of the individual state—it is a matter of international responsibility and concern. This is the principle on which Amnesty International is founded, and the concept that lies behind the creation of international human rights standards and mechanisms to monitor and enforce those standards. To promote international standards, to strengthen them and to try to ensure effective means of enforcing them are important aspects of Amnesty International's work, particularly through the United Nations (UN), but also through other international and regional bodies. . . . The purpose of this report is to record the efforts Amnesty International made to protect individuals in the diverse situations where their inalienable rights were transgressed. This is a report about people, not statistics.

SECTION II: A CENTURY OF HOLOCAUST

The Nuclear Age

On August 6, 1945, the world entered the nuclear age with the detonation of the atomic bomb over the city of Hiroshima, Japan. Persuaded by the argument that such use would ultimately save Allied lives, President Truman ordered another bomb dropped on Nagasaki two days later. The Japanese surrendered and the race was on to match America's technological achievement. The selections below relate the events, from Albert Einstein's famous letter to President Roosevelt proposing the possibility of such a weapon, to U.S. attempts at responsibly controlling the destructive power it had unleashed. Jonathan Schell's eerie description of the effects of a nuclear attack on contemporary New York City follows.

The Theory: Letter
to President Roosevelt (1939)

ALBERT EINSTEIN

Albert Einstein
Old Grove Rd.
Nassau Point
Peconic, Long Island

August 2nd, 1939

F. D. Roosevelt,
President of the United States,
White House
Washington, D.C.

Sir:

Some recent work by E. Fermi and L. Szilard, which has been communicated to me in manuscript, leads me to expect that the element uranium may be turned into a new and important source of energy in the immediate future. Certain aspects of the situation which has arisen seem to call for watchfulness and, if necessary, quick action on the part of the Administration. I believe therefore that it is my duty to bring to your attention the following facts and recommendations:

In the course of the last four months it has been made probable—through the work of Joliot in France as well as Fermi and Szilard in America—that it may become possible to set up a nuclear chain reaction in a large mass of uranium, by which vast amounts of power and large quantities of new radium-like elements would be generated. Now it appears almost certain that this could be achieved in the immediate future.

This new phenomenon would also lead to the construction of bombs, and it is conceivable—though much less certain—that extremely powerful bombs of a new type may thus be constructed. A single bomb of this type, carried by boat and exploded in a port, might very well destroy the whole port together with some of the surrounding territory. However, such bombs might very well prove to be too heavy for transportation by air.

The United States has only very poor ores of uranium in moderate quantities. There is some good ore in Canada and the former Czechoslovakia, while the most important source of uranium is the Belgian Congo. . . .

I understand that Germany has actually stopped the sale of uranium from the Czechoslovakian mines which she has taken over. That she should have taken such early action might perhaps be understood on the ground that the son of the German Under-Secretary of State, von Weizsacker, is

Albert Einstein's Letter to President Roosevelt, August 2, 1939. Reprinted by permission of The Hebrew University of Jerusalem, Israel.

attached to the Kaiser-Wilhelm-Institut in Berlin where some of the American work on uranium is now being repeated.

Yours very truly,
(Albert Einstein)

The Reality: Announcement of the Destruction of Hiroshima (August 6, 1945)

HARRY S. TRUMAN

Sixteen hours ago an American airplane dropped one bomb on Hiroshima, an important Japanese Army base. That bomb had more power than 20,000 tons of T.N.T. It had more than two thousand times the blast power of the British "Grand Slam" which is the largest bomb ever yet used in the history of warfare.

The Japanese began the war from the air at Pearl Harbor. They have been repaid many fold. And the end is not yet in sight. With this bomb we have now added a new and revolutionary increase in destruction to supplement the growing power of our armed forces. In their present form these bombs are now in production and even more powerful forms are in development.

It is an atomic bomb. It is a harnessing of the basic power of the universe. The force from which the sun draws its power has been loosed against those who brought war to the Far East.

Before 1939, it was the accepted belief of scientists that it was theoretically possible to release atomic energy. But no one knew any practical method of doing it. By 1942, however, we knew that the Germans were working feverishly to find a way to add atomic energy to the other engines of war with which they hoped to enslave the world. But they failed. We may be grateful to Providence that the Germans got the V-1's and V-2's late and in limited quantities and even more grateful that they did not get the atomic bomb at all. . . .

We are now prepared to obliterate more rapidly and completely every productive enterprise the Japanese have above ground in any city. We shall destroy their docks, their factories, and their communications. Let there be no mistake; we shall completely destroy Japan's power to make war. . . .

I shall recommend that the Congress of the United States consider promptly the establishment of an appropriate commission to control the production and use of atomic power within the United States. I shall give further consideration and make further recommendations to the Congress as to how atomic power can become a powerful and forceful influence towards the maintenance of world peace.

Public Papers of the President, Harry S. Truman, 1947 (Washington, D.C.: Government Printing Office, 1963), pp. 197–200.

The Control of Atomic Energy (1946)

BERNARD BARUCH

We are here to make a choice between the quick and the dead.

This is our business.

Behind the black portent of the new atomic age lies a hope which, seized upon with faith, can work our salvation. If we fail, then we have damned every man to be the slave of Fear. Let us not deceive ourselves: We must elect World Peace or World Destruction.

Science has torn from nature a secret so vast in its potentialities that our minds cower from the terror it creates. Yet terror is not enough to inhibit the use of the atomic bombs. The terror created by weapons has never stopped man from employing them. For each new weapon a defense has been produced, in time. But now we face a condition in which adequate defense does not exist. . . .

The United States proposes the creation of an International Atomic Development Authority, to which should be entrusted all phases of the development and use of atomic energy, starting with the raw material and including—

1. Managerial control or ownership of all atomic-energy activities potentially dangerous to world security.
2. Power to control, inspect, and license all other atomic activities.
3. The duty of fostering the beneficial uses of atomic energy.
4. Research and development responsibilities of an affirmative character intended to put the Authority in the forefront of atomic knowledge and thus to enable it to comprehend, and therefore to detect, misuse of atomic energy. To be effective, the Authority must itself be the world's leader in the field of atomic knowledge and development and thus supplement its legal authority with the great power inherent in possession of leadership in knowledge.

I offer this as a basis for beginning our discussion. . . .

We of this nation, desirous of helping to bring peace to the world and realizing the heavy obligations upon us arising from our possession of the means of producing the bomb and from the fact that it is part of our armament, are prepared to make our full contribution toward effective control of atomic energy.

When an adequate system for control of atomic energy, including the renunciation of the bomb as a weapon, has been agreed upon and put into effective operation and condign punishments set up for violations of the rules of control which are to be stigmatized as international crimes, we propose that—

Department of State Bulletin (June 23, 1946), pp. 1057–1062.

1. Manufacture of atomic bombs shall stop;
2. Existing bombs shall be disposed of pursuant to the terms of the treaty; and
3. The Authority shall be in possession of full information as to the know-how for production of atomic energy. . . .

Let me repeat, so as to avoid misunderstanding: My country is ready to make its full contribution toward the end we seek, subject of course to our constitutional processes and to an adequate system of control becoming fully effective, as we finally work it out.

The bomb does not wait upon debate. To delay may be to die. The time between violation and preventive action or punishment would be all too short for extended discussion as to the course to be followed.

The Destruction of New York City

JONATHAN SCHELL

One way to begin to grasp the destructive power of present-day nuclear weapons is to describe the consequences of the detonation of a one-megaton bomb, which possesses eighty times the explosive power of the Hiroshima bomb, on a large city, such as New York. Burst some eighty-five hundred feet above the Empire State Building, a one-megaton bomb would gut or flatten almost every building between Battery Park and 125th Street, or within a radius of four and four-tenths miles, or in an area of sixty-one square miles, and would heavily damage buildings between the northern tip of Staten Island and the George Washington Bridge, or within a radius of about eight miles, or in an area of about two hundred square miles. A conventional explosive delivers a swift shock, like a slap, to whatever it hits, but the blast wave of a sizable nuclear weapon endures for several seconds and "can surround and destory whole buildings" (Glasstone). People, of course, would be picked up and hurled away from the blast along with the rest of the debris. Within the sixty-one square miles, the walls, roofs, and floors of any buildings that had not been flattened would be collapsed, and the people and furniture inside would be swept down onto the street. . . . As far away as ten miles from ground zero, pieces of glass and other sharp objects would be hurled about by the blast wave at lethal velocities. In Hiroshima, where buildings were low and outside the center of the city, were often constructed of light materials, injuries from falling buildings were often minor. But in New York, where the buildings are tall and are constructed of heavy materials, the physical collapse of the city would certainly kill millions of people. The streets of New York are narrow ravines running between the high walls of the city's buildings. In a

Jonathan Schell, *The Fate of the Earth* (New York: Alfred A. Knopf, 1982), pp. 47–50, 52. Reprinted by permission of the publisher.

Explosion of the atomic bomb over Nagasaki, Japan (August 8, 1945). (*U.S. Air Force Photo*)

nuclear attack, the walls would fall and the ravines would fill up. The people in the buildings would fall to the street with the debris of the buildings, and the people in the street would be crushed by this avalanche of people and buildings. At a distance of two miles or so from ground zero, winds would reach four hundred miles an hour, and another two miles away they would reach a hundred and eight miles an hour. Meanwhile, the fireball would be growing, until it was more than a mile wide, and rocketing upward, to a height of over six miles. For ten seconds, it would broil the city below. Anyone caught in the open within nine miles of ground zero would receive third-degree burns and would probably be killed; closer to the explosion, people would be charred and killed instantly. From Greenwich Village up to Central Park, the heat would be great enough to melt metal and glass. Readily inflammable materials, such as newspapers and dry leaves, would ignite in all five boroughs . . . and west to the Passaic River, in New Jersey, within a radius of about nine and a half miles from ground zero, thereby creating an area of more than two hundred eighty square miles in which mass fires were likely to break out.

If it were possible (as it would not be) for someone to stand at Fifth Avenue and Seventy-second Street (about two miles from ground zero) without being instantly killed, he would see the following sequence of events. A dazzling white light from the fireball would illumine the scene, continuing for perhaps thirty seconds. Simultaneously, searing heat would ignite everything flammable and start to melt windows, cars, buses, lamp-posts, and everything else made of metal or glass. People in the street would immediately catch fire, and would shortly be reduced to heavily charred corpses. About five seconds after the light appeared, the blast wave would strike, laden with the debris of a now nonexistent midtown. Some buildings might be crushed, as though a giant fist had squeezed them on all sides, and others might be picked up off their foundations and whirled uptown with the other debris. On the far side of Central Park, the West Side skyline would fall from south to north. The four-hundred-mile-an-hour wind would blow from south to north, die down after a few seconds, and then blow in the reverse direction with diminished intensity. While these things were happening, the fireball would be burning in the sky for the ten seconds of the thermal pulse. Soon huge, thick clouds of dust and smoke would envelop the scene, and as the mushroom cloud rushed over-head (it would have a diameter of about twelve miles) the light from the sun would be blotted out, and day would turn to night. Within minutes, fires, ignited both by the thermal pulse and by broken gas mains, tanks of gas and oil, and the like, would begin to blow in the direction of the blast. As at Hiroshima, a whirlwind might be produced, which would sweep through the ruins, and radioactive rain, generated under the meteorological conditions created by the blast, might fall. Before long, the individual fires would coalesce into a mass fire, which, depending largely on the winds, would become either a conflagration or a firestorm. In a conflagration, prevailing winds spread a wall of fire as far as there is any compustible material to sustain it; in a firestorm, a vertical updraft caused by the fire itself sucks the surrounding air in toward a central point, and the fires therefore converge in a single fire of extreme heat. A mass fire of either kind renders shelters useless by burning up all the oxygen in the air and creating toxic gases, so that anyone inside the shelters is asphyxiated, and also by heating the ground to such high temperatures that the shelters turn, in effect, into ovens, cremating the people inside them.

In this vast theatre of physical effects, all the scenes of agony and death that took place at Hiroshima would again take place, but now involving millions of people rather than hundreds of thousands. Like the people of Hiroshima, the people of New York would be burned, battered, crushed, and irradiated in every conceivable way. The city and its people would be mingled in a smoldering heap. And then, as the fires started, the survivors (most of whom would be on the periphery of the explosion) would be driven to abandon to the flames those family members and other people who were unable to flee, or else to die with them. Before long, while the ruins burned, the processions of injured, mute people would begin their slow progress out of the outskirts of the devastated zone. However, this time a much smaller proportion of the population than at Hiroshima would have a chance of escaping. In general, as the size of the area of devastation increases, the possibilities for escape decrease.

A description of the effects of a one-megaton bomb on New York City gives us some notion of the meaning in human terms of a megaton of nuclear explosive power, but a weapon that is more likely to be used against New York is the twenty-megaton bomb, which has one thousand six hundred times the yield of the Hiroshima bomb. The Soviet Union is estimated to have at least a hundred and thirteen twenty-megaton bombs in its nuclear arsenal, carried by Bear intercontinental bombers. In addition, some of the Soviet SS-18 missiles are capable of carrying bombs of this size, although the actual yields are not known. Since the explosive power of the twenty-megaton bombs greatly exceeds the amount necessary to destroy most military targets, it is reasonable to suppose that they are meant for use against large cities. If a twenty-megaton bomb were air-burst over the Empire State building at an altitude of thirty thousand feet, the zone gutted or flattened by the blast wave would have a radius of twelve miles and an area of more than four hundred and fifty square miles. . . .

The Cold War: Origins and Development

The term "Cold War" has been used to describe the era of uneasy relations between the western Allies and the Soviet Union after World War II. Each was competing for influence in Europe and did so through propaganda as much as through troop placement. In the first excerpt, the Soviet leader Joseph Stalin offered a glimpse of the ideological combat that was to be waged in the future. A month later, Winston Churchill, who had largely directed the British war effort, warned the West of the deceptive Soviet Union in his famous "Iron Curtain" speech.

The Soviet Victory: Capitalism versus Communism (February 1946)

JOSEPH STALIN

It would be wrong to believe that the Second World War broke out accidentally or as a result of the mistakes of some or other statesmen, though mistakes certainly were made. In reality, the war broke out as an inevitable result of the development of world economic and political forces on the basis of modern monopoly capitalism.

Marxists have stated more than once that the capitalist system of world economy conceals in itself the elements of general crisis and military clashes, that in view of this in our time the development of world capitalism takes place not as a smooth and even advance but through crises and war catastrophes.

The reason is that the unevenness of the development of capitalist countries usually results, as time passes, in an abrupt disruption of the equilibrium within the world system of capitalism, and that a group of capitalist countries which believes itself to be less supplied with raw materials and markets usually attempts to alter the situation and re-divide the "spheres of influence" in its own favour by means of armed force. . . .

This results in the splitting of the capitalist world into two hostile camps and in war between them.

Perhaps the catastrophes of war could be avoided if there existed the possibility of re-distributing periodically raw materials and markets among the countries in accordance with their economic weight—by means of adopting coordinated and peaceful decisions. This, however, cannot be accomplished under present capitalist conditions of the development of world economy. . . .

As to our country, for her the war was the severest and hardest of all the wars our Motherland has ever experienced in her history.

But the war was not only a curse. It was at the same time a great school in which all the forces of the people were tried and tested. The war laid bare all the facts and events in the rear and at the front, it mercilessly tore off all the veils and covers which had concealed the true faces of States, governments, and parties, and placed them on the stage without masks, without embellishments, with all their shortcomings and virtues.

. . .

And so, what are the results of the war? . . .

Our victory means, in the first place, that our Soviet social system has won, that the Soviet social system successfully withstood the trial in the flames of war and proved its perfect viability.

Embassy of the U.S.S.R., Speech Delivered by J. V. Stalin at a Meeting of Voters of the Stalin Electoral Area of Moscow (Washington, D.C.: Governement Printing Office, 1946).

It is well known that the foreign press more than once asserted that the Soviet social system is a "risky experiment" doomed to failure, that the Soviet system is a "house of cards," without any roots in life, imposed upon the people by the organs of the "Cheka," [secret police] that a slight push from outside would be enough to blow this "house of cards" to smithereens.

Now we can say that the war swept away all these assertions of the foreign press as groundless. The war has shown that the Soviet social system is a truly popular system, which has grown from the people and enjoys its powerful support, that the Soviet social system is a perfectly viable and stable form of organisation of society.

More than that, the point is now not whether the Soviet social system is viable or not, since after the objective lessons of the war no single skeptic now ventures to come out with doubts concerning the viability of the Soviet social system. The point now is that the Soviet social system has proved more viable and stable than a non-Soviet social system, that the Soviet social system is a better form of organisation of society than any non-Soviet social system.

"Iron Curtain" Speech (March 1946)

WINSTON CHURCHILL

I now come to the . . . danger which threatens the cottage home and ordinary people, namely tyranny. We cannot be blind to the fact that the liberties enjoyed by individual citizens throughout the United States and British Empire are not valid in a considerable number of countries, some of which are very powerful. In these states control is forced upon the common people by various kinds of all-embracing police governments, to a degree which is overwhelming and contrary to every principle of democracy. The power of the state is exercised without restraint, either by dictators or by compact oligarchies operating through a privileged party and a political police. It is not our duty at this time, when difficulties are so numerous, to interfere forcibly in the internal affairs of countries whom we have not conquered in war, but we must never cease to proclaim in fearless tones the great principles of freedom and the rights of man, which are the joint inheritance of the English-speaking world and which, through Magna Carta, the Bill of Rights, the habeas corpus, trial by jury, and the English common law find their famous expression in the Declaration of Independence. . . .

A shadow has fallen upon the scenes so lately lighted by the Allied victory. Nobody knows what Soviet Russia and its Communist international

Congressional Record, 79th Congress, 2nd session, pp. A1145–A1147.

organization intends to do in the immediate future, or what are the limits, if any, to their expansive and proselytizing tendencies. . . . From Stettin in the Baltic to Triest in the Adriatic, an iron curtain has descended across the continent. Behind that line lie all the capitals of the ancient states of central and eastern Europe. Warsaw, Berlin, Prague, Vienna, Budapest, Belgrade, Bucharest, and Sofia, all these famous cities and the populations around them lie in the Soviet sphere and all are subject, in one form or another, not only to Soviet influence but to a very high and increasing measure of control from Moscow. Athens alone, with its immortal glories, is free to decide its future at an election under British, American, and French observation.

In a great number of countries, far from the Russian frontiers and throughout the world, Communist fifth columns are established and work in complete unity and absolute obedience to the directions they receive from the Communist center. Except in the British Commonwealth, and in the United States, where communism is in its infancy, the Communist parties and fifth columns constitute a growing challenge and peril to Christian civilization. These are somber facts for anyone to have to recite on the morrow of a victory gained by so much splendid comradeship in arms and in the cause of freedom and democracy, and we should be most unwise not to face them squarely while time remains. . . .

On the other hand, I repulse the idea that a new war is inevitable, still more that it is imminent. It is because I am so sure that our fortunes are in our own hands and that we hold the power to save the future, that I feel the duty to speak out now that I have occasion to do so. I do not believe that Soviet Russia desires war. What they desire is the fruits of war and the indefinite expansion of their power and doctrines. But what we have to consider here today while time remains, is the permanent prevention of war and the establishment of conditions of freedom and democracy as rapidly as possible in all countries.

Our difficulties and dangers will not be removed by closing our eyes to them; they will not be removed by mere waiting to see what happens; nor will they be relieved by a policy of appeasement. What is needed is a settlement, and the longer this is delayed, the more difficult it will be and the greater our dangers will become. From what I have seen of our Russian friends and allies during the war, I am convinced that there is nothing they admire so much as strength, and there is nothing for which they have less respect than for military weakness. For that reason the old doctrine of a balance of power is unsound. We cannot afford, if we can help it, to work on narrow margins, offering temptations to a trial of strength. If the western democracies stand together in strict adherence to the principles of the United Nations Charter, their influence for furthering these principles will be immense and no one is likely to molest them. If, however, they become divided or falter in their duty, and if these all-important years are allowed to slip away, then indeed catastrophe may overwhelm us all.

The Truman Doctrine (March 1947)

HARRY S. TRUMAN

In the first months of 1946, President Truman received urgent requests from the Greek government for economic assistance, which, it was hoped, would put an end to the chaos and strife hindering its recovery from the war. Hoping to forestall Communist dissidents who were threatening the stability of the government, Truman appealed to Congress to appropriate such financial assistance. He also asked for military as well as economic aid to Turkey. The controversial Truman Doctrine, as it came to be called, committed the United States to an active policy of promoting ideological divisions between it and the Soviet Union, and further escalated Cold War tensions. The Marshall Plan of 1947, which advocated the rebuilding of West Germany after the war, is an example of this policy of Soviet containment.

One of the primary objectives of the foreign policy of the United States is the creation of conditions in which we and other nations will be able to work out a way of life free from coercion. This was a fundamental issue in the war with Germany and Japan. Our victory was won over countries which sought to impose their will, and their way of life, upon other nations.

To ensure the peaceful development of nations, free from coercion, the United States has taken a leading part in establishing the United Nations. The United Nations is designed to make possible lasting freedom and independence for all its members. We shall not realize our objectives, however, unless we are willing to help free peoples to maintain their free institutions and their national integrity against aggressive movements that seek to impose upon them totalitarian regimes. This is no more than a frank recognition that totalitarian regimes imposed upon free peoples, by direct or indirect aggression, undermine the foundations of international peace and hence the security of the United States.

The peoples of a number of countries of the world have recently had totalitarian regimes forced upon them against their will. The Government of the United States has made frequent protests against coercion and intimidation, in violation of the Yalta agreement, in Poland, Rumania, and Bulgaria. I must also state that in a number of other countries there have been similar developments.

At the present moment in world history nearly every nation must choose between alternative ways of life. The choice is too often not a free one.

One way of life is based upon the will of the majority, and is distinguished by free institutions, representative government, free elections,

Public Papers of the President, Harry S. Truman, 1947 (Washington, D.C.: Government Printing Office, 1963), pp. 177–180.

guarantees of individual liberty, freedom of speech and religion, and free-dom from political oppression.

The second way of life is based upon the will of a minority forcibly imposed upon the majority. It relies upon terror and oppression, a con-trolled press and radio, fixed elections, and the suppression of personal freedoms.

I believe that it must be the policy of the United States to support free peoples who are resisting attempted subjugation by armed minorities or by outside pressures.

I believe that we must assist free peoples to work out their own destinies in their own way.

I believe that our help should be primarily through economic and financial aid which is essential to economic stability and orderly political processes.

The world is not static, and the *status quo* is not sacred. But we cannot allow changes in the *status quo* in violation of the Charter of United Nations by such methods as coercion, or by such subterfuges as political infiltration. In helping free and independent nations to maintain their freedom, the United States will be giving effect to the principles of the Charter of the United Nations. . . .

The seeds of totalitarian regimes are nurtured by misery and want. They spread and grow in the evil soil of poverty and strife. They reach their full growth when the hope of a people for a better life has died.

We must keep that hope alive.

The free peoples of the world look to us for support in maintaining their freedoms.

If we falter in our leadership, we may endanger the peace of the world—and we shall surely endanger the welfare of this Nation.

Great responsibilities have been placed upon us by the swift movement of events.

I am confident that the Congress will face these responsibilities squarely.

The Marshall Plan (June 1947)

GEORGE C. MARSHALL

The truth of the matter is that Europe's requirements for the next three or four years of foreign food and other essential products—principally from America—are so much greater than her present ability to pay that she must have substantial additional help or face economic, social, and political dete-rioration of a very grave character.

Department of State Bulletin (June 15, 1947), pp. 1159–1160.

The remedy lies in breaking the vicious circle and restoring the confidence of the European people in the economic future of their own countries and of Europe as a whole. The manufacturer and the farmer throughout wide areas must be able and willing to exchange their products for currencies the continuing value of which is not open to question.

Aside from the demoralizing effect on the world at large and the possibilities of disturbances arising as a result of the desperation of the people concerned, the consequences to the economy of the United States should be apparent to all. It is logical that the United States should do whatever it is able to do to assist in the return of normal economic health in the world, without which there can be no political stability and no assured peace. Our policy is directed not against any country or doctrine but against hunger, poverty, desperation, and chaos. Its purpose should be the revival of a working economy in the world so as to permit the emergence of political and social conditions in which free institutions can exist. Such assistance, I am convinced, must not be on a piecemeal basis as various crises develop. Any assistance that this Government may render in the future should provide a cure rather than a mere palliative. Any government that is willing to assist in the task of recovery will find full cooperation, I am sure, on the part of the United States Government. Any government which maneuvers to block the recovery of other countries cannot expect help from us. Furthermore, governments, political parties, or groups which seek to perpetuate human misery in order to profit therefrom politically or otherwise will encounter the opposition of the United States.

It is already evident that, before the United States Government can proceed much further in its efforts to alleviate the situation and help start the European world on its way to recovery, there must be some agreement among the countries of Europe as to the requirements of the situation and the part those countries themselves will take in order to give proper effect to whatever action might be undertaken by this Government. It would be neither fitting nor efficacious for this Government to undertake to draw up unilaterally a program designed to place Europe on its feet economically. This is the business of the Europeans. The initiative, I think, must come from Europe. The role of this country should consist of friendly aid in the drafting of a European program and of later support of such a program so far as it may be practical for us to do so. The program should be a joint one, agreed to by a number, if not all, European nations.

An essential part of any successful action on the part of the United States is an understanding on the part of the people of America of the character of the problem and the remedies to be applied. Political passion and prejudice should have no part. With foresight, and a willingness on the part of our people to face up to the vast responsibility which history has clearly placed upon our country, the difficulties I have outlined can and will be overcome.

Soviet Objections to NATO (1949)

Distrust and tension between the United States and the Soviet Union continued to mount in 1948 as the Russians stopped all traffic, including food transports, into their zone of German occupation. From June 1948 to May 1949, the United States airlifted supplies to the people of Berlin and defied Soviet heavy-handedness. The Cold War escalated again when the United States formed the North Atlantic Treaty Organization (NATO) in March and April 1949. This was a mutual defense pact which maintained that an attack on any one of the members of the alliance was an attack on all and that retaliation would be a united effort. By September 1949, the Soviet Union had detonated its first atomic bomb. The Soviet response to the formation of NATO follows.

The statements contained in the North Atlantic treaty that it is designated for defense and that it recognizes the principles of the United Nations organization serve aims which have nothing in common either with the tasks of self-defense of the parties to the treaty or with real recognition of the aims and principles of the United Nations organization. Such great powers as the United States, Great Britain and France are parties to the North Atlantic treaty.

Thus the treaty is not directed either against the United States of America, Great Britain or France.

Of the great powers only the Soviet Union is excluded from among the parties to this treaty, which can be explained only by the fact that this treaty is directed against the Soviet Union. . . .

The North Atlantic pact is designed to daunt the states which do not agree to obey the dictates of the Anglo-American grouping of powers that lay claim to world domination, though the untenability of such claims was once again affirmed by World War II which ended in the debacle of Facist Germany, which also had laid claim to world domination.

Among the participants in the North Atlantic treaty are also countries whose Governments expect to benefit at the expense of the richer parties to this treaty and made various plans with regard to obtaining new credits and other material advantages.

At the same time one cannot but see the groundlessness of the anti-Soviet motives of the North Atlantic treaty, inasmuch as it is known to all that the Soviet Union does not intend to attack anyone and in no way threatens the United States of America, Great Britain or the other parties of the treaty.

The conclusion of the North Atlantic treaty and establishment of a new

"Text of the Soviet Memorandum on the Atlantic Pact" (April 1, 1949). Reprinted by permission of The Associated Press.

grouping of powers is motivated by the weakness of the United Nations organization.

It is perfectly evident, however, that the North Atlantic treaty does not serve the cause of consolidating the United Nations organization but on the contrary leads to the undermining of the very foundation of this international organization because establishment of the above grouping of powers is far from corresponding to the aims and principles of the United Nations organization and runs counter to the Charter of this organization.

An Assessment of Communism (1953)

THEODORE WHITE

By 1950, it was natural to begin assessing the events that had transpired during the first half of the century and to speculate on developments for the future. In 1953, the Soviet leader Joseph Stalin died, and many wondered how this might change the face of Communism and subsequently the nature of the Cold War. Theodore White, a journalist who had spent much of his early career in China and became famous for his political analysis of the presidency, offered this view of Communism in 1953.

Americans are so frightened by the evil in communism that they fail to see that the greatest danger is not the evil but the attraction in it. Only Americans live in a society in which communism can seduce no healthy mind. Most of our senior Allies and the myriad-man countries who live outside our Alliance are made of people who stand transfixed by fear of communism and its sinister charm at the same time.

The magic appeal in the Communist faith is simple. It is the belief that pure logic applied to human affairs is enough to change the world and cure it of all its human miseries. It is buttressed by the belief that the processes of history are governed by certain "scientific" laws, which automatically guarantee the triumph of communism when the situation is ripe, if only its protestants have the courage to strike and act.

This simple credo carries an almost irresistible attraction to two kinds of people everywhere in the world: first, to small coteries of able and ambitious young men hungry for the ecstasy of leadership, and, secondly, to larger masses of ignorant people who have just begun to hope.

To both these schools of converts, the fatal flaw in the Communist faith is neither apparent nor important. This fatal flaw is embedded in the nature of human beings whenever they gather politically. Human beings

Theodore H. White, *Fire in the Ashes* (New York: William Sloane Associates Publishers, 1953), pp. 318–320.

tend to be illogical. The logic of which communism boasts is never certain, therefore, of success in any political operation unless simultaneously it imposes so rigid a discipline as to make ordinary people mere bodies in the sequence of their masters' planning. Logic cannot succeed if its premises are to be shaken over and over again by vagrant human emotions allowed freely to express themselves in all their passion and frailty. Any political organization which sets out to be totally logical thus calls for total discipline; total discipline inevitably requires police, and police bring terror.

But the weakness of communism lies less in the calculated immorality of terror than in the inevitable internal appetite of the discipline. The discipline feeds on itself; it shrinks the area of discussion and decision into ever narrower, ever tighter, ever more cramped circles. Fewer and fewer men have less and less access to the raw facts which are necessary for wise judgment. The discipline they control and impose inevitably sneaks back to weaken them, to blind or deafen them into stupidity and error.

To those who come to communism out of ambition or out of misguided intelligence, this flaw is not immediately apparent. Each of this type of convert cherishes the illusion until too late that the ever-shrinking circle of discipline will leave him safe at its center of creative leadership, rather than crushed and tortured as discipline contracts about his own soft human body. To the second category of converts, those who come to it out of hunger and ignorance, this flaw in communism (even if it could be explained to them) seems unimportant. They have always been excluded from decision and control over their own lives. Communism promises them simply "more"; they are ready to believe. The hungrier and more ignorant they are, the more difficult it is to explain to them that their own hopes and welfare are directly dependent on the freedom of creative minds, with which they are unfamiliar, to think independently of all discipline.

To the Western world, so challenged by communism, this flaw in the adversary presents a grotesque problem. Communism's prison-logical system of human organization grows in strength decade by decade even as its leadership becomes less and less capable of wise and sensible decision. For all its dynamism and strength, the Communist world falls into blunders with increasing frequency, blunders which are only rectified by great wrenchings of policy that shake the world with disaster. To deal with communism, one must recognize both its strength and its blunders clearly. . . .

Such an event as the death of Stalin, by shaking the superstructure of discipline, by admitting for a brief moment the clash of several opinions and the consequent opportunity for a slightly larger area of discussion at the summit, has given the Communist machinery of politics a momentary opportunity to review some of its errors. But, unless communism ceases to be communism, the process of discipline calls for a new tightening of control, a new struggle to apply the logic of a single man to a world of dark and uncertain phenomena.

Self-Renewal: The Attack on Stalin (June 1956)
NIKITA KHRUSHCHEV

After Stalin's death in 1953, the power vacuum was eventually filled by Sergeyevich (Nikita) Khrushchev. At the 20th Communist Party Congress, Khrushchev quite unexpectedly attacked Stalin and his legacy of fear. The Soviets were looking for a new beginning.

Comrades, in the report of the Central Committee of the Party at the 20th Congress, in a number of speeches by delegates to the Congress . . . quite a lot has been said about the cult of the individual and about its harmful consequences.

After Stalin's death the Central Committee of the Party began to implement a policy of explaining concisely and consistently that it is impermissible and foreign to the spirit of Marxism-Leninism to elevate one person, to transform him into a superman possessing supernatural characteristics akin to those of a god. Such a man supposedly knows everything, sees everything, thinks for everyone, can do anything, is infallible in his behavior.

Such a belief about a man, and specifically about Stalin, was cultivated among us for many years. . . .

Stalin originated the concept "enemy of the people." This term automatically rendered it unnecessary that the ideological errors of a man or men engaged in a controversy be proven; this term made possible the usage of the most cruel repression, violating all norms of revolutionary legality, against anyone who in any way disagreed with Stalin, against those who were only suspected of hostile intent, against those who had bad reputations. This concept, "enemy of the people," actually eliminated the possibility of any kind of ideological fight or the making of one's views known on this or that issue, even those of a practical character. In the main, and in actuality, the only proof of guilt used, against all norms of current legal science, was the "confession" of the accused himself; and, as subsequent probing proved, "confessions" were acquired through physical pressures against the accused.

This led to glaring violations of revolutionary legality, and to the fact that many entirely innocent persons, who in the past had defended the Party line, became victims.

We must assert that in regard to those persons who in their time had opposed the Party line, there were often no sufficient serious reasons for their physical annihilation. The formula, "enemy of the people" was specifically introduced for the purpose of physically annihilating such individuals. . . .

Thus, Stalin had sanctioned in the name of the Central Committee of

Congressional Record, 84th Congress, 2nd session, pp. 9390–9402 (June 4, 1956).

the All-Union Communist Party (Bolsheviks) the most brutal violation of Socialist legality, torture and oppression, which led as we have seen to the slandering and self-accusation of innocent people.

Speech to the 22nd Communist Party Congress (1962)
NIKITA KHRUSHCHEV

Although there may have been hope that the fears of the Cold War would be reduced, the decade from 1955 to 1966 was especially intense in its rhetoric and ideological conflict. As Khrushchev menacingly said of capitalist states in 1956, "Whether you like it or not, history is on our side. We will bury you!" This was the era of Senator Joseph McCarthy, who played on the fears of Americans with his deceitful rantings that Communists had infiltrated the highest echelons of government. It was during this time (1961) that the Berlin Wall was built, sealing off the city into Communist and democratic sectors—a symbolic as well as practical measure. And finally, in 1962, the two superpowers nearly went to nuclear war as President Kennedy demanded the removal of Soviet missiles from Cuba. The following excerpt is from Khrushchev's speech to the 22nd Congress of the Communist party. Note the argument carefully.

The most rabid imperialists, acting on the principle of "after us the deluge," openly voice their desire to undertake a new war venture. The ideologists of imperialism, intimidating the peoples, try to instill a kind of philosophy of hopelessness and desperation. Hysterically they cry: "Better death under capitalism than life under communism." They do not like free peoples to flourish, you see. They fear that the peoples in their countries too will take the path of socialism. Blinded by class hatred, our enemies are ready to doom all mankind to the catastrophe of war. The imperialists' opportunities to carry out their aggressive designs, however, are becoming smaller and smaller. They behave like a feeble and greedy old man whose powers have been exhausted, whose physical capacity has weakened, but whose avid desires remain. . . .

As long as the imperialist aggressors exist, we must be on guard, keep our powder dry, improve the defense of the socialist countries, their armed forces and the state security agencies. If, in the face of common sense, the imperialists dare attack the socialist countries and plunge mankind into the abyss of a world war of annihilation, this mad act of theirs would be their last, it would be the end of the whole system of capitalism. (*Applause.*)

Our party clearly understands its tasks, its responsibility, and will do everything in its power to see to it that the world socialist system continues to grow stronger, gathers fresh strength and develops. We believe that in

Current Soviet Policies, IV (New York, 1962), pp. 44–45, 50, 77. Reprinted by permission of *The Current Digest of The Soviet Press.*

the competition with capitalism socialism will win. (*Prolonged applause.*) We believe that this victory will be won in peaceful competition and not by way of unleashing a war. We have stood, we stand and we will stand by the positions of peaceful competition of states with different social systems; we will do everything to strengthen world peace. (*Prolonged applause.*)

The most important component of our party's foreign policy activities is *the struggle for general and complete disarmament.* The Soviet Union has been waging this struggle for many years now, and doing so firmly and perseveringly. We have always been resolutely opposed to the arms race, since rivalry in this sphere in the past not only saddled the peoples with a terrible burden but inevitably led to world wars. We are even more resolutely opposed to the arms race now that there has been a colossal technical revolution in the art of war and the use of today's weapons would inevitably entail the deaths of hundreds of millions of people.

The stockpiling of these weapons, proceeding as it is in a setting of cold war and war hysteria, is fraught with disastrous consequences. All that has to happen is for the nerves of some fellow in uniform to crack while he is on duty at a "push-button" somewhere in the West, and things may happen that will bring more than a little misfortune upon the peoples of the whole world.

Naturally, when we put forward a program of general and complete disarmament, we are talking not about the unilateral disarmament of socialism in the face of imperialism or vice verse, but about universal renunciation of arms as a means of solving problems at issue among states. . . .

The example of the Soviet Union inspires all progressive mankind. Never has the great vital forces of Marxist-Leninist teaching been so clearly evident as in our days, now that socialism has triumphed fully and finally in the Soviet Union, the cause of socialism is winning new victories in the countries of the world socialist commonwealth, and the international Communist and workers' movement and the national liberation struggle of peoples are growing and expanding tempestuously.

The revolution awakened the great energy of peoples, which is transforming the world on the principles of socialism and communism. Colossal changes are taking place and will take place throughout the world under the influence of the successes of communism.

The victory of communism is inevitable! (*Stormy applause.*)

The great army of Communists and of Marxist-Leninists acts as the vanguard of the peoples in the struggle for peace, for social progress and for communism, the bright future of mankind. New and ever newer millions of people will assemble and rally under the great banner of communism. The cause of progress, the cause of communism will triumph! (*Stormy applause.*)

Long live the great and heroic Soviet people, the builders of communism! (*Stormy applause.*)

Long live the indestructible unity and fraternal friendship of the peoples of the world socialist camp! (*Stormy applause.*)

Long live the heroic party of the Communists of the Soviet Union, created and tempered in struggle by the great Lenin! (*Stormy applause.*)

Long live the indestructible unity of the international Communist and workers' movement and the fraternal solidarity of the proletarians of all countries! (*Stormy applause.*)

Long live peace the world over! (*Stormy applause.*)

Under the all-conquering banner of Marxism-Leninism, under the leadership of the Communist Party, forward to the victory of communism! (*Stormy, prolonged applause, turning into an ovation. All rise.*)

America's Foreign Policy (1983)

GEORGE SHULTZ

During the 1970s, the Soviet Union and United States, under the respective leadership of Leonid Brezhnev and Richard Nixon, demonstrated cooperation through cultural exchanges and even negotiated a Strategic Arms Limitation Treaty (SALT) in 1972. This policy of détente, as it was called, was a hopeful sign that the world was becoming a more secure place in which to live. But during the Carter presidency, the Soviet Union invaded the sovereign state of Afghanistan (December 1979), an act that drew international criticism and contributed to the Carter Doctrine of January 1980: Any threat upon American oil interests in the Persian Gulf would be considered provocative and tantamount to war. In 1981, Ronald Reagan was inaugurated as president, having won the election in part on a "get-tough" stance toward the U.S.S.R. His verbal attacks characterized the Soviet Union as "the evil Empire" and "the focus of evil in the world." Such rhetoric did little to encourage cooperation between the two nations. It was only late in 1985, during Reagan's second term, that a summit conference was held. George Shultz, Secretary of State, offered this assessment of American foreign policy in 1983.

Americans are, by history and by inclination, a practical and pragmatic people—yet a people with a vision. It is the vision—usually simple and sometimes naive—that has so often led us to dare and to achieve. President Reagan's approach to foreign policy is grounded squarely on standards drawn from the pragmatic American experience. As de Tocqueville pointed out, "To achieve its objective, America relies on personal interest, and gives full reign to the strength and reason of the individual." That is as true now as when it was said 150 years ago. Our principal instrument, now as then, is freedom. Our adversaries are the oppressors, the totalitarians, the tacticians of fear and pressure.

On this foundation, President Reagan's ideas and the structure of his foreign policy are so straight forward that those of us enmeshed in day-to-

George Shultz, Speech delivered before the United Nations, September 30, 1983.

day details may easily lose sight of them. The President never does; he consistently brings us back to fundamentals. Today, I will talk about those fundamentals. They consist of four ideas that guide our actions.

- We will start from realism.
- We will act from strength, both in power and purpose.
- We will stress the indispensable need to generate consent, build agreements, and negotiate on key issues.
- We will conduct ourselves in the belief that progress is possible, even though the road to achievement is long and hard.

Reality

If we are to change the world we must first understand it. We must face reality—with all its anguish and all its opportunities. Our era needs those who, as Pericles said, have the clearest vision of what is before them, glory and danger alike, and, notwithstanding, go out to meet it.

Reality is not an illusion nor a sleight of hand, though many would have us believe otherwise. The enormous, grinding machinery of Soviet propaganda daily seeks to distort reality, to bend truth for its own purposes. Our world is occupied by far too many governments which seek to conceal truth from their own people. They wish to imprison reality by controlling what can be read or spoken or heard. They would have us believe that black is white and up is down.

Unpleasant Reality

Much of present day reality is unpleasant. To describe conditions as we see them, as I do today and as President Reagan has over the course of his presidency, is not to seek confrontation. Far from it. Our purpose is to avoid misunderstanding and to create the necessary preconditions for change. And so, when we see aggression, we will call it aggression. When we see subversion, we will call it subversion. When we see repression, we will call it repression.

- Events in Poland, for example, cannot be ignored or explained away. The Polish people want to be their own master. Years of systematic tyranny cannot repress this desire, and neither will martial law. But in Poland today, truth must hide in corners.
- Nor can we simply turn our heads and look the other way as Soviet divisions brutalize an entire population in Afghanistan. The resistance of the Afghan people is a valiant saga of our times. We demean that valor if we do not recognize its source.
- And Soviet surrogates intervene in many countries, creating a new era of colonialism at the moment in history when peoples around the globe had lifted that burden from their backs. . . .

Strength

America's yearning for peace does not lead us to be hesitant in developing our strength or in using it when necessary. Indeed, clarity about the magnitude of the problems we face leads inevitably to a realistic appreciation of the importance of American strength. The strength of the free world imposes restraint, invites accommodation, and reassures those who would share in the creative work that is the wonderful consequence of liberty.

Strength means military forces to insure that no other nation can threaten us, our interests, or our friends. But when I speak of strength, I do not mean military power alone. To Americans, strength derives as well from a solid economic base and social vitality at home and with our partners. And, most fundamentally, the true wellspring of strength lies in America's moral commitment.

Military Strength

The bulwark of America's strength is military power for peace. The American people have never accepted weakness, nor hesitancy, nor abdication. We will not put our destiny into the hands of the ruthless. Americans today are emphatically united on the necessity of a strong defense. This year's defense budget will insure that the United States will help its friends and allies defend themselves—to make sure that peace is seen clearly by all to be the only feasible course in world affairs. . . .

Economic Strength

The engine of America's strength is a sound economy. . . . The United States, with its vast resources, can survive an era of economic strife and decay. But our moral commitment and our self-interest require us to use our technological and productive abilities to build lasting prosperity at home and to contribute to a sound economic situation abroad. . . .

Moral Strength

The bedrock of our strength is our moral and spiritual character. The sources of true strength lie deeper than economic or military power—in the dedication of a free people which knows it responsibility. America's institutions are those of freedom accessible to every person and of government as the accountable servant of the people. Equal opportunity; due process of law; open trial by jury; freedom of belief, speech, and assembly—our Bill of Rights, our guarantees of liberty and limited government—were hammered out in centuries of ordeal. Because we care about these human values for ourselves, so must we then be concerned, and legitimately so, with abuses of freedom, justice, and humanitarian principles beyond our borders. This is why we will speak and act for prisoners of conscience, against terrorism, . . . This is why we are anxious to participate in periodic reviews of the human rights performance of ourselves as well as others. We welcome scrutiny of our own system. We are not perfect, and we know it, but we have nothing to hide.

Our belief in liberty guides our policies here in the United Nations as elsewhere. Therefore, in this forum the United States will continue to insist upon fairness, balance, and truth. We take the debate on human rights seriously. We insist upon honesty in the use of language; we will point out inconsistencies, double standards, and lies. We will not compromise our commitment to truth. . . .

Progress

Perhaps the most common phrase spoken by the American people in our more than two centuries of national life has been: "You can't stop progress." Our people have always been imbued with the conviction that the future of a free people would be good.

America continues to offer that vision to the world. With that vision and with the freedom to act creatively, there is nothing that people of goodwill need fear.

I am not here to assert, however, that the way is easy, quick, or that the future is bound to be bright. There is a poem by Carl Sandburg in which a traveler asks the sphinx to speak and reveal the distilled wisdom of all the ages. The sphinx does speak. Its words are: "Don't expect too much."

That is good counsel for all of us here. It does not mean that great accomplishments are beyond our reach. We can help shape more constructive international relations and give our children a better chance at life. It does mean, however, that risk, pain, expense, and above all endurance are needed to bring those achievements into our grasp.

We must recognize the complex and vexing character of this world. We should not indulge ourselves in fantasies of perfection or unfulfillable plans or solutions gained by pressure. It is the responsibility of leaders not to feed the growing appetite for easy promises and grand assurances. The plain truth is this: We face the prospect of all too few decisive or dramatic breakthroughs; we face the necessity of dedicating our energies and creativity to a protracted struggle toward eventual success.

That is the approach of my country—because we see not only the necessity, but the possibility, of making important progress on a broad front.

The High Stakes of Civilization

After the development of nuclear weapons, new defense strategies had to be devised. Conventional weapons still exist, of course, and remain the primary implements of active war. But our experience with nuclear weapons is limited, and thus nuclear war is based on abstractions and potentials of "what might happen if. . . ." It is difficult to develop defense strategies if no one knows whether missile systems will actually function as they are intended. As more and more weapons are built and they become more complex, are they more prone to mechanical failure and, worse yet, failure in human judgment? There is a growing concern that nuclear proliferation will result in an eventual disaster—one that would prove fatal for the human race. Thus, there are those who would advocate complete disarmament, others a "freeze" in existing numbers with no further manufacturing of missiles, some a reduction of nuclear weapons and a commitment only to conventional conflict (nuclear pacifism). Many politicians and scientists subscribe to a defense theory called MAD—Mutual Assured Destruction. This theory maintains that if there exists a rough nuclear parity, then neither side will attack for fear of imminent and massive retaliation. In essence, the nuclear arsenals of each nation hold the corresponding populations "hostage." The following excerpts give voice to some of these arguments.

Nuclear Pacifism (1962)

H. STUART HUGHES

The trouble with the phrase "unilateral disarmament" is that it suggests an all-or-nothing stance. It seems to convey the impression that we are going to strip right down to our underwear shorts without enticing hesitations along the way. Scarcely any unilateralist would advocate this; such a position is rather that of the doctrinaire pacifists, with whom people like myself work in harmony on specific issues but with whom they differ on the wider question of the role of force in human affairs.

Unilateralism as I conceive it necessarily proceeds by stages—with pauses to give our potential adversaries the opportunity to respond in kind. Actually, the first moves might entail little risk as all. The main point is that *something* must be done right away to prove that we are in earnest about disarmament. Yet the logic of the unilateralist position lies ultimately in the complete renunciation of nuclear weapons. . . . In short, I believe that we and our allies should eventually restrict our defense to conventional weapons alone.

I well know the awful risks that such a decision would involve. Every conscientious unilateralist has spent countless hours of worry over the implications of what he recommends: he can never be sure that he is right. We face a choice of evils—a choice of risks. All we can say is that to us the risks involved in depriving our country of nuclear weapons loom less threat-

H. Stuart Hughes, excerpted from *An Approach to Peace*, pp. 71–73, 75–80, 87. Copyright © 1962 H. Stuart Hughes. Reprinted by permission of Atheneum Publishers, a division of Macmillan, Inc.

eningly than the dangers of going on with the arms race; we agree with Sir Charles Snow that if matters continue on their present course, there is almost a mathematical certainty that some of the bombs or missiles will sooner or later go off. In this world of ghastly insecurity, we would rather take our chances on nuclear defenselessness and trust to the more primitive devices by which free men in earlier ages have safeguarded their liberty. That is what next needs to be explained.

As this point of the argument people who think as I do are usually confronted with the now classic question, "Would you rather be red than dead?" I object strongly to such a formulation: it is one chosen by our adversaries to put us in the worst possible light; it eliminates all intermediate possibilities and shades of meaning. . . . If our adversaries want to phrase the issue that way, I see no alternative to accepting the challenge: the only possible answer is a thunderous "Yes." Certainly I would rather be red than dead—in the sense that I choose life over senseless slaughter. But should there be a chance of a meaningful death, then I might make the other choice. This is why I do not think an affirmative answer to this crude and primitive question is the same thing as "surrender."

Today a handful of men are indeed free to choose, in that they hold the power of decision over whether or not to push the fatal button. But they have only a vague idea of what will be the consequences of their act—even though they must be aware that these will extend far, far beyond anything they can possibly intend or imagine. War in this new sense has grown beyond the proportions of humanity. The problem for those of us who do not renounce force entirely is to return it to a human scale.

Does this mean "surrender"? Does it mean "to invite the conquest of the world" or to offer ourselves "on a platter" to our putative enemies? I do not think so. I do not believe that a unilateral American renunciation of thermonuclear deterrence would make nearly so much of a difference as most of my countrymen suppose. It has yet to be proved that our "deterrent" has deterred anybody from anything. I do not think it has been the threat of thermonuclear retaliation that has kept the Soviet Union out of Western Europe. What has given the Russians second thoughts about occupying West Germany or France has been the conviction that they would find themselves most unwelcome there.

The point, then, is to make military occupation too expensive a matter--both physically and morally—to be worthwhile for the attacker.

The prime need is to develop a pattern of defense by conventional weapons alone that would be "credible" (to us another arms control phrase) both to ourselves and to our potential enemies. . . . My proposal would involve a drastic reduction of our country's present overseas commitments. It would mean the liquidation of a number of our alliances. For it implies that we would come to the defense of *those nations alone which had sufficient social and political solidity* to organize and support a territorial-militia or guerrilla-resistance type of defense—that is, those nations which, without necessarily conforming to *our* definition of democracy, were based on a bond of trust between government and people strong enough to hold out against trials and temptations of unprecedented magnitude.

·   ·   ·

If this "modest proposal" has far-reaching implication for our present alliance system, it has still wider consequences for our society at home. I am under no illusions as to the radical—indeed, rethinking of nearly all the assumptions, stated or tacit, of our current policy. In terms of the "sacrifices" that our leaders so often and so hollowly call on us to make, what I am proposing demands far more individual dedication than a mere raising of taxes or contraction of consumer goods—for it implies that every able-bodied American will have to equip himself to serve as a citizen-soldier in the old-fashioned sense of the term. It means something much more strenuous than the rather perfunctory part-time military training that only a small minority of young Americans are currently receiving. It entails a tangible and personal commitment to an ideal—not just passive assent to an abstract call to greatness. It means that every American will be obliged to consider war as something close at hand, rather than as an indistinct menace whose very magnitude and remoteness make for escapism or fatalistic acceptance or moral callousness; he will need to decide when and how and for what concrete and visible loyalties he is willing to lay down his life.

That is what I mean by returning war to a human scale. The militia or guerrilla type of defense I am proposing would close the gap between rhetoric and actuality in our national behavior. It would constitute a policy that both our allies and our potential enemies could understand and act on. . . . It would restore the honored practice of resistance to oppression on the part of voluntary collectives and spontaneous self-sustaining groups. This tradition in earlier centuries ranked as the chief support of Western liberty. . . .

If the colonial wars of liberation over the past decade and a half have taught us nothing else, they have at least demonstrated that in the contemporary world a superiority in arms does not necessarily mean final victory. First in Indochina, then in Algeria, small bodies of men, poorly armed but familiar with the countryside and supported by the local population, have tied up for years the regular army of a major power. The native people have known what they were fighting for; the Europeans have been disoriented, far from home, and uncertain of their cause. The relevance of this example for a Western democracy facing Communist "conquest" should be apparent to all. It is a lesson that we Americans need to ponder.

·   ·   ·

The proposal I have made for the non-nuclear defense of our own country and our allies will, I hope, never have to be applied. I think of it as a final deterrent to aggression—a real deterrent, as opposed to the abstract deterrent of our hydrogen bombs, which is too gruesome to be fully credible.

Why Strategic Superiority Matters (1983)

ROBERT JASTROW

I left nuclear research in 1958 when I joined NASA. I did not think much about it, or about nuclear bombs, for the next twenty years until, three years ago, I happened to come across an . . . article on nuclear weapons and SALT by Daniel Patrick Moynihan. . . . In reading Senator Moynihan's article, I became aware for the first time that the policies of the United States for protecting its citizens from destruction are based on a flawed premise.

The premise is that the Soviet Union will be deterred from a surprise nuclear attack on the United States by the knowledge that such an attack would trigger a devastating American counterattack. And, of course, *we* are deterred from an attack on the USSR by the knowledge that the Soviets maintain a similar arsenal. The result is a nuclear standoff, and world peace.

In other words, each side holds the other side's civilian population as hostages. Holding hostages, and threatening their massacre, are time-honored methods for achieving one's objectives in war, but they have never been suggested before as a means of keeping the peace. The proposal of mass exchange of hostages is a simple but brilliant strategy conceived by American intellectuals who were trying to figure out a solution to a terrible problem: how does the U.S. protect itself from nuclear destruction in an age in which missiles vault the oceans and the concept of Fortress America no longer has meaning?

The academicians who thought up this idea called it Mutual Assured Destruction, or sometimes simply MAD. It makes very good sense, as you would expect, since the policy was formulated by some of the most brilliant scientists and academicians who have ever served in an advisory capacity to our government. The trouble is that MAD is a theory, and like all theories, it depends on an assumption. This assumption has turned out to be false.

The assumption behind the theory of Mutual Assured Destruction is that both the United States and the USSR will freely offer up their populations for massacre. But this requires that each country give up all attempts to defend its own people. In other words, the two countries must agree that neither will have a civil-defense program, and neither side will try to shoot down the other side's missiles. . . .

Actually, MAD is a logical response to the problem of nuclear war, and it could have worked, *if* the Russians had been reasonable and seen matters

Reprinted from Robert Jastrow, "Why Nuclear Superiority Matters," *Commentary*, Vol. 75, no. 3 (March, 1983), pp. 27–28, 31–32, by permission; all rights reserved.

our way—if they had been willing to offer up their people as hostages, just as we have done. But the Soviet Union saw things differently.

It is now clear—in fact it has been clear for a decade—that while for many years the American government adopted the strategy of Mutual Assured Destruction proposed by our scientists and academicians, the Soviet government rejected it. The USSR undertook to do exactly what our strategists say it is supposed not to do: it implemented large programs for defending its citizens from nuclear attack, for shooting down American missiles, and for fighting and winning a nuclear war. The result, as Senator Moynihan has said, is "a policy in ruins," and the greatest peril our nation has faced in its 200-year history.

In the course of time, technology will improve the accuracy of our submarine-launched nuclear missiles to the point where they will have a hard-target "kill" capability, and the American deterrent will be restored. According to present estimates, that should happen by the end of the 1980's. The intervening four to five years will be, as Dr. Kissinger has said, "a period of vulnerability such as we have not experienced since the early days of the Republic."

If the nuclear-freeze movement is successful, the period of vulnerability will be extended into the 1990's. Assuming that does not happen, how will the Russians make use of the four or five years of nuclear superiority they will still enjoy?

The Persian Gulf is the most likely target of a Soviet move. Imagine a Soviet-instigated outbreak of violence in Saudi Arabia with American businessmen taken hostage, and a pro-Soviet regime installed, backed by Russian guns and Cuban mercenaries. With a substantial part of the oil flow to Western Europe under Soviet control, and the Middle East in upheaval, the United States will be tempted to intervene with conventional forces. If the Soviets respond by sending in their own troops, and conventional war breaks out, we cannot prevail. The USSR has constructed five airfields in southern Afghanistan, bringing the Persian Gulf within range of its fighter aircraft. The Soviet navy heavily outnumbers the American navy in surface ships and attack submarines. As a consequence, we will probably not be able to maintain our supply lines to the Gulf and the Mediterranean and simultaneously protect our sea lanes in Atlantic and Asian waters. Defeat will be almost certain.

Could we threaten to escalate to the nuclear level? Only this threat could hope to save us from defeat in the Persian Gulf. But now the Soviet superiority in nuclear weapons becomes the decisive factor. The United States has gone on a nuclear alert three times in the past—in 1948 in the Berlin crisis, in 1962 in the Cuban missile crisis, and in 1973 when the Russians threatened to intervene in the war between Egypt and Israel. We prevailed in each confrontation. In the first two cases we had strategic superiority, and in the third a rough parity. Today, this is no longer true. We would not dare to threaten the use of our nuclear weapons, because of the circumstances I have described.

What about a Soviet move into Western Europe? In Europe, the superiority of conventional Soviet forces would be overwhelming: approximately 45,000 tanks on the Soviet side against 17,000 in NATO; a Soviet superiority of 2 to 1 in aircraft, 2 to 1 in artillery, and 3 to 1 in missile launchers. NATO forces would not be able to withstand a massive Soviet thrust into Western Europe.

But a direct attack would not be necessary. Threats, accompanied by a general escalation of tension, would probably suffice to bring all of Western Europe under Soviet hegemony. Alexander Solzhenitsyn has described how it would happen:

> At one time there was no comparison between the strength of the USSR and yours. Then it became equal—Perhaps today it is just greater than balance, but soon it will be two to one. Then three to one. Finally it will be five to one. . . . With such a nuclear superiority it will be possible to block the use of your weapons, and on some unlucky morning they will declare: "Attention. We're marching our troops to Europe, and if you make a move, we will annihilate you." And this ratio of three to one, of five to one, will have its effect: you will not make a move.

Twenty years ago, or even ten years ago, the American nuclear arsenal would have been sufficient to deter a Soviet attack on Western Europe, but that is no longer the case.

When will the Russians make their move? Leonid Brezhnev supplied the timetable a few years ago, in a speech to Communist leaders in Prague:

> We are achieving with detente what our predecessors have been unable to achieve using the fist. . . . By 1985 . . . we will have achieved most of our objectives in Western Europe. . . . Come 1985, we will be able to extend our will wherever we need to. . . .

And so we finally see why strategic superiority matters. We see how it is that, as Senator Moynihan has said, he who can blow the world up three times has more power than he who can blow it up only twice.

"Pacem in Terris" (1963)

POPE JOHN XXIII

The papacy, which played such an important role in the Middle Ages, declined in international authority after the Protestant Reformation. However, with the emergence of twentieth-century leaders such as John XXIII, Paul VI, and John Paul II, the papacy has played an important role in international affairs apart from the 800 million Catholics it represents. For example, John Paul II (1978–   ) was a formidable figure in defying Soviet

Pope John XXIII, *Pacem in Terris* (New York: Paulist Press, 1963), pp. 38–40.

threats to invade his native Poland in 1980; his knowledge of languages and frequent travel have made him a vital force, especially in Third World countries. The encyclical presented below, translated as "Peace on Earth," was issued by Pope John XXIII in 1963. It speaks to the issue of nuclear arms escalation and is indicative of the active papacy of the late twentieth century.

It is with deep sorrow that We note the enormous stocks of armaments that have been and still are being made in more economically developed countries, with a vast outlay of intellectual and economic resources. And so it happens that, while the people of these countries are loaded with heavy burdens, other countries as a result are deprived of the collaboration they need in order to make economic and social progress.

The production of arms is allegedly justified on the grounds that in present-day conditions peace cannot be preserved without an equal balance of armaments. And so, if one country increases its armaments, others feel the need to do the same; and if one country is equipped with nuclear weapons, other countries must produce their own, equally destructive.

Consequently, people live in constant fear lest the storm that every moment threatens should break upon them with dreadful violence. And with good reason, for the arms of war are ready at hand. Even though it is difficult to believe that anyone would deliberately take the responsibility for the appalling destruction and sorrow that war would bring in its train, it cannot be denied that the conflagration may be set off by some unexpected and obscure event. And one must bear in mind that, even though the monstrous power of modern weapons acts as a deterrent, it is to be feared that the mere continuance of nuclear tests, undertaken with war in mind, will prove a serious hazard for life on earth.

Justice, then, right reason and humanity urgently demand that the arms race should cease; that the stockpiles which exist in various countries should be reduced equally and simultaneously by the parties concerned; that nuclear weapons should be banned; and that a general agreement should eventually be reached about progressive disarmament and an effective method of control. In the words of Pius XII, Our Predecessor of happy memory: *The calamity of a world war, with the economic and social ruin and the moral excesses and dissolution that accompany it, must not be permitted to envelop the human race for a third time.*

All must realize that there is no hope of putting an end to the building up of armaments, nor of reducing the present stocks, nor, still less, of abolishing them altogether, unless the process is complete and thorough and unless it proceeds from inner convictions: unless, that is, everyone sincerely cooperates to banish the fear and anxious expectation of war with which men are oppressed. If this is to come about, the fundamental principle on which our present peace depends must be replaced by another, which declares that the true and solid peace of nations consists not in equality of arms but in mutual trust alone. We believe that this can be brought to pass, and We consider that it is something which reason requires, that it is eminently desirable in itself and that it will prove to be the source of many benefits.

In the first place, it is an objective demanded by reason. There can be, or at least there should be, no doubt that relations between States, as between individuals, should be regulated not by the force of arms but by the light of reason, by the rule, that is, of truth, of justice and of active and sincere cooperation.

Secondly, We say that it is an objective earnestly to be desired in itself. Is there anyone who does not ardently yearn to see war banished, to see peace preserved and daily more firmly established?

And finally, it is an objective which will be a fruitful source of many benefits, for its advantages will be felt everywhere, by individuals, by families, by nations, by the whole human family. The warning of Pius XII still rings in our ears: *Nothing is lost by peace; everything may be lost by war.*

SECTION III: REFLECTIONS ON HUMANITY IN THE TWENTIETH CENTURY

A Portrait of Albert Einstein: "As Long As There Will Be Man, There Will Be Wars"

PHILLIPPE HALSMAN

One of the most fertile and influential scientific minds in history belonged to Albert Einstein. Besides his contributions to the field of physics, Einstein was also a great humanist who believed in man's ability to change society and progress toward international cooperation. It is ironic that it was Einstein who brought the destructive potential of nuclear energy to the attention of President Roosevelt in 1939. In this excerpt, Phillippe Halsman, one of the most famous photographers of distinguished people, describes his meeting with Einstein in 1947.

I admired Albert Einstein more than anyone I ever photographed, not only as the genius who singlehandedly had changed the foundation of modern physics, but even more as a rare and idealistic human being.

Personally, I owed him an immense debt of gratitude. After the fall of France, it was through his personal intervention that my name was added

Phillippe Halsman, *Halsman Sight and Insight* (Garden City, N.Y.: Doubleday, 1972), p. 8.

to the list of artists and scientists who, in danger of being captured by the Nazis, were given emergency visas to the United States.

After my miraculous rescue I went to Princeton to thank Einstein and I remember vividly my first impression. Instead of a frail scientist I saw a deep-chested man with a resonant voice and a hearty laugh. The long hair, which in some photographs gave him the look of an old woman, framed his marvellous face with a kind of leonine mane. He wore slacks, a grey sweater with a fountain pen stuck in its collar, black leather shoes, and no socks.

On my third visit I had the courage to ask him why he did not wear any socks. His secretary, Miss Dukas, who overheard me, said, "The professor never wears socks. Even when he was invited by Mr. Roosevelt to the White House, he did not wear any socks." I looked with surprise at Professor Einstein.

He smiled and said, "When I was young I found out that the big toe always ends up by making a hole in the sock. So I stopped wearing socks." As slight as this remark was, it made an indelible impression on me. This detail seemed symbolic of Einstein's absolute and total independence of thought. It was this independence that gave him the courage when he was an unknown twenty-six-year-old patent clerk to publish a scientific paper which overthrew all the axioms held sacrosanct by the greatest physicists of his time.

The question of how to capture the essence of such a man in a portrait filled me with apprehension. Finally, in 1947, I had the courage to bring on one of my visits my Halsman camera and a few floodlights. After tea, I asked for permission to set up my lights in Einstein's study. The professor sat down and started peacefully working on his mathematical calculations. I took a few pictures. Ordinarily, Einstein did not like photographers, whom he called *Lichtaffen* (light monkeys). But he cooperated because I was his guest and, after all, he had helped to rescue me.

Suddenly, looking into my camera, he started talking. He spoke about his despair that his formula $E = mc^2$ and his letter to President Roosevelt had made the atomic bomb possible, that his scientific search had resulted in the death of so many human beings. "Have you read," he asked, "that powerful voices in the United States are demanding that the bombs be dropped on Russia now, before the Russians have the time to perfect their own?" With my entire being I felt how much this infinitely good and compassionate man was suffering from the knowledge that he had helped to put in the hands of politicians a monstrous weapon of devastation and death.

He grew silent. His eyes had a look of immense sadness. There was a question and a reproach in them.

The spell of this moment almost paralysed me. Then, with an effort, I released the shutter of my camera. Einstein looked up, and I asked him, "So you don't believe that there will ever be peace?"

"No," he answered, "as long as there will be man, there will be wars."

The Doctrine of the Sword

MAHATMA GANDHI

When one thinks of power, authority, influence, and the forces that promote change in society, violence and coercion are often inevitable factors in the equation. But nonviolent resistance has been a proven source of power. Mahatma Gandhi (1869–1948) and Martin Luther King, Jr. (1929–1968) each practiced it as a creed essential to the success of a free India in 1948 and an integrated America in 1968. It is indeed ironic that both men were shot to death by assassins. The first selection contains excerpts from the writings of Mahatma Gandhi. They give the essence of his philosophy of nonviolence. The second selection by Mulford Sibley, a political scientist, contends that pacifism need not require surrender or martyrdom, but is the basis for civilized progress and justice in the world.

I do believe that, where there is only a choice between cowardice and violence, I would advise violence. Thus when my eldest son asked me what he should have done, had he been present when I was almost fatally assaulted in 1908, whether he should have run away and seen me killed or whether he should have used his physical force which he could and wanted to use, and defended me, I told him that it was his duty to defend me even by using violence. Hence it was that I took part in the Boer War, the so-called Zulu Rebellion and the late war [World War I]. Hence also do I advocate training in arms for those who believe in the method of violence. I would rather have India resort to arms in order to defend her honour than that she should, in a cowardly manner, become or remain a helpless witness to her own dishonour.

But I believe that non-violence is infinitely superior to violence, forgiveness is more manly than punishment. Forgiveness adorns a soldier. But abstinence is forgiveness only when there is the power to punish; it is meaningless when it pretends to proceed from a helpless creature . . . But I do not believe India to be helpless. I do not believe myself to be a helpless creature. Only I want to use India's and my strength for a better purpose.

Let me not be misunderstood. Strength does not come from physical capacity. It comes from an indomitable will . . . I am not a visionary. I claim to be a practical idealist. The religion of non-violence is not meant merely for the *rishis* [holy men] and saints. It is meant for the common people as well. *Non-violence* is the law of our species as violence is the law of the brute. The spirit lies dormant in the brute, and he knows no law but that of physical might. The dignity of man requires obedience to a higher law—to the strength of the spirit.

Ronald Duncan, ed., *Selected Writings of Mahatma Gandhi* (London: Faber & Faber, Ltd., 1951), pp. 53–54, 56, 58, 60, 66. Reprinted by permission of the Navajaivan Trust.

I have therefore ventured to place before India the ancient law of self-sacrifice. . . . The *rishis,* who discovered the law of non-violence in the midst of violence, were greater geniuses than Newton. They were themselves greater warriors than Wellington. Having themselves known the use of arms, they realized their uselessness, and taught a weary world that its salvation lay not through violence but through non-violence.

Non-violence in its dynamic condition means conscious suffering. It does not mean meek submission to the will of the evil-doer, but it means the pitting of one's whole soul against the will of the tyrant. Working under this law of our being, it is possible for a single individual to defy the whole might of an unjust empire to save his honour, his religion, his soul, and lay the foundation for that empire's fall or its regeneration. . . .

The next point, that of *ahimsa* [non-violence], is more abstruse. My conception of *ahimsa* impels me always to dissociate myself from almost every one of the activities I am engaged in. My soul refuses to be satisfied so long as it is a helpless witness of a single wrong or a single misery. But it is not possible for me—a weak, frail, miserable being—to mend every wrong or to hold myself free of blame for all the wrong I see. The spirit in me pulls one way, the flesh in me pulls in the opposite direction. There is freedom from the action of these two forces, but that freedom is attainable only by slow and painful stages. I can attain freedom not by a mechanical refusal to act, but only by intelligent action in a detached manner. This struggle resolves itself into an incessant crucifixion of the flesh so that the spirit may become entirely free. . . .

I have not the capacity for preaching universal non-violence to the country. I preach, therefore, non-violence restricted strictly to the purpose of winning our freedom [India's freedom from British rule] and therefore perhaps for preaching the regulation of international relations by non-violent means. But my incapacity must not be mistaken for that of the doctrine of non-violence. I see it with my intellect in all its effulgence. My heart grasps it. But I have not yet the attainments of preaching universal non-violence with effect. I am not advanced enough for the great task. I have yet anger within me, I have yet [a] duality in me. I can regulate my passions, I keep them under subjection, but before I can preach universal non-violence with effect, I must be wholly free from passions. I must be wholly incapable of sin. Let the revolutionary pray with and for me that I may soon become that. But meanwhile let him take with me the one step to it which I see as clearly as daylight, i.e. to win India's freedom with strictly non-violent means. And then you and I shall have a disciplined, intelligent educated police force that would keep order within and fight raiders from without, if by that time I or someone else does not show a better way of dealing with either. . . .

Not to believe in the possibility of permanent peace is to disbelieve in godliness of human nature. Methods hitherto adopted have failed because rock-bottom sincerity on the part of those who have striven has been lacking. Not that they have realized this lack. Peace is unattainable by part performance of conditions, even as chemical combination is impossible without complete fulfilment of conditions of attainment thereof. If recognized leaders of mankind who have control over engines of destruction were wholly to renounce their use with full knowledge of implications, permanent peace can be obtained. This is clearly impossible without the great powers of the earth renouncing their imperialistic designs. This again seems impossible without these great nations ceasing to believe in soul-destroying competition and to desire to multiply wants and therefore increase their material possessions. It is my conviction that the root of the evil is want of a living faith in a living God. It is a first-class human tragedy that peoples of the earth who claim to believe in the message of Jesus whom they describe as the Prince of Peace show little of that belief in actual practice. It is painful to see sincere Christians . . . limiting the scope of Jesus's message to select individuals. I have been taught from my childhood, and I have tested the truth by experience, that primary virtues of mankind are possible of cultivation by the meanest of the human species. It is this undoubted universal possibility that distinguishes the human from the rest of God's creation. If even one great nation were unconditionally to perform the supreme act of renunciation, many of us would see in our lifetime visible peace established on earth.

The Quiet Battle (1963)

MULFORD Q. SIBLEY

It is difficult to see how anyone with a concern for morality can possibly defend modern war and policies based on its threat. From the viewpoint of the morality of the means—and accepting the fact that these are important distinctions between their economic and political systems—there would seem to be little difference between Communism and Western Democracy in practice: both of them resort to threats of mass annihilation and both seem to be willing to shatter the whole structure of civilized society in the name of some abstraction which neither can define with precision. Each claims it is "defending" itself when it resorts to the most horrible preparations for mass slaughter. How any civilized human beings can support either side, in view of these considerations, is difficult to understand. If the world does somehow survive, men in a future generation will look back to our time with both amazement and loathing: amazement that so many millions, East and West, tamely submitted themselves to be slaughtered; loathing at the rank hypocrisy involved in the whole process, with each side proclaiming its devotion to the highest civilized values. Just as we inquire today how millions of Germans could have submitted their fates to the commands of an immoral dictatorship, so will our descendants ask how millions of human beings professing "Christian" moral ideals could with scarcely a murmur build up stockpiles of bacteria, H-bombs, and missiles to kill their fellow men and women.

. . .

What else can we do? It is at this point that the advocate of non-violent power has most to say. For he is asserting, essentially, that the development of an organized movement against both war and invasion, together with widespread commitment to completely unarmed defense, would be most likely to accomplish such widely proclaimed objectives as the frustration of invasion and defense of basic freedoms.

Before turning to the implication of non-violence for war and invasion, it might be well to point out that the fear of invasion is in some measure a groundless one, particularly insofar as it refers to the possibility of the Soviet Union or China occupying the United States or the United States invading the Soviet Union or China. For the Soviet Union to "control" the vast territory of the United States would be a very difficult task, even without military or formally organized non-violent resistance. The center of control would be remote from those to be controlled. Even today the Soviet Union has difficulties with its Eastern European satellites who are relatively close to it and who, moreover, resemble it in many ways. Any attempted invasion of the United States with the purpose of control would magnify these difficulties enormously. As Ambassador Kennan puts it, Americans seem not to recognize how hard it is to operate "far-flung lines of power" or to see that there are definite "limits to the effective radius of political power from any center in the world." . . .

We should never forget, of course, that a policy of non-violent resistance to invasion would entail a price. Not only would there have to be rigorous training and discipline beforehand but there would and could be no guarantee of success or of immunity from suffering. At a minimum, the scheme would involve: a table of alternative leadership, so that leaders hanged or imprisoned would automatically be succeeded by their understudies; thousands of hard-core Satyagrahis [practioners of non-violence] who would be in the forefront of non-cooperation and civil disobedience campaigns; thorough preparation for psychological resistance, so that the general population would respect the persons of the invaders while refusing, in concert, to cooperate with their acts; and careful planning for food supplies. Unarmed resistance, as a matter of fact, requires at least as much planning as military defense.

Whatever the practical advantages of non-violent opposition . . . the moral superiority of non-violence consists in the fact that while under it we might have to suffer injustice (disruption of ordinary ways of life, physical injury, torture, or even death), we do not commit it (we do not deliberately kill, we confine coercion to that which does not seriously injure, and we constantly seek avenues for negotiation). And in the last analysis the advocate of non-violent resistance believes, with Socrates, that it is always better to suffer injustice than to commit it. . . .

It is not certain that civilization will not use its violent instruments to destroy its non-violent achievements and frustrate its aspirations. In the name of protecting the values of non-violent ends, elaborate and sensitive social organization and technology may be employed to defeat those ends through the use of violence as means. If this is not to be the outcome of our contemporary madness, it will be because men discover in time that they can neither attain nor defend the ends of non-violence and democracy by the methods of violent power: any apparent success is more than counterbalanced by the evil ends set up by the means.

Once they make this discovery, human beings will turn to the doctrine of non-violence and to the discipline and practice of non-violent resistance. Without regarding non-violent resistance as the only key to an ideal society, they will see in it, nevertheless, a form of power somewhat compatible with the goals they profess. Their means will have been brought measurably into harmony with their ends; and they will find that in repudiating the immorality of killing they will also have discovered a far more useful method than violence for the attainment of justice.

South African Apartheid (1983)

ARCHBISHOP DESMOND TUTU

One of the most influential factors in Western Civilization has been racism. It has been used to justify imperialism and to inspire genocide. The 20th century has indeed seen its share of racism at the hands of Adolf Hitler, the Ku Klux Klan and other white supremicist groups. Still, there have been significant strides to correct the injustices of the past. The civil rights movement in the United States during the mid-1960's, as well as affirmative action programs and Supreme Court decisions, give evidence to a continuing effort to achieve racial equality. Yet the problem still persists. South Africa remains a bastion of racial segregation in its advocacy of apartheid—or enforced, legal segregation.

One of the most outspoken critics of this policy is South African Archbishop Desmond Tutu. In the following excerpt, he discusses the South African policy of "population removal." Tutu argues that the Black majority are barred from living in the affluent cities and are forced into "homelands" or townships where they provide an inexpensive labor force to be exploited by the White minority. By focusing world opinion on the abuses of Anglo-Boer rule, Tutu hopes to elicit sanctions and other restrictive measures from the world community.

Desmond Tutu, *Hope and Suffering: Sermons and Speeches* (Grand Rapids, Mich.: William B. Eerdmans Publishing Company, 1984), pp. 90–91, 95 –102. Copyright © 1983 by Desmond Tutu. Reprinted by permission of Desmond Tutu.

1948 and After

When the [South African] Nationalists came to power in 1948 they resur-rected their ideal of the Boer republics of the late nineteenth century and early twentieth century. They developed discriminatory legislation that was to hand, and initiated their own amazing creativity—the Race Classifica-tion, the Job Reservation, Mixed Marriages, Immortality and other racist laws . . . Basically, the South African crisis is one that hinges on political power, for it is this, if you have it, which commands access to other kinds of power—economic well-being, social amenities and facilities. That is why it is such a charade to talk about improving the quality of life of Blacks in their own areas, in talking about the so-called changes which have been wrought in the matter of sport, the creation of international hotels and restaurants, in the removal of discriminatory signs. It is a charade because no matter how wonderful the improvements in the Black person's lot may be (and I don't doubt that there will be very significant improvements) these will always be mere concessions that are always at risk, and vulnerable because they depend on the whim of those who have political power. When they deem it convenient for themselves they will withhold these privileges and when they think otherwise they will dole them out lavishly, or not, from their bounty.

Basically it is a question of how you can maintain political power in the hands of a White Oligarchy. Perhaps there is a preliminary stage—how do you, as a White minority outnumbered five to one, survive in a continent that has on the whole shown itself hostile to White presence? And the answer which the imperialistic Europeans decided upon with almost un-canny unanimity was to subjugate the native peoples and to retain most power in White hands. And so Africa in particular, but much of the so-called Third World in general, found itself ruled by these White for-eigners. In time most of this colonial empire came to throw off the yoke of oppression. Southern Africa has been tardy in joining the liberation move-ment, but the waves of freedom have now washed away most White minor-ity rule even in this sub-continent, the latest to fall being that in Zimbabwe, where we had famous last words from Mr. Ian Smith [former Prime Minis-ter of Rhodesia (Zimbabwe)], such as that it would not happen during his lifetime or only over his dead body and not in a thousand years.

During our period it has been quite clear that the Whites were deter-mined to keep political power in their hands exclusively. It did not strike them as at all odd (at least, the majority of them) that the way they were going about things was totally at variance with the accepted meaning of that democracy whose virtues they extolled so much, as they vilified Commu-nism and Marxism.

On accession to power the Nationalist Party made no bones about their determination to maintain White domination with policies that were nakedly racist. They had stepped into the corridors of political power on the waves of White apprehension of the so-called Black peril . . . and they did not conceal this from anybody. . . .

And the Total Strategy is a developing one. Some very specially blessed Blacks (urban Blacks) will also be part of this "gravy train." Their quality of life will be significantly enhanced, their children are likely to go to good White schools, they will get very good salaries, etc. etc., and they will be co-opted into the system as a Black middle class to be a buffer between the *have*-Whites and the *have-not*-Blacks, and being so greatly privileged they will be supporters of the status quo such as you cannot ever hope to find anywhere. That is the new strategy of the Nationalist Government. The bitter pill is very significantly coated with sugar. Those who will belong to this core economy and society will be numerically insignificant, and will pose hardly any threat to the power-wielding White group. But what of the rest—the hapless *hoi polloi?* They will be, and are being, relegated to the outer darkness, the limbo of the forgotten. They must get out . . . Nobody repudiated Mr. Mulder when he pointed out in Parliament that the logical conclusion of apartheid was that there would be no Black South Africans.

And to get to that conclusion, they have with very little compunction moved nearly two million Blacks. They have moved them often from places where they had reasonably adequate housing, where they were able to work—some in the informal sector, as casual labourers, within walking or reasonable distance of their places of work. They have moved them, dumped them as if they were potatoes, in largely inhospitable areas, often with no alternative accommodation. . . .

People are starving in most of these resettlement camps. I know, for I have seen it. They are starving not because of an accident or a misfortune. No, they are starving because of deliberate Government policy made in the name of White Christian civilization. They are starving; a little girl can tell you that when they can't borrow food, they drink water to fill their stomachs. This is the solution the Nationalists have decided upon. Many can't work, not because they won't work but because there is no work available. So they sit listlessly while we reap the benefits of a soaring gold price and our boom, which makes us want to import skilled labour from overseas. They are there as a reservoir, deliberately created, of cheap labour. When Black labour is needed, the laws forced Blacks into town when they were often well-to-do farmers. They had to become wage earners in order to pay the taxes levied on them. Now they are not really wanted, so they are endorsed out. There are probably two million Blacks unemployed and another million likely to lose their jobs, but they are out of sight and so are out of mind. . . .

The Cost

The cost in terms of human suffering is incalculable. Undernourishment, starvation and malnutrition have serious consequences in growing children. They may suffer irreversible brain damage . . . But how do we compute the cost in the legacy of bitterness, anger, frustration and indeed hatred which we are leaving behind for our children? In the body of this paper I have described many things that have happened to us Blacks in this country during the several decades of our oppression and exploitation and deprivation. It is, I believe, a miracle of God's grace that Blacks still talk to Whites, to any Whites. It is a miracle of God's grace that Blacks still say that we want a non-racial South Africa for all of us, Black and White together. It is a miracle of God's grace that Blacks can still say they are committed to a ministry of justice and reconciliation and that they want to avert the blood-bath which seems more and more inevitable as we see little bending and give on the crucial issue of power-sharing. We are told that the Afrikaners [White, South African minority of Dutch extraction] have found it very difficult to forgive, certainly difficult to forget what the British did to them in the concentration camps. I want to say that Blacks are going to find it difficult, very difficult, to forgive, certainly difficult to forget what Whites have done and are doing to us in this matter of population removals.

All Blacks live in a constant state of uncertainty. Even I, a bishop in the Church of God and General Secretary of the South African Council of Churches, have no security. The township manager could in his wisdom decide that my continued presence in Soweto [impoverished black suburb of Johannesburg] was detrimental to its good ordering and peace, and by the stroke of his pen would withdraw my permission to reside there, just like that. We each have such a sword of Damocles hanging over our heads. I don't suppose many Whites know this or, if they do, care too much about it. . . .

What the Church Can Do

The solutions are both long-term and short-term. The short-term strategy is to oppose all removals. We suggest that representations are made to the authorities to persuade them to desist forthwith. If we know about any removals likely to happen then let us do all we can to oppose them. If all our efforts to dissuade the authorities fail, then we should be there, physically present as the witnessing and caring Church. We must use all non-violent methods to hinder the act of demolition.

We should support those in resettlement camps, providing them with as much relief that they will need as possible—food, blankets, etc. And the Church should help to rehabilitate these shocked persons by being a serving Church, helping to develop a community spirit and helping the people help themselves. . . .

In the long term, the solution must be political. There are not two ways about it. Either there is going to be power-sharing or there is not. If not, then we must give up hope of a peaceful settlement in South Africa. If the Government is determined to go ahead with its Balkanization of South Africa on ethnic lines, and depriving Blacks of their South African citizenship, then we have had it, the ghastly alternative will be upon us. Population removals must stop immediately if we are to be able to work for a new kind of South Africa, and the Church should be in the forefront to prepare all of us for this new South Africa.

There is still a chance, but if we let it slip then it will be gone for ever. Neither the most sophisticated arsenal nor the best army or police force will give White South Africa true security, for that will come and come automatically when all of us, Black and White, know we count as of equal worth in the land of our birth, which we love with a passionate love. Please God, we pray you, let them hear us, let them hear us before it is too late.

White South Africa, please know that you are deluding yourselves, or you are allowing yourselves to be deluded, if you think that the present ordering of our society can continue. Blacks will be free whatever you do or don't do. That is not in question. Don't let the *when* and the *how* be in doubt. Don't delay our freedom, which is your freedom as well, for freedom is indivisible. Let it be now, and let it be reasonably peaceful. . . .

Poverty and Mercy

DOROTHY DAY

One of the most widespread problems of the twentieth century is not modern at all. Poverty has been a motivating force for revolution and historical change for centuries. Yet in the modern world, because of technological advances in communication, the plight of the poor can be revealed with greater accuracy and less abstraction. Class divisions have always been a part of individual societies, but now world divisions have become more evident. The wealth of "First World" countries, such as the United States, Great Britain, and France, are more readily compared to the developing "Third World" nations in Latin America and Africa. Relief organizations, such as the Peace Corps, "Save the Children," and CARE have struggled with international poverty for years. Independent support has also come from popular rock musicians and entertainers who have garnered funds through "Live Aid" concerts to relieve Ethiopian famine victims and to protest South African apartheid policy. Still, true progress in this sphere does not come from "flash" awareness, but rather through a long-term commitment to helping others on an individual basis.

One of the most influential advocates of social reform in the twentieth century was Dorothy Day (1897–1980). A founder of the Catholic Worker movement in 1936, Day established over fifty Houses of Hospitality and farming communes across the United States where the hungry are fed and the homeless welcomed. She espoused a life of voluntary poverty and for years administered to the destitute on Manhattan's Lower East

Robert Ellsberg, ed., *By Little and By Little: The Selected Writings of Dorothy Day* (New York: Alfred A. Knopf, 1983), pp. 93–94, 109–111.

Side, working "little by little" to restore their dignity and self-respect. A self-proclaimed anarchist and pacifist, Dorothy Day offers in her writings an ecumenical solution to a world problem.

"And There Remained Only the Very Poor" (1940)

[The above quotation] were the words contained in a news account of the evacuation of Paris. But they apply to New York in the summer. The poor cannot get away. There is always a residue of the destitute which remains in the city like mud in a drained pond. You see them in the parks, you see them lying on the sidewalk in broad daylight along the Bowery, that street of forgotten men. You see them drifting about the city, from one end to the other.

They come to us in droves: eight hundred every morning on the coffee line; one hundred and twenty-five for lunch and again for supper. It is an informal crowd at noon. They start gathering in the yard, men who have passed the word along to other transients, homeless ones, that perhaps there is food to be had. Many days the soup runs short and then there is only coffee and cake (thanks to Macy's, which gives us their leftovers every morning).

Many days go by with no money coming in at all. Right now our telephone is shut off, but the man in the candy store next door calls us to his phone for messages. Today we expect the gas and electricity to go. What to do? We can borrow a few oil stoves and continue to cook and feed those who come. Vegetables are contributed, soup bones, fish. But we must buy the coffee, sugar, milk, and bread. As long as we are trusted the bills continue to mount. Even the printer is letting us go to press with $995 owing this summer.

And there is the children's camp on Staten Island, donated by a friend. It holds eight children—forty can be cared for during the summer—and they can spend their days on the beach and sleep at night to the rustle of wind in the maples around the camp. The most beautiful sound in the world is the sound of little waves on a hot beach. And the sweetest sight is Viola, aged four, who lives on Grand Street in a six-flight walk-up, one of eight children, who is playing in the sand and waves on the beach these days. Or perhaps it is Rosemary and Barbara, Italian and Negro, with their arms around each other's necks as they pose for a picture on the shore.

There is poverty and hunger and war in the world. And we prepare for more war. There is desperate suffering with no prospect of relief. But we would be contributing to the misery and desperation of the world if we failed to rejoice in the sun, the moon, and the stars, in the rivers which surround this island on which we live, in the cool breezes of the bay, in what food we have and in the benefactors God sends.

The heat wave which is a misery to some is to us a joy. We remember the bitter cold of the winter, and those who have to sleep under the stars nestle into the warmth of the hot pavements.

Our greatest misery is the poverty which gnaws at our vitals, an agony to the families in our midst. And the only thing we can do about it is to appeal to you, our readers, begging your help. We are stewards, and we probably manage very badly in trying to take care of all those who come, the desperate, the dispossessed. Like St. Peter, they say, "To whom else shall we go?" and they are our brothers in Christ. They are more than that: they are Christ, appealing to you.

So please help us to keep going. Help these suffering members of the sorrowing Body of Christ.

"Little By Little" (1953)

Poverty is a strange and elusive thing. I have tried to write about it, its joys and its sorrows, for twenty years now; I could probably write about it for another twenty years without conveying what I feel about it as well as I would like. I condemn poverty and I advocate it; poverty is simple and complex at once; it is a social phenomenon and a personal matter. It is a paradox.

St. Francis was "the little poor man" and none was more joyful than he; yet Francis began with tears, with fear and trembling, hiding in a cave from his irate father. He had expropriated some of his father's goods (which he considered his rightful inheritance) in order to repair a church and rectory where he meant to live. It was only later that he came to love Lady Poverty. He took it little by little; it seemed to grow on him. Perhaps kissing the leper was the great step that freed him not only from fastidiousness and a fear of disease but from attachment to worldly goods as well.

Sometimes it takes but one step. We would like to think so. And yet the older I get, the more I see that life is made up of many steps, and they are very small affairs, not giant strides. I have "kissed a leper," not once but twice—consciously—and I cannot say I am much the better for it.

The first time was early one morning on the steps of Precious Blood Church. A woman with cancer of the face was begging (beggars are allowed only in the slums) and when I gave her money (no sacrifice on my part but merely passing on alms which someone had given me) she tried to kiss my hand. The only thing I could do was kiss her dirty old face with the gaping hole in it where an eye and a nose had been. It sounds like a heroic deed but it was not. One gets used to ugliness so quickly. What we avert our eyes from one day is easily borne the next when we have learned a little more about love. Nurses know this, and so do mothers.

Another time I was refusing a bed to a drunken prostitute with a huge, rouged mouth, a nightmare of a mouth. She had been raising a disturbance in the house. I kept remembering how St. Therese said that when you had to refuse anyone anything, you could at least do it so that the person went away a bit happier. I had to deny her a bed but when that woman asked me to kiss her, I did, and it was a loathsome thing, the way she did it. It was scarcely a mark of normal human affection.

We suffer these things and they fade from memory. But daily, hourly, to give up our own possessions and especially to subordinate our own impulses and wishes to others—these are hard, hard things; and I don't think they ever get any easier.

You can strip yourself, you can be stripped, but still you will reach out like an octopus to seek your own comfort, your untroubled time, your ease, your refreshment. It may mean books or music—the gratification of the inner senses—or it may mean food and drink, coffee and cigarettes. The one kind of giving up is not easier than the other. . . .

But the fact remains that every House of Hospitality is full. There is a breadline outside our door, every day, twice a day, two or three hundred strong. Families write us pitifully for help. This is not poverty; this is destitution. . . .

But I am sure that God did not intend that there be so many poor. The class structure is of our making and by our consent, not His, and we must do what we can to change it. So we are urging revolutionary change.

So many sins against the poor cry out to high heaven! One of the most deadly sins is to deprive the laborer of his hire. There is another: to instill in him paltry desires so compulsive that he is willing to sell his liberty and his honor to satisfy them. We are all guilty of concupiscence, but newspapers, radios, television, and battalions of advertising men (woe to that generation!) deliberately stimulate our desires, the satisfaction of which so often means the degradation of the family.

Because of these factors of modern life, the only way we can write about poverty is in terms of ourselves, our own personal responsibility. The message we have been given is the Cross. . . .

On Human Nature (1930)

SIGMUND FREUD

Among the most controversial figures of the twentieth century was the Austrian physician and psychoanalyst Sigmund Freud (1856–1939). Freud sought to apply the critical methods of science to the understanding of the human unconscious. His research centered on sexuality and the interpretation of dreams in his explanation of human motivation. He portrayed the mind as an area in which the irrational, amoral instincts (*id*) struggled with the restrictive demands of society (*superego*). The *ego* sought to reconcile these conflicting forces in order to maintain a stable existence. Freud's work led to a revolution in human understanding. Humanity was stripped of the privacy of its inner nature.

One of Freud's most revealing works on the antagonisms between the

Reprinted from *Civilization and Its Discontents* by Sigmund Freud, translated by James Strachey, pp. 58–61, 92, by permission of W. W. Norton & Company, Inc. Copyright © 1961 by James Strachey.

demands of instinct and the restrictions of human society is *Civilization and Its Discontents* (1930). In the excerpt below, Freud describes the destructive nature of human beings.

The element of truth behind all this, which people are so ready to disavow, is that men are not gentle creatues who want to be loved, and who at the most can defend themselves if they are attacked; they are, on the contrary, creatures among whose instinctual endowments is to be reckoned a powerful share of aggressiveness. . . . Anyone who calls to mind the atrocities committed during the racial migrations or the invasions of the Huns, or by the people known as Mongols under Ghengis Khan and Tamerlane, or at the capture of Jerusalem by the pious Crusaders, or even, indeed, the horrors of the recent World War [1914–1918]—anyone who calls these things to mind will have to bow humbly before the truth of this view.

The existence of this inclination to aggression, which we can detect in ourselves and justly assume to be present in others, is the factor which disturbs our relations with our neighbour and which forces civilization into such a high expenditure [of energy]. In consequence of this primary mutual hostility of human beings, civilized society is perpetually threatened with disintegration. The interest of work in common would not hold it together; instinctual passions are stronger than reasonable interests. Civilization has to use its utmost efforts in order to set limits to man's aggressive instincts and to hold the manifestations of them in check. . . . Hence, therefore, the use of methods intended to incite people into identifications and aim-inhibited relationships of love, hence the restriction upon sexual life, and hence too the ideal's commandment to love one's neighbour as oneself—a commandment which is really justified by the fact that nothing else runs so strongly counter to the original nature of man. In spite of every effort, these endeavours of civilization have not so far achieved very much. It hopes to prevent the crudest excesses of brutal violence by itself assuming the right to use violence against criminals, but the law is not able to lay hold of the more cautious and refined manifestations of human aggressiveness. The time comes when each one of us has to give up as illusions the expectations which, in his youth, he pinned upon his fellow-men, and when he may learn how much difficulty and pain has been added to his life by their ill-will. At the same time, it would be unfair to reproach civilization with trying to eliminate strife and competition from human activity. These things are undoubtedly indispensable. But opposition is not necessarily enmity; it is merely misused and made an *occasion* for enmity.

The Communists believe that they have found the path to deliverance from our evils. According to them, man is wholly good and is well-disposed to his neighbour; but the institution of private property has corrupted his nature. The ownership of private wealth gives the individual power, and with it the temptation to ill-treat his neighbour; while the man who is excluded from possession is bound to rebel in hostility against his oppressor. If private property were abolished, all wealth held in common, and everyone allowed to share in the enjoyment of it, ill-will and hostility would disappear among men. Since everyone's needs would be satisfied, no one would have any reason to regard another as his enemy; all would willingly undertake the work that was necessary. I have no concern with any economic criticisms of the communist system; I cannot enquire into whether the abolition of private property is expedient or advantageous. But I am able to recognize that the psychological premises on which the system is based are an untenable illusion. In abolishing private property we deprive the human illusion. In abolishing private property we deprive the human love of aggression of one of its instruments, certainly a strong one, though certainly not the strongest; but we have in no way altered the differences in power and influence which are misused by aggressiveness, nor have we altered anything in its nature. Aggressiveness was not created by property. It reigned almost without limit in primitive times, when property was still very scanty, and it already shows itself in the nursery almost before property has given up its primal, anal form; it forms the basis of every relation of affection and love among people. . . . If we do away with personal rights over material wealth, there still remains prerogative in the field of sexual relationships, which is bound to become the source of the strongest dislike and the most violent hostility among men who in other respects are on an equal footing. If we were to remove this factor, too, by allowing complete freedom of sexual life and thus abolishing the family, the germ-cell of civilization, we cannot, it is true, easily foresee what new paths the development of civilization could take; but one thing we can expect, and that is that this indestructible feature of human nature will follow it there. . . .

The fateful question for the human species seems to me to be whether and to what extent their cultural development will succeed in mastering the disturbance of their communal life by the human instinct of aggression and self-destruction. It may be that in this respect precisely the present time deserves a special interest. Men have gained control over the forces of nature to such an extent that with their help they would have no difficulty in exterminating one another to the last man. They know this, and hence comes a large part of their current unrest, their unhappiness and their mood of anxiety. . . .

The Responsibility of the Individual (1956)

JEAN PAUL SARTRE

Existentialism has been an important philosophical movement in the twentieth century. Its premier spokesman, Jean Paul Sartre, in his book

Jean Paul Sartre, *Existentialism and Human Emotions* (New York: Philosophical Library, 1957), pp. 52–54, 56–57. Copyright © 1957 by the Philosophical Library Inc. Reprinted by permission of the Philosophical Library Inc.

Being and Nothingness, contends that man is condemned to be free and that with freedom comes responsibility for one's choices and actions. Such responsibility for war, life, and death is a burden that cannot be shirked and is not easily borne.

The essential consequence of our earlier remarks is that man being condemned to be free carries the weight of the whole world on his shoulders; he is responsible for the world and for himself as a way of being. . . . Thus there are no *accidents* in a life. . . . If I am mobilized in a war, this war is *my* war; it is in my image and I deserve it. I deserve it first because I could always get out of it by suicide or by desperation; these ultimate possibilities are those which must always be present for us when there is a question of envisaging a situation. For lack of getting out of it, I have *chosen* it. This can be due to inertia, to cowardice in the face of public opinion, or because I prefer certain other values to the value of the refusal to join in the war (the good opinion of my relatives, the honor of my family, *etc.*). Anyway you look at it, it is a matter of a choice. This choice will be repeated later on again and again without a break until the end of the war. . . . Thus, totally free, undistinguishable from the period for which I have chosen to be the meaning, as profoundly responsible for the war as if I had myself declared it, unable to live without integrating it in *my* situation, engaging myself in it wholly and stamping it with my seal, *I must be without remorse or regrets as I am without excuse; for from the instant of my upsurge into being, I carry the weight of the world by myself alone without anything or any person being able to lighten it.*

Love and Human Existence (1955)

ERICH FROMM

Sanity becomes an important commodity in a world that often seems to be ripping apart. Psychoanalyst Erich Fromm, in his book *The Sane Society*, offers love as the key to being sane and being human.

There is only one passion which satisfies man's need to unite himself with the world, and to acquire at the same time a sense of integrity and individuality, and this is *love. Love is union* with somebody, or something, outside oneself, *under the condition of retaining the separateness and integrity of one's own self.* It is an experience of sharing, of communion, which permits the full unfolding of one's own inner activity. The experience of love does away with the necessity of illusions. There is no need to inflate the image of the other person, or of myself, since the reality of active sharing and loving permits me to transcend my individualized existence, and at the same time to experience myself as the bearer of the active powers which constitute the act of loving. What matters is the particular *quality* of loving, not the object. Love is in the experience of human solidarity with our fellow creatures, it is in the erotic love of man and woman, in the love of the mother for the child, and also in the love for oneself, as a human being; it is in the mystical experience of union. In the act of loving, I am one with All, and yet I am myself, a unique, separate, limited, mortal human being. Indeed out of the very polarity between separateness and union, love is born and reborn. . . . Love, paradoxically, makes me more independent because it makes me stronger and happier—yet it makes me one with the loved person to the extent that individuality seems to be extinguished for the moment. In loving I experience "I am you," you—the loved person, you—the stranger, you—everything alive. In the experience of love lies the only answer to being human, lies sanity. . . .

.   .   .

And the end of all our exploring, will be to arrive where we started, and know the place for the first time.

T. S. Eliot

STUDY QUESTIONS

Section I: A Century of Progress

1. Explore some of the moral questions that arise from medical research. When you replace someone's internal organs, do you change his or her very being? Do the potentials of genetic engineering bother you? Scientists have developed the birth control pill, made possible test tube babies, and are investigating the possibilities of cryogenic preservation. Are these valid areas of scientific research, or are these steps toward the creation of "Frankenstein's monster"?

2. Read the selections on John Glenn's flight carefully. Why was it important for his flight to succeed? What does this say about progress?

3. Do you agree with Eric Hoffer on his assessment of the moon landing? Should the vast funds that are spent for space exploration be channeled into feeding the poor or sheltering the homeless of the world? Where do your priorities lie?

4. World War I (1914–1918) shattered all illusion of civility and augured an era of total war in which civilians as well as soldiers died and the boundaries of destruction ceased to have meaning. Analyze the articles of the Hague Convention of 1907. Are "laws of war" so unrealistic? Which of the articles do you respect the most? Note the treaty of 1922 concerning submarines and poisonous gas. Are both these weapons immoral? Poisonous gas was not used in World War II by mutual consent—yet this was a "total war." Does total war preclude "laws of humanity"?

5. In his book *Why War?* (Paris, 1933), the great physicist Albert Einstein wrote, "Mankind can only gain protection against the danger of unimaginable destruction and wanton annihilation if a supranational organization has alone the authority to produce or possess [nuclear] weapons . . . and the legal right and duty to solve all the conflicts which in the past have led to war." What is your reaction to this opinion? To what extent are organizations like the United Nations and Amnesty International useful and effective? Would it make a difference if they did not exist?

Section II: A Century of Holocaust

6. Do you think that President Truman was justified in his use of the atomic bomb on Hiroshima and Nagasaki? The Baruch Plan was the first comprehensive package for the control of atomic energy. Is this a responsible document? Why? Does it make Truman's use of "The Bomb" easier to accept?
7. What did Stalin mean in his speech of February 1946 by the phrase, "Soviet victory"? What policy was Churchill advocating in his "Iron Curtain" speech? Was he pessimistic or optimistic about the possibility of war?
8. According to Theodore White, why is Communism successful and what are its weaknesses? What are the main points about capitalism and Communism that Khrushchev stressed in his speech to the 22nd Communist Party Congress? After analysis of this document, do you agree or disagree with White's assessment of Communism?
9. What did Secretary of State George Schultz say about progress in his speech on American foreign policy? Are you optimistic or pessimistic about U.S.-Soviet relations in the future? Why?
10. What is the basis of the MAD theory of nuclear defense? Are you persuaded by Jastrow's article on strategic superiority? What do you think of the idea of "nuclear pacifism" as argued by H. Stuart Hughes?
11. Two atomic bombs were dropped in 1945, the first and only time nuclear weapons have been directed against human beings. Today we live under the "abstraction" of nuclear holocaust, as evidenced by Jonathan Schell's description of an attack on New York City. For those born after 1945, can the terror of that event long ago maintain our allegiance toward arms control, or must we have an example of an atomic explosion every generation or so in order to promote the seriousness of negotiation? Will people forget the horrors of Hiroshima the further they are removed by time from the experience? Is a nuclear war "winnable"?

Section III: Reflections on Humanity in the Twentieth Century

12. According to Mahatma Gandhi, is violence always to be avoided? What did he mean when he said, "I am a practical idealist"? How difficult is it to achieve nonviolence? If one must struggle to obtain a nonviolent attitude, does this mean that violence is a dominant characteristic of human nature?

How does the selection of Mulford Sibley strike you? Is he too idealistic in his beliefs?

13. According to Archibishop Desmond Tutu, what is the "strategy" of the white Nationalist government toward blacks in South Africa? How does Tutu use religion as a base of appeal? Is racism an inherent aspect of human nature, or is it an aberration that must be taught and cultivated through education and societal reaffirmation? To what extent has the United States progressed in its race relations?

14. What was Sigmund Freud's view of human nature? Do you agree with this view? Compare Freud's ideas with the attitudes of Dorothy Day, Erich Fromm, and Mahatma Gandhi. Is humanity disposed more toward respecting life and granting mercy or toward aggression?

15. According to Jean Paul Sartre, why are there no "accidents" in life? Why has existentialism often been called a "depressing philosophy"? If being "free" is usually considered an advantageous human condition, why does the existentialist believe that he is "condemned to be free"?

16. After you have read through this chapter on the contemporary world, what are your impressions? How do you define the concept "progress," and what seems to be its key ingredient? Is it love, God, or the unfettered researches and discoveries of pure science? Is nonviolence a practical alternative to violence? What will form the basis of humanity's advancement or destruction in the future? Will we continue to live in a world dominated by the dichotomy of progress and holocaust?

Aspects of Western
civilization : problems and
sources in history